WOMEN
AND THE MAKING
OF AMERICA

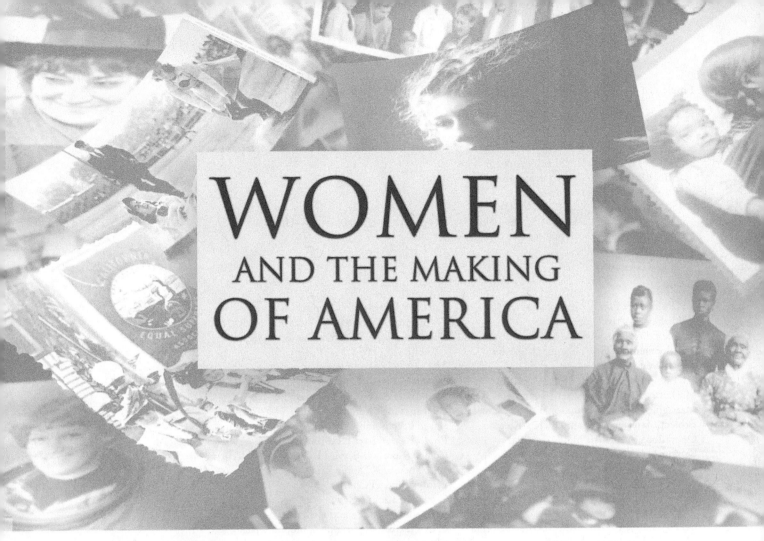

WOMEN
AND THE MAKING
OF AMERICA

VOLUME 2

MARI JO BUHLE
Brown University

TERESA MURPHY
George Washington University

JANE GERHARD
Mount Holyoke College

PEARSON

Prentice
Hall

Library of Congress Cataloging-in-Publication Data

Buhle, Mari Jo
    Women and the making of America / Mari Jo Buhle, Teresa Murphy, Jane Gerhard.
        p. cm.
    Includes bibliographical references and index.
    ISBN-13: 978-0-13-183916-8 (combined, vols. 1 and 2)
    ISBN-13: 978-0-13-812688-9 (vol. 1)
    ISBN-13: 978-0-13-812687-2 (vol. 2)
    1. Women's studies—United States—History. 2. Feminism—United States—History. I.
Murphy, Teresa. II. Gerhard, Jane F. III. Title.
    HQ1181.U5B84 2008
    305.40973—dc22

                                                                            2008015611

VP/Publisher: Priscilla McGeehon
Publisher: Charlyce Jones Owen
Senior Editorial Assistant: Maureen Diana
Developmental Editor: Carolyn Viola-John
Executive Marketing Manager: Sue Westmoreland
Marketing Assistant: Athena Moore
Managing Editor (Production): Lisa Iarkowski
Project Manager: Marianne Peters-Riordan
Operations Specialist: Maura Zaldivar
Senior Art Director: Maria Lange
Interior Design: Ilze Lemesis
Cover Design: Maria Lange
Cover Illustration/Photo: (From bottom center): Audette Scott/Corbis/Sygma; Courtesy of the Library of Congress (b-e, h, j-l); California Historical Society; Bettmann/CORBIS; Franklin D. Roosevelt Library.

Cover Art Creation: Cory Skidds
AV Project Manager: Mirella Signoretto
Director, Image Resource Center: Melinda Patelli
Manager, Rights and Permissions: Zina Arabia
Manager, Visual Research: Beth Brenzel
Manager, Cover Visual Research & Permissions: Karen Sanatar
Image Permission Coordinator: Craig A. Jones
Photo Researcher: Julie Tesser
Composition/Full-Service Project Management: Emily Bush/S4Carlisle Publishing Services
Printer/Binder: Courier
Credits and acknowledgments borrowed from other sources and reproduced, with permission, in this textbook appear on appropriate page within text or on page C-1.

Pearson Education LTD., London
Pearson Education Singapore, Pte. Ltd
Pearson Education, Canada, Ltd
Pearson Education–Japan
Pearson Education Australia PTY, Limited

Pearson Education North Asia Ltd
Pearson Educación de Mexico, S.A. de C.V.
Pearson Education Malaysia, Pte. Ltd
Pearson Education, Upper Saddle River, New Jersey

8 9 10 V092 16 15

ISBN-13: 978-0-13-812687-2
ISBN-10:   0-13-812687-9

Brief Contents

Chapter 1   Worlds Apart, to 1700   2

Chapter 2   Contact and Conquest, 1500–1700   32

Chapter 3   Eighteenth-Century Revolutions, 1700–1800   64

Chapter 4   Frontiers of Trade and Empire, 1750–1860   98

Chapter 5   Domestic Economies and Northern Lives, 1800–1860   130

Chapter 6   Family Business: Slavery and Patriarchy, 1800–1860   164

Chapter 7   Religion and Reform, 1800–1860   196

Chapter 8   Politics and Power: The Movement for Woman's Rights, 1800–1860   228

Chapter 9   The Civil War, 1861–1865   260

Chapter 10   In the Age of Slave Emancipation, 1865–1877   294

Chapter 11   The Trans-Mississippi West, 1860–1900   330

Chapter 12   New Women   362

Chapter 13   The Woman Movement, 1880–1900   398

Chapter 14   The New Morality, 1880–1920   432

Chapter 15   The Progressive Era, 1890–1920   464

Chapter 16   The Jazz Age, 1920–1930   502

Chapter 17   The Great Depression, 1930–1940   540

Chapter 18   World War II Home Fronts, 1940–1945   576

Chapter 19   The Feminine Mystique, 1945–1965   616

Chapter 20   Civil Rights and Liberal Activism, 1945–1975   652

Chapter 21   The Personal Is Political, 1960–1980   688

Chapter 22   Endings and Beginnings, 1980 to 2008   724

Contents

About the Authors   xxvii

Preface   xxix

Introduction   xxxiv

CHAPTER 1   WORLDS APART, TO 1700   2

Women in the Americas   5
  Hunting and Gathering   5
  Cultural Differences   7
  Marriage, Family, and Gender Identities   10
  Exercising Power   11
  Women's Lives: *LADY XOC*   13

European Women   13
  Flexible Labor Force   14
  Patriarchal Societies   15
  Women's Voices: LIVING AS A MAN   16
  Women's Voices: LOVE AND MONEY   18
  Challenges to Patriarchy   19

African Women   21
  Work and Power   21
  Women's Lives: *Idia, First Iyoba of Benin*   22
  Family Economies   23
  Dependence and Freedom: Slavery in Africa   24

The Gendered Dynamics of Contact   25
  Discovering New Worlds   26
  Sexuality and Claims of Civilization   27
  Gender and the Emergence of the Slave Trade   28

CHAPTER 2   CONTACT AND CONQUEST, 1500–1700   32

Spanish Conquest in the Southwest   35
  Immigration and Work   35
  Captivity and Kinship   36
  Women's Lives: *Doña Marina*   37
  Religion and Conquest   38
  Witchcraft, Resistance, and Revolt   39

Trading Ventures in the North   40
  The Fur Trade   41
  Catholicism and Conversion   42

Women's Voices: CONFLICTS WITH THE HURON   43
Marriage, Sex, and Survival in the Middle Ground   44
New Netherland Trade   45

Plantation Societies of the Southeast   46
The Tobacco Economy   47
Wealthy Widows and Serving Wenches   48
Slavery, Race, and Intermarriage   50
Women's Lives: *Pocahontas*   51
Anxious Patriarchs   52

Godly Societies of New England   53
Goodwives   54
Women's Voices: A GOODWIFE   55
Family Government   55
Female Piety   57
Witchcraft and Danger   58

CHAPTER 3   EIGHTEENTH-CENTURY REVOLUTIONS,
1700–1800   64

The Market Revolution   67
Cities of Women   67
A New World of Goods   68
Issues of Inequality   69
Slavery in a Market Economy   70

Family Relations and Social Responsibilities   72
Passions and Patriarchal Authority   72
Women's Voices: LETTER TO A FATHER   73
Disorderly Women: The Challenge of the Great Awakening   74
Female Companions: The Gendered Enlightenment   75

Declaring Independence   77
Daughters of Liberty   78
Loyalist Wives   80
Women's Lives: *Mercy Otis Warren*   81
Fighting the War   81
Seize the Day: Indian and Slave Women of the Revolution   83
Women's Voices: CONCERNS OF AN INDIAN MATRON   85
Female Citizens   86
Women's Lives: *Phillis Wheatley*   87

A Virtuous Republic   88
  Republican Mothers and Virtuous Wives   89
  Educated Women   90
  A Limited Revolution   92

CHAPTER 4   FRONTIERS OF TRADE AND EMPIRE,
              1750–1860   98

Indian Country   101
  Multiple Meanings of Captivity   103
  Seneca Households: "A Perfect Equality"   104
  Shawnee Society and the Incorporation of Strangers   106
  Inheritance and Power among the Cherokee   107
  Women's Voices: A CHEROKEE LEADER   108

Slavery and Freedom in Louisiana   111
  The Traffic in Women   112
  Women's Lives: *Sacagawea*   113
  New Orleans and Urban Slavery   115
  Gens de Couleur Libre   116

Western Frontiers   117
  Texas: The Challenges of Settlement   117
  New Mexico Women and Trading Networks   119
  Women's Lives: *Gertrudis Barcelo*   121
  California Missions   122
  The Overland Trails   124
  Women's Voices: A MISSIONARY'S PERSPECTIVE   125

CHAPTER 5   DOMESTIC ECONOMIES AND NORTHERN LIVES,
              1800–1860   130

Industrial Transformations   133
  Factory Families   133
  Independent Mill Girls   134
  Family Wage Economy   136

Town and Country   137
  Seamstresses, Servants, and Shopgirls   138
  Sex for Sale   140
  Butter and Eggs   141

Private Lives: Defining the Middle Class   142
  Hidden Economy of Housework   142
  Cult of Domesticity   143

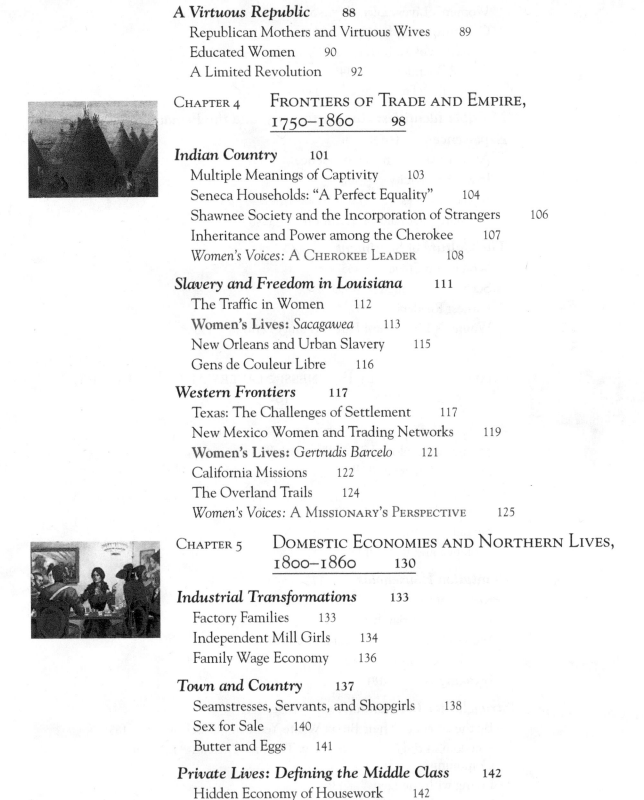

Women's Lives: *Lilly Martin Spencer*   144
Courtship and Marriage   146
Women's Voices: MOTHERLY DISCIPLINE   147
Sexual Boundaries   148
Controlling Family Size   149

Multiple Identities: Race, Ethnicity, and the Female Experience   150
African American Independence   151
Irish Domesticity   152
Women's Voices: AN IRISH IMMIGRANT   153
German Guardians of Tradition   154

The Culture of Sentiment   155
Women on Stage   155
Scribbling Women   156
Earnest Readers   157
Women's Lives: *Sara Parton (Fanny Fern)*   158

CHAPTER 6   FAMILY BUSINESS: SLAVERY AND PATRIARCHY, 1800–1860   164

Antebellum Slavery   167
Strong as Any Man: Slave Women's Work   168
Status and Special Skills   170
Family Life   171
Women's Voices: A SLAVE'S PLEA   173
Sexual Demands of Slavery   174
Violence and Resistance   175

Plantation Households   177
Keeper of the Keys   177
Defense of Patriarchy   178
Women's Lives: *Mary Randolph Randolph*   179
Family Networks   180
Breaking Ties   181

Struggles for Independence   183
By the Sweat of Their Brow: White Yeoman Households   183
Freedom in the Midst of Slavery: The Free African American Community   184
Living with the Law   185
Women's Lives: *Elizabeth Keckley*   186

Representing the South   188
  Constructing Virtue: Slave Women   188
  Plantation Novels   189
  Fighting for the South   190
  Women's Voices: A DEFENSE OF THE SOUTH   192

CHAPTER 7   RELIGION AND REFORM, 1800–1860   196

Revivals and Religious Virtue   199
  Gendered Revivals in the North   199
  Evangelical Commitments in the South   201
  Mothers and Missionaries   201
  Preaching the Word   203
  Women's Voices: RECEIVING THE CALL TO PREACH   204

Religion and Family Authority   205
  Quakers, Spiritualists, and Female Autonomy   205
  Reform Judaism and Gender Hierarchies   206
  Power and Danger in Catholic Convents   207

Controlling the Body, Perfecting the Soul   209
  Celibacy of Shakers   209
  Bible Communism: Complex Marriage in the Oneida Community   210
  Moral Reform Societies: Combating the Sex Trade   211
  Women's Voices: REFORMING THE MEN   212
  Bodily Purification and the Dangers of Drink   213
  Women's Lives: *Mary Gove Nichols*   214
  Curbing Domestic Violence   215

Contesting the Nation: Social and Political Reforms   217
  Working Women and Labor Protests   217
  Protesting Indian Removal   218
  Women's Lives: *Sarah Bagley*   219
  Race, Hierarchy, and the Critique of Slavery   220
  Politics and Gender in the Antislavery Movement   222

CHAPTER 8   POLITICS AND POWER: THE MOVEMENT FOR
             WOMAN'S RIGHTS, 1800–1860   228

Life, Liberty, and Property   231
  Communitarian Experiments in Family and Property   231
  Family Assets: Married Women's Property Laws   233
  Women's Lives: *Frances (Fanny) Wright*   234
  Work and Wages   236

Challenging the Doctrine of Separate Spheres   238
Promoting Female Seminaries   238
Confronting Educational Barriers   239
Women's Voices: THE IMPORTANCE OF COLLEGE   240
Demands for Divorce   241

Woman's Influence versus Woman's Rights   243
The Beecher-Grimke Debate   243
Political Participation   244
Women's Lives: *Jane Cazneau*   246
From Moral Suasion to Political Action   247

Forging a Movement   248
Seneca Falls and Other Conventions   248
The Female Citizen   250
Women's Voices: A RELIGIOUS DEFENSE OF WOMAN'S RIGHTS   250
Aren't I a Woman?   252
Reaching Out   253
Marriage and Divorce   254

CHAPTER 9   THE CIVIL WAR, 1861–1865   260

The Northern Home Front   263
Woman's National Loyal League   264
Bonnet Brigades   265
United States Sanitary Commission   266
Women's Voices: WORKING FOR THE U.S. SANITARY COMMISSION   268
Freedmen's Aid Societies   269
Wartime Employments   270

On the Battlefields   272
Army Nurses   272
Women's Voices: A CONFEDERATE NURSE'S STORY   275
Soldiers   276
Spies   277

Plantation Society in Turmoil   279
Unflinching Loyalty to the Cause   279
Plantations without Patriarchs   280
Camp Followers and Contrabands   282
Women's Lives: *Harriet Tubman*   284

A Woman's War   286
A Moral Crusade to End Slavery   286
Women's Lives: *Elizabeth Stuart Phelps*   287
Memoirs and Memories   288

CHAPTER 10   IN THE AGE OF SLAVE EMANCIPATION, 1865–1877   294

Reconstructing Southern Households   298
The Meaning of Freedom   298
Women's Voices: A SLAVE'S CHILD REMEMBERS THEIR QUEST FOR FREEDOM   300
Negotiating Free Labor   301
White Women on the Old Plantation   302
"Freedom Was Free-er" in Towns and Cities   303

Woman's Rights Reemerge   305
"The Negro's Hour"   306
Organizing for Woman Suffrage   309
The Notorious Victoria C. Woodhull   309
Women's Voices: LECTURING ON WOMAN'S RIGHTS   310
The New Departure   313

Woman's Right to Labor   314
Women's Clubs   314
Women's Lives: *Myra Colby Bradwell*   317
Associations for Working Women   318
Trade Unions   319
Women's Lives: *Jennie Collins*   320

The Woman's Crusade   321
"Baptism of Power and Liberty"   321
Frances E. Willard   322
Home Protection   323

CHAPTER 11   THE TRANS-MISSISSIPPI WEST, 1860–1900   330

On the Range and in Mining Communities   333
Home on the Range   333
The Sporting Life   334
Domesticity on the Mining Frontier   335

Mormon Settlements   337
The Doctrine of Plural Marriage   338
"The Mormon Question"   339
The Woman's Vote in Utah   339
Women's Voices: AN ANONYMOUS MORMON SPEAKS HER MIND   341

Spanish-Speaking Women of the Southwest   342
Landowning Elite   343
Communal Villagers   344
Urban Householders   345

Building Communities in the Heartland   346
   The Homestead Act and Immigration   346
   Woman's Work, Never Done   347
   Women's Lives: *Laura Ingalls Wilder*   349
   Turning Wilderness into "Civilization"   350
   The Patrons of Husbandry   351

Indian Women, Conquest, and Survival   351
   The Nez Perce   352
   Plains Indians   353
   Women's Voices: LEAVING FOR THE MISSION SCHOOL   354
   The Southern Ute   355
   Women's Lives: *Susan La Flesche Picotte, M.D. and Susette La Flesche Tibbles*   356

CHAPTER 12   NEW WOMEN   362

New Industries, New Jobs   365
   Manufacturing   366
   Retail Sales and Office Work   367
   Women's Voices: THE FIRST DAY ON THE JOB   368
   Domestic Service   370

New Immigrants   370
   Chinese   371
   Italians   373
   Eastern European Jews   374

The New South   376
   Tenant Farming and Sharecropping   376
   Domestic Service   377
   Textiles and Mill Villages   378

New Professions   380
   Education   380
   Medicine   381
   Women's Lives: *M. Carey Thomas*   382
   Women's Lives: *Marie Elizabeth Zakrzewska*   383
   Ministry   384
   Visual Arts   386

The New Woman at Home   387
   Smaller Families, Better Babies   387
   Women's Voices: DESCRIBING WOMEN'S PLACE IN THE ART WORLD   388

Woman's Sphere Transformed   389
From Production to Consumption   391

CHAPTER 13   THE WOMAN MOVEMENT, 1880–1900   398

Cross-Class Alliances   402
Young Women's Christian Association   402
Women's Lives: *Grace Hoadley Dodge*   403
Christian Homes for African American Women Workers   404
Women's Educational and Industrial Union   406
Illinois Woman's Alliance   407

Spanning the Nation   408
National Woman's Christian Temperance Union   408
National American Woman Suffrage Association   410
Women's Voices: SUFFRAGE VISIONARY   411
General Federation of Women's Clubs   413
National Association of Colored Women   414

Campaigns of the 1890s   416
Populism   416
Women's Lives: *Mary Elizabeth Lease*   417
Woman Suffrage in the West   418
Antilynching Crusade   419
The Spanish American War   421

Woman's Empire   422
Women's Foreign Mission Movement   423
Women's Voices: OVERSEAS MISSIONARY   424
World WCTU   425
Outposts of the YWCA   426

CHAPTER 14   THE NEW MORALITY, 1880–1920   432

Urban Pleasures, Urban Dangers   435
"Women Adrift"   435
Women's Voices: WEIGHING MARRIAGE AGAINST CAREER   436
Cheap Amusements   437
"Charity Girls"   439

Changing Relations of Intimacy   440
Courtship and Marriage   440
Divorce   441
Women's Lives: *Kate O'Flaherty Chopin*   442
Female Friends and Women Lovers   443

Curbing "Social Evils"   445
Social Purity Campaigns   445
Crusading against Prostitution   446
Legislating against Miscegenation   449

Women's Bodies and Reproduction   450
Designed for Motherhood   450
Controlling Reproduction   451
The Birth Control Campaign   452
Women's Lives: *Margaret Sanger*   453

Rebels in Bohemia   454
Living the New Morality   454
Women's Voices: "RED EMMA" CRITIQUES MARRIAGE   456
Heterodoxy and Feminism   457
Art and Politics   458

CHAPTER 15   THE PROGRESSIVE ERA, 1890–1920   464

"Municipal Housekeeping"   467
Jane Addams and Hull-House   467
The Settlement Movement: A Community of Women   468
"A Power for Good": Neighborhood Activism   470

The Era of Women's Strikes   472
Women's Trade Union League   472
Uprising in the Garment Industry   474
"Bread and Roses": The Lawrence Textile Strike, 1912   476
Protective Labor Legislation   477
Women's Voices: SURVIVING THE TRIANGLE FIRE   478

"Mother-Work"   479
Women's Lives: *Charlotte Perkins Gilman*   480
Juvenile Courts   481
Mothers' Pensions   481
The Children's Bureau   482

World War I   484
Wartime Employment   484
The Women's Peace Movement   485
In National Defense   486
Keeping Men Fit to Fight   487

Votes for Women   489
Out of the Doldrums   489
Women's Lives: *Carrie Chapman Catt*   490

Southern Strategy   491
Winning Campaign   492
Women's Voices: A Suffrage Militant   493
Nineteenth Amendment, 1920   494

Chapter 16   The Jazz Age, 1920–1930   502

"Revolution in Manners and Morals"   505
Courtship in Transition   506
Women's Lives: *Georgia O'Keeffe*   507
Women's Voices: "Young Women Seek Advice About Petting"   509
The Companionate Marriage   510
Invention of the Lesbian Threat   512

Women and Work   513
Married Women Workers   513
Pink-Collar Workers   514
Professional Workers   516

Beyond Suffrage   517
Feminist-New Style   518
The League of Women Voters   518
Women's Voices: "Feminist-New Style"   519
The Equal Rights Amendment   521
The Sheppard-Towner Act   522

Women's Activism   524
"Race Women" and Pan-Africanism   524
The Anti-Lynching Crusade   526
Ku Klux Klan   528

The Culture of Modernity   530
Dance Crazes   531
The Harlem Renaissance   532
Singing the Blues   533
Women's Lives: *Gertrude "Ma" Rainey*   534

Chapter 17   The Great Depression, 1930–1940   540

Facing the Depression   543
The Economics of Running a House   544
Postponing Marriage and Children   545
Women's Voices: Dust Bowl Diary   546
Gender and the Politics of Providing   547

Activism   551
   Appalachian Women in the Textile Industry   551
   Chinese Women in San Francisco's Garment Industry   553
   Latinas and the California Canning Industry   555

Women and the New Deal   556
   Eleanor Roosevelt and the Women's Network   556
   Women's Lives: *Mary Williams (Molly) Dewson*   559
   Women in the New Deal   560
   Gender in the Welfare State   562
   Women's Voices: DISCRIMINATION IN THE WORKS PROJECT
   ADMINISTRATION   565

Cultures of the 1930s   566
   Representing Gender in New Deal Public Art   566
   Documenting the Depression   567
   Regulating Hollywood   569
   Women's Lives: *Mae West*   571

CHAPTER 18   WORLD WAR II HOME FRONTS, 1940–1945   576

Women at Work on the Home Front   579
   Working for Victory   580
   For the Duration   582
   Double V Campaign   584

Gender and Wartime Popular Culture   586
   Advertising the War   586
   Women's Voices: LIFE ON THE HOMEFRONT   588
   Hollywood's War   589
   Women's Lives: *Rita Hayworth*   590
   Wartime Fashion   591
   All-Girl Players   592
   Women's Voices: JOINING THE BAND   594

Wartime Domesticity   595
   Feeding a Family   595
   Housing Shortages   596
   Homemaking in the Internment Camps   597
   Women's Lives: *Mine Okubo*   600
   Parenting during the Crisis   601

Creating a Woman's Army   602
   The Women's Army   603
   Gender Anxieties in the Women's Army Corps   605

Women's Air Force Service Pilots   607
Prejudice in the Women's Army   608
Demobilization   610

CHAPTER 19   THE FEMININE MYSTIQUE, 1945–1965   616

***Beyond Domesticity*   619**
Rosie Does Not Go Home   619
Working Mothers   621
Challenging Segregation at Work   622

***Cold War Mothering*   624**
Bringing Up Baby   625
Momism   626
The Black Mother and Racism   627
Women's Lives: *Mamie Phipps Clark*   628

***Remaking the American Home*   629**
The Suburb   630
Chinatown   632
The Barrio   634

***The Heterosexual Imperative*   635**
Women's Voices: WOMEN CAN NO LONGER BE TAKEN FOR GRANTED   636
Beauty Icons   637
Sexual Brinkmanship   638
Women's Lives: *Mary Steichen Calderone*   640
Beats and Bohemians   641
Writing Womanhood   642

***Sexual Dangers*   643**
Back-Alley Abortion   643
The Homosexual Menace   645
Lesbian Subcultures   646
Women's Voices: BUTCH IN THE 1950S   647

CHAPTER 20   CIVIL RIGHTS AND LIBERAL ACTIVISM, 1945–1975   652

***The Civil Rights Movement*   655**
Challenging Segregation   655
Women's Lives: *Fannie Lou Hamer*   659
Freedom Struggles   660
Coming of Age in Mississippi   662
Women's Voices: FIGHTING SEGREGATION: AN ORAL HISTORY   663

A Movement Takes Shape   665

Labor Activism   665

The President's Commission on the Status of Women   667

Building a Movement   667

Women's Lives: *Shirley Chisholm*   669

The National Welfare Rights Organization   671

Women's Voices: "WELFARE IS LIKE A SUPERSEXIST MARRIAGE"   672

Agenda for Reform   673

Legislating Equality   674

Education and Athletics   676

Women's Lives: *Patsy Matsu Takemoto Mink*   678

Reproductive Freedom   679

Media and the Movement   680

CHAPTER 21   THE PERSONAL IS POLITICAL, 1960–1980   688

Sexual Revolutions   691

Liberation for All   691

Obscenity Redefined   694

Gay Liberation   695

Women's Voices: LESBIANS IN THE CIVIL RIGHTS MOVEMENT   696

Women's Liberation   696

Women of the New Left   697

Women's Voices: A VIETNAM WAR NURSE WRITES HOME   699

Black Feminism   700

"We Called Ourselves 'Feministas'"   701

Women's Lives: *Audre Lorde*   702

The Woman Warrior   703

Personal Politics   705

Rethinking Heterosexuality   705

Lesbian Feminism   707

Women's Lives: *Kate Millett*   708

The Feminist Art Movement   710

The Women's Health Movement   712

Abortion Activism   714

Family Life, One Day at a Time   715

Women at Work   715

The "Second Shift"   716

Marriage and Divorce   717

The Feminization of Poverty   718

Chapter 22   Endings and Beginnings, 1980 to 2008   724

The New Right   727
    The STOP ERA Campaign   727
    The Pro-Family Movement   729
    Moral Panics and Culture Wars   731
    Embattled Feminists   733
    Women's Lives: *Sandra Day O'Connor*   735
    The Antiabortion Movement   739

Work and Family in the 1990s   741
    Work and Welfare   741
    Gender Gaps   743
    Women's Lives: *Hillary Rodham Clinton*   744
    Caring for the Elderly   747

Global America   748
    New Faces, New Families   749
    The Gulf Wars   751
    Terrorism at Home and Abroad   753
    Global Feminism   755
    Third-Wave Feminism   757
    Women's Voices: A Third-Wave Feminist Analyzes Beauty   758
    Women's Voices: On the Twenty-Fifth Anniversary of *Roe* v. *Wade*   760

    Appendix   A-1

    Glossary   G-1

    Photo Credits   C-1

    Index   I-1

Maps, Tables, and Figures

Maps

1-1 North American Culture Areas, c. 1500   8

1-2 Atlantic Trade Among the Americas, Great Britain, and West Africa during the Seventeenth and Eighteenth Centuries   25

2-1 New Mexico in the Seventeenth Century   35

2-2 New France in the Seventeenth Century   41

2-3 European Colonies of the Atlantic Coast 1607-1639   47

3-1 Demonstrations against the Stamp Act in 1765   77

3-2 North America After the Treaty of Paris 1783   89

4-1 Southern Indian Cessions and Removals 1830s   102

4-2 Louisiana Purchase   112

4-3 Overland Trails 1840s   124

5-1 Lowell, Massachusetts in 1832   135

5-2 American Cities in 1820   138

5-3 American Cities in 1860   139

6-1 Population of the South in 1850   168

6-2 Expansion of Slave States During the Antebellum Period   182

9-1 Union and Confederate States   263

10-1 Dates of Former Confederate States Readmitted to the Union   298

11-1 Land Accession, Treaty of Guadalupe Hidalgo   342

12-1 Patterns of Immigration, 1820-1914   371

13-1 The American Domain, C.A. 1900   422

15-1 Woman Suffrage by State   495

16-1 The Great Migration and the Distribution of the African American Population in 1920   525

17-1 The Dust Bowl   545

Tables

2-1 Life Expectancy at Age 20 for Whites in British North America: North vs. South   56

3-1 Four Largest Cities in British North America   67

5-1 Wages of Lowell Factory Workers   136

10-1 African-American Population during Reconstruction in the States Subject to Congressional Reconstruction   297

12-1 Growing Urban Population   365

12-2 Women Enrolled in Institutions of Higher Education, 1870-1920   380

14-1 Premarital Pregnancy Rate Eighteenth-Nineteenth Century   445

17-1 Median Income of Black Families Compared to the Median Income of White Families for Selected Cities, 1935-1936   547

Overview Tables

Conflicts and Conquest   59

British Measure Leading to the Revolution   78

Acquisition of Territories by British North America and the United States (1760-1860)   101

Types of Women's Work   150

Types of Slave Labor   172

Antebellum Reform Movements   223

Different Approaches to Women's Exercise of Power   248

Amendments to the Constitution and Federal Legislation during Reconstruction, 1865–1875   307

Women's Organizations Formed 1868-1876   315

Major Legislation   676

Abortion Time Line   737

Figures

16-1 Annual Immigration to the US, 1860-1930   508

17-1 Unemployment, 1925-1945   550

18-1 Women's Wartime Work   581

18-2 Women Serving in the American Military   603

20-1 Percentage of Women in Poverty by Race, 1960-1990   671

20-2 Women and the Professions   677

WOMEN'S LIVES

Lady XOC 13

Idia, First Iyoba of Benin 22

Doña Marina 37

Pocahontas 51

Mercy Otis Warren 81

Phyllis Wheatley 87

Sacagawea 113

Gertrudis Barcelo 121

Lily Martin Spencer 144

Sara Parton (Fanny Fern) 158

Mary Randolph Randolph 179

Elizabeth Keckley 186

Mary Gove Nichols 214

Sarah Bagley 219

Frances (Fanny) Wright 234

Jane Cazneau 246

Harriet Tubman 284

Elizabeth Stuart Phelps 287

Myra Colby Bradwell 317

Jennie Collins 320

Laura Ingalls Wilder 349

Susan La Flesche Picotte, M.D. and Susette La Flesche Tibbles 356

M. Carey Thomas 382

Marie Elizabeth Zakrzewska 383

Grace Hoadley Dodge 403

Mary Elizabeth Lease 417

Kate O'Flaherty Chopin 442

Margaret Sanger 453

Charlotte Perkins Gilman 480

Carrie Chapman Catt 490

Georgia O'Keeffe 507

Gertrude "Ma" Rainey 534

Mary Williams (Molly) Dewson 559

Mae West 571

Rita Hayworth 590

Mine Okubo 600

Mamie Phipps Clark 628

Mary Steichen Calderone 640

Fannie Lou Hamer 659

Shirley Chisholm 669

Patsy Matsu Takemoto Mink 678

Audre Lorde 702

Kate Millett 708

Sandra Day O'Connor 735

Hillary Rodham Clinton 744

Women's Voices

Living as a Man   16

Love and Money   18

Conflicts with the Huron   43

A Goodwife   55

Letter to a Father   73

Concerns of an Indian Matron   85

A Cherokee Leader   108

A Missionary's Perspective   125

Motherly Discipline   147

An Irish Immigrant   153

A Slave's Plea   173

A Defense of the South   192

Receiving the Call to Preach   204

Reforming the Men   212

The Importance of College   240

A Religious Defense of Woman's Rights   250

Working for U.S. Sanitary Commission   268

A Confederate Nurse's Story   275

A Slave's Child Remembers Their Quest for Freedom   300

Lecturing on Woman's Rights   310

An Anonymous Mormon Speaks Her Mind   341

Leaving for the Mission School   354

The First Day on the Job   368

Describing Women's Place in the Art World   388

Suffrage Visionary   411

Overseas Missionary   424

Weighing Marriage Against Career   436

"Red Emma" Critiques Marriage   456

Surviving the Triangle Fire   478

A Suffrage Militant   493

"Young Women Seek Advice About Petting"   509

"Feminist—New Style"   519

Dust Bowl Diary   546

Discrimination in the Works Project Administration   565

Life on the Homefront   588

Joining the Band   594

Women Can No Longer Be Taken for Granted   636

Butch in the 1950s   647

Fighting Segregation: An Oral History   663

Welfare is Like a Supersexist Marriage   672

Lesbians in the Civil Rights Movement   696

A Vietnam War Nurse Writes Home   699

A Third-Wave Feminist Analyzes Beauty   758

On the Twenty-Fifth Anniversary of *Roe v. Wade*   760

About the Authors

Mari Jo Buhle

Mari Jo Buhle is William R. Kenan Jr. University Professor and Professor of American Civilization and History at Brown University, specializing in American women's history. She received her B.A. from the University of Illinois, Urbana–Champaign, and her Ph.D. from the University of Wisconsin, Madison. She is the author of *Women and American Socialism, 1870–1920* (1981) and *Feminism and Its Discontents: A Century of Struggle with Psychoanalysis* (1998). She is also coeditor of *Encyclopedia of the American Left*, second edition (1998). Professor Buhle held a fellowship (1991–1996) from the John D. and Catherine T. MacArthur Foundation.

Teresa Murphy

Teresa Murphy is Associate Professor of American Studies at George Washington University. Born and raised in California, she received her B.A. from the University of California, Berkeley and her Ph.D. from Yale University. She is the author of *Ten Hours Labor: Religion, Reform, and Gender in Early New England* (1992) and is currently completing a study about the origins of women's history in the late eighteenth and early nineteenth centuries. She is the former Associate Editor of *American Quarterly*.

Jane Gerhard

Jane F. Gerhard is a visiting assistant professor of History at Mount Holyoke College, specializing in American women's history and the history of sexuality in America. She received her B.A. from Hampshire College in Amherst, Massachusetts, and her Ph.D. from Brown University. She is the author of *Desiring Revolution: Second Wave Feminism and the Rewriting of American Sexual Thought, 1920 to 1982* (2001).

PREFACE

Women and the Making of America writes—and rewrites—the history of women and gender in the United States from the era of the first cultural contact between indigenous peoples and Europeans in the fifteenth century to the new globalism of the twenty-first century. This narrative is organized around an exploration of the dynamics of power—between women and men, as well as among different women. As a result, the chapters in this book return repeatedly to the meaning of diversity in American history; the meaning of sexuality; and the changing nature of gender, of definitions of masculinity and femininity, in the history of the United States. This is an approach that builds on recent interpretive trends that have moved beyond the "separate spheres" paradigm that governed the scholarship in women's history during its formative years in the 1970s. Rather than focusing on the status of women in the shifting relationship between the ostensibly "private" affairs of the family and the "public" dimensions of society and politics, this book recognizes that women cannot be studied apart from the world of politics and diplomacy. Women and issues of gender have been deeply enmeshed in the creation of both society and the political order in the United States.

Women and the Making of America explores the lives of a broad spectrum of women because it recognizes that diversity is a central factor in the history of women and gender. Each chapter explores, in one way or another, how relationships among women were determined by differences of race, ethnicity, class, age, region, or religion. Hierarchies and inequalities occurred within families, communities, and the nation. These differences affected both personal encounters, such as among friends and family, and major institutions, such as education and the labor market. For example, at the end of the nineteenth century, groups of reform-minded white women in the western United States, filled with the fervor of evangelical Protestantism, extended aid and protection to groups of women who shared few of their values or enjoyed little of their power: Chinese prostitutes in San Francisco and Mormon plural wives in Utah. The story that comes into focus is complex, situating missionary women and their clients within a historical context that highlights competing notions of sexuality and agency. This sort of attention to diversity reveals the power dynamics among various groups of women that were central to the overlapping—mutually constitutive—hierarchies that have shaped all women's lives.

Women and the Making of America not only highlights these power dynamics but pays special attention to the history of social activism that addressed inequalities. Women of all groups participated—albeit to varying degrees and in distinctive ways—in political affairs that extended from family to community to nation. By the end of the eighteenth century, groups of women began to form their own organizations for social betterment. By the end of the nineteenth century, many of these organizations came together to create a variety of social movements that made women's diverse voices heard. Even before the passing of the Nineteenth Amendment to the Constitution, which granted women the right to vote, many women found ways to challenge existing dynamics of power and to represent their own interests as members of communities and as women. These more informal challenges necessarily figure prominently in the chapters ahead, recognizing power in the most personal and intimate relationships between men and women and among women themselves.

Women and the Making of America explores the power of these intimate relationships in the historical realm of sexuality. As seen through various lenses—reproduction, health, pleasure, reigning definitions of normality and deviancy, laws, and reform agendas, sexuality serves as an enduring benchmark for assessing power dynamics. From the early-nineteenth-century "passionless" republican mothers to the sexually expressive "women adrift" during the Progressive Era to the celebrants of the 1960s sexual revolution, women often relied on sexuality for their authority. This book explores the meaning of these forms of sexual expression, as well as exploring the female subcultures organized around sexuality. The development of lesbian subcultures in the twentieth century, for example, provides opportunities for exploring the links between gender, sexuality, and social hierarchies.

Women and the Making of America underscores the significance of the United States as a "nation of immigrants." From the appearance of the first European explorers and settlers in the fifteenth century to the recent upsurge and shifting patterns of immigration in the twenty-first century, women have taken part in a larger world system of global exchange in people, trade, and ideas. A continental perspective additionally emphasizes the great expanse of the nation, including shifting boundaries and territorial acquisitions that add to population diversity. Equally important, the rise of the United States as a global power plays a major role in the nation's history, engaging women in military actions and war and forcing them into an international market for goods and services. Within such context, several chapters raise questions about the sources of influence and control within the family, the market economy, and nation state and necessarily foreground issues of citizenship.

Women and the Making of America ultimately explores both the political economy and the sphere of reproduction to shape a narrative. Changing patterns of women's labor, household as well as market, and the relationship of both to issues of power within the family and society at large are central to the stories of diverse groups of women. The achievements of women, individually and collectively, in fields ranging from the arts and sciences, education, and humanitarian reform to politics broadly defined illustrate various dimensions of power. At the same time, conventional signposts in the history of the United States figure prominently. Students new to the study of American history will find these signposts helpful as context; advanced students will find ways to reconstruct and reshape the familiar historical narrative.

SPECIAL FEATURES

Introduction A separate introductory chapter summarizes various approaches to the study of women and gender in history, provides an overview of historiography focused on the scholarship since the 1970s, and introduces the concept of power and explains it as the principal category of analysis. It also provides examples of diversity, sexuality, and global perspective that shape the overall narrative.

Chapter Opening Each chapter begins with a short first-person account that sets the scene for the major themes considered.

Women's Lives Each chapter has two short biographies, which all together highlight the themes of diversity, sexuality, and global perspective. These biographies demonstrate the way the history presented in the main body of the chapter affected individuals.

Women's Voices Each chapter has two primary source excerpts from letters, personal diaries, public statements, or first-person accounts that offer perspectives of well-known or ordinary women on the events considered in the chapter.

Maps, Graphs, Charts, and Tables Maps in each chapter situate the history of women spatially in the United States. Most chapters offer a graph, chart, or table to suggest longer trends.

Overview Tables These special tables provide students with a summary of complex issues.

Photos and Illustrations Each of the photos and illustrations date from the historical period under discussion and aid the student in visualizing the world in which women have lived and the relationships in which they were engaged.

Time Lines Each chapter includes a time line that integrates major events in U.S. history and the special events of women's history.

Review Questions Review questions at the end of each chapter help students review, reinforce, and retain the material in each chapter and encourage them to relate the material to broader issues in American history.

Recommended Reading The works in the short, annotated Recommended Reading list at the end of each chapter have been selected with the undergraduate college student in mind.

Additional Bibliography The Additional Bibliography contains additional readings for both instructors and students interested in pursuing topics in women's history in more depth.

Glossaries A Glossary of Key Terms provides definitions of key concepts.

SUPPLEMENTARY MATERIAL

Instructor's Manual with Test Item File The *Instructor's Manual* contains everything instructors need for developing and preparing lecture presentations, including chapter outlines and overviews, lecture topics, discussion questions, and information about audiovisual resources. It also includes a Test Item File of over 1,500 multiple-choice, short-answer, and essay questions.
ISBN: 0-13-2278040-5; 978-0-13-2278040-9

Test Generator This computerized test management program, available for Windows and Macintosh environments, allows instructors to design their own exams by selecting items from the Test Item File. The Test Generator software is available by download from the Pearson Instructor Resource Center. http://www.prenhall.com/irc

Primary Sources in Women's History A collection of 300 primary source documents and images organized by the content of the chapters in the text.
ISBN: 0-13-227842-1; 978-0-13-227842-3

Prentice Hall and Penguin Bundle Program Prentice Hall and Penguin are pleased to provide adopters of *Women and the Making of America* with an opportunity to receive significant discounts when orders for the text are bundled together with Penguin titles in women's history.

 **http://www.myhistorykit.com** Prentice Hall's exclusive *MyHistoryKit™* offers unique tools and support that make it easy for students and instructors to integrate this online study guide with the text.

Instructors can elect to use a gradebook to monitor student assignments. This helpful student resource is organized according to the main subtopics of each chapter.

 **Research Navigator™** Prentice Hall's Research Navigator™ helps your students make the most of their study and research time. From finding the right articles and journals to citing sources, drafting and writing effective papers, and completing research assignments, Research Navigator™ simplifies and streamlines the entire process.

Complete with extensive help on the research process and three exclusive databases full of relevant and reliable source material including EBSCO's *ContentSelect* Academic Journal Database, the *New York Times* Search by Subject Archive, and Best of the Web Link Library, Research Navigator™ is the one-stop research solution for your students. Take a tour on the Web at http://www.researchnavigator.com.

ACKNOWLEDGMENTS

We wish to thank our collaborators at Pearson/Prentice Hall: Charlyce Jones Owen, Publisher; Charles Cavaliere, Executive Editor; Sue Westmoreland, Executive Marketing Manager; Marianne Peters-Riordan, Production Editor; Carolyn Viola-John, Development Editor, Maureen Diana, Editorial Assistant; Emily Bush, Project Editor.

We wish to also thank the reviewers for providing insightful comments:

Carli Schiffner, *SUNY Canton*

Elizabeth Hayes Turner, *University of North Texas*

Nancy Rosenbloom, *Canisius College*

Kathleen A. Laughlin, *Metropolitan State University*

Michael Goldberg, *University of Washington, Bothell*

Louise Newman, *University of Florida*

Angela Boswell, *Henderson State University*

Margaret A. Spratt, *California University of Pennsylvania*

Joyce L. Broussard, *California State University, Northridge*

Alice Kessler-Harris, *Columbia University*

Jimmie McGee, *South Plains College*

Thomas Dublin, *SUNY Binghamton*

Karen Blair, *Central Washington University*

Margaret Lowe, *Bridgewater State College*

Richard Godbeer, *University of California, Riverside*

Sharon Hartman Strom, *University of Rhode Island*

John McClymer, *Assumption College*

Marguerite Renner, *Glendale Community College*

We authors shared equally in the writing of *Women and the Making of America*. Although we take collective responsibility for the book, we each authored specific chapters. Teresa Murphy wrote chapters 1–8; Mari Jo Buhle wrote chapters 9–15; and Jane Gerhard wrote chapters 16–22.

For assistance in research, our thanks go to John O'Keefe, Laurel Clark, Karen Inouye, Nicole Eaton, and Laura Prieto.

We thank our friends and family for their support: Jean Wood; Susan Smulyan; Paul Buhle; David Stern; and Joel, Max, Nicholas, and Grace Kuipers.

INTRODUCTION

WRITING U.S. WOMEN'S HISTORY
Why History?
Origins of the Field
Standard Approaches to Women's History

FRAMEWORKS OF WOMEN'S HISTORY
The Social Construction of Gender
Public/Private and Separate Spheres
Identity and Diversity

**FUNDAMENTAL ASSUMPTIONS AND
PREMISES OF THIS BOOK**

CLASSIFIED

ACTIVISM

WOMEN
OWNED
BUSINESSES

WHAT'S
NEW

RESOURCES
AND LINKS

E-MAIL

ARTICLES AND
SPEECHES

FEMINIST.
COM♀

WOMEN'S
HEALTH ISSUES

While students today may think it obvious that women have a history worth studying, it was not always the case. Historians of women, beginning at the turn of the twentieth century, had to win a place for their field by establishing that conventional histories neglected women's contributions to U.S. society and too often left out the experiences of ordinary people in the United States. Along with scholars of African American and Native American histories, historians of women participated in larger trends in academic life that altered the definition of what counted as "history."

Home page of Feminist.com website. (Reprinted with the permission of the Women's College Coalition.)

This introduction looks at the origins of the field of women's history, but it does more than historicize the field. It also introduces three central frameworks used by historians to analyze women's diverse experiences: the social construction of gender, public/private spheres, and the category of woman. Last, it introduces the organization and layout of the textbook, highlighting what students can expect to see, read, and learn as they use it.

WRITING U.S. WOMEN'S HISTORY

The field of U.S. women's history has ties to movements for social change, specifically the broad social and political movement—Progressivism—that flourished in the United States between 1890 and 1920 and the protest movements of the 1960s and 1970s. At both moments, teachers and students discovered that the study of history connected them not only to the past but to the future.

Anarchist Emma Goldman, an early advocate for feminism, called for women to be as free as their male counterparts, demanding in a 1897 speech that women required "freedom of action, freedom in love and freedom in motherhood."

Why History?

In 1916, Caroline F. Ware enrolled in Vassar College, where she met a remarkable group of faculty. Her teachers, representatives of the first generation of women to support themselves as "professional" historians, took pride in their rigorous course offerings in historical methodology. They also taught their students, Ware recalled later in life, that the study of history could serve as the "prelude to responsible social action."

Ware's mentor was Lucy Maynard Salmon, who in 1897 published *Domestic Service*, a detailed examination of household workers in the United States. Salmon and her Vassar students had gathered mountains of data on wages, hours, conditions of labor, and relationships with employers—all for the specific purpose of finding remedies for the "social disadvantages" borne by the many women who worked as servants. Although the bulk of the study focused on contemporary conditions, Salmon opened with a lengthy historical review and explained to her readers that insights into the current situation depended on an understanding of the past.

Salmon, who helped to pioneer the new field of women's history, insisted that her own historical research effectively guided her down the path of social reform. Through the administrative offices of the American Historical Association, the major professional society in the field, she worked to promote the study of history in the public school system. She also campaigned steadily for woman's rights, serving on the boards of several suffrage organizations. Much to the dismay of Vassar's president, Salmon encouraged students to demonstrate their own dedication to the cause by holding suffrage meetings on the campus. Meanwhile, Salmon played an active role in civic betterment in the surrounding community of Poughkeepsie, New York.

Carolyn F. Ware, who proudly admitted that she "got her education at Vassar," learned these lessons well. As an undergraduate, she excelled in her coursework and, following Salmon's advice, interned during her junior year at a social service organization in New York. Later, at Harvard University, she chose to write a dissertation on the first modern industry to employ women, cotton textile manufacturing in early New England. Then, after receiving her doctorate, Ware returned to Vassar to instruct yet another generation of women students in the "service ideals" that she had imbibed from her own mentors.

The field of women's history emerged at the turn of the twentieth century as a distinct product of scholar-activists like Salmon and Ware. Wedded to the social idealism of the Progressive Era, these historians determinedly studied various aspects of women's past—work, family, and politics—to provide the requisite knowledge necessary for planning the future, a future when the relationships between men and women would be more equitable than they were during their own times. Despite their innovations and accomplishments, their project had come to a near halt in the late 1920s when first-wave feminism, the movement for woman suffrage that began with the historic meeting at Seneca Falls, New York, in 1848 went into retreat.

In the late 1960s, with the emergence of second-wave feminism, often referred to as the *women's liberation movement*, the field of women's history revived. A new generation of scholars eagerly embraced the mantle of the scholar-activist and set themselves, in their own words, to "constructing usable pasts." This time around, they enlarged the research agenda in new and exciting ways.

In 1969, Roxanne Dunbar unwittingly echoed her predecessors in insisting that, for feminists, "It is not enough that we take collective action. We must know where we come from historically and personally and how we can most effectively break the bonds." Unlike Ware, Dunbar had not found someone like Salmon to inspire her to study history. To the contrary, by the time she had come of age, there were few courses being taught by women professors and none that focused on the history of women. Dunbar instead came to this conclusion through her political activism.

In the 1960s, when Dunbar moved from her home in Oklahoma to the San Francisco Bay Area in California, she found her inspiration in a vibrant movement for social change. This inspiration deepened after she moved to Boston, where she met a group of women who were deeply involved in the women's liberation movement. Together they founded the radical feminist Cell 16 and published *No More Fun and Games: A Journal of Female Liberation*. Ultimately, it was her political activism that led her to deepen her study of history. After receiving a doctorate from UCLA, Dunbar took a position at California State University–Hayward, where she helped to found programs in Native American studies, ethnic studies, and women's studies.

Dunbar and Ware, working in different historical moments, each found a synergy between her study of history and her political hopes. For these two women, history provided new ways to approach pressing contemporary social questions. While individuals studied the history of women in the early years of the century, a critical mass of interested scholars grew in the 1970s, enabling the field of women's history to grow rapidly and achieve a place in the academic world.

Origins of the Field

After nearly a half century of quiescence, the academic study of women across several disciplines took off. In 1969, U.S. colleges and universities offered only seventeen courses on women. A year later, there were more than one hundred women's studies courses; and by 1973 there were more than two hundred. No single feminist organization directed this growth. The courses cropped up spontaneously all over the country, with some campuses implementing new programs in response to sit-ins and strikes conducted jointly by students and faculty. In other places, faculty women privately pressured their departments to sponsor women's studies classes. The first women's studies program was established in 1970 at San Diego State College after a year of intense organizing.

Activist and scholar Catherine Stimpson later recalled that for both faculty and students, the discovery of women's studies was exhilarating and challenging as it often "began with a sense of rupture and estrangement from accepted knowledge" in their academic disciplines. Professional organizations for feminist scholars formed. Journals for feminist scholarship came into existence, including *Signs*, *Frontiers*, and *Feminist Studies*, which worked in tandem with programs and conferences to build the field of women's history. Ann Calderwood, the first editor of *Feminist Studies*, recalled that the journal "grew out of the women's movement at its early, spontaneous and energetic phase, bringing together political commitment and scholarship. Then merely to assert that women should be studied was a radical act."

According to the American Historical Association, the concentration in women's history and gender studies is currently one of the fastest-growing areas of the discipline. Several colleges and universities now offer advanced degrees in women's history, and courses in the area are now offered at most colleges and universities in the United States.

Standard Approaches to Women's History

Perhaps the most long-lived approach to women's history is what scholars in the field term "compensatory." Historians readily acknowledge that women have played only a minor role in history as conventionally defined by men's achievements. For the most part, women have not served as heads of state; generals in armies; or leaders of business, religion, or the arts. However, a few exceptional women have stood out for their distinctive accomplishments.

Many of us have grown up reading biographies about these famous—and occasionally infamous—women. It is now nearly common knowledge that: beginning in 1804, the teenage Sacagawea of the Shoshone tribe helped to guide the Lewis and Clark expedition; in the mid-nineteenth century, activist Dorothea Dix first brought the plight of the mentally ill to public attention and helped create the first generation of U.S. mental asylums; Martha Jane Canary, better known as Calamity Jane, achieved fame as a gunslinger and cross-dresser; and Amelia Earhart drew international attention in 1933 as the first woman to fly unaccompanied across the Atlantic Ocean. However entertaining and rich as appealing anecdotes, biographies of such "women worthies" often tell very little of the lives of the majority of women. To the contrary, such biographies tend to emphasize their subjects' unique or quaint qualities as well as remarkable achievements.

"Contribution" history, a variation on this theme, builds on the premise that women have played important roles in history that have not yet been sufficiently recognized. A popular example of this category, the history of women's participation in social reform, dutifully records their activities in movements ranging from antislavery to the social settlements to civil rights. In such studies, biographies—of Sojourner Truth, Jane Addams, and Ella Baker, for example—once again figure prominently to highlight the activities of the leaders of these important movements.

Like "compensatory" history, a focus on women's contributions sheds little light on the majority of women. We may come to appreciate that a group of women led by Jane Addams and her friend and colleague Ellen Gates Starr in 1889 founded Hull House, the leading social settlement of the Progressive Era. Usually, what we do not learn is the means by which these women managed such an extraordinary feat at a time when the majority of women not only lacked even the right to vote but held no public office outside the realm of local school boards.

In other words, "contribution" history tends to focus narrowly on women's previously unrecognized role in, for example, reform movements but typically fails to examine the ways these women made their way past the many barriers against their participation in the masculine realm of politics. That they devoted much of their lives to improving women's condition usually remains unexamined, figuring only incidentally among their achievements in promoting social betterment in general. In sum, the main "story" of history remains centered on familiar events, such as wars, politics, and presidents' administrations, and men continue to serve as the principal actors. What is unique to the "contribution" approach is the recognition that women have played at least a small role in the standard story of U.S. history.

Perhaps the most enduring topic in the model of contribution history is the woman suffrage movement. Recent U.S. history textbooks provide some coverage of the struggle for the vote, noting its beginning at the Seneca Falls, New York, meeting in 1848 and celebrating its conclusion in the ratification of the Nineteenth Amendment to the Constitution in 1920. The participants themselves in this great campaign inaugurated this tradition by crafting numerous books and essays on the subject dearest to their heart. Moreover, these novice historians did this work not just to gather recollections but to supply future generations with the requisite knowledge to carry on the struggle.

The leading example, still an invaluable resource, is the massive collection of documents compiled over forty years by Elizabeth Cady Stanton, Susan B. Anthony, Matilda Joslyn Gage, and Ida Husted Harper. The unwieldy six-volume *History of Woman Suffrage*, which the editors described as an "arsenal of facts," warrants its prominent status among the "classics" in the field of women's history. Shortly before women won the right to vote, a sympathetic reviewer praised the collection for offering "glowing records of as wonderful women as the world ever saw." Other prominent suffragists also supplied memoirs that

Pilot Amelia Earhart became a celebrity in the 1920s when she became the first woman to cross the Atlantic Ocean in a plane, an act that challenged the ideas that women were too weak for demanding physical and mental tasks.

included vivid descriptions of the campaigns they led. Since 1920, scholars have been building on these early efforts to produce an abundance of excellent books on the topic. Still, especially in U.S. history textbooks, the history of women begins and ends with the campaign for the ballot, thereby relegating to the margins the many other facets of a broader—and unending—movement to expand woman's rights and excluding the history of the majority of women who did not join in the struggle.

Since the late 1960s, when the field of women's history revived alongside second-wave feminism, scholars have created for themselves a much more ambitious agenda. Neither content with the results of "compensatory" or "contribution" histories nor satisfied by the noble accounts of the campaign for suffrage, they have aspired to create a framework suitable for encompassing the lives of women who, for the most part, have been absent in our stories of the past. This ambitious project required a reassessment of the measure of historical significance and what the main story line would ultimately be.

FRAMEWORKS OF WOMEN'S HISTORY

Since the 1960s, historians have created new frameworks for the writing of U.S. women's history. Three frameworks have proved most important to the field. The first is a framework that emphasizes that gender is a product of society and culture, not only biology. The second is that the division of social life into public and private realms simplifies what is in fact a far more complex and dynamic field of social relations. Last is the understanding that women have multiple identities that are rooted in race, class, sexuality, and religion, as well as gender.

The Social Construction of Gender

Historians of women drew from a range of disciplines and none proved more useful than anthropology. Feminist anthropologists gave historians of women an approach to the study of the social construction of gender. Anthropologists demonstrated the wide variety of social roles women played across time and place, including public and private roles. They demonstrated that societies create gender differences differently in different places; that a great variety existed in women's social roles and powers, their public status, and their cultural definitions of femininity; and that the nature, quality, and social significance of women's activities vary more than had previously been assumed. In short, anthropologists offered historians tools for analyzing the links between work, status, and gender.

One crucial insight came from Michelle Zimbalist Rosaldo in her groundbreaking introduction to the anthology *Women, Culture and Society*, published in 1974. Rosaldo set out important distinctions between biological sex and the social construction of gender. She argued that while biology dictates that women lactate and bear children, societies construct—and thus can change—the meanings attached to those biological facts. She and other feminist anthologists argued that woman's ability to

Portrait of Camille Clifford in 1906, the woman who inspired illustrator Charles Gibson's "Gibson Girl," an idealized representation of white femininity that appeared in magazines at the turn of the 20th century.

bear children must be uncoupled from a set of assumptions about woman's nature—assumptions that have gained the appearance of universal truth and have been used to justify women's subordination. Rosaldo wrote, "That women have been seen as wives and more particularly mothers; that their lives have been defined in terms of reproductive functions; that their personalities have been shaped by ties with 'mothers' who in turn are women—all of these are human products that we feel account for women's secondary status."

Rosaldo and other feminist anthropologists found help in the work of Margaret Mead. Mead's study of adolescence and sexuality in *Coming of Age in Samoa* (1928) and *Sex and Temperament in Three Primitive Societies* (1935) demonstrated varieties in the social construction of gender and in women's status. Mead herself was very much a product of the sea change in U.S. gender roles that took place in the 1910s and 1920s, particularly the gains women made in education and in the professions. She graduated from Barnard College in 1923 and was among the first graduates of Columbia University to earn a doctorate in anthropology, which she completed in 1929. Until 1933, Mead studied in New Guinea where she observed three specific cultures: Arapesh, Mundugumor, and the Tchambuli. Each culture displayed distinctive gender roles. In one culture, both the women and men were cooperative; in the second, they were both ruthless and aggressive; and in the Thambuli culture, the women were dominant and the men more submissive. These findings led Mead to propose that masculine and feminine characteristics reflected cultural conditioning (or socialization), not fundamental biological differences. She wrote in *Sex and Temperament* that "If those temperamental attitudes which we have traditionally regarded as feminine—such as passivity, responsiveness, and a willingness to cherish children—can so easily be set up as the masculine pattern in one tribe, and, in another, be outlawed for the majority of women as for the majority of men, we no longer have any basis for regarding aspects of such behavior as sex linked."

While Rosaldo claimed Mead as an important forerunner, she and her peers strove to explain the deeper structures that shaped what they understood as the persistent, cross-cultural devaluation of women. She agreed with Mead that women engaged in a variety of social behaviors. Yet, cross-cultural studies indicated that, despite such variations, women's responsibility for child rearing was so commonplace as to be nearly universal. The conflation of childbearing and child rearing was a situation that tied most women to the "private" sphere of the family while at the same time freed men for "public" activities of society. Rosaldo concluded that "the opposition between domestic and public orientations provides the necessary framework for an examination of male and female roles in any society."

While the structure of private/public spheres explained much, Rosaldo and her peers were keenly aware of the role that ideology played in the production of gender. Saturated in the U.S. world of television, movies, and advertisements on the one hand and that of sermons, marriage experts, doctors, and advice columnists on the other, this generation of feminists appreciated that the representations of gender mattered to men's and women's understanding of themselves as much as did the economic and political dimensions of society. They argued that it was not only the actual division between "public" and "private" but the meanings people express about it that mattered. Rosaldo ultimately concluded that "woman's place in human social life is not in any direct sense a product of the things she does, but of the meaning her activities acquire through concrete social interaction." Building on this insight, feminist anthropologists offered historians of women an important framework for thinking about the public/private distinction as firmly rooted in both material and ideological realms.

Public/Private and Separate Spheres

The public/private distinction and its relationship to gender—the associations between men, masculinity, and the public sphere and those between women, femininity, and the private sphere—gave historians a pliable framework for examining change and continuity in women's history. It enabled historians to examine the ongoing connection of women to domesticity, or the private sphere, which has remained strong, while assessing the significant changes in women's economic, political, and legal opportunities. As the field took off in the 1960s, historians of women wrote accounts of ordinary women in their daily lives framed by their familial roles and responsibilities. They aimed to return both women and the importance of private life to the historical record.

The field of social history, which also took shape in the mid-1960s, proved to be the defining characteristic of recent scholarship on women's history. In choosing topics of everyday life and the experiences of "ordinary" people, social historians contributed new information about the history of the "private" sphere as well as its connection to the public. By using census data and court records, for example, they shed light on the historical dimensions of sex ratios, fertility rates, family size, and various life-cycle patterns, such as age of first marriage, births of first and last children, first menstruation and menopause, and death. They told of the food people ate and the way they procured and prepared it. They provided literacy rates and documented the rise of school systems and coeducation. All of these new explorations shed new light on the "private" sphere of the family and allowed women's historians to redirect the beam to the social relations between the sexes.

Private life, however, comprised more than motherhood and food. Thanks to insights gained from the second wave of feminism, historians of women understood the private realm as one also of conflict and violence as much as pleasure and satisfaction. Historians introduced such topics as birth control and abortion, women's physical and mental health, childbirth and child rearing, sexual pleasure, rape, and domestic violence. That personal and private events, events that took place typically in the home and outside of the purview of public notice, could be part of the historical record drew on and embodied the famous feminist slogan "the personal is political." Personal life and issues of identity had roots in social life and as such could not be classified as merely "personal." To answer questions concerning women's subjective experiences that cannot be found in published sources, historians turned to diaries, letters, memoirs, and other literary sources. Recovering women's voices from the past became a central part of rebuilding a historical record, including the most intimate details, of women's lives. These explorations developed more nuanced accounts of women's difference from men as well as from each other. Historians of women discovered a distinctive culture of women.

Yet, the view of men and women as living in separate and distinctive worlds was also a product of nineteenth-century gender ideology. Historians of the private realm found the notion of "separate spheres" in published essays, diaries, and sermons and adopted it as a way to explain nineteenth-century women's experiences as well as their understandings of themselves as women. Separate spheres neatly mapped gender on to the public/private divide. Men ruled the public world of work and politics, women the private world of home. Yet, so tight was the mapping of gender on to the categories of public and private that the trope, or metaphor, of separate spheres threatened to obscure its function as a discourse of gender. Women never existed purely in the private realm, historians ultimately concluded, and neither were the issues of politics or economy separate from the home.

Women's historians did not study gender as a feature only of the "private" realm. They also studied the role gender played in the public world of work, economics, and politics. Historians demonstrated that the association of women with the realm of family, home, and children affected the entire course of U.S. economic history. From the onset of industrial capitalism in the late eighteenth century through the era of deindustrialization that shaped the last half of the twentieth century, the presumed natural or biological differences between men and women served as the ideological foundation for what has become known as the family wage, the notion that societies thrive only when men earn wages sufficient to meet the needs of their family. A corollary to the family wage is the belief that societies run best when women stay home and tend to the domestic needs of families. Yet, the ideal of the family wage, with its deeply gendered scripts of male breadwinner and female caretaker, rarely captured the complex reality of women's wage work. From the first textile mills of the early nineteenth century to the service occupations that have increasingly sustained the U.S. economy since World War II, women have worked outside the home. Indeed, by the first years of the twenty-first century, women in every age group, from twenty to seventy and more, are much more likely to be working than they were twenty years ago; while men in their prime, that is, between the ages twenty to fifty-four, are less likely to be employed. Still, the nexus of "woman" and "family" remains strong.

New studies of the gendered dimensions of the public sphere underscore that gender is not a concept with relevance only to the private sphere. Rather, it is an analytic tool that casts light on the ways that ideas about masculinity and femininity shape economic, legal, and political systems, not only individuals.

Identity and Diversity

A fundamental building block of U.S. women's history has been the idea that women, in addition to their class, racial, and religious differences, share a common experience of being "women." While central to the enterprise of writing women's history, the category of "woman" has nonetheless been controversial. In the 1970s, feminists argued that women faced a uniquely gendered form of discrimination. This view of women's shared experiences of femininity and of subordination affirmed the idea of the connectedness of women across time and culture. It identified the common and unifying feature of women to be the female body. The female body did not "cause" women's secondary status, but the meanings attached to the female body nearly universally emphasized women's subordination to men. Ironically, the female body—the physical difference between men and women—was understood by many second-wave feminists as the point of origin for both women's oppression and feminist activism. Just as women's biological difference from men served to justify the historical subordination of women to men, that same biological difference, in the hands of feminists, justified political action undertaken to dismantle women's subordination.

Initially, the sense of a shared female identity across culture and history was empowering. However, in asserting the idea that women were oppressed as women and that, therefore, women should band together regardless of other kinds of differences among them, led second-wave feminists into uncomfortable discussions about alternative forms of identity to which women lay claim (such as race, religion, and nation). It raised thorny questions about the essential or fundamental nature of women that held the category together and justified its existence. By the mid-1970s, women of color and Chicana feminists had pioneered an alternative politics of identity that shaped the practice of both feminism and women's history. Feminists of color demanded that activists and scholars alike address the simultaneous and interlocking forms of inequality that shaped women's experiences. Poverty, racism, homophobia, and sexism converged in powerful ways, they insisted, and could not be ranked and ordered.

As a result of minority feminist theory and activism, the field of U.S. women's history questions accounts of women's lives that segregate gender identities from those forged in and through race, class, and sexuality. For example, women in the antebellum South experienced their womanhood in markedly different ways. Enslaved women may have shared the material space of the plantation with their white mistresses, but their experiences of femininity, from childbirth to death, were not at all similar. While free African American and enslaved women tended to children and the needs of their families, they had little control over the material conditions of their lives or that of their children. White women, rich and poor, had more options but often found their privileges undercut by their dependency on men.

Similarly, women's historians have shown that individuals have harnessed notions of womanhood to a wide variety of political aims. When African American Sojourner Truth, a former slave and abolitionist, famously explained in 1851 that "nobody helps me into carriages or over puddles or gives me the best place—ain't I a woman?" she challenged her listeners to come to terms with the different value placed on the femininity of white and black women, of poor and landed whites, of freed and bonded African American women. For Truth, laying claim to respectable womanhood was a savvy political tactic. Elizabeth Cady Stanton, who also blended abolitionism with woman's rights activism, embraced a different tactic. She found that the answer to women's secondary status lay in casting off the limits womanhood placed on woman's rights and choices. In recognition of the nation's 1876 centennial, Stanton proposed that "woman was made first for her own happiness, with the absolute right to herself— to all the opportunities and advantages life affords for her complete development; and we deny the dogma of the centuries, incorporated in the codes of all nations—that woman was made for man—her best interests, in all cases, to be sacrificed to his will." As an educated, white, middle-class woman, Stanton rejected contemporary notions of womanhood as a limitation on her agency and thereby stood in stark contrast to Truth who viewed these notions as a potential resource to be mobilized.

Unity among women, then, is no longer assumed by historians of women. As a field of inquiry, U.S. women's history examines the relationships of power between groups of women at the same time it continues to emphasize the reality that women, as women, face historically specific experiences and oppressions. Far from being a natural difference or biological fact, womanhood is an experience saturated with history and politics.

FUNDAMENTAL ASSUMPTIONS AND PREMISES OF THIS BOOK

In their different ways, both Truth and Stanton would have endorsed a principle that has guided scholars: the importance of recognizing that women were agents of change rather than compliant victims of oppressive circumstances or restrictive ideology. For example, when the first textile factories appeared in the late eighteenth century, women and children constituted the first workforce; and as the system of industrial production expanded in subsequent decades, women continued to staff the mills and assess their situation. In the early 1820s, women weavers in Pawtucket, Rhode Island, protested their low wages and poor conditions, leading to what is considered to be the first strike of factory workers in the United States. Within the family, women also acted forcefully. One historian has gone so far as to trace the rise of "domestic feminism" as evidenced in the declining size of families of the white, urban, middle class in the nineteenth century. Without relying on new contraceptive techniques or mechanisms, women were gaining more control over reproduction, this historian concluded, by assuming the right to determine the timing and frequency of sexual intercourse within marriage. As a consequence, over the course of the nineteenth century, the average number of children per family dropped from seven to four.

In the late 1940s, one of the most distinguished historians in the United States, Mary R. Beard, warned against using "oppression" or "subjection" as a baseline for writing women's history. Such a formulation does disservice to the rich historical record, she insisted. Beard made her case vividly in *Woman as Force in History*, a book illustrating the way "civilization" has depended on women's work and contributions, especially in the realm of private life. It was women, whose primary role has always been the preservation of life, who, in essence, nurtured the development of society from its beginning. Beard emphasized not only women's achievements but went to great lengths to document their enormous contributions to community life that other historians had overlooked in their misguided focus on the nation-state and its male leaders.

Recently, historians of women have continued down this path, once again examining the tremendous role that women have played within their communities. Lacking access to the formal mechanisms of power, women instead formed their own networks of kin and friends to take responsibility for the welfare of the poor and the indigent, the mentally or physically disabled, the unemployed and uprooted, and especially dislocated women and their children. By the early twentieth century, the organizations and institutions they had established were so extensive and well-rooted that they formed the basis of what historians would later term the "welfare state."

The main narrative line of this book builds on these premises, viewing the division between "private" and "public" as important primarily in a rhetorical sense, that is, as a language of gender rather than a description of material reality. Instead, agency or *power* emerges as a central category of analysis. This category facilitates a study of relationships between men and women (rather than a study of women in isolation) as well as relationships among women, either as friends or relatives, and as antagonists. The category *power* also prompts a consideration of the changing nature of those relationships, thereby making gender—masculinity as well as femininity—a central feature of the narrative. Finally, this category recognizes that these relations of *power* are structured as well by other factors. The relationships among women—as determined, for example, by differences of race, ethnicity, class, age, region, and religion—are part of a dynamic history of hierarchy and inequality within families, communities, and nation. This textbook examines how women of varying backgrounds have negotiated their differences both in personal encounters and institutional movements. The category *power* is used to examine the social relationships between men and women, specifically within the realm of sexuality. In line with recent scholarship, sexuality emerges as a major dimension in the history of women and gender. A focus on sexuality, defined through reproduction, women's health, reigning definitions of sexual normality and deviance, and as an enduring benchmark for measuring gender equality, provides an important means through which to analyze changes in women's lives. From the early-nineteenth-century "passionless" republican mothers to sexually expressive African American blues singers of the 1930s, notions of ideal or deviant womanhood often rely on sexuality for their authority. Lesbian subcultures also serve as analytic opportunities to explore the relationship between gender and sexuality.

Photographers and journalists documented the impact of the Depression on communities across the country, like this photo of a breadline in Harlem, New York, in the early 1930s. Such images also record the racial and gendered hierarchies involved in relief efforts.

This book deploys *power*, then, as an expansive category. Individual chapters cover familiar topics, such as the shift of production of goods from home to factory, as events that affected the power dynamics within the family, that is, between husband and wife as well as between parents and children, and as events that reconfigured relationships among women of different social standings, particularly among those who earned wages for their labors, either in the home or in the factory, and those who did not. Individual chapters also highlight topics that have more recently come to the fore of scholarship, such as the role of U.S. women in establishing an imperialist agenda for the United States in the late nineteenth century. Within such contexts, this textbook raises questions about the sources of influence or control within the family, the market economy, the community, and the nation state. Moreover, the analysis of power necessarily emphasizes issues of gender, class, race, and citizenship and illustrates the fluidity between what are conventionally distinguished as the "private" and "public" arenas.

In using power as a category of analysis, this textbook develops a narrative focused on both the sphere of reproduction and the political economy. Of special interest are the changing patterns of women's labor, household as well as market, and the relationship of both to issues of power within the family and society at large. A large component of the text concerns activism and political organization, including such conventional topics as voting rights and unionism. Moreover, the achievements and contributions of women, individually and collectively, serve not so much to lionize these pioneers but to illustrate various dimensions of the operation of power in U.S. society.

However, despite the analytical emphasis on power, the conventional signposts in the history of the United States figure prominently. These signposts provide background for the novice and at the same time serve to orient more advanced students to events encountered in other contexts or courses.

The stories thus unfold in several major sections: the era of exploration and colonization; the American Revolution and the creation of a new nation; the industrialization of the economy and expansion of territories; the Civil War and the abolition of slavery; the expansion of the nation both within the North American continent and overseas; the push toward reform and the increasing participation of women in the labor market; and the consolidation of mass consumer society as shaped by the major events of the twentieth century, including the Great Depression, World War II, the cold war, and the civil rights movements that led up to second-wave feminism. However, at the heart of this organization is a mix of methodologies—an examination of the changing social relationships that constitute the history of women as well as a consideration of social constructions, that is, of gender.

RECOMMENDED READING

Julie Des Jardins. *Women and the Historical Enterprise in America: Gender, Race, and the Politics of Memory, 1880–1945*. Chapel Hill: University of North Carolina Press, 2003. A detailed examination of women in the profession of history, which includes a highly informative chapter on the first women to write and teach on U.S. women's history.

Nancy A. Hewitt. "Beyond the Search for Sisterhood: American Women's History in the 1980s." *Social History* 10 (1985): 299–321. Warns against assuming that what women share in common supersedes the differences based in class and racial inequalities.

Evelyn Brooks Higginbotham. "African-American Women's History and the Metalanguage of Race." *Signs* 17 (Winter 1992): 251–74. A key text on theoretical and methodological issues concerning the place of race in women's history.

Joan Kelly-Gadol. "The Social Relations of the Sexes: Methodological Implications of Women's His-tory." *Signs* 1 (Summer 1976): 809–82. One of the first essays to specify the theoretical dimensions of the project of women's history.

Linda K. Kerber. "Separate Spheres, Female Worlds, Woman's Place: The Rhetoric of Women's History." *Journal of American History* 75 (1988): 9–39. Argues against the notion that men and women actually lived in "separate spheres" and replaces it with an emphasis on rhetoric.

Denise Riley. *"Am I That Name?": Feminism and the Category of "Women" in History*. Minneapolis: University of Minnesota Press, 1988. Offers an analysis of the way rhetorical conventions have helped to fashion our understanding of gender differences, especially as embodied in the term "woman."

Joan Wallach Scott. "Gender: A Useful Category of Historical Analysis." *American Historical Review* 92 (December 1986). Argues that not just women's history but all history can be retold if gender is used as the primary means of analysis.

ADDITIONAL BIBLIOGRAPHY

Mary R. Beard. *Woman as Force in History: A Study in Traditions and Realities*. New York: The Macmillan Company, 1946.

Berenice A. Carroll, ed. *Liberating Women's History: Theoretical and Critical Essays*. Urbana: University of Illinois Press, 1976.

Blanche Wiesen Cook. "The Historical Denial of Lesbianism." *Radical History Review* 20 (Spring/Summer 1979): 60–65.

Martin Duberman, Martha Vicinus, and George Chancey, eds. *Hidden from History: Reclaiming the Gay and Lesbian Past*. New York: NAL Books, 1989.

Lisa Duggan. "The Discipline Problem: Queer Theory Meets Lesbian and Gay History." *Gay and Lesbian Quarterly* 2 (1995): 179–91.

Judith Grant. *Fundamental Feminism: Contesting the Core Concepts of Feminist Theory*. New York: Routledge, 1993.

Mary S. Hartman and Lois Banner, eds. *Clio's Consciousness Raised: New Perspectives in the History of Women*. New York: Harper & Row, 1974.

Nancy Isenberg. "Second Thoughts on Gender and Women's History." *American Studies* 36 (1995): 93–105.

Joan Kelly. "The Doubled Vision of Feminist History." *Feminist Studies* 5 (Spring 1979): 216–27.

Gerda Lerner. *The Majority Finds Its Past: Placing Women in History*. New York: Oxford University Press, 1979.

_____. *Why History Matters*. New York: Oxford University Press, 1997.

Tessie Liu. "Teaching the Differences among Women from a Historical Perspective: Rethinking Race and Gender as Social Categories." *Women's Studies International Forum* 14, no. 4 (1991): 265–76.

Patrice McDermott. *Politics and Scholarship: Feminist Academic Journals and the Production of Knowledge*. Urbana: University of Illinois Press, 1994.

Sue Morgan, ed. *The Feminist History Reader*. London; New York: Routledge, 2006.

Louise M. Newman. "Dialogue: Critical Theory and the History of Women: What's at Stake in Deconstructing Women's History." *Journal of Women's History* 2 (Winter 1991): 58–68.

Karen Offen, Ruth Roach Pierson, and Jane Rendall, eds. *Writing Women's History: International Perspectives*. Bloomington: Indiana University, 1991.

Benita Roth. *Separate Roads to Feminism: Black, Chicana, and White Feminist Movements in America's Second Wave*. Cambridge, UK; New York: Cambridge University Press, 2004.

Daniel Scott Smith. "Family Limitation, Sexual Control, and Domestic Feminism in Victorian America." In *Clio's Consciousness Raised: New Perspectives on the History of Women*, edited by Mary Hartman and Luis W. Banner, New York: Harper & Row, 1974, 119–36.

Carroll Smith-Rosenber. "The Female World of Love and Ritual: Relations between Women in Nineteenth Century America." *Signs* 1 (1975): 1–29.

Manuela Thurner. "Subject to Change: Theories and Paradigms of U.S. Feminist History." *Journal of Women's History* 9 (Summer 1997): 122–46.

Barbara Welter. "The Cult of True Womanhood, 1820–1860." *American Quarterly* 18 (1966): 151–74.

THE TRANS-MISSISSIPPI WEST, 1860–1900

ON THE RANGE AND IN MINING COMMUNITIES
Home on the Range
The Sporting Life
Domesticity on the Mining Frontier

MORMON SETTLEMENTS
The Doctrine of Plural Marriage
"The Mormon Question"
The Woman's Vote in Utah

SPANISH-SPEAKING WOMEN OF THE SOUTHWEST
Landowning Elite
Communal Villagers
Urban Householders

BUILDING COMMUNITIES IN THE HEARTLAND
The Homestead Act and Immigration
Woman's Work, Never Done
Turning Wilderness into "Civilization"
The Patrons of Husbandry

INDIAN WOMEN, CONQUEST, AND SURVIVAL
The Nez Perce
Plains Indians
The Southern Ute

HOW DID the skewed sex ratio on the range and mining frontier affect the position of women?

HOW DID gender relations among Mormons differ from those of other settlers?

WHAT WERE the effects of incorporation on Spanish-speaking women?

HOW DID men and women distribute the work of managing a household on the plains?

WHAT WAS the impact of the Dawes Severalty Act on the status of Indian women?

When courage to look around had at last been mustered, I found that my new home was formed of two wall tents pitched together so the inner one could be used as a sleeping and the outer one as a sitting room. A calico curtain divided them, and a carpet made of barley sacks covered the floor. In my weary state of mind and body the effect produced was far from pleasant. The wall tents were only eight feet square, and when windowless and doorless except for the one entrance, as were those, they seemed from the inside much like a prison.

As I lay in bed that night, feeling decidedly homesick, familiar airs, played upon a

Oglala Sioux performing the Ghost Dance at Pine Ridge, South Dakota, illustration by Frederic Remington, Harper's Weekly, December 6, 1890. (The Granger Collection, New York)

very good piano, suddenly sounded in my ears. It seemed impossible that there could be a fine musical instrument such a distance from civilization, particularly when I remembered the roads over which we had come, and the cluster of tents that alone represented human habitation. The piano, which I soon learned belonged to our captain's wife, added greatly to her happiness, and also the pleasure of us all, though its first strains only intensified my homesick longings.

This lady and myself were the only women at the post, which also included, besides our respective husbands, the doctor and an unmarried first lieutenant. The latter, as quartermaster and commissary, controlled all supplies, could make us either comfortable or the reverse, as he chose. . . .

My housekeeping was simplified by absolute lack of materials. I had, as a basis of supplies, during the succeeding two years, nothing but soldiers' rations, which consisted entirely of bacon, flour, beans, coffee, tea, rice, sugar, soap, and condiments. Our only luxury was dried apples, and with these I experimented in every imaginable way until toward the last my efforts to disguise them utterly failed, and we returned to our simple rations.

Source: Mrs. Orsemus Boyd. Cavalry Life in Tent and Field (New York: J. Selwin Tait & Sons, 1894), as reprinted in Christiane Fischer, ed., Let Them Speak for Themselves: Women in the American West, 1849–1900 (New York: E. P. Dutton, 1978), 11–12, 16.

Frances Mullen Boyd (1848–1926) was one of many Euro-American women who left their childhood homes to journey to the western states and territories in the decades after the Civil War. Just a few months after marrying in October 1867, she joined her husband, a recent graduate of West Point, at Camp Halleck, Nevada, where they set up housekeeping.

Fannie Boyd was just one woman in what was, up until that time, the largest mass migration in history. The discovery of gold in California in 1849 sparked a movement of thousands of people from all parts of the world, making the West the most ethnically diverse region of the United States. Moreover, new communities formed at such an unprecedented rate that by the end of the century nearly one-quarter of the U.S. population lived west of the Mississippi River. The new settlers carved a niche for themselves in the expanding western industries—mining, cattle ranching, and agriculture—and helped to make the western states and territories a crucial element in the growing national economy by furnishing both capital and raw materials.

But contrary to the image of the West popular among some easterners, the trans-Mississippi West was not an unsettled wilderness. The newcomers interrupted and often displaced established communities and helped to destroy centuries-old ways of life. They sparked warfare, brought poverty and disease, and altered the natural environment at the same time that they helped to make the United States the leading industrial nation in the world.

After the completion of the transcontinental railroad in 1869, the trip westward became easier than the one Fannie Boyd endured. Nevertheless, the challenge of making a home in unfamiliar, often harsh surroundings persisted. Some women never adjusted. Other Euro-American women, like Boyd, who had grown up in New York City, demonstrated courage and resourcefulness and adapted to the new setting. Whether they found themselves living, as Boyd did, in the primitive dwellings of an army camp, the complex households of a ranching community, or the hurriedly constructed houses that dotted the plains and prairie, most of these women tried to create and maintain their homes in the wilderness. The doctrine of separate spheres became a prime marker of not only a stable community but "civilization," as measured by their own precepts (see chapter 5). However, their domestic ideals often conflicted with those of other women who were struggling to hold on to their own households amid the aggressive westward expansion of the United States.

ON THE RANGE AND IN MINING COMMUNITIES

The industries that flourished in the trans-Mississippi West—cattle driving, mining, freighting, and lumbering—attracted a disproportionate number of men and encouraged the growth of towns and cities that appeared virtually overnight to cater to their needs and interests. Dodge City, Kansas, and Butte, Montana, for example, were "wide-open" towns where gambling, drinking, and prostitution prospered and where "respectable" women were in short supply. The few women who settled in the region often found fault with its "masculine" character. "The more I see of men," one complainer wrote, "the more I am disgusted with them . . . this is the Paradise of men—I wonder if a Paradise for poor *Women*, will ever be discovered—I wish they would get up an exploring expedition, to seek for one." However, some women relished the opportunity to take on the challenge of a rough and often rowdy environment. Through a combination of luck and hard work, they achieved a degree of financial independence and status rare among their contemporaries back East.

Home on the Range

The two decades after the Civil War witnessed the creation of a spectacular cattle market that produced not only a steady supply of beef for eastern consumers but the legendary Wild West. The muscular cowboy dressed in leather chaps and a broad-brimmed Stetson hat, with a pair of silver-handled pistols strapped to his narrow hips, played the starring role. A few women tapped into this imagery: Annie Oakley was the most famous. Born in 1860 in a log cabin on the Ohio frontier, Oakley was such a skilled sharpshooter by age nine that she was supporting her entire family. In 1885, she joined "Buffalo Bill's Wild West" touring company; and, billed as "Little Sure Shot," she soon became the main attraction. Oakley, like Buffalo Bill himself and his troop of fancy-dressed cowboys, had little to do with cowpunching. They found their niche as well-paid entertainers.

The popular image of cowboys and cowgirls obscured the reality of an exhausting and tedious job that only men performed. Driving a herd several hundred miles from Texas to the stockyards of Wichita or Abilene, Kansas, took a toll on even the strongest young men who made up the workforce. Most cowboys hung up their spurs after only one run. Except for the prostitutes who worked in trailside "hoghouses," very few women made the long drive. Sally Redus once accompanied her cattleman husband, riding side saddle and carrying her baby on her lap all the way from Texas to Kansas. In 1871, Mrs. A. Burks made the journey in a little buggy while her

In this 1900 photograph, Annie Oakley (1860–1926) is shown with some of the many medals she won for sharp-shooting. At the time, she was traveling with Buffalo Bill Cody's Wild West show. Women flocked to see her perform.

husband led a group of Mexican vaqueros. Despite the dangers of stampedes and confrontations with rustlers, she relished both the excitement and her special status as the only woman in camp. "The men rivaled each other in attentiveness to me," she reported, "always on the lookout for something to please me, a surprise of some delicacy of the wild fruit, or prairie chicken, or antelope tongue." Wives of prosperous ranchers, Redus and Burks were in no danger of becoming one of "the fellers."

Back on the ranch, a familiar division of labor prevailed, although most wives crossed over to do men's work when necessary. "The heavy work of the ranch naturally falls to men," a Wyoming woman explained in 1899, "but I think most ranch women will bear me out in saying that unless the women . . . be always ready to do anything that comes along, . . . the ranch is not a success." Not infrequently, husband and wife worked as a team. After her husband died, Elizabeth Collins turned their ranch into such a prosperous business that she became known as the "Cattle Queen of Montana."

For the majority of ranch wives, the daily routine was far more conventional and often very demanding. Women handled the "inside work," that is, the usual domestic chores of housekeeping and tending children. However, if their ranch was large, so too was their household, encompassing perhaps dozens of servants, hired hands and their wives, and perhaps a tutor or schoolteacher for the children, as well as a stream of visitors.

Not all women, especially those who were recent migrants to the West, possessed the emotional or physical stamina for this work. Angie Mitchell, who lived on a ranch near Prescott, Arizona, kept a pistol on the trunk near her bed in response to the regular nocturnal invasion of skunks. More frightening, however, were the bands of stampeding cattle that threatened her insubstantial homestead. "We took a firm hold of our sheets flapped them up & down & ran forward yelling as loud as we could," she reported, while her friends beat a tin pan with a stick and waved their aprons. The cattle, which had been startled by coyotes, swerved just past their flimsy shack before crossing the creek to safety. Two nights later, the cattle panicked again, this time in response to the screaming of mountain lions. Once again, the women rallied and diverted the stampede. "A few more nights of this sort of business," Mitchell concluded, "& we'll all be crazy."

Their daughters, however, often thrived in the wide-open spaces. Rejecting sunbonnets and petticoats for wide-brimmed hats and split skirts, they worked alongside their fathers and brothers, riding horses "clothespin style," roping calves and branding cattle, and shooting guns. One young woman reported that her grandmother, after visiting their ranch near Laramie, Wyoming, complained that her father was "making a boy out of me." However, such fears did not hold back the many young women who relished "outside work."

The Sporting Life

As many as fifty thousand women in the trans-Mississippi West sold companionship as well as sex in burgeoning cities like San Francisco and Denver and in the many small, makeshift towns and mining camps. Although few conformed to the myth of the racy madam who made a fortune or the dance-hall girl with a heart of gold, prostitutes did play important parts in shaping the culture and institutions of western cities. A vivid example of the division of labor by gender, their trade nevertheless undermined some of the treasured tenets of the doctrine of separate spheres by making certain behaviors usually associated with marriage major items of commerce.

With men far outnumbering women in mining camps, on the range, at military forts, and in the towns that sprang up along the freight routes, prostitution supplied women with the largest source of employment outside the home. Prostitutes traveled first from Mexico, Brazil, and Peru and later from other regions of the United States and from Europe, Australia, and China. As the lyrics of a mining song from Butte, Montana, where the first hurdy-gurdy house opened in 1878, attested: "First came the miners to work in the mine./ Then came the ladies to live on the line."

Chinese prostitutes, often kidnapped as girls or sold by their impoverished fathers to procurers, served the nearly thirty-five thousand Chinese men who had immigrated to the American West in search of the "Gold Mountain." Called "Chiney ladies" or "she-heathens" by their white patrons, and "wives to a hundred men" by their Chinese patrons, these women worked in big cities like San Francisco but also in the remote mining towns. The Page Law of 1875, implemented by the federal government in response to rising anti-Chinese prejudice, targeted prostitutes and effectively halted the immigration of all Chinese women. Nevertheless, as late as 1880, nearly half of the prostitutes in the mining town of Helena, Montana, were Chinese.

In general, prostitutes represented a stratified, ethnically diverse, and youthful population. The most impoverished Indian women turned to prostitution after mining operations encroached on their settlements and drove them to the brink of starvation. However, the majority of prostitutes were native-born white women. Prostitutes ranged in status from the lowest, the women who plied their trade on the street, to the higher-class ladies who worked in brothels. Yet, the majority of prostitutes remained flexible, picking up paying customers wherever they could. Having grown up in poverty, many accepted hard work, even servitude, as their fate.

Although prostitutes routinely practiced some form of birth control, such as the use of pessaries and douches, and frequently terminated pregnancies by abortion, many gave birth. However, motherhood was rare. Local authorities would not allow children to live in the red-light districts, even if it meant sending them to the county poor farm.

A few "soiled doves" managed to become rich as well as notorious by running profitable bordellos. A successful Denver madam explained, "I went into the sporting life for business reasons and for no other. It was a way for a woman in those days to make money and I made it." In addition, the "summer women," the prostitutes who moved into the mining camps or cattle towns during the busy season, could earn wages in just a few months that far exceeded the annual income of local retail clerks or domestic servants.

Although highly publicized, such success stories were rare and became increasingly so by the turn of the century. By that time, town officials had responded to the demands of the "respectable" citizenry and forced many prostitutes out of business. The majority of prostitutes responded to diminishing opportunities and increasing threats of arrest by quitting. Those who chose to persevere often turned for protection to men who, for a large cut of their earnings, acted as pimps and solicitors. Addicted to drugs or alcohol, often infected with syphilis or tuberculosis, many had little choice but to live out their lives in the trade. Prostitutes commonly lived in destitution and faced an early, sometimes violent death. Suicide rates were especially high.

Domesticity on the Mining Frontier

The discovery of gold in California in 1848 encouraged a huge number of men and very few "respectable" women to seek their fortune in the West. Women and children made up less than 5 percent of the newcomers to the region. Most wives, known as "gold rush widows," stayed home waiting for their husbands' case of "gold fever" to run its course. Some wives, however, refused to be left behind. In the 1860s and 1870s, when reports of new rushes in Colorado, Montana, and Idaho spread eastward as far as Europe, these women decided to brave the harsh conditions of the mining frontier. They risked arrest by putting on men's trousers, grabbed a pick or a drill, and joined their husbands in the pursuit of Eldorado.

However, the majority of these adventurers were neither prospectors nor prostitutes but housekeepers, although distinctions were not sharply drawn. In the central Arizona mining district, for instance, where in the 1860s small towns sprang up around the goldfields, Mexican women adapted a long-standing folk custom and became the temporary companions of either Mexican or Anglo miners. In contrast, the Anglo women who lacked a tradition of informal unions rarely cohabited with men who were not their husbands and even more rarely crossed racial lines to do so. However, in either case, transgressions were easily overlooked. "We never ask women where they come from or what they did before they came to live in our neck of the woods," one Montana woman explained. "If they wore a wedding band and were good wives, mothers, and neighbors that was enough for us to know."

In the early days of settlement, mining camps and towns afforded women opportunities to bridge the customary division of labor by gender. In Helena, Montana, for example, one of every five adult women in 1870 worked for wages outside the home. Many took advantage of their domestic skills to run boardinghouses and restaurants, to work as shopkeepers, and to teach school. In many communities, they often competed with the Chinese men who had gained a toehold in the laundry business. "True there are not many comforts and one must work all the time and work hard but [there] is plenty to do and good pay," one woman wrote home from Nevada City. "It is the only country that I ever was in where a woman received anything like a just compensation for work." But even on the mining frontier, the overwhelming majority of married women preferred the familiar role and "kept house."

Housework, however, rarely provided the satisfaction of a job well done. The dirt and grime of makeshift towns proved implacable enemies, and even basic supplies like soap and butter were often in short supply. Equally important, in towns where nine of every ten residents moved within a decade, and where men outnumbered women five to one, many housewives found it very difficult to recreate the circle of female friends and family that in other regions made domesticity a social enterprise. "I never was so lonely and homesick in all my life," a young wife of a Denver prospector complained. However, most housewives eventually learned to cope with such unfavorable conditions, often by becoming more inventive and self-reliant.

On the mining frontier, as throughout the trans-Mississippi West, marriages dissolved at a higher rate than in other parts of the United States. Hard-rock miners faced both erratic employment and extremely dangerous conditions, and many women were abandoned by restless husbands or widowed early. Contemporaries routinely commented on the "very liberal" divorce laws in the new states and territories, noting that men and women rarely stayed married against their wills. In 1867, in one county in Montana, divorces actually outnumbered marriages.

In the face of such uncertainties, women looked outward to their communities and established various civic institutions to protect their families. In the 1880s, in Candelaria, Nevada, known as a "good sporting town," the miners supported thirteen saloons and not a single church. Fistfights and even murders were common. No wonder that women organized themselves to impose some semblance of order. In Helena,

The discovery of gold in 1897 in the Yukon region of Canada prompted as many as 100,000 fortune-seekers to head for the region. One in ten participants in the Klondike Gold Rush, as this movement was called, was a woman. As one adventurer reported: "when our fathers, husbands and brothers decided to go, so did we, and our wills are strong and courage unfailing. We will not be drawbacks nor hindrances, and they won't have to return on our account."

Montana, for example, at least half of the pioneering generation of women supported some kind of reform society. They campaigned vigorously for temperance and against prostitution, sponsored schools and libraries, and formed religious and benevolent societies. One woman reporting from Virginia City in 1869 claimed that "the entire religious and social life of Nevada is conducted by the ladies." "The lords of creation," she insisted, were "mere money-making machines, with apparently no other human attributes than a hasty appreciation of a good dinner, the hope of a fortune, and a home 'at the bay' [San Francisco], or in the dimly remembered East." The second generation of women advanced even more rapidly to leadership positions in their communities, often forsaking marriage and family to work full time for civic betterment.

Greatly outnumbered during the early days of settlement, women eventually made an impact on their communities and often explored opportunities for self-support that would have been unavailable to them in other regions of the country. Western expansion fostered such possibilities for some women, but it also placed new restrictions on established communities, especially those with households that varied from the emerging norms.

MORMON SETTLEMENTS

In the 1840s, Joseph Smith, the founder of the Church of Jesus Christ of Latter-day Saints, claimed an angel had told him that it is "the will of Heaven that a man have more than one wife." After newspapers exposed and ridiculed this revelation, Mormons became the targets of persecution and violent physical attacks. Forced to abandon their prosperous settlement in Nauvoo, Illinois, a group led by Brigham Young migrated to the Great Salt Lake Basin in 1846. In the Utah wilderness, they rebuilt their exclusive community. By 1870, Mormon missionaries had recruited settlers from the East and from as far away as Scandinavia, and their population exceeded eighty-seven thousand. And unlike other western territories, Utah could boast a sex ratio that was nearly equal.

plural marriage The Mormon custom of taking more than one wife in order to maximize the number of children.

Plural marriage quickly became one of the defining characteristics of the Mormon community. Brigham Young, the first territorial governor and president of the Church of Jesus Christ of Latter-day Saints, wedded twenty-seven women and fathered fifty-six children. However, even at its peak, polygamy was practiced by no more than 15 percent of Mormon families, and the majority of male practitioners took only two wives. Nevertheless, plural marriages affected all members of the community, always remaining a possibility and serving as an important symbol of their spiritually unique way of life.

The Doctrine of Plural Marriage

As sanctioned by their faith, Mormon families were strictly patriarchal, and a woman's spiritual salvation depended on her relation to her husband. If their marriage were "sealed" as a "celestial marriage," it would last through eternity and qualify both husband and wife for the highest degree of spiritual glory, exaltation. However, all Mormons bore a unique responsibility: to serve the needs of the ethereal spirits who required a mortal body to prove themselves worthy of salvation. Brigham Young proclaimed it "the duty of every righteous man and every woman to prepare tabernacles for all the spirits they can." Thus, a woman's spiritual destiny was determined in part by the number of "tabernacles"—that is, children—she brought into this world. In turn, men aspired to take at least two wives, each ideally bearing between seven and eight children.

Among the minority of Mormons who practiced polygamy (more precisely, polygyny, for only men were allowed more than one spouse), families functioned much like families in other regions of the West. Wives sometimes shared a single home, each keeping her own bedroom and together sharing common household chores and child rearing. Occasionally, if the husband were sufficiently wealthy, his wives lived in separate homes and even in different towns. Plural wives sometimes formed strong bonds, although it was not unknown for jealousy to figure into these relationships, especially if their husband favored one wife over others. However, in other aspects of family life, such as fertility and divorce rates, Mormons deviated little from the average.

Like other newcomers to the western territories, women expected to work hard. Women spun and wove cloth, made clothing, and tended household gardens. In the face of the enormous challenge of growing crops in the semiarid land, women joined men in planting and harvesting and often in the vital work of irrigation. It was not uncommon for a wife, particularly a first wife, to manage the household in her husband's absence and often for long periods. Church leaders explicitly encouraged women to be competent and to teach their daughters to be self-reliant.

The church invited women to work outside the home as a means to strengthen the local economy. By the late 1860s, women were running cooperative stores for the sale of homemade products; eventually, they were overseeing a successful silk manufacturing industry. Women also formed female relief societies, which sponsored religious programs, such as Bible readings and lectures, and administered local charities.

"The Mormon Question"

By the time of the Civil War, the population of the Utah territory was growing quickly enough to warrant a bid for statehood; from the perspective of the Christian Northeast, the prospect of a new state that promoted polygamy—allegedly a "relic of barbarism"—was intolerable. The popular press and government officials likened polygamy to slavery and portrayed plural wives as hapless victims of male lust. In 1862, Congress passed the **Morrill Anti-Bigamy Act**, which made plural marriage a federal crime. Nevertheless, because Mormons did not publicly record second or subsequent marriages, and because juries in Utah typically refused to enforce the new law, the Morrill Act had little impact on Mormon communities.

Morrill Anti-Bigamy Act Passed by Congress in 1862, this legislation made plural marriage a federal crime.

With the completion of the transcontinental railroad in 1869, which brought new settlers to the territory, Mormon marriage practices once again attracted national attention. President Ulysses S. Grant pledged to eradicate polygamy; and his successors—Hayes, Garfield, and Arthur—concurred, all taking up the "Mormon Question" in their annual messages to Congress.

The bulk of the commentary focused on Mormon women. The former abolitionist Harriet Beecher Stowe equated polygamy and slavery and waged a new campaign "to loose the bonds of a cruel slavery whose chains have cut into the hearts of thousand of our sisters." The popular Civil War orator Anna Dickinson, who visited Salt Lake City in 1869, returned to the East with a new lecture in her repertoire, "White Sepulchers," in which she described the debasement of plural wives by sexually craven men. Like many other critics, she alleged that Mormon women had been either seduced or tricked into a relationship no better than prostitution.

Mormon women refuted these charges. In 1870, when Senator Shelby M. Cullom of Illinois introduced a bill in Congress that would strip Mormon men of the bulk of their rights as citizens should polygamy continue to prevail in Utah, Mormon women staged mass demonstrations to protest this "mean, foul" legislation. One spokeswoman praised the outpouring of women for giving "lie to the popular clamour [sic] that the women of Utah are oppressed and held in bondage." To those who would abolish the Mormon way of life, she charged: "[W]herever monogamy reigns, adultery, prostitution, free-love and foeticide [abortion], directly or indirectly, are its concomitants. . . ." Mormon women, she insisted, look upon polygamy as a "safeguard" to these common evils.

The Woman's Vote in Utah

The protest by Mormon women had also undermined a novel plan to curtail the practice of polygamy. Several members of Congress proposed enfranchising Utah's women, assuming that Mormon women, if given a chance, would use their votes to eradicate polygamy. The "great indignation meeting" of five thousand angry women protesting the **Cullom Bill** quickly put this plan to rest. However, for their own purposes, the Mormon-controlled territorial legislature gave the ballot to the women of Utah in February 1870.

Cullom Bill Introduced into Congress in 1870 to strengthen the provisions of the Morrill Anti-Bigamy Act, which had been largely ignored during the Civil War.

Within the week, according to Brigham Young, twenty-five women voted in municipal elections in Salt Lake City, proving to the world that Mormon women were no slaves to a religious patriarchy. Moreover, these women wielded their new political power primarily to show themselves as willing participants in plural marriage. Equally significant, by placing women on the roster of eligible voters, Mormons had increased their representation in territorial elections to more than 95 percent.

A leading suffragist and longtime friend of Susan B. Anthony, Emmeline Blanch Wells (1828–1921), front and center, poses with five sister wives. Wells played a prominent role in the Salt Lake City Relief Society and served as editor of the Women's Exponent, *a journal that vigorously defended the practice of plural marriage.*

These events took the national woman suffrage movement off guard. The leaders greeted the enfranchisement of Utah women as a major victory for their side. Elizabeth Cady Stanton and Susan B. Anthony made a long journey to Utah in 1871 to celebrate; a representative of the American Woman Suffrage Association likewise visited Salt Lake City. Yet, all this goodwill could not obscure the fact that most suffrage leaders detested the association of their cause with plural marriage. With Victoria Woodhull whipping up controversy by advocating free love, neither the NWSA nor the AWSA could afford to be linked to yet another heterodox position on marriage.

In 1882, after Congress passed the Edmunds Act outlawing "bigamous cohabitation," a major movement for the disfranchisement of Utah women gained force. Antisuffragists insisted that Mormon women, in casting their votes, simply obeyed their husbands' dictates, thus proving that women in general were unprepared to take on responsibilities of citizenship. Meanwhile, several Mormon women who had abandoned their faith and former plural wives—including a woman known as "The Rebel of the Harem," an estranged plural wife of Brigham Young—added fuel to the fire by publishing shocking accounts of sexual bondage. Finally, in 1887, Congress passed the **Edmunds-Tucker Act,** simultaneously disincorporating the Mormon church and disenfranchising the women of Utah.

Although suffragists formally protested the antisuffrage clause of the Edmunds-Tucker Act, they did so only halfheartedly. The *Woman's Journal* called woman suffrage in Utah a "sham of freedom." Moreover, suffragists adamantly refused the requests of Mor-

Edmunds-Tucker Act
Legislation disincorporating the Mormon church and disenfranchising supporters of polygamy, including women.

WOMEN'S VOICES

AN ANONYMOUS MORMON SPEAKS HER MIND

The editor of the Anti-Polygamy Standard, *Jennie Anderson Froiseth, collected stories by apostate Mormon women, that is, by women who had abandoned their faith to illustrate the abuse and degradation they allegedly endured under the system of plural marriage. "If the wives and mothers of America could only be made aware of the extent and character of this degradation of their sex . . ." she explained, "the onrushing tide of public sentiment, once set in motion, would sweep away the curse of polygamy in a single year."*

My husband and self became converted to Mormonism in the Eastern State through the preaching of a traveling missionary. We were both enthusiastic converts, and speedily removed to Zion, bringing with us two little ones and a fair share of this world's goods. While on the plains, we heard of the doctrine of polygamy; but I was in such an abnormal state of mind, being so completely infatuated with the new religion, that I received the announcement of the revelation with comparatively little astonishment. . . .

Of course, after we had been in Zion for awhile my husband was admonished to "live his religion." When I found the cross likely to come home to me, although I began to feel very different about it, I had still sufficient faith in the system as a divine principle, not to violently oppose my husband. I told him it would break my heart to see another supersede me in his affections; but that I loved him too well to peril his future glory, and prevent his exaltation in the next world, consequently I would sacrifice my own feelings, and not oppose him, if he would promise me solemnly that I should always be first in his esteem and regard. . . .

The young bride was brought home to my house, and became one of our family, no provision for separate housekeeping being made for her. I tried to feel kindly toward her; for after I had consented to the marriage, I was woman enough to try and treat her well; although, at times, the very sight of her at my table, or sitting in my little sewing-room with my husband at her side, almost drove me wild with jealousy, even before I perceived that she was using all her arts, and every means at her command, to win his affections from me. She was a true daughter of her father, a man who stepped on hearts as if they were stones, and little by little, I discovered how she was ensnaring my husband, getting him so completely in her power, and under her control, that he seemed to have no thoughts for any one but her. In less than six months, her influence over him became so strong that he did her bidding as if he were a mere child, while wife and little ones were totally neglected. When he entered the house, he would rush off to her apartment, unmindful of me, or the children whom he had always met with a smile and a kiss. I cannot describe the change that came over our home in those few months; and when I found that I, his true and loyal wife, who had left home, friends, and kindred to follow him to the promised land, was being neglected and almost totally discarded for a girl whose name we did not even know one short year before, I became nearly insane with grief and remorse. I suffered the bitterest kind of remorse, for in reality I was more to blame in the outset than he; and I could not disguise from myself the fact that I had dug a grave, and buried my happiness with my own hands.

Source: *Jennie Anderson Froiseth, ed.,* The Women of Mormonism: Or, The Story of Polygamy as Told by the Victims Themselves *(Detroit: C. G. G. Paine, 1882), 77–78.*

Questions

1. How does the selection of the "second wife" take place, according to this report?

2. How do we interpret this document given its purpose to expose the evils of plural marriage?

mon women to defend plural marriage. By this time, the woman's vote in Utah had become a liability to the suffrage movement—just as polygamy had become a liability to the Mormon Church. In 1887, the Mormon leadership announced that the church would no longer sanction plural marriage, thus clearing the way for admission of Utah to statehood.

After enjoying voting rights for seventeen years, Utah women would not give up the ballot graciously. The most militant formed the Utah Territory Woman Suffrage Association and spearheaded a vigorous campaign. When the state was finally admitted to the Union in 1896, Utah women regained the right to vote and won the right to hold public office.

SPANISH-SPEAKING WOMEN OF THE SOUTHWEST

"My life is only for my family," wrote Adina de Zavala in 1882. "My whole life shall be worth while [sic] if I can render happy and comfortable the declining years of my parents and see my brothers safely launched on life's troubled seas." This San Antonio matron paid tribute

MAP 11-1 LAND ACCESSION, TREATY OF GUADALUPE HIDALGO

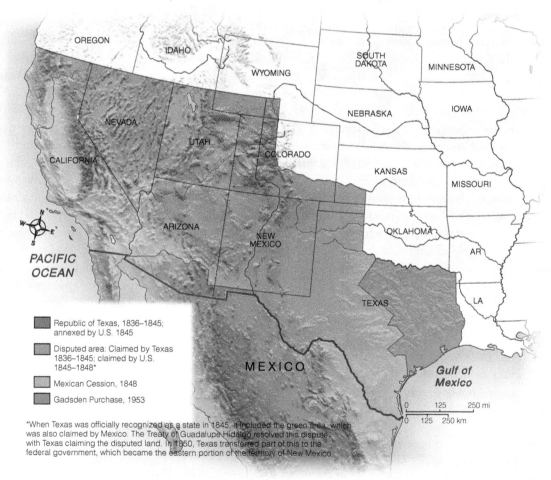

By the terms of the Treaty of Guadalupe Hidalgo, which marked the end of the war between the United States and Mexico in 1848, Mexico ceded large parts of its land to the United States.

to *la familia,* that is, the enduring bonds of affection and duty extending from biological kin to close friends that characterized Mexicano settlements in the region that came to be known as the American Southwest. They respected the authority of their husbands—*machismo*—and revered marriage and motherhood as the primary source of a woman's self-affirmation and esteem. However, in daily life, the actual behavior of Spanish-speaking women often diverged from these ideals. Moreover, by the 1880s, Anglos were settling in the Southwest in such great numbers that old mores could not survive intact.

> **la familia** Spanish expression denoting the enduring bonds of affection and duty extending from biological kin to close friends.

During the last half of the nineteenth century, Spanish-speaking women were drawn into the processes of incorporation into the United States (see chapter 4). In 1848, the Treaty of Guadalupe Hidalgo, which marked the end of a war between the United States and Mexico, granted to the United States half of all Mexican territory—what would become the states of California, Arizona, Nevada, and Utah, most of New Mexico, and parts of Colorado and Wyoming. In 1853, the United States purchased an additional strip of land between El Paso and the Colorado River that rounded off the accession of all the land north of the Rio Grande River. The Mexicanos who lived in this region were formally guaranteed the "free enjoyment of their liberty and property" as citizens of the United States, although Anglo developers and land speculators soon took over the local economy. By the 1880s, Anglo-owned industries, including rairoads, lumber mills, and mines, and the transformation of subsistence agriculture into a thriving commercial enterprise had effected dramatic changes that encompassed *la familia* and women's role within the Mexicano household.

Landowning Elite

Through the 1870s, elite Spanish-speaking women continued to benefit from the well-established practice of intermarriage with Anglos as well as from the customary right to accumulate property jointly with their husbands and to inherit and maintain property in their own names (see chapter 4). Following the United States–Mexican War, this long-standing Spanish tradition was incorporated into the legal system of several southwestern states, including Texas, where big cattle ranches flourished. Several wealthy Texan widows took their place among the largest landowners in the state, registering their own cattle brands as well as filing homestead claims with the county courts.

One Texan woman profited immensely from these customs and stood out among the wealthiest citizens of the state. Salome Balli had come from a large landowning family, and during the years of her marriage to an ambitious Anglo, John Young, she expanded her holdings many times over. In 1860, newly widowed but still a young woman of twenty-nine, Balli owned the title to land worth more than one hundred thousand dollars, a veritable fortune at the time.

However, only the wealthiest women benefited from this system. The majority of women, like their male contemporaries, fared less well with the rise of Anglo-owned commercial ranching and agriculture. In the Lower Rio Grande Valley, for example, where Mexicanos outnumbered Anglos, they lost the bulk of their property to Anglos who were better equipped to manipulate the new court system. While their husbands and sons found themselves herding cattle or tending sheep and goats for Anglo landowners,

A woman of the Mexican upper class, as this portrait indicates, had access to fine clothing and expensive jewelry. Her personal finery marked her family's status in the community.

Mexicanas worked as domestic servants, cooks, gardeners, or field hands. It was not uncommon for whole families to join the ranks of migrant workers, finding a meager source
of income as pickers in the cotton fields of South Texas.

Communal Villagers

Well before the United States–Mexican War, in an effort to encourage settlement in
what had then been the northern outpost of the nation, the Mexican government had
conferred communal property rights to groups that petitioned for land. After the accession of this region by the United States, thousands of Mexican families continued
to live and work in villages scattered throughout the mountains and deserts of northern New Mexico and part of Colorado. The women who lived in these communal villages of small-scale cattle and sheep herders enjoyed similar benefits of inheritance
and property rights but nevertheless lived very different lives from those of the elite
landowners.

As in other agricultural communities, Mexicanas cared for the home and maintained nearby a small garden plot and perhaps a patch of land reserved for a few graz-
ing sheep and goats. Their husbands in turn took responsibility for the heavy outdoor
labor, such as herding sheep and cattle and plowing the fields. The community as a
whole shared the principal resources, including the large pastures and water supply,
and took collective responsibility for their maintenance. Men and women also pooled
their labor. Women often worked in groups to prepare foodstuffs, spin wool, and plas-
ter their adobe homes, an annual chore; and men worked together in the physical and
seasonal labor typical of agricultural economies. Men also managed the external trade,
selling grain and livestock on the open market.

By the 1880s, the transcontinental railroads that passed through this region served as
a catalyst of change in the work of men and women. Anglos came in great numbers, bringing new commercial opportunities for men. Mexicanos took advantage of a growing cash
economy, finding jobs on the railroads and in the mines. They also worked for Anglo
ranchers, digging irrigation ditches and herding sheep and cattle. While the actual tasks
were often familiar, the location and exchange of labor for cash were not. Men now left
their villages for long stretches of time, hoping to earn enough money to keep up with rising taxes and household expenses. Left behind, women assumed more responsibilities.

Although religious and ethnic traditions continued to support the patriarchal authority invested in *machismo*, the new economic arrangements worked against old customs. With men absent for months at a time, women gained power in their family and
community. Women took on the work of herding sheep or tending the communal
fields. Equally important, they strengthened their own networks.

Women's networks, which were rooted in kin relationships, extended far into the
tightly knit neighborhoods. For example, most married women maintained very strong
ties with parents and in-laws. Grandparents customarily served as godparents for a
family's first- and second-born children; they were called *comadres* and *copadres*, and
their responsibilities often included child rearing. Godparents not only officiated at
christening services, a common Catholic custom, but also acted as surrogate guardians.
Maternal grandparents usually served as godparents for the first child, paternal grandparents for the second, and then other relatives and friends assumed these important
roles. In this fashion, kin and kith became links in a network of reciprocal obligations,
which in the absence of men became women's sole domain.

While men were away, women also took responsibility for the physical and spiritual well-being of the village. Some older women whose children were grown served as midwives, delivering babies, caring for new mothers, and acting as counselors to the whole village. Even within the male-dominated Roman Catholic Church, the locus of spiritual life from baptism, feast days, weddings, and burial, village women played unusually prominent roles. Although men sustained the *Penitentes*, a religious and mutual aid society known for its flagellant practices, women carried out their own rituals and formed auxiliaries to men's societies. They prevailed in religious ceremonies during May, the month devoted to the Blessed Virgin Mary. In general, **Mariolatry** muted the masculine character of many rituals and legitimated women's participation in church affairs. So, too, did the chronic shortage of priests.

As Anglos encroached on their land and drew more and more villagers into the market economy, even the determination of women could not save the community. Whole families began to pull up stakes, heading for the burgeoning towns and cities where women joined men in the expanding system of wage labor.

Mariolatry Worship of the Virgin Mary as religious practice within the Roman Catholic Church.

Urban Householders

In the decades following the United States–Mexican War, the new Anglo settlers drove out many longtime Mexican residents, reducing the Hispanic population by as much as half in southwestern cities such as San Antonio, Texas. However, by the end of the century, this trend had reversed. Expanding trade and industry worked like a magnet, attracting not only Mexicanos from the communal villages but also many immigrants from Mexico. Single women and widows in particular took advantage of expanding opportunities for wage work, flocking to Texas cities as well as to well-established urban enclaves such as Santa Fe, Albuquerque, Tucson, and Denver. They moved in such numbers that before the century ended, the majority of Mexican Americans had become urban dwellers.

Upper-class Spanish-speaking women often came from families that had lived in these cities for generations; they considered themselves distinct from the growing populations of *mestizos*, Mexicans of mixed Spanish and Indian blood; and they tended to identify with Spain rather than Mexico (see chapter 4). They maintained their high status by spearheading the emerging consumer culture, although by the 1880s even women in the communal villages had access to sewing machines, cook stoves, and manufactured furniture. Wealthy women, however, ordered their furnishings and fashions from prominent retailers, such as Bloomingdale's in New York. If they enjoyed a status comparable to that of the Amadors family in Las Cruces, New Mexico, they sent their children to English-language schools and perhaps traveled to Chicago to take in the World's Fair of 1893.

At the other end of the social scale were the women who had fled rural poverty to build a better life for themselves and their family in the city. They lacked the means to enjoy the new consumer goods and instead found themselves barely able to scrape by on the wages they could earn as cooks, domestic servants, seamstresses, or laundresses for wealthy Anglo or Hispanic families. Old customs died hard, however, and many of the newcomers supplemented their wages by maintaining small backyard gardens. Mexicanas staffed the open markets, selling produce, bowls of chili, baked goods, and handicraft. Overall, though, few women earned more than subsistence and, as a group, far less than men. The move to the city usually made Mexicanas dependent on their husbands for support, unraveled the networks that had sustained them in the communal village, and ultimately reduced their power within both the family and community.

Despite such setbacks, Mexicanas continued to play important roles in preserving old traditions, including their allegiance to the Roman Catholic Church. Their families continued to baptize their children, celebrate the feast day of their patron saints, mark the transition from girlhood to womanhood at age fifteen by the *Quinceañera*, and marry according to prescripts of the church. National holidays of Mexico, such as *Cinco de Mayo*, which marked the Mexican victory over French invaders in 1862, continued to give the community distinctive reasons to celebrate its heritage.

BUILDING COMMUNITIES IN THE HEARTLAND

Homestead Act of 1862
Legislation allowing a household head, male or female, to obtain land in the public domain to establish a family farm.

"The average farmer's wife is one of the most patient and overworked women of the time," one writer proclaimed in 1884 in *The American Farmer*. Many European-born and Euro-American women who settled the western territories, including the nation's heartland, may have agreed with this sentiment. They tended to put aside the drudgery and tedium that often characterized life in the wilderness and instead took pride in their contribution to the welfare of their family and community. Women worked hard to create a home and sought to reestablish old ways, including familiar patterns of love and labor. In the 1880s, for the three of every four people who lived in rural areas, the most enduring element was the household, the primary site of production that required the labor of all able-bodied members.

South Dakota, which became a state in 1889, advertised free land for homesteading in this poster prepared for the Columbian Exposition, held in Chicago in 1893. Although the early days of settlement were over, the state continued to encourage the formation of new communities.

The Homestead Act and Immigration

The **Homestead Act of 1862** made landowning a possibility for adventurous, free-spirited Euro-American women. The Act allowed a household head, male or female, to file for a quarter section (160 acres) of the public domain with the option of buying it at a bargain price at the end of six months' residence or owning it outright after five years of improving the land. Legally subordinate to her husband, a married woman could not qualify as a household head.

Unmarried women, however, were eligible to file claims. Wyoming homesteader Elinore Pruitt Stewart insisted that "any woman who can stand her own company, can see the beauty of the sunset, loves growing things, and is willing to put in as much time and careful labor as she does over the washtub, will have independence, plenty to eat all the time and a home of her own in the end." Few women accepted Stewart's invitation. Women filed less than 15 percent of all claims, and those who did file were more often than not acting as proxies for sons or brothers who for some reason failed to meet the terms of the Homestead Act. Only rarely did women homesteaders farm or ranch on their own. Stewart herself fudged on the details of her own, highly publicized success story: one week after filing her claim, she married the rancher who lived on the adjacent lot, thus securing for the newlyweds enough acreage to support a household.

Although land speculators took the greatest advantage of the Homestead Act, the completion of the transcontinental railroad in 1869 encouraged many prospective farmers and ranchers to head west in droves. At the same time, marketing campaigns describing the rich bounties to be had in the American West targeted Europeans, many of whom lacked access to land in their home countries. Promotional literature often emphasized the opportunities available to women in particular, underscoring the possibility of attending school, earning a living, and holding property. By the end of the century, more than two million Europeans—from Germany, Scandinavia, Poland, Ireland, Russia, and many smaller countries—had relocated to the Great Plains, remapping the region as a potpourri of tightly knit ethnic communities.

A few African American families took advantage of the Homestead Act and left the South in the hope of becoming farmers. At the close of Reconstruction, as many as fifteen thousand black people, known as **Exodusters**, moved to Kansas, where they formed a handful of distinct communities. A smaller number moved to Indian Territory, which later became Oklahoma, while others scattered throughout the Great Plains and Rocky Mountains. Meanwhile, white farming families—known as "Yankees" to both European immigrants and African Americans—created a steady stream of migrants from states bordering the Mississippi River.

Exodusters A term for the nearly 15,000 African Americans who moved to Kansas at the close of Reconstruction.

The Homestead Act helped to bring ethnic diversity to most regions of the nation's heartland. It was not unusual for neighbors to lack even a common language. Nevertheless, despite such diversity, the basic patterns of women's lives varied little from group to group.

Woman's Work, Never Done

A familiar division of labor governed most farm households. Men tended the fields and outbuildings; women performed their customary tasks, such as sewing and knitting, preserving and preparing food, and cleaning the house, as well as the especially burdensome chore of laundering clothes. Although these everyday jobs fell to married women nationwide, housekeeping could prove especially challenging to even the most dedicated farm wife. For instance, because so few trees grew on the plains, settlers typically used bricks of compacted soil instead of lumber to build their houses. "Soddies," as they were called, provided sufficient protection from most elements of nature, although not the bugs and snakes that made their own home in the walls. Moreover, the walls of sod houses continuously shed bits of dirt while the ceilings let in rain, and the mud that formed eventually ruined most carpets and furniture. In addition to the Herculean chores of housekeeping, women took responsibility for several outdoor tasks. They tended chickens and gathered eggs, milked cows, and maintained a vegetable garden to keep their household supplied with produce.

Although farm communities readily acknowledged the importance of women's labor in the family economy, it is unclear if women's status was commensurate with their contribution. For example, rural isolation forced husbands and wives to rely on one another for companionship, but this situation could either foster a more egalitarian marriage or make a woman more vulnerable to domestic violence. However, men continued to enjoy the privilege of both custom and law in making major decisions, such as buying more property and equipment or pulling up stakes altogether. Also, the seasonal nature of men's work gave them an advantage. Men enjoyed enough leisure to make trips to town, where politics and fraternal activities eased the tedium of their routine. In contrast, women's work was unremitting, especially when it came to the care of children.

Children grew up with these role models before them, working alongside their mothers and fathers at gender-specific chores. "I assist Mother in household duties which are various," one young woman wrote. "She is preparing me for a Farmer's wife," that is, for a life of hard work.

Farm wives did find ways to contribute to the family economy that were often more satisfying than the ceaseless rounds of cooking, cleaning, and washing. Many women ran small-scale businesses. By selling baked goods such as breads, pies, and cookies, they could earn a small amount of cash; or they could barter for needed supplies, such as trading eggs and butter for household items like soap, linens, and clothing produced by neighboring women.

There were times, however, when the customary division of labor broke down. Men pitched in to help with the housework and child care, typically when their wives were recovering from illness or childbirth. In turn, women were prepared to take over when their husbands were called away to scout out new land, herd cattle, or take crops to market and, in such cases, assumed responsibility for the entire farming enterprise for weeks or months at a time. It was not unknown for farm wives to take on outdoor work, such as helping with the planting and harvesting, digging cellars, and building barns and sheds. However, as soon as cash could be spared to hire male helpers, most wives retreated to the home. The U.S. Department of Agriculture, in its 1872 annual report, affirmed the status quo, specifically advising farmers to encourage their wives to stick to the occupations "essentially feminine," such as the "household arts in which women are qualified by nature to excel" and not to "hold the plow or dig ditches, or build fences."

The Chrisman sisters are shown in front of their sod house in 1886, a year before Lizzie, the eldest, filed her homestead claim in Custer County, Nebraska. Eventually, all but the youngest acquired land under the provisions of the Homestead Act.

WOMEN'S LIVES

LAURA INGALLS WILDER

Laura Ingalls Wilder grew up in a pioneering family constantly on the move. Her father, Charles Ingalls, loved the open space of the prairie, and convinced his wife, Caroline Ingalls, and their four daughters to try homesteading in various locations throughout the Midwest and Plains states. When Laura was thirteen, the family settled in De Smet, a market town in the Dakota Territory with a population not much more than eighty. In later life, at age sixty-five, Laura began to use her memories of these small towns, such as Pepin, Wisconsin, where she was born, and Independence, Kansas, as settings for seven historical novels, the "Little House" books that have been read and savored by children across the generations.

Based in part on childhood memories, her stories capture the joys and hardships of rural life. *The Long Winter*, for example, dramatically depicts a winter of extremely harsh temperatures and ferocious snowstorms that brought her family to the brink of starvation because trains could not cut a passage to bring the needed provisions. In contrast, *These Happy Golden Years* offers a joyful conclusion to her series of stories, recounting her own stint as a young schoolteacher and, finally, her engagement and marriage.

The youthful Laura's imagination did not, however, preclude a childhood that was typical for girls growing up in the nation's heartland. Necessity often compelled Laura to assist her father in outdoor chores, serving, as she later recalled, as his "right-hand man." Nevertheless, her stories feature the heroic role of her otherwise stoic mother, who worked relentlessly to create for her family a comfortable home in the wilderness. The "Little House" books, with their tender details of domestic life, exalt the contribution of women to community building and family preservation, even under the most adverse circumstances. Indeed, whatever success Pa achieved could be attributed to the perseverance and talent of Ma, as he knew all too well. These were the lessons that Ma passed on to her daughters, depicted by Laura in careful and loving detail: making cheese and butter, preserving fruits and meats, and cooking meals over an open fire; knitting socks and gloves, sewing shirts and dresses by hand, and weaving straw into hats; cleaning house, lugging buckets of water for laundry, and carrying in wood for the fireplace.

These skills served the adult Laura Ingalls, who became a homesteader herself. In 1885, she married Almanzo Wilder, who shared her love of the rural life, and they soon had a baby daughter, Rose. However, misfortune followed this happy beginning. A son died shortly after birth, and a fire destroyed their home and barn. Laura and her husband nearly succumbed to diphtheria, and Almanzo never fully recovered. After a series of moves to escape drought and debt, they created a new home for themselves in a log cabin in Mansfield, Missouri, in 1894. A decade of hard work ended in prosperity, and the couple enjoyed a good life in the farming of poultry, dairy products, and fruit.

At the prompting of her daughter, Rose Wilder Lane, who herself became a successful writer and fled the rural life as soon as she was able, Laura began to fashion her childhood experiences into memorable and best-selling works of fiction. *Little House on the Prairie* appeared in 1935. ■

Immigrant women, in comparison to native-born farm wives, were more likely to pitch in whenever and wherever needed. "Among us Yankees," one Iowan observed, "the German habit of working women in the field was the sure mark of the 'Old Countryman.'" Whereas many such "Yankees" viewed immigrant farm wives as they did the women of many Indian tribes, as victims of lazy men, most immigrants considered the absence of Anglo women in the fields a sign of degeneracy. Coming from the European peasantry and accustomed to farm labor, most immigrant women simply assumed they would tend the fields and dairies and then, when time and energy allowed, tackle housekeeping. For similar reasons, immigrant farm families tended to be larger than those among the native-born families because they viewed children as an asset, as essential components of the household labor pool and insurance to parents in old age.

Turning Wilderness into "Civilization"

"I feel quite lonesome & solitary," one woman complained to in her diary. "My spirits are depressed. I have very little female society." Frequent moves made friendships fragile, and many women new to the region yearned for the friends and family left behind. To ease the isolation, settlers often built their homes on the adjacent corners of their allotments. Even strongly held prejudices did not keep some women from seeking female companionship from neighbors of different ethnicities or races from themselves. Mothers and daughters often found their relationship develop into an enduring friendship. While sons moved on to greener pastures, daughters were more likely to stay close to their mothers, often marrying local farmers and remaining in the community.

Farm wives typically turned to their neighbors and friends as much for help with chores as for companionship. Planting and harvesting brought neighbors together as did the occasional work of building new houses or barns. Quilting bees were popular forms of amusement for women, while county fairs attracted whole families. Childbirth summoned neighboring women to serve as midwives and supporters.

After the initial period of settlement, men and women broadened their range of social contacts beyond their families and neighbors and began to build the basic institutions of the small town or village. First came the school, which was built by men and staffed by women. The church was not far behind. As in other regions, western women formed auxiliaries and involved themselves in missionary activities. They organized Sunday schools and carried the gospel to nearby Indian reservations. Men and women alike joined clubs, although usually along gender-exclusive lines. Men organized themselves into fraternal associations and sporting clubs; women constructed a network of voluntary associations and benevolent societies as well as clubs devoted to education and culture.

Men and women often nurtured diverging aspirations for their communities. Men looked to the town to provide services relevant to both their business and their leisure. They promoted the establishment of banks, saloons, and brothels. Women more typically sought to impose order and morality, favoring Sunday-closing laws for retail establishments and financial institutions and the abolition of drinking, gambling, and prostitution altogether. As in other regions of the country, women assumed their role as moral guardians, an ideal that was affirmed in print media, church sermons, and public lectures.

Temperance rallied the largest number of women. The Woman's Crusade of 1873–74 recruited women across the West, from the mining frontier as well as from numerous towns of the plains and prairie. The first president of the national WCTU, Annie Turner Wittenmyer, hailed from the farming state of Iowa. Although native-born women provided the bulk of WCTU membership, some immigrant groups, Swedes in particular, formed their own chapters and sponsored a variety of programs to discourage the use of alcohol.

The Patrons of Husbandry

The household basis of the farm economy was reflected in the region's largest organization, the Patrons of Husbandry, better known as the Grange (a word for "farm"). The **Grange** began as a secret fraternal society in 1867 and grew in the 1870s to some 1.5 million members. For men and women alike, the Grange became the center of social life, the chief sponsor of picnics in the summer and holiday dances in the winter. The Grange organized cooperatives to sell grain and to buy equipment and household items and promoted state legislation to regulate shipping rates.

Grange The popular term for the Patrons of Husbandry, an organization of family farmers that formed in 1867.

From its inception, the Grange set itself apart from most other fraternal societies by inviting both women and men to join. "The Grange door swings inward as readily at the gentle knock of woman," one Granger announced, "as to the ruder knock of man." Grangers thus emphasized the distinctive and complementary roles of farm husbands and wives. One woman explained that the Grange resembled a healthy family, with the husband supplying "rude and vigorous force" and the wife adding "the refinement of her more sympathetic impulses to his energy." Only men served on the committees dealing with cooperatives or lobbying legislatures, while women managed the educational, charitable, and social activities of the order.

The order's 1874 Declaration of Purposes called for a "proper appreciation of the abilities and sphere of woman." In their newspapers and at their meetings, Grangers thoroughly addressed issues of rural domesticity, exchanging tips on housework and cooking as well as child rearing. They also acknowledged the repetitive, exhausting nature of these tasks and identified the farm woman's plight as one of drudgery. The Patrons of Husbandry emerged as one of the few national organizations to endorse woman's suffrage and saluted the WCTU as a kindred organization and required all members to take a vow of abstinence.

INDIAN WOMEN, CONQUEST, AND SURVIVAL

Ravaged by disease and pressured by the onslaught of Euro-American traders, prospectors, and homesteaders, Native American tribes nevertheless survived in far greater numbers than they did east of the Mississippi (see chapter 7). At the close of the Civil War, approximately 360,000 Indian people lived in this region, the majority on eight reservations where white Christian missionaries taught them to speak English, convert to Christianity, and become farmers. Greater changes lay ahead. In response to lobbying by white settlers and corporate interests, the federal government drastically reduced the land allotments that had earlier been promised to native peoples "for as long as the grass grows and the water runs." Large-scale war broke out, marked by intermittent bloody conflicts that lasted until 1886, when the Apache warrior Geronimo surrendered in Skeleton Canyon, Arizona, to the U.S. Army.

All the while, groups of Christian reformers were lobbying the federal government to implement more humane assimilationist policies on the reservations. The noted author Helen Hunt Jackson was one of the most influential. Her book, *A Century of Dishonor* (1881), exposed the cruelties that had been inflicted on Indian peoples and became to Indian reformers what Harriet Beecher Stowe's *Uncle Tom's Cabin* was to

Women's National Indian Association
Founded in 1879 to promote assimilationist policies among Native American women.

Dawes Severalty Act
Also called the Indian Allotment Act, this 1887 legislation divided reservation land in an effort to assimilate tribal members into the general American population as "responsible farmers."

abolitionists. Jackson was also active in various reform organizations, including a branch of the **Women's National Indian Association** (WNIA), which had formed in 1879. The WNIA raised money to promote assimilationist programs, sponsoring teachers, missionaries, and physicians to work among various Indian tribes. It also staged a massive petition campaign, urging Congress to phase out the reservation system, to make homesteaders of individual Indian families, and to establish a school system for children.

The WNIA was the chief force behind the **Dawes Severalty Act** (1887), named after the senator who sponsored it, which allowed the United States to convert communal tribal lands to individual ownership. The government distributed allotments of 160 acres to heads of households, that is, to Indian men who agreed to be "severed" legally from their tribes and to become farmers; in return, they could petition to become citizens of the United States. Indian women were to relinquish their roles as producers to become farm wives and care primarily for home and children. In sum, the Dawes Severalty Act strengthened the authority of the federal government to prescribe a nuclear family system and to proselytize the doctrine of separate spheres as the chief means to assimilate Indian men and women into "civilization."

The Nez Perce

According to tribal lore, it was a woman who facilitated the first friendly contact between white explorers and her tribe. Wet-khoo-weis was so grateful to a white woman for rescuing her from captivity by rival Indians that when the Lewis and Clark Expedition arrived in Nez Perce territory in 1806 she persuaded tribal leaders to "do them no harm." From this point on, the Nez Perce regarded themselves as friends to white traders and settlers.

Living on the plateau where Idaho, Washington, and Oregon now meet, the Nez Perce remained on good terms with the U.S. government until the 1860s, when, following the discovery of gold, they were forced to cede nearly nine-tenths of their land. A substantial portion of the tribe refused assignment to a reservation and, in 1877, followed Chief Joseph to search for sanctuary in Canada. During the long journey, Nez Perce women performed the essential tasks of setting up and dismantling the camps and caring for the wounded warriors. When their husbands were killed in battle, women occasionally retrieved the guns, mounted their horses, and joined the fight. United States troops finally forced Chief Joseph's band to surrender in northern Montana, just thirty miles from the Canadian border.

Meanwhile, those Nez Perce women who had accepted reservation status became enmeshed in assimilationist programs based on the doctrine of separate spheres. In 1869, President Ulysses S. Grant put Christian missionaries in charge of reservations, and the Presbyterians who volunteered to work among the Nez Perce did more than instruct the tribe in the tenets of their religion. The missionaries pleaded with tribal members to abide by the sexual division of labor deemed appropriate to "civilization." For example, they advised the Nez Perce to replace their tipis with the wooden-frame houses typical of sedentary American farmers. Such houses, which could comfortably accommodate only a few people, would undermine the prevailing extended-family living arrangements and induce the Nez Perce to live as nuclear families, or so the missionaries believed. Moreover, the missionaries insisted that men construct the new homes, thereby displacing the women who customarily built the tipis and thereby served as the chief providers of housing.

The missionaries had less success, however, in pursuading women to reject traditional clothing styles and functions. Used to fashioning buffalo skins into ornately beaded garments, Nez Perce women welcomed the sewing machine and woven textiles traded by the Euro-Americans. Even in the building of tipis, they readily switched from buffalo hides to canvas. However, they were reluctant to follow the advice of missionaries to forsake highly decorated clothing, which the Protestants denounced as "heathen" and wasteful. Viewing clothing as an important marker of identity and status, most Nez Perce women continued to savor beaded leggings, feathered hats, and shell jewelry.

However, Nez Perce women did adapt to farming as a way of life, although in ways that undoubtedly surprised their Protestant instructors. Men resisted the role of farmer because, traditionally, gardening among the Nez Perce was "women's work." In contrast, women readily accepted basic farm chores as routine. But contrary to the missionaries' wishes, Nez Perce women also took on the heavy outdoor work of cultivating, threshing, and harvesting. At first, they used horses to drag the equipment; later they drove tractors. The women also refused to stay put on their own farms and instead continued the customary practice of working in groups, even pitching tents in the field and spending the night together. In the few instances when the missionaries convinced men to farm, their wives still refused to retreat to the home and instead hired out, earning wages by sifting and winnowing wheat.

Plains Indians

The role and status of Plains women underwent similarly dramatic changes as a result of the U.S. government's determination to turn Indians into self-sufficient farmers. By the 1870s, the buffalo, which had inhabited the plains for thousands of years, were on the verge of extinction, a consequence of reckless slaughter by white overland traders wielding powerful new weapons. Various tribes, with the mainstay of their livelihood disappearing, agreed to cede large portions of their land in return for the right to live in security in Indian Territory or on a reservation. Believing that the prospects for "civilizing" these tribes lay in the hands of women, federal agents and missionaries then began to implement vigorous programs to transform Indian women into homemakers.

Such was the case of the Sioux women who lived on the Devil's Lake Reservation in North Dakota, which had been established in 1867. More quickly than the Nez Perce, it seemed, Sioux men accepted responsibility for agricultural production. Federal agents persuaded them to take up what had traditionally been "women's work" by offering such incentives as kerosene,

The 1891 photograph by the J.C. H. Grabill shows the wife of the Lakota Sioux chief American Horse with several other Indian women sitting in an encampment tipi, probably at the Pine Ridge Reservation, South Dakota.

WOMEN'S VOICES

LEAVING FOR THE MISSION SCHOOL

Gertrude Simmons Bonnin, who wrote under her chosen name Zitkala-Sa (Red Bird), trained as a musician and devoted much of her life to pan-Indian activism. She was born and raised on the Yankton Sioux Reservation in South Dakota until she enrolled, at age eight, in the Quaker mission school in Wabash, Indiana. In this autobiographical piece, she recalls her mother, Ellen Simmons, whose Yankton-Lakota name was Taté Iyòhiwin (Every Wind or Reaches for the Wind).

My Mother

A wigwam of weather-stained canvas stood at the base of some irregularly ascending hills. A footpath wound its way gently down the sloping land till it reached the broad river bottom; creeping through the long swamp grasses that bent over it on either side, it came out on the edge of the Missouri.

Here, morning, noon, and evening, my mother came to draw water from the muddy stream for our household use. Always, when my mother started for the river, I stopped my play to run along with her. She was only of medium height. Often she was sad and silent, at which times her full arched lips were compressed into hard and bitter lines, and shadows fell under her black eyes. Then I clung to her hand and begged to know what made the tears fall.

"Hush; my little daughter must never talk about my tears"; and smiling through them, she patted my head and said, "Now let me see how fast you can run today." Whereupon I tore away at my highest possible speed, with my long black hair blowing in the breeze.

I was a wild little girl of seven. Loosely clad in a slip of brown buckskin, and light-footed with a pair of soft moccasins on my feet, I was as free as the wind that blew my hair, and no less spirited than a bounding deer. These were my mother's pride,—my wild freedom and overflowing spirits. She taught me no fear save that of intruding myself upon others. . . .

Setting the pail of water on the ground, my mother stooped, and stretching her left hand out on the level with my eyes, she placed her other arm about me; she pointed to the hill where my uncle and my only sister lay buried.

"There is what the paleface has done! Since then your father too has been buried in a hill nearer the rising sun. We were once very happy. But the paleface has stolen our lands and driven us hither. Having defrauded us of our land, the paleface forced us away."

"Well, it happened on the day we moved camp that your sister and uncle were both very sick. Many others were ailing, but there seemed to be no help. We traveled many days and nights; not in the grand happy way that we moved camp when I was a little girl, but we were driven, my child, driven like a herd of buffalo. With every step, your sister, who was not as large as you are now, shrieked with the painful jar until she was hoarse with crying. She grew more and more feverish. Her little hands and cheeks were burning hot. Her little lips were parched and dry, but she would not drink the water I gave her. Then I discovered that her throat was swollen and red. My poor child, how I cried with her because the Great Spirit had forgotten us!"

"At last, when we reached this western country, on the first weary night your sister died. And soon your uncle died also, leaving a widow and an orphan daughter, your cousin Warca-Ziwin. Both your sister and uncle might have been happy with us today, had it not been for the heartless paleface."

My mother was silent the rest of the way to our wigwam. Though I saw no tears in her eyes, I knew that was because I was with her. She seldom wept before me.

Source: *Zitkala-Sa (Gertrude Bonnin), American Indian Stories (Washington, DC: Hayworth Publishing House, 1921), 7–11.*

Questions

1. How does Zitkala-Sa, who left the reservation when she was a young child, describe her relationship with her mother?

2. In this work of fiction, how much do you think Zitkala-Sa draws from her own experiences?

tools, and clothing and even plots of land for the most adept farmers. Eventually, some Sioux men became very successful wheat farmers. With their husbands now acting as chief breadwinners of the family, women left the fields and tended only small gardens for domestic consumption.

The reservation boarding schools, established in the 1870s to "uplift" the Indians, reinforced this arrangement. Immediately upon arrival, children had their long, straight hair shorn and their distinctive tribal clothing stripped away, while their Christian teachers attempted to refashion them in the style of Anglo boys and girls. The teachers promoted acculturation by establishing curricula clearly delineated by gender. They taught Sioux boys agricultural methods, as well as other vocational skills such as carpentry and blacksmithing with the expectation that as adults they would take on the role of chief breadwinner of the family. In contrast, girls prepared for a life of economy dependency. They studied and practiced the homemaking arts, including cooking and baking; housecleaning; and quilting, crocheting, and knitting. In addition, Sioux girls received a heavy dose of moral training to prepare for their future role in sustaining a Christian home. However, a small number of girls flourished in the new educational setting and went on to become doctors, writers, and teachers themselves.

Ultimately, the majority of Sioux women lost considerable status as tribal members. At one time highly skilled in tailoring and decorating buffalo hides, tribal women adapted readily to the new forms of needlework; and quilting soon emerged as major decorative art on the reservations, and quilts were important items for sale or exchange. However, women's handicraft and homemaking activities did not carry the same weight as men's contribution to the livelihood of family and tribe alike. Women retained some traditional prerogatives, such as the right to dissolve a marriage and to participate in ceremonies and rituals. However, women were no longer consulted about intertribal dealings; nor could they negotiate with federal agents who recognized only men as heads of household.

A small group of Sioux women faced their greatest trial in 1890. Their land area reduced by the federal government, the Sioux could no longer sustain their tribes and suffered for want of food and other necessities. Many believed that the day of judgment was near, and they joined an ecstatic spiritual movement, the Ghost Dance, which swept the plains and simultaneously provoked federal officials who interpreted it as a war dance. In December, representatives of various Sioux tribes gathered at the Wounded Knee Creek near the Pine Ridge and Rosebud reservations in South Dakota and on December 19 were massacred by the 7th U.S. Cavalry. At least forty-four women and eighteen babies died in the **Wounded Knee Massacre** considered the final armed conflict between Native Americans and the federal government.

Wounded Knee Massacre The attack by the US 7th Calvary on December 29, 1890 that resulted in the deaths of nearly 190 Indians, the majority of whom were women and children.

The Southern Ute

At one time, the Southern Ute lived by hunting and foraging in a wide region spanning the Rocky Mountains and the Great Basin; and by the early nineteenth century, they had become powerful actors in a flourishing trade economy among other Indians, Mexicans, and Anglos. However, when the land they occupied became part of the United States in 1848, the Ute started down a path that ultimately led to reservation status. By the terms of the Dawes Severalty Act, the reservation became an administrative unit of the Office of Indian Affairs (OIA), which, along with missionary and reform organizations, acted to undermine the remaining vestiges of the Ute's collectivist society and egalitarian gender system.

WOMEN'S LIVES

SUSAN LA FLESCHE PICOTTE, M.D. AND SUSETTE LA FLESCHE TIBBLES

A few remarkable Indian women took on important roles as cultural mediators. Such was the case of two Omaha sisters, Susan and Susette La Flesche. Both their parents were children of intermarriage with French traders, but the family's identity as Omaha was secure across the generations. Their father, Joseph La Flesche, also known as Iron Eye, had served as tribal chief until shortly after Susan's birth, a time when the Omaha, like other Plains Indians, were up against the era of the reservation. Disease and malnourishment plagued the small tribe, and their father represented the faction promoting partial acculturation over its likely alternative, extinction. He himself had given up the lodge home and traditional clothing and had converted to Christianity.

Susan and Susette, who was older by eleven years, from early childhood acquired traditional skills by working beside their mother, and they learned English and other academic subjects from the teachers at the mission boarding school. The Presbyterian-run school closed in 1869, and both Susette and Susan continued their formal education at the Elizabeth Institute for Young Ladies in New Jersey. In 1884, Susan joined, as she put it, other "happy seekers after knowledge" at an industrial boarding school, the Hampton Institute in Virginia, where she was trained to teach "civilization" and bring Christianity back to the reservation. However, both Susan and her sister wanted to do more, and they used their education to become cultural brokers or mediators.

Susette returned to the reservation and taught for a short time before emerging as a prominent activist for Indian rights. In 1878, she and her future husband, Thomas Henry Tibbles, became forceful advocates for the destitute Ponca tribe, which had been forcibly re-moved from Dakota Territory to the increasingly crowded Indian Territory. Acting as a translator for Ponca chief Standing Bear, Susette conducted a dramatic speaking tour of the eastern states. Until her death, she offered a counterpart to those reformers who aspired to "civilize" the Indians, arguing forcefully instead for citizenship rights and protection of the law.

Susan, in contrast, took to heart the lessons she had learned at school and pledged herself to help the Indians progress toward "civilization." However, like her sister, she herself refused to embrace the idealized role of homemaker and continued her education at the Woman's Medical College in Philadelphia. The first Indian woman to receive a medical degree, she accepted an appointment from the Office of Indian Affairs and in 1889 returned to Omaha as physician to the students who attended the government-run boarding school. Within a short time, she was supplying medical services to the entire tribe. Although she took a few years off to recuperate from her challenging and time-consuming responsibilities to marry and to give birth to two sons, until her death Susan La Flesche Picotte, M.D., practiced medicine among her people. ■

The Carlisle Indian School in Pennsylvania opened in October 1879 to assimilate Indian children to white ways. This photograph, taken at the turn of the century, shows young women attending the "breakfast lesson" in home economics. More than 10,000 Indian children were educated at Carlisle before the school closed in 1918.

Prior to the reservation, Ute men achieved status in the highly masculine role of raider and warrior, while women derived their authority from the responsibility of guarding the camp and protecting the children. On occasion, when the fighting neared their home territory, armed women joined the men in battle, scalping their enemies and carrying back the spoils. In the victory ceremonies, women received their share of the honor.

Like other Indian women, Ute women found it increasingly difficult to hold on to their customary roles in the aftermath of the Dawes Severalty Act. The terms of the Act decreed their husbands the head of the household, and the Office of Indian Affairs similarly assumed that political leadership on the reservation belonged to men alone. Government agents therefore dealt only with all-male councils on matters ranging from allotments to educational programs.

Ute women resisted these changes in governance and continued to participate in tribal-sponsored forums about various aspects of reservation policy. For example, Ute women, reluctant to send their children to boarding schools that had high rates of contagious disease, forced the OIA to open a day school in 1886. Four years later, 150 women presented their opinions at a major meeting about tribal finances. Within their families, they preserved their authority to make decisions about the care of their children and the welfare of their household. They also served as liaisons with Ute families in other jurisdictions, thereby helping to maintain the regional tribal community. And given the stringencies on the reservation, especially the prevalence of disease, the tribe had little choice but to value women's contributions.

CONCLUSION

In 1890, the director of the U.S. Census declared that the nation's "unsettled area has been so broken into by isolated bodies of settlement that there can hardly be said to be a frontier line." The trans-Mississippi West had been incorporated into the United States. Americans had brought to this region their political, legal, and economic systems, as well as their cultural and social institutions. For women, this transformation had pivoted on the doctrine of separate spheres, foremost the tenets of domesticity.

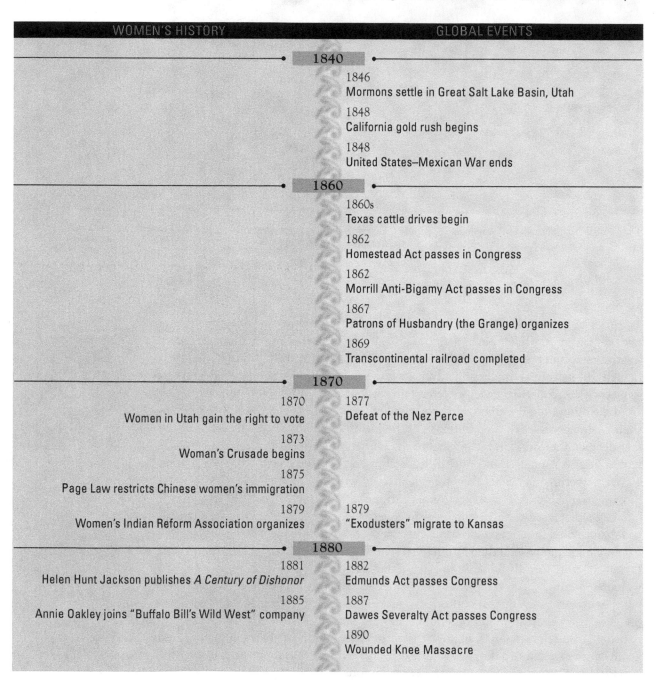

WOMEN'S HISTORY	GLOBAL EVENTS
1840	
	1846 Mormons settle in Great Salt Lake Basin, Utah
	1848 California gold rush begins
	1848 United States–Mexican War ends
1860	
	1860s Texas cattle drives begin
	1862 Homestead Act passes in Congress
	1862 Morrill Anti-Bigamy Act passes in Congress
	1867 Patrons of Husbandry (the Grange) organizes
	1869 Transcontinental railroad completed
1870	
1870 Women in Utah gain the right to vote	1877 Defeat of the Nez Perce
1873 Woman's Crusade begins	
1875 Page Law restricts Chinese women's immigration	
1879 Women's Indian Reform Association organizes	1879 "Exodusters" migrate to Kansas
1880	
1881 Helen Hunt Jackson publishes *A Century of Dishonor*	1882 Edmunds Act passes Congress
1885 Annie Oakley joins "Buffalo Bill's Wild West" company	1887 Dawes Severalty Act passes Congress
	1890 Wounded Knee Massacre

Even as the federal government marked the closing of the frontier, the trans-Mississippi West served as home to more and more women whose cultures intersected, often clashed, and encouraged new meanings for traditional practices. They found themselves enmeshed in a continuous struggle that would define ethnic, racial, and class hierarchies in this region while they simultaneously reconsidered established practices of women's work and markers of women's status within their families and their communities. In other words, domesticity served as a major site of contest, an arena for asserting power and establishing identity, and a measure of civilization over wilderness.

REVIEW QUESTIONS

1. What factors promoted the imbalanced sex ratio in the states and territories west of the Mississippi?

2. Why did woman suffrage come first to the western territories and states?

3. How did the incorporation of Mexican lands into the United States affect the lives of Spanish-speaking women?

4. How did men and women manage their households on the plains and prairies?

5. How did Indian women respond to the assimilationist programs sponsored by the U.S. government and carried out by missionaries?

RECOMMENDED READING

Kathryn M. Daynes. *More Wives Than One: Transformation of the Mormon Marriage System*. Urbana: University of Illinois Press, 2001. A 150-year study of polygamy in Manti, Utah, this book provides an especially vivid portrait of plural marriage in this locality during the last half of the nineteenth century.

Sarah Deutsch. *No Separate Refuge: Culture, Class, and Gender on an Anglo-Hispanic Frontier in the American Southwest 1880–1940*. New York: Oxford University Press, 1987. Traces and analyzes the increasing marginality of Hispanic women as their communities moved into Anglo areas to the north of their original communal villages of New Mexico.

Deborah Fink. *Agrarian Women: Wives and Mothers in Rural Nebraska, 1880–1940*. Chapel Hill: University of North Carolina Press, 1992. Centered on Boone County, Nebraska, this well-researched book explores the lives of farm wives and mothers with an eye on their roles in a family economy dominated by their husbands.

Dee Garceau. *The Important Things of Life: Women, Work, and Family in Sweetwater County, Wyoming, 1880–1929*. Lincoln: University of Nebraska Press,

1997. Emphasizes ethnic diversity and studies in close detail the roles of women in both mining and ranching communities across two generations.

Caroline James. *Nez Perce Women in Transition, 1877–1900*. Moscow: University of Idaho Press. 1996. Based in part on forty-six interviews with Nez Perce women, this book covers many facets of reservation life in the process of acculturation and supplements a rich narrative with extraordinary photographs.

Elizabeth Jameson and Susan Armitage, eds. *Writing the Range: Race, Class, and Culture in the Women's West*. Norman: University of Oklahoma Press, 1997. A collection of essays emphasizing the cultural diversity of the American West and highlighting the interconnections of gender, class, race and ethnicity in four centuries of history in this region.

Katherine Osburn. M.B., *Southern Ute Women: Autonomy and Assimilation on the Reservation, 1887–1934*. Albuquerque: University of New Mexico Press, 1998. Provides compelling evidence that Southern Ute women resisted many of the assimilationist programs imposed by the Dawes Severalty Act and continued to participate in tribal affairs well into the twentieth century.

Benson Tong. *Unsubmissive Women: Chinese Prostitutes in Nineteenth-Century San Francisco*. Norman: University of Oklahoma Press, 1994. Tells a complicated story of the women who came from China to work in the burgeoning commercial sex industry. Less a study of victimization than one of survival in a new land.

ADDITIONAL BIBLIOGRAPHY

General Histories and Historiography

Susan Armitage and Elizabeth Jameson, eds. *The Women's West*. Norman: University of Oklahoma Press. 1987.

Elizabeth Jameson. "Toward a Multicultural History of Women in the Western United States," *Signs* 13 Summer 1988, 761–91.

Julie Roy Jeffrey. *Frontier Women: "Civilizing the West? 1840–1880*. New York: Hill and Wang, Revised Edition 1998.

Sandra L. Myres. *Westering Women and the Frontier Experience, 1800–1915*. Albuquerque: University of New Mexico Press, 1982.

Glenda Riley. *Women and Indians on the Frontier, 1825–1915*. Albuquerque: University of New Mexico Press, 1984.

Lillian Schlissel, Vicki L. Ruiz, and Janice Monk, eds. *Western Women: Their Land, Their Lives*. Albuquerque: University of New Mexico Press, 1988.

Quintard Taylor and Shirley Ann Wilson Moore, eds. *African American Women Confront the West*. Norman: University of Oklahoma Press, 2003.

On the Range and in Mining Communities

Anne M. Butler. *Daughters of Joy, Sisters of Mercy: Prostitutes in the American West, 1865–90*. Chicago: University of Illinois Press, 1985.

Marion S. Goldman. *Gold Diggers and Silver Miners: Prostitution and Social Life on the Comstock*. Ann Arbor: University of Michigan Press, 1981.

Lucie Cheng Hirata. "Free, Indentured, Enslaves: Chinese Prostitutes in Nineteenth-Century American," *Signs*, 5 Autumn 1979, 3–29.

Ruth B. Moynihan, Susan Armitage, and Christiane Fischer Dichamp, eds. *So Much to Be Done: Women Settlers on the Mining and Ranching Frontier*, 2d ed., New Haven: Yale University Press, 1983, 1998.

Paula Petrik. *No Step Backward: Women and Family on the Rocky Mountain Mining Frontier, Helena, Montana, 1865–1900*. Helena: Montana Historical Society, 1990.

Sally Zanjani. *A Mine of Her Own: Women Prospectors in the American West, 1850–1950*. Lincoln: University of Nebraska Press, 1997.

Mormon Communities

Maureen Ursenbach Beecher, and Lavina Fielding Anderson, eds. *Sisters in Spirit: Mormon Women in Historical and Cultural Perspective*. Urbana: University of Illinois Press, 1987.

Jessie L. Embry. "Effects of Polygamy on Mormon Women," *Frontiers*, 7, #3. 1984, 56–61.

Sarah Barringer Gordon. *The Mormon Question: Polygamy and Constitutional Conflict in Nineteenth-Century America*. Chapel Hill: University of North Carolina Press, 2002.

Jeffrey Nichols. *Prostitution, Polygamy, and Power: Salt Lake City, 1847–1918*. Urbana: University of Illinois Press, 2002.

Spanish-Speaking Women of the New Southwest

Teresa Palomo Acosta, and Ruthe Winegarten. *Las Tejanas: 300 Years of History*. Austin: University of Texas Press, 2003.

Darlis A. Miller. "Cross-Cultural Marriages in the Southwest: The New Mexico Experience, 1846–1900, *New Mexico Historical Review*, 57 October 1982, 335–59.

Vicki Ruiz, and Susan Tiano, eds. *Women on the United States-Mexico Border: Responses to Change*. Westminster, Mass.: Allen and Unwin, 1987.

Building Communities in the Heartland

Sheryll Black-Patterson. "Women Homesteaders on the Great Plains Frontier, *Frontiers: A Journal of Women Studies*, Vol. 1, No. 2 (Spring, 1976), pp. 67–88.

Katherine Harris. *Long Vistas: Women and Families on Colorado Homesteads.* Niwot, Co.: University of Colorado Press, 1993.

Norman Juster. *So Sweet to Labor: Rural Women in America, 1865–1895.* Norman: University of Oklahoma Press, 1979.

H. Elaine Lindgren. "Ethnic Women Homesteading on the Plains of North Dakota," *Great Plains Quarterly,* 9, 1989, 157–73.

Sally McMurry. *Families and Farmhouses in Nineteenth Century America.* New York: Oxford University Press, 1988.

Donald B, Marti. *Women of the Grange: Mutuality and Sisterhood in Rural America, 1866–1920.* Westport: Greenwood Press. 1991.

Indian Women

Patricia Albers. and Beatrice Medicine. *The Hidden Half: Studies of Plains Indian Women.* Washington, DC: University Presses of America, 1983.

Evelyn Blackwood. "Sexuality and Gender in Certain Native American Tribes: The Case of Cross-Gendered Females," *Signs,* 10 Autumn 1984, 27–42.

Lisa Emmerich. "Right in the Midst of My Own People': Native American Women and the Field Matron Program," *American Indian Quarterly,* 15 Summer 1991, 201–16.

Margaret D. Jacobs. *Engendered Encounters: Feminism and Pueblo Cultures, 1879–1934.* Lincoln: University of Nebraska Press, 1999.

Devon Abbott Mihesuah. *Cultivating the Rosebuds: The Education of Women at the Cherokee Female Seminary, 1851–1909.* Urbana: University of Illinois Press, 1997.

Theda Purdue, ed. *Sifters: Native American Women's Lives.* New York: Oxford University Press, 2001.

Jane E., Simonsen. *Making Home Work: Domesticity and Native American Assimilation in the American West, 1860–1919.* Chapel Hill: University of North Carolina Press, 2006.

Mary C. Wright. "The Woman's Lodge: Constructing Gender on the Nineteenth-Century Pacific Northwest Plateau," *Frontiers,* 24, #12003, 1–18.

Memoirs, Diaries, Autobiographies and Biographies

Maureen Ursenbach Beecher. *Life Writings of Frontier Women,* 5 vol. Salt Lake City: University of Utah Press.

Isabella Bird. *A Lady's Life in the Rocky Mountains.* Norman: University of Oklahoma Press, 1883, 1971.

Rachel Calof and J. Sanford Rikoon. *Rachel Calof's Story: Jewish Homesteader on the Northern Plains.* Bloomington: Indiana University Press, 1995.

Cheryl J. Foote. *Women of the New Mexico Frontier, 1846–1912.* Niwot: University Press of Colorado, 1990.

Kay Graber, ed. *Sister to the Sioux: The Memoirs of Elaine Goodale Eastman, 1885–1891.* Lincoln: University of Nebraska Press, 2004.

Elizabeth Hampsten. *Read This Only to Yourself: The Private Writings of Midwestern Women, 1880–1910.* Bloomington: Indiana University Press, 1982.

Joan Mark. *A Stranger in Her Native Land: Alice Fletcher and the American Indians.* Lincoln: University of Nebraska Press, 1988.

Valerie Mathes. *Helen Hunt Jackson and Her Indian Reform Legacy.* Austin: University of Texas Press, 1990.

Darlis A. Miller. *Mary Hallock Foote: Author-Illustrator of the American West.* Norman: University of Oklahoma Press, 2002.

Lillian Schlissel. *Women's Diaries of the Westward Journey.* New York: Schocken Books. 1982, 1992.

Lillian Schlissel and Catherine Lavender, eds. *The Western Women's Reader: The Remarkable Writings of Women Who Shaped the American West, Spanning 300 Years.* New York. HarperPerennial, 2000.

Patty Barlett Sessions. *Mormon Midwife: The 1846–1888 Diaries of Patty Barlett Sessions.* Logan: Utah State Univesity Press, 1997.

Elinor Pruitt Stewart. *Letters of a Woman Homesteader.* Boston: Houghton Mifflin Co., 1914.

Benson Tong. *Susan La Flesche Picotte, M.D.: Omaha Indian Leader and Reformer.* Norman: University of Oklahoma, 1999.

Sally Zanjani. *Sarah Winnemucca.* Lincoln: University of Nebraska Press, 2001.

NEW WOMEN

NEW INDUSTRIES, NEW JOBS
Manufacturing
Retail Sales and Office Work
Domestic Service

NEW IMMIGRANTS
Chinese
Italians
Eastern European Jews

THE NEW SOUTH
Tenant Farming and Sharecropping
Domestic Service
Textiles and Mill Villages

NEW PROFESSIONS
Education
Medicine
Ministry
Visual Arts

THE NEW WOMAN AT HOME
Smaller Families, Better Babies
Woman's Sphere Transformed
From Production to Consumption

HOW DID the increasing pace of industrial growth affect women's role in the nation's cities?

WHAT FACTORS account for the differing experiences among New Immigrant women?

HOW DID race and racism affect the working lives of women in the New South?

WHICH PROFESSIONS proved to be the most amenable to women's advancement?

HOW DID new patterns of consumption affect the role of middle-class women in the home?

Brooklyn, 9/12/84

My dear Marie,

A long, long time ago it was that we left Hamburg, and in this time you, dear Marie, have often been expecting a letter from me. You mustn't be angry that I am only now writing, because in a foreign country you have all sorts of things to think about at the beginning. Oh, if only we could sit together for a while, then I could tell you many a little tale of adventure, but the endlessly vast ocean calls for writing. . . .

"The Cotton Pickers" 1876 Winslow Homer (American, 1836–1910) oil on canvass, 24 1/16 × 38 1/8 in Los Angeles County Museum of Art.

On August 8 we had the dumb luck of both getting a job together in a very fine private house in Brooklyn. This town is only separated from New-York by water, you can go across in 5 minutes with the ferry, and most of the quality folks who have their business in New York live here, since Brooklyn is much prettier and the air is much healthier. Anna is the scullery maid and I'm the cook, we each get 12 dollars a month (50 marks)—what do you thin, dear Marie, don't you have the slightest desire to come to *Kamerika*?

There's more work, of course, since Americans live very lavishly, they eat 3 hot meals a day, and then we have to do all the laundry in the house, since it's so awfully expensive to send it out, we even have to iron the shirts and cuffs, here you have to understand everything, we do our best, but we can do things when we want, the *Ladys* don't pay much attention to the household, they don't do anything but dress up themselves 3–4 times a day and go out. . . .

Please write and tell me when you get this letter. Oh blast it, I forgot to tell you what wonderful fruit there is in *Kamerika*, every day we eat peaches, melons and bananas, and then I also wanted to tell you if you have an old shoe or boot, don't throw it away, tie a red or blue bow on it and hang it on the wall in your room. You may think I'm crazy, but you out to know, dear Marie, that here in America, that's what they call an antique.

I can't find the Fritz Stellen you told me about since there's no town hall here, for we live here like wild folks here in the land of freedom, we haven't needed any papers yet, no one has asked us about our names and origin.

But that's enough for now, if there's anything else you want to know about, just ask what you want to know and then I'll write and tell you what you want to know.

Source: Published in News From the Land for Freedom: German Immigrants Write Home, *ed. Walter D. Kamphoefner, Wolfgang Helbich, and Ulrike Sommer, trans. Susan Carter Vogel (Ithaca, N.Y.: Cornell University Press, 1991), 95–97.*

*I*n her own way, Wilhelmine Wiebusch marked the rise of the New Woman, a concept more commonly associated with the youthful representatives of the middle class but nevertheless elastic enough to encompass a diversity of women exploring possibilities—either by choice or by necessity—outside the familial home. A large proportion were recent arrivals and, like Wiebusch, they helped to form the biggest wave of immigration in the nation's history. They often found themselves not only living in a strange land but doing unfamiliar work.

After the Civil War, immigrant women from Ireland, Germany, and Scandinavia together accounted for nearly half of all household workers. Demand was so high for their services that by the turn of the century New York City alone sponsored nearly 170 employment agencies to list openings in domestic service alone. Immigrant women from southern or eastern Europe, in contrast, filled the growing ranks of factory operatives and retail clerks.

Even in the South, where King Cotton continued to dominate the economy, the development of industries like textiles drew both black and white women from the countryside to burgeoning towns and cities. Although marriage continued to pull women back into the household, even those women who continued to work primarily in their homes caring for their families saw their roles transformed by the emergent consumer economy. In light of these changes, contemporaries in the final decades of the nineteenth century began to discuss the arrival of the "New Woman" and acknowledged that she appeared in many guises—middle as well as working class; native-born as well as immigrant—and in virtually every part of the country.

NEW INDUSTRIES, NEW JOBS

The New Woman owed a great deal to the **second industrial revolution** that reshaped the U.S. economy in ways unimaginable just a generation earlier. A revolution in technology, including the development of electricity as a replacement for steam power; a breathtaking expansion in transportation systems; and the emergence of mass production all helped the nation ascend, in terms of productivity, from fourth to first place in the world. By the turn of the century, Americans were manufacturing one-third of all the world's goods. And much of this activity was taking place in the nation's big cities. Unlike antebellum manufacturing, which took place mainly in the countryside, in the new factory towns like Lowell, Massachusetts, the second industrial revolution transformed the old commercial cities of Baltimore, New York, Boston, and Philadelphia into gigantic urban areas, replete with growing suburbs. Manufacturing also pushed westward, making major urban centers of Cleveland, Chicago, Milwaukee, and St. Louis.

In 1870, scarcely one in eight women was working for wages; in 1910 one in four women was gainfully employed. Women were also moving into new jobs, rejecting domestic service whenever possible to work in manufacturing, retail sales, business, and education. Although a significant number of married women earned wages, particularly African American women who tended to work throughout their adult lives, the overwhelming majority of women wage earners were unmarried and young, usually between the ages of fourteen and twenty-four. Wage earning gave

second industrial revolution The major advances in the technical aspects of industrial production, including consumer goods, that occurred in the last half of the nineteenth century.

TABLE 12-1   Growing Urban Population

	1860	1870	1880	1890	1900
U.S. Population	31,444,000	38,558,000	50,156,000	62,947,000	75,995,000
Urban Population	6,217,000	9,902,000	14,130,000	22,106,000	30,160,000
Percent Urban	19.8	25.7	28.2	35.1	39.7
Percent Rural	80.2	74.3	71.3	64.9	60.3

Figures have been rounded to the nearest thousand.

Source: Robert G. Barrows, "Urbanizing America," in Charles W. Calhoun, ed., The Giladed Age (Wilmington, DE: 1996), 93, 95. As reprinted in Rebecca Edwards, New Spirits: Americans in the Gilded Age, 1865–1905 (NY: Oxford Univ Press, 2006), p. 13.

Despite the quickly growing urban population, the United States remained primarily a rural nation until 1920.

these New Women just enough time, space, and pocket change to experiment beyond the range of their parents' supervision before marriage pulled them back into the domestic circle.

Manufacturing

labor segmentation A practice by employers that governs the corporate labor market, opening up jobs to only specific groups by race, ethnicity, or gender.

The second industrial revolution helped secure a process that became known as **labor segmentation** by race and sex. The best-paying jobs remained firmly in the hands of white male workers. Women displaced men in a few occupations, such as in the manufacture of shoes, and occasionally worked in different divisions of the same industry, such as in cigar making. But only rarely did women find jobs in premium trades like steel production or transportation. Instead, women worked for low wages in mainly light manufacturing.

By 1900, of all women wage earners, 38 percent native-born white women, 21 percent foreign-born women, but less than 3 percent African American women worked in manufacturing. They could be found making artificial flowers, straw hats, umbrellas, and gloves; working as operatives in textile mills; preparing horsehair cushions for sofas and putting cane-bottom seats in chairs; painting flowers on pottery and glassware; and assembling paper boxes.

In garment manufacturing, as early as 1860, women outnumbered men, and they continued to prevail as the industry grew in response to consumer demand. By 1900, more than two hundred thousand workers were producing an ever-expanding array of

The documentary photographer Lewis Hine used his camera to educate the American public about the poor conditions in sweatshops and tenements of New York City. Here, in this 1911 photograph, he shows two women, one with a baby in her lap, making lace collars on the subcontract system.

ready-made clothing. Men worked as skilled cutters or tailors, while women handled the bulk of simple stitching and piecework, such as the sewing of collars and cuffs and buttonholes and buttons. In general, men produced the finer grades of clothing, such as suits and cloaks, while women contributed to the production cheaper items like skirts, shirtwaists (blouses), and underwear.

Centered in New York, Philadelphia, Boston, and Chicago with smaller operations in St. Louis, Cleveland, and Baltimore, the garment industry employed large numbers of foreign-born women, with Jews clustering in women's wear and Italians in men's wear. The majority of these women worked in large "inside shops" that employed as many as several hundred workers and produced entire garments. However, a sizable number worked in the "outside shops" that had characterized the garment industry since the antebellum era.

In the small "outside" shops, women assembled precut pieces of garments through a system known as subcontracting. These jobs were easy to get, even for "greenhorns." Newly arrived immigrants in New York had only to go to the "Pig Market" (an ironic name as one could buy everything but pork) at Essex and Hester streets on the predominantly Jewish Lower East Side to be greeted by a contractor in need of "hands." However, many contractors preferred to hire their *landsleit*, friends and family from the Old Country. Gathering six or seven women in tenement shops, they paid these workers by the piece and then charged the merchants or manufacturers who bought the final products a price large enough to ensure themselves a profit. Contractors also tapped the pool of needy women whose household responsibilities kept them at home; these women worked at very low rates, often by hand and with the help of their children. By the end of the century, the garment industry had become notorious for its **sweatshop** conditions.

sweatshop A workshop is supervised by a middleman, the sweater, whose employees produce mainly clothing under harsh conditions.

These conditions surprised Angelina, a sixteen-year-old Italian immigrant who had come to America to make and wear beautiful clothes. She had acquired some dressmaking skills in the Old Country, but her cousin warned that "it was altogether different here, where each person makes but one special part of the dress and work is so scarce one has to take whatever can be found." On her second day in the United States, with her cousin's help, Angelina found a job in a garment factory where she pressed corset covers at three cents a dozen, a wage too low to purchase a simple shirtwaist, which cost more than a dollar. Angelina soon began to look forward to marriage as a way out of the shop.

Other workers, however, found the sociability of the factory a source of personal satisfaction and emotional support. For the first time, they were able to reach beyond the small circles of their family and neighborhood to make new friends in the shops.

Retail Sales and Office Work

For white women fluent in English, department stores and offices offered alternatives to the factory. Although supervision was intense and chances for advancement virtually nil, the work was cleaner and often steadier, the hours shorter and the pay just a little bit better. African American women, however, could find such jobs only within their own communities; managers of big department stores like Macy's hired African American women to operate elevators or to stock shelves in the storeroom but rarely to sell the merchandise. At the turn of the century, the vast majority of women in clerical work and retail sales—in some cities upward of 80 percent—were native born and white.

WOMEN'S VOICES

THE FIRST DAY ON THE JOB

Rahel Gollup (1880–1925) immigrated from Russia in 1892, when she was twelve years old, and settled with her family in New York City. She soon took a job in one of the sweatshops of the Lower East Side's booming garment industry. The passage that follows is from her autobiography.

About the same time that the bitter cold came father told me one night that he had found work for me in a shop where he knew the presser. I lay awake long that night. I was eager to begin life on my own responsibility but was also afraid. We rose earlier than usual that morning for father had to take me to the shop and not be over late for his own work. I wrapped my thimble and scissors, with a piece of bread for breakfast, in a bit of newspaper, carefully stuck two needles into the lapel of my coat and we started.

The shop was on Pelem Street, a shop district one block long and just wide enough for two ordinary sized wagons to pass each other. . . . Now only I felt frightened, and waiting made me nervous, so I tried the knob. The door yielded heavily and closed slowly. I was half way up when it closed entirely, leaving me in darkness. I groped my way to the top of the stairs and hearing a clattering noise of machines, I felt about, found a door, and pushed it open and went in. A tall, dark, beardless man stood folding coasts at a table. I went over and asked him for the name (I don't remember what it was). "Yes," he said crossly. "What do you want?"

I said, "I am the new feller hand." He looked at me from head to foot. My face felt so burning hot that I could scarcely see.

"It is more likely," he said, "that you can pull bastings than fell sleeve lining." Then turning from me he shouted over the noise of the machine: "Presser, is this the girl?" The presser put down the iron and looked at me. "I suppose so," he said, "I only know the father."

The cross man looked at me again and said, "Let's see what you can do." He kicked a chair, from which the back had been broken off, to the finisher's table, threw a coat upon it and said raising the corner of this mouth: "Make room for the new feller hand."

One girl tittered, two men glanced at me over their shoulders and pushed their chairs apart a little. By this time I scarcely knew what I was about. I laid my coat down somewhere and pushed by bread into the sleeve. Then I stumbled into the bit of space made for me at the table, drew in the chair and sat down. The men were so close to me on each side I felt the heat of their bodies and could not prevent myself from shirking away. The men noticed and probably felt hurt. One made a joke, the other laughed and the girls bent their heads low over their work. All at once the thought came: "If I don't do this coat quickly and well he will send me away at once." I picked up the coat, threaded my needle and began hastily, repeating the lesson father impressed upon me. "Be careful not to twist the sleeve lining, take small false stitches."

My hands trembled so that I could not hold the needle properly. It took me a long while to do the coat. But at last it was done. I took it over to the boss and stood at the table waiting while he was examining it. He took long, trying every stitch with his needle. Finally he put it down and without looking at me gave me two other coats. I felt very happy! When I sat down at the table I drew my knees close together and stitches as quickly as I could. . . .

All day I took finished work and laid it on the boss's table. He would glance at the clock and give me other work. Before the day was over I knew that this was a "piece work shop," that there were four machines and sixteen people were working. I also knew that I had done almost as much work as "the grown-up girls" and that they did not like me. I heard Betsy, the head feller hand, talking about "a snip of a girl coming and taking the very bread out of your mouth."

Source: *Rose Cohen*, Out of the Shadow: A Russian Jewish Girlhood on the Lower East Side *(New York: George H. Doran Co., 1918) 108–11.*

Questions

1. What does Rose Gollup Cohen's reminiscences tell us about gender relations in the turn-of-the-century garment industry?

2. Why does she think the older workers do not like her?

Jobs behind the counters of the nation's department stores became a major source of employment for white working-class women. Marshall Field's in Chicago, Macy's in New York, Filene's in Boston, and Wanamaker's in Philadelphia, among others, hired women at such a fast pace that the number of women working in sales leaped from less than eight thousand in 1880 to more than fifty-eight thousand just ten years later.

In the nation's offices, women began to replace the men who had customarily filled the positions of bookkeeper, copier, and clerk. During the Civil War, the federal government first hired women to clip treasury bills at wages lower than those paid to men; after the war ended, federal law set a precedent by establishing maximum salaries for women at one-half to two-thirds that of men. By the end of the century, in tandem with the expansion of the federal bureaucracy, women filled one-third of all the federal office jobs in Washington, D.C. Meanwhile, private industry nationwide began to hire women to handle the increasing number of records of business transactions.

New technologies facilitated the employment of women in the office. Calculators, dictaphones, and stencil and mimeograph machines, as well as bookkeeping and billing machines, simplified many office tasks, leading to a greater division of labor as well as more tedium on the job. In this way, office work was becoming akin to light manufacturing, a sector already associated with women. However, no machine became so quickly and so completely tagged as "feminine" as the typewriter, which was widely introduced in the 1880s. Stenographer-typist soon became the first office position to be dominated by women.

The expansion of office work provided many clerical jobs for middle-class women. This photograph by the famed western photographer William Henry Jackson, circa 1902, shows the typing department at the National Cash Register factory (Dayton, Ohio), which manufactured a range of office equipment, including adding machines.

Saleswomen and office workers epitomized the working-class New Woman. Required by their employers to dress simply but smartly, they cut stylish figures as they headed to their downtown offices. Women in retailing often lived apart from their families, skimping on groceries to pay the rent in a fashionable neighborhood. Better-educated than their factory-working peers and inclined to see themselves as "business women" rather than "operatives," they set a standard for working-class respectability.

Domestic Service

With business and industry offering more desirable alternatives, the proportion of women working in domestic service began to shrink. In 1870, one of every two female wage earners worked as a domestic servant; by 1910, the proportion had declined to one of four. However, the growing urban middle class created such a huge demand that the absolute number of domestic servants in the United States doubled in the half century after 1870 to nearly two million.

The supply of servants never came close to meeting the demand. Prospective employers complained about the so-called "servant problem." As one matron put it, "Thoroughly competent girls for general housework are not to be had 'for love of money' in some places. Girls rush into stores and shops as 'salesladies' and go half-starved, half-clothed, and half-housed, and wear themselves out in soul and body rather than 'degrade themselves' by going out as servants."

Young women did not want to work as servants. It was not so much the wage scale or even the actual labor, repetitive and strenuous as it was. The major disincentives were the hours, which were virtually unlimited, and the mistress's intrusive supervision. Domestic servants resented being forced to wear livery, for example, and being addressed by their first names. "I am Mary to every guest in the house," one worker complained, "and every stranger who appears at the kitchen door; in fact, how can I respect myself when no one else shows me any!"

By the turn of the century, Irish, German, and Scandinavian immigrants dominated the field, with Irish women representing more than half of all servants. Twenty years later, while white women moved on to better jobs, African American women were catching up, representing nearly 40 percent of all servants. In contrast, Jews, Russians, Poles, and Italians rarely worked as domestic servants.

NEW IMMIGRANTS

Between 1880 and 1924, the peak years of immigration, approximately twenty-five million people landed on American shores. The majority of these so-called "new immigrants" were peasants or farmers displaced from their land; others were handicraft workers whose jobs had been taken over by factories. Whatever their background, new immigrant women, like their male contemporaries, avoided the nation's countryside, and very few settled south of the Mason-Dixon Line. Instead, they headed to the big manufacturing centers.

Irish and Scandinavian women often traveled alone, but most other women made the journey with their husbands. Occasionally, a married man came in advance to secure work and a place to live, but he usually sent for his family as soon as possible, perhaps encouraging siblings and even parents to join him. Immigrant women quickly reconstituted their households and acceded to such traditions as arranged marriages. Nevertheless,

MAP 12-1   Patterns of Immigration, 1820–1914

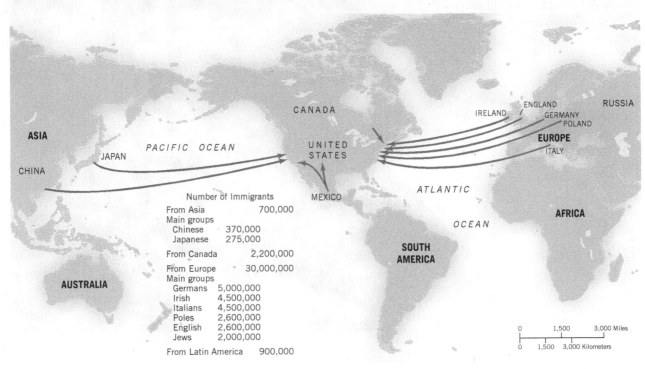

Number of Immigrants

From Asia	700,000
Main groups	
Chinese	370,000
Japanese	275,000
From Canada	2,200,000
From Europe	30,000,000
Main groups	
Germans	5,000,000
Irish	4,500,000
Italians	4,500,000
Poles	2,600,000
English	2,600,000
Jews	2,000,000
From Latin America	900,000

Between 1880 and 1920, nearly 25 million people immigrated to the United States. These so-called "new immigrants" came mainly from southern and eastern Europe and settled in the nation's cities.

many women sought more than mere escape from the poverty of their Old World village. As one observer of immigrant life noted, wives routinely warned their husbands that in America things will be different, for women have more power there."

Chinese

Between 1848, when the gold rush began, and 1882, when the Chinese Exclusion Act was passed by Congress, as many as three hundred thousand Chinese, mostly from the Pearl River delta of Guangdong province, entered the United States, but very few of this number were women. In the mid-nineteenth century, the majority of Chinese men who worked as itinerant laborers in railroad construction or mining simply lacked the resources to provide for a wife and family. Nor did they want to subject family members to the intense racism they had to endure. Chinese customs also impeded women's immigration. A married woman was duty bound first not to her husband but to her children and her parents-in-law, and she therefore stayed behind to serve them. Those few young women who did immigrate to the United States often did so because their fathers had sold them into domestic service or prostitution. The Page Act of 1875 and the Chinese Exclusion Act of 1882 brought the immigration of Chinese women to a virtual halt (see chapter 11). In no other immigrant group did men come to outnumber women to such an extent: twenty to one.

For nearly a half century, the Chinese population in the United States was frozen in this state of gender imbalance. The number of Chinese women remained too small to replenish the population, and **antimiscegenation laws**, introduced in 1880, prevented

antimiscegenation laws State legislation enacted to prevent interracial marriage.

Immigrants from China were often detained for several weeks at the immigration station at Angel Island, which opened off the coast of San Francisco in 1910. At this time, court decisions in reference to the Chinese Exclusion Act allowed only those women who were the wives or children of Chinese merchants and U.S. Citizens. Between 1882 and 1943, approximately 40,000 Chinese women were admitted to the United States.

men from marrying outside their ethnic group. Many men, however, had wives and children living in China, and they visited them intermittently. For the most part, Chinese men lived in bachelor communities.

Approximately four thousand Chinese women per year immigrated to the United States during this period, usually to join their merchant husbands or fathers. More often than not, they settled on the West Coast in exclusive ethnic enclaves known as Chinatowns. San Francisco was the most popular destination; at the turn of the century, nearly half of all Chinese women in the country lived there. Like other immigrant women, Chinese women managed the household and cared for the children; when the family economy demanded it, they also worked with their husbands in running laundries, grocery stores, and restaurants.

The wives of wealthy merchants rarely left their homes. The hostility of white Americans provoked sufficient fear to keep wives from venturing out alone; and Confucian philosophy, which deemed women inferior and justified male domination, allowed them few freedoms. Foot binding, still practiced among the upper classes, reinforced these ideals by making walking painful and mobility nearly impossible. "When I came to America as a bride," one merchant's wife recalled, "I never knew I was coming to a prison. . . . I was allowed out of the house but once a year. That was during New Years when families exchanged . . . calls and feasts. . . . Otherwise, we seldom visited each other; it was considered immodest to be seen too many times during the year." Isolated in the home, confined to their community, Chinese women had far less opportunity to develop an independent spirit than immigrant women of other ethnic groups. Nevertheless, although many customs survived the Pacific crossing, Chinese women did benefit from the disruption of arranged marriages and extended families. "It's better to be a woman in America," one San Francisco resident declared.

Their daughters, like those of other ethnic groups, were yet more successful in resisting the constraints of Old World customs. Daughters learned both ethnic pride and housekeeping from their mothers and, like their mothers, envisioned their roles as cultural bearers. They nevertheless often challenged parental authority to make their own decisions about vocation and marriage. However, although daughters could refuse to give in to some of their parents' demands, they could not overcome the racism of mainstream society. Women could now work outside the home and even outside their communities, but they often found themselves on the bottom rungs of the occupational ladder. Only in the 1920s were Chinese women able to secure retail and clerical jobs outside their communities.

Italians

Between 1880 and 1920, Italians immigrated to the United States in record numbers. Of the nearly five million newcomers, the majority from southern Italy, men outnumbered women by three to one. Most of these men were "birds of passage." They came to the United States to make money and then bring their earnings back to their families in their homeland. Overall, between 20 and 30 percent of all Italians returned permanently to Italy. Only after 1900 did Italians immigrate mainly as families. In keeping with Old World customs, women usually made the trans-Atlantic journey with their husbands; if they made the trip alone, they did so to be reunited with husbands or fathers.

After recovering from the stressful ocean crossing, immigrant wives quickly reestablished their households, often in crowded tenements near their kin and in cities concentrated in the Northeast and mid-Atlantic states, near the port of entry. In much smaller proportions, Italians settled in California, while sizable communities also developed in New Orleans, Chicago, and Detroit. Italian parents expected sons and daughters to pitch in, as had been the practice in rural Italy where family survival depended on the participation of all its members. So it would be in the American city, where, because of widespread prejudice against them, the vast majority of Italian men could secure only low-paying jobs in manual labor. Little children helped their mothers with such tasks as gathering firewood or hanging clothes; older children left school to work in factories.

Compared to other new immigrant women, Italian wives rarely worked outside the home, except in cities where light industry was both plentiful and inviting. This is not to say that they did not help to stoke the family coffers. Because their husbands earned such low wages, wives often contributed more than half of a family's income. Seasonal work in canneries provided an occasion to earn money; piecework at the kitchen table supplied more regular wages; and the money paid by boarders helped greatly to make ends meet. In New York City, for example, a government report estimated that 98 percent of home garment

The overwhelming majority of Italians who came to the United States were men who planned to work for a few years and then return to Italy. Between 1900 and 1910, nearly 40 percent of more than 2 million Italians eventually went back to their homeland. Those married men who chose to stay usually sent for their wives and children. The family appearing in this photograph circa 1910 gathered at Ellis Island, the major port of entry for Italians.

finishers were Italian women. In other cities, such as Chicago and Baltimore, where the men's clothing trade flourished, Italian women could also be found in the factories. But the income derived from these labor-intensive activities did not dispel the idea that married Italian women were first and foremost wives and mothers.

Their daughters, however, did not follow directly in their mothers' footsteps. The overwhelming majority did eventually marry and establish their own households, often not far from their parents' homes. Nevertheless, after an early childhood of helping their mothers with chores and doing their share of the piecework—stringing rosary beads and stemming artificial flowers were common tasks easily learned by youngsters—daughters took a big step and looked for jobs in factories and offices.

By age fourteen, most Italian girls had quit school to join the ranks of wage earners. Dutiful daughters handed their wages to their mothers. Government reports showed that girls actually contributed a greater amount to the family income than did boys. "You know how it is with a boy," one mother explained. "He wants things for himself." However, peer culture often pushed girls to tamper with tradition and withhold a portion of their pay for themselves. One young woman described receiving her first paycheck: "I'll never forget the time I got my first pay, you know. . . . I went downtown first, and I spent a lot, more than half of my money . . . I just went hog wild, I guess." Control of a daughter's wage became a major source of conflict between the generations. An Italian mother summed up the situation: "It is my money, they assert, and therein lies the greatest change."

Daughters tended to marry later than their mothers had and often continued to work until the birth of children. They also gained more authority within their marriages. "Now I am an American girl," one woman exclaimed as a way to insist upon respect from her husband.

Eastern European Jews

As part of the second largest ethnic group among the new immigrants, Jewish women from Eastern Europe hoped to find greater opportunities in America as well as freedom from the religious persecution sweeping across their homeland. Beginning in the 1880s, pogroms terrorized Jews and imposed many new restrictions. Before the outbreak of World War I, two million Jews—men and women in nearly equal number—sought refuge in the United States; and, unlike many other new immigrants, they had no intention of returning.

Ellis Island Located in the New York Harbor, the main port of entry for immigrants in the late nineteenth and early twentieth centuries.

Like Italians, Jews entered through **Ellis Island**, and a very large proportion remained on the East Coast. In 1920, the majority lived between Boston and Baltimore, and nearly half lived in New York. Resettled close to their *landsleit* in ethnic enclaves such as New York's Lower East Side and sections of Brooklyn and the Bronx, Jewish women set about making a new life for themselves and their families.

Jewish women came to the United States with considerable experience in wage earning. Married women who hailed from peasant villages had worked alongside their children in agricultural labor while their husbands ran small businesses in nearby towns or worked in shops of various kinds. A far larger number of women came from manufacturing centers and, by force of necessity, had turned to the handicraft trades or factories as a source of income. The garment industry in particular had offered respectable employment to women, married or single. In the Old Country, then, it was common for husbands and wives to share the responsibility of bread-winning, and most mothers trained their daughters in a marketable skill.

Although many Jewish women found a warm welcome from kin upon their arrival and even secured a familiar job in the garment industry, they also discovered much that was new and unexpected. The actual living conditions of the ethnic neighborhood quickly deflated many dreams of what the New World held in store. Dark and dingy tenements, families crowded into tiny rooms—such realities hardly matched the stories they had heard in the Old Country. In America, it was said, the sidewalks were paved with gold! Marie Ganz, later a prominent Jewish activist, described the disappointment her mother experienced when, after a two-year wait, she finally joined her husband in the United States. Her mother quickly surveyed the "two miserable rooms" that her husband had rented in a rear tenement and compared them to the "comfortable farmhouse" she had left behind in Galicia, then an autonomous province of Austria-Hungary. In disgust, she exclaimed: "So, we have crossed half the world for this!" But knowing they were going to stay, Jewish women coped with their disappointments and helped to reestablish what has been described as "a family culture of work." Like Italians, Jews assumed that everyone in the household would help to sustain it.

Marie Ganz (1891–1968) grew up in New York City's Lower East Side, a working-class neighborhood populated mainly by Jewish immigrants from Eastern Europe. She had emigrated in 1896 with her mother and younger brother from a farm in Galicia, Poland and joined her father, who had settled in the United States two years earlier. Marie's father soon died, and by the time she was eight years old she was helping her mother support the family by doing piecework at home.

Although Jewish men were likely to earn higher wages than Italian men by working in industry or running a small business, they, too, found it nearly impossible to support their families on their own. Nevertheless, Jewish immigrant wives broke with Old Country traditions and rarely worked outside the home. Instead, families depended on income provided by boarders and wages paid to older children. Most immigrant wives found the care of small children in the big city and housekeeping in a dingy tenement more than they could easily manage. In time, the immigrant community ceded the breadwinner role to men and measured a family's respectability by the wife who stayed at home. However, such was not the case for daughters.

By age sixteen, most single Jewish women were working for wages. Jennie Matyras, a Russian Jew, remembered: "My ambition in life was to get to be a good worker because being the oldest daughter, it was my job to do the dressmaking for the family." At age fourteen, she started as a "learner" in the clothing trade.

Although most Jewish daughters, like their Italian contemporaries, accepted the responsibility to help support their family, many also dreamed of the education denied them in Russia, where Czarist law restricted schooling to wealthy Jews. "My whole hope was coming to this country to get an education," Fannie Shapiro remembered, "I heard so much about America a free country for the Jews and you . . . didn't have to pay for schooling, so I came." Yet, although Jews valued education in general and considered it a major mark of accomplishment for men, they saw schooling beyond the elementary grades as irrelevant for girls destined for domesticity or, worse, as a luxury that would spoil them for marriage. Jewish parents therefore expected their daughters to put aside such aspirations for themselves and instead to earn money to help pay for their brothers' education. Despite such discouragement, daughters persisted. More than any other ethnic group, Jewish women had the highest rates of attendance at the evening classes sponsored by the New York public school system; by the 1920s, they could make comparable claims for college attendance.

By working outside the home and attending school, Jewish daughters adapted to American mores much more rapidly than their mothers did. They soon gave up their Old World names and quickly learned English. From their peers in the shops and schoolrooms, they learned to fashion themselves in the latest clothing and hairstyles. Popular amusements, such as movies and stage plays, reinforced these lessons. Mary Antin remembered entering that "dazzlingly beautiful palace called a 'department store,'" where she and her sister "exchanged [their] hateful home-made European costumes . . . for real American-made garments, and issued forth glorified in each other's eyes." Leah Stern recalled that by high school she imagined a life for herself that was far different from her mother's. "I didn't mean to go to work at fourteen or fifteen, marry at sixteen, be a mother at eighteen and an old woman at thirty," she recalled. To the contrary, Stern imagined herself a New Woman.

THE NEW SOUTH

The surge of industrial development that drew large numbers of women into the workforce in northern cities did not happen in the South. The majority of southern women, along with their families, remained bound to the single-crop agricultural system—cotton, tobacco, sugar, or rice—that persisted as the mainstay of the regional economy. Nevertheless, despite the small scale of development, by the 1880s the prospect of a boom in industry—a New South—had sparked optimism not only among white male boosters, the vocal heads of the chambers of commerce and mayors of growing cities, but among the region's women.

Toward the end of the century, several important manufacturing sectors—furniture, cigarettes and cigars, and textiles—offered white women unprecedented opportunities for employment. Towns and cities sprang up around new factories, drawing African American women into a growing service economy. As women came to earn their own income, as small as it was, family dynamics began to change, particularly as young wage earners demanded more personal autonomy and power within relationships.

Tenant Farming and Sharecropping

For African Americans, 90 percent of whom lived in the South, the promises of the new era rang especially hollow, and the majority continued to endure a harsh routine that was reminiscent of slavery. Too often, it seemed, women of sharecropping families found themselves, with children in tow, working alongside their husbands in the fields. Like farm women everywhere, they also brought in a little cash by marketing crops from the family garden or selling eggs and butter. But even those women who had special skills, such as midwives, usually bartered their services or earned just small amounts of money. The promises of the New South were few, and poverty remained their lot in life.

Forced to rent a one- or two-room log cabin with shabby furnishings and to pay steep prices for supplies, tenant families often remained trapped for generations in a vicious cycle of dependency. The best a family could do was to reckon accounts at the end of the year, give the white landowner his share of the crop (usually between one-third and one-half), pay their debts, and move on while hoping for better luck on another plantation.

Despite high rates of mobility, African American women maintained a relatively stable network of kin. Tenant families frequently moved in groups, a custom that allowed women to pool their labor. Most women found it nearly impossible to manage single-handedly such demanding tasks as caring for children and the infirm alongside outdoor labor like hoeing or chopping cotton.

One consequence of persistent poverty was a sharp decline in fertility. Although farm families tended to be larger than average, with children an asset when many hands were needed, African American families were an exception. Poor nutrition and disease promoted infertility, miscarriages, and stillbirths—as well as early death. The life expectancy of African American men and women was thirty-three years.

The situation of poor white women was not much better. By the turn of the century, with fully one-third of all white farmers working as tenants, these farm women also juggled domestic responsibilities and outdoor labor. During harvest time, one woman explained, "The women down this way go to the field 'bout as reg'lar as the men. Cotton will be openin' now in four weeks, and that'll be the last of the house except for cookin' and washin' and ironin' till it's all picked." However, their families tended to be larger than those of neighboring black women. Indeed, white southern farm women had the highest birthrate in the nation, bearing an average of six children.

Despite women's important role in the family economy, men held the reins of power. In both black and white families, men negotiated with the landowner, squared away the accounts at the end of the year, took the crops to market, and managed the income from the sale. Men also assigned the chores and decided when and where to move.

Black and white women in farm families knew little beyond the boundaries of the countryside, and most admitted that southern rural life—especially as the price of cotton declined as the century came to a close—was unremittingly hard. But they could always hope for better lives for their children, particularly if their sons and daughters took advantage of the emerging urban economy. As one observer noted, "The young girls and boys are hastening to the towns and cities."

Domestic Service

Discriminatory practices in hiring prevented black women's jobs from showcasing the modernity of the New South. "When a Southerner speaks of servants," a white Virginian woman commented, "negroes are always understood. Irish biddy, English Mary Ann, German Gretchen, and Scandinavia maids are as yet unknown factors. . . . Black Dinah holds the fort." In 1900, upward of 90 percent of all African American women working for wages in the South did so as domestic servants.

Girls not yet in their teens hired out as nursemaids, while older girls and unmarried women often worked as live-in maids or housekeepers for white families. Servants were in such short supply, though, that married women could limit their hours and refuse to sleep on the premises. For example, African American cooks, who earned the highest wages of all household workers, usually returned to their own homes after preparing the evening meal.

Laundry work did not pay nearly as well as housekeeping but provided more flexibility. Workers typically carried huge bundles of soiled clothing and bedding back to their own neighborhoods, where they set up laundries outside their homes or shared

In 1908, when Lewis Hine took this photograph, nearly one-quarter of the work-force in southern textile mills were children. Girls worked primarily in the spinning room, which was also known as the "Children's Department." (Lewis Hine (American 1874–1940), "A Carolina Spinner," 1908. Gelatin silver print, 4¾ x 7 in. Milwaukee Art Museum, Gift of the Sheldon M. Barnett Family. M1973.83)

common space—as well as conversation and even child care—with other washer-women. Although vital to their families, their wages were so low that even white working-class families could afford to hire at least one black washerwoman. As a consequence, laundry work reigned as the largest single category of household service for African American women.

By the turn of the century, some African American women were rejecting domestic service to reap a small amount of what the New South had to offer. Even dirty, low-paying jobs like shucking oysters or stemming tobacco seemed preferable to cleaning a white woman's house or doing her laundry. Better yet was work in dressmaking and millinery. Skilled seamstresses responded aggressively to white women's growing demand for fancy clothing by establishing their own retail shops.

Textiles and Mill Villages

African American women made little headway in the textile mills, where white women were determined to prevail. In 1897, more than a thousand white textile operatives in Atlanta walked off their jobs to protest the hiring of twenty black women. The mill owner responded by assuring the strikers that he had tried first to hire white women for the new positions and, moreover, that he shared the strikers' feelings. "I do not mind having my dinner served by a colored cook," he stated, "but I don't say that they should sit down to my table." The strike ended after the mill owner discharged all African American women except scrubwomen. In turn, the white workers agreed to make up for the loss of hands by working longer hours.

For white men, women, and children, textiles, the New South's premier industry, offered new opportunities for wage earning. By the turn of the century, the number of operatives neared one hundred thousand, two-thirds of them working in the Carolinas alone. Textile production flourished in the Piedmont, a region that had once been the South's backcountry. Bolstered by hundreds of new, well-equipped factories and burgeoning mill villages and even a few sizable cities, the Piedmont now surpassed New England in the production of yarn and cloth.

For many poor white women, a move to a mill village came as a long-awaited escape from the diminishing returns of tenant farming. For others, it held out the possibility of combining the two. Some Piedmont families worked seasonally at farming; then, once the crops were harvested, they relocated to factory towns until spring planting. Other families sent off their older daughters to earn cash wages in what southern farmers called **"public work."** Sons, however, usually stayed behind to work the fields; or, if they could be spared, the older boys sought the better-paying jobs in extractive industries, like mining and timber, or in railroad construction. However, many families pulled up stakes altogether, loaded their few belongings onto a small cart, and headed for the mills.

Like the first spinning factories in New England, southern mills relied on the **family system of labor** (see chapter 5). Because employers paid very low wages, children as young as seven or eight joined their parents in the mills. Employers even accommodated the schedules of nursing mothers. They sometimes allowed them to return home intermittently during the day to tend to their babies, but it was not unknown for a nursing mother to keep her baby in a box to the side of her machine. Despite such complications, mill owners preferred to hire women for the simple reason that they paid them about 60 percent of the wages paid to men. Mill hands worked long hours: twelve-hour days, six days a week.

Mill families lived in small houses that they rented from the mill owner. Without electricity or running water, these simple, wood-frame houses were usually no better and no worse than the cabins provided to tenant farmers. However, the mill superintendent usually extended his watch from factory to village, policing the behavior of the mill hands at both locations. A woman pausing to smoke a cigarette on her own porch could earn a reprimand from a vigilant superintendent.

Despite these restrictions, unmarried women found more opportunities for courtship than they did in the countryside. By their mid-teens, most of the boys and girls in the village were working in the mills and determinedly intermingling beyond the watchful eyes of parents. "My wife worked in the spinning room," one husband recalled. "We met, and it must have been love at first sight because it wasn't very long after we met that we married. She was a spinning room person, and I would go, when I could, up to the spinning room, and we'd lay in the window and court a little bit. We decided then just to get married." Such freedom would have been much more difficult to achieve on the farm, where parents put a high premium on a daughter's labor. In the mill village, where less was at stake, daughters had more control over the circumstances of their marriage, including the choice of husband.

Nor were their marriages patterned on those of their parents. Their fathers had once enjoyed a high degree of authority as head of a complex family enterprise; their own husbands, mill operatives like themselves, could not claim the privileges enjoyed by the patriarch of a farm family. Moreover, married women, through their domestic networks of kith and kin, fortified their ties to the larger community, while their husbands, lacking the opportunity to work collectively with male neighbors, stood at a greater distance from the social affairs of the village. Although poverty haunted the second generation of mill women, they found a modicum of comfort and security and a degree of friendship that had eluded their mothers. In their own way, they had joined the ranks of New Women.

"public work" A common phrase for wage labor in the postbellum South.

family system of labor The practice of employing entire families, including young children, common in the production of textiles.

NEW PROFESSIONS

The surest sign of the New Woman was women's increasing visibility in professional occupations. By 1920, nearly 12 percent of employed women enjoyed professional status. Although the overwhelming majority—nearly 75 percent—worked in two occupations long associated with domesticity, teaching and nursing, a sizable number had moved into professions that had been, for the most part, previously closed to women. More than a few became renowned for their achievements in higher education, medicine, the ministry, and visual arts.

Education

After the Civil War, women were hired specifically to carry into the nation's schools the "feminine" attributes of purity and piety—at approximately half the salary paid to male teachers. At the elementary level, women frequently entered the classroom with no more than a sixth-grade education themselves. However, a rapidly expanding school system, especially in the western states, created such an enormous demand for teachers that college graduates soon joined their less-educated peers. By the turn of the century, two-thirds of all professional women worked in education, and women represented 75 percent of the nation's teachers. However, turnover was high; most school boards required women to resign when they married.

Barred from most other professions, African American women pursued careers in teaching. After the Civil War, approximately six hundred thousand former slaves, adults as well as children, enrolled in elementary schools, many organized by the Freedmen's Bureau and run by Northerners. From this beginning, a black school system staffed mainly by southern African American women gradually developed. Four universities were founded in part to train black teachers: Howard University in Washington, D.C.; the Hampton Institute in Hampton, Virginia; Morehouse College in Atlanta; and Fisk University in Nashville. The Atlanta Female Baptist Seminary,

TABLE 12-2 Women Enrolled in Institutions of Higher
Education, 1870–1920

Year	Number of Women Enrolled (thousands)	Percentage of All Students Enrolled
1870	11	21.0
1880	40	33.4
1890	56	35.9
1900	85	36.8
1910	140	39.6
1920	283	47.3

(*Source: Mabel Newcomer*, A Century of Higher Education for American Women (*New York: 1959*), *p. 46*.)

After American colleges and universities opened their doors to women, the percentage of women students grew quickly, such that by 1920 they represented nearly one-half of the student body.

founded in 1881 and renamed Spelman Seminary in 1884, made teacher training the core of its academic program and sent its students into communities that lacked even a single elementary school. A 1906 survey conducted reported that nearly 90 percent of Spelman alumnae had worked as teachers at some point in their lives.

Overall, according to census reports, in 1910, more than 22,500 black women were teaching nationwide, three times the number of black men in the profession. Respected for their ability to provide students with the benefits of literacy and other skills, these teachers frequently became community leaders. Nevertheless, a highly discriminatory pay scale forced many African American teachers to supplement their meager salary by working during weekends and summer months, usually as washerwomen or seamstresses.

During this period, white women made headway at the secondary level, although white men continued to hold the best-paying positions in the nation's high schools. A much smaller number, mainly those with graduate degrees, found positions in higher education as professors, deans, or administrators, although primarily in the women's colleges. Only on rare occasion did state or private coeducational institutions appoint women at faculty rank.

In the environment of the women's college, however, women professors and administrators thrived. Some educators, such as M. Carey Thomas who presided over Bryn Mawr, abjured marriage to devote their lives to their career, although they often forged partnerships with other women who shared their dedication to the college. Several women's colleges, such as Mt. Holyoke, provided apartments for faculty, replete with communal kitchens and dining rooms as well as strictly enforced curfews. Relieved of the most burdensome domestic tasks, these women could pursue their scholarship and enjoy the companionship of their colleagues.

Medicine

The educator Ella Flagg Young remarked that "every woman is born a doctor. Men have to study to become one." Although male physicians admitted that the practice of medicine was as much an art as a science, they nevertheless did not believe that women could make good doctors. As a consequence, aspiring female physicians found the doors to the mainstream medical colleges closed to them and trained instead at the "irregular" schools that specialized in various brands of **sectarian medicine**, such as homeopathy, water cure, or botanics. As late as 1893, only 37 of 105 "regular" medical colleges, such as those affiliated with major state universities, admitted women.

Pioneering physicians such as Marie Zakrzewska and Elizabeth Blackwell favored coeducational training and established their own colleges and clinics only after female applicants were repeatedly denied admission to the existing medical colleges. The Woman's Medical College of the New York Infirmary, which Elizabeth Blackwell and her physician sister, Emily, founded in Manhattan in 1868, introduced a rigorous three-year curriculum that combined laboratory and clinical training in advance of many other medical colleges. By the turn of the century, nineteen women's medical colleges and nine women's hospitals had been established; by that time, many public universities admitted women, beginning with the University of Michigan in 1869. Women took advantage of these new opportunities, and the number of female physicians increased from only two hundred in 1860 to approximately seven thousand by the end of the century, when they represented 5 percent of all physicians in the United States. The American Medical Association admitted its first female member, Sarah Hackett Stevenson, in 1876.

sectarian medicine Originated as an alternative to the harsh or "heroic" practices of mainstream or "allopathic" medicine and included such movements as homeopathy, hydrotherapy, and eclecticism.

WOMEN'S LIVES

M. CAREY THOMAS

By the turn of the century, M. Carey Thomas was the most renowned woman educator in the United States. Born in Baltimore, Martha Carey Thomas, who preferred to be called Carey, grew up in a Quaker family with activist leanings. Her mother, a temperance advocate, encouraged her daughter to test the waters of higher education and suggested she enroll in Vassar, one of the new private women's colleges that had opened since the Civil War. Although the founders of these schools promised to give women the first-rate education that men received in the Ivy League, Thomas decided to try out coeducation. She enrolled in Cornell University, which had begun to admit women in 1875. After earning a bachelor degree in 1877, she pursued graduate study at Johns Hopkins University, of which her father was a trustee; but, in order to earn a doctoral degree, she found herself sojourning in Europe and ultimately matriculating from the University of Zurich.

While studying abroad, Thomas was drawn into plans for a new women's college outside Philadelphia and, because of her European training, began to envision herself as the leader of the endeavor that in 1885 became Bryn Mawr College. After returning to the United States, she served as dean and professor of English while aspiring to take over as the college's second president. In preparation, she toured the women's colleges—Vassar, Smith, Wellesley, and the Harvard Annex (Radcliffe)—hoping to draw selectively from their examples to shape Bryn Mawr into a superior institution. Thomas then formulated her ideas about admissions, curriculum, residential policy, and faculty standards. "The president of a new college . . .," she explained, "should be like the architect of a building and make every part in keeping." On September 1, 1894, M. Carey Thomas began her twenty-eight-year term as president of Bryn Mawr College.

Although Thomas published only one book on women's higher education, she reigned as the leading authority of the era. Above all, she believed that women and men were entitled equally to the same education, preferably grounded in the liberal arts. "Women while in college ought to have the broadest possible education. This college education should be the same as men's, not only because there is but one best education, but because men's and women's effectiveness and happiness and the welfare of the generation to come after them will be vastly increased if their college education has given them the same intellectual training and the same scholarly and moral ideals."

Thomas, in insisting that Bryn Mawr offer both undergraduate and graduate degrees to women, encouraged her students to use their education to advance in the professions. A large proportion of the early graduates of Bryn Mawr—perhaps as many as 45 percent between 1889 and 1908—never married. Thomas herself spent her private life in the company of women. ■

WOMEN'S LIVES

MARIE ELIZABETH ZAKRZEWSKA

One of the most determined of her generation, Marie Zakrzewska founded one of the most important institutions to foster women's medical training. Born in Berlin, Germany, the oldest of five daughters, Zakrzewska had assisted in her mother's midwifery practice before she began, at age twenty, formal training in the largest hospital in Prussia. She graduated in 1851 and soon became a professor and chief midwife in the hospital. Convinced that the United States offered more opportunities to practice medicine, she immigrated in 1853 only to discover that she had been mistaken in her assumption.

Disappointed but not defeated, Zakrzewska soon met Dr. Elizabeth Blackwell, the first licensed woman physician in the United States, who helped secure her admission to the Cleveland Medical College. Tutored in English and supplied with textbooks by the well-connected physician, and supported financially by women affiliated with the local ladies' physiological society, Zakrzewska became one of four women in a student body of more than two hundred. After completing her training, Dr. Zakrzewska returned to New York, where she intended to establish a private practice. Turned away by wary landlords and rejected by prospective patients, she soon found herself on the staff of the New York Infirmary for Women and Children, which Blackwell had founded in 1857.

After working without salary for two years, Zakrzewska decided she had paid her debt to her mentor and moved to Boston to join the staff of the New England Female Medical College. She soon quarreled with the hospital administrator; and with the assistance of the women members of its board, broke away to establish a training hospital, the New England Hospital for Women and Children, in 1862.

Zakrzewska made Boston a major center for the practice of medicine by women and for women. With solid financial backing from the New England Women's Club, Zakrzewska created an all-women staff, and she herself served actively as attending physician. "My coworkers were young and inexperienced, looking up to me for wisdom and instruction," she later recalled, "while the public in general watched with scrupulous zeal in order to stand ready for condemnation." Despite such handicaps, under her inspiring but rigorous discipline, her residents completed their internships to become some of the most able practitioners of medicine of their generation. While in training, her physicians gained valuable hands-on experience serving a large clientele, mostly charity cases of poor women and their children.

(continued)

By 1878, the New England Hospital for Women and Children had successfully trained so many physicians that a group was ready to form the first women's medical society in the United States, the New England Hospital Medical Society. Belatedly in 1884, after the years of pressure, the Massachusetts Medical Society voted to admit women. Meanwhile, Tufts Medical School began to admit women in such large numbers that by the turn of the century women represented 42 percent of its graduates. By this time, women accounted for nearly one in five of the city's doctors.

Meanwhile, Dr. Zakrzewska, who had stepped down as attending physician in 1887, was ready to close her private practice. In 1899, she retired. Three years later, she died, proud of her achievement but nevertheless disappointed that the record of the New England Hospital did result in the opening of "Harvard College to such women as desire entrance there." ∎

Several cities served as major centers of professional activity. Chicago hospitals, for example, extended privileges to both male and female physicians. In Boston, by 1890s, nearly one in five physicians was a woman. In Washington, D.C., Howard University, which had opened its medical department in 1868, invited both black and white women to apply for admission. However, once enrolled, female students endured so many discriminatory practices that groups of Howard graduates set up their own clinics to train women.

African American women, who matriculated from medical schools at a higher rate than white women, confronted more postgraduation obstacles. Male-run hospitals excluded them entirely from clinical and research posts; and women's hospitals, which did offer residencies to black women, were too few in number to meet the demand. For example, none of the clinics founded by white women doctors in Washington, D.C., enrolled African American women in their training programs by the end of the century. A larger proportion of black women physicians used their medical diplomas, not as a credential to practice medicine but to secure a position in another profession, most commonly in education.

Ministry

Through much of the nineteenth century, the ministry, along with law, reigned as one of the most respected professions in the United States; and the nation's largest denominations—Roman Catholic, Episcopalian, Lutheran, Presbyterian, and Baptist—denied women ordination and the right to preach. Women nevertheless provided the bulk of membership, taught Sunday school, and performed the essential social services for their parishes. Their auxiliaries raised the funds to establish and maintain such important institutions as parochial schools, hospitals, orphanages, and asylums for prostitutes or unwed mothers. Women raised the funds to send hundreds of thousands of male missionaries to the West and around the world and to provide scholarships to train young men for the ministry. Yet, despite the impassioned pleas of such luminaries as WCTU president Frances Willard, who wrote a timely book entitled *Women in the Pulpit*, most denominations acknowledged women's service but refused them a position in the church hierarchy. Only by relying on their own networks within organized religion did women forge religious careers and avocations for themselves—mainly along the periphery of established churches.

African American women excelled in creating a vast social ministry and were especially active within the black Baptist Church. In the 1880s, they began to organize their own conventions at the state level and targeted education and missionary work. They also formed local Bible study classes for their own enlightenment; and although they made no claim on the right to ordination, women did become increasingly vocal in church governance as well as in the interpretation of doctrine.

In 1900, Nannie Helen Burroughs built on this legacy, appearing before the National Baptist Convention held in Richmond, Virginia, to proclaim the "righteous discontent" of black women with their role within the church. Her speech, "How the Sisters Are Hindered from Helping," stirred the women in attendance to form the Woman's Convention, Auxiliary to the National Baptist Convention. The **Woman's Convention**, separate from the all-male governing structure of the Baptist Church, became the largest representative body of black women and a major catalyst for social activism.

Within the Roman Catholic Church, religious communities of women continued to staff charitable institutions, including hospitals and orphanages. After 1880, women entering religious orders—mainly French, Irish, German, and French-Canadian immigrants—helped to develop a system of parochial schools in the major cities and, with virtually no training, became the principal teaching staff. For the most part, they did not aspire to take on larger diocesan roles or become priests. To the contrary, nuns, who lived communally in convents, took vows of celibacy, poverty, and obedience.

Within the major Protestant denominations, however, women demanded the right to become ordained ministers. One such challenger was Anna Howard Shaw, who enrolled in Boston University to prepare for the ministry only to discover that she, the only woman in the class, would have a tougher time than her relatively well-to-do male peers. Lacking in funds, she depended on the local chapter of the Woman's Foreign Missionary Society to provide nourishing meals and a weekly allowance. After she graduated, she became a minister on Cape Cod; but because the New England Conference of the Methodist Episcopal Church refused to ordain her, she could not administer the sacraments to her parishioners. Ever determined, she applied for ordination to the Protestant Methodist Church and in 1880 became its first woman minister. However, Shaw soon tired of her small and remote ministry, returned to Boston University, this time to its medical school, and earned a medical degree in 1885. By 1892, she was working full time as president of the National American Woman Suffrage Association, a position she held until 1913.

Shaw's contemporaries found a smoother path to the ministry within the small denominations and emerging sects. The Quakers, Universalists, Unitarians, Free-Will Baptists, and Christian Congregationalists, for example, allowed and occasionally encouraged women to serve as ministers. In 1870, women represented only five of the slightly more than six hundred clergy affiliated with Universalists and Unitarians; by 1890, the number of women ministers in these two liberal sects had grown to about

At age twenty-one, Nanny Helen Burroughs (1879–1961), the daughter of a preacher and domestic servant, inspired the formation of the Woman's Convention, auxiliary to the National Baptist Convention. Within a few years after its formation in 1900, the Woman's Convention, which conducted its affairs as a social ministry, became the largest black women's organization in the United States, claiming 1.5 million members by 1907.

Woman's Convention
Organized by women to carry out their social service within the black Baptist Church.

seventy. The Unitarians took pride in the size of their delegation to the World Parliament of Religions, held in conjunction with the Columbian Exhibition of 1893 (Chicago World's Fair), particularly the number and prestige of the women who spoke from their platform. One reporter at the meeting insisted that "most of the Unitarian ideas were voiced by women," a group that included the aged Julia Ward Howe and the famed suffragist Elizabeth Cady Stanton.

In the so-called "new" religions of the late nineteenth century, women found the space to carve out leadership positions for themselves. Spiritualism continued to thrive, for example, and women excelled as well-paid mediums or trance speakers, that is, as conduits for the spirits to communicate their messages to people still alive on Earth (see chapter 7). Such was true, too, for Theosophy, an occult sect made wildly popular by the Ukrainian-born Helena Petrovna Blavatsky. In 1875, Madame Blavatsky, as she was known, founded the Theosophical Society. Under her tutelage, her devoted followers prepared to introduce other Americans to unfamiliar Eastern religions, particularly Hinduism and Buddhism.

Of the "new" religions, New Thought and Christian Science developed in response to women's leadership. Much like Theosophy, both metaphysical movements aimed to make people aware of the creative power of their minds, particularly their ability to heal the sick through prayer. Mary Baker Eddy, who published the key text, *Science and Health*, in 1875 took credit for founding Christian Science. In 1879, she organized the Church of Christ (Scientist) in Boston and two years later opened a metaphysical college where she charged very large sums for lessons in spiritual healing. By the time of her death in 1910, the Christian Science movement had grown to perhaps as many as ninety thousand members, and she herself died a millionaire. New Thought, meanwhile, which remained a movement of loosely affiliated sects, provided a large forum for women to emerge as lecturers, teachers, writers, and publishers of mind cure philosophy.

Visual Arts

Women began to train at established arts schools and academies in 1844 when the Pennsylvania Academy of the Fine Arts opened its doors to them. Nevertheless, only in the 1870s were women allowed to enroll in classes using nude subjects; and even then women were segregated into "ladies' life classes," which supposedly preserved their modesty and protected their reputation by sparing them exposure to the human anatomy in the presence of mixed company. The prestigious National Academy of Design enforced this policy well into the 1930s.

Much like women set on a career in medicine, those who could afford to study abroad chose Europe as their destination. Harriet Hosmer, who excelled as a neoclassical sculptor, studied in Rome; Mary Cassatt, who braved realism and sexuality as artistic themes, made France her permanent home. The great majority, as in the case of other aspiring professionals, relied on women's institutions. The Philadelphia School of Design for Women, founded in 1844, and the Woman's National Art Association, formed in 1866, became the first links in an emerging network of professional women artists.

By the 1880s, women artists, much like women educators and physicians, had created a place for themselves in their profession that was determined as much by their gender as by their work. In an effort to mesh domestic responsibilities and vocational aspirations, some aspiring artists literally transformed their homes into studios. Increasingly, though, marriage seemed incompatible with artistic accomplishment. "There *is* no *art* for a woman who marries," proclaimed illustrator Mary Hallock Foote, who chose painter Helena de Kay Gilder as her domestic companion. In the company of other women, artists created both private and public institutions to foster their professional ambitions. By the turn of the century, a plethora of art clubs encouraged both amateurs and professionals and staged exhibitions of their work. In Chicago, New York, and Philadelphia—all major centers of art—women established regional associations and additionally affiliated with the National Association of Women Painters and Sculptors, which sponsored its first exhibition in 1891.

No group of professional women garnered as much respect and admiration as artists. Yet, like other professionals, women artists triumphed mainly in their own, separate circles or on the periphery of the larger profession. Like the women educators and administrators who thrived mainly at women's colleges,

Mary Hallock Foote (1847–1938) studied fine art at Cooper School of Design in New York City. Reluctantly, she accompanied her husband to western states and territories and worked primarily as a short-story writer and illustrator. "Crest of the Bluff" provided graphic imagery for a short story by the famed New England local colorist Mary Wilkins Freeman, which was published in The Century *in 1891.*

and like the women physicians who created their own outstanding medical colleges and hospitals, a small cadre of artists broke professional ground. The overwhelming majority, much like grammar school teachers, homeopathic physicians, and practitioners of "new" religions, made little headway in the major genres of the fine arts, such as the historical or landscape painting that brought fame to male artists. Women found greater prospects for careers in the applied or decorative arts.

THE NEW WOMAN AT HOME

Despite the increasing number of women earning wages, and despite their impressive advances into professional occupations, the overwhelming majority of women continued to work exclusively within "woman's sphere." As late as 1920, 75 percent of women identified themselves as full-time homemakers, fulfilling their seemingly timeless roles as wives, mothers, and housekeepers.

However, in urban areas and especially among the middle classes, home and family life had changed so dramatically since the Civil War that homemakers, in their own way, had joined the ranks of the New Woman.

Smaller Families, Better Babies

American families had shrunk in size over the course of the nineteenth century, so much so that by 1900 a middle-class household rarely comprised more than four or five members. In rural areas, families tended to be a little larger, as were those among

WOMEN'S VOICES

DESCRIBING WOMEN'S PLACE IN THE ART WORLD

Born in Philadelphia, Anna Lea traveled to Europe shortly after the Civil War to study art. In 1871, she settled in England, where she later married Henry Merritt, a fellow artist and critic, who died just three months after their wedding. Anna Lea Merritt established herself as a successful portrait painter and developed strong feelings about the place of women in the world of professional artists.

It is now twenty-seven years since I have lived by my brush. The great interest in art and the development of influential exhibitions and schools in America I have watched with keen interest and with the regret that I had not their aid in early life. Born in America grafted on England, each country has a hand. . . . As a woman artist, I may consider it a little from the woman's point of view, but there has never been any great obstacles for women to overcome. Our work in England from the first has found its place in the general body of art work, and modern conditions affect men and women equally. . . .

Is it possible that women are differently from men affected by all these modern circumstances?

Women artists have been fairly treated in the exhibitions; there was never any exclusion.

Recent attempts to make separate exhibitions of women's work were in opposition to the views of the artists concerned, who knew that it would lower their standard and risk the place they already occupied. What we so strongly desire is a place in the large field: the kind ladies who wish to distinguish us as women would unthinkingly work us harm. . . .

But the inequality observed in women's work is more probably the result of untoward domestic accidents. Some near relative may be ill, and a woman will give her care and thought where a man would not dream of so doing, where no one would expect it from him. By many smaller things a woman's thoughts are distracted when a man's more easily keep on the course. Women who work must harden their hearts, and not be at the beck and call of affections or duties or trivial domestic cares. And if they can make themselves so far unfeminine, their work will lose that charm which belongs to their nature, and which ought to be its distinction.

The chief obstacle to a woman's success is that she can never have a wife. Just reflect what a wife does for an artist:

Darns the stockings;

Keeps his house;

Writes his letters;

Visits for his benefit;

Wards off intruders;

Is personally suggestive of beautiful pictures;

Always an encouraging and partial critic.

It is exceedingly difficult to be an artist without this time-saving help. A husband would be quite useless. He would never do any of these disagreeable things.

Another feminine defect is a tendency to over-thriftiness and over-industry. For instance, in the spring, when our pictures are sent in, when the birds are singing, when "a young man's fancy (we are told) lightly turns to thoughts of love," to what does every true woman turn? To spring cleaning, of course. A man does not: he goes away.

We working women do not amuse ourselves, we are apt to be working always. Constant industry becomes plodding and monotonous. Some of us even make a dress occasionally. But this thriftiness is a great mistake, for ideas are begotten—and observation is acute in moments of leisure—far from the tools of craft. Only look how incessant industry has injured one class of little people whom it has been too much the habit to extol: I allude to the busy bee. . . .

Save us from the modern tendency to turn art into an organized industry. This is woman's tendency—to deny herself frivolity or rest, to work over-hard, to lose in consequence freshness and spontaneity, and to become like the miserable bee. . . .

Art in all its branches is a profession as open to women as to men. For women of exceptional ability there have always been interest and employment. In painting and in sculpture, in enamelling, in house decoration, bookbinding, and that most enchanting art, landscape gardening, many succeed and gain cordial recognition. There ought to be a lady member in every firm of domestic architects, for mere men have a way of forgetting coal cellars and linen cupboards. Doubtless women would think of many improvements in domestic convenience while not overlooking the beautiful. Home-making is their specialty.

Source: Anna Lea Merritt, "A Letter to Artists: Especially Women Artists," Lippincott's Monthy Magazine 64 (March 1900): 463–69.

Questions

1. According to Anna Lea Merritt, what are the best chances for women's success in the art world?

2. Does she believe that women and men have different kinds of talents or merely unequal opportunities to develop them?

African Americans and new immigrants. In the growing metropolis, however, disparities among various groups and regions lessened.

Smaller family size did not necessarily translate into more time for nondomestic pursuits. In a book published in 1909, the Swedish writer Ellen Key heralded *The Century of the Child*, capturing the essence of the new era. Poor families and rural mothers continued to regard their children as extra hands, sending them into the factories or fields as necessary; in contrast, urban middle-class mothers worked harder themselves to provide their children a beneficial emotional environment from the moment of birth. Such mothers no longer simply "tended" to their children's basic needs but "reared" them. They encouraged them along a developmental path, which was based on the most up-to-date scientific findings rather than common sense or folk wisdom.

A wealth of new literature on "scientific motherhood" appeared by the turn of the century, warning mothers to go beyond "instinct and mother love" and to follow the new precepts. The popular advice book, *Infant Care* (1914), for example, instructed mothers to begin toilet training when their child reached the age of two or three months. The author acknowledged that such early training demanded "much time and patience" on the part of the mother but insisted that proper toilet habits adopted at an early age would be "of untold value to the child, not only in babyhood, but throughout the whole of life." She also advised mothers to weigh their infants before and after each feeding to make certain they received the proper nourishment. By 1920, women were skimping more on household chores than their counterparts a half century earlier but devoting many more hours to child care and to shopping.

Woman's Sphere Transformed

The second industrial revolution transformed the way women handled their domestic chores. In comparison to the open hearth, the cast-iron stove not only used less fuel but made cooking easier and safer. After the turn of the century, gas replaced wood and coal in the newest designs of cook stoves, while electricity gradually took the place of gas as a source of indoor lighting in urban homes. For the middle-class housekeeper, electricity also powered a widening range of appliances, including some models of stoves and such luxuries as automatic dishwashers, ironing machines, and vacuum cleaners. By 1912, when the price of electricity became more affordable, about 16 percent of residences had electric service; by 1920, 37 percent did. Farm women, however, had to wait until the 1930s for rural electrification under the New Deal.

Perhaps no technology lightened the load of the housekeeper or marked the differences between the classes as much as indoor plumbing. Hauling water for cooking, laundry, cleaning, and bathing the entire family—and then carrying out the slops—was one of the housekeeper's most backbreaking chores. At the turn of the century, a sizable proportion of middle-class homes had indoor plumbing; for rural and working-class households, back-porch water faucets or nearby hydrants and outdoor privies remained the norm.

Middle-class housekeepers welcomed the new labor-saving technology, although as a whole it did little to reduce the amount of time spent in housework. Full-time and especially live-in servants disappeared at nearly the same rate that the new technologies came in. As a consequence, the matron of the house took on most of the chores that in earlier times a domestic "helper" or maid would have done. At the same time, domesticity, much like child care, achieved a new aura as reformers and experts proclaimed it a science.

Since the publication of *The American Woman's Home: Or, Principles of Domestic Science, Being a Guide to the Formation and Maintenance of Economical, Healthful, Beautiful, and Christian Homes* (1869) by sisters Catharine E. Beecher and Harriet Beecher Stowe, the topic of housekeeping kept many pens in motion. In the late 1860s, Melusina Fay Peirce proposed a scheme of cooperative housekeeping, whereby women would pool their efforts to reduce what she described as "the dusty drudgery of house ordering." She convinced a group of women in Cambridge, Massachusetts, to rent a neighborhood facility where they collectively managed all the cooking, baking, sewing, and laundry that they ordinarily performed in their individual homes, and then charged their husbands the going market rate for such services. The experiment ultimately failed, a fate Peirce attributed to "HUSBAND-POWER." Charlotte Perkins Gilman, writing nearly forty years later, came up with a variation on this scheme. In *Women and Economics* (1898), she advocated the integration of household chores into modern industry. Meal preparation, laundry, cleaning, and even child care would all become commercial enterprises. Like Peirce, Gilman advocated the removal of chores from individual homes; unlike her forerunner, she did not assume that only women would perform them.

Contrary to the expectations of visionaries like Peirce and Gilman, the home remained the site of women's domestic labor, and, much like child rearing, domesticity developed into a vocation demanding both dedication and training. The first public universities that admitted women in the 1860s and 1870s made **home economics** central to the curriculum designed for women, while groups of reformers established cooking schools for adult women and campaigned to introduce cooking and sewing classes into the public schools.

African American women's colleges encouraged students to learn cooking and sewing, viewing mastery of the domestic arts as a means of establishing respectability.

home economics
Originated in the 1880s as an academic discipline devoted to the care of home and family.

At Spelman, for example, all senior women took turns, in groups of five, living in the Practice College, learning these arts by doing their own housekeeping, meal planning, and cooking. The educators did not envision this program as training for domestic service but as preparation for managing the home. Southern public schools, however, required black female students to study home economics specifically as preparation for future jobs as servants.

In 1908, the American Home Economics Association (AHEA) was organized to make home economics for girls what industrial education was for boys. Under the leadership of Ellen Swallow Richards, the first woman to receive a degree from the Massachusetts Institute of Technology and the first woman to serve on its faculty, the AHEA promoted the scientific study of nutrition and housekeeping. Richards herself aspired to make home economics a career track for the college woman who would then apply scientific principles "not only in her own home, but in all work for the amelioration of the condition of mankind." By the second decade of the twentieth century, when many secondary schools embraced vocational education, home economics became a staple in the curriculum. By 1920, one-third of all female high school students were enrolled in home economics courses, the majority preparing not to become researchers or teachers like Richards but full-time housewives.

From Production to Consumption

"Housekeeping," Ellen Richards explained, "no longer means washing dishes, scrubbing floors, making soap and candles; it means spending a given amount of money for a great variety of ready-prepared articles and so using the commodities as to produce the greatest satisfaction and the best possible mental, moral, and physical results." Indeed, over the course of the nineteenth century, commercial industries gradually took over the production of more and more items that women customarily made at home. Canned and prepared foods, toiletries and pharmaceuticals, soap and candles, clothing and bedding of all kinds were not only readily available in urban shops or through mail-order catalogs but were often cheaper and better than similar items made at home. Rural and urban working-class families nevertheless continued to regard their homes as active workplaces where butter could be churned before brought to market or where shirts could be stitched before collected by the contractor. Middle-class families, however, viewed their homes as distinct from the marketplace and assumed that homemakers would become the primary purchasers of basic necessities as well as luxuries.

Legions of advertisers stepped forward to persuade women to embrace a new identity—consumer. By the 1880s, national advertising agencies were selling their services to manufacturers, promising to create a demand among housewives for all kinds of brand-name products ranging from packaged cereals to patent medicines and cigarettes. Vast displays of advertisements supported the publication of a host of new magazines devoted to domesticity, such as *Ladies' Home Journal*, which interwove short stories and advice columns about women's role as consumer.

Montgomery Ward began as a mail-order business in 1872, advertising a wide variety of goods in its sales catalog. By 1908, when this advertisement appeared, Ward's enormously popular "wish book" weighed more than four pounds and promoted the latest fashions to American women everywhere, even those who lived in remote rural districts.

Mass retailers also helped to shape this new identity. Having debuted in the 1870s, department stores quickly grew into palaces of consumption, enticing women with an ever-expanding array of goods as well as providing them with a pleasant destination. For the middle-class consumer, work merged into leisure. Retailers such as Filene's in Boston, Marshall Field's in Chicago, Wanamaker's in Philadelphia, and Macy's in New York seemed to spare no expense in constructing grand, well-lighted buildings and in staging magnificent displays for their wares. Huge plate-glass windows filled with the latest fashions lured women inside. Elaborately decorated aisles marked seasonal holidays like Christmas and Easter or provided an imaginary escape to such exotic places as "the streets of Paris" or a Japanese garden. The department store offered a host of amenities: restaurants, travel bureaus, beauty parlors, writing rooms, post offices, libraries, butcher shops, and even roof gardens and child-care facilities. To make purchasing easy, by 1902, the major department stores offered charge accounts to their customers.

Department stores catered to an urban clientele of women, whereas the chain stores reached the small towns and mail-order catalogs reached the countryside. Montgomery Ward, founded in 1872, built its mail-order business by marketing to the Patrons of Husbandry; Sears, Roebuck & Company, by offering a nearly endless line of goods, became Ward's chief competitor in the 1890s. By this time, chain stores such as Woolworth's had begun to cut into the small-town market for cheap variety items, while supermarkets like A&P competed with independent grocers by offering a greater range of items at lower prices.

Not all married women embraced this new identity with equal fervor. Many immigrants were either too poor or bound to traditional ways. Many men simply refused to turn over their wages to their wives, thus curtailing their ability to shop. Yet, for most women with the means to do so, shopping became an important social ritual, a reason to meet friends for lunch or tea, and, equally important, a major domestic responsibility.

CONCLUSION

"The destiny of the world today lies in the hearts and brains of her women," pronounced Mary Seymour Howell in 1887. "The world can not travel upward faster than the feet of her women are climbing the paths of progress." Seymour's prognosis was shared by many of her contemporaries who had witnessed significant changes in women's work since the Civil War. Whether women now earned a small pittance in the nation's factories or fields, or commanded a sizable salary as the first generation to make a significant inroad into the professions, the most optimistic believed women were breaking sharply with the circumscribed life of the past. Nevertheless, the majority eventually withdrew from the world of work to marry and care for a family. But even then, their activities within the home bore only a superficial resemblance to their mothers'. The ideology of separate spheres, still resilient, had begun to break down under the challenge of the New Woman.

1840

1844
Philadelphia School of Design for Women opens

1857
New York Infirmary for Women and Children opens

1860

1862
New England Hospital for Women and Children opens

1866
Woman's National Art Association forms

1868
Woman's Medical College of the New York Infirmary established

1875
Page Act prohibits entry of women for prostitution
Madame Helene Blavatsky founds the Theosophical Society

1878
Boston physicians form first women's medical society

1879
Mary Baker Eddy organizes Church of Christ (Scientist) in Boston

1872
Montgomery Ward begins as a catalog-order business

1880

1880
Anna Howard Shaw ordained as first woman minister in Methodist Episcopal Church

1881
Atlanta Female Baptist Seminary, renamed Spelman, opened

1897
White women protest the hiring of black women in Atlanta textile mill

1898
Charlotte Perkins Gilman publishes *Women and Economics*

1882
Chinese Exclusion Act halts Chinese immigration

1893
Columbian Exhibition (Chicago World's Fair) held
World Parliament of Religions convenes

1900

1900
Woman's Convention of the National Baptist Church formed

1908
American Home Economics Association formed

1909
National Training School for Women and Girls established

1914
Infant Care published

1915
American Medical Associations admits women for the first time

REVIEW QUESTIONS

1. Why did women prefer jobs in manufacturing over those in domestic service?
2. Why did Jewish immigrant women predominate in the garment trades?
3. How did the rise of the southern textile industry affect race relations between women?
4. Why did women often rely on their own networks and create separate institutions to pursue careers in the professions?
5. How did child care change at the turn of the century?

RECOMMENDED READING

Susan Porter Benson. *Counter Cultures: Saleswomen, Managers, and Customers in American Department Stores, 1890–1940*. Urbana, IL: University of Illinois Press, 1986. A three-way study of department stores with keen attention to the dynamics of class as well as gender. Fascinating analysis of the operation of women's culture in the workplace.

Virginia G. Drachman. *Hospital with a Heart: Women Doctors and the Paradox of Separatism at the New England Hospital 1862–1969*. Ithaca: Cornell University Press, 1984. Traces the career of Dr. Marie Zakrzewska as founder of the long-lived women's hospital and insightfully examines the history of the hospital within the larger context of a general shift from gender separatism to integration and especially the consolidation of medicine as a profession.

Susan A. Glenn. *Daughters of the Shtetl: Life and Labor in the Immigrant Generation*. Ithaca: Cornell University Press, 1990. Glenn makes a powerful case for the impact of wage-labor on immigrant women's behavior and expectations. A brilliant, well-researched study of Jewish New Women.

Jacquelyn Dowd Hall, et. al. *Like a Family: The Making of a Southern Cotton Mill World*. Chapel Hill: University of North Carolina Press, 1987. Based in part on oral histories, this book examines the transformation of the Piedmont into a center of industrial production.

Evelyn Brooks Higginbotham. *Righteous Discontent: The Women's Movement in the Black Baptist Church, 1880–1920*. Cambridge, MA: Harvard University Press, 1993. A rich narrative tracing the rise of the Woman's Convention of the black Baptist Church, highlighting women's role in social activism and in establishing a place for themselves in church governance and interpretation of theology.

Tara W. Hunter. *To 'Joy My Freedom: Southern Black Women's Lives and Labors after the Civil War*. Cambridge, MA: Harvard University Press, 1997. A study of African American women who worked in household service in the New South. Hunter's research extends well beyond the workplace to consider neighborhood life as well as commercial amusements as focal points for women's fight for dignity and self-respect.

Sarah Abigail Leavitt. *From Catharine Beecher to Martha Stewart: A Cultural History of Domestic Advice*. Chapel Hill: University of North Carolina Press, 2002. An insightful and compelling survey of the major trends in tips to homemakers and in the setting of standards for domesticity.

Laura R. Prieto. *At Home in the Studio: The Professionalization of Women Artists in America*. Cambridge, MA: Harvard University Press, 2001. A close study of the emergence of professional identity among women artists, their use of domestic and "feminine" metaphors to break into the art world and the contradictions that such practices bequeathed to future generations.

Beryl Satter. *Each Mind a Kingdom: American Women, Sexual Purity, and the New Thought Movement, 1875–1920*. Berkeley: University of California Press, 1999. A deeply researched and highly engaging study of women's leadership in the New Thought movement. Satter links the role of women as mind-cure healers and the turn-of-the-century woman's movement.

Sharon Hartman Strom. *Beyond the Typewriter: Gender, Class, and the Origins of Modern American Office Work, 1900–1930.* Urbana, IL: University of Illinois Press, 1992. Examines the processes by which women became the prime targets for recruitment to office work in the early twentieth century. Strom vividly illustrates the office hierarchy and the place of scientific management in maintaining male dominance.

Diane C. Vecchio. *Merchants, Midwives, and Laboring Women: Italian Migrants in Urban America.* Urbana, IL: University of Illinois Press, 2006. Makes a strong case that Italian immigrant women often worked outside the home, depending on the local economy. The author compares labor force patterns in Milwaukee, Wisconsin, a heavy-industry town, and Endicott, New York, a center of light manufacturing.

Judy Yung. *Unbound Feet: A Social History of Chinese Women in San Francisco.* Berkeley: University of California Press, 1995. Chooses the theme of foot binding to frame her remarkable study of social change. Yung begins with the cloistered lives of nineteenth-century immigrant women and ends with the activism of the World War II generation.

ADDITIONAL BIBLIOGRAPHY

Wage-Earning Women

Sarah Eisenstein. *Give Us Bread But Give Us Roses: Working Women's Consciousness in the United States, 1890 to the First World War.* London, Boston: Routledge & K. Paul, 1983.

Lisa M. Fine. *The Souls of the Skyscraper: Female Clerical Workers in Chicago, 1870–1930.* Philadelphia: Temple University Press, 1990.

David M. Katzman. *Seven Days a Week: Women and Domestic Service in Industrializing America.* New York: Oxford University Press, 1978.

Joanne J. Meyerowtiz. *Women Adrift: Independent Wage Earners in Chicago, 1880–1930.* Chicago: University of Chicago Press, 1988.

Priscilla Murolo. *The Common Ground of Womanhood: Class, Gender, and Working Girls' Clubs, 1884–1928.* Urbana, IL: University of Illinois Press, 1997.

John L. Rury. *Education and Women's Work: Female Schooling and the Division of Labor in Urban America, 1870–1930.* Albany: State University of New York Press, 1991.

Leslie Woodcock Tentler. *Wage-Earning Women: Industrial Work and Family Life in the United States, 1900–1930.* New York: Oxford University Press, 1979.

Immigrant Women

Betty Boyd Caroli, Robert F. Harney, and Lydio F. Tomasi. *The Italian Immigrant Woman in North America: Proceedings of the Tenth Annual Conference of the American Italian Historical Association Held in Toronto. Ontario (Canada) October 28 and 29, 1977 in Conjunction with the Canadian Italian Historical Association.* Toronto: Multicultural History Society of Ontario, 1978.

Miriam Cohen. *Workshop to Office: Two Generations of Italian Women in New York City, 1900–1950.* Ithaca, NY: Cornell University Press, 1993.

Elizabeth Ewen. *Immigrant Women in the Land of Dollars: Life and Culture on the Lower East Side, 1890–1925.* New York: Monthly Review Press, 1985.

Huping Ling. *Surviving on the Gold Mountain: A History of Chinese American Women and their Lives.* Albany, NY: State University of New York Press, 1998.

Janet A. Nolan. *Ourselves Alone: Women's Emigration from Ireland, 1885–1920.* Lexington: University Press of Kentucky, 1989.

Maxine Schwartz Seller, ed. *Immigrant Women.* Revised Second Edition. Albany: State University of New York Press, 1994.

Judith E. Smith, *Family Connections: A History of Italian and Jewish Immigrant Lives in Providence, Rhode Island, 1900–1940.* Albany, NY: State University of New York Press, 1985.

Sydney Stahl Weinberg. *The World of Our Mothers: The Lives of Jewish Immigrant Women.* Chapel Hill: University of North Carolina Press, 1988.

Virginia Yans-McLaughlin. *Family and Community: Italian Immigrants in Buffalo, 1880–1930.* Ithaca, NY: Cornell University Press, 1977.

Judy Yung. *Chinese Women of America, A Pictorial History.* Seattle: University of Washington Press, 1986.

New South

Edward L. Ayers. *The Promise of the New South: Life After Reconstruction.* New York: Oxford University Press, 1992.

Marie Johnson. *Southern Ladies, New Women: Race, Region, and Clubwomen in South Joan Carolina, 1890–1930.* Gainesville: University Press of Florida, 2004.

Barbara Ellen Smith, ed., *Neither Separate Nor Equal: Women, Race, and Class in the South.* Philadelphia: Temple University Press, 1999.

Professional Women

Virginia G. Drachman. *Sisters in Law: Women Lawyers in Modern American History.* Cambridge, MA: Harvard University Press, 1998.

Roberta Frankfort. *Collegiate Women: Domesticity and Career in Turn-of-the-Century America.* New York: New York University Press, 1977.

Penina Migdal Glazer and Miriam Slater. *Unequal Colleagues: The Entrance of Women into the Professions, 1890–1940.* New Brunswick, NJ: Rutgers University Press, 1987.

Lynn D. Gordon. *Gender and Higher Education in the Progressive Era.* New Haven: Yale University Press, 1990.

Barbara J. Harris. *Beyond Her Sphere: Women and the Professions in American History.* Westport, CT: Greenwood Press, 1978.

Darlene Clark Hine. *Black Women in White: Racial Conflict and Cooperation in the Nursing Profession, 1890–1950.* Bloomington: Indiana University Press, 1989.

Miriam R. Levin. *Defining Women's Scientific Enterprise: Mount Holyoke Faculty and the Rise of American Science.* Hanover: University Press of New England, 2005.

Gloria Moldow. *Women Doctors in Gilded-Age Washington: Race, Gender, and Professionalization.* Urbana: University of Illinois Press, 1987.

Regina Markell Morantz-Sanchez. *Sympathy and Science: Women Physicians in American Medicine.* New York: Oxford University Press, 1985.

Susan M. Reverby. *Ordered to Care: The Dilemma of American Nursing, 1850–1945.* New York: Cambridge University Press, 1987.

Stephanie J. Shaw. *What a Woman Ought to Be and To Do: Black Professional Women Workers during the Jim Crow Era.* Chicago: University of Chicago Press, 1996.

Kirsten Swinth. *Painting Professionals: Women Artists and the Development of Modern Art, 1870–1930.* Chapel Hill: University of North Carolina Press, 2001.

Mary Roth Walsh. *"Doctors Wanted: No Women Need Apply": Sexual Barriers in the Medical Profession, 1835–1875.* New Haven: Yale University Press, 1977.

Women's Work at Home

Elaine S. Abelson. *When Ladies Go-A-Thieving: Middle-Class Shoplifters in the Victorian Department Store.* New York: Oxford University Press, 1989.

Dolores Hayden. *The Grand Domestic Revolution: History of Feminist Designs for American Homes, Neighborhoods, and Cities.* Cambridge, MA: MIT Press, 1981.

William R. Leach. "Transformations in a Culture of Consumption: Women and Department Stores, 1890–1925," *Journal of American History,* 71 (September 1984), 319–342.

Jane Bernard Powers. *The "Girl Question" in Education for Young Women in the Progressive Era.* Washington, D.C.: Falmer Press, 1992.

Susan Strasser. *Never Done: A History of American Housework.* New York: Pantheon Books, © 1982.

Biographies, Autobiographies, and Memoirs

Mary Antin. *The Promised Land.* North Stratford, N.H.: Ayer Press, 2000, 1969.

Joyce Antler. *Lucy Sprague Mitchell: The Making of a Modern Woman.* New Haven: Yale University Press, 1987.

Rose Cohen. *Out of the Shadow.* New York: George H. Doran Co. 1918.

Gillian Gill. *Mary Baker Eddy*. Reading, MA: Perseus Books, 1998.

Elizabeth Hasanovitz. *One of Them*. Boston: Houghton Mifflin Co., 1918.

Marie Hall Ets. *Rosa: The Life of an Italian Immigrant*. Minneapolis: University of Minnesota Press, 1970.

Rose Schneiderman, with Lucy Goldwaite. *All for One*. New York: P.S. Eriksson, 1967.

Arleen Marcia Tuchman. *Science Has No Sex: The Life of Marie Zakrzewska, M. D.* Chapel Hill: University of North Carolina Press, 2006.

Cynthia Grant Tucker. *A Woman's Ministry: Mary Collson's Search for Reform as a Unitarian Minister, a Hull House Social Worker, and a Christian Science Practitioner*. Philadelphia: Temple University Press, 1984.

THE WOMAN MOVEMENT, 1880–1900

CROSS-CLASS ALLIANCES

Young Women's Christian Association

Christian Homes for African American
Women Workers

Women's Educational and Industrial Union

Illinois Woman's Alliance

SPANNING THE NATION

National Woman's Christian
Temperance Union

National American Woman
Suffrage Association

General Federation of Women's Clubs

National Association of Colored Women

CAMPAIGNS OF THE 1890S

Populism

Woman Suffrage in the West

Antilynching Crusade

The Spanish American War

WOMAN'S EMPIRE

Women's Foreign Mission Movement

World WCTU

Outposts of the YWCA

WHAT STRATEGIES
DID *various women's
organizations develop to
address the needs of
wage-earning women?*

HOW DID *federation
improve the ability of
organized women to
wage their campaigns?*

LACKING THE
VOTE, HOW DID
*women participate in
the great political cam-
paigns of the 1890s?*

WHAT ROLE DID
*women play in the
missionary movements
of the late nineteenth
century?*

Let me then frankly say that I believe we should organize a miniature council in every town and city, confederating these in every State, and instructing the State Council to send delegates to the National Council. [The President of the council] should have power to choose her own cabinet from the seven ablest women of the country, representing the industries, education, professions, philanthropies, reforms, and the religious and political work of women. We should thus have within the National Government, as carried on by men, a republic of women, duly

Women of Plymouth, 1893 *Lucia Fairchild Fuller (American, 1872–1924) Mural, Women's Building, 1893 World's Exposition* organized and officered, not in any wise antagonistic to men, but conducted in their interest as much as in our own, and tending toward such mutual fellowship among women, such breadth of knowledge and sympathy as should establish solidarity of sentiment and purpose throughout the Nation of women-workers, put a premium upon organized as against isolated efforts for human betterment, minify the sense of selfhood and magnify that of otherhood, training and tutoring women for the next great step in the evolution of humanity, when men and women shall sit side by side in Government and the nations shall earn war no more. . . .

We have long met to read essays, make speeches and prepare petitions; let us hereafter meet, in this great Council, to *legislate* for Womanhood, for Childhood and the Home. Men have told us solemnly, have told us often and in good faith, no doubt, that "they would grant whatever the women of the National asked." Our time to ask *unitedly* has waited long, but it is here at last. . . . what end have we in view? Is it fame, fortune, leadership? Not as I read women's hearts, who have known them long and well. It is for love's sake—for the bringing in of peace on earth, good-will to men.

Source: "Speech by Frances E. Willard to the National Council of Women of the United States, Assembled in Washington, D.C., Feb. 23, 1891." In Transactions of the National Council of Women of the United States, Assembled in Washington, D.C., February 22 to 25, 1891 *(Philadelphia, PA: J. B. Lippincott & Co., 1891), 27, 31.*

National Council of Women Formed in 1888 in commemoration of the fortieth anniversary of the woman's rights meeting at Seneca Falls, New York, as a representative body of women's reform organizations.

International Council of Women Formed in 1888 as a counterpart to the National Council of Women with delegates representing women activists from nine nations.

rances Willard outlined this plan to create a "republic of women" within the United States at the first meeting of the **National Council of Women** (NCW). As president of the new organization, she used her office to push the delegates to think boldly about their prospects for power.

In the early 1880s, Elizabeth Cady Stanton and Susan B. Anthony had proposed an international meeting of suffragists to commemorate the fortieth anniversary of the first woman's rights meeting at Seneca Falls, New York. As the anniversary approached, leaders from various women's organizations decided to broaden the agenda by extending an invitation to "women workers along all lines of social, intellectual, moral or civic progress and reform . . . whether they be advocates of the ballot or opposed to women's suffrage."

In March 1888, representatives from fifty-three women's organizations gathered in the nation's capital to celebrate the progress of women. The railroads offered reduced fares to travelers from across the country, while steamships brought delegates from as far away as England, Finland, and Germany. After more than a week of meetings, the delegates adopted a platform that, to Stanton's dismay, did not include woman suffrage but instead listed its "cardinal tenet" as woman's right to "equal wages for equal work." Moreover, the delegates chose to honor Willard for her outstanding leadership in the Woman's Christian Temperance Union by naming her, rather than Stanton, as president of the new organization. The meetings concluded with the formation of the **International Council of Women** (ICW), which would

The National Council of Women, organized in 1888, comprised the presidents of national organizations of women dedicated to the advancement of women's work in education, philanthropy, reform, and social culture. Pictured here are the general officers in the early 1890s.

build trans-Atlantic bridges between women activists and the NCW, which would link American organizations.

The formation of the ICW and the NCW marked a high point in what the delegates referred to as the "woman movement." Deeply involved in public affairs, the rising generation of women continued to rely on single-sex voluntary organizations to advance their goals, and activists were less invested in the right to vote than in the imperative to reform society. Organized women would—in the words of one of the speakers—"plead for freedom for themselves in the name of and for the good of humanity."

However, this devotion to "the good of humanity" did not dispel the biases and prejudices of the era. While white activists reached out to their working-class "sisters," they rarely crossed the lines of race, ethnicity, or religion. Nor did white activists do much to protest the rise of Jim Crow and the increasing violence waged against African Americans. Moreover, although strongly committed to democratic ideals, they associated much of the merit of their "civilization" with the Anglo-Saxons who predominated. Nor did women unite in opposition to the imperialism that took the nation into the overseas war that resulted in new territories and new populations under the rule of the United States.

CROSS-CLASS ALLIANCES

In 1887, the social reformer Helen Stuart Campbell published *Prisoners of Poverty*, a compilation of melodramatic short stories about the hardships women endured in trying to earn a living wage in the New York garment industry. A few years later, the U.S. Commissioner of Labor, Carroll D. Wright, echoed her sentiments, publishing his own volume to reassure the public that, despite their impoverishment, "the working women of the country are as honest and as virtuous as any class of our citizens." During final decades of the nineteenth century, a large number of middle- and upper-class women activists agreed with this assessment and helped to create a vast array of social services specifically for wage-earning women.

This enterprise, however well meaning, failed to bridge a growing gap between the classes or to ameliorate poverty. In an era marked by labor strife and massive strikes, by social dislocations caused by a huge wave of rural black migration into industrializing cities and European immigration, and by poverty growing in the wake of a major depression, inequality grew larger rather than smaller. Nevertheless, despite these limitations, the ICW's commitment to "equal wages for equal work" drove the work of these organizations.

Young Women's Christian Association

Young Women's Christian Association
Formed in several cities shortly after the Civil War to offer social services to young wage-earning women.

Shortly after the Civil War, the **Young Women's Christian Association** (YWCA) organized as an offshoot of the Ladies' Christian Union, which had formed in New York City in 1858 to assist "young women who are dependent on their own exertions for support." Bringing souls to Christ was their primary goal, but the Protestant women who founded the YWCA also aspired to instill in young women a respect for labor and to encourage them to develop their talents to the fullest. "It is manifestly the arrangement of Providence," one director wrote, "that a large proportion, not of men only but also of women, should procure the necessities of life by labor, in some of its various forms, bodily or mental, with hands or brain." Many of the well-to-do founders also envisioned their task as bridging "the gulf that divides the favored from the less fortunate."

By 1875, when twenty-eight associations had formed in the nation's major cities and on several college campuses, more than half of the local chapters maintained employment committees to help newcomers to the city secure reputable employment, and the majority sponsored inexpensive housing. One of the early directors asked rhetorically what the association could do for young women separated from their families. The obvious answer was: "It can build them a home—not a boardinghouse—with cheerful warmth, baths, public parlors, a library with stimulating books for leisure, morning and evening worship."

The leaders of the YWCA aimed to improve women's skills so they could compete more effectively in a labor market dominated by men. The New York YWCA offered the first class in typewriting in 1870. Most YWCAs ran training schools for domestic servants and helped to place them with respectable families. Because most women preferred to work in manufacturing or retail trades, classes in dressmaking, millinery, and stenography were the most popular. In smaller numbers, women also studied woodworking, industrial drawing, and upholstery. Programs in calisthenics and gymnastics grew in number from their introduction in the late 1870s, while the advanced classes on anatomy and hygiene prepared women to become teachers of physical training in the

WOMEN'S LIVES

GRACE HOADLEY DODGE

In 1881, Grace H. Dodge helped to organize a club of working women in New York City. The daughter of a very wealthy philanthropist, she and a silk weaver who had attended her Sunday school class together outlined a program based on three main principles: cooperation, self-government, and self-support.

At the time, there were several well-established institutions such as the YWCA and settlement houses that helped working women make their way in the city. The working girls' clubs would supplement their programs and, equally important, provide a closer relationship between the wealthy patrons and the members. Keen on building such an alliance, Dodge invited several of her well-to-do friends to join her in sponsoring this novel endeavor in "working *with* not *for*" club members. Meanwhile, nearly two hundred wage-earning women joined the first club.

Dodge soon found herself at the head of a growing network of working girls' clubs with affiliates in Boston, Philadelphia, and as far west as Chicago and St. Louis. In 1890, the Association of Working Girls' Societies held its first convention; by 1894, when the second convention took place, approximately one hundred clubs represented a combined membership of more than eleven thousand.

Dodge believed that one of the strongest links in this cross-class alliance was the common ideal of self-improvement. She herself had been taught by mainly private tutors and, unlike other young women of her means, she did not attend college. She nevertheless regarded her work in social service as equivalent to a profession—her salary, she joked, "paid in advance" by her wealthy parents. In sponsoring the working girls' clubs, Dodge aimed to impart the principal lessons of her privileged upbringing to wage-earning women.

The notion of "respectability" was a shared goal. The names of various clubs reflected this aspiration: "Endeavor," "Enterprise," and "Steadfast." Dodge published an anthology of members' writings—*Thoughts of Busy Girls, Who Have Little Time for Study Yet Find Much Time for Thinking* (1892), which contains essays with titles such as "What Constitutes an Ideal Womanhood and How to Attain it" and "Purity and Modesty: Two Words of Value."

By the mid-1890s, sisterly sentiments began to falter, especially as club members took an increasing interest in labor reform and trade unionism. In 1896, Dodge stepped aside, leaving the working-class leaders to reinvent their association as the National League of Women Workers, which supplemented its social and educational programs with campaigns to improve the conditions of women's labor.

(continued)

Dodge's philanthropic work did not end here, however. While directing the Association of Working Girls' Societies, she also worked to introduce the household arts to public schoolchildren. She established the Industrial Education Association, which encouraged the training of vocational education teachers. This project brought her a greater appreciation of the importance of good teaching, and she provided the main source of funds for the establishment of the institution that became in 1892 the Teachers College of Columbia University.

Dodge's interest in working women took a different form after the turn of the century, when she became the president of the National Board of the YWCA in 1906. The following year, she organized the New York Travelers' Aid Society to protect young women new to the city, which, under her leadership, grew into national and international organizations. ■

city's public schools. By the end of the century, the educational component had become so successful that many local Ys converted residential rooms into classrooms.

The advertisement for this book, which was published in 1901, read: "A Book Giving Full Information on all the Mysterious and Complex Matters pertaining to Women." Dr. Mary R. Melendy, a devotee of the WCTU, advised women on maternal health and well-being and child-rearing.

The YWCA did not operate as a charity, although local associations covered much of their operating expenses through endowments maintained by wealthy women affiliated with Protestant churches. Residents paid for room and board. The superintendent supplied additional services, such as laundry, cleaning, and even visiting nurses and physicians if necessary. They also maintained a library and encouraged the young women to organize reading clubs. Of course, the board of managers deemed no class as important as the weekly Bible study. Each resident, as a professed Christian, was expected to attend a church of her choice every Sunday and was "affectionately invited," although not required, to participate in evening devotional services. By 1906, more than six hundred local chapters had affiliated with the National Board of the YWCA.

By this time, the YWCA had become an international organization. The World's YWCA organized in 1894, with headquarters in London and thriving chapters in Norway and Sweden. Although the British YWCA dated only to 1885, it had deep roots in women's social services and soon joined Americans to add affiliates in countries such as India, Argentina, France, Italy, Japan, and China.

Christian Homes for African American Women Workers

The YWCA at first opened membership to African American women; but toward the end of the century, as the black urban population grew and as Jim Crow took hold, the all-white boards encouraged the formation of racially segregated facilities. In 1893, in Dayton, Ohio, the first black YWCA formed, followed by similar associations in Philadelphia, Baltimore, Harlem, Brooklyn, and Washington, D.C. In the South, black Ys formed mainly on college campuses. The black branches operated separately and subordinately to the white YWCAs in their localities but offered similar programs inspired by the determination to provide Christian influence and protection to young working women.

In addition to the YWCA, and occasionally in association with the local branch, African American women in northern communities created their own array of organizations to address the plight of young working women, particularly displaced southerners. In 1897, Victoria Earle Mathews, president of the Brooklyn Women's Club, helped to establish the **White Rose Home and Industrial Association** to "protect self-supporting colored girls who were coming to New York for the first time." Incorporating the symbolism of purity and virtue into its name, the White Rose Home offered temporary room and board to job seekers. Mathews also organized groups of women to meet newcomers at the train and boat depots, hoping to protect them from the unscrupulous recruiters who tried to lure the naive young women into less-than-honorable jobs, including prostitution. The sponsors of the White Rose Home offered instruction in domestic skills as well as in etiquette and "proper" dress and also sponsored a kindergarten for working mothers.

African American women in other cities founded dozens of similar institutions. In 1895, clubwomen established the **Sojourner Truth Home for Working Girls** in Washington, D.C. Around the same time, a group of prominent black Chicago clubwomen organized to protect young African American women from the "Human vultures ever ready to destroy young womanhood" and in 1908 opened the **Phyllis Wheatley Home.** The home provided temporary lodging to more than three hundred young women during its first seven years and secured reputable employment for more than five hundred.

In 1905, in Philadelphia, the Association for the Protection of Colored Women offered similar services, in one year dispensing aid to more than thirteen hundred young black women. From this small beginning, the **National League for the Protection of Colored Women** formed in 1906. The League coordinated activities among affiliated chapters and reached out to southern organizations, such as church groups and women's clubs, for help in distributing information about securing employment and lodging in northern cities.

A little later, Jane Edna Hunter played a similar role. A daughter of sharecroppers who had left the South to find a better life for herself in Cleveland, Hunter understood the difficulties of finding suitable housing and employment. "Sometimes I feel I've just been living my life for the moment when I can start things moving toward a home for poor Negro working girls in the city," she later recalled. In 1911, she invited a group of black domestic servants to join together in establishing the Phillis Wheatley Association and within a year they established a boardinghouse. The association and home quickly became a prominent institution within Cleveland's black community, supported by funds or the local sweat power of local

White Rose Home and Industrial Association Formed in 1897 to assist African American women coming to New York in search of work.

Sojourner Truth Home for Working Girls Formed in 1895 for African American working women.

The daughter of sharecroppers, Jane Edna Hunter (1882–1971) managed to graduate from college and train as a nurse. Despite her professional standing, after she moved to Cleveland in 1905 she could not find a decent place to live because of segregation laws and practices. In 1911 she founded the Phillis Wheatley Association to provide room and board and other social services to young African American women coming to the city in search of work.

Phyllis Wheatley Home Named after the famous African American poet, homes that were established to assist African American working women searching for work and residences.

National League for the Protection of Colored Women Formed in 1906 as a federation of organizations established to assist young African American women migrating to northern cities.

Women's Educational and Industrial Union Founded in 1877 to help women support themselves by offering social services and practical vocational training.

cross-class alliance A concept referring to the joint projects of middle- and upper-class women and working-class women based on the assumption of "sisterhood."

African American women. Eventually Hunter tapped the goodwill of prominent whites, including those who benefited directly from her programs to improve the skills of domestic servants. By the 1930s, the Phillis Wheatley Home had provided the model for similar homes across the country, as far away as Seattle and Atlanta.

Women's Educational and Industrial Union

As early as 1868, the members of the New England Women's Club asked themselves what they could do to better the conditions of the growing number of women working in Boston. The needle trades had provided work to many women since the early part of the nineteenth century, but the Civil War had given the industry a major boost, making Boston the major manufacturing city of cheap, ready-to-wear garments. Alongside the garment industry, other branches of light manufacture and retail sales grew. Domestic service continued to employ large numbers of women. Thousands upon thousands of women from New England, Canada, the South, and Europe sought positions in the city with the highest ratio of servants per family of any northern city.

After conducting an extensive investigation of working conditions in these industries, a committee of the New England Women's Club recommended a plan of action that called for the establishment of boardinghouses, the creation of vocational schools, and a program to assist new arrivals in the city. Little came of this plan until 1877, when a group of clubwomen found the resources to inaugurate the **Women's Educational and Industrial Union** (WEIU) with the intention of forming "a Union of all classes and conditions of women." This time the idea caught on, and within a year the WEIU managed to recruit four hundred members; within the next decade, membership tripled.

The WEIU, known as the "most cherished plan" of the NEWC, became an umbrella for a wide assortment of programs that were similar in design to those operated by Christian voluntary organizations. The Industrial Department operated a retail establishment where house-bound women could sell their handiwork or prepared foods. The Employment Committee maintained a job registry; the Reception Committee kept open its large headquarters, which included offices and a well-stocked reading room and library; and the Lunch Committee managed an inexpensive restaurant for women who worked in downtown stores and offices. The Protective Committee recruited lawyers who worked *pro bono* to help women gain wages withheld by dishonest employers. The Befriending Committee oversaw a mutual sick benefit program that helped women get through periods when they were too incapacitated to work and a second program to assist newcomers to Boston.

Even more than YWCA officials, the WEIU directors promoted their institution as a **cross-class alliance** of women. "We meet," the Boston president insisted, "not purse to purse or talent to talent or acquirement to acquirement, but heart to heart . . . on the common ground of humanity." Although the services offered to wage-earning women were the most extensive, the WEIU sponsored programs aimed specifically at women embarking on professional careers. The Lecture Committee employed the talents of such veteran reformers as Lucy Stone and Mary Livermore. The Committee on Moral and Spiritual Development encouraged dozens of women, including Julia Ward Howe, to develop their ministerial talents in one of the few venues available to them; its Sunday afternoon meetings provided a pulpit to aspiring women preachers.

The WEIU thrived in at least a dozen other cities, including Buffalo, Providence, Cleveland, and San Francisco. Hundreds of smaller societies with similar agendas proliferated in many other communities. The Woman's Union for Good Works of Haverhill, Massachusetts, which dated to 1891, operated a home for young working women; the Flower Festival Society of Los Angeles, which organized in 1885, hosted an annual exhibition of flowers and used the proceeds to fund a boarding home for working women.

Illinois Woman's Alliance

Like Boston, Chicago offered women many jobs in domestic service, retail sales, and light manufacturing and in the last decades of the nineteenth century pushed ahead to become the nation's foremost industrial city. By 1890, the size of its garment industry surpassed that of Boston, and eight thousand women—more than half of the total female workforce in manufacturing—worked in the production of clothing. Moreover, Chicago was home to the most vibrant sector of the labor movement at this time, and its thriving immigrant community ensured a sharp radical edge. As a consequence of this unique combination of industrial conditions and local politics, women with allegiance to the labor and socialist movements spearheaded the efforts to befriend the working woman.

This wood engraving appeared in Frank Leslie's Illustrated Newspaper *in November, 1888, just as the Illinois Woman's Alliance was taking up the campaign against the exploitative practices common to sweatshops.*

In 1888, a group of women activists led by British-born Elizabeth Morgan formed the **Illinois Woman's Alliance** (IWA). Morgan, whose husband headed the local Trades and Labor Assembly and the Socialist Labor Party, was one of the first women to join the Knights of Labor and went on to become the main organizer for the local **Ladies' Federal Labor Union,** which took in workers from various trades and which affiliated with the American Federation of Labor. Morgan's associate was Corinne Brown, who had worked for thirteen years as a teacher and principal in the Chicago public school system. Brown, like Morgan, considered herself a socialist; but as a wife of a prominent banker, she also moved comfortably within the circles of the prestigious Chicago Woman's Club. The two activists secured delegates from thirty local women's organizations and the Trades and Labor Assembly to form the IWA, which took as its motto "Justice to Children, Loyalty to Women."

Illinois Woman's Alliance Formed in 1888 to assist working women and their children.

Ladies' Federal Labor Union Chicago union of women working in several trades that did much of the campaigning for the passage of the Illinois Factory Inspection Act of 1893.

The IWA announced its intention "to prevent the moral, mental, and physical degradation of women and children as wage-workers by enforcing the factory ordinances and the compulsory education law" as well as "to secure the enactment of such new laws as may be found necessary." The IWA also conducted clothing drives for the poor, managed to persuade the city government to establish public bath houses in working-class households, and campaigned against police harassment of prostitutes.

Although the IWA lasted only six years, the coalition of Chicago women's organizations had a major impact on public policy in Illinois. Its most important venture was an attack on the "sweating system" in the garment industry, an unhealthy, poorly paid system of outwork located in tenement buildings.

In response to their campaign, in 1893, the Illinois legislature passed the most important sweatshop legislation of the decade that limited the hours of labor for women and children to eight. To enforce compliance with the new law, the governor appointed Florence Kelley as the state's chief factory inspector.

Opposed to the new legislation, employers organized the Illinois Manufacturers' Association and successfully challenged several key aspects of the law. In 1894, the Illinois Supreme Court struck down the **Illinois Factory Inspection Act,** and the IWA soon dissolved. Yet, despite this reversal, the IWA had managed to take an important step in securing the commitment of the state to the principles of social justice.

Illinois Factory Inspection Act Passed in 1893, this landmark act specified conditions of labor in sweatshops in the state of Illinois; it was declared unconstitutional the following year.

SPANNING THE NATION

Lacking the right to vote, rebuffed by the major political parties, women activists continued to rely on single-sex voluntary associations. Weaving these organizations into a vast network, they spread their influence, spanning the nation and ultimately reaching across the oceans to distant lands and new constituencies.

By the end of the century, more than a dozen national organizations consolidated the power of American women. Some were relatively small, such as the National Council of Jewish Women, created in 1893; others, such as the National Congress of Mothers, formed in 1897, grew quickly to become the Parent-Teachers Association, which continues to review policy in schools across the country. By the turn of the century, the largest organizations had established branches overseas.

National Woman's Christian Temperance Union

The WCTU had become the single largest organization of women in the United States by the time Frances Willard took over the presidency in 1879. For ten years, she traveled across the country, averaging one meeting per day, and recruited many members. By the mid-1890s, a sizable army of organizers assisted her in this ceaseless work, forming new chapters and energizing those that had lost their steam.

The WCTU became the first women's organization to build a base in the South. Willard, regarded as a "foreigner" by most southerners, conducted a successful four-month tour of the region in 1881. Sallie Chapin of Charleston, South Carolina, quickly grabbed the reins, forming so many chapters that by the end of the decade the South, previously considered a missionary field, had become fully integrated into the national organization and capable of supporting its own cadre of organizers. The southern WCTU nevertheless set its own standards, for example, by refusing to endorse woman suffrage and by maintaining separate chapters for black and white members.

By 1890, the National WCTU wielded considerable power and influence. Local chapters organized parallel to the established legislative districts, a strategy that allowed temperance activists to pressure their state representatives effectively. They lobbied for bills limiting or abolishing the sale of alcoholic beverages, imposing high license fees on retail establishments, or enacting local option laws. It was, however, Willard's **"do-everything" policy** that transformed the WCTU into an organization with far-reaching goals.

"do-everything" policy This policy provided an umbrella for the promotion of a multitude of programs beyond temperance.

In 1881, Willard first advised WCTU members to "do everything" necessary to restrict the sale and consumption of alcohol. A decade later, her appeal referred less to tactics than to goals. For example, at the 1889 National WCTU convention, delegates

These women were all members of Frances Willard's "army of women," the national WCTU, which by the end of the nineteenth century had organized women throughout the United States to address many issues related to the status of women and children, including the right to vote.

passed an antivivisection resolution and voted to petition Congress to prohibit the manufacture of cigarettes. They also decided to appeal to the Russian Czar for the humane treatment of Siberian exiles and to lobby state legislatures to establish free kindergartens. Delegates additionally affirmed their commitment to work for the establishment of separate reformatories for women and for the employment of police matrons and women administrators in women's correctional institutions. Issues of health and hygiene also figured prominently on their agenda. Willard herself campaigned for the use of whole-wheat flour in the baking of bread and better regulation of drugs prescribed by physicians. The *Union Signal,* the WCTU newspaper, urged women to fight for local ordinances to guarantee smoke-free environments. By 1896, the National WCTU had created thirty-nine departments, twenty-five of which involved women in social activism that did *not* involve temperance.

The Chicago WCTU, Willard's home chapter, emerged as a model of the "do-everything" policy. The Chicago union maintained two day nurseries, two Sunday schools, a vocational school for young people, a mission that sheltered four thousand homeless or destitute women within a twelve-month period, a free medical dispensary that treated more than sixteen hundred patients per year, and a lodging house for men that included a low-cost restaurant. The National WCTU also supported a temperance hospital in Chicago, a thirty-five room facility dedicated to treating all diseases without the use of alcohol.

"Were I to define in a sentence, the thought and purpose of the Woman's Christian Temperance Union," Willard offered, "I would reply: *It is to make the whole world*

HOMELIKE." By 1890, membership topped 150,000; including auxiliaries, such as the Young Women's Christian Temperance Union, that figure grew to more than 200,000. A few years later, the WCTU had collected dues sufficient to support a twelve-story national headquarters in Chicago, known as the Woman's Temple. By this time, the fruits of international organizing, which had begun shortly after the WCTU formed, had also ripened into the World WCTU, the strongest, most vital international organization of women. Willard had succeeded in transforming the WCTU from a single-issue campaign against drink to a massive organization with a multifaceted agenda for social change.

National American Woman Suffrage Association

In contrast to the WCTU, which had early on endorsed the woman's ballot, both the NWSA and the AWSA advanced very slowly. By 1890, women enjoyed the right to vote in a few western territories, and they had gained partial suffrage in nineteen states. Kansas women, for example, had won the right to vote in school board and municipal elections in 1887. But these few victories could not disguise the fact that the prospect of full voting rights was no brighter than it had been at the end of the Civil War. Between 1870 and 1890, eight states held suffrage referenda, and all eight were defeated. At the federal level, the situation was even gloomier. In 1882, the House of Representatives and the Senate both created committees on woman suffrage. Their hearings, however, went nowhere; and in January 1887, the Senate voted to quash the measure and end discussion.

The differences between the NWSA and the AWSA during the Reconstruction era now seemed insignificant compared to their shared failure to bring women to the ballot box. It was time, advised Alice Stone Blackwell, the activist daughter of Lucy Stone and Henry Blackwell, for the NWSA and the AWSA to put aside these differences and maximize their resources by merging the two organizations.

National American Woman Suffrage Association Formed in 1890 to promote the ballot for women.

After three years of negotiations and with steady encouragement from Susan B. Anthony, a convention held in February 1890 marked the formation of the **National American Woman Suffrage Association** (NAWSA). Initially, the old guard reigned over the new organization, with Elizabeth Cady Stanton serving as the first president. After just two years, Stanton turned over the office to Anthony, who determinedly nurtured a new generation of activists. Anthony held on to the presidency until 1900 and remained dedicated to the movement until her death in 1906.

At annual NAWSA conventions, delegates continued to argue among themselves about the surest route to woman suffrage, that is, state *versus* federal strategies. Meanwhile, state campaigns went forward. Between 1870 and 1910, suffragists waged 480 campaigns in thirty-three states, most west of the Mississippi, but they managed to get referenda before the voters only seventeen times. Even more discouraging, all but two went down in defeat. These years became known, rightly so, as "the doldrums."

Although victory remained elusive, even at the state level, the NAWSA itself thrived. The new leadership streamlined operations and planned national conventions along more formal lines. With the induction of a sizable number of new members, the NAWSA became a truly national and diverse organization. Recent college graduates, many employed outside the home, represented a growing constituency. Some very wealthy women added their luster to the new organization. In California,

WOMEN'S VOICES

SUFFRAGE VISIONARY

Mary Seymour (1844–1913) was born and raised in Livingston County, New York. After her marriage to George Howell, a Presbyterian minister, she moved to Albany, where she became a leader in the woman suffrage movement. She also was a very popular speaker on the NAWSA campaign circuit and for the WCTU. In this address, "The Dawning of the Twentieth Century," she expressed her optimism about the times ahead, when women would achieve full political rights and use them to improve society and the world.

We stand today in the dying light of the nineteenth century and in the dawning of the twentieth. If you and I could have chosen when to have existed I think there would have been no more inspiring time than now. Look back fifty years, and from the dim twilight of the tallow candles of those days we stand now in the brilliant electric light of this year eighteen hundred and ninety-three . . . With the prejudice of the ages confronting her on every hand [woman] has pushed steadily forward and the stone way of opposition is beginning to crumble. Indeed, now it is tottering and we must get out of the way, the stone still standing, before the full dawn of the twentieth century is here. Ever since woman began to think for herself, ever since woman took life in her own hands, the dawning of a great light has flooded this world. We are the mothers of men. Show me the mothers of a country and I will tell you of its sons.

The destiny of the world today lies in the hearts and brains of its women. This world can not travel upward faster than the feet of its women are climbing the paths of progress. Put us back if possible, veil us in harems, take from us all knowledge, back to the Dark Ages. The nineteenth century is closing over a world arising from bondage. It is the sublimest closing of any century the world has ever beheld. The nations of the earth have seen and are still looking at that luminous writing in the heav-

ens, "the truth shall make you free," and for the first time are gathering to themselves the true significance of liberty. . . . The dying light of the nineteenth century beholds it in the dawning rays of the twentieth, because the mothers of men are, for the first time, putting on the beautiful garments of liberty. We need, and the world needs, our political freedom. Even our social and religious liberty is worthless without political liberty. Let us this morning dedicate ourselves anew to our labor for woman, and go forth with braver souls, cleaner brains and more solute purpose to our work for these years.

I would have the women of our country so aroused to the greatness of the work and the few years that are left us in this century; so filled with zeal, determination and enthusiasm that the Congress of the United States and our legislatures may know and understand that our freedom must be fully granted to us by 1900, so that the twentieth century shall dawn on a "government of the people, for the people and by the people." Now it is a government of the men, for the men, and by the men. God bless the men.

It is the evening of the nineteenth century, but its twilight is clearer than its morning. I look back and I see each year improvement and advancement. I see woman gathering up her soul and personality and claiming them as her own against all odds and the world. I see her now asking that that personality be felt in her nation. I see old prejudices giving way. All reforms for the elevation of humanity have the great woman heart in them. Have I been too radical? Would you have me more conservative? What is conservatism? It is the dying faith of a closing century. What is fanaticism? It is the dawning light of a new era. Yes my friends, a new era for the world will dawn with the twentieth century. I look forward to that time with beating heart and bated breath. I lean forward to it with an impatient eagerness. I catch the first faint rays of that beautiful

(continued)

morning. In the East the star has appeared and soon the full dawn of the twentieth century will be upon us. I see a race of men, strong, brave and true, because the mothers of men are free, and because they gave to their sons the pure blood of liberty.

Source: *Mary Seymour Howell, "The Dawning of the Twentieth Century," in Mary Kavanaugh Oldham Eagle, ed., The Congress of Women Held in the Woman's Building World's Columbia Exposition (Chicago: American Publishing House, 1894), 679–80.*

Questions

1. Why is Howell so optimistic about the future in terms of women's status in the United States?

2. In what ways do her observations reflect her faith in women's participation in social reform movements and organizations?

3. Why does she argue for woman's rights by referencing their maternal roles?

"southern strategy" Attempt by the NAWSA in the 1890s to broaden its constituency by appealing, often on racist grounds, to southerners.

Mrs. Leland Stanford, wife of the railroad magnate, made generous financial contributions; in Illinois, Mrs. Potter Palmer played a similar role. Working-class women also emerged as a powerful force for suffrage. In the mid-1880s, the Knights of Labor, then at its peak, endorsed woman suffrage.

The NAWSA had far less success in the South. In 1892, heeding Laura Clay's warning that the movement would go down in defeat "unless you bring in the South," the organization named the prominent Kentucky suffragist the chair of a new "Southern Committee" charged with organizing below the Mason-Dixon Line.

The NAWSA's **"southern strategy"** had a dramatic impact on the organization. To gratify the white southern delegation, the NAWSA chose Atlanta as the site of its 1895 convention. Anthony followed up by asking the elderly but still devoted Frederick Douglass to forgo the meeting. Abiding her request, Douglass was spared the insult of hearing the band play "Dixie" and the subsequent round of rebel yells. Nor did he hear Henry Blackwell, his erstwhile ally from antislavery campaigns, advocate woman suffrage on the grounds that "in every state save one there are more educated women than all the illiterate voters, white and black, native-born and foreign." In 1903, in the keynote address to the NAWSA convention held in New Orleans, Belle Kearney made the case yet more explicitly and expediently. Appealing to white male voters, she predicted that women's enfranchisement would "insure immediate and durable white supremacy, honestly attained."

The NAWSA's southern strategy advanced the racist drift of the organization but did little to further the suffrage cause. Southern white men proved intractable, preferring to deny the vote to black men rather than enfranchise any women, including their wives and daughters. Admitting defeat, the NAWSA leadership that succeeded Anthony decided simply to abandon the South. Meanwhile, the NAWSA's reliance on racist tactics drove away many African American suffragists.

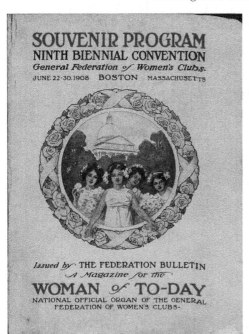

Every two years, local women's clubs sent representatives to the convention of the General Federation of Women's Clubs, which were elaborate affairs covered extensively in the society pages of local newspapers. Despite its motto, "Unity in Diversity," the GFWC at the turn of the century did not welcome black women to their ranks.

Proportionately more committed to woman suffrage than their white contemporaries, black women chose to campaign for the ballot under the auspices of their separate WCTU chapters, church societies, or women's clubs. A few black leaders attended the annual NAWSA conventions and, on occasion, addressed the assembly. In 1900, club leader Mary Church Terrell appeared, mainly to condemn the NAWSA's racist policies.

General Federation of Women's Clubs

In the two decades after the formation of Sorosis and the New England Women's Club in 1868, women's clubs spread to cities and towns across the United States. Professionally employed women continued to join, but they were eventually outnumbered by middle-class homemakers. Self-improvement remained a central theme of club activities, but suffrage and civic improvement became increasingly prominent in the programs of most clubs. By the early 1880s, so many women's clubs had formed that federation seemed a necessary step to maximize resources.

In preparation for the twentieth anniversary of Sorosis, Jennie Croly and her colleagues proposed a plan for federation modeled after the WCTU. They envisioned the formation of a central governing board, representing local clubs, and the establishment of a series of departments for specialized work. The following year, in April 1890, representatives from ninety-seven clubs met in New York City to breathe life into Croly's dream and proudly announced the formation of the **General Federation of Women's Clubs** (GFWC).

The leaders of the GFWC stepped into their national roles with a great deal of fanfare. They themselves were already prominent members of society; the first treasurer, for example, was Phoebe Hearst, wife of a wealthy U.S. Senator and mother of William Randolph Hearst of newspaper fame. These women captured the limelight at the biennial conventions of the GFWC, which took place in various major cities and lasted for several days. Given the social composition of the leadership, it was not surprising that descriptions of the meetings—as well as of the sumptuous settings, elaborate dinners and lavish entertainments, and elegant gowns and precious jewelry of the attendees—appeared prominently in the society pages of local newspapers.

However, at the local level, the second generation of club members advanced not as celebrities but as community leaders. They tended to place greater emphasis on home life than their predecessors did and developed programs to help women become better mothers and homemakers. But as New Women, often college-educated themselves, they took up this work in a systematic manner. Committees formed to survey the problems associated with home sanitation; nutrition, including food preparation; and the management of servants. Some of the most ambitious clubs established schools of domestic science and, in the wake of their success, persuaded local school boards to incorporate their programs into the standard curriculum for high school girls.

From this point, women's clubs commonly branched out into educational reform, for example, by urging the creation of kindergartens within the public school system and presenting members as candidates for local school boards or as truant officers. Local women's clubs also worked with other organizations, such as the Association of Collegiate Alumnae and the WCTU, to secure better equipment for classrooms and higher salaries for teachers. Some clubs endowed scholarships in the women's colleges. The Rhode Island Women's Club worked relentlessly to create the women's college at Brown University, later known as Pembroke.

General Federation of Women's Clubs Formed in 1890 as a federation of local women's clubs.

Club leaders, while still interested in literature and the arts, aspired to take on the larger problems facing their communities. As one writer explained, "The period of the old-fashioned culture club was one of incubation. Women had to turn in on themselves and learn to know each other before they dared or knew how to turn outward. . . ." By the 1890s, it was common for clubs to sponsor courses on politics for its members and to maintain at least one civic committee to foster the beauty, cleanliness, and morality of their towns or cities. "We prefer Doing to Dante, Being to Browning. . . . We've soaked in literary effort long enough; today nothing but an orgy of philanthropy will satisfy us."

Shortly after the formation of the GFWC, statewide federations organized to coordinate activities at the local level and to pool their resources for civic betterment. The New Hampshire Federation, for example, saved the forests of the White Mountains from the "vandals who would convert them into lumber and paper." Each state federation sponsored a committee on the Industrial Condition of Women and Children, which investigated conditions of labor, including wages. The Massachusetts Federation collected so much data on the "dangerous trades" that the committee conducting this work secured an official investigation by the Board of Health. The New York State Federation, which began with ninety-nine clubs in 1895, grew so quickly that two years later more than two hundred clubs had affiliated, representing twenty-five thousand women.

Although at the time the GFWC represented no more than half of all the women's clubs in the United States, the national organization succeeded in showcasing women's involvement in civic reform. Indeed, as one club member observed, clubwomen were especially suited to these kinds of engagements, not least because "women's function, like charity, begins at home and then, like charity, goes everywhere." However, the generosity of the GFWC did not extend to women of color.

National Association of Colored Women

African American organizers built on a long tradition of women's activism in women's benevolent societies affiliated with various black churches, and by the late 1880s they had organized their own clubs to address the many problems facing their communities. The foundation for a national organization was laid by the Colored Women's League, founded in 1893 by Mary Church Terrell, Anna Julia Cooper, and Mary Jane Patterson. The league claimed 113 branches in cities as scattered as Boston, Washington, Chicago, and St. Louis. Two years later, *The Women's Era,* a magazine dedicated to strengthening the network of black women activists, called a convention, and delegates concluded their meetings by forming a second organization, the National Federation of Afro-American Women. Then, in 1896, the two national organizations decided to unite as the **National Association of Colored Women** (NACW). The new federation adopted the motto "Lifting as We Climb."

National Association of Colored Women Established in 1896 as the merger of the National Federation of Afro-American Women and the National League of Colored Women.

Mary Church Terrell served ably as the first president of the NACW. Born in 1863, the year of the Emancipation Proclamation, she had grown up in a middle-class family in Memphis. She graduated from Oberlin College in 1884 and spent two years studying languages in Europe before returning to Oberlin for a master's degree. After teaching for a short while at Wilberforce University in Xenia, Ohio, she took a teaching position at the distinguished M Street High School in Washington, D.C., where she met and later married Robert Heberton Terrell, a fellow teacher who also practiced law. As president, Mary Terrell developed into one of the most popular lecturers and writers in the NACW.

The NACW built on a long tradition of voluntary associations. Its leaders passionately embraced the cause of racial uplift while developing programs of self-improvement for members. "The old notion that woman was intended by the Almighty to do only those things that men thought they ought to do is fast passing away," clubwoman Fanny Barrier Williams noted. "In our day and in this country, a woman's sphere is just as large as she can make it and still be true to her finer qualities of soul." Mainly middle-class, college-educated women, often the wives of successful professional or businessmen and teachers themselves, club leaders prided themselves on being both good Christians and highly respectable members of their communities.

Like their white counterparts, black clubwomen designed programs to educate mothers, strengthen the family, and advocate temperance. Terrell, for example, condemned segregation with the same force she extolled motherhood and home life. "Nothing lies nearer the heart of colored women," she once declared, "than the children." She encouraged the local clubs to support kindergartens, day nurseries, and orphanages, as well as homes for the aged and hospitals.

Some NACW leaders also believed that women were better suited than men to lead the battle for racial justice. Frances Ellen Watkins Harper, for example, appealed to women to embrace their responsibilities, insisting that women evinced little of men's "lust for power" and instead were "grandly constructive" in their work. Women, in her opinion, displayed a higher morality and could therefore serve better as ambassadors of the race.

The NACW also formed in part as a response to their exclusion from white women's organizations. Especially as Jim Crow tightened its grip on the nation, most tenaciously in the South, the majority of white women's clubs refused to admit black women or to cooperate with them in campaigns. In 1900, for example, Josephine St. Pierre Ruffin traveled to the fifth biennial convention of the GFWC in order to represent the Massachusetts Federation of Women's Clubs (as its single black member), the New England Woman's Press Club, and the Woman's Era Club of Boston. Upon her arrival, white women became visibly upset by her request to be seated as a delegate from the Woman's Era Club, which the Executive Committee had admitted to the federation before realizing that it was an all-black club. The controversy erupted into a huge debate. In the end, the GFWC granted Ruffin a seat but only as a delegate from the Massachusetts Federation and the New England Woman's Press Club. Unable to represent the Woman's Era Club, Ruffin refused to participate.

Although the Colored Women's League had sent a representative to the 1895 meeting of the NCW, it was not until 1900 that the NCW granted delegate status to the NACW. African American clubwomen accepted the invitation to join because they shared the goal, according to Adella Hunt Logan, of promoting "the welfare of all women in the country." They also sought recognition for their important and ongoing contributions to the temperance and suffrage campaigns. In 1904, Terrell served as the American delegate to the International Congress of Women meeting in Berlin, speaking to the assembly in English, as well as in German and French.

The strength of the NACW continued to center in the Northeast, with Boston and Washington, D.C., the most active chapters. In 1897, the association claimed five thousand members; by 1904, the NACW represented fifteen thousand women from thirty-one states. As the association grew in size, so did its range of programs. By 1904, the NACW boasted twelve departments of work, which reflected the interests of women in literature and culture as well as in professional occupations such as business, medicine, and the law.

CAMPAIGNS OF THE 1890S

While women poured their energies into various single-sex organizations designed to redress the growing inequalities in American society, a large number joined men in the protest movements that took shape during the 1890s, especially as hard times worsened with the Depression of 1893. Even without the vote, women began to participate in local and state electoral politics, hoping they could wield their moral authority as guardians of the home to make government more responsive to the needs of women and children. Several achieved renown as national figures or regional leaders in an uphill battle to halt the increasingly racist and imperialist tenor of the nation and to revive and extend the democratic and egalitarian principles that inspired its foundation. However, the presidential election of 1896, which established the expansionist, probusiness administration of Republican William McKinley, put a damper on this heated contest over who ruled America.

Populism

Farmers' Alliance Organized in the 1880s as the political wing of the Granger movement and became the backbone of Populism by the end of the decade.

Populism Radical agrarians who sought political office in the 1890s to challenge corporate control.

Organized first into local chapters of the **Farmers' Alliance,** women in the country's heartland joined their menfolk in creating a new political movement—**Populism.** The movement forcefully challenged the reigning corporate monopolies that were destroying the family farmer's way of life. Populists, men and women alike, looked to redress the extreme imbalance of power and demanded such major reforms as an overhaul of the monetary and banking systems, a progressive income tax, and public ownership of the railroads. Compared to Republicans and Democrats, Populists encouraged women to participate in the movement. "If politics means anything," one Populist contended, "It concerns women."

Throughout the trans-Mississippi West, the Grange had prepared women for political action (see chapter 11). In the growing commercial centers, the WCTU wielded even more influence, organizing masses of women to collect temperance pledges and encouraging them to join their male counterparts in the Good Templars in statewide campaigns for prohibition legislation. The Kansas Farmers' Alliance, for example, built on this legacy and recruited between thirty thousand and fifty thousand women, who represented 30 percent of the membership. Women often performed customary services, such as providing food for picnics. They also sewed banners with such timely slogans as "Death to the Monopolies" and "The Farmer Is All."

The most prominent Populist women were not farm wives but middle-class women with experience in either women's clubs or the WCTU. Annie Diggs, for example, played well on the lecture circuit. She promised that women, if given the ballot, would work hand in hand with men to usher in prohibition and abolish poverty. In Diggs's mind, Populists would fulfill Willard's aspiration for the WCTU: home protection.

Like their male counterparts who sought alliances with such organizations as the Knights of Labor and urban reformers, the Populist women located in commercial centers reached out to scores of other women's associations. Building bridges to local WCTU and suffrage chapters proved easy in most cities and towns outside the

WOMEN'S LIVES

MARY ELIZABETH LEASE

Populist Mary E. Lease was one of the most famous political orators of the late nineteenth century, a proud proponent of woman's rights, and a distinguished member of the first generation of women lawyers in the United States. She used her talents to educate the public on the "Woman Question" but also worked ceaselessly with men to promote various causes for social justice. Her unbounded dedication allowed her to become one of the few women of the era to wield power within a major political party. Yet, for all her accomplishments, Lease was also the author of a profoundly racist tract, "The Problem of Civilization Solved," wherein she advocated the colonization of all "inferior races" somewhere in the tropics.

The daughter of Irish immigrants, the famed Populist orator grew up in a poor Catholic family in western Pennsylvania. In 1870, she moved to Kansas to become a teacher at the Osage Mission and met and married Charles Lease, a local druggist. The Panic of 1873 brought them to the brink of financial ruination, and the young couple relocated to Texas, where two of their six children died. In the mid-1880s, the family moved back to Kansas, where Mary Lease emerged as a political activist of international renown.

In 1884, Lease took her first public stand as a proponent of temperance and woman suffrage. She began by writing a series of articles on woman's rights for the local newspaper and by organizing a local woman's club. Two years later, she founded the Wichita Equal Suffrage League and became its first president. Meanwhile, she studied law and, after passing the bar exam, started a small practice with another woman lawyer.

Like many other women activists of her generation, Lease did not restrict her involvement to women's concerns. By the end of the 1880s, she had become a leading light in the local labor movement

and a rising star within the Farmers' Alliance. It was within this political milieu that she perfected her talent for oratory. She promised that the men and women working together in the Populist movement would complete the mission put forth by Frances Willard and place "the mothers of this nation on an equality with the fathers."

With the formation of the Populist movement, Lease became one its leading speakers. Beginning in 1890, she set herself to campaign across the country, engendering hostility from both her Republican and Democratic opponents, who characterized her as a "petticoated smut-mill." Despite such aspersions, she became one of the most quoted women in U.S. history by advising Kansas farmers to "raise less corn and more hell." Actually, one of her coworkers is said to have coined the phrase, but Lease accepted the attribution because, she later admitted, it was "a right good piece of advice."

(continued)

By this time, Lease's reputation had reached its peak. Admired by suffragists, Lease was drafted to run for the U.S. Senate, but, despite Susan B. Anthony's support, she declined to enter the race. Instead, she accepted the governor's appointment to become the first woman to preside over the Kansas State Board of Charities. The crucial 1896 elections, which brought the resounding defeat of the Populist presidential candidate, William Jennings Bryan, cut short her political career. In 1897, she left her husband in Wichita and moved to New York City, where she supported herself and her children as a journalist and as a lecturer. In the 1920s, she joined the National Woman's Party and served for a time as president of the National Birth Control Society. ■

conservative South. Populist women also sent delegations to meetings of the NAWSA, the ICW, and the NCW.

In Kansas, a group of urban Populist women tried to launch a **National Woman's Alliance.** They published a monthly newspaper, *The Farmer's Wife*, which promoted the "natural unity" of temperance, suffrage, labor, and agrarian movements and claimed representation in at least twenty-six states.

However, the National Woman's Alliance lived longest on paper and foundered when the Populists, meeting in convention in 1892, revealed the limits of their goodwill toward women. Following the path of other national party organizations, the assembly voted to form the People's Party and, at the same time, refused to endorse the woman's ballot. Willard, who attended the meeting, left in despair. A few die-hard loyalist women continued to serve alongside men on important committees, militantly expressed their views at conventions, and on occasion even ran for local office. However, in the West, local Populists played a major role in revitalizing the state campaigns for woman suffrage.

National Woman's Alliance A short-lived organization led by Populist women and their allies in the temperance and suffrage movements.

Woman Suffrage in the West

As early as 1869, the Wyoming legislature granted the right to vote to the twelve hundred women who were living in the territory at the time. In 1890, Wyoming achieved statehood, becoming the first state to enfranchise women. Waving the suffrage flag, boosters began to invite women from across the nation to settle in this "promised land." Three years later, Colorado, a state since 1876, became the first state to pass a popular referendum entitling women to vote.

The Colorado campaign showcased a remarkable alliance among various Populist, labor, and women's organizations. Earlier, on the eve of Colorado statehood, suffragists had spearheaded a vigorous but unsuccessful campaign. In its disappointing aftermath, the new state legislature effected a fifteen-year moratorium on popular referenda for women's enfranchisement. Undaunted, suffragists marshaled their forces and worked mainly within the WCTU and various voluntary associations to build a sizable network of activists. Then, in the late 1880s, suffragists were ready to take advantage of the burgeoning Populist movement. Although the national party refused to endorse the woman's ballot, Colorado Populists followed their electoral victory in the state by calling for a referendum.

The recently formed Colorado Equal Suffrage Association invited the NAWSA's star organizer, Carrie Chapman Catt, to join them. After kicking off the campaign with a huge Labor Day rally in Denver, Catt won the favor of local trade unionists and Populists and then headed off on a thousand-mile tour. Leonora Barry (Lake), famed organizer for the Knights of Labor, also stumped the state, and the president of the Colorado WCTU conducted her own five-month speaking tour.

With the endorsement of many newspapers and ultimately all major parties, the suffrage referendum passed 55 to 45 percent statewide and did even better in counties where Populists were strong. Eighteen days later, the Populist Governor Davis Waite presented a proclamation granting women the right to vote. In 1894, an estimated 40 to 50 percent of Colorado's women cast ballots for the first time in state elections. After celebrating their victory, the leaders of the Colorado campaign traveled to Utah to help local women, who had been disfranchised since passage of the Edmunds-Tucker Act in 1887, win back the right to vote. In 1896, Utah and Idaho joined the small constellation of woman suffrage states.

Ida B. Wells-Barnett (1862–1931), a leading activist in the black community, helped to build several organizations, including women's clubs in Chicago. She is best known for her leadership in the anti-lynching crusade that took shape in the 1890s.

The victorious resolutions to the campaigns in Wyoming, Colorado, Utah, and Idaho did not prepare suffragists for the "doldrums" ahead. Overwhelming defeats in Kansas in 1894 and California in 1896 proved far more indicative of popular sentiment. In these two states, a coalition of suffragists, WCTU activists, and clubwomen waged well-organized campaigns, but they could not counter their opposition. Worse, suffragists' associations with the radical Populist insurgency began to work against them. Following the 1896 national election of William McKinley, Republicans became firmly entrenched in both the White House and Congress, and politicians in the new conservative era felt no need to court women's vote. Instead of riding the crest of a Populist victory, suffragists instead sank with their erstwhile allies. Only in 1910 did suffragists' fortunes turn brighter. Western states again led the way. Referenda passed in Washington (1910); California (1911); Kansas, Oregon, and Arizona (1912); and Montana (1914).

Antilynching Crusade

Virginia clubwoman Janie Porter Barrett remarked perceptively on the upsurge in racial discrimination and violence in the 1890s. "No one can deny that the Negro race is going through the most trying period in its history. Truly these are days when we are 'being tried as by fire.'" In the South, African Americans were losing their hard-won civil liberties as new laws regulating employment contracts and crop liens virtually bound them to the land or sent them to prison. New poll taxes and property and literacy qualifications robbed black men of the right to vote in most southern states. In 1883, the Supreme Court overturned the Civil Rights Act of 1875 and thereby allowed private and public establishments, including schools and libraries, to turn away African Americans. The era of Jim Crow gained official sanction in 1896 when the U.S. Supreme Court, in its **Plessy v. Ferguson** decision, upheld segregation by condoning "separate but equal" facilities for black and white people.

Groups of black women took strong stands against the escalating terror. In 1898, race riots broke out in the small town of Phoenix, South Carolina, and in Wilmington,

Plessy v. Ferguson
The 1896 Supreme Court decision that established "Jim Crow" as the law of the land by condoning "separate but equal" facilities for black and white people

North Carolina. In 1900, four days of rioting in New Orleans killed as many as a dozen African Americans. Lynching, which was widespread in rural areas, took an even greater toll. Between 1889 and 1898, more than eleven hundred African American men, women, and children were murdered by lynch mobs. In 1892, the year that lynching peaked, African American women mobilized to form an antilynching crusade.

At the forefront of this movement was Ida B. Wells, a journalist who had been born a slave in Holly Springs, Mississippi, in 1862. In 1892, a series of lynchings in Memphis, which included the brutal killing of a close friend, prompted her to write a series of scathing editorials condemning the acts. While a white mob destroyed her newspaper office and threatened to kill her, Wells fled first to Philadelphia and then to New York, where she became the most vocal antilynching crusader in the nation.

Wells made her case against lynching in her widely circulated pamphlet, *Southern Horrors: Lynch Law in All Its Phases*, which was published in 1892. Describing the South as a "white man's country," she refuted the most commonplace myths about lynching. The majority of incidents involved accusations of murder, not rape, she insisted; and, moreover, as far as illicit sexual encounters went, white women were often the initiators. The more common perpetrators of sexual violence, Wells countered, were the white men who formed the lynch mobs, and *their* victims were primarily black women and little girls.

Wells made antilynching an international campaign. On her highly publicized trip to England in 1894, she gained the support of the British press and reformers who condemned lynching as not only barbaric but a disgrace to white civilization. After returning to the United States, Wells embarked on a year-long lecture tour to publicize the facts of lynching and to rally Christian churches to take a stand against mob violence. Although white southerners condemned her tactics and many African Americans found her approach too militant, she persisted in documenting consensual sex across the color line and in keeping the issue of lynching in the news.

The politics of lynching nearly split apart the WCTU. In 1893, Willard persuaded delegates at the annual convention to pass an antilynching resolution but nevertheless suggested, contrary to Wells's argument, that black men were culpable of ghastly crimes against white women. The next year, at the twentieth anniversary of the WCTU meeting in Cleveland, Willard restated her position. "It is my firm belief," she announced, "that in the statement made by Miss Wells concerning white women having taken the initiative in nameless acts between the races she has put an imputation upon half the white race in this country that is unjust, and, save in the rarest exceptional instances, wholly without foundation." In holding firm to this position, Willard became, in the minds of many black women, such as Boston clubwoman Josephine St. Pierre Ruffin, an "apologist" for lynching.

The politics of lynching also had a direct impact on the tenor of black women's organizations. In 1895, Wells published a book-length exposé of lynching, *The Red Record*, that provoked vitriolic attacks not only on Wells but on black womanhood in general. A white newspaper editor in Missouri, James W. Jacks, published a public letter impugning the character of all African Americans and describing black women as prostitutes, natural liars, and thieves. In July, the First National Conference of the Colored Women of America assembled in Boston gave Wells its "unanimous endorsement," agreed to continue her crusade against lynching, and also pledged to prove the respectability of African American women by making "purity" a major item on its educational agenda.

The Spanish American War

The nineteenth-century woman movement peaked just as the United States embarked on its first major imperialist venture, the **Spanish American War.** Ostensibly fought to liberate Cuba from the tightening grip of the Spanish Empire, this "splendid little war," as it was called, ended with the acquisition of territories beyond the nation's continental border and the prospect of new and highly desirable markets. The war, especially the jingoism that propelled it, also promised to enhance American manhood through the rigors of combat and simultaneously to encourage women to embrace their roles as helpmates. For example, Theodore Roosevelt, who led several major military campaigns, eulogized the imperialist endeavor as an appropriate means to make men stronger in their capacity for self-government.

Since the mid-1890s, Americans, dedicated to the spread of democracy abroad, had called upon their government to aid the Cuban nationalists in their struggle for independence from Spain. Finally, the tide turned when, on February 15, 1898, a huge explosion sank the *USS Maine*, a battleship that had been dispatched to the Havana harbor ostensibly to protect American citizens on the island. Clara Barton, who was in Havana directing the Red Cross effort to bring supplies to the beleaguered civilian population, described the scene. "They had been crushed by timbers, cut by iron, scorched by fire, and blown sometimes high in the air, sometimes driven down through the red hot furnace room and out into the water," she reported. The American press capitalized on her lurid description and, along with patriotic groups, clamored for retaliation (although, it was later learned, the explosion had actually resulted from an accident): "Remember the Maine, to Hell with Spain." On April 25, the U.S. Congress issued a formal declaration of war.

Amid the surge of patriotism, many women turned to relief work. "Will the women of our state falter or fail when they are needed? No! A thousand times no!" read a leaflet of the Massachusetts Woman's Relief Corps. More than 320 chapters formed in just this one state. Women set themselves to rolling bandages, collecting donations, preparing food for the troops, and tending to the wounded in the hospitals. However, the mobilization was short-lived. The fighting ended after just 113 days.

The war that began to liberate Cuba from Spain set the United States firmly on the path to empire. The United States not only occupied Cuba until 1902 and annexed Puerto Rico and Guam but also fought one of the bloodiest wars in the nation's history to colonize the Philippines.

The ranks of the woman movement split on this issue. Elizabeth Cady Stanton and Susan B. Anthony both favored the overseas missions, envisioning them as benevolent acts to bring democracy and "civilization" to "backward" nations. "I am strongly in favor of this new departure in American foreign policy," Stanton remarked. "What would this continent have been if left to the Indians?" Anthony, a Quaker, ultimately resigned herself to the war as a means to pacify the Philippine rebels. But for those women in the WCTU, the GFWC, and the NCW, who for decades had been lobbying for peace and international arbitration, the Spanish American War represented a catastrophe in world affairs.

Indeed, there were numerous women who agreed with the premises of the jingoist argument for war as an opportunity to revivify manhood: armed combat was the apogee of masculinity. However, they did not condone this development, and the

Spanish American War A short war between Spain and the United States in 1898 that liberated Cuba and the Philippines from Spanish rule.

most militant became leading members of the Anti-Imperialist League. Mary Livermore took a strong stand, while Jane Addams condemned the war for its especially brutish character. Nevertheless, despite their fervor, Livermore and Addams represented a small minority within the turn-of-the-century woman movement, which for the most part embraced the principles—if not all the practices—of U.S. imperialism.

WOMAN'S EMPIRE

Throughout the nineteenth century, American missionary women advanced what one historian termed "beneficent imperialism." They ventured to distant outposts to bring Christianity as well as the alleged benefits of their own civilization, which they deemed superior to all others. By the end of the century, as the United States entered into an age of aggressive territorial expansion, the missionary impulse quickened, sending ever larger numbers of women to foreign lands. With the approval of the U.S.

MAP 13-1 THE AMERICAN DOMAIN, CA. 1900.

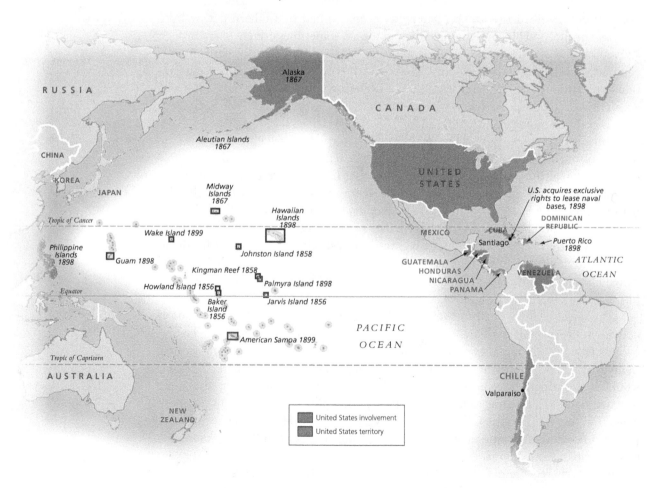

The United States claimed jurisdiction over several islands in the South Pacific and Caribbean and the Alaskan territory.

government, women missionaries often came to wield considerable power, especially in realms concerning the welfare of women and children.

These missionaries shared the prevailing assumption that women's status was a key indicator of "civilization," and they believed that Christianity was the only religion that acknowledged the dignity and worth of womanhood. Among the heathen, one missionary wrote, woman is still regarded "as a scandal and a slave, a drudge and a disgrace, a temptation and a terror, a blemish and a burden." To remedy this situation, they identified three general areas for improvement—education, family, and sexuality.

Women's Foreign Mission Movement

In the last half of the nineteenth century, middle-class women transformed missionary service into a major female avocation. Wives of male ministers continued to play important roles, but, in weighing the multiple problems of managing households in foreign lands, the missionary societies decided to enlist unencumbered single women instead. Bred on exciting stories of travel abroad, many of these women responded enthusiastically to the call and found a career potentially more exciting and definitely more challenging than teaching school at home.

In 1861, the Woman's Union Missionary Society of America for Heathen Lands formed as a nondenominational organization to recruit never-married or widowed women to serve in foreign lands. By 1873, all the major evangelical denominations had created their own women's boards, making **"Woman's Work for Woman"** a guiding spirit for both fund-raising and active service. New magazines, such as the *Heathen Woman's Friend* (Methodist), appeared to publicize this activity, featuring letters, stories,

"Woman's Work for Woman" A phrase representing the agenda of the Woman's Foreign Missionary Society.

By the turn of the century, women represented about 60 percent of American foreign missionary service. Emily S. Harwell, who graduated from Mt. Holyoke College in 1876, stands alongside her Chinese students at the Foochow Mission in 1902. She wrote letters describing the difficulty Chinese women had in walking to church with their bound feet and the hardships they endured from their powerful mothers-in-law.

WOMEN'S VOICES

OVERSEAS MISSIONARY

Amanda Berry Smith (1837–1915) achieved an international reputation as a charismatic holiness preacher and dedicated missionary. In 1879, she embarked for India to deliver sermons on the gospels. In Bombay and Calcutta, she attracted sizable audiences who were curious to see an African American woman who had been born in slavery. In 1881, she traveled to Liberia, which she called "the land of my forefathers," a nation that had been settled in the 1820s by former slaves and free African Americans. Suffering from both malaria and arthritis, she stayed for eight years, conducting Christian missionary work and organizing temperance societies. Here, she relates her experiences at an orphanage in Colar, India, in 1880.

Miss Anstea had invited me to come to Colar and visit her mission. So, on my way from Bombay, I stopped at Colar for a week. Colar was a large native town, and Miss Anstea's mission covered a large area, in which she had a chapel, and a very nice, commodious mission house, large, comfortable apartments for the boys and girls, separate, and several very comfortable houses for missionaries, all nicely situated and well furnished.

I held meetings in the little chapel every night. Our morning prayer was similar to a service; at the ringing of the bell the boys and girls would file in and take their seats, and we would have prayers before they went to work.

The Lord gave us great blessings during the week's services. At night the church would be crowded; large numbers of the heathen from the outside came in; many of them seemed to be deeply interested. The Lord wonderfully helped me to speak to them every night; and several of the children professed to be converted.

One Sabbath morning as we were at prayers at the Mission House, a poor woman came and sat on the veranda, outside, with a beautiful baby in her arms, about three or four months old. When prayers were over, she was asked what she wanted. . . .

[S]he said that she had had nothing to eat for two days, and she was starving, and she wanted her to take her baby; she had come a very long way from a native town; she said she had three other children, and had nothing for them to eat; and if she would give her fifty cents and keep the baby, she would go and get something for the other children; but she could not bear to see the baby starve to death before her eyes.

It was a beautiful child, a little girl. By that time we were all around her. Miss Anstea questioned her in every possible way to find out if her story was true.

She told her she was afraid she had taken somebody's baby and wanted to pass it off for her own; but at this the poor woman wept bitterly and declared the baby was her own, but that they were starving, and it was her last resort to save her baby, to bring it to the Mission; the others, she said, were older, and somebody might help them; but nobody wanted the baby. . . .

One of Miss Anstea's Christian girls said she would look after it. I think Miss Anstea offered to pay her a small sum; or some of the rest suggested that; another said they would milk the goat so the baby would have milk. I said, "I will give the woman the fifty cents"; but I gave her a little more than fifty cents.

She laid the baby down on the mat. Of course, they have no clothes on them; they are perfectly naked. She put her hand on her heart and sighed, and then ran away out of the compound. When she got to the gate she turned and looked back; poor thing! she was so thin, and looked just like what she had said, that she was starving to death; you could see she was weak; but, oh, that look when she got to the gate! I shall never forget it; it was full of a mother's love and tenderness for her baby. My heart ached for her; and to save my life I could not keep back the tears.

How often the missionary in different foreign fields comes up against heart rending scenes, before which they often stand helpless. All they can do is to weep with them that weep, and pray with them that don't know how to pray for themselves.

We took the baby in, and Miss Anstea adopted it, and we named it "Amanda Smith."

Source: *Mrs. Amanda Smith*, An Autobiography (*Chicago: Meyer & Brother, 1893*), 318–20.

Questions

1. What did Smith hope to accomplish in Liberia?

2. Why does she work primarily among women and children?

3. Why does she simultaneously conduct Christian missionary work and temperance agitation?

poetry, graphics, and didactic essays like "Girl Life in the Orient" and "High-Caste Women in India." Several of these magazines achieved readerships of nearly twenty-five thousand. By the end of the century, women missionaries in foreign lands outnumbered men, representing more than 60 percent of active missionaries.

Women missionaries, like their male counterparts, performed evangelical work and, if trained in medicine, brought health services to the mission field. For the most part, women focused on educational programs, building and maintaining schools from the elementary grades through college. The American teachers took pride in their pupils' accomplishments, claiming at times that the proficiency of the young girls in their care outdistanced that of their male peers or even their American counterparts. In most countries, women missions aimed to prepare girls and young women for public service, to train them as teachers, nurses or physicians, and administrators of schools, hospitals, and orphanages. In China, missionaries established schools for girls far in advance of government-supported institutions and simultaneously aided the locally run campaigns to abolish the custom of foot binding. However, most missionaries anticipated that ultimately these girls would grow to women fully prepared to make a Christian marriage and keep a Christian home. Child marriages and polygamy therefore became special targets of their efforts.

By the turn of the century, the small towns and rural areas of the Midwest were supplying the majority of women missionaries. Usually with the encouragement of their parents, who themselves were usually involved in some kind of church work, these women turned to missionary work as an alternative to teaching and as a means to achieve a modicum of independence and status for themselves outside marriage. In China, for example, by 1920, unmarried and married women served in equal numbers, the former living together in all-women residences.

World WCTU

By 1892, it was said that the sun never sets on the WCTU. By that time, the organization enjoyed at least nominal representation in every continent except Antarctica and claimed forty national affiliates. Although the United States accounted for the

World WCTU Organized in 1891 as a federation of national affiliates of the WCTU to proselytize temperance and woman's rights throughout the world.

largest number of members, representing about 50 to 60 percent worldwide, the WCTU was proportionately just as strong in Japan and Australia. The **World WCTU** functioned as a major emissary of Protestant morality and Anglo-American culture, including a strong commitment to women's rights. It had, in sum, realized Frances Willard's aspiration "to belt the globe, and join the East and West."

Temperance missionary Jessie Ackerman traveled for seven years as a temperance missionary before returning to the United States in 1895. In that time, she had traveled around the world twice, and she took equal pride in her temperance accomplishments and personal exploits. When traveling by sea, she boasted, she like to climb the mastheads to hail other vessels, a dangerous practice that once landed her in the Indian Ocean during a fierce storm. Similarly, the Kalahari Desert and the Himalaya mountains presented minor physical obstacles. One July 4th found her celebrating on an iceberg inside the Arctic Circle. She spent six weeks deep in the interior of China, dressed in Chinese clothing and eating nothing but boiled rice.

Ackerman was one of thirty-five women who served between 1888 and 1924 as round-the-world missionaries for the WCTU. Another thirty-four worked on short-term assignments to countries outside the United States; and perhaps another twenty-five did ancillary work. After 1900, Canada and Great Britain also sent women abroad.

Temperance missionaries organized WCTU chapters wherever they went, winning local women to temperance but also addressing unique issues. They preached against foot binding in China, for example, and for dress reform and physical fitness in Japan. Despite their Protestant zeal, these missionaries proved very tolerant of non-Christian religions. The World WCTU meeting in 1892 voted to remove "heathen" from all descriptions of non-Christian lands and identified a "great virtue" in Islam in its aversion to the consumption of alcohol. The *Union Signal* featured a chart of the world great religions—Buddhism, Hinduism, and other faiths—as links in a great chain of "one supreme being." However, few temperance missionaries ever doubted the superiority of Christianity, especially in regard to women. The most "civilized" nations, in their opinion, were those that promoted evangelical Christianity.

The WCTU became the prime mover for woman suffrage in Anglo-American settlements throughout the world. In Australia and New Zealand, for example, the WCTU led the campaign that resulted in women's enfranchisement by the turn of the century. Indeed, the WCTU emerged as such a powerful force for woman suffrage that many women with scant interest in temperance joined local chapters to work for enfranchisement.

Outposts of the YWCA

World YWCA The U.S. YWCA extended its representation around the world to improve the conditions of women by providing social services and education.

The **World YWCA** held its first convention in 1898 and quickly became so successful that the American association in 1906 divided into two, coordinating home and foreign services, and undertook to train women for service overseas. By the mid-1920s, when overseas work reached its peak, the YWCA had mobilized more than one thousand women as lay missionaries. Aspiring to achieve "the evangelization of the world in this generation," these women were especially eager to experience the excitement of foreign service.

In 1894, the American YWCA assigned its first agent on overseas duty. Agnes Hill, despite her university education, arrived in India with only superficial knowledge of the country and its caste system. Although the British YWCA had begun to pave the way as early as the 1870s, Hill got off to a rough start. For example, she attempted to export the Y's physical fitness programs, which were very popular in the United States, to a population that equated exercise with manual labor and sought to avoid it. Moreover, Hill faced an uphill battle proselytizing Christianity among women who were mainly Muslim or Hindu. Hill, however, was unwilling to give up. She established the administrative structure for the Indian National Association, which became a model for federation within the World YWCA. Working for the YWCA, Hill stayed in India until 1942.

YWCA missionaries to China received elaborate rounds of welcome from huge, well-established delegations from various European and Asian nations, as well as from the American business and missionary communities. In contrast, the Chinese often expressed strong anti-Western feelings, which had erupted dramatically in the Boxer Rebellion of 1900. Nevertheless, YWCA missionaries persisted, targeting the condition of women and speaking out on such issues as arranged and plural marriages, foot binding, prostitution, and the opium trade. They established chapters in the leading cities and recruited Chinese women to serve on boards and to staff the organization. After meeting with initial resistance, the Y missionaries established thriving physical fitness programs and dress reform. They also played an instrumental role in introducing hygiene programs to combat the contagious diseases like malaria, tuberculosis, and typhoid, which were deadly and prevalent. Like missionaries affiliated with various Protestant denominations, the agents of the YWCA stressed education for Chinese girls and women as a station on the path to Christianity.

During the 1890s, the YWCA in major urban areas began to develop programs for foreign-born women. By 1910 nearly sixty branches were sponsoring special activities, including bilingual classes. This poster, which dates to 1919, celebrates the international outlook of the Y.

CONCLUSION

"The cruel kindness of the old doctrine that women should be worked for, and should not work, that their influence should be felt, but not recognized, that they should hear and see, but neither appear nor speak," wrote Julia Ward Howe in 1891, "—all this belongs now to the record of things which, once measurably true, have become fabulous." The many women who had joined Howe in activism would have agreed with her statement, measuring their accomplishments in terms of the massive national and international organizations that made up the woman movement. They would have shared her optimism about the future, anticipating a prominent role in the massive protest and political movements of the 1890s. If their success was cut short during the tumultuous decade, they could take solace in having built a foundation that would blossom into social activism during the Progressive Era that lay ahead. However, the majority of these activists— white, native-born, and Protestants—had yet to deal with the reality that along with power came responsibility. The increasing racism of their society, fueled in part by imperialist ventures, dimmed the prospects for the "sisterhood" they so fervently extolled.

WOMEN'S HISTORY	GLOBAL EVENTS

1860

1861
Woman's Union Missionary Society forms

1869
Wyoming territorial legislature grants
women the right to vote
National Woman Suffrage Association formed
American Woman Suffrage Association formed

1877
Women's Educational and Industrial Union forms

1879
Frances E. Willard assumes WCTU presidency

1880

1881
Willard introduces "Do-Everything" Policy
at WCTU annual meeting
WCTU Southern organizing drive

1882
U.S. Senate and House create committees
on woman suffrage

1887
Kansas women vote in school board
and municipal elections
Helen S. Campbell publishes *Prisoners of Poverty*

1888
National and International Council of Women
Illinois Woman's Alliance forms

1883
U.S. Supreme Court overturns Civil Rights Act of 1875

1889
Populists organize

1890

1890
WCTU membership tops 150,000
General Federation of Women's Clubs forms
AWSA and NWSA merge to form the
National American Association of Woman Suffrage
Wyoming becomes first state to enfranchise women

1892
Ida B. Wells publishes *Southern Horrors*

1893
National Council of Jewish Women forms
First African American YWCA organizes in Dayton, Ohio
Colorado grants women the right to vote

1894
World YWCA organizes

1893
Illinois Factory Inspection Act passed
Economic depression spreads nationwide

1896
William McKinley elected President
Plessy v. Ferguson upholds segregation

1898
Spanish American War declared in April

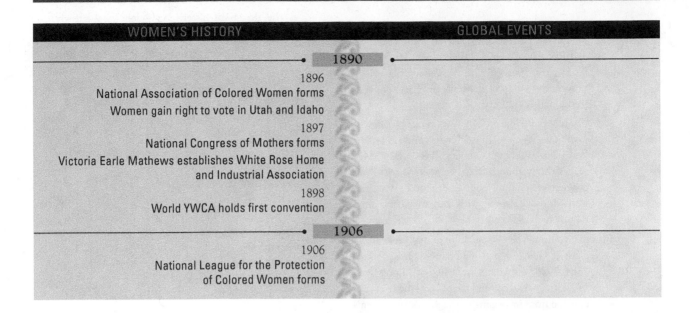

WOMEN'S HISTORY	GLOBAL EVENTS

1890

1896
National Association of Colored Women forms
Women gain right to vote in Utah and Idaho

1897
National Congress of Mothers forms
Victoria Earle Mathews establishes White Rose Home
and Industrial Association

1898
World YWCA holds first convention

1906

1906
National League for the Protection
of Colored Women forms

REVIEW QUESTIONS

1. How did racial tensions and animosities affect the various campaigns waged by the late-nineteenth-century woman movement?

2. What role did imperialism play in shaping the programs of women activists?

3. Discuss the importance of national and international federations of women in the 1890s.

4. How successful were women activists in bridging class differences?

5. How effective was volunteerism in providing women access to power outside the realms of government and business controlled by men?

RECOMMENDED READING

Gail Bederman. *Manliness and Civilization: A Cultural History of Gender and Race in the United States, 1880–1917*. Chicago and London: University of Chicago Press, 1995. A wide-ranging analysis, conducted through a series of biographical case studies, of the related discourses of gender, race, and society. Bederman offers a thorough interpretation of the masculinist perspectives of Theodore Roosevelt as well as an insightful analysis of the use of "civilization" by the antilynching reformer Ida B. Wells.

Rebecca Edwards. *Angels in the Machinery: Gender in American Party Politics from the Civil War to the Pro-*

gressive Era. New York: Oxford University Press, 1997. Edwards demonstrates, in the era of "separatism as strategy," many women played important roles in the major partisan parties and in movements such as Populism. She pays close attention to regional variations.

Jane Hunter. *The Gospel of Gentility: American Women Missionaries in Turn-of-the-Century China*. New Haven: Yale University Press, 1984. An evocative study, based on letters and diaries, of the experiences of American women who sought to convert the "heathen" Chinese to Christianity.

Kristin L. Hoganson. *Fighting for American Manhood: How Gender Politics Provoked the Spanish-American and Philippine-American Wars.* New Haven: Yale University Press, 1998. An imaginative and provocative study of the representation of gender in the politics of imperial warfare.

Rebecca J. Mead. *How the Vote Was Won: Woman Suffrage in the Western United States, 1868–1914.* New York: New York University Press 2004. Mead places the woman suffrage campaigns within the context of regional politics, including race relations and coalitions with other reform movements, such as Populism.

Priscilla Murolo. *The Common Ground of Womanhood: Class, Gender and Working Girls' Clubs, 1884–1928.* Urbana: University of Illinois Press, 1997. Traces the rise and fall of a unique cross-class alliance from its origins in the 1880s to its demise as the dream of sisterhood faded in the early decades of the twentieth century.

Louise Newman. *White Women's Rights: The Racial Origins of Feminism in the United States.* New York: Oxford University Press, 1999. An iconoclastic treatment of well-known women, as a few lesser-known, in the late-nineteenth century woman's rights movement.

Ian Tyrrell. *Woman's World, Woman's Empire: The Woman's Christian Temperance Union in International Perspective, 1880–1930.* Chapel Hill: University of North Carolina Press, 1991. Tells a fascinating story of the emergence of the WCTU as major force in making temperance as well as the woman movement an international endeavor. Tyrrell provides an integral chapter in the larger history of U.S. expansion.

ADDITIONAL BIBLIOGRAPHY

Women's Organizations

Karen Blair. *The Clubwoman as Feminist: True Womanhood Redefined 1968–1914.* New York and London: Holmes & Meier, 1980.

Anne Ruggles Gere, Anne Ruggles. *Intimate Practices: Literacy and Cultural Work in U.S. Women's Clubs, 1880–1920.* Urbana: University of Illinois Press, 1997.

Anne Meis Knupfer. Anne Meis. *Toward a Tenderer Humanity and a Nobler Womanhood: African American Women's Clubs in Turn-of-the-Century Chicago.* New York: New York University Press, 1996.

Joan Marie Johnson, Joan Marie. *Southern Ladies, New Women: Race, Region, and Clubwomen in South Carolina 1890–1930.* Gainesville: University Press of Florida, 2004.

Kathleen D. McCarthy, Kathleen D. ed. *Lady Bountiful Revisited: Women, Philanthropy, and Power.* New Brunswick: Rutgers University Press, 1990.

Dorothy Salem. *To Better Our World: Black Women in Organized Reform, 1890–1920.* New York: Carlson Publishers, 1990.

Anne Firor Scott. *Natural Allies: Women's Associations in American History.* Urbana: University of Illinois Press, 1991.

Stephanie Shaw. "Black Club Women and the Creation of the National Association of Colored Women," *Journal of Women's History,* 3 (Fall 1991): 10–25.

Anastatia Sims. *The Power of Femininity in the New South: Women's Organization and Politics in North Carolina, 1880–1930.* Columbia: University of South Carolina Press, 1997.

Elizabeth Hayes Turner. *Women, Culture, and Community: Religion and Reform in Galveston, 1880–1920.* New York: Oxford University Press, 1997.

Marshal Wedell. *Elite Women and the Reform Impulse in Memphis, 1875–1915.* Knoxville: University of Tennessee Press, 1991.

Campaigns of the 1890s

Jean J. Baker, ed. *Votes for Women: The Struggle for Suffrage Revisited.* New York: Oxford University Press, 2002.

Beverly Beeton. *Women Vote in the West: The Woman Suffrage Movement, 1869–1896.* New York: Garland Publishing, 1986.

Michael Lewis Goldberg. *An Army of Women: Gender and Politics in Gilded Age Kansas.* Baltimore: Johns Hopkins, 1997.

Elna C. Green. *Southern Strategies: Southern Women and the Woman Suffrage Question.* Chapel Hill: University of North Carolina Press, 1997.

Donald B. Marti. *Women of the Grange: Mutuality and Sisterhood in Rural America, 1866–1920*. Westport: Greenwood Press, 1991.

Francesca Morgan. *Women and Patriotism in Jim Crow America*. Chapel Hill: University of North Carolina Press, 2005.

Woman's Empire

Nancy Boyd. *Emissaries: The Overseas Work of the American YWCA 1895–1970*. New York: The Woman's Press, 1986.

Joan Jacobs Brumberg. "Zenanas and Girlless Villages: The Ethnology of American Evangelical Women, 1870–1910," *Journal of American History*, 69 (September 1982): 347–71.

Carol C. Chin. "Beneficent Imperialists: American Women Missionaries in China at the Turn of the Twentieth Century," *Diplomatic History*, 27 (June 2003): 327–52.

Elizabeth K. Eder. *Constructing Opportunity: American Women Educators in Early Meiji Japan*. Lanham: Lexington Books, 2003.

Patricia Grimshaw. *Paths of Duty: American Missionary Wives in Nineteenth-Century Hawaii*. Honolulu: University of Hawaii Press, 1989.

Patricia R. Hill. *The World Their Household: The American Woman's Foreign Mission Movement and Cultural Transformation, 1870–1920*. Ann Arbor: University of Michigan Press, 1985.

Dana L. Robert. *American Women in Mission: A Social History of Their Thought and Practice*. Macon: Mercer University Press, 1998.

Maina Chawla Singh. *Gender, Religion, and Heathen Land: American Missionary Women in South Asia, 1860s to 1940s*. New York: Routledge, 1999.

Laura Wexler. *Tender Violence: Domestic Visions in an Age of U.S. Imperialism*. Chapel Hill: University of North Carolina Press, 2000.

Rumi Yasutake. *Transnational Women's Activism: The United States, Japan, and Japanese Immigrant Communities in California, 1859–1920*. New York: New York University Press, 2004.

Memoirs, Diaries, Autobiographies, and Biographies

Marion K. Barthelme, ed. *Women in the Texas Populist Movement: Letters to the Southern Mercury*. College Station: Texas A. & M. University Press, 1997.

Ruth Bordin. *Frances Willard: A Biography*. Chapel Hill: University of North Carolina Press, 1986.

Paul E. Fuller. *Laura Clay and the Woman's Rights Movement*. Lexington: University Press of Kentucky. 1992, 1975.

Abbie Graham. *Grace H. Dodge, A Biography*. New York: The Woman's Press, 1926.

Adrienne Lash Jones. *Jane Edna Hunter: A Case Study of Black Leadership, 1910–1930*. Brooklyn, NY: Carlson Publishers, 1990.

Jane Taylor Nelson, ed. *A Prairie Populist: The Memoirs of Luna Kellie*. Iowa City: University of Iowa Press, 1992.

Patricia A. Schechter. *Ida B. Wells-Barnett and American Reform, 1880–1930*. Chapel Hill: University of North Carolina Press, 2001.

Kathryn KishSklar. *Florence Kelley and the Nation's Work*. New Haven: Yale University Press, 1995.

Mary Church Terrell. *A Colored Woman in a White World 1940*. New York: Ransdell Company, 2005.

Joan Waugh. *Unsentimental Reformer: The Life of Josephine Shaw Lowell*. Cambridge: Harvard University Press, 1997.

Frances E. Willard. *Glimpses of Fifty Years; The Autobiography of an American Woman*. Chicago: Woman's Temperance Publication Association, 1889.

The New Morality, 1880–1920

URBAN PLEASURES, URBAN DANGERS
"Women Adrift"
Cheap Amusements
"Charity Girls"

CHANGING RELATIONS OF INTIMACY
Courtship and Marriage
Divorce
Female Friends and Women Lovers

CURBING "SOCIAL EVILS"
Social Purity Campaigns
Crusading against Prostitution
Legislating against "Miscegenation"

WOMEN'S BODIES AND REPRODUCTION
Designed for Motherhood
Controlling Reproduction
The Birth Control Campaign

REBELS IN BOHEMIA
Living the New Morality
Heterodoxy and Feminism
Art and Politics

WHY WERE working-class women at the forefront in changing sexual relations at the turn of the century?

WHAT WAS the relationship between changes in hetero- and homosocial relations?

WHAT EFFORTS were advanced to effect new controls on sexual relationships?

HOW AND why did women seek to limit their fertility?

WHAT IS the relationship between the new morality and feminism?

As long as I believed, in harmony with my early teaching, that sex was a degrading and disgusting phenomenon which men enjoyed but to which women submitted only because it was a part of wifely duty, the appeal of celibacy and independence was enhanced. But with the biology and psychology courses of college and university, sex took on a new meaning. It was probably as much of a shock to me to learn that women had their share of sexual instincts and emotions as it was to many of my classmates to come into contact with philosophical doubts concerning the

Sunday, Women Drying Their Hair, *1912 John Sloan (American, 1871–1951) Oil on canvas, 25½ × 31½ 1938.67, Museum Purchase Addison Gallery of American Art © ARS, NY, Phillips Academy, Andover, Mass.*

religious views which they had unquestioningly accepted. My own churchgoing had been at a minimum, indulged in purely at my own whim and inclination, so that I was able to slough off what little superstition I had acquired without any sense of discomfort. But to readjust my ideas and my philosophy to a world which had suddenly lost its feminine integrity, and in which women needed men even as men needed women, was a serious matter.

It took many hours and days of reading to furnish me with a background against which I could evolve a new philosophy to settle this conflict. Westermarck, Crawley, Freud, Adler, Jung, Havelock Ellis, and Ellen Key became my daily familiars. At last I emerged with a modified viewpoint. The necessity of a normal sex life for women was a scientific fact, and I must bow to the truths established by science. I was not, however, compelled to accept the institution of marriage, which was plainly a lineal descendant of primitive rites and ceremonials having its beginnings in ideas of magic later carried over into the folkways and mores. I could recognize that I had normal sex emotions but I need not give up my freedom and independence by submitting to any such religious or legal ceremony.

Phyllis Blanchard

Source: Elaine Showalter, ed., These Modern Women: Autobiographical Essays from the Twenties (*New York: The Feminist Press,* 1989): 107–8.

hyllis Blanchard eventually married in 1925 at age thirty, but rather than settling into the conventional role of wife and mother, she became a prominent child psychologist. With a doctorate in psychology from Clark University, she easily found an intellectual rationale for her rejection of customary gender roles. As she notes, she discovered the works of an assortment of European writers who, in various ways, were exploring the tenets of a "new morality."

Like others in her milieu, Blanchard read the newly translated works of Sigmund Freud who, in developing the theory of psychoanalysis, had established the centrality of the sexuality to the human psyche. Woman's desire in this realm equaled that of men, he noted, and it was only because sexuality was a subject shrouded in silence that women suffered from an "artificial retardation" of their sexual instinct. The British sexologist Havelock Ellis, who figured prominently on Blanchard's list, surpassed Freud in condemning the current restraints on sexual expression. Sex, he wrote, is, simply, "ever wonderful, ever lovely."

Sexual enthusiasts, the "new moralists" endorsed the "repeal of reticence" that was, in fact, sweeping the nation and much of Europe. They wrote novels, plays, and various treatises on the subject; carried their convictions into new forms of art; and spearheaded political campaigns, such as the birth control movement. However, others disagreed with their assessment and rejected their prognosis for a better future. To the contrary, they fewed with alarm the rising divorce rate and the spread of prostitution. The "promiscuous mingling" of the city's youth at dance halls and amusement parks especially offended the sensibilities of those who stubbornly held on to the old ideas about the piety and purity of womanhood. Nevertheless, despite very strong differences in opinion, it was without doubt, as one commentator noted, "sex o'clock" in America. Whether the changes represented a revolution in manners and mores or merely a variation on a theme, no one could yet determine.

Urban Pleasures, Urban Dangers

"No amusement is complete in which 'he' is not a factor," commented Belle Israels, a reformer who keenly observed the behavior of young working women out with their boyfriends. From her vantage point in New York City, she could see that the city provided these women, many of them from immigrant families, with unparalleled opportunities to shed the role of dutiful daughter and mingle with the opposite sex. These women may have earned paltry wages, but the shortened workday—less than ten hours a day or sixty hours a week by 1910—left enough time for not only leisure but also romance.

"women adrift"
Common reference to women who set up households outside marriage or family.

Young working women determinedly explored the delights of the city—amusement parks, movies, restaurants, and department stores—and did so, as often as possible, in the company of men. They forged a path, embracing the emerging consumer-oriented culture and fashioning new social relationships that brought men and women closer together—heterosociality, which would become the hallmark of modernity.

"Women Adrift"

In the nation's cities, one-fifth of all wage-earning women lived apart from their families, kin, and employers, and many took advantage of their residential independence to establish new codes of sexual conduct. Not a few of these **"women adrift,"** as they were called, had fled their hometowns because their fathers had refused to let them go out with boys. Others resented turning over their earnings to their parents. "I wanted more money for clothes than my mother would give me . . . " one young woman explained. "We were always fighting over my pay check. Then I wanted to be out late and they wouldn't stand for that. So I finally left home." Some young women simply found the family farm or small town unbearably dull compared to the attractions of the big city.

The low wages that women earned could rarely cover more than a small, simply furnished room with a private family. Some landladies were sensitive to the disadvantaged position of wage-earning women and charged them lower rent than they did male lodgers, often in return for help with household chores or child care. However, the majority of wage-earning women did not seek a "home away from home" and instead favored contractual tenant relationships with their landladies or landlords. "A place like that should have a strictly hotel basis," one young Irish woman commented,

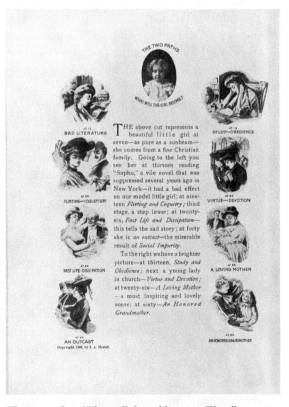

The two paths—What will the girl become? This illustration from Social Purity, a book published in 1903, is meant to warn young women against the dangers of the "new morality" while commending the virtues of old-fashioned notions of womanhood.

WOMEN'S VOICES

WEIGHING MARRIAGE AGAINST CAREER

Raised on a farm in Colorado, Jessie Haver entered Smith College in 1906 and after her graduation worked as a statistician, first in Boston and, later, in Washington, D.C. Determined to forgo marriage, she finally relented and married Hugh Butler in 1920. Here, in an oral history interview conducted in 1972, she recalls her equivocation.

Everything completely changed when I left Boston. Frankly, I was worried because I wasn't meeting any men. I had had a rigid rule in college that I would make no dates because I was getting educated, as my mother told me to do. But now I was twenty-five years old. At this point, I was beginning to wonder if I was ever going to marry. . . . Underneath everything else, what I really wanted was to have a baby. And that meant I had to get married.

I had never taken any interest in boys, except for my brother who was my pal. For some reason I felt superior to them intellectually. I finally did have a boy invite me to the junior prom in high school. My high school teacher got him to do it, I think. He sent me some red carnations. By that time I was seventeen years old. I didn't know how to talk to boys. I was awkward and ill at ease. That's why I wanted to go to a college where there were no men, where I would learn to communicate with ease.

Of course, when I was at Smith there was Horace Lyon. He came to Colorado to get me to marry him after I graduated. He was just a perfect darling, very good-looking and very faithful, fine young man. The trouble was I did not love him. I tried, but it was no good. Within half an hour, I couldn't think of anything to talk about. Imagine that! Well, you can't marry somebody without love—at least I couldn't. I knew I'd never get a chance like that again. My family had a fit at the way I treated him.

In Boston I began to see that I was in an environment where I'd never meet any attractive men, the kind of men I'd like. In boarding houses and places like that, you don't. I was lonely. I had no home and I needed companionship. I liked this Portuguese at a boarding house. He was a handsome fellow. He was the one that aroused me sexually. I was twenty-four years old then. He was very interested in men, really, and is the one who taught me how to swim, but he was never with me for weekends. He would go back down to southern Massachusetts, where his family lived. He said that his father was a drunkard and would come home and beat up his mother, and so he had to be there to protect her. That was the story he told. He hadn't asked me to marry him, but I think he wanted to. Then I had a dream that he had a girl down there that his mother had picked for him to marry. He was a good boy wanting to do what his family said, but was terribly upset trying to decide what to do. When he came back one Monday, I told him about the dream. He never showed up again and I never heard a word from him. That was the end of that. Soon after that, I went to Washington. That's how a dream saved me.

When I went to Washington, everything changed. I'd landed a tremendous job and a good salary and I had prestige and loved my job. Why get married? . . .

So I was getting to be in no hurry to marry. Then I met Hugh. He didn't want to marry either. So I had a boyfriend at last. We went out to dinner every night, Dutch treat. That was a new idea. Women working in offices were new, too. If you were working and he was working, it was natural. I think I was getting a bigger salary than he was, or as big. . . .

I think my job had a lot to do with the attitudes I was developing toward marriage. I had an important job. I saw that being like a man had its value, instead of being like a woman. Then also, there was this friend whom I visited repeatedly. She had three children. I thought she was in a horrible position. Her husband had a high position at Yale University and was a wealthy man. But there she was, glued to this home and children and cooking and everything. I thought, Thank God! I'm free.

Source: *Sherna Gluck, ed., From Parlor to Prison: Five American Suffragists Talk about Their Lives* (New York: Vintage Books, 1976), *98–103.*

Questions

1. How does Jessie Haver Butler respond to the desire for male companionship and her careeer ambitions?

2. What role does sex play in her strivings?

"no Christian stuff; and a decent name." Lodging houses, more common after the turn of the century, offered fewer amenities, such as meals, but more freedom from the oftentimes strained intimacy of the small boardinghouse.

Apartments in large cities were beyond the reach of the average working woman, although by 1910 small groups began to pool their resources to rent flats or even entire houses. One of the most highly publicized adventures in "cooperative housing" was the Chicago **Jane Club,** named after settlement director Jane Addams. Established with her financial backing during a strike in 1892, the club housed a small group of factory workers, each paying room and board and contributing one hour per week to housekeeping chores. "The social spirit was just as cooperative as the financial relationship," recalled one early member. "We enjoyed doing things together." Unlike the YWCA, the Jane Club posted no curfews and did not monitor sexual behavior.

Jane Club The Chicago cooperative housekeeping arrangement for a group of working women who wished to avoid boardinghouses.

The neighborhoods known as furnished room districts provided a setting where the youthful and usually transient residents could defy conventions with impunity. It was not uncommon for women to invite men to their rooms for casual sexual encounters or for others to share their space with "women sweethearts." Although the majority lived "adrift" for only a few years, usually until they married, the experience allowed young women to make the transition from childhood to adulthood without direct parental supervision.

Cheap Amusements

Whether they lived alone or with parents or friends, young women frequented the growing number of commercial entertainments. Employers complained that wage-earning women played so hard during the weekend that they came to work on Monday morning "worn to a frazzle." Then, throughout the workday, they chatted over the din of the machines, recounting their adventures or sharing their romantic fantasies. As soon as the shift ended, young women quickly discarded their practical shirtwaists for fancy clothes—earrings, large hats, dancing slippers, and even feather boas and artificial hairpieces—and embarked on yet another evening on the town.

Fashion became a major preoccupation and for immigrant women a means to identify as American. At work, wage-earning women talked incessantly about the latest trends in clothing and hairstyles and traded cosmetics. To put a damper on such activities, strict employers posted rules prohibiting the "excessive use" of face powder and rouge. Determined to "put on style," most women were undaunted by such restrictions. "A girl must have clothes," one garment worker explained, "if she is to go into high society at Ulmer Park or Coney Island or the theater. A girl who does not dress well is stuck in a corner, even if she is pretty." The rapid expansion of ready-made clothing at the turn of the century made cheap but fancy garments and accessories readily available at pushcarts, neighborhood stores, and the bargain basements of the large department stores. During the slow season, garment workers used their sewing machines to make summer outfits from the remnants.

The main topic of conversation, however, was "gentlemen friends." One middle-class observer commented that at Macy's there was "more smutty talk in one particular department than in a dance hall." While their parents scrupulously avoided the subject of sex, young working women eagerly offered advice. One Jewish woman recounted that she learned the "facts of life" from a coworker. "From that time on I began to look at life differently," she recalled: "I started to make the acquaintance of young men."

During the warm-weather months, young working-class men and women flocked to the new amusement parks, such as Coney Island in New York and Riverview in Chicago, which opened in 1904. Just two years later, there were more than fifteen hundred amusement parks nationwide. Traveling by trolley, boat, or elevated railway, as many as five hundred thousand New Yorkers and an equal number of Chicagoans reached the popular resorts on summer weekends. The boardwalks provided scores of games and attractions, including strong jets of air that blew women's skirts to shocking heights, exposing ankles and even knees! The popular roller-coaster rides encouraged young couples to hold each other tight, while the tunnel of love provided a darkened environment where kissing could take place beyond watchful eyes. The amusement parks charged little for either admission or the numerous attractions, in all making for a cheap date for white working-class youth. Most of these new parks, including Atlanta's "White City," barred African Americans.

Dancing was perhaps the favorite pastime. In New York City, the more than five hundred public dance halls proved, according to reformer Belle Israels, that "the town is dance mad." Some of the largest dance palaces accommodated between five hundred and three thousand patrons, the majority of whom were factory or office workers.

The dance halls provided women the best opportunity to elude their parents' control of dating and courtship, to experiment with new styles, and to meet men on their own. The etiquette of the dance

By 1897, when this photograph was taken, Coney Island had become a popular destination for day-trippers from Manhattan. These young women wear the latest design in bathing suits, now constructed with swimming and physical activity in mind.

hall encouraged relaxed intermingling. Women, paying reduced admission fees, often attended with friends or coworkers and readily accepted invitations to dance from strangers. Casual encounters, especially with the help of a few cocktails, could advance quickly into intimacy, if only for the duration of the evening. One middle-class observer reported that "most of the younger couples were hugging and kissing . . . [and] almost every one seemed to know one another and spoke to each other across the room."

Popular dance styles further encouraged such behavior. "Spieling" brought men and women into close, rigid contact as they spun rapidly around the dance floor. "Tough dancing," which included the turkey trot, the bunny hug, the dip, and the grizzly bear, allowed yet more physical contact, particularly in the pelvic region, and often simulated sexual intercourse.

Many of these new dance forms originated in southern cities, where "jook joints" and "dives" encouraged young African American men and women to reclaim their bodies as instruments of pleasure rather than manual labor. One of the most popular dances was the "slow drag," which one observer described: [C]ouples would hang onto each other and just grind back and forth in one spot all night." Other dances, such as fanny bump and ballin' the jack, also depended on pelvic movements and other erotic gestures capitalizing on the rhythmic beats of ragtime and the blues, the "lowdown" music that was becoming increasingly popular in urban areas across the United States.

The movies, which cost only a nickel, provided a darkened setting where heterosexual romance could blossom. "Note how the semi-darkness permits a 'steady's' arm to encircle a 'lady friend's' waist," one observer pointed out. But it was not just young wage-earning women who attended the picture shows. By 1910, when women represented 40 percent of the working-class movie audience, older married women were going to their neighborhood theaters just as frequently as young wage-earning women. Married couples and mothers with babies in arms sat in the dark alongside the many young couples on dates. In 1909, every Sunday, up to five hundred thousand people attended the more than 340 nickelodeons in New York's Lower East Side. At the same time, African Americans in Atlanta flocked to the cheap, all-black or segregated movie theaters lining Decator Street, the center of the city's commercial entertainment district.

In watching the early silent films, working-class women across the generations could see the beautiful Mary Pickford portraying a young woman who leaves her small town for the big city. The movie heroine at first tries to earn a livelihood working in an office but soon secures better wages and more excitement as a chorus line dancer in a cabaret. The story ends on a happy note: Pickford's character picks up a handsome man who, after treating her to numerous urban delights, proposes marriage. At the same time, in a nearby theater, the Jewish film star Theda Bara and the Italian-born idol Rudolph Valentino were making the silver screen sizzle with their bold projections of sexual desire. In various ways, motion picture shows and other commercial entertainments encouraged young women to imagine a relationship as romantic as that celebrated on the screen.

"Charity Girls"

To pay for the new fashions and entertainments, wage-earning women often went without lunch or saved carfare by walking to and from work. Just as frequently, they relied on the largess of their male companions. The higher wages paid to men, as well as long-standing customs, encouraged women to depend on men for an evening on the town. Men paid for dinner, perhaps tickets to a movie or dancehall, and even a few luxuries such as gifts of perfume or flowers. "Pleasures don't cost girls so much as they do young men," one saleswoman explained. "If they are agreeable they are invited out a good deal, and they are not allowed to pay for anything."

"Charity girls" earned their reputations in this fashion, venturing unescorted to amusement parks and dance halls to "pick up" strangers who would then "treat" them, perhaps to drinks and dinner at a cabaret. In return, the women provided companionship and favors ranging from a brief kiss good night to fondling and even sexual intercourse. These women "draw on their sex as I would on my bank account," one man complained, "to pay for the kind of clothes they want to wear, the kind of shows they want to see."

A charity girl expected nothing more from a night on the town than a good time, or she could hope to strike it lucky and find a boyfriend or even a future husband. However, her plans for marriage, more often than not, included the joys and pleasures that she came to know during courtship.

"charity girls" A reference used in the early twentieth century for young women who traded sexual favors for treats and amusements.

CHANGING RELATIONS OF INTIMACY

The British new moralist Edward Carpenter optimistically predicted that "marriage shall mean friendship as well as passion, that a comrade-like equality shall be included in the word love." In the United States, a generation of women stood poised to test his hypothesis. At the turn of the century, 85 percent of American women over the age of twenty-five were married, widowed, or divorced, and many had nurtured an expectation for companionship in marriage that far exceeded that of their mothers. At the same time, the generation born between 1865 and 1895 produced the highest proportion of never-married women in U.S. history, and a sizable portion of this number formed loving relationships with members of their own sex. But neither group, it seemed, had much use for the time-worn ideology of "female passionlessness."

Courtship and Marriage

With the flow of European immigrants into the United States and the migration of African Americans to northern cities, marriage customs in any one location varied tremendously from group to group. Many African Americans, for example, continued to practice serial monogamy and often preferred common-law marriages to those sanctioned by church or state. One woman in Mississippi commented that "a man is your husband if you live with him and love each other . . . [M]arriage is something for the outside world." Meanwhile, the new immigrant populations brought their own traditions. Some groups such as Chinese and Jews did their best to preserve the Old-World custom of arranged marriage against the wishes of increasingly resistant daughters. "I didn't come to America to have to marry someone like him," one rebellious daughter protested. Other immigrant parents, like Italians, allowed daughters to select their future husband but assumed the right to approve their choice.

For many working-class women, despite the allure of romance, marriage offered foremost the possibility of escaping the deadening routine of factory work. A stanza in a Jewish folk song went: "Day and night and night and day,/ And stitching, stitching,

stitching!/ Help me, dear God, may my handsome one come along,/ and take me away from this toil." Many young women nevertheless sought a husband who would be both friend and lover as well as provider.

Advice experts encouraged this trend. One of the most popular physician-writers disputed the older notion of female passionlessness (see chapter 5) and endorsed sexual pleasure as "normal" for both men and women. "It is a false notion and contrary to nature that . . . passion in a woman is a derogation of her sex," asserted Dr. George Naphey in *The Physical Life of Woman: Advice to the Maiden, Wife, and Mother* (1869).

One of the earliest surveys of women's sexual attitudes and behavior revealed that many white middle-class women agreed. Clelia Duel Mosher, a physician affiliated with Stanford University, collected data on forty-five women, 80 percent born between 1850 and 1880, and found that two-thirds admitted to sexual desire and enjoying sexual in-

By the turn of the century, most American-born women chose to wear white wedding gowns as a symbol of their innocence and virginity. The wedding itself had become an elaborate—and expensive—affair. In 1900, the median age at first marriage for women was 21.9 years and 25.9 years for men.

tercourse. "I consider this appetite as ranking with other natural appetites," one woman explained, "to be indulged legitimately and temperately." The majority in Mosher's sample nevertheless named reproduction as the primary and proper purpose of intercourse.

Divorce

Rising expectations for marriage, including sexual compatibility, accompanied an accelerating rate of divorce. By 1900, in any one year, nearly one marriage in six ended in divorce, giving the United States the highest divorce rate in the world. A distinguished professor at Columbia University attributed this shocking trend to the "emancipation of women." Because many women could now support themselves, he argued, they no longer felt compelled to stay in a marriage that brought them unhappiness or, in some cases, personal injury.

"Restlessness! Restlessness!" exclaimed the popular author Margaret Deland, writing in the *Atlantic Monthly* in 1910. "And as it is with the young woman, so it is with the older woman." Middle-class homemakers, another observer noted, had their appetites "whetted for more abundant and diverting interests than the mere humdrum of household duties." Men, too, put a larger stake in finding a compatible partner. The advice columnist Dorothy Dix, writing in 1915, noted that the young man's ideal mate was a "husky young woman who can play golf all day and dance all night, and drive a motor car, and give first aid to the injured if anybody gets hurt, and who is in no more danger of swooning than he is." Sex appeal and companionship outscored good housekeeping skills. Men and women were demanding more from relationships than their

WOMEN'S LIVES

KATE O'FLAHERTY CHOPIN

Of French Creole extraction, Kate Chopin grew up in luxury and in 1870 married well. Her husband, a cotton broker, brought her from St. Louis to New Orleans, where they mingled with the Creole upper class and summered at Grande Isle, a fancy resort area off the Louisiana Gulf Coast. After bearing six children in short order, Chopin saw her fortunes sink. Her husband's business failed in 1879; he died in 1883. The young widow returned to her mother's home in St. Louis and began to write. With the publication of her first short story in 1889, her fortunes turned again, and she found herself on the road to literary acclaim.

After publishing more than a hundred short stories, Chopin published *The Awakening* (1899), an extraordinary and highly controversial novel. The story follows the twists and turns in the life of a white woman vacationing with her businessman husband and two young sons at a seaside resort outside New Orleans. The protagonist becomes increasingly unresponsive to her husband's nagging complaints that she is neglecting her duties to the family. Edna Pontellier decides to "do as she likes and to feel as she likes." Husband Leonce quickly concludes that his wife is ill, but the narrator explains that Edna was actually "becoming herself and daily casting off that fictitious self which we assume like a garment."

Chopin then sympathetically depicts Edna as she begins to toy with the idea of adultery. At the resort, she shamelessly flirts with one young man, accompanying him without a chaperone on a day-long outing, and she approaches a sexual relationship with another, a known rake. Edna also explores new sensations of sensuality. She relishes the feeling of the tropical sun, luscious water, and soft breezes; luxuriates in long naps and delicious dinners; and revels in her own, too-long-neglected body, discovering and savoring "the fine, firm quality and texture of her flesh."

Chopin also shows this restless wife and mother searching for a way to escape the confines of her domestic role. Although she has little natural talent, Edna aspires to become a painter. It soon becomes clear to her, however, that society does little to accommodate even those women whose skills equal their ambition. Despite her disillusionment, Edna refuses to retreat. Her two small children, the narrator explains, "appeared before her like antagonists who had overcome her; who had overpowered and sought to drag her into the soul's slavery for the rest of her days." Edna tells a friend: "I would give up the unessential; I would give my money, I would give my life for my children; but I wouldn't give myself."

Chopin's protagonist clearly overstepped the bounds of propriety in several key ways, and yet the author offered no judgment. One critic dismissed *The Awakening*, Chopin's third novel, as "gilded dirt"; another called the novel "sensual and devilish." Not until the 1960s, when themes of women's restlessness and sexuality became acceptable, did *The Awakening* resurface, according to one literary historian, as "a most important piece of fiction about the sensual life of a woman." Chopin succumbed to a cerebral hemorrhage and died in St. Louis at the age of fifty-three. ■

parents did and were more willing to end a marriage if their mates failed or refused to live up to their expectations.

However, the majority of Americans, fearing the demise of the family, continued to view divorce with disfavor. State legislatures tightened up the existing divorce laws and enacted new ones. New York, for example, limited divorce only to cases of adultery; South Carolina barred divorce altogether. Despite these restrictions, marriages continued to break down at an alarming pace.

Female Friends and Women Lovers

Quite a few self-supporting women resisted the pressure to marry and instead pursued the companionship of other women. During their college years, many had become love struck with a classmate or a teacher and engaged in the popular practice of "smashing." Frances Willard's sister Mary said of her experiences at North Western Female College: "So when I first left home to attend a boarding school, I was willing in my loneliness to have a 'little friendship.' So I fell in love just like a boy, and wooed and won, as a friend and a good one, a sweet tempered, sweetfaced girl." It was in this setting that Frances Willard herself found the first of the "little friendships" that would sustain her throughout her adult life.

In the last half of the nineteenth century, **"Boston marriages"** were very common. Same-sex couples set up households together and established networks of other women who also lived independently of men. They sometimes bought houses jointly, vacationed and celebrated holidays together, and shared the parenting of adopted children.

Such was the case with settlement worker Jane Addams and her forty-year partner Mary Rozet Smith; with Bryn Mawr College president M. Carey Thomas and Mary Garrett; and with Frances Willard and Anna Gordon. The friendship between the prominent author Sarah Orne Jewett and Annie Adams Fields, the wife of her publisher, developed into a loving, long-term relationship following the death of Fields's husband. In Annie Fields's absence, Jewett wrote letters expressing the emotional pain she endured upon their separation. "Dearest Fuff," she wrote in 1886, "I long to see you and say all sorts of foolish things . . . and kiss you ever so many times and watch you going about. . . . " Such expressions of endearment were common within their circle of artists, writers, and stage performers. Annie Fields's own sister, Lissie Adams, for example, also chose another woman as her life's companion.

It is unclear if these relationships were sexual in a physical sense or principally romantic and spiritual. Earlier in the century, the ideology of female passionlessness did little to encourage women to carry out their bodily desires with either men or women. However, as pleasure and self-expression emerged as markers of heterosexual intimacy, the love between women undoubtedly took on erotic dimensions, at least for some couples.

By the end of the century, physicians and researchers had begun to create a taxonomy of sexual behavior, fashioning a spectrum ranging from "normal" to "morbid" and establishing the modern categories of "heterosexuality" and "homosexuality," which they positioned at the opposite ends of a continuum. The British sexologist Havelock Ellis, for example, published *Sexual Inversion* in 1897 and, using the terms "homosexual" and "lesbian," designating as "abnormal" those women who loved only other women, particularly those women who dressed or acted like men. In this context, the notion of an intensely romantic yet entirely sexless relationship between two women lost much of its credibility, especially if one partner matched the new stereotype of the "mannish lesbian."

"Boston marriage" A term popular in the late nineteenth century that referred to women who set up housekeeping together and lived in a marriage-like relationship.

Jane Addams, the founder of Hull-House, and Mary Rozet Smith, one of its chief financial benefactors, were devoted companions. Smith managed much of Addams's social affairs and took care of her personal needs. Their letters to one another reveal an emotional intimacy typical of the "Boston marriages" or romantic friendships of the era.

Popular magazines and newspapers carried accounts of "sexual deviancy," including the sensationalistic 1892 murder trial of Alice Mitchell in Memphis, Tennessee. Mitchell, who was just nineteen years old, was accused of murdering her lover, seventeen-year-old Freda Ward. Their families at first viewed their relationship as typical of the romantic friendship commonplace among teenage girls. But when Freda's brother discovered their plan to elope, with Alice cross-dressing and assuming the name of "Alvin," he forced Freda to return the engagement ring. After Freda took up with a couple male suitors, Alice took her revenge and killed her. The court judged Alice "not guilty by reason of insanity" and committed her to an asylum, where she died six years later.

With the help of both the scientific and popular presses, "homosexuality" and "heterosexuality" emerged as broad categories by which individuals could identify and be identified. "In many large cities," one contemporary observer noted, "the subjects of the contrary sexual impulse form a class by themselves and are recognized by the police." Cross-dressing men known as "fairies" and "queer creatures" patronized their own resorts and cabarets and sponsored masquerade or "drag" balls. "Certain smart clubs," one investigator reported, "are well-known for their homosexual atmospheres." Women were less visible in these emerging gay communities, but they managed to stake out a presence in all the major cities. And many couples, despite the new stigma attached to same-sex intimacy, persisted in their relationships.

CURBING "SOCIAL EVILS"

Society shall rise to "higher levels," Frances Willard predicted in 1885, "by holding men to the same standard of morality . . . and by punishing with extreme penalties such men as inflict upon women atrocities compared with which death would be infinitely welcome." Willard responded to changes in sexual behavior, as did large sectors of the public, with a combination of displeasure and fear. Women—that is, white women—seemed too vulnerable, in their opinion, in a society where men held power. The era of the new morality therefore ushered in a second trend—a growing number of prohibitions and regulations of both speech and behavior, which were increasingly maintained with the force of law. In different ways, the social purity campaigns, the movement against prostitution, and the legislation regulating interracial sex all struck out at men's alleged licentiousness.

Social Purity Campaigns

Social purity advocates targeted the so-called double standard of morality, which granted men sexual license while demanding purity from women. By bringing men into line with the prevailing standards for women, they aspired to create controls over sexual behavior that would ensure women's safety and establish stringent penalties for the male violators. Reformers went so far as to insist that sexual activity in marriage occur only under conditions of mutual assent.

Legal efforts to advance social purity dated to 1873 when Anthony Comstock drafted the Act for the Suppression of Trade In and Circulation of Obscene Literature and Articles of Immoral Use. Better known as the **Comstock Act of 1873,** the federal law made it a criminal act to send through the mail "obscene, lewd or lascivious materials" as well as items intended "for any indecent or immoral use," that is, information or devices for contraception or abortion. Comstock succeeded not only in silencing Victoria Woodhull and Tennessee Claflin but in securing for himself a special appointment in the U.S. Post Office that authorized him to pursue violators (see chapter 10).

Despite Comstock's visibility, it was the WCTU that mobilized masses of women to promote social purity. Frances Willard secured the establishment of the WCTU's Department of Social Purity in 1885 and enthusiastically endorsed its major program,

social purity The ideal of a single standard of sexual morality for both men and women, advocating abstinence before marriage and restrained behavior after.

Comstock Act of 1873 Federal law that made it illegal to send any "obscene, lewd, and/or lascivious"—specifically including contraceptive devices and information—materials through the mail.

TABLE 14-1   Premarital Pregnancy Rate Eighteenth–Nineteenth Century

1681–1720	14%
1721–1760	21%
1761–1800	27%
1801–1840	18%
1841–1880	10%
1881–1910	23%

(Based on pregnancies of under 8 1/2 months from date of marriage in Daniel Scott Smith and Michael S. Hindus. "Premarital Pregnancy in America 1640–1971: An Overview and an Interpretation," Journal of Interdisciplinary History, *Vol 5, No. 4, (Spring, 1975) pp. 538, 561).*

Premarital pregnancy serves well as a measure of change in sexual behavior.

"The White Life for Two." Local branches sponsored mothers' meetings, lobbied to obtain instructional programs in the public schools, and on occasions joined Comstock to advance a vigorous censorship campaign of books and other printed materials. The WCTU also formed the White Shield campaign, which enrolled hundreds of thousands of women who pledged to lead a "pure life." The White Shield became the popular "sister" society of the all-male White Cross, which had organized with the support of Protestant churches and the YMCA.

The WCTU crusaded against various forms of "immorality," such as prostitution, rape, and the sexual exploitation of children. One of its most successful campaigns targeted the **age of consent,** the age at which a girl could legally agree to "carnal relations with the other sex." Most states had fixed the age of consent at the common-law practice of ten years. Delaware had the lowest, age seven. A massive petition drive spearheaded in 1886 with assistance from the Knights of Labor resulted in new congressional legislation raising the age of consent from ten to sixteen years in all territories and the District of Columbia. A decade later, the majority of states had raised the age of consent to sixteen or, in a few cases, eighteen, making men who had consensual sex with a woman under that age liable for arrest and prosecution for statutory rape.

age of consent Phrase referring the minimum age at which a person is considered capable of giving informed consent to any contract or behavior, with particular reference to sexual acts.

Although the National Association of Colored Women did not become actively involved in the campaigns to raise the age of consent, fearing that young black women would be unfairly targeted and arrested, the organization strongly endorsed the broader goals of the social purity movement. The NACW had formed partially in response to a slanderous letter printed in a British newspaper in 1895. The letter, written by the president of the Missouri Press Association to the secretary of the Anti-Lynching Society of England, described African Americans as a race bereft of morality and labeled black women as thieves, liars, and prostitutes. Although such derogatory commentary was not unusual in the white press, leading African American women found these allegations especially outrageous. According to Margaret Murray Washington, black women were "suddenly awakened by the wholesale charges of the lack of virtue and character." Club women instructed their members to guard their reputations and to strive to present themselves as exemplars of purity. In 1904, delegates to the national convention of the NACW endorsed "temperance, educational mothers' meetings, and the elimination of immoral literature."

In the first decade of the twentieth century, Fritz Guerin became a famed photographer of women, often posed in only partial dress, who appeared to delight in their personal beauty and sensuality. Images such as this one, which circulated through newspaper tabloids and postcards, drew the ire of social purity reformers.

Crusading against Prostitution

During the Civil War, venereal disease spread so rampantly among soldiers that several prominent physicians pro-

The White Cross: I Promise by the Help of God

1. To treat all women with respect, and endeavor to protect them from wrong and degradation.
2. To endeavor to put down all indecent language and coarse jests.
3. To maintain the law of purity as equally binding upon men and women.
4. To endeavor to spread these principles among my companions, and to try and help my younger brothers.
5. To use every possible means to fulfill the command, "Keep THYSELF pure."

The White Shield: I Promise by the Help of God

1. To uphold the law of purity as equally binding upon men and women.
2. To be modest in language, behavior and dress.
3. To avoid all conversation, reading, pictures and amusements which may put impure thoughts into my mind.
4. To guard the purity of others, especially the young.
5. To strive after the special blessing promised to THE PURE OF HEART.

posed a licensing program of prostitutes modeled on the recently enacted Contagious Diseases Act in England. After the war, the president of the American Medical Association endorsed this plan as a public health measure. While the New York legislature considered several bills, the municipality of St. Louis instituted an official licensing plan that required regular medical inspections of prostitutes. The program lasted for scarcely four years, from 1870 to 1874, when a coalition of clergy and women reformers forced the city to end it.

Social purity advocates, as well as many suffragists, sought not to regulate but to eradicate prostitution by "rescuing" fallen women and "punishing" sinful men. "There is no escape from the conclusion that while woman's want of bread induces her to pursue this vice," Susan B. Anthony reasoned, "man's love of the vice itself leads him there."

One of the largest organizations to conduct "rescue" work was the **Florence Crittenton Mission**, founded by merchant-philanthropist Charles Crittenton and named for his beloved daughter who had succumbed to scarlet fever at age four. The first Crittenton mission opened in April 1883 on Bleecker Street, a few doors away from one of the most notorious brothels in New York City. The mission's volunteer workers formed "rescue bands" to comb the nearby streets, inviting prostitutes and their clients to attend the regular midnight services conducted in the mission chapel. A half century later, a chain of more than sixty-five Florence Crittenton homes offered assistance to women, primarily unmarried mothers who lacked a place to live.

Florence Crittenton Mission A refuge for prostitutes and safe haven for women without homes named for the recently-deceased daughter of founder Charles Crittenton.

By the end of the century, virtually every large city and many small towns were sponsoring "houses of refuge" of various kinds. For example, a group of Presbyterian women opened the Chinese Mission Home in San Francisco in 1874 to provide "shelter and protection" to those Chinese women who had been sold into a "slavery worse than death." The mission's all-white staff aspired to teach these women sufficient skills so that they could redeem themselves through "honest labor." However, most of the prostitutes who moved into the mission home did so only after they became engaged to marry. Settled into the mission for a term up to one year, which was financed by their prospective husbands, these women immersed themselves in an intensive course of instruction on the domestic

"Who would have prophesied a century ago that today like hardware and groceries the daughters of the people would be bought and sold," asked state's attorney and Chicago reformer Clifford G. Roe in his popular book on white slavery, published at the height of the scare in 1911.

"white slavery panic"
A moral panic based on the assumption that thousands of young women were being lured into prostitution and held against their will.

Mann Act Also known as the White-Slave Traffic Act of 1910, banned the interstate transport of women for "immoral purposes."

arts so that they could prepare to keep a Christian home. By the turn of the century, the Chinese Mission Home was "rescuing" approximately eighty prostitutes a year.

The high point of rescue work occurred between 1908 and 1914, when the **"white slavery panic"** swept the country. Reformers told melodramatic tales of white slavers luring unsuspecting young women and girls into dance halls or amusement parks, forcefully drugging or seducing them, and then holding them in bondage in houses of prostitution. In response to such lurid tales and high-pressured lobbying, Congress passed the **Mann Act** in 1910, making it a federal crime to take a woman across state lines for "immoral purposes." Meanwhile, settlement houses, Chicago's Immigrants' Protective League, and the National Council of Jewish Women launched programs to protect young women from the snares of procurers. In addition to organizing international conferences on white slavery, they sent volunteers to the the major ports of entry and immigration centers, such as Ellis Island and Angel Island, to offer assistance to newcomers traveling alone. "Beware of those who give you addresses, offer you easy, well-paid work, or even marriage," read one of their broadsides, which was printed in three languages.

Civic-minded men joined women reformers in the accelerating crusades against prostitution. Together they proposed the establishment of municipal vice commissions and special grand juries, first, to gauge the extent of prostitution and, second, to prescribe a remedy. More than forty cities and states set up investigative committees that collectively uncovered, as one reformer put it, "the debauchery of tens of thousands of both sexes." A major cause of prostitution, they concluded, was the inability of many women to support themselves. They also blamed parents for failing to supervise their children amid the many temptations that accompanied spread of commercial amusements. However, it was organized vice, they concluded, that bore the major responsibility for turning approximately two hundred thousand women nationwide into prostitutes.

These well-intended efforts made little headway against the commercialized prostitution that did indeed flourish in virtually every city, large or small, and among all classes of men. In New York, in the middle-class price range, there were twice as many brothels as the fifty-cent cribs that working-class men could afford, and boys of both classes commonly turned to prostitutes for their first experience in sexual intercourse. In 1912, there were fourteen brothels in the small town of Janesville, Wisconsin, nearly thirty in midsize Lancaster, Pennsylvania, and more than eighteen hundred in metropolitan New York, where no less than fifteen thousand prostitutes plied their trade. "Sporting guides" and "blue books" mapped the city's red-light districts, describing the various specialties of individual prostitutes and the prices they charged.

Legislating against Miscegenation

Laws banning interracial marriage dated to the mid-seventeenth century, but only with the abolition of slavery did states begin to tighten and enforce such legislation as a means to control race relations and to bolster white supremacy. One white southerner expressed his fear of race mixing, or **miscegenation,** a term popularized in the early 1860s: "If we have intermarriage we shall degenerate; we shall become a race of mulattoes . . . ; we shall be ruled out from the family of white nations. Sir, it is a matter of life and death with the Southern people to keep their blood pure." The laws enacted after the Civil War carried harsh penalties; the "antimiscegenation" law in Alabama, for example, stipulated imprisonment or a sentence of hard labor for not less than two nor more than seven years.

Relationships between white women and black men provoked the most censure, although such liaisons had been tolerated to some degree among poor southerners before the Civil War. The "blood" of white women must remain "absolutely pure," one postbellum writer pronounced, "and it is the inflexible resolution of the South to preserve that purity, no matter how dear the cost."

In the South shortly after the Civil War, the Ku Klux Klan provided extra-legal force to this conviction (see chapter 10). The Klan terrorized white women who violated the code of behavior and inflicted horrifying abuse on their black partners that ranged from tar-and-feathering, torture, genital mutilation, and severe beatings, to burning and lynching. "If the negro marries an outcast white woman . . . ," white supremacist Hinton Rowan Helper opined in 1867, "both he and she ought to be hung three minutes after the conclusion of the ceremony, or as soon thereafter as the necessary preparations could be made."

In contrast, interracial marriage and sexual relations between white men and black women continued to draw little more than scorn or ridicule because such liaisons mirrored and reinforced the existing patterns of race and gender domination. White men, for example, frequently kept black women as mistresses. The new laws, moreover, did little to protect black women from sexual abuse by white men. To the contrary, following the demise of slavery, the brutal assault and rape of black women increased, serving as a commonplace "weapon of terror."

By the turn of the century, states throughout the South and West had adopted some form of "antimiscegenation" laws. Legislatures, for example, forbade marriages between Indians and whites. In California, white Americans raised the spectre of the "Yellow Peril" to convince legislators to amend the state's civil code in 1880 to prohibit marriage between a white person and a "Negro, Mulatto, or Mongolian." Ultimately, twelve states or territories banned marriages between "Orientals" and whites.

This legislation made marriage virtually impossible for an entire generation of Chinese men in the United States. The **Page Act of 1875,** the first federal law to restrict

In 1912 Seaborn Roddenbery (Dem., GA) proposed an amendment to the U.S. Constitution to "prohibit forever" interracial marriage within the United States. A response to the African American heavyweight champion Jack Johnson's highly publicized marriages to white women, Roddenbery's bill failed but not before prompting a flurry of similar legislative activity in several states where interracial marriage was legal. Although only one new "anti-miscegenation" law passed at the state level in 1913, in Wyoming, from 1913 to 1948 thirty states enforced the laws already in place.

miscegenation A term introduced into the United States in 1863, refers to an alleged mixing of "races" through sexual relations and provided the basis for laws prohibiting interracial marriage and cohabitation.

Page Act of 1875 Enacted by the U.S. Congress to restrict immigration from Asian countries, especially women identified as prostitutes.

immigration by prohibiting the entry of prostitutes, effectively singled out women from China (see chapter 12). Within just two years, the number of Chinese women disembarking in San Francisco, the major point of entry, had fallen by as much as 80 percent. By the end of the century, this restriction caused a severe imbalance in the sex ratio. The number of Chinese women in the United States did not rise above five thousand and represented just 7 percent of the entire Chinese population. Although repeatedly challenged, the U.S. Supreme Court upheld the constitutionality of these state laws, a decision that was not reversed until 1967.

While social purity activists were striking out against "illicit" sexual behavior, other reformers were organizing to expand the range of "normal" activities and "proper" attitudes. After the turn of the century, these two groups stood firmly in opposition to each other. However, they touched common ground in rejecting the double standard of morality. But whereas social purity activists hoped to bring men into women's realm of purity and restraint, others aspired to grant women more of the privileges that men had been enjoying for centuries.

WOMEN'S BODIES AND REPRODUCTION

By the time Margaret Sanger stepped forward to proclaim the birth control movement as "the most far-reaching social development of modern times," groups of reformers had already incited what Sanger described as "the revolt of woman against sex servitude." Experts ranging from physicians and educators to the president of the United States weighed in on this subject, delivering a strikingly wide range of opinions. Controversies erupted with such fervor that it seemed as if the fate of the nation depended on the future of the female body, particularly its ever-mysterious and awesome capacity to bear children.

Designed for Motherhood

It was as if, a male physician contended, "the Almighty, in creating the female sex, had taken the uterus and built up a woman around it." In the last half of the nineteenth century, most physicians assumed that a woman's reproductive organs connected directly to the central nervous system and thereby controlled the actions of all other organs and systems in her body. Consequently, in their opinion, menstruation and ovulation had a dramatic impact on women's health, emotions, and behavior and, to a large extent, worked in concert to prepare her for motherhood and, by extension, for domesticity.

The emergence of the New Woman caused great concern among the medical community and spawned an outpouring of commentary on this subject. Physicians warned that puberty, when the reproductive organs were just beginning to function, made girls peculiarly vulnerable to all kinds of stress. Dr. Edward H. Clarke, a former professor at the Harvard Medical School, warned that "brain-work" and menstruation were incompatible. The combination, he claimed, resulted in "monstrous brains and puny bodies; abnormally active cerebration, and abnormally weak digestion; flowing thought and constipated bowels; lofty aspirations and neuralgic sensations." He therefore advised mothers to keep their daughters from nerve-draining intellectual work, especially the rigors of higher education.

Clarke's treatise, *Sex in Education: Or, a Fair Chance for Girls* (1873), which described female college graduates as "mannish maidens," generated considerable criticism.

The physician Mary Putnam Jacoby refuted Clarke's contentions, saying that she had found scant evidence that the menstrual cycle affected women's mental or physical abilities. Administrators at the women's colleges, likewise determined to refute Clarke's claims, responded by establishing fitness programs to complement the intellectually demanding academic curriculum. Nevertheless, even decades after the publication of Clarke's book, Bryn Mawr president M. Carey Thomas noted that her students "were haunted . . . by the clanging chains of that gloomy little specter."

Thomas's students were justified in their suspicions that higher education may jeopardize their chances for a healthy motherhood. In 1904, the psychologist G. Stanley Hall still insisted that girls must be educated "primarily and chiefly for motherhood." Meanwhile, the British biologist and popular writer Grant Allen, publishing in an American magazine, described woman as "the sex sacrificed to reproductive necessities."

Controlling Reproduction

Dedicated to ensuring a smooth path to reproduction, the mainstream medical profession contributed little to the idea of family limitation. When physicians had begun to carve out the specialty field of gynecology, the physiology of conception was largely unknown, but those who wrote on the subject commonly condemned any form of contraception. They insisted that the widespread practice of *coitus interruptus*, or withdrawal, had an injurious effect on a woman's delicate nervous system. Rather, the antebellum physician William A. Alcott advised "the submissive wife" to "do everything for your husband which your strength and a due regard to your health would admit." In late 1860s, medical societies passed formal resolutions condemning birth control practices and abortion.

At the same time, a few courageous reformers flaunted expert opinion to speak out on "voluntary motherhood," that is, the right of women to control their fertility. In the early 1870s, both Elizabeth Cady Stanton and Victoria Woodhull wrote and lectured on the topic (see chapter 10). They, too, rejected contraceptives, fearing that "artificial" methods would allow men to demand yet more sex from their wives. However, they did insist, in line with social purity advocates, that women had the absolute right to determine the frequency, timing, and form of sexual relations within marriage.

In a trend that one historian has termed **"domestic feminism,"** American women appeared to gain more power over marital relationships. Among white women surviving to menopause, the average number of children born fell from 7.04 in 1800 to 3.54 a century later. The drop for urban middle-class women was even sharper because immigrant and rural women brought up the average by bearing more children. But even for African American women, the majority of whom still lived in rural areas, the fertility rate dropped by one-third between 1880 and 1920. For many Americans, two children represented the ideal number.

By the turn of the century, middle-class women were using the variety of methods to control fertility that dated to the early nineteenth century (see chapter 5). While many encouraged their husbands to practice withdrawal, an increasing number of women relied on contraceptive devices like condoms, sponges, and pessaries. In Mosher's sample, 42 percent of the women who used contraceptives listed douching as their preferred method and named sulphate of zinc, alum, alcohol, soap suds, and plain water as solutions of choice. Still other women used the rhythm method, some carefully charting their menstrual cycles in a special diary. However, most of these methods were

"domestic feminism" Coined by historian Daniel Scott Smith, refers to the increasing power of married women to control reproduction.

either unreliable or inefficient. As a last resort, women turned to an underground network of abortionists.

Educated white women achieved the lowest fertility rates of all women, simply by marrying later than average or choosing not to marry at all. For example, more than half of the women who graduated from Bryn Mawr between 1889 and 1908 never married; for Wellesley and the University of Michigan, the percentages were just a bit lower, 43 percent and 47 percent, respectively. Three-quarters of all women who received doctoral degrees between 1877 and 1924 remained unwed. Highly educated women who did marry tended to have fewer children than the average or none at all.

The drop in fertility among educated white women was so striking that some worried citizens predicted an impending crisis for the nation. Their fear dated to 1870 when the Massachusetts census bureau reported higher birthrates among the immigrant population than among the native-born Americans and among poor people than among the affluent. In 1903, no less than the president of the United States, Theodore Roosevelt, cautioned that the low birthrate among white Anglo-Saxon Protestants was sure to result in **"race suicide."** His advice—breed larger families—found few takers.

"race suicide" A phrase attributed to President Theodore Roosevelt heralding the demise of "civilization" caused by the dropping birth rate among Americans of Anglo-Saxon ancestry.

The Birth Control Campaign

The campaign launched by Margaret Sanger targeted the masses of working people. A neo-Malthusian, she believed that working people, by limiting family size, could utilize their meager resources more efficiently and put themselves in a better position to foment revolution—or at least to demand higher wages. In endorsing these principles, Sanger won support of large numbers of socialists and anarchists, who became the backbone of the birth control movement in its first years.

In 1915, following William Sanger's arrest, the most talented radical activists headed a widespread campaign. The labor agitator Elizabeth Gurley Flynn spoke at dozens of meetings sponsored by the Industrial Workers of the World (IWW). Flynn sent words of encouragement to Margaret Sanger, then in exile, and described the upbeat mood of the crowds that turned out to hear about birth control. The socialist Kate Richards O'Hare reported from the Midwest that her newspaper, the *National Rip Saw*, had been "flooded" with letters from women demanding the secret to family limitation.

The most prominent agitator was Emma Goldman, who was by then well known as an anarchist and a free lover. Like Sanger, Goldman had worked as a nurse in New York's Lower East Side and understood well the urgency of getting birth control information to the burgeoning population of poor immigrant women. She decided to test the limit of the Comstock laws by giving graphic descriptions of contraceptive techniques in her public lectures. After a cross-country tour, Goldman was finally arrested in New York City on February 11, 1916.

Hundreds of people stormed Carnegie Hall to hear Goldman defend herself. "I have simply given to the poorer women in my audiences information that any wealthy woman can obtain secretly from her physician who does not fear prosecution," she explained. "I have offered them

"*Marriage and love have nothing in common; they are as far apart as the poles; are, in fact, antagonistic to each other.*" So wrote the famed anarchist Emma Goldman (1869–1940) in 1911. She envisioned a new society where men and women would be free to express themselves in all realms, including the sexual realm, without the constraints of institutions. Believing that marriage was nothing more than legalized prostitution, she took many lovers and wrote passionate letters about her sexual desires and feelings.

WOMEN'S LIVES

MARGARET SANGER

In 1910, Margaret Sanger found herself the mother of three small children and a housewife feeling increasingly stifled by the "complacent suburban attitude" of her Westchester, New York, surroundings. Luckily, her artist-architect husband felt the same. The family moved to New York City, where Margaret and William Sanger found the stimulation they craved. They joined a circle of Greenwich Village bohemians and radicals. They made friends with the likes of Eugene V. Debs, John Reed, Upton Sinclair, and Emma Goldman and spent many evenings at the salon of Mabel Dodge talking about art, revolution, and sex. Sanger soon became an active member of the local women's committee of the Socialist Party and helped to evacuate and care for the workers' children during the famous textile strike at Lawrence, Massachusetts, in 1912.

Sanger also resumed a career in public health, working as a visiting nurse mainly in New York's immigrant Lower East Side and specializing in obstetrical care. She later claimed that one woman, desperate to avoid another pregnancy, related that her doctor's only advice was to have her husband sleep on the roof. The woman, Sadie Sachs, died shortly from an attempted abortion. Sanger's own mother, a devout Catholic, died prematurely at age fifty after giving birth to eleven children. These two tragic events, Sanger insisted, caused her "to seek out the root of the evil, to do something to change the destiny of others whose miseries were as vast as the sky."

In March 1914, Sanger began to publish a monthly newspaper, the *Woman Rebel*, emblazoned with the masthead "No Gods, No Masters." After three issues, the Comstock Act caught up with her, and the newspaper was banned for violating postal obscenity laws by discussing and advocating the use of contraception, or what Sanger had termed "birth control." Fleeing imprisonment, she made her way to England where she deepened her study of sexuality and contraception. In the meantime, friends began to distribute a sixteen-page pamphlet, "Family Limita-

tion," in which she explicitly described a variety of contraceptive devices and techniques. William Sanger was soon jailed for distributing the pamphlet.

In October 1915, Margaret Sanger returned to the United States to face trial, hoping that the proceedings would provide a public forum to garner support for the cause. The court dropped the charges, however, following the sudden death of her five-year-old daughter. By this time, Sanger had managed to inspire a net of activists who sponsored her on a nationwide tour. When Sanger returned to New York, she went on to open the first birth control clinic in the United States, in Brownsville, a predominantly Jewish and Italian section of Brooklyn. Arrested again, in October 1916, she now had an entire organized movement in place to push for birth control. Sanger herself stayed with the campaign, playing a major role in organizing the Planned Parenthood Federation in 1942 and living long enough to witness the 1965 Supreme Court decision, *Griswold v. Connecticut*, which removed the last legal obstacle for married women to gain access to birth control. ■

advice as to how to escape the burden of large families without resorting to illegal operations." Goldman's highly publicized trial and incarceration in the workhouse prompted Margaret Anderson, the editor of the *Little Review*, to write: "Emma Goldman was sent to prison for advocating that women need not always keep their mouths shut and their wombs open."

National Birth Control League Founded in 1916 to advocate changes in legislation that restricted the dissemination of birth control information and devices.

American Birth Control League Founded in 1921 to provide services to women in need; later became Planned Parenthood.

Meanwhile, a group of middle-class women and men moved to the forefront of the movement. Several in New York City formed the **National Birth Control League** (NBCL), directed by suffragist Mary Ware Dennett. The NBCL built a campaign not by appealing to working-class women but by enjoining physicians and wealthy individuals to demand a repeal of the existing state and federal laws that designated birth control information and devices as "obscene." Dissatisfied with the singular legislative approach, Margaret Sanger organized the rival **American Birth Control League** (ABCL), which by the mid-1920s boasted a membership of more than thirty-seven thousand. The ABCL also promoted legislative reform and depended on professionals for leadership but provided practical services, such as educational programs and clinics, and funded research and conferences to attract international affiliates.

By the end of the 1910s, groups of African American women were actively campaigning for the creation of birth control clinics in black communities. In 1918, the Women's Political Association of Harlem initiated a series of lectures on the subject, and several years later Margaret Sanger spoke to black audiences in the Bronx. In 1925, at the request of the Urban League, the ABCL began to lay plans for a clinic in Harlem, which opened in 1929.

REBELS IN BOHEMIA

"We were healthy animals and we were demanding our right to spring's awakening," one college woman recalled. Between 1910 and 1914, this idea inspired small circles of radicals and so-called "bohemians" to insist on greater honesty in sexual relations and an end to the double standard. They gave testimony to this aspiration not only through their social activism and artistic works but through the way they lived out their personal lives. It was within this context that a new, distinctively modern form of politics emerged.

Living the New Morality

In the late-1870s, small groups of radicals began to challenge Anthony Comstock's anti-"obscenity" laws by publicly denying that marriage was the only proper context for sexual relations. Like Victoria Woodhull, they proudly proclaimed themselves to be free lovers (see chapter 10). Theirs was an uphill and unpopular battle. For more than twenty years, Ezra and Angela Heywood published *The Word* in an attempt to break what they believed was a conspiracy of silence about all topics related to human sexuality; Moses Harman and Lois Nichols Waisbrooker did the same with *Lucifer, the Light-Bearer*.

After the turn of the century, a new generation of mostly middle-class women and men took advantage of the greater freedom they discovered amid the diverse populations of the nation's big cities. They typically congregated in the furnished room districts and immigrant neighborhoods, forming distinctive enclaves that became famous for their "bohemian" character. In the environs of Chicago's Bug House Square and San Francisco's North Beach, these adventurers tampered with the moral values prescribed by their parents and attempted to create a new lifestyle wherein men and women lived together honestly and loved freely as equals.

The low-rent neighborhood of Greenwich Village, located on the west side of downtown Manhattan, became the most celebrated bohemian mecca. Mabel Dodge's nearby salon on Fifth Avenue provided a forum for discussions of sexuality, enlivened by the preachings of Margaret Sanger, who served, according to her host, as "an ardent propagandist for the joys of the flesh." Sanger and her companions felt no compunction in denigrating chastity for either men or women and instead insisted on the right to sample various pleasures on the way to marriage. Some chose to avoid the institution altogether, while others condemned the artificial restraints imposed by monogamy. Louise Bryant and John Reed, both journalists and political activists, and Susan Glaspell and her husband George Cram Cook, both playwrights and novelists, were only the most prominent denizens of "Bohemia" who attempted to live by the precepts of the new morality.

If they married, bohemian women refused to sacrifice their independence. They continued to pursue careers and shunned domesticity. A few couples joined together in cooperative housekeeping arrangements, sharing cooking, cleaning, and child care; others chose to live in a comparatively barren flat rather than a fully funished house that demanded constant upkeep. In the fashion world, bohemians became known as trendsetters. Women abandoned the popular body-molding corsets for the comfort of loose-fitting garments, men avoided business suits for casual wear, and in warm weather both put aside clunky shoes for sandals. Women often smoked and drank as freely as men. A favorite meeting place was the "Working Girls Club," not a charity home but a saloon in Greenwich Village. Young men were drawn to the defiant woman, the writer Floyd Dell later recalled, because she "was comparatively freed from the home and its influence; because she took the shock and jostle of life's incidents more bravely, more candidly and more lightly."

One such rebellious woman was Ida Rauh. Born to a well-to-do Jewish family in New York City, Rauh as a young, adventurous woman decided to move downtown "to find out about life." There, in 1907, she met Max Eastman, who would become the editor of the radical magazine *The Masses* and her future husband. Eastman remembered her then as a woman who "had renounced so hotly all the frills and luxuries of bourgeois life that she lived almost like a pauper. She would bring one informal garment, a simple, self-made unobtrusively becoming garment and lie . . . reading or sleeping all day." Like Kate Chopin's fictional character Edna Pontellier in *The Awakening*, Rauh claimed the right to revel in sensuous languor.

Eventually, Rauh married Eastman—for the sake of convenience, she insisted. The couple continued to list their names separately on the mailbox of their Greenwich Village flat. Gradually, however, like so many other relationships conceived in Bohemia, noble aspirations proved insufficient for the long haul. Rauh and Eastman soon separated and finally divorced in 1922.

"Open marriage," or free love, proved far more attractive as an ideal than as an actual practice. A customary prerogative for men, multiple sexual partners continued to place women at a disadvantage, not least by raising the chances of unwanted pregnancy.

"open marriage" Refers to an agreement that recognizes the right of husbands and wives to engage in extramarital sexual relationships without the stigma of infidelity.

WOMEN'S VOICES

"RED EMMA" CRITIQUES MARRIAGE

Emma Goldman issued some of the most forceful critiques of the institution of marriage. Born in Lithuania, she had immigrated to the United States when she was seventeen, married briefly, and then devoted her life to anarchism. Goldman also promoted free love and published a popular "little magazine," Mother Earth. Known as "Red Emma," she was deported for her incendiary views during World War I and spent the remainder of her life in the Soviet Union.

The popular notion about marriage and love is that they are synonymous, that they spring from the same motives, and cover the same human needs. Like most popular notions this also rests not on actual facts, but on superstition.

Marriage and love have nothing in common; they are as far apart as the poles; are, in fact, antagonistic to each other. No doubt some marriages have been the result of love. Not, however, because love could assert itself only in marriage; much rather it is because few people can completely outgrow a convention. There are today large numbers of men and women to whom marriage is naught but a farce, but who submit to it for the sake of public opinion. At any rate, while it is true that some marriages are based on love, and while it is equally true that in some cases love continues in married life, I maintain that it does so regardless of marriage, and not because of it. . . .

Marriage is primarily an economic arrangement, an insurance pact. It differs from the ordinary life insurance agreement only in that it is more binding, more exacting. Its returns are insignificantly small compared with the investments. In taking out an insurance policy one pays for it in dollars and cents, always at liberty to discontinue payments. If, however, woman's premium is a husband, she pays for it with her name, her privacy, her self-respect, her very life, "until death doth part." Moreover, the marriage insurance condemns her to life-long dependency, to parasitism, to complete uselessness, individual as well as social. Man, too, pays his toll, but as his sphere is wider, marriage does not limit him as much as woman. He feels his chains more in an economic sense. . . .

From infancy, almost, the average girl is told that marriage is her ultimate goal; therefore her training and education must be directed towards that end. Like the mute beast fattened for slaughter, she is prepared for that. Yet, strange to say, she is allowed to know much less about her function as wife and mother than the ordinary artisan of his trade. It is indecent and filthy for a respectable girl to know anything of the marital relation. Oh, for the inconsistency of respectability, that needs the marriage vow to turn something which is filthy into the purest and most sacred arrangement that none dare question or criticize. Yet that is exactly the attitude of the average upholder of marriage. The prospective wife and mother is kept in complete ignorance of her only asset in the competitive field—sex. Thus she enters into life-long relations with a man only to find herself shocked, repelled, outraged beyond measure by the most natural and healthy instinct, sex. It is safe to say that a large percentage of the unhappiness, misery, distress, and physical suffering of matrimony is due to the criminal ignorance in sex matters that is being extolled as a great virtue. Nor is it at all an exaggeration when I say that more than one home has been broken up because of this deplorable fact.

If, however, woman is free and big enough to learn the mystery of sex without the sanction of State or Church, she will stand condemned as utterly unfit to become the wife of a "good" man, his goodness consisting of an empty head and plenty of money. Can there be anything more outrageous than the idea that a healthy, grown woman, full of life and passion, must deny nature's demand, must subdue her most intense craving, undermine her health and break her spirit, must stunt her vision, abstain from the depth and glory of sex experience until a "good" man comes along to take her unto himself as a wife? That is precisely what marriage means. How can such an arrangement end except in failure? This is one, though not the least important, factor of marriage, which differentiates it from love.

Source: Emma Goldman, Anarchism and Other Essays, *(New York: Mother Earth Publishing Association, 1911) 233–45.*

Questions

1. How does Emma Goldman make her argument for free love and against marriage?

2. What role does sex play in her critique of contemporary marriage practices?

Moreover, even the most determined and well-educated woman found it nearly impossible to secure employment that would bring her financial security—or allow her to raise children without depending on a husband for support. Nevertheless, many women were willing to pay a steep emotional price for their experimentation and took comfort in the sense that they were helping to seal the fate of the culture of separate spheres.

Heterodoxy and Feminism

In New York, a self-described "little band of willful women, the most unruly and individualistic you ever fell upon," came together in 1912 to form an innovative women's club, **Heterodoxy.** In its thirty-year history, the club admitted only a little more than one hundred members, but its small roster listed some of the most eminent professional women of the time. This "club for unorthodox women" rebuffed philanthropy and instead served as a forum for women to air their opinions on an endless range of topics. Its biweekly luncheons attracted scores of bohemian women such as Ida Rauh, her sister-in-law Crystal Eastman, Susan Glaspell, Henrietta Rodman, and Mabel Dodge Luhan. Most of the members were trying to sustain their careers while taking pleasure in personal relationships. Perhaps as many as one-quarter of Heterodoxy members were lesbians.

As individuals, the members of Heterodoxy maintained strong political profiles. Rauh, for example, frequently supported trade union campaigns among working women and stood at the forefront of the woman suffrage movement. She also enjoyed the comradeship of her husband, Max Eastman, who shared dedication to Socialism and much of her political work. Eastman stood on the front lines of the birth control agitation and also headed the Men's League for Woman Suffrage. Heterodoxy members like Rauh all had strong opinions on politics, including socialism, anarchism, syndicalism, and progressivism, as well as the Republican and Democratic parties. But what set them apart from their contemporaries was a determination to give their personal lives a political dimension.

The members of Heterodoxy were among the first women to use the term **"feminism,"** which appeared in the United States around 1910 as a French import. "We have grown accustomed . . . to something or other known as the Woman Movement.

Heterodoxy A club of "unorthodox women" formed by Marie Jenny Howe in 1912 that included the cream of New York's literary, artistic, and political activists.

"feminism" A term introduced into the United States around 1910 to augment the demands for voting rights and economic equality with a psychological dimension akin to "self-realization."

That has an old sound," one journalist noted. "Therefore, no need to cry it down. But Feminism!" Was it possible that the century-long campaign for women's emancipation could take on an astonishingly new dimension? The answer was a resounding YES!

Despite the enthusiasm for the new term, a precise definition eluded most enthusiasts. They understood that "feminism" was not the same as the demand for the ballot, equal wages, or access to higher education and the professions. The founder of Heterodoxy, Marie Jenny Howe, insisted that feminism of course included all these endeavors. In 1913, Crystal Eastman and Henrietta Rodman sponsored the Feminist Alliance precisely to demand "the removal of all social, political, economic, and other discrimination which are based upon sex." But in addition to these familiar aspirations, Howe pointed out, feminism stood for the "social revaluation of outgrown customs." Howe offered a simple definition of feminism as an "appropriate word to register . . . woman's effort toward development," which included foremost a "changed psychology, the creation of a new consciousness in women."

Feminists continued to work for women's advancement, and they played an especially vital role in the birth control movement. They tended, however, to emphasize the highly personal and individualistic goal of self-realization. Much like Kate Chopin's protagonist in *The Awakening*, Edna Pontellier, they focused not so much on gains in the public sphere as achieving satisfaction in the interstices of private life, that is, in their relationships. Intimacy and sexual freedom therefore ranked very high on their agenda. For feminists, the personal was, indeed, political.

Art and Politics

Many feminists found that the questions they foremost sought to answer were best posed through the medium of art. Kate Chopin was merely one of dozens of women who turned to writing to explore the social and psychological realities of women's lives. Ellen Glasgow, Willa Cather, and Mary Austin all created complex fictional protagonists who challenged the orthodoxy of the day. Edith Wharton's *The House of Mirth* (1905) detailed the outworn marriage customs of New York's high society and the emotional damage they inflicted on women. Her ravishing yet financially needy protagonist, Lily Bart, refused to marry for money but at the same time knew that love alone would not satisfy her craving for luxuries. In 1921, Wharton was awarded a Pulitzer Prize for *The Age of Innocence* (1920), which also explored the themes of love, marriage, and divorce among the upper classes.

The Greenwich Village bohemians excelled in contributing a satiric dimension to the feminist critique of love and marriage. Cornelia Barnes, a cartoonist on the staff of *The Masses*, drew a playful cover for the magazine that featured two modern women in conversation. One is saying: "My Dear, I'll be economically independent if I have to borrow every cent!" Susan Glaspell wrote and produced equally wry plays, several parodying her own circle of friends. She tapped her friends to act in her plays, which she staged in Lower Manhattan or on Cape Cod, where she and her husband helped to sponsor a little theatrical company, the Provincetown Players. Glaspell's female protagonists invariably resembled women in her milieu, all expressing a "diffused longing for an enlarged experience" that usually involved sex.

The dancer Isadora Duncan made waves both in the United States and abroad by attaching her revolutionary politics to freeing the female body from conventional constraints. Developing what would later be called modern dance, Duncan rejected classical ballet for a style of dance based on natural, expressive movements. She also rejected corsets, petticoats, and stockings for a loose-fitting, sheer tunic that emphasized the contours of her body. "Spectators in the front rows gasped when they saw the famous barefoot dancer leaping forward . . . clad only in the lightest, scantiest, and most translucent silk," one reviewer observed. "One glance sufficed to show that beneath this airy raiment . . . nature was unadorned. . . . Anthony Comstock himself would have been surprised."

The poet Gladys Oaks offered perhaps the most succinct summary of feminism and the new morality. She not only affirmed woman's sexuality but celebrated her right to express it in her short poem entitled simply "Climax":

I had thought that I could sleep

After I had kissed his mouth

With its sharply haunting corners

And its red.

But now that he has kissed me

A stir is in my blood,

And I want to be awake

Instead.

Isadora Duncan (1877–1927) sought to emancipate the female body from all artificial constraints and to free dance from its mooring in nineteenth-century ballet. Her choice of costume, usually a tunic secured at the breast and hips, became emblematic of her philosophy of modern dance. "It has never dawned on me to swathe myself in hampering garments or to bind my limbs and drape by throat," she explained, "for am I not striving to fuse soul and body in one unified image of beauty?"

CONCLUSION

By the turn of the century, a new morality had swept much of urban America, pushing aside the remaining vestiges of "female passionlessness" and affirming not only the existence but the merits of the female sexual drive. Working-class women played a large role in this process, providing an inspiration to many other women who were attempting to break away from the middle-class mores of their parents. At the same time, the era ushered in a new "heterosociality," signifying a companionship between men and women that superseded the old ideology of "separate spheres." In sum, the era heralded a great change in the relations between the sexes, one that was bringing men and women closer together in all aspects of life, including sexual companionship.

Yet, these monumental changes, which one historian has grouped together under the heading of the "first sexual revolution," did not come easily or without the introduction of new restrictions on sexual behavior. To the contrary, sexuality became subject to increasing scrutiny, as medical and other experts codified behavior into "normal" and "deviant," as legislators outlawed interracial relationships, and as large sectors of the public attempted to bring men into the fold of the presumably pure. Indeed, what would become known as "sexual modernism" would prove to be a highly contested arena.

WOMEN'S HISTORY	GLOBAL EVENTS
1865	
1869 Dr. George Naphey's *The Physical Life of Woman* published	
1873 Dr. Edward H. Clarke publishes *Sex in Education*	1873 Comstock Act passed by Congress
1875 Page Act prohibits immigration of prostitutes	
1880	
1883 First Florence Crittenton mission opens in New York City	
1885 The WCTU establishes Department of Social Purity	
1886 Age of Consent campaign	
1890	
1892 Jane Club established in Chicago Alice Mitchell tried for murder	1897 Havelock Ellis published *Sexual Inversion*
1896 Alice B. Stockham publishes *Karezza, Ethics of Marriage*	
1899 Kate Chopin's *The Awakening* published	
1900	
	1903 President Theodore Roosevelt speaks on "race suicide"
1905 Edith Wharton's *The House of Mirth* published	1905 Riverview, Chicago amusement park, opens
	1909 Freud lectures at Clark University
1910	
1911 Emma Goldman publishes "The Traffic in Women"	1910 Divorce rate reaches rate of one marriage in six dissolved in any one year Mann Act passed by Congress
1912 White slavery panic peaks Heterodoxy forms	
1914 Margaret Sanger publishes *Woman Rebel*	

| WOMEN'S HISTORY | GLOBAL EVENTS |

1915

1915
William Sanger arrested for distributing
"Family Limitation"

1916
Emma Goldman arrested for lecturing on birth control

1920
Edith Wharton's *The Age of Innocence* published

REVIEW QUESTIONS

1. What was the role of working-class women in advancing heterosocial relationships? What was the importance of leisure time and the spread of amusement parks, dance halls, and movie theaters?

2. With the decline of "female passionlessness," how did middle-class marriage change? What was the impact on same-sex relationships?

3. What were the causes and effects of the panic over white slavery?

4. Was the birth control movement successful in reaching its goals?

5. What did contemporaries mean by "feminism"?

RECOMMENDED READING

Karen Abbott. *Sin in the Second City: Madams, Ministers, Playboys, and the Battle for America's Soul.* New York: Random House, 2007. An engrossing study of the Everleigh Club, the most infamous brothel in Chicago at the turn of the century, managed by two sisters who prospered from the sex trade.

Crista DeLuzio. *Female Adolescence in American Scientific Thought, 1830–1930.* Baltimore: Johns Hopkins University Press, 2007. A groundbreaking study of expert opinion on "femininity" and psychological development. DeLuzio covers the scholarship from several fields of medical and behavior science that defined "normality" in terms of the "adolescent girl."

Elizabeth Francis. *The Secret Treachery of Words: Feminism and Modernism in America.* Minneapolis: University of Minnesota Press, 2002. A brilliant study of a group of Bohemians who combined their quest for women's liberation with an affirmation of revolutionary politics. Francis offers an insightful analysis of Isadora Duncan's ideas about the liberated female body.

Linda Gordon. *Woman's Body, Woman's Right: Birth Control in America.* New York: Grossman/Viking

1976, rev. 1990. A sweeping overview of Margaret Sanger's career within a political context.

Martha Hodes. *White Women, Black Men: Illicit Sex in the Nineteenth-Century South.* New Haven and London: Yale University Press, 1997. Focused on sexual liaisons between white women and black men, Hodes's book traces a history of relative tolerance for such relationships during the slavery era to the extreme taboo and violent enforcement of the postbellum South.

Peggy Pascoe. *Relations of Rescue: The Search for Female Moral Authority in the American West, 1874–1939.* New York: Oxford University Press, 1990. An intercultural study of the home mission movement at the turn of the twentieth century. Pascoe examines the efforts of Prostestant women in the American West to "rescue" Chinese prostitutes, Mormon polygamous wives, unmarried women, and Indian women.

Kathy Peiss. *Cheap Amusements: Working Women and Leisure in Turn-of-the-Century New York.* Philadelphia: Temple University Press, 1986. The classic study of commercial entertainments as a setting for the emergency of heterosocial relationships, pioneered by working-class men and women.

Ruth Rosen. *The Lost Sisterhood: Prostitution in America, 1900–1918*. Baltimore: The Johns Hopkins University Press, 1982. Examines both the campaigns to curtail prostitution and the experiences of the women who practiced it.

Christine Stansell. *American Moderns: Bohemian New York and the Creation of a New Century*. New York: Metropolitan Books, 2000. Stansell paints a detailed portrait of the new lifestyle radicalism that flourished in Greenwich Village during the 1910s. In discussing the interrelation of art and politics, she makes a strong and vivid case for the influence of women.

Emily Toth. *Unveiling Kate Chopin*. Jackson: University Press of Mississippi, 1999. A full biography of Chopin, with special attention to her fiction as well as to her career.

ADDITIONAL BIBLIOGRAPHY

Urban Pleasures, Urban Dangers

Nan Enstad. *Ladies of Labor, Girls of Adventure: Working Women, Popular Culture and Labor Politics at the Turn of the Twentieth Century*. New York: Columbia University Press, 1998.

Randy D. McBee. *Dance Hall Days: Intimacy and Leisure among Working-Class Immigrants in the United States*. New York: New York University Press, 2000.

Joanne J. Meyerowitz. *Women Adrift: Independent Wage Earners in Chicago 1880–1930*. Chicago: University of Chicago Press, 1988.

Lauren Ravinovitz. *For the Love of Pleasure: Women, Movies, and Culture in Turn-of-the-Century Chicago*. New Brunswick: Rutgers University Press, 1998.

Sharon E. Wood. *The Freedom of the Streets: Work, Citizenship, and Sexuality in a Gilded Age City*. Chapel Hill: University of North Carolina Press, 2005.

Changing Relations of Intimacy

George Jr. Chauncey. "From Sexual Inversion to Homosexuality: Medicine and the Changing Conceptualization of Female 'Deviance,'" *Salmagundi*, 58/59Fall/Winter 1983, pp. 114–46.

Carl Degler. "What Ought to Be and What Was: Women's Sexuality in the Nineteenth Century," *American Historical Review*, 79(1974), 1467–1490.

Lisa Duggan. *Sapphic Slashers: Sex, Violence, and American Modernity*. Durham: Duke University Press, 2000.

Trisha Franzen. *Spinsters and Lesbians: Independent Womanhood in the United States*. New York: New York University Press, 1996.

Karen Lystra. *Searching the Heart: Women, Men, and Romantic Love in Nineteenth-Century America*. New York: Oxford University Press, 1989.

Elaine Tyler May. *Great Expectations: Marriage and Divorce in Post-Victorian America*. Chicago: University of Chicago Press, 1980.

James R. McGovern. "The American Woman's Pre-World War I Freedom in Manners and Morals," *Journal of American History*, 55 September 1968, 315–33.

Curbing Social Evils

Nicola Beisel. *Imperiled Innocents: Anthony Comstock and Family Reproduction in Victorian America*. Princeton: Princeton University Press, 1997.

Mark Thomas Connelly. *The Response to Prostitution in the Progressive Era*. Chapel Hill: University of North Carolina Press, 1980.

Frederick K. Grittner. *White Slavery: Myth, Ideology, and American Law*. New York & London: Garland Publishing, Inc., 1990.

Barbara Meil Hobson. *Uneasy Virtue: The Politics of Prostitution and the American Reform Tradition*. New York: Basic Books, 1987.

Martha Hodes ed. *Sex, Love, Race: Crossing Boundaries in North American History*. New York: New York University Press, 1999.

Margaret D. Jacobs. "The Eastmans and the Luhans: Interracial Marriage between White Women and Native American Men, 1875–1935," *Frontiers*, 23: 2002, 29–54.

Rachel F. Moran. *Interracial Intimacy: The Regulation of Race & Romance*. Chicago: University of Chicago Press, 2003.

Alison M. Parker. *Purifying America: Women, Cultural Reform, and Pro-Censorship Activism, 1873–1933*. Urbana: University of Illinois Press, 1997.

David J. Pivar. *Purity Crusade: Sexual Morality and Social Control, 1868–1900*. Westport: Greenwood, 1973.

Peggy Pascoe. "Race, Gender, and Intercultural Relations: The Case of Interracial Marriage," *Frontiers*, 12 1991: 5–18.

David J. Pivar. *Purity Crusade: Sexual Morality and Social Control, 1868–1900*. Westport: Greenwood, 1975.

Leigh Ann Wheeler. *Against Obscenity: Reform and the Politics of Womanhood in America, 1873–1935*. Baltimore: The Johns Hopkins University Press, 2004.

Women's Bodies and Reproduction

Janet Farrell Brodie. *Contraception and Abortion in Nineteenth-Century America*. Ithaca: Cornell University Press, 1994.

Susan Cayleff. *Wash and Be Healed: The Water-Cure Movement and Women's Health*. (Temple University Press, 1987), 7–25.

Ellen Carol DuBois and Linda Gordon. "Seeking Ecstasy on the Battlefield: Danger and Pleasure in Nineteenth-Century Feminist Thought," *Feminist Studies*, 9 (Spring 1983), 7–25.

David M. Kennedy. *Birth Control in America: The Career of Margaret Sanger*. New Haven: Yale University Press, 1970.

Rachel P. Maines. *The Technology of Orgasm: "Hysteria," the Vibrator, and Women's Sexual Satisfaction*. Baltimore: Johns Hopkins University Press, 1999.

James Mohr. *Abortion in America: The Origins and Evolution of National Policy, 1800–1900*. New York: Oxford University Press, 1978.

James W. Reed. *From Private Vice to Public Virtue: The Birth Control Movement and American Society since 1830*. New York: Basic Books, 1978, 1984.

Carroll Smith-Rosenberg. *Disorderly Conduct: Visions of Gender in Victorian America*. New York: Oxford University Press, 1985.

Andrea Tone. *Devices and Desires: A History of Contraceptives in America*. New York: Hill and Wang, 2001.

Martha H. Verbrugge. *Able-Bodied Womanhood: Personal Health and Social Change in Nineteenth-Century Boston*. New York: Oxford University Press, 1988.

Sue Zschoche. "Dr. Clarke Revisited: Science, True Womanhood, and Female Collegiate Education," *History of Education Quarterly*, 29 Winter 1989, 545–569.

Rebels in Bohemia

Martin Blatt. *Free Love and Anarchism*. Urbana: University of Illinois, 1989.

Adele Heller and Lois Palken Rudnick, eds. *1915, The Cultural Moment: The New Politics, the New Woman, the New Psychology, the New Art and the New Theatre in America*. New Brunswick: Rutgers University Press, 1991.

Judith Schwarz. *Radical Feminists of Heterodoxy: Greenwich Village 1912–1940*. Lebanon: New Victoria Publishers, 1982.

Hal D. Sears. *The Sex Radicals: Free Love in High Victorian America*. Lawrence: Regents Press of Kansas, 1977.

June Sochen. *The New Woman: Feminism in Greenwich Village, 1910–1920*. New York: Quadrangle Books, 1972.

Ellen Kay Trimberger. "Feminism, Men, and Modern Love: Greenwich Village, 1900–1925," in Ann Snitow, et. al., eds., *Powers of Desire: The Politics of Sexuality*. New York: Monthly Review Press, 1983.

Biographies and Memoirs

Margaret Anderson. *My Thirty Years' War: An Autobiography*. New York: Covici, Friede, 1930.

Linda Ben-Zvi. *Susan Glaspell: Her Life and Times*. New York: Oxford University Press, 2005.

Neith Boyce and Carol DeBoer-Langworthy, ed. *The Modern World of Neith Boyce: Autobiography and Diaries*. Albuquerque: University of New Mexico Press, 2003.

Isadora Duncan. *My Life*. New York: Norton, 1927.

Emma Goldman. *Living My Life*. 2 vols. New York: Dover Publications, Inc., 1931.

Mabel Dodge Luhan and Lois Palken Rudnick, ed. *Intimate Memories: The Autobiography of Mabel Dodge Luhan*. Albuquerque: University of New Mexico Press, 1999.

Margaret Sanger. *An Autobiography*. New York: W. W. Norton, 1971(1938).

Ellen Kay Trimberger. *Intimate Warriors: Portraits of a Modern Marriage, 1899–1944*. New York: The Feminist Press, 1991.

Alex Wexler. *Emma Goldman: An Intimate Life*. New York: Pantheon Books, 1984.

Eileen Whitfield. *Pickford: The Woman Who Made Hollywood*. Toronto: Macfarlane Walter & Ross, and University of Kentucky, 1997.

THE PROGRESSIVE ERA, 1890–1920

"MUNICIPAL HOUSEKEEPING"
Jane Addams and Hull-House
The Settlement Movement: A Community of Women
"A Power for Good": Neighborhood Activism

THE ERA OF WOMEN'S STRIKES
Women's Trade Union League
Uprising in the Garment Industry
"Bread and Roses": The Lawrence Textile Strike, 1912
Protective Labor Legislation

"MOTHER-WORK"
Juvenile Courts
Mothers' Pensions
The Children's Bureau

WORLD WAR I
Wartime Employment
The Women's Peace Movement
In National Defense
Keeping Men Fit to Fight

VOTES FOR WOMEN
Out of the Doldrums
Southern Strategy
Winning Campaign
Nineteenth Amendment, 1920

HOW DID women transform their domestic concerns into public issues?

WHAT ROLE did cross-class alliances play during the Progressive Era?

WHAT IMPACT did "maternalism" have on progressive reform?

WHAT CHANGES did World War I bring to American women?

HOW DID women finally win the right to vote?

Several days before Christmas 1896 one of my Irish playmates suggested that I go with her to a Christmas party at Hull-House. I told her that I never went to Christmas parties.

"Why not?" she asked.

"I do not go anywhere on Christmas Day," I said.

"But this party will not be on Christmas Day. It will be on the Sunday before Christmas Day," she said.

I repeated that I could not go and she persisted in wanting to know why. Before I could think, I blurted out the words: "I might get killed."

"At the Emancipated Women's Club," Puck, February 26, 1896.

"Get killed!" She stared at me. "I go to Hull-House Christmas parties every year, and no one was ever killed."

I then asked her if there would be any Jewish children at the party. She assured me that there had been Jewish children at the parties every year and that no one was ever hurt.

The thought began to percolate through my head that things might be different in America. . . .

My friend and I arrived at Hull-House and went to the coffee shop where the party was being held. There were many children and their parents seated when we arrived. . . .

People called to each other across the room. Then I noticed that I could not understand what they were saying. It dawned on me that the people in this room had come from other countries. Yet there was no tension. Everybody seemed to be having a good time. There were children and parents at this party from Russia, Poland, Italy, Germany, Ireland, England, and many other lands, but no one seemed to care where they had come from, or what religion they professed, or what clothes they wore, or what they thought. . . .

Then Jane Addams came into the room! It was the first time that I looked into those kind, understanding eyes. There was a gleam of welcome in them that made me feel I was wanted. She told us that she was glad we had come. Her voice was warm and I knew she meant what she said. . . .

We were all poor. Some of us were underfed. Some of us had holes in our clothes. But we were not afraid of each other. What greater service can a human being give to her country than to banish fear from the heart of a child? Jane Addams did that for me at that party.

Source: Hilda Satt Polacheck, I Came a Stranger: The Story of a Hull-House Girl, edited by Dena J. Polacheck Epstein (Urbana: University of Illinois Press, 1989), 51–52.

ilda Satt Polacheck emigrated from Poland in 1892 when she was ten years old and settled with her family in Chicago just four doors down from Hull-House. By the time she met Jane Addams, the founder of the most famous social settlement in the nation, she had already taken a job, along with her sister, in a nearby knitting factory, where she put up with what she described as the "monotony of work" for far too many years. Unlike those immigrants who mistrusted reformers, Polacheck revered Addams, not as a "lady bountiful," as she was sometimes called, but as a friend and mentor.

At Hull-House, Polacheck enjoyed a host of leisure activities and soon found herself an active member of the settlement community, starting out as a receptionist and guide and advancing to a teacher of English. Hull-House became for her, as its charter mandated, a center for "higher civic and social life." Like Addams, she attended rallies for woman suffrage and passed out leaflets. Although her involvement with Hull-House ended in 1912 when she married and moved to Milwaukee, its imprint lasted. During World War I, Polacheck joined the peace movement and, like Addams, made it a lifelong commitment.

The Progressive Era represented a great age for women as political actors. They joined other like-minded Americans in seeking solutions to the many problems caused by unbridled social and economic changes, particularly the excesses associated with the second industrial revolution and the tremendous growth in urban—mainly immigrant—populations. Child labor, poor working conditions, impure food and water, overcrowded and dirty neighborhoods, and inefficiency and corruption in government were just a few of the issues that propelled them toward activism. At the national level, progressive reformers, as they were called, demonstrated their strength in the 1912 presidential election, when four candidates ran on similarly reformist platforms. But lacking the right to vote and to hold public office in most states, women reached out first to their own networks.

Although women reformers relied on many of the organizations and institutions that dated to the late nineteenth century, they embraced a new strategy. They realized that the solutions to the poverty and injustices overflowing in urban America demanded more resources than women could provide in their separate voluntary associations. Following in the footsteps of Florence Kelley, who had fought for legislation in the 1890s that made the Illinois state government accountable for the working conditions in factories, women reformers now joined forces to demand that the state—that is, government at all levels—take on broad responsibility for the welfare of its citizens, especially its women and children.

During the Progressive Era, the collective influence of women was greater than at any previous time in American history and not equaled again until the resurgence of the women's movement in the mid-1960s. Ultimately, it was the claim to power that brought the majority of women into the suffrage camp. If women were to be the vanguard in transforming the state in the service of social justice, they needed to participate fully in the political process. In short, women needed the ballot foremost as an instrument of reform.

"MUNICIPAL HOUSEKEEPING"

"Women's place is Home," Rheta Childe Dorr explained, "but Home is not contained within the four walls of an individual home. Home is the community." Reformers like Dorr took it upon themselves to make the nation's urban neighborhoods the center of the **Progressive movement**. Theirs was a loose coalition of activists who sustained a long tradition of involvement in civic betterment and, at the same time, pressured the government to take responsibility for matters that had been primarily the province of the family, the church, or voluntary associations. During the Progressive Era, they succeeded in transforming many domestic or private concerns into public issues while insisting on women's right to play a major advocacy role.

Progressive movement A broad coalition of reformers who advocated efficiency in government and various legislative measures to alleviate the social injustices that accompanied the second industrial revolution.

Jane Addams and Hull-House

Jane Addams (1860–1935), the founder of Hull-House, succeeded Frances Willard as the most celebrated woman of her era. Born to the most prosperous family in Cedarville, Illinois, she graduated from the Rockford Female Seminary in 1881 feeling fully prepared for an activist life. She had hoped to attend Smith College for a year and then medical school, but in both cases illness intervened. Addams found herself at home, experiencing what she later described as "the nadir of my nervous depression and a sense of maladjustment." Finally, in 1887, a trip to Europe lifted her spirits and provided the inspiration she needed to escape "the family claim."

While touring Europe with her former classmate, Ellen Gates Starr, Addams found herself, she later recalled, "irresistibly drawn to the poor quarters of each city."

In England, she visited Toynbee Hall, the first settlement house in the slums of London's East End. An instant convert to this new "religion of humanity," Addams returned to the United States determined to create a settlement that, like Toynbee Hall, would recruit university students and college graduates to improve the lives of the poor. With this idea in mind, Addams convinced Starr to join her in Chicago. "Let's love each other through thick and thin," she wrote to her close friend, "and work out a salvation."

Using her substantial inheritance and donations from wealthy Chicagoans, Addams purchased an old, dilapidated mansion in the city's Near West Side, a bustling working-class community of immigrants, and named it **Hull-House**. After a round of renovations, in September 1889, the two young women opened their doors and invited their neighbors to spend their evenings with them. Soon, they attracted other college-educated women who joined them in this novel endeavor and who also took up residence in Hull-House. They began to organize several series of programs, including vocational classes, social services, and cultural events; and, within a few years, more than one thousand people were regularly signing up. By 1907, Hull-House had grown into a thirteen-building complex covering an entire city block. It served as a major center of progressive reform, combining philanthropy, political action, and social science research.

A large component of Hull-House programs catered to children and their mothers. The complex included a day nursery, kindergarten, playground, gymnasium, and medical dispensary. An extensive array of programs served the adult immigrant population. Respectful of the unique cultural practices of the various ethnic groups yet convinced of the benefits of assimilation, Hull-House offered English-language classes; employment referral services; a boardinghouse, library, and art studio; instruction in cooking and housekeeping; and even a post office.

Addams never envisioned Hull-House as merely a social and educational center. She understood that the solutions to the most pressing problems such as chronic poverty and inadequate housing could not be solved within the neighborhood alone. She therefore promoted the settlement as a base for political action.

In the name of social justice, Addams and her coworkers tackled problems large and small, from garbage collection in the neighborhood to corruption in city politics. Hull-House reformers like Florence Kelley bravely took on the local political machines and rallied the community to demand legislation abolishing child labor and making school attendance compulsory. In recognition of Hull-House's many accomplishments, Addams was chosen to second the nomination of Theodore Roosevelt for president on the 1912 ticket of the Progressive Party, which incorporated many of Hull-House's reform measures into its national platform. By 1920, Hull-House reigned as the most famous of nearly five hundred other social settlements.

Hull-House One of the first settlement houses in the United States, founded in Chicago in 1889 by Jane Addams and Ellen Gates Starr.

The Settlement Movement: A Community of Women

For a sizable number of college-educated women like Addams and Kelley, the settlement house provided a meaningful alternative to marriage, teaching, or missionary work. As early as 1890, when settlements had been formed in Boston and New York, as well as Chicago, the overwhelming majority of residents were women, and almost all had attended college.

The women's colleges sent a disproportionate number to the settlements. The founders and administrators aimed to graduate women who would contribute to the public good. The motto of Smith College expressed this imperative: "Add to your virtue, knowledge." In addition to instilling in their students a sense of mission, Smith, Wellesley, Vassar, and Bryn Mawr established innovative curriculums highlighting the new social sciences. Their students studied political economy and systems of government and grappled, often at close range, with the problems of poverty and labor unrest. Undergraduate students also formed small but tight-knit communities that respected in equal measure intellectual achievement and social service. Upon graduation, these young women refused to be, in Jane Addams's words, "smothered and sickened with advantages" typical of their middle-class upbringing and took their mission to the nation's cities.

Unlike other forms of benevolence, settlements functioned as homes for activists. While the few male settlement workers at Hull-House rented rooms in nearby houses, the longest-term workers were the women residents who, according to Addams, were held together by the "companionship of mutual interests." Florence Kelley, for example, in waging the campaign for the Illinois Factory Inspection Act, found not only political allies but intimate friends among her coresidents at Hull-House. Addams herself lived at Hull House until her death in 1935. At the **Henry Street Settlement** on the Lower East Side of New York City, a

Nurse takes a short cut across tenement roofs to visit a patient, circa 1908. In 1893, Lillian Wald and Mary Brewster founded the Henry Street Visiting Nurse Service to provide health care to the poverty-stricken immigrants who populated Manhattan's Lower East Side. By 1917, when their staff of nurses made more than 266,000 home visits in New York City alone, the program had spread to cities nation-wide.

In 1895, Lillian Wald opened the Henry Street Settlement, which served as headquarters for her visiting nurses and organized many programs for neighborhood children. The settlement opened one of the city's earlies playgrounds, sponsored summer camps and offered a wide range of educational activities. This photograph, taken by Lewis Hine in 1910, shows girls in a knitting class at the settlement.

group of women, under the leadership of Lillian Wald, lived and worked together for more than a half century. Some of the friendships developed into "crushes" or long-lasting romantic attachments, such as Addams's relationship first with Starr and later with Mary Rozet Smith. In most cases, such companionship provided the emotional nourishment that allowed these women to dedicate their lives to political activism.

By living in the heart of the city's working-class and mainly immigrant neighborhoods, settlement residents gained an intimate knowledge of the problems of the poor that most other reformers lacked. "I can see why life in a settlement house seemed so great an adventure," recalled Alice Hamilton, who had moved to Hull-House in 1897. "It was all so new, this exploring of a poor quarter of a big city. The thirst to know how the other half lived had just begun to send people pioneering in the unknown part of American life." From this vantage point, settlement workers gained the knowledge, skills, and constituencies they needed to effect change and, in several cases, to rise to positions of national leadership.

"A Power for Good": Neighborhood Activism

Not all women who targeted the community as the locus of their reform activism lived in settlements. To the contrary, married women who lived with their families in their own homes served, through various women's organizations, as the rank-and-file of the progressive movement. Settlement workers were careful to nurture their relationships with these dedicated activists. Hull-House, for example, worked closely with the dynamic Chicago Woman's Club and additionally depended on other local women's organizations such as the WCTU and the YWCA.

Club women were the principal sponsors of settlements among African Americans, who in most locations were excluded from the racially segregated mainstream settlement houses. Lugenia Burns, an activist in the Southeastern Federation of Colored Women's Clubs, founded the **Neighborhood Union**, a settlement directed and financed by African Americans. Born in St. Louis, Hope had lived and worked for awhile at Hull-House before she married and then moved to Atlanta with her husband, who became the president of Morehouse College. "People living in slums do not have to die in slums," she concluded, "nor do slums have to continue to be slums." In 1908, Burns began to recruit activists from the local black women's clubs and other voluntary organizations, divided the city into districts, and established a network of community-based programs all affiliated with the Neighborhood Union. Like Hull-House, the Neighborhood Union served as a center for cultural events, educational programs, and political action. The injustices caused by segregation guided most campaigns, with the public school system of Atlanta, sanitary and health facilities, and employment and transportation at the top of their agenda.

To carry out their campaigns of **"municipal housekeeping,"** African American club women depended on larger networks of black reformers. In Chicago, as in many other northern cities, they allied themselves with the men who ran the local branches of the Urban League and the National Association of Colored People (NAACP). In southern cities, however, Jim Crow had effectively pushed black men to the sidelines of politics, and clubwomen found their most seasoned allies among churchwomen.

The **Women's Convention of the Black Baptist Church**, numerically the most significant Protestant sect among African Americans, responded to the spread of Jim Crow in a variety of ways, not least by building institutions as alternatives to the pub-

Henry Street Settlement Founded in New York City in 1893 by Lillian Wald to provide social and health services to mainly immigrant families.

Neighborhood Union A social settlement founded in Atlanta in 1908 by Lugenia Burns Hope in response to the impoverished conditions of African Americans.

"municipal housekeeping" A phrase popular during the Progressive Era to connote the extension of women's domestic skills to urban affairs.

Women's Convention of the Black Baptist Church The locus of the women's movement within the Black Baptist Church.

Nannie Burroughs, photographed here with other women of the Woman's Convention, auxiliary to the National Baptist Convention, opened the Training School for Women and Girls in Washington, D.C., 1909. Like other settlement houses, the Training School offered a range of educational courses, including vocational training in several trades and instruction in the humanities. Students were also required to study black history and the Bible.

lic spaces reserved for whites only. Clubwomen and churchwomen played the leading roles in opening schools, establishing libraries, sponsoring cultural events such as concerts, providing recreational facilities such as playgrounds, and organizing vocational training programs in their communities. In 1913, the Women's Convention opened a settlement house in Washington, D.C., which sponsored a variety of programs including a soup kitchen and medical clinic.

Southern white women also took up the gauntlet to improve their own communities, although more slowly than their northern counterparts. For example, in Memphis, the Nineteenth Century Club had organized only in 1890 and then as a literary and cultural endeavor. By the turn of the century, Memphis clubwomen responded to the reform fervor sweeping the nation and inaugurated projects more political and public in nature. For example, the club formed a special committee to secure police matrons who would protect women prisoners from sexual abuse in the city's jails. Similarly, in El Paso, Texas, women organized to study literature before broadening their horizons to spearhead the formation of a Civic Improvement League, which took on the huge task of cleaning up the frontier community. By 1914, the local newspaper commended the El Paso Woman's Club for outstripping all other local organizations working for "civic improvement."

Clubwomen, white and black, North and South, rallied to improve public health and sanitation, and in at least forty cities local activists formed **women's health protective associations** (WHPAs). The WHPA of Galveston, Texas, for example, did heroic work in the aftermath of the hurricane of 1900, which nearly demolished the city. They continued their work throughout the Progressive Era, securing trash cans in public places, urging residents to burn their garbage, demanding cleaner streets and alleys, and sponsoring a "Swat the Fly" effort to curb the spread of contagious diseases like typhoid. The Philadelphia association campaigned for the construction of functional

women's health protective associations
Local groups that sponsored public health initiatives and raised money for building and maintaining hospitals.

filtration systems for the local water supply and, in league with the County Medical Society, inaugurated a program of medical inspection in the schools. The WHPAs raised money for building and maintaining hospitals, predominantly for the treatment of tuberculosis, a leading cause of illness and death that was especially rampant in urban slums. Determined "municipal housekeepers," clubwomen conducted the major campaigns to secure the passage and enforcement of pure food and milk acts.

THE ERA OF WOMEN'S STRIKES

"[W]e have now a trade-union truism, that 'women make the best strikers.'" So proclaimed Helen Marot of the New York Women's Trade Union League. Marot wrote in the aftermath of the largest strike of women in American labor history, the "uprising" of the city's shirtwaist makers that capped nearly a decade of slow but steady mobilization spearheaded by women trade unionists and their middle- and upper-class allies. Not just in New York but in other centers of manufacturing, cross-class alliances of women formed to investigate the shops and to report on the conditions they found there. They made the public keenly aware of the injustices associated with the factory system, such as low wages and long hours, unsanitary working conditions, and the problems caused by unsafe buildings. Equally important, they worked together to transform the image of the "working girl." No longer simply the victim of the excesses of industrial capitalism but a hero in her own right, from "the outcast of today," as one writer put it, to "the pioneer of tomorrow."

Women's Trade Union League

Following the decline of the Knights of Labor in the 1890s, wage-earning women found few opportunities to organize. The leaders of the American Federation of Labor (AFL), which was founded in 1885 and succeeded the Knights as the premier labor organization, chose to focus on highly skilled white men and did little to welcome women to their ranks. In northern cities, groups of seasoned women reformers tried to fill the void. Settlement workers, for example, invited wage-earning women to use their facilities as a meeting place to organize trade unions. When striking garment workers in Boston needed help in forming a union, the leaders turned not to the AFL but to Denison House, a settlement in the city's South End.

Meanwhile, various women's organizations supplied the personnel and resources to form consumers' leagues. For example, the Women's Educational and Industrial Union and the New England Women's Club issued the invitation for the founding meeting of the Boston consumers' league, while the Working Women's Society played a similar role in New York. Consumers' leagues campaigned against sweatshops and sponsored investigations of labor conditions in factories employing women and children. They also created a "White List" of stores and factories that maintained fair standards in wages and hours and a sanitary environment and advised shoppers to patronize only these establishments. In 1899, several local leagues affiliated as the **National Consumer's League** (NCL); one year later, Florence Kelley left Hull-House for New York to head the NCL, a position she held until her death in 1922.

In 1903, wage-earning and middle-class women allied to form one of the most successful cross-class alliances in American history, the **National Women's Trade Union League** (NWTUL) in 1903. The constitution of the new venture specified that mem-

National Consumer's League Founded in 1899 by a group of women affiliated with Hull-House to lobby for improved conditions in the manufacture of consumer goods.

National Women's Trade Union League Founded in Boston in 1903 to "assist in the organization of women wage workers into trade unions."

bership include both workers and their "allies," that is, middle- and upper-class women who were committed to trade unionism, and additionally specified that wage-earning women hold the majority on the executive board. Within a decade, the alliance proved successful, and the NWTUL stood at the forefront of a campaign to organize unions in trades where women predominated. The most active branches were located in New York, Chicago, and Boston, while at least a dozen other cities claimed small organizations.

Leonora O'Reilly stepped forward to become one of the most influential working-class members. Head resident at a Brooklyn settlement house when she joined, she also held impeccable labor credentials. She had begun working in a garment factory at age eleven and, along with her mother, had been active in the Knights of Labor in the late 1880s. After the demise of the Knights, she tried to work with several other unions and helped to form the Working Women's Society. Having benefited greatly from the assistance of settlement-house workers, she was now eager to cast her lot with the new cross-class alliance of women.

Rose Schneiderman, a twenty-three-year-old cap maker, soon joined O'Reilly and became the New York branch's first full-time organizer. Schneiderman had emigrated from Poland with her Orthodox Jewish parents and had lived in New York City since she was eight, except for a couple years in Montreal where she learned about trade unionism. When she joined the WTUL in 1905, the women's local of the United Cloth Hat and Cap Makers' Union, which she had helped to organize, boasted several hundred members, and Schneiderman was known as a skilled organizer.

Meanwhile, O'Reilly recruited Margaret Dreier, the eldest daughter of a wealthy German-American family and an activist in Progressive Era reforms. Dreier served as the president of the New York WTUL until 1905, when she married a fellow reformer, Raymond Robins, and moved with him to Chicago where she took over as president of both the Chicago branch and the National WTUL. In New York, she was succeeded by her sister, Mary Dreier. The Dreier sisters successfully recruited scores of activists from women's organizations and the settlements, including many college-educated women and some very wealthy society women.

Born in Poland, Rose Schneiderman (1882–1972) immigrated to the United States with her family in 1890. By 1895, following her father's death, she was working to help support her mother and brothers. Living and working in Manhattan's Lower East Side, she met radicals and trade unionists who supported her efforts to organize women into a capmakers' union. Schneiderman joined the New York branch of the Women's Trade Union soon after its founding and quickly became one of its star organizers. She stayed with the WTUL until 1950, when the organization disbanded.

League tactics reflected the complexity of its membership. The WTUL sponsored "sociables" for working women with the intention of combining the discussion of unionism with the drinking of tea. More successful in attracting new members, however, were daily street meetings. During the lunch break, WTUL speakers would set up a platform, fly their banner, and, according to O'Reilly, preach "the gospel of trade unionism at and near the factory door." In this fashion, the WTUL managed to increase the number of wage earners in its ranks, recruiting successfully among the young Jewish and Italian immigrants who predominated in the garment trade as well as among retail clerks, textile operatives, and even laundresses and waitresses.

League members often referred to themselves as a "sisterhood," insisting that what they shared as women could override the differences of class. "Are we not all sisters of one another," Leonora O'Reilly asked, "and should not a woman's heart thrill at being called upon for help?" Like their settlement peers, WTUL activists formed strong networks based in friendship and mutual dedication to reform. Mary Dreier wrote to O'Reilly: "A strange and beautiful mixture of personal and impersonal is my relationship to you and I love you." Mary Dreier also found her life's companion, reformer Frances Kellor, among league members. Still, such relationships, especially those that bridged large differences of wealth and education, were far from easy, and members could never agree if the WTUL was foremost an arm of the labor movement or a branch of the women's movement.

Uprising in the Garment Industry

In 1907, Leonora O'Reilly wrote to "ally" Helen Marot: "We are looking forward to a revolution in New York among working women." Just two years later, her prediction came true, and the New York WTUL experienced its greatest moment amid the shirtwaist makers' strike, the so-called **"Uprising of 30,000."**

"Uprising of 30,000" Popular name for the strike of the shirtwaist makers who shut down the New York garment industry for several months beginning in November 1909.

The 1909 strike had been preceded by a series of sporadic strikes, almost all short and unsuccessful, and by fitful attempts to establish a viable union in the garment trade. Workers had repeatedly protested unsanitary shop conditions; unlimited hours of overtime in the busy season and no work—and no pay—during the summer months; extreme variations in wages from one shop to another; and a wage system that included charges for electricity, needles, and thread. But at the heart of their grievances was the expanding system of subcontracting.

The subcontracting system, which depended on large firms putting out work to smaller firms, had caused a nearly intolerable "speedup" in piecework throughout the industry. In response, the shirtwaist strikers demanded a standardized wage system and a fifty-two-hour workweek. To enforce these policies, they insisted on the right to establish a union industrywide and named their bargaining agent as Local 25 of the **International Ladies' Garment Workers' Union** (ILGWU).

International Ladies' Garment Workers' Union Founded in Chicago in 1905, the "Wobblies" represented the radical wing of the labor movement and organized workers into "one big union" without regard to skill.

The strike, which began on November 23, 1909, made heroes of the thousands of teenage Jewish women who predominated in the garment trades. They had gathered the night before in Cooper Union in the Lower East Side and listened while a series of speakers addressed the crowd in English and Yiddish. Mary Dreier represented the WTUL, and even Samuel Gompers, president of the AFL, put in an appearance. Finally, Clara Lemlich from Leiserson's shop, which had already been on strike for eleven weeks, stood up. "I have listened to all the speakers," she cried in Yiddish, "and I have no further patience for talk. I am one who feels and suffers for the things pictured. I move we go on a general strike!" The crowd jumped to its feet, stomping and cheering. The next morning, the New York newspapers reported this event as the "Revolt of the Girls" and designated Lemlich its Joan of Arc.

Close to thirty thousand shirtwaist makers, three-quarters of them Jewish, walked out of nearly five hundred shops. Although a number of employers settled within a few days, the large manufacturers held out, pushing the strike into the bitter cold of December. The WTUL helped the strikers maintain their picket lines against frequent assaults and arrests. They also organized marches and planned rallies and recruited volunteers from the settlements, the NCL, various women's organizations, and northeastern women's colleges to join the picket lines and to staff the twenty halls that served as organizational headquarters. "Friends, let us stop talking about sis-

In the winter of 1909–1910, mostly young immigrant women—90 percent Jews and Italians—strikers in New York's shirtwaist industry stunned both male trade unionists and the general public with their militancy and determination. Members of the WTUL helped to provide support services and fostered sympathy among other women's organizations. The strikers proved that unskilled women workers considered "unorganizable" by the established craft unions could wage a general strike and spearhead a drive to create lasting organizations in their trade.

terhood," one appeal read, "and MAKE SISTERHOOD A FACT!" News of the strike dominated the front pages of the city's newspapers and spilled over to the society pages.

The strikers eventually won many of their demands, but they deadlocked with the largest manufacturers on the issue of union recognition. In mid-February, the ILGWU called an end to the strike.

Despite this disappointing outcome, the shirtwaist strikers had scored major victories. Local 25 signed up nearly twenty thousand new members to become the largest local in the ILGWU. The strikers thus proved that women could not only strike courageously but organize themselves into a union and achieve positions of leadership. Moreover, their actions inspired hundreds of thousands of women workers in cities across the nation.

The shirtwaist strike immediately spread to Philadelphia following an attempt by New York manufacturers to shift production there. By 1910, workers in the menswear industry in Chicago, representing a variety of Eastern European immigrants, joined the protest against the subcontracting system. Led by young Hannah Shapiro, forty thousand men and women walked off their jobs, closing down the city's garment industry. Garment strikes spread to Cleveland, Milwaukee, Kalamazoo, and St. Louis and on to

San Francisco. In ladies' apparel, the strikes continued intermittently until 1916, when the famous Protocol of Peace established for the first time the principle of collective bargaining in the industry.

"Bread and Roses": The Lawrence Textile Strike, 1912

On January 11, 1912, a bitterly cold, snowy day in Lawrence, a group of Polish women weavers at the Everett Cotton Mill opened their pay envelopes to find that their wages had been cut as a result of new legislation in Massachusetts that reduced the weekly maximum hours of work for women and children from fifty-five to fifty-four hours. The cut amounted to only thirty cents, but even this small sum was more than their already tight family budgets could bear. "Better to starve fighting than to starve working," they concluded. The workers promptly fled the factory, calling others to join them. They linked arms with fellow Italian and Lithuanian workers and carried their appeal to mills throughout the city. Two days later, nearly thirty thousand workers—men, women, and children representing forty nationalities—shut down Lawrence's great textile industry.

The wives of millworkers joined the outpouring. Women who worked mainly at home—some pregnant, others with babies in arms—carried signs reading "We Want Bread and Roses, Too," joined the picket lines and soon turned the strike into a community struggle. Because three-quarters of the city's eighty-five thousand people depended on the textile industry for their livelihood, the impact of the strike spread across the multiethnic working-class neighborhoods. The corner grocery store, the tenement stoop, and the streets became meeting points where news from the mills blended into discussions of family welfare. Housewives ran soup kitchens for the strikers from their homes and cared for children while their parents marched on the picket line. They also took to the streets, linked arms to form an "endless chain," and paraded through the neighborhoods to jeer at scabs, police, and city officials. The more aggressive of their number carried scissors to cut the uniforms of the "gray wolves," that is, the National Guard troops stationed to protect the property of the mill owners. Testifying in court, the district attorney estimated that "one policeman can handle ten men, while it takes ten policemen to handle one woman."

The size of the strike and the militancy of the strikers and their community allies attracted attention throughout the country. The radical **Industrial Workers of the World** (IWW), rival to the AFL, sent organizers to Lawrence. The IWW, which had formed just a few years earlier, in 1905, aimed to organize all workers, regardless of craft or trade, race, ethnicity, or gender, into one big union and ultimately to overthrow the employing class. One of the IWW's most charismatic speakers, the youthful "Rebel Girl," Elizabeth Gurley Flynn, enthralled crowds with appeals for solidarity. Understanding just how important women were to the strike, she also paid particular attention to housewives and addressed their needs, for example, by helping them get credit from local shopkeepers.

Flynn also headed the famous **"children's crusade."** In talking to some of the strikers, she had learned that it was common in France and Italy to send the children of strikers to sympathizers in other villages in

Industrial Workers of the World Founded in Chicago in 1905, represented the radical wing of the labor movement and orga-nized workers into "one big union" without regard to skill.

"children's crusade" Plan to send the children of the textile strikers to temporary homes outside Lawrence.

Known as "The Rebel Girl," Elizabeth Gurley Flynn (1890–1964) joined the Industrial Workers of the World in 1906 and within a year had become a full-time organizer. She was one of the most forceful and popular speakers in the labor movement. This photograph shows her in 1913 addressing silk workers who were on strike in Paterson, New Jersey.

order to keep them out of harm's way. Flynn began to organize a similar plan for the children of Lawrence strikers. Margaret Sanger traveled from New York to fetch children and transport them to temporary homes in, for example, New York, Philadelphia, and Barre, Vermont. The children's exodus generated so much favorable publicity on behalf of the strikers that the mill owners and city officials tried to put a stop to it, sending out the police who proceeded to beat children and women, including a pregnant Italian woman who later miscarried. Public reaction was swift and strong. Finally, after eight weeks, the beleagured mill owners began to negotiate with strike leaders; and on March 12, at a mass meeting, the strikers accepted the new wage offer and voted to go back to work. The IWW leader Bill Haywood announced that "the women won the strike."

Protective Labor Legislation

The WTUL played a minimal role in the Lawrence strike. Affiliated with the AFL, the WTUL leadership stayed clear of strikes led by the rival IWW—not that the AFL had provided a warm welcome. Although the WTUL organized a sizable number of women into AFL-affiliated unions and trained scores of outstanding women for leadership positions, the league faced the fact that even after the heroic garment strikes, according to one activist, women had "no place and no power and mostly no voice" in the mainstream labor movement. The WTUL held to its pledge to organize women into unions, but disillusionment and frustration pushed many members to shift their focus to campaigns for woman suffrage and protective labor legislation.

The National WTUL's support of protective legislation dated at least to 1908, when the U.S. Supreme Court, in its ruling on **Muller v. Oregon**, upheld Oregon's law limiting women to ten hours of work in factories and laundries. Florence Kelley, who had helped to prepare the brief, called on the WTUL to join the NCL in lobbying for additional regulatory legislation. The two organizations cooperated in campaigning for shorter-hours bills as well as a state-regulated "living wage."

The movement for protective legislation gained force in 1911 in the aftermath of the tragic fire that engulfed the Triangle Shirtwaist Factory and took the lives of 146 workers in New York City. Several reform organizations, including the NCL and the WTUL, held hearings that concluded in proposals for expanded legislation to prevent not only industrial accidents and injuries but occupational diseases, such as lead poisoning. Rose Schneiderman, at first doubtful about the efficacy of such legislative work, soon joined the board of the New York State Factory Investigating Commission and, like many other activists in the NCL and the WTUL, she began to focus her political energies on securing broader protective labor legislation for wage-earning women at both at the state and federal levels.

If implemented, many of the proposed laws would improve conditions for both male and female workers by mandating better lighting and seats for workers, industrial safety and fire regulations, and the appointment of factory inspectors. However, the most controversial were restrictive or prohibitive laws that, like *Muller v. Oregon*, affected women alone. With the support of both the WTUL and the NCL, individual states passed hundreds of such laws.

By 1917, all but nine states had limited the number of hours a woman could work in specific occupations. "Women's physical stature and the performance of maternal functions place her at a disadvantage," the Supreme Court declared in upholding this

Muller v. Oregon The landmark U.S. Supreme Court ruling that upheld Oregon state law restricting the hours a woman may work on the grounds that the state has an interest in protecting a woman's health.

WOMEN'S VOICES

SURVIVING THE TRIANGLE FIRE

Rosey Safran, a young Jewish immigrant from Galacia, had been working at the Triangle Shirtwaist Company for two and a half years when a deadly fire broke out. More than 140 young garment workers, many in their teens, died in the fire or jumped to their deaths. The WTUL, which joined Local 25 of the ILGWU to prepare a mass funeral march for the victims, immediately began an investigation into working conditions and consolidated its campaign for protective labor legislation.

I, with a number of other girls, was in the dressing room on the eighth floor of the Asch Building, in Washington place, at 4.40 o'clock on the afternoon of Saturday, March 25, when I heard somebody cry! "Fire!" I left everything and ran for the door on the Washington place side. The door was locked and immediately there was a great jam of girls before it. The fire was on the other side, driving us away from the only door that the bosses had left open for us to use in going in or out. They had the doors locked all the time for fear that some of the girls might steal something. . . .

The fire had started on our floor and quick as I had been in getting to the Washington place door the flames were already blazing fiercely and spreading fast. If we couldn't get out we would all be roasted alive. The locked door that blocked us was half of wood; the upper half was thick glass. Some girls were screaming, some were beating the door with their fists, some were trying to tear it open. There were seven hundred of us girls employed by the Triangle Waist Company, which had three floors, the eighth, ninth and tenth, in the Asch Building. On our floor alone were two hundred and thirty. Most of us were crazy with fear and there was great confusion. Some one broke out the glass part of the door with something hard and heavy—I suppose the head of a machine—and I climbed or was pulled thru the broken glass or was and ran downstairs to the sixth floor, where some one took me down to the street.

I got out to the street and watched the upper floors burning, and the girls hanging by their hands and then dropping as the fire reached up to them. There they were dead on the sidewalk. It was an awful, awful sight, especially to me who had so many friends among the girls and young men who were being roasted alive or dashed to death. I can't describe how I felt as I stood watching. I could see the figures, but not the faces—the police kept us all too far back. We hoped the fire nets would save some, but they were no good for persons falling so far. One girl broke thru the thick glass in the sidewalk and fell down into a cellar. That shows with what force they came down from the ninth floor.

One girl jumped from the ninth floor and her clothing caught on a hook that stuck out from the wall on the eighth. The fire burned thru her clothing and she fell to the sidewalk and was killed. Another girl fell from the eighth to the sixth floor, when a hook supporting a sign caught her clothes and held her. She smashed the window of the sixth floor with her fist and got in the shop and went down to the street, saving herself. One of my friends, Annie Rosen, was an examiner on the ninth floor. She was near a window when the cry of fire was raised. She tried to open the window to get out. It stuck, but she got it open and climbed on a little fire escape. The fire was coming up from the eighth floor and in getting from the ninth to the eighth her hat and her hair were burned. She doesn't know how she got to the eighth; maybe she fell. She was going to jump to the ground, but the people who were watching her from the street shouted not to do it, and somehow she got thru the flames. She fell from the eighth to the sixth floor on the fire escape and then she was carried down to the street and taken to Bellevue Hospital, where there were many of her companions. She is out now, but pale as a ghost; she does not think that she will ever be strong again. She has lost her nerve and is afraid all the time.

Source: Rosey Safran, "The Washington Place Fire," The Independent 70 (April 20, 1911): 840–41.

Questions

1. The Asch Building, the site of the Triangle Fire, was considered one of the safest buildings in New York City. In Safran's description, who is responsible for the tragedy, the owners of the building or the managers of the factory?

2. In what ways do Safran's descriptions of the Triangle Fire provide data for arguments for protective labor legislation?

legislation. Many states passed legislation barring women from working at night, for example, arguing that women needed those hours to care for their families. Night work, the framers of these new laws added, also exposed women to the "moral" dangers that mounted following sundown. At the same time, only a handful of states instituted minimum wage laws, in effect "protecting" women while reducing their salary and restricting their options for employment.

Asked why women were being treated as children, one AFL writer answered: "Because it is to the interest of all of us that female labor should be limited so as not to injure the motherhood and family life of a nation." The WTUL leadership echoed this argument: such laws were necessary "to permit efficient motherhood and healthy children."

"MOTHER-WORK"

"Some of us who are not really mothers in the narrow sense," Leonora O'Reilly, explained, "express the mother instinct in the sense of social motherhood." By giving a public dimension to women's traditionally private work of child care, she identified the premise of an important aspect of progressivism that historians have labeled **"maternalism."** O'Reilly, like many other activists, hoped to transfer to the state the nurturing qualities associated with mother love. In a less sentimental fashion, she also assumed that women would play active, even leading roles as policymakers in an emerging **welfare state** that expanded the responsibilities of government to ensure the social and economic security of its citizens through state-supported programs and services such as protective labor legislation, public schools, health care, and pensions for the elderly.

The majority of the lobbyists for social legislation were white middle-class women. African American women had little reason to place their trust in any government that allowed Jim Crow to flourish, and most black and working-class activists continued to focus on building institutions within their own communities. Nevertheless, the new agencies that were established during the Progressive Era reached far and wide to families across the nation.

"maternalism" A term used by historians to describe the emphasis of Progressive Era reformers on the health and welfare of women and children.

welfare state Reference to a system of government in which the state assumes primary responsibility for the *welfare* of its *citizens* and accords them services as a matter of entitlement.

WOMEN'S LIVES

CHARLOTTE PERKINS GILMAN

At the turn of the century, Charlotte Perkins Gilman reigned as the nation's chief writer on the "woman question." A scion of the prominent Beecher family, she had grown up in poverty but received steady encouragement from her parents to pursue her intellectual ambitions. She attended the Rhode Island School of Design, becoming skilled as an illustrator and proficient at gymnastics. At age twenty-one, she married Charles Walter Stetson, a fellow artist. Marriage, however, did not suit her temperament, motherhood even less so. Four years later, after suffering severe depression, she divorced Stetson and allowed him custody of their infant daughter. A life of activism then lay ahead.

In the 1890s, Gilman began to reach her stride as a self-supporting woman and prolific writer. She joined numerous women's organizations, advocated woman suffrage, and embraced Bellamy Nationalism. She also worked on what would be her most acclaimed treatise, *Women and Economics*, which was published in 1898. Basing her argument in theories of social evolution, which were popular at the time, she deemed sexual inequality a detriment not only to women but to the progress of civilization. Women, she insisted, were just as capable as men at performing the world's work but had been restricted by custom and masculine prerogative to the sphere of domesticity and child care. If the world of work were reorganized to utilize the best talents of individuals regardless of gender, she reasoned, women and men could meet on common ground and proceed to make the world a better place for all.

As the maternalist movement took shape, Gilman supplied her own vision of motherhood. Men, she wrote, "have wasted women's lives like water, and the children of the world have been sacrificed to [their] sins. Now we will have a new world, new-born, new-built, a mother-world as well as a father-world in which we shall not be ashamed or afraid to plant our children." But in mapping her plans for this mother-world, Gilman did not project women into singularly nurturing roles. To the contrary, she rejected the maternalists' idealization of motherhood and advocated instead the socialization of both housework and child care so that women would be free to pursue work that best suited their talents and interests. She refused to endorse pensions for mothers on the grounds that such a program would only buttress women's role as the primary caretakers of children and continue to force their isolation in the home. "Only as we live, think, feel, and work outside the home," Gilman explained, "do we become humanly developed, civilized, socialized."

Gilman married a second time in 1900 and went on to publish a number of books. In 1909, she began *The Forerunner*, a magazine that she owned and edited and filled entirely with her own writings for the next seven years. Diagnosed with breast cancer in 1932, she spent her last year with her daughter and her family. Facing imminent death, Charlotte Perkins Gilman took her own life in August 1935. ■

Juvenile Courts

The Chicago Woman's Club played the leading role in lobbying for one of the first social welfare measures in the United States, the juvenile court system. For decades, socially prominent club members had been involved in charitable work in the city's slums and responded with alarm to the growing rate of juvenile delinquency in the 1890s. They tried a variety of measures to help working-class children keep out of trouble, from establishing kindergartens in poor neighborhoods to conducting mothers' classes focused on child-rearing practices to campaigning for child labor and truancy laws.

Members of the Chicago Woman's Club tried, too, to help children arrested and detained for petty crimes. Often in conjunction with the local WCTU, they worked to establish matrons in the city's jail, placed teachers there to conduct classes, and supported legislation to establish a separate reformatory for girls. Their steady demand that children be tried quickly and separately from adults finally formed the basis for statewide legislation, and in 1899 Illinois became the first state to legislate juvenile courts. Pushed by women's organizations, particularly the General Federation of Women's Clubs (GFWC), twenty-two more states enacted similar legislation by 1920.

As the campaign gained momentum, men and women reformers worked in tandem to secure new social legislation. They also enlarged women's professional opportunities, winning for them appointments as police and probation officers and even as judges. For example, Hull-House, which had supported the Illinois legislation, became the center of the probationary system in Chicago.

In claiming to protect and rehabilitate working-class offenders, the **juvenile court system** treated boys and girls differently. Whereas the majority of boys were picked up for thievery, disorderly conduct, or crimes against property and frequently placed on probation, girls were arrested primarily as sex delinquents and detained. For example, in Alameda County in northern California, nearly three-quarters of the girls who appeared before the courts between 1910 and 1920 admitted to sexual relations with men. Often it was their own parents who initiated the proceedings in an effort to impose traditional moral codes on daughters determined to assert their autonomy. Reformers aspiring to make "the State as near as possible a real mother to the girls," according to one California Progressive, advocated the construction of temporary detention homes and dozens of reformatories.

juvenile court system
Special courts established to handle children under the age of 18 who commit acts that would be crimes if committed by adults as well as children who run away from home or engage in behaviors dangerous to themselves or others.

The rehabilitation programs focused primarily on domestic skills, with the goal of transforming sexually energetic teenagers into women ready to take on the responsibilities of marriage and motherhood as defined by their middle-class overseers. It was not uncommon for girls to spend several years in these institutions, living in a cottage system that grouped them into small "families." In Los Angeles, for example, the juvenile courts remanded girls arrested at age fourteen to an average stay of 3.7 years. The juvenile court movement, along with the development of the reformatory system, improved conditions of incarceration for teenage "delinquents" and at the same time facilitated the surveillance of female sexual behavior by the state.

Mothers' Pensions

The majority of reformers who spearheaded the juvenile court movement believed that the increasing incidence of juvenile delinquency resulted from mothers working outside the home. Recognizing that necessity rather than a selfish desire for a career drove these mothers to wage earning, they promoted a second measure: **mothers' pensions**.

mothers' pensions
State legislation established to subsidize the domestic work of poor women with dependent children.

The activist Mary Ritter Beard observed that "more women have agreed on the wisdom of mothers' pensions than on any other single piece of social legislation." And once again, Illinois was in the vanguard, passing in 1911 the first statewide legislation that, in effect, subsidized the domestic work of impoverished women with dependent children. Within two decades all but two states had passed similar legislation, making mothers' pensions one of the most successful programs of the Progressive Era.

National Congress of Mothers Founded in 1897, the organization promoted education for child-rearing and infant health; later became the Parent-Teaching Association.

The **National Congress of Mothers** (NCM)—now known as the PTA, along with local affiliates of the General Federation of Women's Clubs, played a leading role in making child rearing a major item of Progressive Era politics. In 1897, two thousand women, mostly members of local mothers' clubs, attended the organizational meeting that laid the basis for a movement that would grow to nearly two hundred thousand by 1920. Devoted to family life and persuaded that mothers possess near-absolute power over their children's development, the NCM encouraged women to educate themselves in order to fulfill their maternal responsibilities. The NCM also placed its faith in the state to assist mothers by itself acting as "a wise and gentle and kind and loving parent" who embraced the responsibility for the welfare of its citizens.

Although the NCM had long endorsed mothers' pensions, three Hull-House staffers—Julia Lathrop, Sophonisba Breckinridge, and Edith Abbott—did much of the research behind the Illinois legislation and helped to shape the new programs, which were run through the juvenile court system. The Mothers' Pensions Division investigated applicants and appointed a probation officer who would handle the benefits, arrange for home visits and evaluate the quality of housekeeping, and monitor the children's school record. In maintaining such standards, the program directors awarded the greatest share of pensions to widows and the least to unmarried mothers, who were categorized as "morally unfit." Other groups were also underserved. In 1913, an addendum to the Illinois legislation restricted entitlements to citizens, thus excluding large numbers of recently immigrated poor mothers. African Americans, who had the highest ratio of female-headed households, made up only a very small portion of those mothers receiving pensions.

Maternalists scored a considerable number of successes in their campaigns for welfare, which laid the foundation for Aid to Families with Dependent Children, the program that would be enacted in the 1930s as part of the New Deal. At the same time, they established notable careers in social service for many college-educated, middle-class women. Ironically, they won their battles by arguing that other women belonged in the home to care for their families. For this reason, they also endorsed the "family wage," by which the male breadwinner earned sufficient wages to support his family without supplementary income from either his wife or his children.

U.S. Children's Bureau Created in 1912 within the federal government to investigate and report *"upon all matters pertaining to the welfare of children and child life among all classes of our people."*

The Children's Bureau

Maternalist reform reached its apex in the creation of the **U.S. Children's Bureau** in 1912. Florence Kelley and Lillian Wald of the Henry Street Settlement came up with the idea of a federal agency and managed to win the endorsement of President Theodore Roosevelt. In 1909, at a White House Conference on the Care of Dependent Children, two hundred prominent activists jumped on the bandwagon;

and three years later, President William Howard Taft signed the legislative bill establishing the Children's Bureau and appointed Julia Lathrop (1858–1932) the first director.

"The first and simplest duty of women," according to Lathrop, who never married or had children, "is to safeguard the lives of mothers and babies, to develop the professional dignity of all motherhood, as motherhood has too long suffered from sheer sentimentality. . . ." As director, she set out to coordinate the activities of women reformers engaged in child-welfare programs across the United States and to assess systematically the needs of the nation's children. Lathrop had prepared well for this assignment. She had graduated from Vassar College in 1880, moved to Hull-House in

Spearheaded by Florence Kelley, Lillian Wald, and Jane Addams, the National Child Labor Committee formed in 1904 with a mission of "promoting the rights, awareness, dignity, well-being and education of children and youth as they relate to work and working." In 1908, the committee hired Lewis Hine to document child labor abuse. Hine took this photograph in 1910 and helped to prepare the way for the creation of the U.S. Children's Bureau in 1912.

1890, and quickly became a hands-on activist in maternalist reform. Lathrop served as an inspector for the Illinois Board of Charities and helped to formulate curricula at the School of Civics and Philanthropy in Chicago, which emphasized the practical aspects of social service. As the first woman to head a federal agency, she assembled a staff of fifteen—all women—to comply with the legislative charge "to investigate and report" on such matters as infant mortality, childhood diseases and accidents, child labor, and juvenile courts.

Lathrop made the health of infants and children the first priority of the Children's Bureau. In its first years, the Children's Bureau published small books and pamphlets of medical advice to mothers and shorter bulletins featuring up-to-date information on nutrition, childhood diseases, and other aspects of baby care. Distribution was wide for these items: nearly 1.5 million copies of *Infant Care* (1914) were circulated by 1921. Meanwhile, Lathrop's staff worked closely with local women's organizations, hosted health conferences, and replied personally to the thousands of mothers who sent letters to the Children's Bureau asking for advice. One of their most successful campaigns, conducted with the help of the GFWC, culminated in the passage of state legislation setting up procedures for registering all births. As a consequence of a systematic collection and review of massive data, the Children's Bureau staff established the close correlation between poverty and infant mortality. Before she stepped down as bureau chief in 1921, Lathrop outlined the Sheppard-Towner Act, the landmark maternity bill that committed federal aid to state governments to protect the health and well-being of all mothers and their dependent children (see chapter 16).

WORLD WAR I

World War I began in August 1914 following the assassination of the heir to the throne of the Austro-Hungarian Empire by a Serbian nationalist. Although many Americans were shocked and saddened by the outbreak of a devastating war that soon engulfed Europe, the United States pledged neutrality. However, as the war raged on, Congress began to prepare, passing the National Defense Act in June 1916, which doubled the size of the army and increased funding for battleships and armaments. Finally, after German U-boats sank seven U.S. merchant ships, President Woodrow Wilson, promising to make the world safe for democracy, signed a declaration of war on April 6, 1917.

While the U.S. army enrolled four million men, sending half to Europe as the American Expeditionary Force, American women responded to the crisis in a variety of ways. The majority, swept up in a wave of patriotism, shifted their volunteer work to efforts to win the war. Other longtime activists resisted this impulse and instead formed a vital peace movement. Meanwhile, the rapid expansion of production during wartime brought new opportunities to wage-earning women, including the hundreds of thousands of African American women who moved from the rural South to industrial cities in the North.

Wartime Employment

With one of every six male workers enrolled in the armed forces and immigration cut off, World War I provided women with new opportunities for wage earning. Nearly one million women joined the labor force for the first time during World War I, while a far greater number already working outside the home were able to quit such low-paying jobs as domestic service for better-paying employment in industry. Women showed up in unfamiliar places—on the assembly lines in munitions plants and chemical plants, behind the switches on train locomotives, on the platforms of streetcars, and under big bags of mail on the city's streets. United States military installations, including hospitals and offices, employed a large number of women in civilian jobs.

African American women took advantage of the new opportunities available to them. Before the war, upward of 90 percent of all black female wage earners worked as either agricultural laborers or domestic servants, mainly in the South. Now, with the incentive of wartime employment, they helped to form the mass exodus from the South known as the **Great Migration**. Between 1916 and 1921, about 5 million African Americans—5 percent of the southern black population—headed for northern industrial cities like New York, Chicago, and Philadelphia.

Great Migration The migration of thousands of African Americans from the rural South to the urban North, which was especially pronounced during World War I when job opportunities opened up.

Many black women took over the domestic and janitorial jobs that white women abandoned for better-paying positions in industry. With the help of African American women's clubs, churches, and the Urban League, they also managed to break into factory work. However, black women were usually assigned to the worst jobs and required to work in separate rooms or on segregated production lines. In Chicago, for example, three thousand African American women found work in the meat-packing plants, performing such unsavory tasks as removing the brains from hogs' heads. Still, even these jobs were better than doing back-breaking labor in the cotton fields back home.

At the end of the war, returning servicemen replaced women in most industrial jobs. White women gained most in fields that they already dominated, such as nursing and clerical work, and only a small portion returned to domestic service. African American women found themselves squeezed out of industrial jobs and taking up the slack in household work.

The upsurge in women's employment in wartime industries had prompted government officials, with the assistance of women reformers, to increase federal oversight of women wage earners. In 1920, the WTUL and other groups called for a continuation of this policy in the form of a permanent Women's Bureau, housed within the Department of Labor. Mary Anderson, longtime member of the WTUL, became the first director and set herself to educational work and the investigation of conditions in trades where women prevailed.

The Women's Peace Movement

"I Didn't Raise My Boy to Be a Soldier," the title of a popular song of 1915, expressed well the sentiments of a segment of American women who opposed the war. Within weeks of the outbreak of the European war, on August 29, 1914, a band of fifteen hundred women—all dressed in black—staged the Woman's Peace Parade on New York's Fifth Avenue. Over the next year, groups of women began to organize against the war, as well as the preparedness movement that was gaining steam in the United States.

In January, 1915, Jane Addams and suffrage leader Carrie Chapman Catt called a meeting in Washington, D.C., in response to a request from European peace activists to rally American women to their cause. Approximate eighty-six delegates representing various women's organizations attended and drew up a platform endorsing international arbitration and woman suffrage. The conference concluded by establishing the **Woman's Peace Party** (WPP), which became the most influential component of the larger peace movement.

Woman's Peace Party Founded in Chicago in 1915 and chaired by Jane Addams, the WPP formed to protest World War I.

Immediately following the outbreak of war in Europe in August 1914, groups of American women began to mobilize on behalf of peace. Within weeks, the prominent suffragsit Fanny Garrison Villard, the daughter of the famous abolitionist William Lloyd Garrison, helped organize the peace parade pictured here. More than 1,500 women, dressed in mourning, staged a "march for civilization" down Manhattan's Fifth Avenue. A few months later, the Woman's Peace Party came into being.

The WPP was headquartered in Chicago with Jane Addams as its head. Addams had advanced the cause of peace for a long time, putting together her thoughts on the subject in *Newer Ideals of Peace*, a book published in 1906. Once the European war broke out, she lectured frequently, speaking forcefully against a U.S. entry. With the formation of the WPP, Adams mobilized peace leaders in each state to form branches. The activists proceeded to deploy maternalism as their campaign strategy, insisting that women's role as nurturers gave them a distinctive perspective on war that men could not readily understand and therefore empowered them to seek solutions to international disputes. Former president Theodore Roosevelt, a prominent promoter of hypermasculinity who, even in peacetime, urged compulsory military training for all men, referred to the WPP as "silly and base," their demands as "hysterical."

Undaunted, the leaders of the WPP quickly moved into the international arena. In April 1915, they sent delegates to an international conference of thirteen hundred women pacifists from twelve nations that met at The Hague, the Netherlands, to protest the mass killing. The delegates endorsed a program similar to the WPP platform, calling for mediation to end war and endorsing woman suffrage. The conference resulted in the formation of the International Women's Committee, which in 1919 became the **Women's International League for Peace and Freedom (WILPF)**. Meanwhile, the delegates designated "envoys" to carry their message to government officials. After returning to the United States, Jane Addams led a delegation to President Wilson, asking him to maintain the nation's neutrality during the European war and to call a conference of other neutrals. When Wilson stalled, Addams turned to automobile magnate Henry Ford and, with his financing, embarked on the Ford Peace Expedition to Stockholm, where international peace advocates met.

Women's International League for Peace and Freedom Formed in 1919, WILPF succeeded the Woman's Peace Party in advocating the end of militarism and world peace.

As the United States moved closer to war, the WPP, along with other peace societies, called for a popular referendum. Once the United States entered the war, in a burst of patriotism, some of the most influential members, such as Catt and Florence Kelley, resigned. The WPP refrained from protesting the war and instead supported the plan for a League of Nations as a forum to settle future disputes among nations. Addams, then president of WILPF, continued to hold that office until 1929 and became honorary president for the remainder of her life. In December 1931, she received the Nobel Peace Prize.

In National Defense

Shortly after the outbreak of the European war, a few courageous American women rushed to France to join the ambulance corps, while others positioned themselves overseas to work with refugees. Following the U.S. entry, American women were allowed, for the first time, to serve in the armed services. Although the majority spent the war working as clerical workers or nurses, more than sixteen thousand women received overseas assignments, mainly in France. For example, three hundred women served as bilingual telephone operators for the army, running switchboards that connected soldiers at the front lines to their commanding officers. However, the armed services refused to commission women as doctors, and those women physicians determined to serve signed up with the French army or with relief agencies, including the Red Cross. The majority of American women stayed home, showing their patriotism through volunteer work with various defense and relief organizations.

The war served to revivify traditional concepts of gender. Men became more manly in fulfilling their military duty to nation, while women in their supportive roles became yet more maternal. Both peace activists and patriots tapped into common rhetoric. The call to form the WPP singled out women and children as "innocent victims of men's unbridled ambitions." Those women lining up with national defense stepped forward in the name of motherhood with equal passion. But rather than opposing armed conflict as a masculinist act of aggression, they reaffirmed their own femininity by embracing sacrifice, even to the extent of giving up their sons for the greater good. They circulated pledges in the name of "patriotic motherhood," encouraging women to promise to make their homes "a center of American ideals . . . and endeavor to teach the children . . . to cherish and revere our country and its history. . . ."

Building on these sentiments, the **Council of National Defense** (CDC) successfully created Women's Committees at the state level, which in turn engaged masses of women to make efficient use of human resources for war. The Red Cross additionally attracted many women. With little more than a hundred chapters when the European war began, the Red Cross comprised more than four thousand chapters by November 1918, when the Armistice was signed. The YWCA offered assistance to the families of men stationed at training centers or recovering in military hospitals and provided temporary housing for single women moving to take advantage of wartime employment.

In southern states, wartime patriotism loosened the grip of Jim Crow on some women's organizations. In North Carolina, for example, the Women's Committees of the CDC integrated black and white volunteers at the county level and achieved considerable success in joint work in the selling of Liberty Bonds. However, most campaigns generated cooperation among organizations that remained segregated in terms of membership, such as women's clubs, churches, and the YWCA. African American women, for example, organized separately to support "colored soldiers" and also collected money, rolled bandages, and assembled first-aid kits for their own auxiliary of the Red Cross. Black and white women active in the YWCA also sponsored separate Hostess Houses and comfort stations, which aimed to keep soldiers away from prostitutes. Nevertheless, for women at the leadership level, the wartime experience suggested a model for the future of women's politics in the South, in particular the organization of women's committees of the Commission on Interracial Cooperation.

This poster, "The Greatest Mother in the World," was created by the muralist Alonzo Earl Forginer to raise funds for the American Red Cross in 1918, after the United States had entered World War I. Suggested by an advertising executive, the image of patriotic maternalism proved immensely and enduringly popular. Ten million copies were distributed at the time, and it became a symbol for the Red Cross well into the 1940s.

Council of National Defense Created by the U.S. Congress during World War I to manage the domestic aspects of the nation's war effort.

Keeping Men Fit to Fight

With the outbreak of World War I, the hysteria around "white slavery" quickly dissipated, and the prostitute emerged as a public enemy, a potential carrier of venereal disease, and therefore a major threat to the nation's fighting troops. Municipal authorities began to crack down on sexual vice in earnest. Even the notorious Storeyville in New Orleans succumbed when the secretary of war warned that the red-light district would be closed by military force if local officials failed to take prompt action.

To safeguard the well-being of men assigned to one of the sixteen "soldier cities" that had been set up by 1918, the federal government created the Commission on Training Camp Activities (CTCA). Keeping soldiers away from alcohol and free of venereal disease was high on the list of priorities. The CTCA officials encouraged sexual abstinence and, as much as possible, policed the sexual activity of enlisted men. For example, if a solider had intercourse while off base, he was required to report to a "prophylactic station" within eight hours of exposure or face charges that could lead to court-martial proceedings.

Chamberlain-Kahn Act Passed in July 1819, this legislation established federal grants for state venereal disease programs aimed to protect men serving in the armed forces.

The **Chamberlain-Kahn Act**, enacted by Congress in July 1918, allowed the states to adopt measures to detain, quarantine, and commit to institutions any "civilian persons" who could carry venereal disease to the military or naval forces. With their wide net, the CTCA swept up nearly thirty thousand women, including many "khaki-mad" girls in their teens whose dates with soldiers could have included sexual intercourse. These women were required to undergo compulsory medical examinations and, if found infected, were quarantined in local hospitals, jails, workhouses, or detention centers until deemed free of disease.

Meanwhile, women reformers rallied foremost to preserve the "purity" of women. The Committee for the Protection of Women and Girls, a federal agency formed in September 1917, at first won the endorsement of such luminaries as Julia Lathrop of the Children's Bureau and recruited Maude Miner, a probation officer with the New York juvenile court system, as director. Miner proposed "protective" programs to prevent what occurred in one town following the construction of a military base: over half of the girls of the senior class at the local high school became pregnant within the year. However, Miner soon found herself forced to abandon educational work for mainly punitive programs directed exclusively at women and girls. After the government approved a huge budget to construct detention homes for "wayward" girls, Miner resigned her position. She and other women complained that the government routinely put the soldiers' interests above those of civilian girls and women.

When the 1918 Armistice was declared, the campaign against sexual vice ended but without establishing the single standard of morality that social purity reformers had been promoting since the late nineteenth century. What had changed from the earlier era was the gender of the perpetrator of illicit sexual encounters. No longer victims of men's wanton behavior, women now carried the full weight of responsibility for their own moral transgressions.

World War I presented many opportunities to women, allowing women to take new jobs, move to new locations, and serve their government in new ways. Nevertheless, like other wars, the "war to end all wars" also reinforced conventional notions of gender by spotlighting men's heroic role in combat and emphasizing women's self-sacrificing role as nurturer. It was therefore a tribute to the shrewd strategy of suffragists that women emerged from World War I on the precipice of a new political era.

VOTES FOR WOMEN

Jane Addams, advocating woman suffrage, reasoned:

> that if woman would fulfill her traditional responsibility to her own children; if she would educate and protect from danger factory children who must find their recreation on the street; if she would bring the cultural forces to bear upon our materialistic civilization; and if she would do it all with the dignity and directness fitting one who carries on her immemorial duties, then she must bring herself to the use of the ballot—that latest implement for self-government. May we not fairly say that American women need this implement in order to preserve the home?

This argument, labeled "expediency" by historians, stressed not the justice of equal rights but the benefits to society that women voters would deliver. By the early twentieth century, as the Progressive Era and, later, World War I drew ever larger numbers of women into reform activities, Addams's argument became ever more appealing. Masses of women had concluded that they required the ballot as an instrument of reform. On this ground, the woman suffrage entered the mainstream.

Out of the Doldrums

After the western state victories of the 1890s, no more states followed, and the federal amendment appeared to be dead. In 1900, the membership of the National American Woman Suffrage Association (NAWSA) barely topped nine thousand, with an average age of members well over forty (see chapter 13). Promising to revive the flagging organization, the energetic Iowan Carrie Chapman Catt stepped forward. Catt served ably as president until 1904, when the NAWSA presidency came into the hands of the popular, dedicated—but inefficient—Anna Howard Shaw.

Shaw did manage to hold on to new constituencies. In 1900, Maud Wood Park and Inez Haynes Gilmore had directed the formation of a College Equal Suffrage League in Boston; and in 1906, the NAWSA made a concerted effort to sign up college women. At the same time, wealthy women new to the cause added a patina of respectability to the movement. Shaw recruited Alva Belmont, a recent divorcée, who financed the move of NAWSA headquarters from sleepy Warren, Ohio, to bustling New York City. The suffrage movement continued to gain cachet, adding a few luminaries, including movie star Mary Pickford. Then, in 1910, women in Washington won the right to vote. With a victory in California in 1911, the NAWSA leaders began to put the period of "doldrums" behind them. Finally, in 1914, delegates to the biennial meeting of the GFWC officially endorsed "the principle of political equality regardless of sex."

Meanwhile, Harriot Stanton Blatch, a daughter of the early woman's rights advocate Elizabeth Cady Stanton, returned from a lengthy stay in England and decided to recruit working women to the suffrage movement. In 1907, true to her belief that "the woman who supports herself has a claim upon the state," she invited college-educated professional women as well as wage-earning women to join the Equality League of Self-Supporting Women. Within a year, the Equality League counted twenty thousand

WOMEN'S LIVES

CARRIE CHAPMAN CATT

The architect of the "winning plan" of the twentieth-century woman suffrage movement, Carrie Chapman Catt emerged as an unrivaled organizer and pragmatic leader. She grew up a feisty child on a farm near Ripon, Wisconsin, and worked her way through college by washing dishes and working in the library. After graduating from Iowa State University in 1880, she became a high-school principal and, two years later, the superintendent of schools in Mason City, Iowa. Marriage, however, cut short her career in education. In 1885, she married Leo Chapman, who died just one year later; and in 1890, she married again. By this time, Catt had joined the woman suffrage movement, representing Iowa at the historic 1890 convention that formed the National American Woman Suffrage Association. Catt and her husband, George William Catt, signed a prenuptial agreement that would allow her to reserve four months of each year for campaigning for woman suffrage.

Catt applied herself, participating in the western state campaigns of the 1890s, and soon rose to national leadership. When Susan B. Anthony retired in 1900, she named Catt her successor as president of the NAWSA. In 1904, Catt stepped down to care for her ailing husband, who died the following year. After a period of recovery, Catt took advantage of her new position as a wealthy widow and returned—now full time—to her reform activities.

In 1902, Catt emerged as the guiding force in the new International Woman Suffrage Alliance; and by 1913, she had presided over its congresses held in Berlin, Copenhagen, Amsterdam, London, Stockholm, and Budapest. Between 1911 and 1913, she conducted a world tour, facilitating the creation of woman suffrage organizations in Africa and Asia.

The growing agitation in New York State also whetted her appetite for organizational work. She served as coordinator of local campaigns and helped form the Woman Suffrage Party in 1910. The magnitude of her skills did not escape the notice of the NAWSA, which brought her back to national leadership in 1916.

As the NAWSA president again, Catt promoted what came to be known as her "winning plan." Since 1912, Alice Paul's Congressional Committee had been advocating exclusive focus on a federal amendment, holding Democrats, the "party in power," as responsible. Catt stood firmly opposed to this strategy, forcing Paul to break with the NAWSA. Catt meanwhile continued to pursue a state-by-state strategy, assuming that key victories—and nonpartisan lobbying—would successfully rally federal legislators. The NAWSA ratified Catt's plan at its 1916 convention.

Catt placed victory at the top of her agenda. She was not above using racist and nativist arguments to promote woman suffrage if she believed the audience would be receptive to such views. After the United States entered World War I, she abandoned her pacifist principles, including her membership in the Woman's Peace Party, which she had helped to found, in the expectation that the NAWSA's support of the war effort would win favor with President Wilson and federal legislatures. She went so far as to serve on the Woman's Committee of the Council of National Defense.

At the final convention of the NAWSA in 1919, Catt proposed the formation of a League of Women Voters, while turning over the reins to a younger generation of women. She revived her pacifist principles and spearheaded the formation of the Committee on the Cause and Cure of War. ■

members, including such prominent reformers as Charlotte Perkins Gilman, Florence Kelley, and Leonora O'Reilly. In 1910, Blatch renamed her organization the Women's Political Union and decided to focus on lobbying politicians. The WTUL soon took up the slack among wage-earning women. In 1912, the NAWSA responded to these promising developments by hiring the prominent trade unionists Rose Schneiderman and Clara Lemlich to attract yet more working-class and wage-earning women to their ranks.

The suffrage movement not only emerged from its doldrums but expanded its ranks considerably. No longer the preserve of white, middle-class Protestant women who were middle age at best, the movement more closely mirrored the diverse society of early twentieth-century America. By the second decade of the century, the movement appeared so powerful that the "anti's" began to mobilize in earnest, forming the **National Association Opposed to Woman Suffrage**. With representation in twenty-five states, this new organization comprising both men and women promoted the idea that women served society best by focusing their energies on the home and family.

National Association Opposed to Woman Suffrage Formed in New York City in 1911 as a federation of state antisuffrage groups, which included both men and women.

Southern Strategy

It was the former abolitionist and husband of Lucy Stone who first proposed that woman suffrage could solve the "Negro problem" in the South. In 1867, Henry Blackwell argued that the number of white voters added by enfranchising women would guarantee the preservation of white supremacy. A generation later, more than a few suffragists were contending that women's enfranchisement would overcome the influence of immigrant voters and were reiterating Blackwell's contention that women's ballots would counter the southern black vote.

In 1895, in an attempt to woo white southern women, the NAWSA chose Atlanta as the site for its convention; in preparation for the meeting, Susan B. Anthony asked the aging but loyal Frederick Douglass to stay away. In 1903, still hoping to appease white southerners, the NAWSA held its convention in New Orleans and, in addition to excluding black women from the assembly hall, invited Belle Kearney of Mississippi to give the keynote address. The prominent suffragist and WCTU activist proceeded to describe the woman's ballot as "the medium to retain the supremacy of the white race over the African." In addition to greeting Kearney's remarks with enthusiasm, the delegates acceded to the southern demand for states' rights and approved a policy that would allow individual states to define the terms of their positions on woman suffrage, which could include the property, literacy, and educational restrictions that already disfranchised most African American men throughout the South.

The NAWSA's "southern strategy" did not pay off. African American women continued to support woman suffrage in proportionally greater numbers than white women. But, continually rebuffed by the NAWSA and required to sit at the back of convention halls or march at the end of parades, they tended to keep to their own organizations and to campaign for universal suffrage. For their part, white southern women managed to overcome much of the deeply embedded hostility to a movement historically linked to abolition and created for themselves a small, racially segregated woman suffrage movement. However, the white southern men who held power remained stubbornly opposed, preferring to protect white supremacy not by adding the votes of their womenfolk but by preventing black men from voting. Recognizing the stalemate, the NAWSA abandoned the South.

Winning Campaign

The widow Catt returned to the presidency in 1915 and transformed the NAWSA into a well-oiled political machine, fully primed to lead the forces to victory. The NAWSA embraced a two-armed strategy: (1) lobbying members of Congress to pass a federal amendment and (2) mobilizing the troops in states that seemed the most likely to approve referenda for woman suffrage. The leadership therefore kept their distance from the suffrage movement in the South, where several state campaigns had ended in failure; they hoped, too, to keep at bay the controversial issue of race.

The Washington, D.C., lobby initially fell to Alice Paul, a young Quaker activist who had recently returned from England. A convert to the militant tactics developed by British suffragettes, Paul had little patience with the educational campaigns typical of the NAWSA or their polite lobbying of politicians. She admired the British suffragettes who took to the streets, staging huge parades, holding open-air meetings, and, on occasion, chaining themselves to lampposts and, when arrested, going on hunger strikes. Paul also liked the way the publicity-seeking British suffragettes directed their message, without restraint, to the party in power. When Woodrow Wilson returned from his presidential inauguration, Paul and her coworkers followed their lead to stage a protest march. Within a short time, the NAWSA leaders, who had pledged themselves to nonpartisanship, grew impatient with Paul's relentless attack on Wilson's administration and, indeed, on all Democrats and pushed out Alice Paul and her Congressional Union, which had formed in 1913.

Paul and her allies such as Lucy Burns appealed to women voters of the western states to join them in forming the **National Woman's Party** (NWP) in 1916. The NWP began to push even more strongly for a federal amendment by targeting the Wilson administration. Even after the United States entered World War I, the NWP continued to heckle Democrats and picket the White House. Like the British suffragettes who inspired them, the NWP protestors were assaulted by passersby and police alike and arrested in droves. Imprisoned, they, too, went on hunger strikes and were forcefed. Their militant tactics did not always generate sympathy for the cause but unfailingly created publicity.

Meanwhile, Catt's **"winning plan,"** which was formally adopted by the NAWSA in 1916, gained speed. Catt herself lobbied on Capitol Hill, crisscrossed the country on speaking tours, and raised huge amounts of money to fund an army of suffrage agitators to work for referenda at the local and state levels. In 1917, New York, long

National Woman's Party Succeeded the Congressional Union as the militant wing of the woman suffrage movement and focused on amending the Constitution.

"winning plan" Formally adopted by the NAWSA in 1916, this strategy introduced targeted key state woman suffrage referenda and simultaneously supported an amendment to the Constitution.

WOMEN'S VOICES

A SUFFRAGE MILITANT

Alice Paul (1885–1977) led the National Woman's Party, a break-away group from NAWSA that embraced militant tactics in the campaign for woman suffrage. In 1917 Paul and her co-workers picketed the White House to protest President Woodrow Wilson's refusal to endorse the ballot. Here, in a letter to Doris Stevens, she recounts her imprisonment in the Occoquan Workhouse in Virginia. Alice Paul was one of the first American suffragists to stage a hunger strike.

However gaily you start out in prison to keep up a rebellious protest, it is nevertheless a terribly difficult thing to do in the face of the constant cold and hunger of undernourishment. Bread and water, and occasional molasses, is not a diet destined to sustain rebellion long. And soon weakness overtook us.

At the end of two weeks of solitary confinement, without any exercise, without going outside of our cells, some of the prisoners were released, having finished their germs, but five of us were left serving seven months' sentences, and two, on month sentences. With our number thus diminished to seven, the authorities felt able to cope with us. The doors were unlocked and we were permitted to take exercise. Rose Winslow fainted as soon as she got into the yard, and was carried back to her cell. I was too weak to move from my bed. Rose and I were taken on stretchers that night to the hospital.

For one brief night we occupied beds in the same ward in the hospital. Here we decided upon the hunger strike, as the ultimate form of protest left us—the strongest weapon left with which to continue within the prison our battle against the Administration. . . .

From the moment we undertook the hunger strike, a policy of unremitting intimidation began. One authority after another, high and low, in and out of prison, came to attempt to force me to break the hunger strike.

"You will be taken to a very unpleasant place if you don't stop this," was a favorite threat of the prison officials, as they would hint vaguely of the psychopathic ward, and St. Elizabeth's, the Government insane asylum. . . .

After about three days of the hunger strike a man entered my room in the hospital and announced himself as Dr. White, the head of St. Elizabeth's. He said that he had been asked by the District Commissioner Gardner to make an investigation. I later learned that he was Dr. William A. White, the eminent alienist.

Coming close to my bedside and addressing the attendant, who stood at a few respectful paces from him, Dr. White said: "Does this case talk?"

"Why would't I talk?" I answered quickly.

"Oh, these cases frequently will not talk, you know," he continued in explanation.

"Indeed I'll talk," I said gaily, not having the faintest idea that this was an investigation of my sanity.

"Talking is our bussiness," I continued, "we talk to any one on earth who is willing to listen to our suffrage speeches."

"Please talk," said Dr. White, "Tell me about suffrage; why you have opposed the President; the whole history of your campaign, why you picket, what you hope to accomplish by it. Just talk freely."

I drew myself together, sat upright, proper myself up for a discourse of some length, and began to talk. The stenographer whom Dr. White brought with him took down in shorthand everything that was said.

I may say it was one of the best speeches I ever made. I recited the long history and struggle of the suffrage movement from its early beginning and narrated the political theory of our activities up to the present moment, outlining the status of the suffrage amendment in Congress at that time. In short, I told him everything. . . .

(continued)

Suddenly it dawned upon me that he was examining me personally; that his interest in the suffrage agitation and the jail conditions did not exist, and that he was merely interested in my reactions to the agitation and to jail. Even then was reluctant to believe that I was the subject of mental investigation and I continued to talk.

But he continued in what I realized with a sudden shock, was an attempt to discover in me symptoms of the persecution mania. How simple he had apparently thought it would be, to prove that I had an obsession on the subject of President Wilson! . . .

It appeared clear that it was their intention either to discredit me, as the leader of the agitation, by casting doubt upon my sanity, or else to intimidate us into retreating from the hunger strike. . . .

But they had by no means exhausted every possible facility for breaking down our resistance. I overheard the Commissioner say . . . ., "Go ahead, take her and freed her."

I was thereupon put upon a stretcher and carried into the psychopathic ward.

Source: Doris Stevens, Jailed for Freedom *(New York: Boni and Liveright, 1920), 220–23.*

Questions

1. How were Alice Paul's tactics different from those used by the majority of suffragists affiliated with the National American Woman Suffrage Association?

2. Why did the doctor who examined her dismiss her arguments for woman suffrage?

considered by suffragists to be the swing state, approved the referendum, with heavily immigrant New York City providing the decisive votes.

By the time the United States entered World War I, the NAWSA membership had swelled to two million, and seventeen states had passed referenda. President Wilson endorsed woman suffrage as a "war measure," that is, to recognize and widen women's contribution to the war effort. The President called upon Congress to pass the Susan B. Anthony Amendment, which would grant women the right to vote. Victory was in sight.

Nineteenth Amendment, 1920

Under pressure from the president, the House of Representatives voted on January 10, 1918, to approve the **Nineteenth Amendment**, which read: "The right of citizens of the United States to vote shall not be denied or abridged by the United States or by any States on Account of sex. The Congress shall have the power by appropriate legislation to enforce the provisions of this article." On June 4, 1919, the U.S. Senate belatedly endorsed the amendment, voting fifty-six to twenty-five, and then sent the amendment to the states for ratification.

Suffragists kept up their campaigning, quickly lining up Illinois, Wisconsin, and Michigan as the first states to ratify the new law. Unsurprisingly, they made little headway in the South, where Georgia and Alabama were the first to deliver negative votes. The anti's also swung into action and succeeded in slowing the process.

Nineteenth Amendment The so-called "Susan B. Anthony Amendment," which granted women the right to vote, was endorsed by the Senate on June 4, 1919 and became law on August 26, 1920.

MAP 15-1   WOMAN SUFFRAGE BY STATE

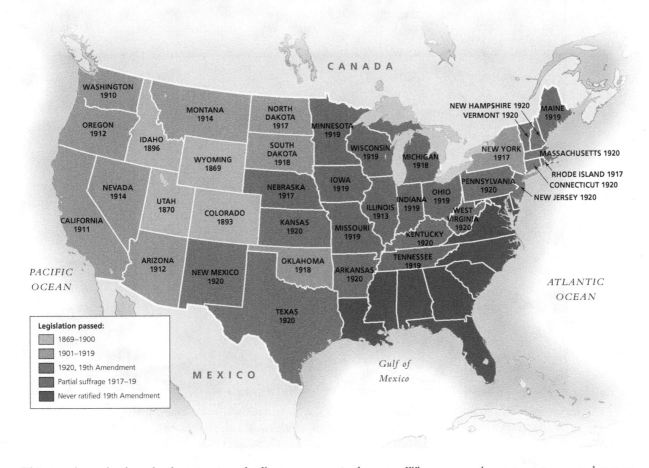

This map shows the dates for the extension of suffrage to women in the states. Whereas several western states granted women the right to vote in the late nineteenth century, a majority of southern states held out and, in addition, refused to ratify the Nineteenth Amendment.

After thirty-five of the required thirty-six states had ratified the amendment, all eyes turned to Tennessee, where the governor, pressured by President Wilson, had called a special session of the state legislature. The vote was scheduled for August 18, 1920. A young man who had stood firm with the anti's until this time surprised everyone by casting the decisive vote in its favor. Echoing the sentiments of many Progressive reformers, he claimed afterward: "I know that a mother's advice is always safest for her boy to follow and my mother wanted me to vote for ratification." But, he added: "I desired that my party in both State and Nation might see it was a Republican from the mountains of East Tennessee, purest Anglo-Saxon section in the world, who made woman suffrage possible."

Supporters gathered to witness Governor Frederick D. Gardner of Missouri sign the document ratifying the Nineteenth Amendment in July 1919. Missouri became the eleventh state to ratify the "Susan B. Anthony Amendment," which granted the right to vote to women. The Nineteenth Amendment became law on August 26, 1920.

On August 26, 1920, the Nineteenth Amendment to the U.S. Constitution became law, in time for women to vote in the upcoming presidential elections.

CONCLUSION

The woman suffrage victory marked the ebbing of women's separate political culture. Women's organizations, such as women's clubs, the WCTU and the WTUL, continued well into the twentieth century, but these organizations could make little headway by claiming that women's domestic and maternal roles provided either the imperative or the justification for their involvement in public affairs. Having learned to work with men in effecting major legislation and in shaping the foundational institutions of the welfare state, the women who spearheaded Progressive Era reform could no longer rally women by appealing to them to become "municipal housekeepers." They had successfully relinquished, for better or worse, a large chunk of those responsibilities to the government. If women were to continue on the path of reform, they would have to find a niche within the halls of government and mainstream politics.

WOMEN'S HISTORY EVENTS	GLOBAL EVENTS
1885	
1889 Jane Addams opens Hull-House	
1895 The NAWSA inaugurates "southern strategy"	
1897 National Congress of Mothers forms	
1898 National Consumer's League forms Charlotte Perkins Gilman publishes *Women and Economics*	1898 Illinois legislates juvenile court system
1900	
1900 College Equal Suffrage League forms in Boston	
1903 National Women's Trade Union League forms	
1907 Equality League of Self-Supporting Women forms	
1908 Lugenia Burns Hope establishes the Neighborhood Union	1908 *Muller v. Oregon* establishes protective labor legislation
1909 Charlotte Perkins Gilman begins *The Forerunner*	1909 New York shirtwaist makers strike
1910	
1910 Chicago garment workers strike	
1911 Illinois passes first mothers' pension law	
1912 U.S. Children's Bureau formed	1912 Textile workers in Lawrence, Massachusetts, strike
1913 Alice Paul forms Congressional Union Woman's Peace Parade protests war The GFWC endorses woman suffrage	1914 World War I begins

(continued)

WOMEN'S HISTORY	GLOBAL EVENTS
1915	
1915	1915
Woman's Peace Party forms	Congress passes National Defense Act
Women's International League for Peace and Freedom forms	The Great Migration begins
1916	1916
Carrie Chapman Catt proposes the "winning plan"	Protocol of Peace signed
1917	1917
National Woman's Party forms	United States enters World War I
Committee for the Protection of Women and Girls formed	1918
Suffrage referendum wins in New York	Chamberlain-Kahn Act enacted
1920	Armistice ends World War I
U.S. Women's Bureau formed	
Nineteenth Amendment ratified	

REVIEW QUESTIONS

1. What is the relationship between women's voluntary organizations and Progressive reform?

2. What is the significance of the garment and textiles strikes to the history of wage-earning women?

3. Why was the notion of "mother-work" so powerful and effective during the Progressive Era?

4. How did the experiences of women vary during World War I?

5. How did the passage of the Nineteenth Amendment affect women's role in politics and reform?

RECOMMENDED READING

Katherine H. Adams and Michael L. Keene. *Alice Paul and the American Suffrage Campaign*. Urbana: University of Illinois Press, 2008. A fine biography and close study of the militant yet nonviolent tactics promoted by suffragist Alice Paul.

Paula Baker. "The Domestication of Politics: Women and American Political Society, 1780-1920," *American Historical Review*, 89 (June 1984): 620–49. Important essay tracing the expansion of

"woman's sphere" into the community. Baker makes a strong case that women's political culture changed dramatically after the Civil War to account for the consolidation of the state.

Nancy Schrom Dye. *As Equals and as Sisters: Feminism, Unionism, and the Women's Trade Union League of New York*. Columbia: University of Missouri Press, 1980. Examines the relationship between workers and "allies" as an important chapter in the history of the women's movement and their collaboration in establishing unions.

Glenda Elizabeth Gilmore. *Gender and Jim Crow: Women and the Politics of White Supremacy in North Carolina, 1896–1920.* Chapel Hill: University of North Carolina Press, 1996. Frames the Progressive Era with the disenfranchisement of African American men, on the one hand, and the increasing power of African American women in their communities, on the other.

Linda Gordon. *Pitied But Not Entitled: Single Mothers and the History of Welfare, 1890–1925.* New York: Free Press, 1994. With the federal welfare policy implemented during the New Deal as its concluding point, this study traces the emergence and development of legislation addressing the needs of single mothers. Gordon documents the role of the activists who shaped welfare policy and assesses the impact of those programs on the mothers they had hoped to serve.

Evelyn Brooks Higginbotham. *Righteous Discontent: The Women's Movement in the Black Baptist Church, 1880–1920.* Cambridge: Harvard University Press, 1993. Argues convincingly that African American women worked principally through the church to establish a powerful reform network and created for themselves positions of power within the black community.

Molly Ladd-Taylor. *Mother-Work: Women, Child Welfare, and the State, 1890–1930.* Cambridge: Harvard University Press, 1994. An interpretive study of "mother-work" in the community, as conducted by such organizations as the National Congress of Mothers, and by the state. Ladd-Taylor offers a penetrating analysis of the U.S. Children's Bureau, mothers' pensions and the Sheppard-Towner Act.

Mary E. Odem. *Delinquent Daughters: Protecting and Policing Adolescent Female Sexuality in the United States, 1885–1920.* Chapel Hill: University of North Carolina Press, 1995. Examines the juvenile justice system with regard to new policies to control female sexuality. Odem provides an acute analysis of the role of the juvenile court and new state reformatories by considering the complex negotiations among women reformers, working-class parents, and teen-age girls.

Anastatia Sims.*The Power of Femininity in the New South: Women's Organizations and Politics in North Carolina, 1880–1930.* Columbia: University of South Carolina Press, 1997. A close study of women's voluntary associations, especially women's clubs, that flourished during the Progressive Era. Sims examines both African American and white women's ventures in "municipal housekeeping" and their contests and conflicts in claiming the mantle of the Southern lady.

Marjorie Spruill Wheeler. *New Women of the New South: Leaders of the Woman Suffrage Movement in the Southern States.* New York: Oxford University Press, 1993. With an emphasis on race and states' rights, this book offers a detailed history of the movement for woman suffrage in the southern states. Wheeler shows that even the most progressive of the elite women she studies did not deviate from the ideas of most white southerners on issues of race and class.

ADDITIONAL BIBLIOGRAPHY

"Municipal Housekeeping"

Blanche Wiesen Cook. "Female Support Networks and Political Activism: Lillian Wald, Crystal Eastman, Emma Goldman," *Chrysalis*, 3 1977, 43–61.

Noralee Frankel and Nancy S. Dye. *Gender, Class, Race and Reform in the Progressive Era.* Lexington: University Press of Kentucky, 1991.

Nancy A. Hewitt. *Southern Discomfort: Women's Activism in Tampa, Florida, 1880s–1920s.* Urbana: University of Illinois Press, 2001.

Cynthia Neverdon-Morton. *Afro-American Women of the South and the Advancement of the Race, 1895–1925.* Knoxville: University of Tennessee Press, 1989.

John P. Rousmaniere. "Cultural Hybrid in the Slums: The College Woman and the Settlement House, 1889–1894," *American Quarterly*, 22 (Spring 1970): 45–66.

Dorothy Salem. *To Better Our World: Black Women in Organized Reform, 1890–1920.* New York: Carlson Publishers, 1990.

Kathryn Kish Sklar. "Hull House in the 1890s: A Community of Women Reformers," *Signs*, 10 (1985): 658–77.

Eleanor J. Stebner. *The Women of Hull-House: A Study in Spirituality, Vocation, and Friendship*. Albany: State University of New York Press, 1997.

Elizabeth Hayes Turner. *Women, Culture, and Community: Religion and Reform in Galveston, 1880–1920*. New York: Oxford University Press, 1997.

Marshal Wedell. *Elite Women and the Reform Impulse in Memphis, 1875–1915*. Knoxville: University of Tennessee Press, 1991.

The Era of Women's Strikes

Ardia Cameron. *Radicals of the Worst Sort: Laboring Women in Lawrence, Massachusetts, 1860–1912*. Urbana: University of Illinois Press, 1994.

Sarah Eisenstein. *Give Us Bread but Give Us Roses: Working Women's Consciousness in the United States, 1890 to the First World War*. London: Routledge, 1983.

Nan Enstad. *Ladies of Labor, Girls of Adventure: Working Women, Popular Culture, and Labor Politics at the Turn of the Twentieth Century*. New York: Columbia University Press, 1999.

Carolyn D. McCreesh. *Women in the Campaign to Organize Garment Workers, 1880–1917*. New York: Garland Publishers, 1985.

Annelise Orleck. *Common Sense and a Little Fire: Women and Working-Class Politics in the United States*. Chapel Hill: University of North Carolina Press, 1995.

Meredith Tax. *The Rising of the Women: Feminist Solidarity and Class Conflict, 1880–1917*. New York: Monthly Review Press, 1979.

Mother-Work

Ruth M. Alexander. *The 'Girl Problem': Female Sexual Delinquency in New York, 1900–1930*. Ithaca: Cornell University Press, 1995.

Sherri Broder. *Tramps, Unfit Mothers, and Neglected Children: Negotiating the Family in Nineteenth-Century* Philadelphia: University of Pennsylvania Press, 2002.

Elizabeth J. Clapp. *Mothers of All Children: Women Reformers and the Rise of Juvenile Courts in the Progressive Era*. University Park: Pennsylvania State University Press, 1998.

Ellen Fitzpatrick. *Endless Crusade: Women Social Scientists and Progressive Reform*. New York: Oxford University Press, 1990.

Linda Gordon, ed. *Women, the State, and Welfare*. Madison: University of Wisconsin, 1990.

Seth Koven and Sonya Michel, eds. *Mothers of a New World: Maternalist Politics and the Origins of Welfare States*. New York, Routledge, 1993.

Kristen Lindenmeyer. *"A Right to Childhood": The U.S. Children's Bureau and Child Welfare, 1912–1946*. Urbana: University of Illinois Press, 1997.

Richard A. Meckel. *Save the Babies: American Public Health Reform and the Prevention of Infant Mortality*. Baltimore: Johns Hopkins University Press. 1990.

Robyn Muncy. *Creating a Female Dominion in American Reform, 1890–1935*. New York: Oxford University Press, 1991.

Theda Skocpol. *Protecting Soldiers and Mothers: The Politics of Social Provision in the United States, 1870s–1920s*. Cambridge: Harvard University Press, 1992.

Jennifer Trost. *Gateway to Justice: The Juvenile Court and Progressive Child Welfare in a Southern City*. Atlanta: University of Georgia Press, 2005.

World War I

Nancy K. Bristow. *Making Men Moral: Social Engineering during the Great War*. New York: New York University Press, 1996.

Carrie Brown. *Rosie's Mom: Forgotten Women Workers of the First World War*. Boston: Northeastern University Press, 2002.

Frances R. Early. *A World without War: How U.S. Feminists and Pacifists Resisted World War I*. Syracuse: Syracuse University Press, 1997.

Lettie Gavin. *American Women in World War I: They Also Served*. Niwot: University Press of Colorado, 1997.

Maurine Greenwald. *Women, War, and Work*. Westport: Greenwood Press, 1980.

Kathleen Kennedy. *Disloyal Mothers and Scurrilous Citizens: Women and Subversion during World War I*. Bloomington: Indiana University Press, 1999.

Tammy M. Proctor. *Female Intelligence: Women and Espionage in the First World War*. New York: New York University Press, 2005.

Carl J. and Dorothy Schneider. *Into the Breach: American Women Overseas in World War I*. New York: Viking-Penguin, 1991.

Linda K. Schott. *Reconstructing Women's Thoughts: The Women's International League for Peace and Freedom Before World War II*. Stanford: Stanford University Press, 1997.

Barbara Steinson. *American Women's Activism in World War I*. New York: Garland, 1982.

Susan Zeiger. *In Uncle Sam's Service: Women Workers with the American Expeditionary Force, 1917–1919*. Ithaca: Cornell University Press, 1999.

The Winning Campaign

Steven M. Buechler. *The Transformation of the Woman Suffrage Movement: The Case of Illinois, 1850–1920*. New Brunswick: Rutgers University Press, 1986.

Mari Jo and Paul Buhle, eds. *The Concise History of Woman Suffrage*, Second Edition. Urbana: University of Illinois Press, 2005.

Susan Englander. *Class Conflict and Coalition in the California Woman Suffrage Movement, 1907–1912: The San Francisco Wage Earners' Suffrage League*. San Francisco: Mellen Research University Press, 1992.

Margaret Mary Finnegan. *Selling Suffrage: Consumer Culture and Votes for Women*. New York: Columbia University Press, 1999.

Linda Ford. *Iron-Jawed Angels: The Suffrage Militancy of the National Woman's Party, 1912–1920*. Lanham, MD: University Press of America, 1991.

Sara Hunter Graham. *Woman Suffrage and the New Democracy*. New Haven: Yale University Press, 1996.

Elna C. Green. *Southern Strategies: Southern Women and the Woman Suffrage Question*. Chapel Hill: University of North Carolina Press, 1997.

Christine A. Lunardini. *From Equal Suffrage to Equal Rights: Alice Paul and the National Woman's Party 1910–1928*. New York: New York University Press, 1986.

Susan E. Marshall. *Splintered Sisterhood: Gender and Class in the Campaign against Woman's Suffrage*. Madison: University of Wisconsin Press, 1997.

Rebecca J. Mead. *How the Vote Was Won: Woman Suffrage in the Western United States*. New York: New York University Press, 2004.

Rosalyn Terborg-Penn. *African American Women in the Struggle for the Vote 1850–1920*. Bloomington: Indiana University Press, 1998.

Biographies, Autobiographies, and Memoirs

Jane Addams. *Twenty Years at Hull-House*. New York: Macmillan, 1910, 1998.

Mary Anderson. *Woman at Work*. Minneapolis: University of Minnesota Press, 1951, 1973.

Helen Camp. *Iron in Her Soul: Elizabeth Gurley Flynn and the American Left*. Pullman: Washington State University Press, 1995.

Lela B. Costin. *Two Sisters for Social Justice: A Biography of Grace and Edith Abbott*. Champaign: University of Illinois Press, 1983.

Allan Davis. *American Heroine: the Life and Legend of Jane Addams*. New York: Oxford University Press, 1973.

Ellen Carol DuBois. *Harriet Stanton Blatch and the Winning of Woman Suffrage*. New Haven: Yale University Press, 1997.

Robert Fowler. *Carrie Catt*. Boston: Northeastern University Press, 1986.

Charlotte Perkins Gilman. *The Living of Charlotte Perkins Gilman*. NY: Arno Press 1933, 1991.

Louise W, Knight. *Citizen: Jane Addams and the Struggle for Democracy*. Chicago: University of Chicago Press, 2005.

Jane Lancaster. *Making Time: Lillian Moller Gilbreth—a Life Beyond Cheaper by the Dozen*. Northeastern University Press, 2003.

Ann J. Lane. *To Herland and Beyond: The Life and Work of Charlotte Perkins Gilman*. New York: Pantheon Books, 1990.

Elizabeth Anne Payne. *Reform, Labor, and Feminism: Margaret Dreier Robins and the Women's Trade Union League*. Urbana: University of Illinois Press, 1988.

Jacqueline Anne Rouse. *Lugenia Burns Hope: Black Southern Reformer*. Athens, Ga., and London: University of Georgia Press, 1989.

Vida Dutton Scudder. *On Journey*. London: JM Dent and Sons, 1937.

Barbara Sicherman. *Alice Hamilton: A Life in Letters*. Cambridge: Harvard University Press, 1984.

Doris Stevens. *Jailed for Freedom*. New York: Boni and Liveright, 1920.

THE JAZZ AGE, 1920–1930

"REVOLUTION IN MANNERS AND MORALS"

Courtship in Transition

The Companionate Marriage

Invention of the Lesbian Threat

HOW DID courtship, marriage, and family life change in the 1920s?

WOMEN AND WORK

Married Women Workers

Pink-Collar Workers

Professional Workers

HOW DID women's work change in the 1920s?

BEYOND SUFFRAGE

Feminist—New Style

The League of Women Voters

The Equal Rights Amendment

The Sheppard-Towner Act

HOW DID winning the vote affect women's political activism?

WOMEN'S ACTIVISM

"Race Women" and Pan-Africanism

The Anti-Lynching Crusade

Ku Klux Klan

WHAT ROLE did consumer culture play in new ideas of women in the 1920s?

THE CULTURE OF MODERNITY

Dance Crazes

The Harlem Renaissance

Singing the Blues

IN WHAT ways did women's activisim express the tension between modernity and traditionalism in America?

Madame C. J. Walker made it possible for black women to straighten their hair and then style it whatever way they wanted to. They say that Madame Walker got the idea of straightening the hair one day when she was ironing clothes, like this: "Hmmmm, if heat will take the wrinkles out of clothes, then maybe heat will take the kinks out of hair." When she discovered that the heat would work, she designed iron combs that you heat on the stove—"hot comb." And she designed "pressers," something like scissors with a knob on the end, which you pull the hair

The Hayden house was a loafing and meeting place" 1919 Arthur Ignatius Keller (1866–1924) Oil on canvas Library of Congress, Washington D.C.

through. . . . There were the shampoos, the oils to straighten with, the treatment for hair troubles. Then she also created a method, which people flocked to study. All of that, put together, was "the Walker System.". . . Mamie (Randolph) taught me. Oh, my, didn't we have fun working on each other's heads. We tried out the Sayman soap mixture, the sage rinses, the egg rinses, the pressing oils, the hair growing pomade, and the special finger movements to make thin hair grow. They worked, too. . . .

Now, we had all the knowledge and all the equipment, but nobody to use them on. So one day I said to Mamie, "Let's go out and find some customers." We took a long streetcar ride that ended up at Mt. Pleasant Street, where there was a big neighborhood of black people. With our two-burner stove and our hot combs, we got off the car and went to the first house. . . . Anyhow, when we worked on the first ladies, the neighbors came to watch, so we worked out of doors the first time, under a tree. Very shortly we had that whole neighborhood, and then we had the next one. We got so many customers until we had to build something to hold them. Finally, Mamie and I set up chairs in our own homes and let the people come to us.

Source: From Mamie Garvin Fields with Karen Fields, Lemon Swamp and Other Places: A Carolina Memoir *(New York: Free Press, 1983).*

ields's memoir of her young adulthood in the 1920s captured the sense of optimism that came to characterize what became known as "the Jazz Age," the years between World War I and the Great Depression of the 1930s. Author F. Scott Fitzgerald coined the phrase to describe the decadent hedonism of the young and the rich who reveled in the new sounds flowing out of New Orleans, Chicago, and New York. Parties where, in the aftermath of Prohibition in 1920, illegal gin flowed and drunken flappers enjoyed the Charlestown dance craze were only the most obvious sign that a new age had dawned. Beyond the speakeasies and jazz clubs, ordinary American women imbibed a popular culture devoted to leisure, consumption, and youth.

Fueled by growth in the national economy, a modern sensibility emerged, encouraging women to express themselves through the many new products pouring into shops and homes across the country. The rapid growth in consumer markets opened new opportunities for savvy business people. Madame C. J. Walker, the first self-made black female millionaire, made a fortune selling beauty products geared specifically to African American women. Having worked hard in the fields of the South as a young girl, she understood laboring women's desires for affordable luxury goods. At the same time, she saw her wealth as a means to help promote economic opportunities for other women. She not only gave women like Fields the chance to work as commissioned agents for her company instead of working long solitary hours as domestics but also put the promise of beauty and sex appeal within reach of ordinary women of color.

The culture of consumption, oriented around the array of new consumer goods, leisure activities, and entertainment venues, had its roots in the second industrial revolution of the 1880s and 1890s and continued to bring profound change to women's lives. Like their counterparts at the end of the nineteenth century, working women in the 1920s found growing opportunities for wage work outside the home and new places to spend their few extra pennies. The leading edge of these social and sexual transformations were in urban centers like New York and Chicago. Yet, unlike the 1890s, this latest "revolution in morals and manners" was broadcast across the country by the emerging mass media: phonograph recordings of popular music, radio shows, magazines, and Hollywood movies. These new forms of popular culture, with their emphasis on individualism and pleasure, linked young women to everything that was new and modern.

Women helped to spur the tremendous upsurge in the U.S. economy, which in the aftermath of World War I was driven by consumer goods. Cities in the Midwest served as hubs for the vast, surrounding farmlands. Cities on the West Coast benefited from the business growth from the opening of the Panama Canal in 1914. By 1926, women did their housework in the nearly sixteen million homes that had electricity and a host of new appliances for those who could afford them. The commercial application of new technologies linked homemakers to advertisers through new products and new modes of address and kept small-town girls informed of new trends in music, fashion, and dating styles taking place in booming cities. Homemakers often worked alongside radios, which by 1929 were selling to the tune of $850 million. Homemakers spent their leisure hours at movie theaters, listening to records, and reading magazines that emphasized consumption, leisure, and, for women, sexual attractiveness. Perhaps the most transformative product in the 1920s for both women and men was the automobile. For young people in particular, the automobile played an important role in the revolution in morals and manners, enabling them to get together and get away from the watchful eyes of their parents.

The consolidating culture of consumption did little to promote political activism. As the United States pulled away from the progressivism of the prewar years, women activists saw their influence fade, their numbers dwindle. The much anticipated women's "voting bloc" never materialized after the passage of women's suffrage, while the reform impulse that had prioritized the human costs of industrialization collapsed under a rising tide of conservatism and nativism. The American Immigration Act of 1924 limited immigration, slowing to a trickle the massive wave of immigration that had been going on since the 1880s. The specter of hordes of immigrant women, who worked long hours and left their children untended on street corners, appeared to threaten the very foundation of American family life. To many Americans, modern woman's primary duty remained to her children and her primary occupation, homemaking, whether she was a flapper or an immigrant.

"REVOLUTION IN MANNERS AND MORALS"

Frederick Lewis Allen's best-selling book, *Only Yesterday*, noted that "a revolution in manners and morals" was sweeping over the country in the 1920s and young women were at its center. Lampooned by editorials and celebrated as a trendsetter for her bobbed hair, makeup, short skirts, and cigarettes, the flapper became one of the pervasive images of the Jazz Age. Popularly, the flapper was portrayed as a free spirit, partying without a chaperone and dancing to hot jazz with her skirt pulled up over her knees. The flapper personified the rejection of the older generation's decorum and restraint. "I mean to do what I like . . . undeterred by convention," announced a fictional flapper in a magazine short story. Many of the changes that began with the new morality at the

Miss Ruth Bennett and Miss Sylvia Clavins captured the playful spirit of the Jazz Age as Representative Thomas McMillian of Charleston, South Carolina watched. Young women, called "flappers," dressed in fashionably short skirts, went out without chaperones to party late into the night. Dance crazes like the Charleston, with roots in black culture, swept across the country.

heterosociality When women and men socialize together, as opposed to single-sex or homosocial settings.

turn of the century extended beyond the working-class women and cultural radicals to the heartlands. The generation of young women coming of age in the 1920s embraced individualism and rejected nineteenth-century notions of collective single-sexed activism as old-fashioned. They embraced **heterosociality**—mixed sexed activities and leisure. In courtship, marriage, and family making, women of the 1920s set a new and decidedly modern course by casting off the old values, dismissed as "Victorian," of selflessness and piety for lives that were not at all like those of their mothers.

Courtship in Transition

In 1924, sociologists Robert and Helen Lynd began their landmark study of Muncie, Indiana, to examine changes in Americans' views of home, work, youth, leisure time, religious and civic beliefs, and behaviors. In *Middletown* (1929), the Lynds found that teenagers had experienced the most change over the previous twenty years. Adolescents moved in their own social world where they could spend unsupervised time together. High school was particularly important. Three-quarters of teenagers attended some high school in the 1920s, providing almost daily opportunities for boys and girls to interact. Teenagers socialized at dances, parties, and in the car where they experimented with new rituals of dating. One commentator estimated that most high school students engaged in behavior that their parents would have seen as scandalous when they were young. Teenagers regularly hugged and kissed on dates, referred to as "petting" or "necking," and a small minority went farther. Rates of premarital intercourse doubled in the 1920s, yet most women reported having restricted coitus to the partner they intended to marry. Opportunity for casual contact between the sexes set this generation apart from their parents and placed them at the leading edge of the changing morality of the 1920s.

With access to cars, to enough extra money to pay for movies and clothes, and ability to attend high school year-round, these young, white, middle-class Americans were free to create and enjoy a youthful subculture. In the rural South, however, poor African American teenagers socialized in mixed generational settings, like at church, festivals, picnics, and at work. One young man complained that there were too few places to take a girl to be alone. "Everyone has their eyes on you and especially on the girl. You can hardly get away with anything."

The heterosociality of teenagers, rich and poor, took place through a growing commodity culture, replete with sexual imagery and advice on attractiveness and romance. Columns in newspapers and women's magazines instructed female readers on the thrill of romantic love and ways to win a man's affection, while advertisement for soap, face creams, and girdles joined romantic success with beauty products. Teenage women of all ethnicities and classes used aspects of the growing consumer culture to teach themselves how to fit in to their peer groups, what to wear to be stylish, and what to say to be popular. For Hispanic immigrants, like those reading the Los Angeles newspaper *La Opinion*, consumption became a major form of assimilation. In 1926, the

WOMEN'S LIVES

GEORGIA O'KEEFFE

Georgia O'Keeffe stands as one of the twentieth century's greatest American artists and one of a few American women to win critical acclaim in a field dominated by men. O'Keeffe's representations of the landscape of the American West stood in stark contrast to the art world's attention to chaos and urban experience in the 1920s.

Georgia O'Keeffe was born in Sun Prairie, Wisconsin, in 1887, the second of seven children. O'Keeffe longed to be an artist from an early age. In 1905, she attended the Art Institute of Chicago and a year later went to study at the Art Students League of New York. She worked briefly as a commercial artist in Chicago before moving to Texas to teach. She made a handful of charcoal drawings, which she sent to a friend in New York. The friend, Anna Pollitzer, showed them to Alfred Steiglitz, a photographer and gallery owner. Moved by the work, he asked Pollitzer without O'Keeffe's consent if he could show them; and without O'Keeffe's knowledge, she had her first exhibition in 1916 at Steiglitz's 291 Gallery. Within two years, Steiglitz had convinced O'Keeffe to move to New York and devote all of her time to painting. From 1923 until his death in 1946, Stieglitz promoted O'Keeffe and her work, organizing annual exhibitions of her art at The Anderson Galleries (1923–1925), The Intimate Gallery (1925–1929), and An American Place (1929–1946). As early as the mid-1920s, when O'Keeffe first began painting large-scale close-up depictions of flowers, which are among her best-known pictures, she had become recognized as one of America's most important and successful artists. In 1924, the two were married, beginning one of the most fruitful and well-known collaborations of the modernist era. In 1929, O'Keeffe took a

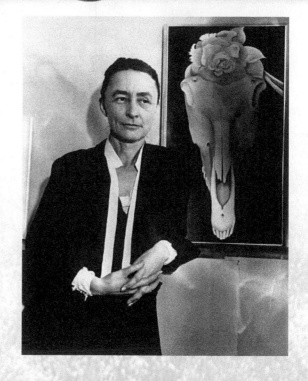

vacation to Taos, New Mexico, that changed the course of her life and work. There, she fell in love with the open skies and sun-drenched landscape. O'Keeffe returned every summer to travel and to paint. When Steiglitz died in 1946, O'Keeffe moved to Taos permanently where she painted New Mexico landscapes. The rich texture of the clouds and sky were similar to her earlier, more sensuous representations of flowers. O'Keeffe continued to work in oil until the mid-1970s, when failing eyesight forced her to abandon painting. Although she continued working in pencil and watercolor until 1982, she also produced objects in clay until her health failed in 1984. She died two years later at the age of ninety-eight. ■

FIGURE 16-1   ANNUAL IMMIGRATION TO THE US, 1860–1930.

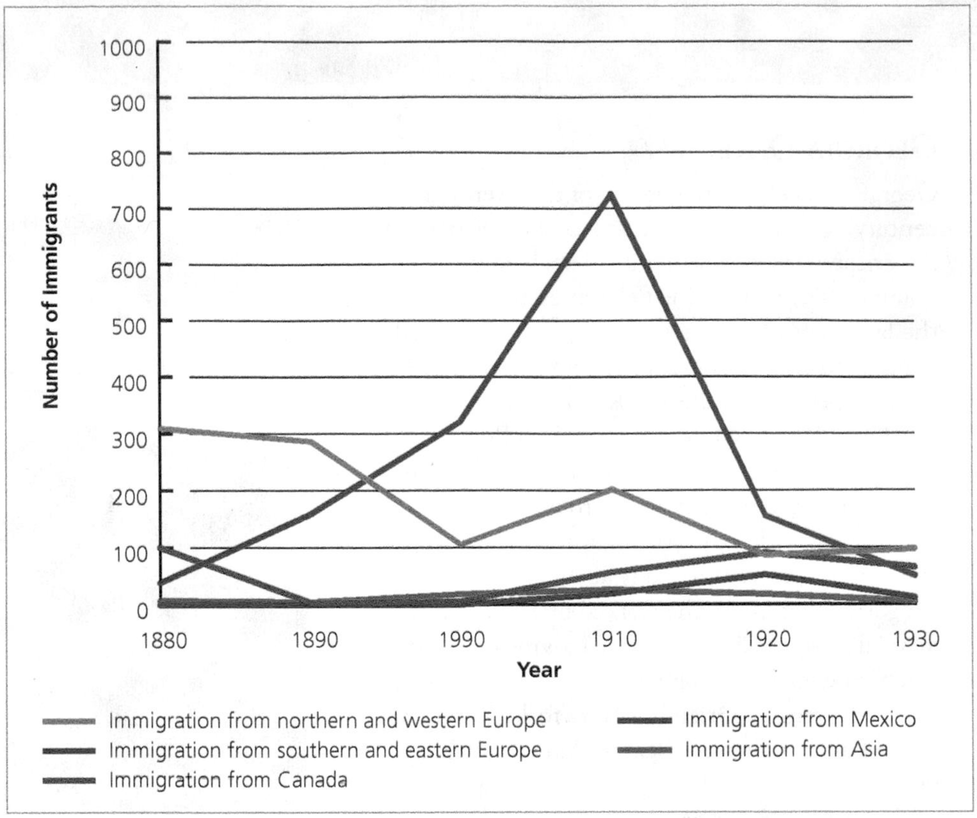

Immigration changed the composition of the American population as newcomers from Southern and Eastern Europe poured into the country looking to start a new life.

paper regularly ran advertisements for clothes and makeup, as well as offering readers tips on teenage dating and advice through quizzes like "How do you kiss?"

Immigrant daughters, like their white counterparts, regularly went to movies and dances, followed fashion trends, attended high school, and participated in school activities. The earlier generation of immigrant daughters who evaded parents and social workers to attend nickelodeons and dance halls pioneered public and urban leisure that by the 1920s had become commonplace. Yet, immigrant women participated in American popular culture against a backdrop of their own community's values, carefully navigating two cultures in an effort to enjoy the freedoms of the new morality while preserving their heritage. In cities such as Los Angeles and San Antonio, where the Mexican population nearly doubled in the 1920s, teenagers regularly clashed with their parents. One Mexican American teenager complained that her mother dressed her as if she were a nun and insisted her daughter have "no makeup, no cream, no nothing."

Worried parents who sought to protect their daughters from dangerous behaviors and dangerous boys found it almost impossible to separate dating from the other aspects of teenage life. Attending public school put new ideas in the minds of teenagers that could lead them to question their family's values. One Chinese teenager in 1924 explained, " My parents always tell me that a girl should be quiet, obedient, and re-

WOMEN'S VOICES

"YOUNG WOMEN SEEK ADVICE ABOUT PETTING"

Not all young women felt comfortable with the "revolution in morals and manners." Some critics denounced women's interest in kissing and dating as immoral, while others found it confusing. In these letters to a newspaper advice column, young women talk about their struggles to navigate the changing social relations in the 1920s and highlight the clash between parents' and peer groups' ideas about a woman's proper behavior.

I've had a feeling that I never intended going out with everyone who cared to take me out, or I never wanted to be kissed by anyone except the one I would some day marry. . . . When I entered high school the rest of my girl friends went out with different boys, but I refused. . . . Now in the office the girls are the same as the ones I knew in high school. They do not think it is wrong to smoke and pet. I myself would never think of doing either, but I want you to understand that I would not look down on those girls, for all they do is their own personal affair.

Sometimes I get the blues so badly that if anyone were there I would do what the rest of my friends do, but, thank goodness, there is something that seems to hold me back. . . . Am I doing right, or have I been in a trance for twenty-one years?

I am not popular. Is it because I won't neck and pet? When the boys ask me for dates I very seldom go, but if I do it ends up by the person I am with being slapped. Then we don't speak for months at a time. I have told these boys again and again I don't care to be necked. Still they insist on having the same thing over every time we go out. The crowd I go with all say I am a "flat tire" because I won't neck. . . . Please tell me what to do.

I should like to meet some of these girls who say how popular they are, but they don't smoke or drink. How they do it is beyond me. I am seventeen and have been going with boys since I was thirteen. I am considered attractive, yet I have to smoke, drink, etc., to secure dates. The boys I go with go to college, and I have yet to find one who does not want a girl to pet the first time he meets her. They take you to the fraternity houses, when we all know it isn't proper. Still the girls go rather than be called poor sports. Many of the boys have apartments. . . . The first thing they do is call up the bootlegger and get gin, etc., to make highballs then put the radio on and dance. Of course petting is a side line to all this. . . . Believe me after you have finished drinking you aren't fit to go home to your parents. But what are we going to do if we want to have a good time? Certainly, if you don't have a good time when you are young you won't get it when you get older.

Which is the better way, I ask you, to behave and stay home or to misbehave and have a great time? . . .

Source: *From Phyllis Blanchard and Carlyn Manasses,* New Girls for Old *(New York: Macaulay Co., 1930), 62–63.*

Questions

1. What do these letters tell us about young women's experience of dating in the 1920s?

2. What are the areas of conflict between parents and peer groups, between the old and the new morality?

spectful to all who are senior to you. But at school, I am told to ask questions and even disagree with teachers. I don't know whom I should listen to." Traditional Chinese families limited their daughters' exposure to American culture by keeping their daughters at home or sending them to work in Chinese homes or businesses to bring in additional income while their brothers attended school (see chapter 12). But with an abundant consumer culture advertising the thrill of falling in love and the melting pot of public high schools bringing teenagers together, parents had more and more difficulty keeping teenagers within traditional ethnic enclaves.

companionate marriage A new style of marriage that emphasized companionship and compatability between spouses, as well as sex education, birth control, and easier access to divorce.

The Companionate Marriage

Marriage experts took note of the "revolution of manners and morals" sweeping over the country. The **companionate marriage**, as it became known, emphasized companionship, compatibility, and mutuality between husband and wife. It called for greater equality between the sexes, easier divorce laws for childless couples, and less formality between partners. According to sociologists, journalists, and educators, young women expected marriage to provide both economic security and sexual satisfaction. In the words of anthropologist Elsie Clews Parson, women demanded "more of marriage than in the days when they had little to expect but marriage."

The companionate marriage rested on a growing ethos of sexual liberalization that reached more and more Americans in the 1920s. Pre–World War I writings of Sigmund Freud, Ellen Key, and Havelock Ellis explored the place of sexuality in men's and women's psychological development and sense of identity (see chapter 15). By the 1920s, their influence extended beyond small groups of radicals and bohemians to doctors, journalists, and marriage counselors and became part of the popular culture. More than two hundred books on Freud's theories appeared in print in the 1920s alone, giving Americans ample opportunity to grow familiar with terms such as *libido, repression, id,* and *ego.* Despite complexity and originality of Freud's theories, popularizers in the United States altered his message into one that simply promoted the healthiness of sexual expression for men and women. Popular magazines bulged with articles on modern marriage, concluding that the distinguishing factors of modern marriage were romantic love and sexual satisfaction.

Experts, however, were not leading the transformation in marriage and sexuality experienced by ordinary women. Rather, they were taking note of a longer change in the sexual views and behavior of women, that had been going on for decades. Social scientist Katherine Bement Davis's pioneering sex survey, "The Sex Lives of Normal Married Women," published in 1929, documented the changes in sexual behavior and attitudes, particularly for young middle-class women, that had occurred since the nineteenth century. Based on lengthy questionnaires completed by single

A new generation of marriage experts published advice in women's magazines like Good Housekeeping *in the 1920s. A new style of marriage that emphasized compatibility between husband and wife and easier divorce laws became popular. The companionate marriage, with its promise of greater equality for women, displaced older ideals of male authority at home.*

and married white women, Davis's survey covered birth control practices, the frequency of intercourse, and factors related to happiness in marriage for women coming of age during and after World War I. She found that 74 percent of her respondents practiced some form of contraception, 40 percent reported masturbating during childhood and adolescence, and 30 percent judged their sexual desires to be as strong as those of their partners. Sex researcher Alfred Kinsey's 1953 report on female sexuality concurred with Davis that women born after 1900 had engaged in twice as much premarital sex as the previous generation. But not all women Davis surveyed were "sex enthusiasts." Many felt confusion and guilt about sexual desires. Four-fifths of those she surveyed felt that premarital sexuality was not acceptable for men or women. Most felt that sexuality ought to be confined to marriage. A quarter of the women reported feeling "repelled" by conjugal relations. Davis concluded that a combination of sex education, physical attraction, and pleasurable sex made for the happiest marriages.

While sexual satisfaction figured more prominently in modern ideas of marriage, marriage itself remained at the center of debates about morality in the 1920s. Colorado judge Ben Lindsey, in his popular 1927 book *Companionate Marriage*, unleashed a storm of controversy when he called for more liberal divorce laws. Lindsey made a name for himself as a Progressive-Era champion of the new juvenile court system. In the mid-1920s, he began to promote his views on marriage through radio addresses, magazine articles, books, and public lectures. He argued that strengthening the institution of marriage was the only way to contain the potentially unruly sexual immorality of the new generation. He called for sex education, greater availability of contraception, and, for childless couples, access to easy divorce. Critics, including religious leaders, attacked Lindsey as a "bolshevic" for his "anti-Christian" ideals. They argued that marriage and civilization were deeply connected and loosening the bonds between husband and wife ultimately threatened the nation. Episcopal bishop William Manning of New York explained, "The family is the most fundamental institution of human life. Civilization depends on the sanctity of the home. The life of our country depends upon this."

Lindsey joined a chorus of voices addressing the growing divorce rate. Despite the new attention to equality within marriage, many Americans felt unease at the new emphasis placed on female sexuality. Traditional marriage, with its idealized vision of gender stability, in which men and women took very clearly defined positions in the family and in the sexual order, remained appealing to many Americans. The escalating divorce rate that had so troubled the Progressive generation continued to rise in the 1920s. In 1922, there were 131 divorces for each one thousand marriages. By 1928, that number had risen to 166. In the 1890s, neglect and failure to provide had been the reasons most frequently given for divorce. But in the 1920s, experts pointed to "the mood of the age," with its "yeasty unrest" as being the root cause. A 1923 *Atlantic* article blamed the speedup of modern life, the higher cost of living, and the over-insistence of women on their rights for driving couples to divorce. Writer Dorothy Dix more sympathetically explained that "people are demanding more of life than they used to. . . . Now . . . we see that no good purpose is achieved by keeping two people together who have come to hate each other." A generation divide opened up between mothers who viewed divorce as unthinkable and daughters who viewed it as unremarkable. A 1924 article in *Woman's Home Companion* concluded that "the age believes in divorce, thinks reticence old-fashioned and false, and holds that getting married is 'only getting married.'" Ironically, it was precisely the concern that the sanctity of marriage was being lost under the new morality that motivated Lindsey and others to update it.

Invention of the Lesbian Threat

As Freudianism entered the popular culture, new aspersions were cast on relationships between women that previously had been seen as unremarkable: female friendships, lifelong partnerships or Boston marriages, and spinsterhood. Psychologists and educators cast female friendships that had once been seen as an ordinary part of girlhood as potential obstacles to marriage and heterosexuality. Women who "resisted" romantic or sexual advances of men were accused of being neurotic at best, or lesbian at worst.

By the 1920s, the term "lesbian" began to circulate alongside the late nineteenth-century term *invert*. This shift in terminology helped to make same-sex love between women more visible. The act of naming contributed to the formation of a new "type" of person and a new way of life: the mannish woman who refused to be economically dependent on men and who willingly desired sexual and emotional partnerships with other women. British author Radcliffe Hall, herself a wealthy mannish lesbian, published *The Well of Loneliness* in 1926, a semiautobiographical novel that detailed the life of an invert, Stephen, who comes to see and express the terrible sense of isolation sexual minorities like herself faced in an intolerant society. The novel was banned in Britain and was released in the United States after a lengthy court battle. Once in print, *The Well of Loneliness* became the most-read lesbian novel in the English language.

Critics singled out female-only institutions such as settlement houses, female academies, and women's colleges as breeding grounds for **sexual inversion**, an early term for same-sex desire. Commentators worried that sexual deviance could spread like a germ among young and impressionable women through the overpowering attentions of disordered teachers or residents. In one novel, *Dance on the Tortoise* published in 1930, a character described the pathology rampant at her same-sex school: "These bunches of women living together, falling in love with each other because they haven't any one else to fall in love with! It's obscene! Take me away!"

The language of sexual deviance also became useful to antifeminists who equated feminism with pathology. Both feminists and lesbians threatened to disrupt the traditional relations between the sexes. Critics of feminism cast feminists as sexually perverse women who desired to usurp men and their roles within the family and society. By casting feminism as a sexual disorder and catching a range of female relationships in its wake, antifeminists narrowed ideas about female sexual and psychological health. They also helped to dismantle the separate and female-dominated spaces where women had once freely gathered, untouched by rumors of sexual scandal.

As ideas about homosexuality and deviance became more widespread, communities of sexual minorities that had existed in ports and urban centers since the eighteenth century continued to grow. Neighborhoods in major urban centers, centered in theater districts, cabarets, speakeasies, and brothels, served as gathering places for women seeking sex with other women. As more women could sustain themselves economically without the support of husbands or family, women began to participate in urban gay life. Public curiosity about homosexuality drew spectators to New York's African American neighborhood of Harlem to witness spectacular drag balls held in the Hotel Astor and the huge Madison Square Garden in the 1920s and 1930s. Officially sanctioned by police and city officials, public drag balls displayed women dressed

sexual inversion An early sexological term for same-sex desire.

as men dancing with women, men dressed as women dancing with men, and a parade of well-dressed men in costume. One Broadway newspaper of the 1920s declared "6000 Crowd Huge Hall as Queer Men and Women Dance."

The sexual modernity of the 1920s afforded women a greater range of sociability and forms of identity. For teenage women, a culture of consumption oriented toward heterosexual romance aided them in their movement away from their parents' traditionalism. For women who desired emotional and sexual romance with women, the 1920s' emphasis on female sexual expression brought both pleasures and dangers. More opportunities for social gatherings and sexual self-knowledge went hand in hand with greater surveillance by doctors, educators, and police.

WOMEN AND WORK

Many of the era's commentators suggested that changes in women's work fueled the "revolution in morals and manners" that characterized the Jazz Age. More women— and more married women—worked for wages. As the economy shifted from production to consumption, new **pink-collar jobs**, done in offices not factories, opened up for young white women. Banks, real estate, insurance offices, publishing houses, and trade and transportation industries required an army of clerks to handle the mountains of paperwork. By 1930, women filled over 52 percent of these clerical positions. A fresh supply of young high-school-educated women from the middle and working classes flooded into offices, newly equipped with typewriters, telephones, and dictating and adding machines. A fascination with the "business woman" in popular culture gave an overlay of glamour to the position of secretary and typist. However, not all women could find work in the nation's offices. The majority of pink-collar jobs remained reserved for white and native-born women. While African American or newly immigrated whites made up 57 percent of all employed women, both groups found the only work open to them was in domestic service or in the garment industry as factory operatives. Job segregation based on race persisted, testifying to all that had not changed in the boom years of the 1920s.

pink-collar job A type of employment traditionally held by women, especially relatively low-paying office work.

Married Women Workers

"The great woman question of to-day," wrote journalist and feminist Crystal Eastman in 1927, is "how to reconcile a woman's natural desire for love and home and children with her equally natural desire for work of her own for which she is paid." Ninteenth-century advocates of women's "right to labor" had understood work as an alternative to marriage, a view born out of the reality that most professional women did not marry and that working women typically left paid work shortly after marrying. By the 1920s, however, American women no longer viewed work and home as mutually exclusive domains. Whereas the typical female worker in 1900 had been single and under twenty-five years of age, by 1930, she was over thirty and married. Married women entered the workforce at five times the rate of other women in the 1920s and constituted 40 percent of the female workforce. One-third of these new workers had children under the age of thirteen.

Women who chose to work for wages outside the home did so for many reasons including economic need, professional aspiration, and what sociologists Robert and Helen Lynd described as a "skyrocketing psychological standard of living." Married women's work enabled some families to meet their basic needs. For others, extra wages enabled families to purchase an array of new consumer products, from fans and refrigerators to silk stockings and automobiles. For other women, social scientist Lorine Pruette summed up the relationship between modernity, consumption, and women's wages in the 1920s when she observed, "As our pleasure philosophy takes deeper hold, as the demand for luxuries, artificially stimulated by advertising, mounts giddily higher, there is no help for it—the women have to go to work . . . the manufacturers need the women as consumers, need the two-wage family and its demands to keep the factories going." Married women increasingly found themselves in the unique position as both wageworker and primary consumer.

Women's role as the family shopper, so important to the growth of new industries, worked against them as they sought work. Ideas about gender and women's proper role in the family limited the kinds of work available to women as well as the wages they earned. Employers believed that women worked for "pin money," or extra money for frivolous expenses, or luxury items that helped to justify the low pay women received relative to men. Women workers earned between 52 and 55 percent of what men earned by being restricted to unskilled jobs classified as "women's work." Racial prejudice also shaped the jobs available to women. While African American or newly immigrated whites made up 57 percent of all employed women, both groups found the only work open to them was in domestic service or in the garment industry as factory operatives. Native-born whites, on the other hand, found work that was cleaner and less physically demanding such as clerical and sales work.

Pink-Collar Workers

Women in the 1920s found new work in the rapidly growing service sector of the economy. The number of service and secretarial jobs expanded rapidly in the 1920s, spurred on by new communication and business technologies. Technological innovations introduced in the late nineteenth century, such as the typewriter, the telephone, and dictating and adding machines, had become commonplace to the office of the 1920s and continued to change the nature and pace of work. Most of the new occupations in the transformed clerical sector were designed for the female employee who had previously been a manufacturing worker. Unlike her counterpart at the turn of the century, the pink-collar worker of the 1920s had a high school diploma and often had taken additional commercial courses. Employers hired typists, stenographers, and office machine operators as they graduated from high school,

Engrained ideas about the inherent skills of women shaped understandings of both office work and office workers. Employers viewed office work as particularly suitable for women, explaining that women could more easily adjust to the routines of the office. Employers saw young women in particular as ideal clerks for what they understood as young women's careful attention to details, their nimble and dexterous fingers, and willing deference to male authority. Employers assumed that women lacked ambition because they worked only until they could marry and raise a family, a belief that neatly folded into the built-in limits of clerking and secretarial work. One account published in the magazine *Delineator* captured the fine line women walked while working in the "male" world of business: "A girl in an office must have distinction without being distinguishable, she must have brains that are disciplined . . . she must have enough force of character to lead a double life and not let its halves interfere with each other; be

The growth of secretarial work offered young white women new employment opportunities in the 1920s. Pink-collar work was cleaner and safer than factory work, and had an overlay of glamour to it. New machines, like this addressograph used by the woman on the left, streamlined tasks and made offices more efficient.

feminine enough to make the man . . . love her and want to marry her, and yet masculine enough to be impersonal and concentrate on what she's doing."

Most women viewed pink-collar work as a step up in status, if not as an increase in the amount of money they earned. Employers expected women to dress in an attractive and feminine manner, a requirement that meant spending more money on clothes. Work in offices often included niceties like recreational lounges for breaks, free meals, medical services, and loans. Despite such perks, pink-collar workers were not paid a wage sufficient enough to support a family. One telephone operator summed up the problem of pink-collar work when she noted that "most of us who retain any sense of independence or self-respect" would prefer salaries sufficient enough for [us] to pay for [our] own lunch and medical expenses. The Women's Bureau reported that the median weekly earnings of women were $13.80, a figure that fell well below the estimates of $20 minimum income needed for city workers.

Pink-collar workers earned only a bit more than did factory operatives and had similarly dead-end careers for the majority of women who did it. Despite the dead-end nature of the work, pink-collar work was clean, safe, and steady and women flocked to it. By 1930, two million women worked in offices and retail sales, outnumbering women in domestic service, teaching, and factory jobs. One-third of these workers were married.

Budget Estimates for a Single Woman Worker by the Ohio Council of Women in Industry, 1925

Boarding and lodging	$5.50
Clothing	$4.50
Laundry	$.75
Carfares	$1.00
Doctors and dentists	$0.38
Church	$0.13
Newspapers	$0.12
Vacation	$0.37
Recreation	$1.50
Savings for reserve	$1.50
Incidentals	$0.75
Organization dues	$0.13
Insurance	$0.37
Self-improvement	$0.25
Total	**$17.25**

Professional Workers

While pink-collar workers labored under the assumption that they were only temporary workers who lacked ambition, college-educated women made inroads into the professions in historic numbers. The peak of the trend of women's ascendancy into the professions, begun in the late nineteenth century, was reached during the 1920s. In the 1920s, women professionals doubled in number. Three-quarters of professional women worked in areas opened up by Progressive-Era reformers, such as social work, medicine, academics, and law. The proportion of doctorates earned by women rose from 10 percent in 1910 to 15 percent in 1930, with women earning one-third of all graduate degrees and making up 30 percent of the nation's college and university faculties. This was a high-water mark that was not reached again until the 1970s. Academic women entered departments of psychology, social science, behavioral science, and anthropology and made important contributions to the study of sex differences, personality development, and intelligence.

Social work, teaching, and nursing remained professional strongholds for women. Female social workers made up 62 percent of the field at the end of the decade. Settlement houses, a haven for college-educated female reformers like Jane Addams and Florence Kelley at the turn of the century, expanded their staffs in the 1920s and consolidated their place in municipal and state public health agencies. Boston's twenty-one settlements alone employed over 150 college-educated women. The field was bolstered by a growing emphasis on graduate training, which included the casework method and resulted in a stronger sense of professional identity. Likewise, women's hold over teaching reached a historic high of 86 percent, or more than eight hundred thousand female teachers, at the beginning of the 1930s. The percentage of female nurses held steady at 96 percent. Salaries for these women-dominated fields were low, making it difficult for women to support themselves or their families on their earnings.

In the field of business, women also made gains. By the end of the decade, a number of women held managerial positions. In Boston, for example, personnel managers, industrial nurses, line forewomen, and other female managers worked in some of the city's largest companies, such as Schrafft Candy, Gillette Razor, Carter's Ink, Winchester Laundry, and dozens of other local businesses. More than sixty of these female industrial "executives," as they called themselves, met as the Boston Forewomen's Council to discuss new management techniques and share strategies for enhancing their new role in the corporate world.

Black women faced unique circumstances in the 1920s as they entered professional occupations. In Boston, African American businesswomen who owned laundries, dress shops, beauty parlors, and groceries formed their own trade associations and social clubs while others served as officers in the Boston Trade Association, the black equivalent of the white-controlled Chamber of Commerce. Such organizations proved to be essential for their members as they weathered economic downturns, providing much needed capital in years when banks routinely refused to extend credit to women. Entering managerial positions or owning a business, however, was no guarantee of equal treatment or equal opportunities. One African American woman qualified thirty-five times for a civil service appointment without being assigned a position. The **National Urban League**, an organization founded in 1910 to improve housing, medical care, and work conditions for African Americans, worked to open managerial opportunities for black women in department stores and secretarial work but met with limited success.

National Urban League A nonpartisan civil rights organization formed to give support to newly arrived migrants from the South to northern cities.

While black professional women constituted a mere 4 percent of all working married women in the 1920s, they became the focus of an anxious discourse on the effects of work on their domestic and community responsibilities. Historically, middle-class African Americans put a premium on women's homemaking duties as a way to resist racist beliefs that cast aspersions on the health and respectability of black families. Black female professionals, who also embraced modern notions of companionate marriage and women's rights, struggled against critics who linked racial uplift to female domesticity and motherhood on the one hand and male authority on the other. Despite such resistance, black women in the 1920s made opportunities for themselves. One such person was Sarah Breedlove, or Madame C. J. Walker, a wealthy African American business woman. By 1917, she had built her business into the largest black-owned company in the country. Walker took great pride that her company afforded a profitable alternative to domestic service for the thousands of black women who worked as commissioned agents for her products. Her agents could earn from five to fifteen dollars a day, in an era when unskilled white laborers were making about eleven dollars a week.

Businesswoman Madam C. J. Walker offered beauty products for African American women at a time when most companies ignored them. The Walker System, which included a broad offering of cosmetics, licensed Walker Agents, and Walker Schools, and offered meaningful employment to thousands of Black women. She built her business into the largest black owned company in the country, with over 3,000 people at its peak.

BEYOND SUFFRAGE

For women active in the suffrage movement, the ratification of the Nineteenth Amendment on August 18, 1920, was a historic moment, long awaited and much anticipated. Yet, the powerful coalition of groups and organizations that had achieved suffrage, each with their different goals for wanting the vote, quickly fragmented upon its passage (see chapter 15). According to seasoned reformer Frances Kellor, "The American woman's movement . . . is splintered into a hundred

fragments under as many warring leaders." Kellor's use of the singular "woman's" movement was precisely what the suffrage victory had destroyed. Throughout the 1920s,
women followed a number of paths toward social reform and activism, many of which
were diametrically opposed to one another. For a younger generation of activists, "self"
or individual consciousness challenged the dominance of "sex" or group consciousness.
Only for the seasoned activists of Progressive-Era fame did maternalism, activism
based on women's roles as mothers, continue to shape their political goals.

Feminist—New Style

With the growth of more commercial places to mingle with men and with the popularity of more daring dress styles (see chapter 14), modern women integrated their public and private identities in ways that demanded a change in feminism. According to
journalist Dorothy Bromley, writing "Feminist—New Style" for *Harpers' Magazine* in
1927, young women had entered a new age of equality. No longer having to choose between personal and professional fulfillment, as had their foremothers, women of the
1920s could look forward to enjoying satisfying work and economic independence, as
well as a life with children and family. Young women frequently characterized former
suffragists and women reformers as overly antagonistic toward men. With their "old-
style" emphasis on building separate institutions from men, suffragists had exacerbated
problems between the sexes. "'Feminism,'" wrote Bromley, "suggests either the old
school of fighting feminists who wore flat heels and had very little feminine charm, or
the current species who antagonize men with their constant clamor about maiden
names, equal rights, women's place in the world and many other causes . . . *ad infinitum*." For this generation, separatism from men was no longer a strategy for political
mobilization. Rather, it was a sign of backward thinking.

For women in their twenties and thirties who did not identify themselves as suffragists, reformers, or activists, the new style of feminism in the 1920s combined a popular mix of antifeminism, a recognition of a de-escalation in women's formal political
activism, and a new attention to heterosociality. The suffrage victory represented more
than the right to vote. It represented women's right to set their own course as individuals. For some of the young women in Bromley's cohort, this meant casting off a life
narrowly scripted by old-fashioned views of women's duty to family or to reform. Bromley explained that a modern American woman knows that it is "her twentieth-century
birthright to emerge from a creature of instinct into a full-fledged individual who is capable of molding her own life. And in this respect she holds that she is becoming man's
equal."

The League of Women Voters

"Feminist—New Style" emphasized women as individuals, free to express themselves
as they wished. The language of individual over group rights dismantled the sense of
solidarity forged during the suffrage campaign, but it did not end women's political activism. The umbrella issue that suffrage had been for a loose coalition of women disappeared and, with it, some of the political energy of those who had participated in its
passage. But for other activist women, long-standing participants in reform, the 1920s
represented the new age of political equality and political involvement for women.

One of the key questions facing politically minded women was what organization to be a part of. Activist women debated among themselves about the merits of

WOMEN'S VOICES

"FEMINIST—NEW STYLE"

Journalist Dorothy Dunbar Bromley (1897–1986) was among a cohort of young women who were more than ready to cast off what they felt were the restrictive preoccupations of an older generation of career suffragists. According to Bromley, "feminist—old style" wore flat heels, disliked men, and chose work over love. "Feminist—new style" enjoyed fashion, looking attractive, and, most importantly, men. Bromley was born on a farm in Ottawa, Illinois, and graduated from Northwestern University. Her first marriage ended in divorce. She remarried and worked as the editor of the women's activities page and wrote a regular column for the New York Herald Tribune. *In this piece, published in 1926, Bromley set out a new vision of feminism that she crafted especially for modern women.*

"Feminism" has become a term of opprobrium to the modern young woman. For the word suggests either the old school of fighting feminists who wore flat heels and had very little feminine charm, or the current species who antagonize men with their constant clamor about maiden names, equal rights, woman's place in the world, and many another cause . . . ad infinitum. Indeed, if a blundering male assumes that a young woman is a feminist simply because she happens to have a job or a profession of her own, she will be highly—and quite justifiably insulted: for the word evokes the antithesis of what she flatters herself to be. Yet she and her kind can hardly be dubbed "old-fashioned" women. . . .

What of the constantly increasing group of young women in their twenties and thirties who are the truly modern ones, those who admit that a full life calls for marriage and children as well as a career? . . . We beg leave to enunciate the tenets of the modern woman's credo. Let us call her "Feminist—New Style."

In brief, Feminist—New Style reasons that if she is economically independent, and if she

has, to boot, a vital interest in some work of her own she will have given as few hostages to Fate as it is humanly possible to give. Love may die, and children may grow up, but one's work goes on forever.

She will not, however, live for her job alone, for she considers that a woman who talks and thinks only shop has just as narrow a horizon as the housewife who talks and thinks only husband and children—perhaps more so, for the latter may have a deeper understanding of human nature. She will therefore refuse to give up all of her personal interests, year in and year out, for the sake of her work. In this respect she no doubt will fall short of the masculine idea of commercial success, for the simple reason that she has never felt the economic compulsion which drives men on to build up fortunes for the sake of their growing families.

Yet she is not one of the many women who look upon their jobs as tolerable meal-tickets or as interesting pastimes to be dropped whenever they may wish. On the contrary, she takes great pride in becoming a vital factor in whatever enterprise she has chosen, and she therefore expects to work long hours when the occasion demands.

But rather than make the mistake that some women do of domesticating their jobs, i.e., burying all of their affections and interests in them, or the mistake that many men make of milking their youth dry for the sake of building up a fortune to be spent in a fatigued middle-age, she will proceed on the principle that a person of intelligence and energy can attain a fair amount of success—by the very virtue of living a well-balanced life, as well as by working with concentration.

Nor has she become hostile to the other sex in the course of her struggle to orient herself. On

(continued)

the contrary, she frankly likes men and is grateful to more than a few for the encouragement and help they have given her.

Source: Dorothy Dunbar-Bromley, *"Feminist—New Style."* Harper's, October 1927

Questions

1. What makes the "Feminist—New Style" distinctive from her foremothers?

2. How does Dunbar understand modern women's obligations to men, marriage, and family?

Rollin Kirby's political cartoon captured the sense of accomplishment many women felt at the passage of the 19th Amendment granting women the right to vote in 1920. After a 72 year-long effort, suffragists succeeding in winning broad support for their cause.

maintaining women's political groups or joining the Democratic and Republican parties. Some older women, raised on the view that women were nonpartisan and ought to stay out of the fray of the rough-and-tumble world of backroom politics, were uncomfortable with the idea of joining the major political parties, fearing it would undermine the special perspective of women that the political system sorely needed. Yet others eagerly jumped into parties politics, like former suffragist Molly Dewson who became a Democratic Party activist, while former antisuffragist Elizabeth Lowell Putnam chose the Republican Party. Others formed new women's organizations. Some followed Alice Paul into the National Woman's Party (NWP), while others followed Maud Wood Park into the newly formed League of Women Voters (LWV). Park, who had served in the National American Women's Suffrage Association (NAWSA), became the first president of the League, the all-white successor organization to the NAWSA, in 1921. The League devoted itself to providing a nonpartisan education that would help women participate who had never been interested in politics. Toward this end, the LWV encouraged women to join political parties and to take on leadership roles in them. Along with the Women's Joint Congressional Committee, a lobbying group made up of fourteen women's organizations, and the Women's Bureau, the LWV continued the maternalist orientation of many of its leaders, lobbied in support of laws that protected women and children, and promoted legislation for worker health and safety. In many ways, the League constituted the attitudes and ongoing activism of the reform-minded mainstream of the suffrage movement.

In the immediate wake of the passage of suffrage, Democrats and Republicans eagerly courted women's vote and incorporated women's issues into their platforms.

Women made inroads into holding offices, particularly on the local and state level, where their devotion to causes such as education and child safety made them particularly well suited to government. Some women took low-level positions in party organizations, and seven women had seats in Congress in 1928. Female officeholders were both empowered and restricted by their close association with "women's issues." Carrie Chapman Catt, the self-described "old suffragist," wrote in 1928 that political equality could not be legislated by amendments, important as they may be. Men, she wrote, "are reconciled, on the whole, to women voters, but not to women in politics."

If men were not reconciled to having women in politics, then neither were the majority of women. The LWV's attempts to get women to vote did not result in the high turnouts they had hoped for to sustain the attention of the two political parties. Only one-third of women voted in the 1920 presidential elections. The much-talked-about "women's bloc" that critics and supporters imagined to be potentially strong enough to elect Progressive candidates and enact Progressive reforms never materialized. Even the LWV's own ranks, which were one-tenth the size of the suffrage organization that preceded it, testified to the declining cohesion of the woman's movement.

The Equal Rights Amendment

In contrast to the nonpartisan efforts of the League of Women Voters, the National Women's Party (NWP), with its eight thousand members, turned its sights on passage of another federal amendment, the **Equal Rights Amendment** (ERA). For Alice Paul, the ERA promised to establish equality between the sexes by ending all legal barriers faced by women on account of sex. Using the language that echoed the 1848 Seneca Falls Declaration of Sentiments, the proposed amendment read: "Equality of rights under the law shall not be denied or abridged by the United States or by any State on account of sex." Feminist Crystal Eastman enthusiastically wrote that the ERA would "sweep out of every dusty court-room, . . . erase from every judge's mind that centuries-old precedent as to women's inferiority and dependence . . . and substitute it at one blow the simple new precedent of equality." The cornerstone of the ERA was full legal equality between the sexes. For ERA supporters, any law that affirmed women's difference from men was seen as an obstacle to women's freedom. According to Paul, "enacting labor laws along sex lines is erecting another handicap for women." With this, she exposed the fundamental fault line dividing political women in the 1920s: women's equality as established by the ERA stood in stark contrast to women's difference from men established in protective legislation.

The "clean sweep" proposed by Eastman, Paul, and others immediately raised the ire of women reformers who had worked for decades to enact protective legislation for women. The success of the protective legislation enacted during the Progressive Era rested on the legal establishment of women's biological difference from men and the government's interest in women's potential motherhood. Such workplace legislation required the state to limit the hours and type of work women could do as a way to ensure a woman's potential for a healthy pregnancy. For these reformers, the ERA represented a threat to all the sex-based protections for women workers they had worked for, undermining their hopes for women's equality based on their difference from men. Mary Anderson, director of the Women's Bureau, a stronghold of protective legislation supporters, called the ERA a "slogan for the insane" introduced by elite women who had little understanding of the lives of working women. Florence Kelley, of the

Equal Rights Amendment (ERA) A proposed constitutional amendment outlawing discrimination "on account of sex.

National Consumers' League, announced that women would always require laws that were "different than those needed by men" because women "cannot be made men" by simply changing the Constitution.

Coming as it did on the heels of the suffrage victory, the proposed ERA played a crucial role in the political atmosphere of the 1920s. While few Americans supported it, the ERA cast a long shadow over legislative struggles related to women and children. The larger debate over how best to promote women's equality went on, even as Congress rejected the proposed amendment in 1923.

The Sheppard-Towner Act

In the heady days in the wake of suffrage, advocates of protective legislation hoped to use women's newfound political clout to direct federal initiatives for special protections for women and children. The Sheppard-Towner Maternity and Infancy Protection Act of 1921 represented the high-water mark for protective legislation activists. Passed when Congress was most eager to curry the favor of women voters, the Sheppard-Towner Act provided matching federal funds to states to provide health services to women and children. The Act was overseen by the Women's Bureau, which established prenatal and child health centers and paid for nurses to visit new mothers at home. The Act seemed to portend the power of women's new presence in the political arena.

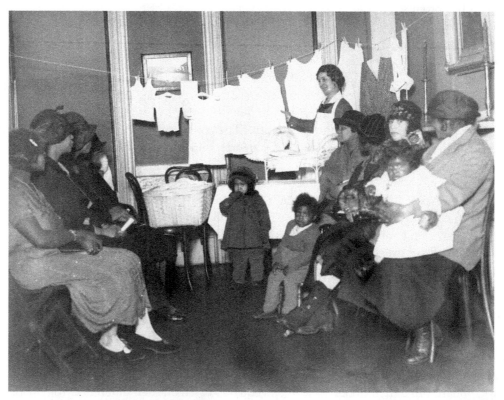

As mothers, women carried the responsibility of caring for the health of their families. Nurses, like this one from the Visiting Nurse Association of Boston in 1925, went to community centers, schools and settlement houses to teach women about sanitation, infant health, and nutrition.

The Sheppard-Towner Act enjoyed the support of a number of women's groups for the tangible help it offered to working women and their children. It brought to a national level many of the local programs women reformers had established in urban centers. It was the first bill that the newly established League of Women Voters supported. It also enjoyed the support of the General Federation of Women's Clubs (GFWC), an organization devoted to improving the work conditions of women and children; the National Consumer League (NCL), headed by political veteran Florence Kelley, that worked toward establishing minimum wage laws; and the Women's Trade Union League (WTUL). For these activists, the Sheppard-Towner Act represented a viable model for using the resources of the federal government to bring improvement to the daily lives of working Americans.

Despite the tremendous effort put forth by women's social welfare activists, a series of setbacks curtailed their attempts to establish safer, cleaner, and healthier conditions for women and children. In 1923, in *Adkins v. Children's Hospital*, the Supreme Court declared a federal minimum wage law for women unconstitutional because it deprived women of the right to bargain directly with their employer. Lawyer Felix Frankfurter used research done by Democratic activist Molly Dewson to argue that low wages and long hours, were linked and if Congress saw fit to regulate hours, then it could regulate wages. However, the majority of the court saw the issue of hours to be related to health and the issue of wages to be potential price-fixing. Further, the Court argued that the Nineteenth Amendment obviated the need for protective legislation. Summing up the paradox of postsuffrage politics, the justices wrote: "We cannot accept the doctrine that women of mature age . . . require or may be subjected to restrictions upon their liberty of contract which could not lawfully be imposed in the case of men under similar circumstances." The Supreme Court also declared unconstitutional the child labor laws passed by Congress in 1918 and 1922. An attempt to pass a federal child labor amendment, approved of by Congress in 1924, ended in defeat when only six states had ratified it by 1930.

In such a climate, the Sheppard-Towner Act, with its ambitious course of maternal and child welfare, faced growing opposition. Since its inception, the Act had faced strong opposition from the American Medical Association whose members did not want federal officials or women reformers involved in the business of health care. Some women activists, most notably birth control advocate Margaret Sanger and the National Women's Party, fiercely criticized the Act. The NWP rejected it because it defined all women as mothers, while Sanger disliked it for not including birth control information or services. The Sheppard-Towner Act, the achievement of which had inspired such confidence in the efficacy of women's activism, by 1929 fell victim to a different reality.

As the country grew more conservative, membership in older women's organizations such as the National Consumers League, the Women's Trade Union League, and the settlement house movement dropped off. Women activists turned their attention to other matters. The League of Women Voters turned to children's issues, and the General Federation of Women's Clubs shifted their attentions to home economics. The coalition of maternalists who had helped pass the nation's first welfare program for women and children fell apart. In this political vacuum, the Sheppard-Towner Act itself was terminated when Congress cut the program's funding despite heavy lobbying efforts by supporters.

WOMEN'S ACTIVISM

By the 1920s, the separate organizational networks that had dominated women's political activism in the nineteenth century no longer dominated. Women actively participated in a variety of mixed-sex political movements and organizations in the 1920s. In Harlem, New York, black women participated in the multinational Pan-African movement headed by the charismatic Marcus Garvey; while in Muncie, Indiana, white women joined the revived nativist Ku Klux Klan (KKK). As more women moved away from women's groups and into groups with men, they faced new battles over authority and direction. While some activists formed separate women's auxiliaries in which they could control their own agendas, as with the Women's KKK, others openly challenged male leadership, as did women in the antilynching campaign. As sex separatism no longer worked as an effective strategy for advancing women's political visions, women had to devise new ways to assert their politics.

"Race Women" and Pan-Africanism

Black women greeted the Nineteenth Amendment with high hopes and registered to vote in large numbers. They faced stiff opposition from whites who worried that women's suffrage would encourage black men to assert their voting rights in the deeply segregated South. In cities and towns across the South, African American women were kept from voting by a number of familiar tactics. Registrars kept them waiting for hours or required payment for a new tax before they could vote. Some women were asked to read and interpret the state and federal constitutions before they could register to vote. Reporting on low turnout, white-owned newspapers reported that black women simply had no interest in voting. African American women activists looked to the National Association for the Advancement of Colored People (NAACP) for help in bringing their complaints to Congress and to national suffrage leaders but received little aid. **"Race women,"** African American female activists, continued to nurture their own political networks and to advance their political goals in city, state, and national antiracist organizations.

One major reform movement was the Universal Negro Improvement Association (UNIA), an international self-help organization, the largest **Pan-African movement** of the twentieth century, founded by Jamaican-born Marcus Garvey in 1917. Commonly known as Garveyism, the movement sought to bring together African American people with people living on the African continent by stressing the need for black people to organize globally for their advancement through Garvey's phrase "One God! One Aim! One Destiny!" Garvey emphasized progress through education and acquiring of skills. By 1923, the UNIA had six million members in nine hundred world branches. When Garvey was arrested on mail fraud in 1923, his second wife Amy Jacques-Garvey became the unofficial leader of the UNIA. Jacques-Garvey had emigrated from Jamaica in 1917, joined the UNIA in 1919, and married Garvey in 1922. Jacques-Garvey brought her belief in women's equality to her Pan-Africanism. As with other race women, Jacques-Garvey understood women's domestic duties to their families as part of racial progress and respectability. But like the new generation of modern women, Jacques-Garvey did not see women's maternal role as precluding their involvement in politics and she herself struck a balance between being a professional woman and wife. Jacques-Garvey served as the associate editor for the international UNIA journal *Negro World* from 1924 to 1927 and wrote a regular column titled "Our

"race women" A term that denoted politically active African American women.

Pan-African movement An international movement to promote unity among people of African nations and of African descent.

MAP 16-1 THE GREAT MIGRATION AND THE DISTRIBUTION OF THE AFRICAN AMERICAN POPULATION IN 1920.

Under 10 percent black population
10 to 29 percent
30 to 49 percent
50 percent and over
● Over 50,000 black people
← African-American migration

African Americans moved from rural southern areas to the urban north and Midwest to escape segregation and take advantage of new work opportunities.

Women and What They Think." Unlike other women's columns in the growing Negro press, this one addressed current issues and politics, demonstrating that "Negro women are great thinkers as well as doers." In more than two hundred editorials, she argued that women's equality was crucial to black liberation. At the same time that she used her column to urge women to actively participate in the Pan-African movement, she paid particular attention to working-class black women whose often unrecognized efforts sustained local communities.

Jacques-Garvey was not alone in her commitment to Pan-Africanism. Led by Margaret Murray Washington, the National Association of Colored Women took an active interest in forging international ties. In 1920, the **International Council of Women of the Darker Races of the World**(ICWDRW) formed and worked with women from other countries to promote the teaching of "race literature," writings by and about African Americans, in schools. Learning the rich traditions of African diaspora was key to the liberation of the race, according to Jacques-Garvey, who wrote that "when the mind is enslaved, physical slavery, in one shape or another, soon follows."

International Council of Women of the Darker Races of the World Founded by African American Mary Talbert in 1922 to promote Pan-African activism.

Amy Jacque Garvey, wife of Marcus Garvey, was a leading Pan-Africanist and Black Nationalist in the 1920s. As a journalist, feminist, and race activist, she embodied both the New Negro and the New Woman of the Jazz Age. From 1924 to 1927, she was the associate editor of the United Negro Improvement Association's newspaper, The Negro World, where she advanced her feminist/nationalist ideas with the inauguration of a new page entitled "Our Women and What They Think."

Commission on Interracial Cooperation (CIC) Established in Atlanta in 1921 the Commission worked with white and black leaders to bring an end to lynching and improve the conditions of poor African Americans.

The deportation of Marcus Garvey in 1927 marked the decline in the UNIA and of Jacques-Garvey's influence in America, as she and her husband returned to Jamaica. Other race women, like Mary Church Terrell, Mary B. Talbert, and Charlotte Atwood, continued to participate in international black activism. They joined the Women's International League for Peace and Freedom, founded by reformers Jane Addams and Emily Greene Balch, where they argued for the necessity for African Americans to join forces with third world people in their fight against oppression (see chapter 15).

The Anti-Lynching Crusade

In the 1920s, lynching remained a tool of political and social intimidation in the South. Lynching, a vigilante practice in which white mobs seized, tortured, and killed their victims, was directed at African American men and women whom perpetrators perceived as having overstepped their place in the social hierarchy of the Jim Crow South by running successful businesses, acquiring a home or car, or not showing deference. By policing the behavior of southern African Americans through the omnipresent threat of lynching, the practice played a key role in the racial and sexual system of Jim Crow. Between 1890 and 1930, more than thirty-two hundred lynchings took place.

Throughout its long history, white southerners justified the practice of lynching as a necessary punishment to protect white women from the mythic black male rapist. Yet, as activists who organized against lynching noted, Americans who had been lynched included women and children. Anxiety over the assertiveness of black soldiers, newly returned from service in Europe where they did not face racial segregation, triggered a new wave of lynchings after World War I. In the wake of seventy lynchings in the immediate postwar years, white southerners hoped that reasserting Jim Crow would end the strife. "We venture to say," opined the Shreveport *Times*, "that fully ninety percent of all the race troubles in the South are the result of the Negro forgetting his place."

African American women, most notably journalist Ida Barnett Wells and activist Mary Church Terrell, worked for years to bring national attention to the crime of lynching (see chapter 13). Yet it took the economic pressure caused by the migration of African Americans out of the rural South in the 1910s and 1920s for southern leaders, black and white, to address lynching as part of a larger system of racial intimidation. In an attempt to stem the flow of workers north, moderate white businessmen and community leaders formed the **Commission on Interracial Cooperation (CIC)** in 1920. The CIC acknowledged and worked with the emergent black middle class in southern cities, yet remained unwilling to challenge Jim Crow segregation by sharing authority with black leaders within the organization. As one white participant explained, "The Negroes draw up a prospectus of what they think they should have in the way of aid and recognition from the whites. The white committee then meets, considers the complaints of the Negroes, and devises means for bettering their condition." Under pressure from the NAACP, however, the CIC became more integrated. At the 1924 annual

On June 24, 1922 a group of African Americans marched in Washington D.C. to protest the govern-ment's inaction on anti-lynching legislation. African American women's clubs raised funds to support the campaign. They worked closely with the National Association for the Advancement of Colored People and the Association of Southern Women for the Prevention of Lynching, a white women's group, to bring na-tional attention to the violent crime.

meeting, twenty-two African American men attended, winning the approval of black leaders, including Pan-Africanist and civil rights leader W. E. B. DuBois.

Incorporating women into the CIC proved harder than integrating it. Bringing African American men and white women together under any circumstances appeared to many white southerners as a threat to southern social relations. Progressive south-ern white women, however, saw themselves as key players in the modernization of southern race relations. In October 1920, the CIC sponsored a southern women's con-ference in Memphis, Tennessee. Ninety-one women from the major Protestant de-nominations, white women's clubs, and the YWCA gathered at the Memphis YWCA and were surprised to find themselves listening to four African American women. The final speaker of the conference, Charlotte Hawkins Brown, electrified the crowd when she placed the responsibility for ending lynching on white women. "The Negro woman of the South lay everything that happens to the members of her race at the door of the southern white woman . . . We all feel that you can control your men . . . so far as lynching is concerned . . . if the white women would take hold of the situation that lynching would be stopped." Brown rejected justifications for lynching that rested on racist myths of the black rapist and the promiscuous black woman whose immorality barred her from protections against sexual exploitation by white men. Linking white racism to everyday practice, she spoke of whites' refusal to address a married black woman as "Mrs.— whether she be cook, criminal or principal of a school." Inspired by all they heard, white listeners remembered the Memphis meeting as transformative. For Brown, the meeting was "the greatest step forward . . . taken since emancipation."

Despite such auspicious beginnings, the new Interracial Woman's Committee quickly reasserted the traditional racial hierarchies the organization hoped to dismantle as white women established segregated groups and assigned to themselves control over state organizations. In many states, local black women's groups found they had no white counterparts with whom to cooperate. With change being slow and interracial cooperation episodic and ritualized in formal meetings only, middle-class black women continued to use their own institutions. In Colored Women's Clubs, church groups, the NAACP, and the YWCA, black women trained themselves in political activism as they worked to improve the lives of people in their communities.

Association of Southern Women to Prevent Lynching (ASWPL)
Founded by Jessie Daniel Ames in 1930 to mobilze white southern women to oppose lynching.

White southern women, like Texas suffragist and businesswoman Jessie Daniel Ames, also grew impatient with the CIC and led Ames and others to form the **Association of Southern Women to Prevent Lynching (ASWPL)** in November 1930. The association organized middle- and upper-class white women into a single-issue movement to oppose lynching. Bringing together lessons learned from their contact with African American women activists and their own experiences as southerners, they denounced a racial system that exploited sexual anxieties to uphold white supremacy. "Public opinion has accepted too easily the claim of lynchers and mobsters that they were acting solely in the defense of womanhood. In the light of facts, we dare not longer permit this claim to pass unchallenged nor allow those bent upon personal revenge and savagery to commit acts of violence and lawlessness in the name of women."

The ASWPL launched a campaign to change the understanding of lynching as not an act of protection but of lawlessness. They urged southerners to recognize how lynching undermined citizens' respect for the law and for law enforcement more generally and called on sheriffs and police officers to protect victims by ending vigilantism. In their first eight years, the ASWPL contributed to a 50 percent reduction in the incidence of lynching in the South.

Ku Klux Klan

In the Midwest the Ku Klux Klan drew a half-million white Protestant women into its ranks in the 1920s to become one of the largest and most politically powerful racist movements in U.S. history. The new Klan, which had grown to five million strong by 1925, filled its secret membership rolls with anxious white Americans in the North and West who feared that their way of life and their values were under assault from groups they considered to be newcomers and troublemakers, particularly religious or political groups that they perceived to have allegiances to foreign leaders, nations, or institutions. Unlike the first Klan who reasserted white rule following Reconstruction (see chapter 10), the new Klan was part of the wave of nativism and anti-immigration that swept the country in the 1920s. Like the old Klan, it targeted anyone who challenged Jim Crow segregation. But the new Klan expanded its list of enemies to include immigrants, Catholics, Jews, and socialists. With its inclusion of boys, girls, and women, the new Klan of the 1920s became, for many, a family affair.

Elizabeth Tyler was the first woman to gain leadership in the new Klan, and she played an instrumental role in the creation of the **Women of the Ku Klux Klan (WKKK)** in 1923. As with many activist women of her generation, Tyler began her political education in the 1910s as a volunteer hygiene worker who visited new mothers living in tenements as part of Atlanta's "better babies" movement. After meeting Edward Clarke, the two organized the Southern Publicity Association and sold their marketing skills to organizations like the Anti-Saloon League and the Salvation Army before landing the KKK as a client. Together, Tyler and Clarke applied modern marketing and advertising techniques to Klan recruitment with impressive results. Tyler's success and the authority she claimed within the organization threatened the all-male leadership of the Klan, which moved her out of the organization by promising her control over a women's organization equal to and separate from the male KKK.

As early as 1922, women, emboldened by the passage of suffrage, protested their exclusion from the Klan. According to one letter to the editor of the Klan publication, *Fiery Cross*, in these "new days of freedom" women wanted to shed their role as the protected and join their men in protecting their homes, families, and communities. Before the WKKK formed, women participated in informal Klan auxiliaries and patriotic societies. These auxiliaries allowed them to do Klan work in large, national organizations like the Ladies of the Invisible Eye and the Queens of the Golden Mask, as well as more local and regional ones such as Atlanta's Dixie Protestant Women's Political

Women of the Ku Klux Klan (WKKK) the women's auxilery of the racist and nativist Ku Klux Klan

Women in the middle west joined the new Ku Klux Klan in record numbers in the 1920s. This photograph, taken in 1924, shows women dressed in the Klan's traditional white robes and hoods. The racist ideology that targeted immigrants, Jews, and African Americans as threatening newcomers provided women a network of social gatherings that bolstered their sense of community pride.

League and Houston's Grand League of Protestant Women. Women's auxiliaries combined white supremacy with social service work. They ran boarding homes and training schools for women looking for work, staffed day-care centers, and collected food for the needy, while opposing racial equality and interracial marriage and advocating a return of the Bible to public schools and immigration restrictions. When the WKKK officially formed in 1923, membership was opened to all white, Gentile, female, native-born citizens over eighteen who had not pledged allegiance to any foreign government or religion and who had been endorsed by two Klanswomen. In 1923, 125,000 women living in the Midwest, Northwest, and the Ozarks region joined the WKKK. Within months, the WKKK reported its membership at 250,000 with followers throughout the country.

Klanswomen had a political agenda through which they blended a new consciousness of women's rights with anti-Catholic, anti-Semitic, and racist beliefs. Many had been active in the temperance and suffrage movements and believed that women's inherent moral natures could clean up government and help rid the nation of the vices of liquor, prostitution, and gambling. They were fierce **nativists** in their hatred of socialists and immigrants and in their support of efforts to root out so-called Jewish influence in the movie industry and to expose rumored conspiracies of the Catholic Church to gain political control of the nation. At the same time and unlike their male counterparts, women of the Klan used the language of suffrage to call for greater equality between Protestant men and women. Paradoxically, through their separate organization, an organization that embraced racist vigilantism, Klanswomen forged a critique of male power that empowered them to move out of their traditional roles.

The inclusion of women and children in the Klan contributed to its normalization during its heyday in the 1920s. The seemingly innocuous family events that participants claimed were "just a way to get together and enjoy" masked the Klan's success in becoming a part of ordinary white Protestant life. Yet, even with the incorporation of bigotry into schools, leisure activities, and homes, the second Klan collapsed rapidly. By 1930, its membership dropped to fewer than fifty thousand men and women. Internally, battles among leaders and disclosure of rampant corruption marred the image of the Klan. Externally, changing social conditions also lessened its appeal. The number of foreign-born residents in the United States declined drastically as immigration laws took effect; and after 1929, the economic depression altered the landscape of national politics. Racism, anti-Semitism, and anti-Catholicism did not disappear in the 1920s, but most white Protestant women no longer looked to the Klan as the vehicle for expressing those sentiments.

nativist A person who supports the interest of native inhabitants against those of immigrants.

THE CULTURE OF MODERNITY

Women in the 1920s both symbolized and struggled to redefine what it meant to be modern. To be a modern woman included a range of new values and activities. Foremost among them was to discover and express oneself in the growing commercial world of new products. Motion pictures and advertising created a visual language of what modern women looked like, how they behaved, and what they bought; while women singers that appeared in cabarets, clubs, and theaters forged a new language for women's aspirations and their disappointments. Running throughout these venues was a new attention to modern women's contrary pulls for romance and independence, work and play, and families and self-expression. Popular culture nurtured these tensions and offered solutions to them in the marketplace of goods.

Dance Crazes

The music of the early 1920s was fast and energetic, and new kinds of dancing evolved along with the new music. The Jazz Age spawned a number of dance crazes that took the nation by storm. In speakeasies, dance halls, and private parties, young Americans took to the dance floor, shaking their upper bodies in the shimmy, gleefully throwing their arms and legs in the air, and hopping or "toddling" every step of the fox-trot. No dance was more popular than the Charleston, a dance named for the city Charleston, South Carolina. Associated with white flappers, the dance became popular after it appeared in the all-black show *Runnin' Wild* in 1923. The dance took its name from "The Charleston," a song written by African American composer James P. Johnson who incorporated popular jazz sounds with rhythms from West Africa. It became a national phenomenon when it was introduced by the dancing girls of the Ziegfeld Follies. Charleston dance contests where hundreds of dancers took the floor for hours were held in dance halls, hotels, and resorts and on street corners. In Hollywood, starlet Joan Crawford made a big splash when she debuted as a flapper who won numerous Charleston contests. The Charleston involved the dancer turning her knees and toes in as she shifted her weight between her legs, intended to mock the "drys," or citizens who supported the Prohibition amendment. The dance was so popular that hospitals reported increasing numbers of people complaining of "Charleston knee." Critics of the new dance disliked its frenetic gestures, and some ballrooms went so far as to post signs that read "PCQ," or "Please Charleston Quietly."

The Black Bottom, a dance that originated in New Orleans in the 1900s, overtook the Charleston in popularity. It was brought to New York City in the theatrical show *Dinah* in 1924 and at the Apollo Theater in Harlem in 1926. Jazz player and composer Jelly Roll Morton wrote the tune "Black Bottom Stomp," which referred to Detroit's Black Bottom area. Another popular dance was the cakewalk, a dance that had its origins in slavery. The dance parodied the formal European ballroom dances. Couples linked at the elbows, lined up in a circle, and danced forward, alternating a series of short hopping steps with a series of very high kicking steps. The Lindy Hop became popular at the end of the decade, named for the American aviator Charles Lindbergh who completed the first solo flight, or "hop," across the Atlantic in 1927.

It seemed that the whole country had dance fever, not only flappers and Hollywood stars. Middle-class families began sending their children to dancing schools like those run by Arthur Murray, where they learned ragtime dances like the One Step and the Tango, made famous by film star Rudolf Valentino. Murry published a long series of "How to Dance" books that, along with new magazines like *The American Dancer* and *Dance Magazine*, promoted the growing popularity of dancing. Yet, the new jazz and jazz dancing were not popular with everyone. Some called the new style "decadent" and "dangerous," and frankly racist reviewers referred to it as "jungle music." Arch conservative Henry Ford loathed jazz and steadfastly continued to promote old-fashioned waltzing and square dances.

The Harlem Renaissance

The new music and dance that filled the nation's speakeasies and ballrooms testified to the importance of black artists to modern America. With its seventy-five thousand black residents, the New York City neighborhood of Harlem had become the "Negro Capital of the World." Between 1910 and 1940, 1,750,000 African Americans left the South, many of them young men and women who had high hopes for a better life in the North. Most southerners who migrated North continued to settle in all-black neighborhoods such as Harlem in New York City, the South Side of Chicago, and Cleveland's East Side. Such segregated neighborhoods created strong communities as well as new sites of cultural and political conflict among African Americans. The black middle class that had long worked to be seen as respectable leaders of the race came into contact with rural and working-class blacks that brought a different set of goals and aspirations.

The artistic and intellectual life that took hold of Harlem in the 1920s grew out of the class politics brought on by the great migration. The writers who became associated with the Harlem Renaissance were often among the black elite, a highly educated group of men and women that included Zora Neale Hurston, Jessie Fauset, and Nella Larson. Hurston, who grew up in Eastonville, Florida, attended Morgan State University, Howard University, and Barnard College. Jessie Fauset came from an affluent family in Philadelphia and graduated Phi Beta Kappa from Cornell University and earned a master of arts degree from the University of Pennsylvania in romance languages.

In their fiction, authors Jessie Fauset and Nella Larson depicted conflicts between a sophisticated urbane black elite and the "folk" of the rural South. Yet, they came out on different sides of the most heated debate taking place among intellectuals, journalists, writers, and artists over the role of art, broadly defined, in the struggle over equality. Fauset, like activist W. E. B. DuBois and intellectual Alain Lock, hoped black literature and arts could change racist stereotypes by promoting positive images of black life. Larson and Hurston, along with poet Langston Hughes and writer Claude McKay, used art to explore the realities of black life and argued that art ought best be measured on its own merits, not by its duty to the race.

The fiction of Nella Larson focused on the contradictions facing women like herself in her novel *Quicksand* (1928). The heroine, Helga, struggles against dominant white definitions of her sexuality as exotic and primitive and, at the same time, the ideas of respectability upheld by the black middle class. Helga is at once drawn to the ways her beauty gives her power over men and dismayed at how quickly she loses that power once she gives herself over to romance. Larson moves her heroine from the racial hothouse of Harlem to the affluence and alienation of her uncle's life in Copenhagen and then to the toil of rural southern life. In each setting, Larson explores the convergence of Helga's race, gender, and sexuality and poses the question, In what ways can black women claim power and pleasure in a life bound by forces that objectify them?

Singing the Blues

The blues, a southern and rural style of music, gained popularity after World War I. It emerged in African American communities from spirituals, rhymed English and Scotch-Irish narrative ballads, and shouts and chants. The use of blue notes and the call-and-response patterns, where the singer calls to the listeners—who then respond, drew from West African musical traditions. In the 1920s, it became a major element of African American and American popular music and reached white audiences. The blues moved from bars to theaters and nightclubs like Harlem's Cotton Club and Beale Street in Memphis. Several record companies, such as the American Records Corporation and Paramount Records, began to record country blues singers like Charlie Patton and Blind Lemon Jefferson. Female singers, like Mamie Smith, Gertrude "Ma" Rainey, Bessie Smith, and Victoria Spivey, sang city or urban blues in the 1920s. Mamie Smith's 1920 "Crazy Blues" sold seventy-five thousand copies in its first month.

In 1923, Bessie Smith began her assent as "the Empress of the Blues" when she signed a contract with Columbia Records. She sang what were commonly known as "race songs," songs that painted a picture of black life. Her first recording included "Downhearted Blues" and "Tain't Nobody's Business if I do." In 1925, she recorded with Louis Armstrong, who said of Smith, "She could phrase a note with a certain something in her voice no other blues singer could get." Smith toured major cities where crowds lined up at clubs to hear her. In her life and her music, Smith represented much of what middle-class blacks most disliked about working-class and southern newcomers. She sang about alcoholism and drank heavily herself; she sang about love and had many lovers; she sang about crime and she personally was drawn to dangerous clubs where, in her words, "the funk was flying." At two hundred pounds, Smith also posed a sizable challenge to the slender ideal of white femininity that became prominent the 1920s, even in Harlem. The famous Cotton Club in Harlem hired only African American dancers who were more than 5'6" tall, less than twenty-one years of age, and of light brown complexion. Smith, Rainey, Ethel Waters, Clara Smith, and Alberta Hunter, many of whom got their start traveling with vaudeville shows and circuses, were among the singers who dominated the blues in the 1920s.

The blues tradition, with its songs of desire and sorrow, seemed to many to be at odds with the black middle-class efforts toward racial progress. If middle-class black activists sought to represent their people as able participants in the life of the nation, they viewed blues singers as confirming all they worked against. Yet, as entertainers whose popularity grew in the 1930s, blues singers like Smith, Rainey, and Waters were at the forefront of a cultural process that advanced notions of equality through the marketplace. By placing a black woman's broken heart at the center of a musical tradition, female blues singers pulled white audiences into an imaginative engagement with their own distinctive way of seeing the world. Blues singers broke down the gaps between white and black, middle class and poor, rural and urban, through their songs, using music to do what many reformers could not: express the distinctive sorrows and joys women felt about love, children, and desire.

WOMEN'S LIVES

GERTRUDE "MA" RAINEY

Gertrude Malissa Nix Pridgett was born on April 6, 1886, in Columbus, Georgia. Drawn to the stage, she made her first public appearance at the age of fourteen in a local talent show called "Bunch of Blackberries." This began a life of performance, first on the vaudeville circuit and later in clubs and recording studios. On tour in 1902, Rainey heard a blues song and she quickly made the style uniquely her own. In February 1904, she married a vaudeville performer known as William "Pa" Rainey, and for several years they toured primarily in the South as a song-and-dance team. They became a popular attraction as part of Tolliver's Circus, The Musical Extravaganza, and The Rabbit Foot Minstrels, where she took a young Bessie Smith under her wing. Rainey had a deep contralto voice that she made into a powerful instrument, the sound of which drew audiences into the emotional world of the singer. In 1923, Ma Rainey made her first phonograph recordings for the Paramount company. Over a five-year span, she recorded some ninety-two songs for Paramount, of which only a few survive: "See See Rider," "Blues Oh Blues," "Oh Papa Blues," and "Trust No Man."

Rainey had romantic relationships with women as well as men. Her bisexuality sometimes appeared in her music, as in "Prove It On Me," recorded by Rainey in 1928 when she sang about going out with crowd of women because "I don't like no men."

The newspaper advertisement that promoted the release of "Prove It On Me" featured Ma Rainey dressed in a man's suit flirting with two other women. Outspoken on women's issues, Rainey was seen as a role model for future women entertainers who took control of their own careers. She continued to sing in public into the 1930s when she retired to Rome, Georgia, where she died of a heart attack on December 22, 1939. ■

1920

1920

The International Council of Women of the Darker Races of the World (ICWDRW) formalizes American women's involvement in the growing Pan African Movement

The Women's Bureau is formed within the Department of Labor

Ratification of the 19th Amendment

The Commission on Interracial Cooperation (CIC) sponsors an interracial women's conference

1921

The Sheppard-Towner Act becomes law

League of Women Voters (LWV) forms

1922

Amy Jacques-Garvey becomes the unofficial leader of the United Negro Improvement Association (UNIA)

Adkins v. Children's Hospital blocks minimum wages for women

ERA introduced

Jazz singer Bessie Smith records her first album

1923

Women of the Ku Klux Klan (WKKK) is formed

The Charleston dance craze begins

1920

Eighteenth Amendment establishes Prohibition

Nineteenth Amendment is ratified

Commerical radio broadcasting begins

1921

First immigration quotas are established

1922

Harlem's Cotton Club opens

1924

Reed-Johnson Immigration Act further tightens immigration quotas

Dawes Plan reduces German reparation payments

1925

1926

Radcliffe Hall publishes *The Well of Loneliness*

1927

Congress renews Sheppard-Towner Act for two years

Judge Ben Lindsey publishes *Companionate Marriage*

October: Journalist Dorothy Bromley writes "Feminist—New Style" for *Harper's*

1928

Seven women served in Congress

Anthropologist Margaret Mead publishes *Coming of Age in Samoa*

Harlem Rennaisance writer, Nella Larson writes *Quicksand*

1929

Sociologists Helen and Robert Lynd publish, *Middletown*

Katherine Bement Davis's pioneering sex survey on women is published

1925

A. Philip Randolph organizes the Brotherhood of Sleeping Car Porters

John T. Scopes is convicted for teaching evolution

1927

Charles Lindbergh makes first solo flight across the Atlantic Ocean

First "talkies" are shown

Marcus Garvey is deported

1929

Stock market crashes

1930

1930

Association of Southern Women to Prevent Lynching (ASWPL) is formed

CONCLUSION

"The word flapper to us means, not a female atrocity who smokes, swears, delights in [movies] like *The Sheik*, and kisses her gentlemen friends goodnight, although there is no particular harm in any of the foregoing," explained a University of Illinois student. "We always think of the flapper as the independent, 'pally' young woman, a typical American product. . . . The Flapper is the girl who is responsible for the advancement of woman's condition in the world."

Whether or not the notorious flapper of the 1920s was as new as critics made out or represented a new age of equality between the sexes as her supporters argued, she nevertheless represented a change in many young women's sense of themselves and their place in society. Young working-class-girls, department store clerks, rural new-comers to cities, and college students insisted that they were different from their mothers and grandmothers, that the world was new and they were at the forefront of the twentieth century.

While the Jazz Age's celebration of modernity and youth and, in particular, its emphasis on individual pleasures changed the ways that Americans entertained themselves, the Jazz Age weakened the Progressive reform impulse of the prewar years. Consumption of a new array of products like cars and radios rose in importance, while anti-immigrant feelings and ongoing Jim Crow segregation spoke the nation's conservative turn in the 1920s. Women activists face apathy from younger women and reform fatigue from former suffragists. The culmination of the nineteenth-century suffrage movement, the passage of the Nineteenth Amendment giving women the right to vote, did not bring about lasting change in the nature of politics that suffragists had imagined.

One of the most important and far-reaching changes of the 1920s was the rising numbers of working women in the fast-growing pink-collar sector of the economy. As consumer spending and service work grew into major engines of economic growth, women found their dual roles as primary shopper and pink-collar worker to be at the heart of modern America.

REVIEW QUESTIONS

1. What made marriage different or modern in the 1920s? What were some of the causes for the companionate marriage?

2. What changes in the economy helped women wage workers? What spurred the growth of the pink-collar job sector?

3. Did winning the vote change women's political activism in the 1920s? In what ways? In what ways did it not?

4. How did women participate in the culture of the jazz age?

RECOMMENDED READING

Beth Bailey. *From Front Porch to Back Seat: Courtship in Twentieth Century America*. Baltimore: Johns Hopkins University Press, 1988. Bailey examines advice literature, youth cultures, popular culture, and American courtship behaviors in this classic study.

Kathleen M. Blee. *Women of the Klan: Racism and Gender in the 1920s*. Berkeley: University of California Press, 1991. Klee, a sociologist, reconstructs the rise and fall of the new Klan of the 1920s in the midwestern U.S. She uses Klan publications and oral histories to analyze the Klan's use of gender and its appeal to white protestant women in their search for equality.

Mari Jo Buhle. *Feminism and its Discontents: A Century of Struggle with Psychoanalysis*. Cambridge: Harvard University Press, 1998. Buhle covers the cultural and intellectual context in which psychoanalytic theory took hold of both American notions of self and feminists' engagement with sexuality, gender, and subjectivity.

Hazel Carby. "'It Jus Be's dat Way Sometime': The Sexual Politics of Women's Blues," Ellen DuBois and Vicki Ruiz, eds., *Unequal Sisters: A Multicultural Reader in U.S. Women's History*. New York: Routledge, 1990. Carby contrasts women in the Harlem Renaissance and female blues singers for their understanding of female sexual desire and its relationship to class differences among African Americans.

Nancy Cott. *The Grounding of Modern Feminism*. New Haven: Yale University Press, 1987. Cott's is an encyclopedic study of women's activism in the years following the 19th amendment. She pays close attention to the transformations between 19th century woman's movement to modern feminism in both ideology and application.

Sarah Deutsch. *Women and the City: Gender, Space, and Power in Boston, 1870–1940*. Oxford and New York: Oxford University Press, 2000. Deutsch's strength in multicultural history is applied to the clashing cultures of class and race in Boston.

Angela J. Latham. *Posing a Threat: Flappers, Chorus Girls, and Other Brazen Performers of the American 1920s*. New York: Oxford University Press, 2000. Latham studies women whose public transgressions of gentile femininity helped open up new styles and attitudes for women in the 1920s.

Rosallyn Terborg-Penn. "Discontented Black Feminists: Prelude and Postscript to the Passage of the Nineteenth Amendment," in Kathryn Kish Sklar and Thomas Dublin, eds., *Women and Power in American History, volume two, from 1870*. New Jersey: Prentice Hall, 1991. Terborg-Penn's account covers the successes and disappointments of black feminists as they join with black men and white suffragists in their efforts to eradicate racism.

ADDITIONAL BIBLIOGRAPHY

Revolution in Manners and Morals

Lillian Faderman. *Odd Girls and Twilight Lovers: A History of Lesbian Life in Twentieth-Century America*. New York: Columbia University Press, 1991.

Vicki Ruiz. "Star Struck: Acculturation, Adolescence, and Mexican American Women, 1920-1950," in Ellen DuBois and Vicki Ruiz, eds., *Unequal Sisters: A Multicultural Reader in U.S. Women's History*. New York: Routledge, 1990, 346–362.

George F. Sanchez. "'Go After the Women': Americanization and the Mexican Immigrant Woman, 1915-1929," in Ellen DuBois and Vicki Ruiz, eds., *Unequal Sisters: A Multicultural Reader in U.S. Women's History*. New York: Routledge, 1990.

Christina Simmons. "Companionate Marriage and the Lesbian Threat," *Frontiers*, IV:3 (1979): 54–59.

John C. Spurlock and Cynthia A. Magistro. *New and Improved: The Transformation of American Women's Emotional Culture*. New York: New York University, 1998.

Women and Work

Susan Porter Benson. "The Work Culture of Sales Clerks in American Department Stores, 1890–1940," in Mary Beth Norton and Ruth Alexander, eds., *Major Problems in American Women's History: Documents and Essays*. Lexington, MA: D.C. Heath and Company, 1989.

Elizabeth Clark-Lewis. "This Work Had an End": African American Domestic Workers in Washington, D.C., 1910–1940," in Carol Groneman and Mary Beth Norton, eds., "To Toil the Live Long Day": *America's Women at Work, 1780–1980.* Ithica: Cornell University Press, 1987.

Evelyn Nakano Glenn. "The Dialectics of Wage Work: Japanese-American Women and Domestic Service, 1905–1940," in Ellen DuBois and Vicki Ruiz, eds., *Unequal Sisters: A Multicultural Reader in U.S. Women's History.* New York: Routlege, 1990.

Jacqueline Jones. *Labor of Love, Labor of Sorrow: Black Women, Work, and the Family, from Slavery to the Present.* New York: Basic Books, 1985.

Barbara Melosh. "The Physician's Hand": Work Culture and Conflict in American Nursing. Philadelphia: Temple University Press, 1982.

Beyond Suffrage

Dorothy M. Brown. *Setting a Course: American Women in the 1920s.* Boston: Twayne Publishers, 1987.

William Chafe. *The American Woman: Her Changing Social, Economic, and Political Roles, 1920–1970.* New York: Oxford University Press, 1972.

Nancy Cott. "Across the Great Divide: Women in Politics Before and After 1920," in Mary Beth Norton and Ruth Alexander, eds., *Major Problems in American Women's History: Documents and Essays.* Lexington, MA: D.C. Heath and Company, 1989.

Evelyn Brooks Higginbotham. "In Politics to Stay: Black Women Leaders and Party Politics in the 1920s," in Ellen DuBois and Vicki Ruiz, eds., *Unequal Sisters: A Multicultural Reader in U.S. Women's History.* New York: Routledge, 1990: 292–307.

Rosalind Rosenberg. *Divided Lives: American Women in the Twentieth Century.* New York: Hill and Wang, 1992.

Lois Scharf and Joan M. Jensen, eds. *Decades of Discontent: The Women's Movement, 1920–1940.* Westport: Greenwood Press, 1983.

Joan G. Zimmerman. "Women's Rights, Feminist Conflict, and the Jurisprudence of Equality," in Mary Beth Norton and Ruth Alexander, eds., *Major Problems in American Women's History: Documents and Essays.* Lexington, MA: D.C. Heath and Company, 1989.

Women's Activism

Hazel Carby. "On the Threshold of Woman's Era: Lynching, Empire, and Sexuality in Black Feminist Theory," in Anne McClintock, Aamir Mufti, and Ella Shohat, eds, *Dangerous Liaisons: Gender, Nation, and Postcolonial Perspectives.* Minneapolis: University of Minnesota Press, 1997: 330–344.

Estelle Freedman. "Separatism as Strategy: Female Institution Building and American Feminism, 1870–1930," *Feminist Studies,* vol. 5, no. 3 Fall 1979: 512–29.

Melanie Gustafson. "Partisan Women in the Progressive Era: The Struggle for Inclusion in American Political Parties," in Ellen DuBois and Vicki Ruiz, eds., *Unequal Sisters: A Multicultural Reader in U.S. Women's History.* New York: Routledge 1990, 242–257.

Jacquelyn Dowd Hall. *Revolt against Chivalry: Jessie Daniel Ames and the Women's Campaign against Lynching.* New York: Columbia University Press, 1979.

Kathryn Kish Sklar, "Why Were Most Politcally Active Women Opposed to the ERA in the 1920s?" in Joan Hoff-Wilson ed., *Rights of Passage: The Past and Future of the ERA.* Bloomington: Indiana University Press, 1986.

Uta Y. Taylor. "'Negro Women are Great Thinkers as well as Doers': Amy Jacques-Garvey and Community Feminism in the United States, 1924–1927," *Journal of Women's History* 12, no. 2 Summer 2000: 104–126.

Deborah Gray White. *Too Heavy a Load: Black Women in Defense of Themselves, 1894–1994.* New York: Norton 1999.

E. Frances White. "Africa on my Mind: Gender, Counter-Discourse, and African American Nationalism," *Journal of Women's History* 2, no. 1 1990: 73–97.

The Culture of Modernity

Angela Y. Davis. *Blues Legacies and Black Feminism: Gertrude "Ma" Rainey, Bessie Smith, and Billie Holiday.* New York: Pantheon Books, 1998.

Thadious M. Davis. *Nella Larsen, Novelist of the Harlem Renaissance: A Woman's Life Unveiled.* Baton Rogue: Louisiana State University Press, 1994.

Ann duCille. "Blues Notes on Black Sexuality: Sex and the Texts of Jessie Fauset and Nella Larsen," John C. Fout and Maura Shaw Tantillo, eds, *American Sexual Politics: Sex, Gender, and Race since the Civil War.* Chicago: University of Chicago Press, 1993: 193–223.

Lewis Erenberg. *Steppin' Out: New York Nightlife and the Transformation of American Culture, 1890–1930.* Chicago: University of Chicago Press, 1981.

Susan Glenn. *Female Spectacle: The Theatrical Roots of Modern Feminism.* Cambridge: Harvard University Press, 2000.

Roland Marchand. *Advertising the American Dream: Making Way for Modernity, 1920–1940.* Berkeley: University of California Press, 1985.

Gaylyn Studlar. *This Mad Masquerade: Stardom and Masculinity in the Jazz Age.* New York: Columbia University Press, 1996.

Memoirs, Autobiographies and Biographies

A'Lelia Bundles. *On Her Own Ground: The Life and Times of Madam C. J. Walker.* New York: Scribner, 2001.

Thadious Davis. *Nella Larson, Novelist of the Harlem Renaissance: A Woman's Life Unveiled.* Baton Rouge: Louisiana State University Press, 1994.

Mamie Garvin Fields with Karen Fields. *Lemon Swamp and Other Places: A Carolina Memoir.* New York: Free Press; London: Collier Macmillan Publishers, 1983.

Zora Neale Hurston. *Dust Tracks on a Road: An Autobiography.* Lincoln: University of Nebraska–Lincoln, 1988.

Nancy Milford. *Zelda: A Biography.* New York: Harper & Brothers Publishers, 1970.

Mary Church Terrell. *A Colored Woman in a White World.* New York: Ransdell Company, 1940.

THE GREAT DEPRESSION, 1930–1940

FACING THE DEPRESSION

The Economics of Running a House

Postponing Marriage and Children

Gender and the Politics of Providing

ACTIVISM

Appalachian Women in the Textile Industry

Chinese Women in San Francisco's Garment Industry

Latinas and the California Canning Industry

WOMEN AND THE NEW DEAL

Eleanor Roosevelt and the Women's Network

Women in the New Deal

Gender in the Welfare State

CULTURES OF THE 1930S

Representing Gender in New Deal Public Art

Documenting the Depression

Regulating Hollywood

HOW DID family life change during the 1930s?

HOW DID working-class women participate in the labor movement?

WHAT IMPACT did women have on the New Deal?

IN WHAT ways did the Depression constitute a crisis of masculinity?

CHAPTER

7

Nov. 30, 1937
Springfield, Mass

Dear Mrs. Roosevelt,

I am a girl sixteen years old. Last May I beg my father to buy an electric refrigerator for mother on Mother's day. We had talked about buying one with her. She thought it was not a very wise thing to do, because we could not afford to pay cash. I wanted it so very bad that my father bought it. He agreed to pay monthly payments of seven dollars and twenty two cents. What mother had said proved to be right. For two weeks after we bought the refrigerator I took sick with a

Rollin Kirby's "Sold Out" "Sold Out" 1929 Rollin Kirby (1875–1952) Illustration, New York World, October 25, 1929

serious kidney ailment which confined me to my bed from May twenty until Nov. twenty-second. I am just recovering from a delicate operation. I came home from the hospital Nov. eighth and my father was layed off after working for the railroad fifteen years. Many a girl of my age is hoping that on Christmas morn they will find a wrist watch, a handbag, or even a fur coat. But my one and only wish is to have father and mother spend a happy Christmas. Mrs. Roosevelt I am asking of you a favor which can make this wish come true. I am asking you to keep up our payments until my father gets back to work as a Christmas gift to me. Though father worked part time for quite a while we never lost anything for the lack of payments. If the refrigerator was taken away from us father and mother would think it a disgrace.

I close hoping with all my heart that my letter will be consider. Mrs. Roosevelt you may rest assure that I have learnt my lesson.

I am respectfully yours

J. B.

Source: Letters to Mrs. Roosevelt: http://newdeal.feri.org/eleanor/jb1137.htm.

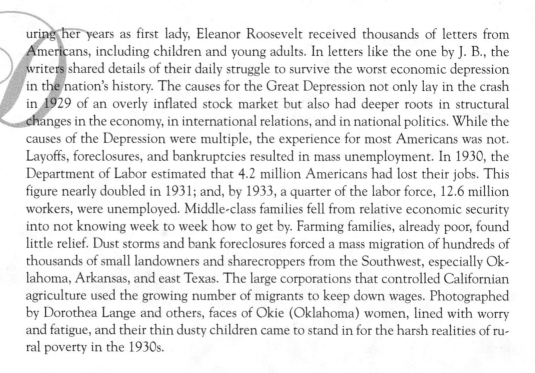

uring her years as first lady, Eleanor Roosevelt received thousands of letters from Americans, including children and young adults. In letters like the one by J. B., the writers shared details of their daily struggle to survive the worst economic depression in the nation's history. The causes for the Great Depression not only lay in the crash in 1929 of an overly inflated stock market but also had deeper roots in structural changes in the economy, in international relations, and in national politics. While the causes of the Depression were multiple, the experience for most Americans was not. Layoffs, foreclosures, and bankruptcies resulted in mass unemployment. In 1930, the Department of Labor estimated that 4.2 million Americans had lost their jobs. This figure nearly doubled in 1931; and, by 1933, a quarter of the labor force, 12.6 million workers, were unemployed. Middle-class families fell from relative economic security into not knowing week to week how to get by. Farming families, already poor, found little relief. Dust storms and bank foreclosures forced a mass migration of hundreds of thousands of small landowners and sharecroppers from the Southwest, especially Oklahoma, Arkansas, and east Texas. The large corporations that controlled Californian agriculture used the growing number of migrants to keep down wages. Photographed by Dorothea Lange and others, faces of Okie (Oklahoma) women, lined with worry and fatigue, and their thin dusty children came to stand in for the harsh realities of rural poverty in the 1930s.

Americans families migrated west looking for work. This family waited in Porterville, California in hopes of picking oranges in one of the area's large farms. Companies hired whole families, paying them poorly and demanding long hours.

Many women found they had few resources to help ward off homelessness and hunger for their children. Yet they did not wait for help to appear. Women organized themselves in as workers, consumers, and renters to pressure employers, landlords, and local officials to address their problems. At the same time, women reformers mobilized to put pressure on the government to address the needs of struggling families. While Roosevelt's New Deal gave much needed aid to poor families, key legislation reinforced the ideal of a family wage paid to men and men alone. The foundation for the liberal welfare state, established in the crucible of the 1930s, rested on the gendered view of women as mothers and fathers as workers, with consequences that profoundly shaped women's status for years to come.

FACING THE DEPRESSION

No era ended as abruptly as did the Jazz Age of the 1920s. In the course of a year, the icons of the 1920s—the flapper, the feminist, and the teenager—went from trendsetters to the very epitome of frivolity. The optimism of the 1920s was first tested by the stock market crash in October 1929 and then strained by President Herbert Hoover's slow response to the crisis. Finally, by the 1932 election, hope had been replaced by fear and despair. Massive layoffs put husbands, brothers, and fathers out of work. Savings were wiped out when banks failed. Foreclosures, eviction, and hunger became commonplace. Women's skills at home were pressed to the limit.

During the Depression, women struggled to keep their families afloat. Some, like these Mexican American women, took in sewing for money, while others took in boarders and laundry. Most women found ways to make whatever they had last longer and stretch further, through canning, recycling, bartering, and ingenuity.

The Economics of Running a House

With money scarce and work unpredictable at best, most American families lived by the credo: "Use it up, wear it out, make it do, or do without." Unlike the 1920s, when women rushed to fill their kitchen and living rooms with marvelous new appliances and radios, the Great Depression forced many women to practice a number of small economies. They bought day-old bread; filled the oven with many dishes to save on gas; relined old coats with old blankets; dropped hems; patched knees, elbows, and sleeves; and cut adult clothes to fit children. If they could afford meat, they bought cheaper cuts; if they had a car, they drove it less; if they could afford an apartment, they moved to smaller ones. Families moved in together to save on rents, creating households of extended families and multiple adults who pooled their wages to keep the family fed and clothed.

Over half the families in the country had incomes of between five hundred and fifteen hundred dollars, which translated into about twenty dollars per week to feed, clothe, and house a family. Deflation had pushed down the cost of goods, meaning that a budget-conscious woman could feed her family on five dollars a week, if she had the money. Two pounds of hamburger sold for twenty-five cents, a quart of milk for ten cents, butter for twenty-three cents. In San Francisco, a Chinese woman with six children explained what a quarter could buy: "A quarter was enough for dinner. With that I bought two pieces of fish to steam, three bunches of vegetables (two to stir fry, one to put in the soup), and some pork for the soup." Women did at home what they had once purchased ready-made. They began canning their own fruits and vegetables; others took up baking their own bread. As families saw their livelihoods dwindle, middle-class homemakers began making dresses, doing laundry, and letting out rooms for much needed money.

The task of maintaining the household became much harder for women during the Great Depression. Families crowded together in small city apartments. Neighbors shared bathrooms, hotplates, stoves, and sinks because of the inadequacy of their individual apartments. They exchanged tasks, such as doing a woman's hair in return for use of her pots and pans or trading bread for a glass of milk. For example, a group of African Americans in Washington, D.C., found innovative ways to meet some of their needs. One Washington, D.C., social worker recounted the actions of "Auntie Jane," a strong, forty-year-old African American woman, who dressed in men's clothes and led a group of women and children into two partially demolished buildings where they gathered firewood for their apartment courtyard.

For women living in the southern Great Plains, endurance and hard work were not enough to let them get by. An environmental crisis, caused by years of drought and large-scale agriculture, triggered massive dust storms. Black blizzards of dust, some reaching over a mile high, blew across the region and left great drifts of dust in their wake. Humans and animals suffered respiratory strain or "dust pneumonia," leaving young children and the elderly particularly vulnerable. With so much topsoil blown away, crops and trees were destroyed; car, truck, and train engines choked with dust often broke down, stranding travelers and closing off commerce. The scale of the storms was unprecedented. A Chicago newspaper reported that a storm on May 10, 1934, dumped 12 million tons of Plains soil on that city. By the next day, the report went on, dust obscured the sun in Washington, D.C., and ships three hundred miles from shore reported dust on their decks. Ann Marie Low kept a diary during the "dirty thirties" of her life in North Dakota. She described the difficulty of staying clean, of keeping house, and of doing the simple tasks of farming. "The mess was incredible! Dirt had blown into the house all week and lay inches deep on everything. Every towel and curtain was just black. There wasn't a clean dish or cooking utensil. . . . It took until 10 o'clock to wash all the dirty dishes. . . . Every room had to have dirt almost shoveled out of it before we could wash floors and furniture."

Postponing Marriage and Children

MAP 17-1   THE DUST BOWL

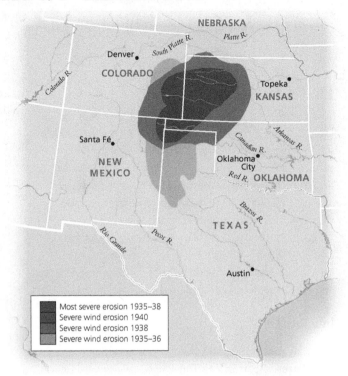

■	Most severe erosion 1935–38
■	Severe wind erosion 1940
■	Severe wind erosion 1938
■	Severe wind erosion 1935–36

After several years of drought conditions, high winds blew up violent dust storms in the mid 1930s. Federal programs sought to improve soil conditions and water management, but years of stripping the landscape of its natural vegetation limited the effectiveness of such efforts.

The strain Americans faced at home placed new importance on women's role as homemaker. Yet, with such economic uncertainty, couples postponed marriage during the Depression, opting to wait it out while they lived at home with parents or family.

The marriage rate fell to new lows in the 1930s. Young couples who could have set off to build a new family, with all its associated expenses, deferred doing so, leaving a generation of Americans who simply missed out on marriage altogether. One estimate claimed that 1.5 million people had postponed marriage. For the cohort of women in their twenties and thirties during the Great Depression, the proportion of single women was 30 percent higher than it had been in the 1920s. Divorce also was out of reach because of the expenses involved in legally dissolving a marriage. Many couples found getting federal relief was easier as a family and so weathered marriages until the crisis passed.

For those couples who did marry, many deferred having children until economic times improved. The U.S. birthrate fell below the replacement level for the first time. The birthrate went from 97.4 births per one thousand women of childbearing age to 75.7 in 1933. Lower birthrates were in part a result of the growing acceptability of birth control. Birth control, long controversial and illegal for all who did not have a doctor's order, became more acceptable as families struggled to feed themselves. Associated with radicalism and women's rights in the 1910s, birth control had by the 1930s

WOMEN'S VOICES

DUST BOWL DIARY

The drought that gripped the Great Plains region of the United States throughout the 1930s not only devastated the land but also changed the life course of many women. Struggling against encroaching poverty, families that chose to stay on their farms found that life was full of sacrifices. For young Americans, it often meant sacrificing wedding plans until economic times improved. Living in North Dakota, college-educated Ann Marie Low kept a diary during the 1930s. In it, she recorded her feelings about the exacting cost of the Depression and the dust bowl on her work and family aspirations.

July 9, 1934

Saturday night Cap and I went to the movies, Claudette Colbert in *The Torch Singer*. Afterward he bought ice cream cones and we sat in the car in front of the store eating them. He brought up the subject of marriage. I reminded him that he promised, if I would go out with him occasionally, he would not mention marriage. I also pointed out the impossibility. He has to run the farm until Sonny is old enough and then will have nothing to start out on his own. I have to work until Ethel gets through college and can help Bud, at least two years. If she doesn't help Bud, we are looking at four years. Though I didn't mention it, in four years Cap will be thirty-six years old. Forget it.

He insisted he wants to get married now. Then I turned shrewish and said I'd seen him leave a dance last year with Joan. If he wants a wife, she would doubtless marry him.

He said he did take her home from a dance once, but there is absolutely nothing between him and Joan and I know it—I am all he wants and I know it.

"Let's not quarrel," I murmured. "Things will work out somehow."

He leaned back against the car seat, saying somberly, "Oh, how I wish it would rain."

The light from the store window was on his face. He is really a handsome man, with a John Barrymore profile and thick wavy auburn hair. Suddenly I seemed to see what his face will be someday—a tombstone on which is written the epitaph of dead dreams. I shivered.

"Oh, Sweetheart, you are cold and have no wrap. I'll take you home."

I didn't tell him I wasn't shivering from the cold.

Source: *Ann Marie Low, Dust Bowl Diary (Lincoln: University of Lincoln Press, 1984), 100.*

Questions

1. Low's feelings toward marrying Cap are complicated by her family obligations as well as her desire for a more romantic hero. What keeps her from marrying him?

2. In what ways does Low's diary reflect the larger issues women faced in the 1930s?

United States v. One Package of Japanese Pessaries This case challenged the Comstock Act and made it legal for medical professionals to ship and receive contraceptives.

become firmly under the control of doctors and professional health-care workers. Many of the clinics that had been forced to close their doors in the 1920s suddenly found their services in great demand.

In 1936, the federal court decision, ***United States v. One Package of Japanese Pessaries***, made obtaining birth control much easier when it overturned all remaining vestiges of the Comstock law, the law that banned the sending and selling of contraceptive information and devices (see chapter 10). The case came about when birth control activist Margaret Sanger decided to import a new type of diaphragm (pessary)

TABLE 17-1 Median Income of Black Families Compared to the Median Income of White Families for Selected Cities, 1935–1936

City and Type of Family	Black	White	Black Income as a Percentage of White Income
Husband–Wife Families			
New York	$980	$1,930	51%
Chicago	$726	$1,687	43%
Columbus	$831	$1,622	51%
Atlanta	$632	$1,876	34%
Columbia	$576	$1,876	31%
Mobile	$481	$1,419	34%
Other Families			
Atlanta	$332	$940	35%
Columbia	$254	$1,403	18%
Mobile	$301	$784	38%

Source: Gunnar Myrdal et al., An American Dilemma (New York: Harper and Brothers, 1944).

designed by a Japanese physician. She had a large number shipped from Tokyo to the United States, where the shipment was seized and confiscated under Section 305 of the Tariff Act, an outgrowth of the Comstock law. Judge Augustus Hand ruled in her favor, stating that if the Congress of the 1870s had possessed the same clinical data on the dangers of pregnancy and the usefulness of contraception that were available in the 1930s, it would never have classified birth control as obscene. By 1940, all states except Massachusetts and Connecticut had legalized the distribution of birth control information to married couples.

The African American birthrate had been steadily dropping since the end of the nineteenth century and continued to do so in the 1930s. For generations, black women had devised methods for birth control and ending unwanted pregnancies that did not require the help of white doctors. During the Depression, the need for planned or deliberate parenthood mobilized support for birth control clinics in black communities, with some advocates linking it to greater autonomy from white doctors and to a larger program of better health services for women and children. Community-sponsored birth control clinics for African Americans opened in Baltimore, New York, Louisville, Fredericksburg, and Boston. These community-based clinics became the foundation in 1939 for the Division of Negro Services in the Birth Control Federation of America.

Gender and the Politics of Providing

During the Depression, more married women and older women entered the workforce, continuing a trend that had begun in 1920s. By decade's end, the median age of the woman worker was over thirty and married women made up 35 percent of all women employed, up from 15 percent in 1900. The growth in the number of working wives testified not to women's desire for self-fulfillment or to the feminist goal of economic equality but to the reality of poverty in the 1930s. Given that half of all American families earned less than twelve hundred dollars annually, married women's work became crucial to the family's ability to weather the economic crisis.

Even as families depended on the wages working wives brought in, many Americans accused working wives of being selfish for taking jobs away from men. Unemployed men became symbolic of national decline—and working men of national strength. States banned married women from local government work in the name of giving work to men. For example, in King County, Washington, the new law gave fifty jobs once held by married women to men, a drop in the sea of the eighty-three thousand unemployed men in that county alone. Banning married women from full-time work missed the reality of the gender-segregated job market, a situation in which the jobs held by women were not jobs men would take. Forcing married women out of their employment strongholds in nursing, clerking, or secretarial work, for example, did little for the unemployed steelworker or automobile factory operative.

Such logic denied the reality of women's occupational location. Working women did not compete for jobs historically reserved for men. Women worked as domestics and in pink-collar work. Ironically, the sex typing of jobs that limited the job opportunities available to women granted women workers a degree of protection from the worst effects of the Depression. The sectors of the economy that lost the most jobs in the 1930s were heavy industry and manufacturing, both strongholds of men's employment. The occupations with the highest concentration of women workers, like clerical, trade, and service jobs, contracted less during the Depression. In reality, men did lose more jobs than did women. Yet, the overall number of men in the workforce had been and remained substantially higher than for women.

Such nuances proved irrelevant to a public looking for quick solutions to widespread unemployment. Legislatures and organizations restricted married women's work opportunities. Married female teachers were hit the hardest. In 1931, a National Education Association that surveyed fifteen hundred schools nationwide found that 77 percent no longer hired married women and 63 percent fired female teachers if they married. Also, 84 percent of insurance companies, 65 percent of banks, and 63 percent of public utilities restricted married women's work, a National Industrial Conference Board survey found. The New England Telephone and Telegraph Company, the Northern Pacific Railway, and the Norfolk and Western Railway Company fired their married women employees in 1931. The federal government followed the same trend. Section 213 of the 1932 National Economy Act outlawed more than one family member from working for the civil service, and women were the ones most often dismissed.

College-educated women and professional women faired particularly poorly in the 1930s. The number of women teachers in elementary and secondary schools fell from 85 percent in 1920 to 78 percent in 1940. For those who remained, promotion to superintendents of schools was rare. While women made up one-third of the nation's college graduates, they comprised only 7.9 percent of college faculties. Women's colleges like Smith and Barnard warned their graduating seniors that few women with bachelor degrees were able to find paid work. Dean Eugenia Leonard of Syracuse University urged female college graduates to focus on volunteer rather than salaried work. The Institute of Women's Professional Relations suggested that women seeking graduate degrees direct themselves to home economics and interior decoration, fields still without male competition.

During the Great Depression, the proportion of all professional women workers fell. Between 1925 and 1945, for example, American medical schools placed a quota of 5 percent on female admissions, making the 1930s the only decade in the twentieth century to post a decline in the percentage of female doctors. Columbia and Harvard law schools refused to accept female applicants throughout the 1920s and 1930s; and as late as 1937, the New York City Bar Association excluded female members, making it illegal for women to practice law in the city. The decline of women in the professions, which began in the 1930s, continued to the 1970s.

While much separated the experience of the female domestic from the female college professor, they shared the ways that a sex-segregated job market shaped their opportunities for work and their earnings. In terms of pay, women across the job spectrum were paid less than men, even when they held identical jobs. Across all industries, women earned 50 to 65 percent of what men were paid. According to the Social Security Administration, in 1937, for example, a woman worker took home an average of $525 per year in contrast to the $1,027 brought home by a man.

Many working women could not meet their basic living costs on such low pay. The Consumers' League of New York reported on the expenses of a woman who earned four dollars a week. After twenty cents for carfare, twenty-five cents for lunch, and twenty-five cents for child care each day, which totaled $3.90 a week, she had ten cents per week to cover all her other expenses. Such realities contradicted the popular notion that women worked primarily for "pin money," that is, to buy luxury items for themselves and not contribute to the bread and butter needed to support a family. As one man wrote, a man who worked "spends his income to support the family while the woman spends for permanent waves, lip sticks. . . . The woman comes home says she works for her money and she will do as she pleases with it which is a fact. . . ." Dislodging such a view seemed all but impossible during the Great Depression.

The public outcry against working married women expressed a tangle of anxieties about manhood, family, and survival in an uncertain time. Working women, historically segregated to lower paying, nonmanagerial, and menial jobs, were not literally taking jobs away from men desperate to work in the 1930s; and neither did married women, a group who made up only 35 percent of all working women. The threat that women workers posed, then, was not to unemployed men but to the ideology of men as the principal breadwinners in the family, a status so important to definitions of healthy masculinity.

Sociologists Robert and Helen Lynd, in the sequel to their 1920s study of Muncie, Indiana, *Middletown in Transition* (1937), noted that although women's domestic roles stayed the same during times of crisis, men's roles changed significantly and in ways that could be psychologically difficult for them. As the primary breadwinners, men measured their success based on what they could provide for their family. A failed economy created a sense of failure in working men who could not fulfill their role as breadwinner. Despite such worries, sociologists found men's authority at home did not wane, even if unemployed. Men and women embraced the ideal of a strong father. Sociologist Mirra Komarovsky, in her 1940 *The Unemployed Man and His Family*, a report on lower-middle-class white families, found that even when unemployed, men did not report losing status in their home. In only one-quarter of her

FIGURE 17-1 UNEMPLOYMENT 1925–1945

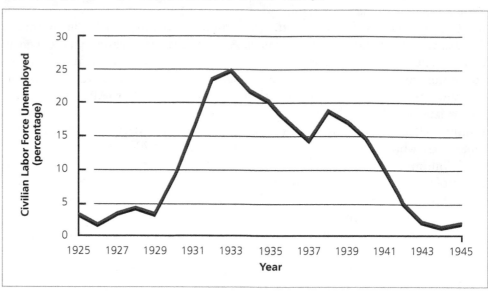

With the collapse of the economy, unemployment soared in the 1930s. The range of New Deal programs that were designed to restore economic activity put some Americans to work but did not end the job shortage. Only with the U.S. entry into World War II would the economy return to full capacity.

respondents did a man report feeling undermined as head of his family from being unemployed. Sociologist Margaret Jarman Hagood, in her study *Mothers of the South* (1939), also demonstrated the independence of male authority from the vicissitudes of the economy. Regardless of their poverty, white tenant farm women upheld the ideal of the male-headed household. According to Hagood, wives willingly yielded to their husbands "the prerogative of planning and managing the farm, of assigning tasks and directing the family's labor on it, of selling the crop at their own discretion and pocketing the proceeds." Hagood concluded that both men and women accepted the "rightness of male dominance."

Concern with the male breadwinner—by sociologists and employers alike—was part of the widespread attention paid throughout the 1930s to traditional gender roles as a bulwark against the uncertainties of the period. Whether or not unemployment damaged men more than women, whether or not women took jobs away from men, the perception of masculinity in crisis was real and had concrete effects. The jobs that women left in federal agencies—teaching and social work—and the lower wages they earned for work in industry might not have helped the majority of unemployed men, but it nonetheless did important ideological work in shoring up the historic authority and dominance of men and masculinity.

ACTIVISM

In the face of growing hostilities toward "the woman worker," working-class women continued to earn wages to support their families. Coming out of class and ethnic traditions of labor unionism, working-class women came together to protect their jobs and protest their falling hours and wages. In 1932, the American labor movement had only 2.8 million union members. Yet, thanks to the unionizing of mass production industries like automobile, steel, rubber, and textiles, union membership hit over 10.5 million by the outbreak of World War II. Changes in the labor movement made it possible for more women to join unions. Historically, the craft-oriented American Federation of Labor (AFL) ignored workers in mass production and unskilled laborers, job classifications in which women dominated. In 1935, a group of more militant AFL union officials and communists committed to workers' rights formed the Committee for Industrial Organization with the goal of organizing mass production workers by industry rather than by craft, a goal that promised to be more friendly to women workers. By 1938, the committee had nearly four million members, withdrew from the AFL, and renamed themselves the **Congress of Industrial Organizations (CIO).** At the same time, women supported the labor movement by joining women's auxiliaries of unions in which their husbands, brothers, or fathers were members. These auxiliaries, like the Women's Emergency Brigade for the 1936 United Automobile Worker strike at two General Motor plants in Flint, Michigan, sent tangible support to striking workers, many of whom occupied factories for weeks at a time. Facing a historic economic crisis, working women demonstrated determination and creativity in their efforts to improve their lives.

Congress of Industrial Organizations (CIO)
The labor union formed in 1935 by John L. Lewis as the result of a dispute with the American Federation of Labor.

Appalachian Women in the Textile Industry

Some regions of the country felt the drag of the economic downturn before the October 1929 stock market crash. By the mid-1920s, Appalachia, once the home of farms and farmers, had been crisscrossed by railroad tracks and dotted with mill villages, and the Piedmont had eclipsed New England as the world's leading producer of yarn and cloth (see chapter 12). By 1933, southern mills produced over 70 percent of the country's cotton and woolen textiles. The cash-wages "public work" done by daughters in textile mills continued to be vitally important to working families. Technological improvements made the mill machines faster, but higher levels of productivity did not translate to higher wages for mill operatives. Overproduction, along with falling need for cotton after World War I, and growing international competition depressed textile workers' already low wages. Factory owners tried to squeeze more work from their employees through what workers called "stretchout," speeding up production by increasing the number of looms assigned to each factory hand, limiting break times, and increasing the number of supervisors to keep workers from slowing down, taking breaks, or leaving work. The stretchout triggered a wave of walkouts throughout the Southeast.

One such walkout took place in 1929 and was led by a group of women. In 1928, two large "artificial silk" or rayon plants operated in the small East Tennessee town of Elizabethton. Town officials had courted the rayon giant, Glanzstoff, by promising the German industrialists that they would have an abundant supply of docile and cheap labor. The first plant, Bemberg, employed 886 men and 384 women; the larger mill, Glanzstoff, employed 1,099 men and 854 women. While all employees worked a fifty-six-hour week, wages for women remained considerably lower than those for men. The women worked ten-hour days winding, reeling, twisting, and inspecting rayon yarn; and their work brought in much-needed wages to families hurt by falling timber yields and failed farms. Teenage women made up 44 percent of the Glanzstoff workforce, most between the ages of sixteen and twenty-one. Like the Lowell textile workers of the nineteenth century (see chapter 7), these daughters of farm families blended home life and work life through bonds of friendship and solidarity as they commuted each day in packed caravans of Model Ts or shared crowded rooms in nearby boardinghouses.

On March 12, 1929, Margaret Bowen, a worker at Glanzstoff, led a walkout of 523 women operatives. Four days later, Bemberg workers struck in sympathy with the Glanzstoff operatives. The workers' protests centered on low wages, unfair promotion policies, and petty regulations that applied only to females. These rules included wearing no makeup, purchasing their own uniforms, and submitting to supervised washrooms where their pay was docked if they lingered too long. "If we went to the bathroom, they'd follow us," Flossie Cole confirmed, "'fraid we'd stay a minute too long." The courts quickly granted injunctions against the strikers, and Tennessee Governor Henry Horton immediately sent two companies of national guardsmen to Elizabethton.

On March 22, a "gentleman's agreement" was reached between the company and the United Textile Workers (UTW) in which the Glanzstoff owners agreed to a new wage scale for "good girl help" and fair treatment of union members. When the raises never materialized and two union leaders were kidnapped and run out of town, a second and more violent phase of the strike began. The women in the Glanzstoff reeling room staged a walkout. "When they blew that whistle everybody knew to quit work," Flossie Cole recalled. "We all just quit our work and rushed out. Some of 'em went to (the nearby plant) Bemberg and climbed the fence. [They] went into Bemberg and got 'em out of there." With both plants closed by what workers called a "spontaneous and complete walkout," the UTW promised support. The plants became fortresses when the national guard arrived with machine guns on the rooftops and armed guardsmen on the ground. The company sent buses manned by soldiers farther up the hollows to recruit new workers and to escort them back to town. Angry workers blocked narrow mountain roads. An estimated 1,250 individuals were arrested in confrontations with the national guard.

As men in the union battled the national guard, women strikers engaged in playful "feminine" actions to advance the strike. Hundreds of "disorderly" working girls from the surrounding hills crowded in taxis and buses and rode through the main street, laughing and pointing at the people watching them. They teased national guardsmen, ridiculed strikebreakers, and disrupted traffic and the flow of goods and workers into plants. Some strikers used theatrical measures. In Elizabethton, twenty-eight-year-old Trixie Perry, a reeler in the Glanzstoff plant, and Texas Bill, a female textile worker, led women who had wrapped themselves in the American flag in front of guardsmen who were forced to present arms each time they passed a flag. At trial, both women continued to use their gender against their accusers in creative ways. When asked if she had blocked a road, Perry answered: "A little thing like me block a big road?" When asked why she was out on the road so early, Texas Bill answered: "I take a walk every morning before breakfast for my health."

Using ordinary language in ways that empowered them and ensnaring the court in its own definition of ladylike behavior, these women and others found novel ways to assert their class-based politics. Leaving family homes for a day or a week and living and working with other women also fostered a gender solidarity that proved instrumental in the textile strikes—if not their outcome. When the strike ended on May 26, 1929, six weeks after it had begun, the women returned to work with little improvement in their wages, hours, or work conditions.

Textile strikes continued, like those at Gastonia in 1929 where the National Guard violently suppressed a strike led by the UTW. Workers initially greeted the

Woman were active in the wave of labor protests that broke out in the 1930s in response to falling wages and violations of labor codes. In the General Textile strike of 1934, shown here, approximately 44,000 million workers in Georgia participated in the protest.

National Recovery Administration (NRA), established in 1933 to reduce overproduction, raise wages, control hours, and guarantee the right of workers to form unions, with optimism. But their optimism faded as the codes created to regulate industries favored owners over workers. New Deal legislation brought some improvement to the conditions in textile factories. However, employers kept the speedup in place, requiring the same amount of work to be done in forty hours as in the previous sixty; and the NRA codes did little to stop it. Frustrated at their union leadership, textile workers pushed for a strike. On Labor Day, September 3, 1934, four hundred thousand workers went on strike and the textile industry was shut down. While the strike did not result in an end to the speedup or improvement in wages, it represented growing power of the labor movement in the 1930s. Ordinary women like Trixie Perry and Texas Bill showed a daring that the UTW or the NRA needed but often lacked.

Chinese Women in San Francisco's Garment Industry

Newly arrived Chinese women found wage work in the small nonunion garment factories near Chinatowns on the East and West coasts. By the 1930s, they were confronting the hard reality of low wages, long hours, and little recourse to improve their work conditions. With the labor movement gaining ground each year of the Depression, the

National Recovery Administration (NRA) The government agency established to coordinate businesses who voluntarily drew up "codes of fair competition" to enhance economic recovery. These codes were intended to help workers by setting minimum wages and maximum hours, and help consumers by setting fair prices.

The International Ladies Garment Workers Union (ILGWU) Formed in 1900 by the amalgamation of seven local unions.

International Ladies Garment Workers Union (ILGWU) hoped to convince Chinese garment workers to join the union.

The ILGWU was one of the first unions to have a primarily female membership and one of the original unions of the CIO (see chapter 12). Founded in 1900 and comprised mainly of Jewish women, the membership of the ILGWU had diversified by the 1930s, reflecting the changing ethnic makeup of the industry's workforce. The union had expanded its ranks 400 percent in the 1930s by opening membership to African American and Mexican American women. In addition to higher wages and shorter hours, the union pioneered benefits such as pension funds, cooperative housing, health care, education, and cultural activities.

Class and ethnic divisions complicated efforts to unionize Chinese garment workers. In San Francisco's Chinatown, the garment industry employed one thousand women in sixty-nine mid- to small-size Chinese-owned factories, most with fewer than fifty workers. The majority of women were foreign born and mothers of young children. San Francisco's Chinese factories paid their workers less that half of what union workers earned and were able to underbid unionized factories. For Chinese contractors who faced chronic racism, underbidding on contracts was the only way to establish a foothold in the highly competitive industry. As with an earlier generation of immigrant women, many of whom worked in the textile factories at the turn of the century, newly arrived Chinese women with few marketable skills had little choice but to accept the harsh work conditions. The ILGWU hoped to either organize the Chinese workers or drive nonunion factories out of business to raise the overall condition of the industry's workers. Despite attention from the ILGWU since the early 1930s, Chinese garment workers remained leery of unionizing.

At first, Chinese women garment workers did not see the union as offering them anything they needed. Chinese neighborhoods were comprised of a web of economic and social relationships that protected their residents through a combination of paternalistic business practices and charities. Associations, churches, and other charity organizations provided help in emergencies, including the *hoi fan*—dinner for a nickel. Chinese businessmen who provided their workers with lunch gave leftover food to needy families, a practice called *wan fan*. There were no breadlines or Hoovervilles, the encampments of cardboard shacks where homeless people lived, in American Chinatowns. Yet, there were also few opportunities for wage work. According to Sue Ko Lee, "You couldn't get out of Chinatown and work anywhere else. You either worked in a laundry, restaurant, or your own barbershop." Women, she recalled, had even fewer opportunities "except to pick shrimp at home. There weren't too many employers."

As conditions worsened under the economic crisis, union organizer Jennie Matyas gained the trust of the Chinese women garment workers. In November 1937, the Chinese Ladies' Garment Workers' Union (LGWU) was chartered and three months later endorsed the ILGWU to be their collective bargaining agent. The following year, the Chinese LGWU launched a strike against the California retailer, the National Dollar Stores. Its owner, Joe Shoong, was one of the wealthiest Chinese businessmen in the country. The store said it paid its workers California's minimum wage of $13.33 for a forty-eight-hour week. Yet, according to the National Dollar Stores workers, 80 percent of whom were immigrant women, the chain never followed either of the state's labor laws. The LGWU and the retailer quickly agreed to wage increases, to a fully unionized workforce, and that all hiring would be decided by the union. Two weeks later, however, National Dollar Stores sold its Chinatown factory to Golden Gate Manufacturing while keeping the retail chain. By selling the Chinatown factory, the company could evade the union contract with the Chinatown workers and use nonunion factories to produce their clothing at much lower costs. The Chinese LGWU called a strike and began picketing both the factory and three of the National Dollar Stores in San Francisco on February 26, 1938.

The strike divided the Chinese in San Francisco, pitting as it did union protestors against Shoong, an active and generous member of the Chinatown community. Chinatown's powerful businesses resented being labeled "capitalists" and turned their back on the strikers. Stores that would have typically given aid to strikers denied them credit, while Chinese organizations offered strikers no support. Class divisions within Chinatown, once covered over by community aid and strong ethnic affiliation, became points of conflict as the Chinese garment workers forged conditional alliances with white female factory workers. Eventually the workers won a closed shop, a 5 percent raise, a forty-hour work week, and an agreement to use Golden Gate Company for a portion of their work.

The 105-day strike was the longest strike in the history of San Francisco's Chinatown. It showed the power of women workers to shape the conditions in which they worked. Yet, at the same time, the strike created less positive results. The Golden Gate Company went of out of business in 1939, one year after union leaders called for the strike. The union helped place workers elsewhere, but shortly after, the Chinese LGWU disbanded. The ease with which low-cost textile factories could be shut down and reestablished left textile workers with little recourse. Despite such vulnerabilities, the ILGWU remained a powerful force. At its height in the 1930s and 1940s, the ILGWU had a membership of three hundred thousand and was one of the most important and progressive unions in the United States.

Latinas and the California Canning Industry

In the fields of California, women agricultural workers began to protest their difficult and worsening work conditions. Relief agencies in California's San Joaquin Valley, for example, did not offer aid to agricultural laborers, and farmers repeatedly reduced the wages they offered workers. The **United Cannery, Agricultural, Packing and Allied Workers of America** (UCAPAWA), founded in 1937 and an affiliate of the CIO, was particularly strong among Mexican and Mexican American workers. The union relied on women's social networks and, as such, cultivated leadership among Mexican women. As union leaders and organizers, women pushed for benefits that aimed to improve the situation of working women such as maternity leave and equal pay for equal work.

In 1939, 430 Mexican American women staged a massive walkout at California Sanitary Canning Company, or Cal San. Earlier in the year, Dorothy Ray Healey, a national vice president of UCAPAWA, had started to recruit Cal San workers. The twenty-four-year-old Healey was already a veteran labor organizer in California's cannery industry. Within weeks of her arrival at Cal San, 400 of the 430 workers had joined the union. The workers began their strike at the height of peach season. The strikers demanded union recognition, elimination of the piece rate system (payment based on the number of fruit picked), and wage increases. The management refused to bargain with the union local, claiming, in error, that it did not represent a majority of workers. Healey immediately organized workers into a number of committees to pressure the company and support the

United Cannery, Agricultural, Packing and Allied Workers of America A labor union that made the greatest inroads with Mexican cannery workers and African American tobacco workers, many of whom were women.

strike. The food committee proved to be the most innovative by winning support of Latino shop owners. Not only did it persuade East Los Angeles grocers to donate staples like flour, sugar, and baby food to the Cal San strikers, it also requested grocers to refuse Cal San products and to remove current stocks from their shelves. If a grocer was unsympathetic, a small band of women picketed the shop during business hours.

After two months of little progress, striking workers took their contract dispute to the affluent neighborhood of Cal San's owners, George and Joseph Shapiro. Reminding onlookers that they were mothers as well as workers, they began round-the-clock picket lines, often including their children who held signs with "Shapiro is starving my Mama" and "I'm underfed because my Mama is underpaid." Such actions forged lines of sympathy across ethnicity and class that worked in the strikers' favor. After several days, the owners met with the union's negotiating team and ended the strike. The workers won a five-cent wage increase and new supervisors who would support the union. Under their own leadership, Mexican American women brought their roles as mother, consumer, and worker together in innovative ways, making the Cal San local the UCAPAWA's second largest.

Women's labor activism reached a historic high point in the 1930s. By 1938, female membership in unions rose to eight hundred thousand, a fourfold increase from 1924. Despite an upsurge in labor activism by women, the downward spiral of the economy and the unevenness of the recovery throughout the 1930s meant working women's efforts to better their situations were limited. Successes in specific industries did much to help those workers in their day-to-day lives, yet for the majority of American workers, male and female, the Depression kept their wages down, their anxieties high, and their belts pulled in tightly. Women workers, however, did have important allies in the administration of Franklin D. Roosevelt.

WOMEN AND THE NEW DEAL

A generation of women reformers who had devoted their professional lives to helping working women, children, and the poor found new ways to implement their social and political goals in the 1930s. From the Progressive Era through the New Deal, women's political activism moved beyond the sphere of voluntary association to lobbying and working within government at all levels to create the public or governmental apparatus to do what women had done in their own societies in the nineteenth century. Caring for the nation's less fortunate citizens, particularly women and children, moved from being a private charity to a public obligation. Like their male counterparts, many women in the New Deal saw the economic situation as a crisis in manhood. And like commentators who blamed men's unemployment on working women, the architects of the New Deal applied a gendered logic to the host of new programs they created. In legislation like the Social Security Act of 1935, assumptions about male wage work and female dependency were written into the new welfare state.

Eleanor Roosevelt and the Women's Network

Democratic women activists, many who lived and worked in New York City and were familiar with President Roosevelt as the former governor, found a powerful friend in the White House: First Lady Eleanor Roosevelt. Women actively involved with nongovernmental organizations such as the Women's Trade Union League, the League of

Women Voters, and the National Democratic Party knew each other and Eleanor Roosevelt professionally and personally and together forged a tight-knit network of female activists within New Deal agencies.

Born on October 11, 1884, to wealthy New York parents, Anna Hall and Elliott Roosevelt, the younger brother of Theodore, Eleanor was orphaned by the age of ten. She lived with her Grandmother Hall until she went to boarding school in London, and there she blossomed both intellectually and socially. She returned to New York City to make her debut in 1902. While traveling from New York City to Grandmother Hall's home, she became reacquainted with her fifth cousin once removed, Franklin Delano Roosevelt. FDR and Eleanor married two years later, and Eleanor's uncle, President Theodore Roosevelt, escorted his niece down the aisle. The couple moved to New York City; and within a year, Eleanor began a decade in which, she later wrote, "I was always just getting over having a baby or about to have one. . . ." In 1911, Dutchess County elected her husband to the New York State senate. The family moved to Albany. In 1913, Eleanor followed FDR to Washington where he served as assistant secretary of the navy. In 1921, FDR was stricken with polio. With the help of Eleanor and close friend

Four months before her husband's inauguration, Eleanor Roosevelt visited a soup kitchen for homeless and unemployed women on December 1, 1932. The worsening economic crisis left thousands of Americans homeless and hungry. In large urban centers like Detroit and Chicago, unemployment reached 50 percent by 1932, fueling political discontentment that led to Franklin D. Roosevelt's overwhelming victory over Herbert Hoover.

Louis Howe, FDR resumed his political career and was elected governor of New York in 1928. This private crisis marked the beginning of Eleanor's political career. In the 1920s and during her husband's years as the governor of New York, Eleanor participated in the four centers of political power open to women in New York State: the Women's Division of the New York State Democratic Committee, the League of Women Voters, the Women's Trade Union League, and the Women's City Club. At the City Club, she met and worked with politically active women such as social workers Lillian Wald and Molly Dewson and labor reformers like Francis Perkins, all of whom were leading reformers during the Progressive era.

As First Lady, Eleanor provided a crucial bridge between female activists and the president. Eleanor assembled a list of women qualified for executive-level appointments, urged the Roosevelt administration to hire them, and, when their suggestions did not get a fair hearing, she did not hesitate to take their ideas to her husband. As Molly Dewson, Director of the **Women's Division of the Democratic National Committee** and avid Roosevelt campaigner, said, "when I wanted help on some definite point, Mrs. Roosevelt gave me the opportunity to sit by the President at dinner and the matter was settled before we finished our soup." As with other Democratic women, Eleanor wanted to see the federal government adopt many of the remedies Progressive women had successfully established on the state level through protective legislation:

Women's Division of the Democratic National Committee The group within the National Democratic Party that organized and coordinated women's volunteer efforts for Democratic candidates.

to ban child labor, to limit the number of hours an employer could force a woman to work, and to remedy the unsafe and exploitative conditions many women faced. The network of women activists who relied on Eleanor in part included women who held top federal jobs in Washington in the 1930s as well as other well-known reformers like Grace Abbott, director of the Children's Bureau, Mary Anderson, director of the Women's Bureau, and Rose Schneiderman, of the Women's Trade Union League.

The network of progressive women of which Eleanor was a part were bound together by emotional ties as well as political ones (see Chapter 15). As with an earlier cohort of reform and professional women, the women who spent their lives working together created affectionate bonds that lasted over a lifetime. Letters often expressed friendships that easily blended work and personal lives. The network of political women connected to Eleanor came of age in the beginning of the century where careers and marriage were seen as irreconcilable and when society still valued female bonding. They lived within circles of women who had devoted themselves to social service and political careers, leaving them in the last remnants of a nineteenth-century woman-centered political and personal world. As with women who graduated from college between 1889 and 1908, for whom rates of marriage hovered at fifty percent, many New Deal women remained unmarried. Although unmarried, they were not single. Among this network of activists were pairs of women committed to each other. Molly Dewson, for example, formed a lifelong relationship with Polly Porter with whom she shared her home and her work for over thirty years. Journalist Esther Lape and Elizabeth Read, Eleanor's personal attorney and financial advisor, and Marion Dickerman and Nancy Cook, both long time Democratic Party activists, also formed "Boston marriages," loving partnerships with each other that sustained them professionally and personally (see Chapter 14).

Eleanor herself had an unconventional marriage. While her relationship with Franklin was successful as a political partnership and the couple raised five children, he had a long-standing romantic relationship with Lucy Mercer, Eleanor's friend and personal secretary, and later with his private secretary, Missy LeHand. Eleanor turned to other important people in her life for emotional intimacy, two specifically. Earl Miller and Lorena Hickok. Her body guard since 1929, Earl Miller was an athletic man who charmed Eleanor with his attention and affection. She also formed a deep and longstanding relationship with journalist Lorena Hickok, whom she met during the presidential campaign of 1932. Hickok, who was covering Eleanor for the Associated Press, became the first lady's close friend and confidante, so much so that Hickok left AP because she could no longer be objective while covering the Roosevelts. Eleanor, who missed the attentions of a loving mother for most of her life, turned to Hickok as a source of emotional support. During their separations, Eleanor wrote ten- and twelve-page letters to Lorena daily, filled with political details and expressions of love. "The nicest time of the day is when I write to you. You have a stormier time than I do but I miss you as much I think. I couldn't bear to think of you crying yourself to sleep. Oh! How I wanted to put my arms about you in reality instead of in spirit . . . Please keep most of your heart in Washington as long as I'm here for most of mine is with you!"

Hickok provided invaluable political and personal advice to Eleanor as the first lady struggled to adjust to Washington politics and her role in the White House. The two women traveled together to vacation spots and on official trips. In 1940, Eleanor invited her to live at the White House. Eleanor's many relationships, including the committed and supportive one with her husband and those of the women's network, sustained her in a variety of ways, enabling her to be the political force in Washington that she was.

WOMEN'S LIVES

MARY WILLIAMS (MOLLY) DEWSON

Nicknamed "the little general" by Franklin D. Roosevelt, Molly Dewson was one of the most effective female party politicians of the twentieth century. As with her friend Eleanor Roosevelt, Dewson's political biography links turn-of-the-century Progressivism to the New Deal. Born in Quincy, Massachusetts, in 1874, Dewson graduated from Wellesley College as a social worker in 1897. For three years, she worked as a research economist for the Woman's Educational and Industrial Union of Boston, after which she became superintendent of the Massachusetts Girls' Parole Department. In 1911, she served also as secretary of the Commission on Minimum Wage Legislation for Massachusetts. In 1915, Dewson joined the Massachusetts suffrage movement. After Red Cross service during World War I, Dewson worked as Florence Kelley's principal assistant in the National Consumers' League campaign for state minimum wage laws for women and children. From 1925 to 1931, she served as president of the New York Consumers' League, working closely with Eleanor Roosevelt, leading the lobbying effort of the Women's Joint Legislative Conference, and playing a central role in the passage of a 1930 New York law limiting women to forty-eight-hour work weeks.

In 1928, she became more active in the Democratic Party, helping in the campaign of Al Smith and FDR's 1930 gubernatorial and 1932 presidential races. Dewson was appointed head of the Democratic National Committee's (DNC) Women's Division.

Dewson understood the importance of women's participation in the Democratic Party machinery and in the government. She worked tirelessly to provide even representation in membership and leadership positions for women on party committees from the precinct level up. Dewson was instrumental in securing the post of secretary of labor for Frances Perkins and placing women high up in the Social Security and National Recovery Administrations. A year after retiring from the DNC in 1936, Dewson became a member of the Social Security Board. She and her lifetime partner, Polly Porter, split their time between New York City and Castine, Maine. Dewson died in Castine in 1962 of complications following a stroke. ∎

Women in the New Deal

By the time the Roosevelts moved into the White House, the economic crisis had worsened. Banks foreclosed on over a thousand homes a day, thirty-eight states had closed their banks, and local governments were unprepared to handle the swelling ranks of the unemployed. An estimated 140,000 women and girls were homeless, and almost four million women were unemployed. Dismayed that no specific program existed to alleviate the suffering of women, Eleanor Roosevelt sponsored a White House Conference on the Emergency Needs of Women in November 1933, which so many of the women's network attended that a reporter quipped that the White House was becoming "Hull House on Pennsylvania Avenue." Harry Hopkins, head of the **Federal Emergency Relief Administration (FERA),** the agency that gave federal money to state governments to fund work and relief programs, worked together with Ellen Sullivan Woodward, head of the Women's Division of the FERA, and Frances Perkins, FDR's secretary of labor, to design work programs for women. The FERA work programs for women used commonplace understandings of "women's work," such as sewing and canning, as well as jobs in clerical, nursing, and teaching fields. By the end of 1933, over three hundred thousand women were employed. By January 1934, every state relief administrator received sixty job descriptions and was ordered to hire a women's division coordinator to recruit women of all races and backgrounds. The **Works Progress Administration (WPA),** the agency that replaced the FERA, was the largest of the New Deal programs and provided recipients work in federally funded programs, including women. The WPA programs built many public buildings, projects, and roads and operated large arts, drama, media, and literacy projects. Over 25 percent of the women employed by the WPA were professionals: teachers, athletic directors, artists, photographers, librarians, nurses, performers, musicians, technicians, and administrators. However, the majority of the women were unskilled and reemployed in domestic services, mattress and bedding projects, surplus cotton projects, or sewing and craft projects. Federal programs paid women less than men and limited their access to better-paying federal work. For example, the administrators of the **Civilian Conservation Corps (CCC),** a relief program designed to combat poverty by giving young men work in construction and conservation projects, barred women from "outside" work and prohibited them from the numerous reforestation and environmental projects. The CCC men received a wage of one dollar a day; women who worked at the camps, feeding and doing laundry, received "an allowance" of fifty cents a week. Women's reemployment was slow. By 1938, over three million women remained unemployed; almost two million women suffered the insufficiency of part-time work.

The first lady's activism and the strong network of political and personal allies made the Roosevelt administration uniquely willing to appoint women to high-level positions in the government. Two women—Frances Perkins and Mary McLeod Bethune—became among the most prominent women in the New Deal. Mary McLeod Bethune headed the Negro Division of the **National Youth Administration,** a program designed to help young people learn skills and wages. Bethune was the undisputed leader of Roosevelt's "Black Cabinet," an informal group comprised of twenty-seven high-ranking men and three women who worked in emergency agencies. The group met every Friday in Bethune's Washington home. Like Eleanor, Bethune connected generations of black women's activism to the New Deal. After years as an

Federal Emergency Relief Administration (FERA) Passed in 1933, the agency gave direct aid to the states, which funneled funds through such local agencies as home relief bureaus and departments of welfare for poor relief.

Works Progress Administration (WPA) A massive federal relief program launched that created paying jobs for unemployed.

Civilian Conservation Corps (CCC) Program was designed to tackle the problem of unemployed young men from ages 18 to 25.

National Youth Administration A program to devise useful work for young people who were on relief in 1935.

educator, Bethune became the leader of the National Association of Colored Women (NACW), the umbrella organization that coordinated black women's clubs. Under her leadership, Bethune tried to turn the focus of the NACW away from self-help and moral uplift and toward broader social issues. When institutional change proved difficult, she formed the **National Council of Negro Women (NCNW)** to coordinate women's efforts to improve African American rights. As with other women active in the New Deal, her friendship with Eleanor granted her access to the president where she could advocate for establishing a Negro division of the National Youth Administration (NYA).

Frances Perkins, the first woman to serve as a cabinet member, served as secretary of labor for all twelve years of the Roosevelt administration. Her political biography demonstrates the deep roots of New Deal liberal reform in Progressive activism. Born in Boston on April 10, 1880, Perkins graduated from Mount Holyoke College in 1903. The following year, she took a teaching job at Ferry Hall, a girls' preparatory school in Lake Forest, Illinois, where she met Dr. Graham Taylor, head of Chicago Commons, one of the city's famous settlement houses. Through him, Perkins learned about trade unionism and met other reform leaders including Jane Addams, Ellen Gates Starr, and Grace Abbott. By the time she returned to the East in 1907, she was firmly committed to social work. In 1910, Perkins became secretary of the New York Consumers' League. Florence Kelley, the NYCL's national director, helped Perkins become a recognized

National Council of Negro Women (NCNW) Founded to bring together many different national and local organizations serving or representing African American women.

Educator and presidential advisor Mary McLeod Bethune chats with first lady Eleanor Roosevelt beside Executive Director Aubrey Williams of the National Youth Administration during the Nation Conference on Youth Problems in 1937. Bethune played a crucial role in directing federal money to young African Americans during the Depression as the head of the Negro Division of the National Youth Administration. She enjoyed a close working relationship with Eleanor Roosevelt.

expert on industrial conditions by assigning her to survey unsanitary cellar bakeries, unsafe laundries, and overcrowded textile sweatshops. On March 25, 1911, Perkins witnessed the Triangle Shirtwaist Company fire, a tragedy that galvanized the city's reform agencies into action (see chapter 15). As secretary of labor, Perkins surrounded herself with a group of women activists who shared her concern for women's issues. One of the most enduring contributions Perkins made was the **Fair Labor Standards Act of 1938.** The Fair Labor Standards Act was a culmination of Perkins's long-standing advocacy for minimum wage and maximum hour legislation. The last of the New Deal's major social measures, this Act covered twelve million workers, immediately raised the pay of three hundred thousand people, and shortened hours for a million more. Child labor, a major concern of Perkins since her days as a social worker, was prohibited in many industries.

Fair Labor Standards Act of 1938 The federal law establishing minimum wages, standards for overtime work and pay, and restrictions on child labor.

modern welfare state Federal and state programs that offer working populations protections against unemployment, sickness, old-age insecurity, and the loss of a family breadwinner. FDR hoped the New Deal would create cradle-to-grave security against "the hazards and vicissitudes of life."

With high-level appointments like those of Perkins and Bethune, women reformers had at last achieved some governmental authority. Women staffed and headed New Deal agencies where their commitment to improving the lives of women and the political power of women could be translated into policies. For some observers, the 1930s were the long-awaited years in which women's activist networks and their attendant commitment to gender equality had at last come into fruition. Through the women's network, governmental and nongovernmental organizations worked in unison to advance the welfare state that had been central to the goals of women reformers during the Progressive Era.

Yet, in casting their lot with the Democratic Party, women reformers turned away from women-run institutions that had for so long supported women's political organizing. As women moved into government, they risked becoming token representatives of equality rather than true political players. For example, Perkins, perhaps the strongest woman after Eleanor Roosevelt in the government, could not parlay the fundamental feminist goal of equal pay for equal work. Integration, or the end of gender separation as a strategy to advance women's causes, had paradoxical outcomes. The appointment of reformers like Perkins and Bethune in the federal government was important. At the same time, as the idea of a powerful women's bloc of voters vanished along with many female-run voluntary organizations, women also lost the infrastructure that had supported and strengthened an organized women's movement for generations.

Frances Perkins, the first woman to serve as a Cabinet member, served as Secretary of Labor for all twelve years of the Roosevelt Administration. As Secretary of Labor, Perkins surrounded herself with a group of women activists who shared her concern for women's issues.

Gender in the Welfare State

The women's political network that helped envision and enact New Deal social programs hoped to use the federal government to help poor and struggling Americans survive the Depression. The network had grander visions as well. The women in the network were among a generation of reformers who hoped to create a social safety net for the poor, sick, and unemployed. Through these women's efforts, the **modern welfare state** was born. At the same time, New Deal policy makers, male and female, brought to their work a set of gendered assumptions about the distinctions between men's and women's work. The attention they paid to the issue of female poverty did not lead them toward programs that would enable working mothers, many who were single or supporting an unemployed husband, to earn better wages and more equitable workplaces. Rather, the relief programs offered by the government rewarded women who stayed at home with their children. Labor Secretary Frances Perkins noted the dangerous cascading impact women's wage work had on families when she testified in 1935 that "you take the mother of a large family, she may be able-bodied and all that, but we classify her as unemployable because if she works the children have got to go to an orphan asylum." By classifying women primarily as homemakers, the government directed its relief efforts to enable women to stay at home and men to earn a living wage.

The government offered two kinds of relief: work and pensions. Public work programs like the Federal Emergency Relief Administration (FERA), the Civil Works Administration (CWA), the Public Works Administration (PWA), and the Works Progress Administration (WPA) hired men and women for federally funded projects that ranged from building libraries and parks through writing state guide books and recording oral histories. These federally funded jobs were the best kind of aid the gov-

Social Security Act of 1935 A governmental program that created pensions for the elderly.

ernment offered because the jobs came with higher wages and, as work-based relief, conferred a level of dignity that public assistance could not. For example, the wages for WPA work in North Carolina were six times higher than the relief granted through a mother's aid grant for one child. However, desirable wage-based relief programs were targeted at men. Of the 1.6 million Americans employed by the federal government in 1934, women made up 11 percent, or 142,000. The CWA hired three hundred thousand women out of four million workers, and the FERA gave women 12 percent of their jobs despite the fact that women made up 25 percent of the unemployed. The women who did receive government jobs were directed into sex-typed jobs. In l936, for example, 56 percent of women on the WPA worked in sewing rooms. The assumptions that male-headed households were the healthiest and that women did not deserve higher-paying jobs as much as men did conspired to make women's unemployment seem less important. Most Americans inside the government viewed the economic crisis as one of men's employment and crafted federal programs to rehabilitate men's jobs, wages, and savings.

The **Social Security Act of 1935,** the pillar of the new welfare program, offered relief by work-based entitlements and by aid to children, widows, the elderly, and the infirm. To address the crisis in male employment, unemployment insurance and old age pensions were based on entitlements and on white masculine employment categories and work patterns such as primarily full-time, preferably unionized, continuous, in-

The Works Progress Administration hired men and women for federally funded projects that ranged from building libraries and parks to writing state guide books and recording oral histories. However, the WPA, like most New Deal Programs, segregated women to sex-typed work. In l936, 56 percent of women on WPA worked in sewing rooms, like this Spanish American woman, weaving a rug in Castillo, New Mexico in 1939.

dustrial breadwinning work. A payroll tax was taken from workers' salaries that was matched by contributions made by their employer, an arrangement that underscored the contributory—and thus more dignified because earned—nature of the program. Retired women workers in jobs covered by the Act took part in the same old age security programs as did men, as long as they met the same work requirements as men. But most women workers did not meet those requirements because most were in jobs that were disqualified from the bill. Workers with low and irregular contributions were seen as unable to contribute enough to provide decent benefits. The program excluded household domestic workers and agricultural laborers, which made up 16 percent of the employed workforce and in which women of color were overrepresented. The program excluded federal, state, and local government jobs (clerical workers and teachers); nonprofits; orphanages; and hospitals—all sectors in which women were heavily represented. The result was that 55 percent of African American workers and 80 percent of all women workers, including 87 percent of African American women workers, were excluded from the program. The NAACP characterized the bill as "a sieve with holes just big enough for the majority of Negroes to fall through."

Aid to Dependent Children (ADC) A program that gave grants to states to use for the support of dependent children.

The Social Security Act included relief for single mothers of children and for children in poverty. The new program, **Aid to Dependent Children (ADC),** absorbed the programs that were once a part of the recently expired Sheppard-Towner bill (see chapter 16), a bill that had provided funds for child and maternal health services throughout the 1920s. While less generous than public work program jobs, ADC relief nevertheless helped keep children with their mothers and a minimum of food on the table for those who received it. It enabled some women to withdraw from paid work and care for their families and homes. The aid, helpful as it was, came at a cost. ADC funds came from both state and federal funds and as such were under the control of state-instituted eligibility guidelines in addition to those required by the federal government. Local administrators could distribute funds, which varied state to state, based on their standards of a "suitable home." Illegitimate children, male friends, alcoholic beverages, boarders, or forms of housekeeping and child rearing deemed alien could be enough to classify a family unfit for aid. Recipients experienced the visits of these local administrators as invasive, often humiliating encounters. The judgments made by the administrators of the program frequently disqualified African American children from support. In Georgia, five years into the program, only 1.5 percent of black children remained on the rolls of ADC as compared to 14.4 percent of white children, and most of the black children lived in Atlanta.

Celebrating strong men as a source of national strength was a major visual theme of New Deal public art. This WPA poster by Isadore Posoff in 1937 highlights the representation of work as the domain of strong men. Administrators of the public art funds hoped to sponsor art that would inspire faith in national values and reassure the country that it would endure the crisis, all through a distinctively American vernacular.

A set of assumptions united welfare policy and gender. The premise of many New Deal social programs was that the health of the nation depended on the quality of its children. Only healthy children could become good citizens and take their proper place in the polity. The preparation of the child for citizenship rested on

WOMEN'S VOICES

DISCRIMINATION IN THE WORKS PROJECT ADMINISTRATION

Racist practices were ingrained in every aspect of American life in the 1930s, including the New Deal relief and welfare programs. Administrators, investigators, and welfare workers on state and local levels were typically white and followed what they referred to as "local practice" of racial segregation. Black families found they were the last to receive relief, the first to be cut off, and the last to be hired for work. Black women wrote to the federal government in an effort to rectify the multitude of injustices they faced.

Millen, GA
R 1, Box 31
February 4, 1935

United States Department of Agriculture
Extension Service
Office of Cooperative Work
Washington, DC

Dear Friends:

I am a widow woman with seven head of children, and I live on my place with a plenty of help. All are good workers and I wants to farm. I has no mule, no wagon, no feed, no grocery, and these women and men that is controlling the Civil Work for the Government won't help me.

Because I am a woman. I want to ask you all to please help me to make a crop this year and let me hear from you on return mail. Yours for business

Mosel Brimson

Please answer me on return mail.

P.S. *These poor white people that lives around me wants the colored people to work for them for nothing and if you won't do that they goes down to the relief office and tell the women—"don't help the colored people, we will give them plenty of work to do, but they won't work." That is the reason poor colored people can't get any help, these poor white people going down to the relief office telling lies. Now I am living on my own land and I am got a plenty of children to make a farm, and all I wants is a chance, and I am not in debt. I wants a mule and feed, and gear and plows, and a little groceries and guano. Please help a poor widow woman one year. Please help me get a start, I will try to keep it.*

Source: WPA Box, Howard University, Washington, D.C. Quoted in Gerda Lerner, ed., Black Women in White America: A Documentary History (New York: Vintage Press, 1972), 399–400.

Questions

1. How did "local practice" operate against Brimson? Why does she appeal to the federal government?

2. How does Brimson use her role as mother to strengthen her case? What other examples of gender can you see in this document?

the quality of home life, and home life, in turn, depended on a mother. Federal programs privileged women's domestic work over women's wage work, preferring to see women as dependents and excluding them from the range of work-based entitlement of the modern welfare state. As the *Washington Evening Star* wrote of Grace Abbott, chief of the Children's Bureau and member of the New Deal women's network, in 1939, "She befriended the mothers of the United States because she realized as few other sociologists did that they hold the fate of the republic in their hands. With similar comprehension she strove for every conceivable advantage for children, appreciating the fact that democracy can survive only with the support of a loyal generation."

Women's efforts to expand federal programs to include work programs for unemployed women and aid to poor mothers and children created the foundations for the modern welfare state. These programs often made the difference between a family going hungry or not. New Deal programs ameliorated some of the worst effects of widespread unemployment and poverty. Yet, the huge sums of money the government pumped into the sagging economy were not enough to end the Depression. It would take the massive industrial output of arming Britain and the Soviet Union in their war against Germany in the late 1930s to bring about an end to the crisis.

CULTURES OF THE 1930S

If the visual imagery of the 1920s focused on the flapper as a sign of gender modernity and a future bright with promise, the 1930s iconography focused on the hardworking mother as the sign of a future infused with nostalgia for a simpler past. Concern with the health and stability of families, along with a restoration of traditional gender roles, appeared not only in sociological discourse and government activism but also in the art sponsored by the government and in Hollywood films. Government funding of the fine arts fell under the Public Buildings Administration, the agency that oversaw the building of hundreds of post offices and courthouses. One percent of funds for federally sponsored public buildings were reserved for embellishments, and these murals, sculptures, and frescos became among the most visible legacies of the New Deal. Another source of government funding came through the **Farm Security Administration (FSA)** and became an unexpected source of work for a generation of photographers and writers as they went into the rural South to document the lives and needs of America's farm communities. Advocates hoped that documenting the lives of poor Americans would play a part in creating a popular consensus on Roosevelt's New Deal. Last, popular culture of the 1930s, particularly motion pictures, relied on funny women rather than sexy ones to amuse audiences. In each arena, shoring up an embattled masculinity through visual images participated in restoring men's sense of authority through containing women in the world of the domestic.

Farm Security Administration (FSA) Created to assist poor farmers during the dust bowl and the Great Depression.

Representing Gender in New Deal Public Art

Administrators of the public art funds hoped to sponsor art that would inspire faith in national values and reassure the country that it would endure the crisis, all through a distinctively American vernacular. The program, which was not intended as relief for unemployed artists, granted commissions through competitions overseen by New Deal administrators and local officials. Between 1934 and 1943, the program sponsored more than 850 artists who produced eleven hundred murals and three hundred sculptures for public buildings. These works appeared in train and air terminals, post offices, federal courthouses, and government offices across the country.

Celebrating strong men as a source of national strength was a major visual theme of New Deal public art. At the same time that the 1930s witnessed widespread unemployment and the de-skilling of industrial labor, public art, in contrast, represented an older view of work as an arena in which men could find autonomy through skill and effort. Public art created images of working men in factories and in the fields that drew attention to the physicality of the male figure while also emphasizing the nobility of work itself. The masculinity of work rested on the autonomy granted by skill and the visibility of productive work as measured by tangible products like baskets of food or automobiles, planes, or machines. It also suggested that the male worker earned enough to support a family. Artist Paul Mays said about his painting for Norristown, Pennsylvania, "I wished to express the meaning of strength—the force and vitality of the working people in this value of factories and furnaces." The attention paid to the male laborer—and, implicitly, the male breadwinner—was achieved by excluding women as wage earners. Images of women wage earners, either in factories or in offices, simply did not exist. By associating wage work with manhood, such images associated a man's wage earning to his rightful authority over his wife and family at home.

This message of the natural authority bestowed on the male breadwinner also appeared in representations of the farm. Images of bountiful harvests, rolling pastures, idealized homes, and the fruits of hard work showed men and women doing sex-specific work for a common goal. Building on and revising the companionate marriage of the 1920s, the representation of farm families showed the importance of women's work while at the same time emphasizing that women's natural place was at the home caring for the family through a round of domestic work like gardening, canning, and child care. The comradely ideal addressed the contemporary crisis in manhood by showing men as strong, capable, and autonomous and emphasizing the natural authority of the husband over his wife, children, and farm. Such iconography used the ideal of a marriage between equally valued partners, each with his or her specific task to do, as a model for an idealized national life.

Through gendered imagery like those of the manly and the comradely ideals, administrators hoped to not only promote the New Deal but also to reassure Americans that the nation was strong enough to weather any crisis. To do so, government-sponsored public art avoided any references to the political and economic crisis of the 1930s. The manly worker of public art echoed with imagery widely used in the Communist and labor movements, yet administrators insisted that no references to labor conflicts, oppressive work conditions, or protest appear in public-funded art. To do so would go against the New Deal program of representing American democracy through nostalgic images of harmonious communities based on autonomous individuals.

Documenting the Depression

Another form of visual iconography, produced in part by New Deal funding, was documentary photography. Akin to the attention social scientists paid to the family during these years, artists and writers explored the causes and the experience of the Depression on ordinary Americans. They too turned their lenses on rural America but, unlike public art, focused more on women than on men. Upholding the long-standing practice of representing the home through women and the nation through men, photographers turned to images of mothers to document the toll of economic hardship. Among the most famous of this genre was the work of Dorothea Lange. In 1935, Roy Stryker, who administered the Historical Section of the Resettlement Administration, hired Lange to be on the staff of the agency's photographers who were sent out to document the effects of the Depression on rural Americans. Lange did most of her work in California. Lange's "Migrant Mother," taken in 1936 in a pea pickers camp, became one of the most memorable images of the despair and resignation of migrant workers. Stryker said of this picture, "When Dorothy took that picture, that was the ultimate. She never surpassed it. To me it was the picture of Farm Security. She has all the suffering of mankind in her, but all the perseverance too. A restraint and a strange courage." While many viewed such pictures uncritically as a simple reflection of human experience, Lange constructed the image by selecting elements and excluding others. In "Migrant Mother," Lange chose to emphasize the woman and only two of her many children and to keep the husband out of the frame, implying that the mother, a hardworking citizen, could lead her family to a better future if she was given the chance.

Margaret Bourke-White, another photographer for the Farm Security Administration, also captured national suffering on the small scale of a single female face. Before the Depression, Bourke-White was known for her industrial photography and was hired by Henry Luce for his new magazine *Fortune* in 1929. In 1935, her editor sent her to cover the Dust Bowl. In her autobiography, *Portrait of Myself*, she wrote, "Here were faces engraved with the very paralysis of despair. These were faces I could not pass by." She began a project to photograph tenant farmers with writer Erskine Caldwell in 1935, which would become the influential *You Have Seen Their Faces* (1937), a de-

Photographer Margaret Bourke White took this famous photo of black flood victims lining up in front of a billboard showing a prosperous white family in a car after the 1937 flood in Louisville, Kentucky. Bourke, who had photographed the human toll of the Dust Bowl, joined the staff of the newly created Life magazine in 1935 where she traveled the country documenting the lives of ordinary Americans.

scription of the harsh day-to-day experience of sharecropping. In 1937, she was hired as one of the first staff photographers of the newly launched *Life Magazine* and shot the first cover. Bourke-White's photos vividly captured the tension between poverty and affluence, none more than the cover photo for *Life* in 1937, which featured black victims of a flood in Louisville, Kentucky, standing in a breadline under a billboard of a smiling white family in a car. The billboard read: "World's Highest Standard of Living. There's no way like the American Way." Bourke-White was affiliated with Communist Party front organizations such as the American Youth Congress and the American League for Peace and Democracy, groups that urged the government to do more to secure economic rights for ordinary Americans.

New Deal images of mothers were useful in justifying the need to create a new governmental safety net to protect mothers and children from the worst effects of poverty. Women, cast solely as mothers in the art and imagery of the New Deal, needed the government's help to do their part in maintaining the strength of the nation. Likewise, images of men as worker-citizens provided a visual language that seemed to promise better days if only the natural gender order was restored. Such imagery worked hand in hand to justify an array of new government initiatives designed to help the male breadwinner and programs to help mothers care for their children.

Regulating Hollywood

The visual language of gender, in which masculinity represented the nation and femininity the domestic, shaped popular culture in the 1930s, most notably in motion pictures. Despite the hard times, 60 percent of Americans went to the movies at least once a week. One of the most common female characters of 1930s films was the spunky heroine who, unlike her flapper predecessor, did not challenge women's primary place in the domestic world. The spunky sidekick took her place among other dominant images of women, including the mother, bifurcated as noble and strong or domineering and henpecking—and briefly by the sexy vamp.

From the earliest years of motion pictures, many critics regarded movies as morally suspect for their display of dancing women and exotic foreigners. In the 1920s, states and cities had formed their own censorship boards that could order the deletion of shots, scenes, and title cards before a film could be shown or, in some instances, ban films outright. By 1922, spurred by several high-profile scandals involving Hollywood celebrities, calls for some type of federal action were heard. In self-defense, motion picture producers passed a succession of moral rules or "codes" intended to guide the content of motion pictures and overseen by former postmaster Will Hays. Although most producers followed these voluntary rules, after a few years the guidelines started to relax as the addition of sound to movies in the late 1920s intensified the filmic treatment of crime, violence, sexual infidelity, profanity, and even nudity. In 1930, a new code—which came to be known as the **Hollywood Production Code**—was written. The industry accepted it nominally, although many movies stretched it to its limits or simply ignored it. Movies made between 1930 and 1934 came to be known as "precode," even though the *Production Code* was theoretically in effect. In 1934, a mechanism was set up to enforce the code. For the next thirty years, virtually every film produced or exhibited in the United States had to receive a seal of approval from the office of Joseph Breen, the head of the Production Code Administration. The language of the 1930 codes testified to the growing power of

Hollywood Production Code "Morality" codes imposed on Hollywood films in the between 1930 and 1960.

mass culture. "It enters intimately into the lives of men and women and affects them closely; it occupies their minds and affections during leisure hours, and ultimately touches the whole of their lives. . . . Wrong entertainment lowers the whole living condition and moral ideals of a race."

In precode films, women initiated sexual encounters and pursued men without being stigmatized as unfeminine or predatory. Female sexuality was granted a degree of expression in *Morocco* (1930), *Trouble in Paradise* (1932), *The Blue Angel* (1930), and *Shanghai Express* (1932). Ginger Rogers, for example, in *Gold Diggers* of 1933, had premarital sex, openly discussed marrying for money, and remained sophisticated if somewhat scandalous. In the wake of more stringent regulation, twin beds for husbands and wives became mandatory and sexuality took place clearly off screen, along with nudity, be it male, female, child, or animal, real or stuffed. Not only did Tarzan and Jane have to cover themselves in the Tarzan films of the 1930s but so did Cheetah and his brethren who wore body stockings. Mae West perhaps faired the worst from the enforcement of the *Production Codes*. Her raunchy talk, peppered with verbal double meanings, paired to great effect with her swaggering body language, all of which had made her a unique filmic presence. With sexuality rendered taboo, she was forced to clean up her image or resign herself to becoming a star of the past.

Postcode films found other ways to express sexual play in acceptable forms. In the surge of wholesomeness, child star Shirley Temple became one of the decade's most beloved stars. Debuting in 1932 at the age of four, Temple's coquettish looks were balanced by her role as the "little mother" who cared for older men. She was a tonic for the hard times the Depression-Era movie audience faced: her perky looks and reassuring manner let them know that everything would eventually be all right. She was the ideal postcode star, with her appeal shrouded in family feeling.

Depression-Era audiences enjoyed screwball and romantic comedies that disguised sexual passion in antagonistic and flirtatious word play. Katherine Hepburn was the queen of such deceit, in films like *Bringing Up Baby* (1938) and *Holiday* (1938), in which she and Cary Grant waged domestic battles as metaphors for sexual attraction. In addition to Hepburn, the stars of screwball included Jean Arthur, Claudette Colbert, Melvyn Douglas, Irene Dunne, Carole Lombard, Myrna Loy, and Ginger Rogers. The screwball comedy involved a number of characteristics that resonated with worried audiences in the 1930s. These comedies poked fun at class snobbery, implying that common folk were superior to the wealthy. Associated with this was the belief that even the wealthy had the potential to exhibit the nobility of ordinary folk. The stories almost always revolved around the idle rich and often came into conflict with the guy who has to work for a living. The screwball comedies frequently depicted a couple that was destined to fall in love but had a difficult time getting together. Divorce and remarriage figured prominently in screwball comedy but always with the reassurance that marriage was ultimately a superior way of life. The best-known screwball comedy of the era was *It Happened One Night* (1934). The mismatched couple in the movie are a snobbish runaway heiress and a gruff out-of-work reporter who is actually looking for a story, helps her, but ends up falling in love. Directed by Frank Capra and starring Claudette Colbert and Clark Gable, it was the first film in history to win all five major Oscars.

Zany screwball comedies, in which silly capable men rescued silly women, entertained Americans in a moment of gender traditionalism. Women in movies pushed the limits of tolerable female behavior to the amusement of the audience at the same time

WOMEN'S LIVES

MAE WEST

Mary Jane West was born in Brooklyn, New York, on August 17, 1893, to parents involved in prize-fighting and vaudeville. Mae studied dance as a child and worked on the stage from the time she was five years old. By the time she was fourteen, she was billed as "The Baby Vamp" for her performances on stage. Although she had not yet matured, the slinky, dark-haired Mae was already performing a lascivious shimmy dance in 1913 and was photographed for a song sheet for the song "Everybody Shimmies Now." West was known for her walk, which was said to have originated in her early years as a stage actress. West had special eight-inch platforms attached to her shoes to increase her height and enhance her stage presence. Eventually, she began writing her own risqué plays using the pen name "Jane Mast." One of those plays, *Sex,* landed her in jail for ten days on obscenity charges in 1926. While incarcerated on Roosevelt Island, she was allowed to wear her silk panties instead of the scratchy prison issue and the warden reportedly took her to dinner every night. She served eight days with two days off for good behavior. Media attention to the case enhanced her career.

Two years later, her play *Diamond Lil* became a huge Broadway success. Mae caught the attention of the Hollywood studios and was given her first movie role with George Raft in *Night after Night* (1932). Although it was a small role, she was able to display a wit that was to make her world famous. Raft himself said of Mae, "She stole everything but the cameras." Movie audiences fell in love with the first woman to make racy comments on film. She became a box-office smash hit, breaking all sorts of attendance records. Her second film, *She Done Him Wrong* (1933), was based on an earlier and popular play that she had written. Nominated for an Academy Award as Best Picture, it also made Cary Grant a star. Her third film later that year was *I'm No Angel* (1933). However, the frank sexuality and seamy settings of her films aroused the wrath of moralists. On July 1, 1934, the censorship of the Production Code began to be seriously and meticulously enforced and her screenplays began to be heavily edited. Her answer was to increase the number of double entendres in her films, expecting the censors to delete the obvious lines and overlook the subtle ones.

By 1936, with *Klondike Annie* (1936) and *Go West Young Man* (1936), she became the highest paid actress in the United States. In 1940, she costarred with W. C. Fields in another film she wrote herself, *My Little Chickadee* (1940). Mae took a respite from the film world, mainly because the censors were getting stricter. She decided she would be able to have greater expression in her work if she went back to the stage. Mae continued to be a success there. Censorship began to relax in the 1960s, and Mae returned to film work in the 1970s. She suffered a series of strokes, which finally resulted in her death at age 87 on November 22, 1980, in Hollywood, California. ■

that they happily embraced domesticity, and gender equilibrium was restored by movie's end. Such movies, with their mixed messages of female autonomy and domesticity and women's power and their dependency, literalized the contradictory pulls of femininity in the 1930s. In ways not unlike the comradely ideal of Section Art, which idealized women at home, and the weary mothers of Dorothea Lange's photographs, screwball comedies worked because they relied on gender normality—in this case, temporarily suspending it—for their humor. The ideology of gender functioned in complex ways to represent security and hope during hard times through the joined images of men hard at work and women happily at home.

CONCLUSION

American women in the 1930s faced the difficult tasks of keeping home intact and family healthy as the country suffered through the long years of economic crisis. Women did what they could to survive—making clothes last, stretching food, bringing in cash in a variety of ways—from taking in boarders and a neighbor's ironing to finding some kind of wage work. They greeted President Roosevelt's New Deal with a mix of gratitude and skepticism. Even though millions of Americans benefited from the alphabet soup of agencies and programs, the New Deal did not end the Depression. It did, however, expand the reach of the federal government and placed it squarely in the daily lives of ordinary Americans.

Women who had long been active in reform politics achieved on the national level many of the social welfare programs they had established on the state level. Eleanor Roosevelt, Frances Perkins, and Mary McLeod Bethune were among a group of committed women activists that made New Deal programs address the problems of poor and unemployed women and minorities, goals they had worked toward during the Progressive Era. Their presence in the federal government proved important to the generations of political women that followed them. Similarly, working women established a place for themselves in male-dominated labor unions. As leaders, organizers, and members, women participated in the surge of labor activism that profoundly shaped the era and its legacy. As the country anxiously watched the gathering storm of war, women were posed to do what was necessary to face the next national crisis.

REVIEW QUESTIONS

1. How did women's lives change during the Great Depression?
2. How did wage-earning women respond to the economic crisis of the 1930s?
3. What kind of activism did women engage in during the 1930s?
4. What did women active in the government accomplish during the New Deal?
5. What role did American popular culture play during the Depression?
6. Did the Depression change Americans' views of gender roles?

WOMEN'S EVENTS	GLOBAL EVENTS
1920	
	1929 Stock market crash
1930	
	1930 Communists to demand government action on rising joblessness Department of Labor estimates 4.2 million unemployed workers
	1931 European banks collapse as the economic crisis spreads
1932 Birthrate drops to all-time low	1932 WWI vets, "the bonus army," marches on Washington D.C. Franklin D. Roosevelt wins landslide victory over Herbert Hoover
1933 Frances Perkins becomes secretary of labor	1933 Adolf Hitler is appointed chancellor of Germany The Twenty-first Amendment nullifies Prohibition Franklin D. Roosevelt sworn into office
	1934 The Federal Emergency Relief Act National Recovery Act Dust storms ravage the western plains states *Hollywood Production Codes* established
1935	
1935 Mary McLeod Bethune heads the Negro Division of the National Youth Administration Dorothea Lange hired by the Resettlement Administration	1935 The U.S. Communist Party supports a "Popular Front" to fight business and fascism Works Progress Administration; Social Security Act passed Committee for Industrial Organization formed
	1936 General Motors employees stage a massive sit-down strike Roosevelt re-elected to a second term
1937 Chinese Ladies' Garment Workers' Union chartered.	1937 Five million workers participate in a variety of labor activism across the nation The "Roosevelt Recession" raises unemployment
1939 430 Mexican American women staged a massive walkout at California Sanitary Canning Company	1938 Fair Labor Standards Act

RECOMMENDED READING

William Chafe. *The Paradox of Change: American Women in the Twentieth Century.* New York: Oxford University Press, 1992. Chafe covers the economic, political, social, and cultural changes in women's lives over the twentieth century. He is particularly masterful in his evaluation of women's work patterns, and their relationship to women's overall status.

Linda Gordon. *Pitied But Not Entitled: Single Mothers and the History of Welfare.* New York: The Free Press, 1994. Gordon's important book set out the contours of what would become a crucial analysis of gender in the origins of the modern welfare state. She combines a history of the progressive women who devoted their lives to helping single mothers from the turn of the century to the New Deal with an analysis of the effects of gender in the creation of, and limitations of social policies.

Alice Kessler-Harris. *In Pursuit of Equity: Women, Men, and the Quest for Economic Citizenship in Twentieth Century America.* New York: Oxford University Press, 2001. Kessler-Harris, long-time scholar of women's wage work, examines the role of "racialized gender" in the construction of economic opportunity, ideas of fairness, and in social policies. Throughout she addresses the role gender played in the ideas about citizenship.

Barbara Melosh. *Engendering Culture: Manhood and Womanhood in the New Deal Public Art and Theater.* Washington: Smithsonian Institution Press, 1991. Melosh's lively and interdisciplinary study documents the art and theatre produced by New Deal art programs. She does so through source materials little used by historians, including agency correspondence with artists and writers, comments by local juries who selected specific works, and the hundreds of other governmental records. Melosh also brings to her work an engaging eye for visual details that strengthen her analysis.

Vicki Ruiz. *Cannery Women, Cannery Lives: Mexican Women, Unionization, and the California Food Processing Industry, 1930–1950.* Albuquerque: University of New Mexico Press, 1987. Ruiz examines the role of Mexican American women in major strikes that led to important changes in the cannery industry. She highlights the role of communities and consumption to the success of labor strikes.

Susan Ware. *Beyond Suffrage: Women in the New Deal.* Cambridge: Harvard University Press, 1981. Ware's study of twenty-eight women examines the network of Democratic activist women who held prominent jobs in the government, and who brought to their work a deep seated commitment to women's issues. Their influence on New Deal programs, and on the Democratic Party itself, represented the institutional pinnacle of first wave feminist political influence.

Blanche Wiesen Cook. *Eleanor Roosevelt, Volume One and Two.* New York: Viking 1992, 1999. Wiesen Cook's biography of Eleanor Roosevelt situates her in a richly developed psychological world as well as the world of women's activism from which ER was a part. Wiesen Cook draws from ER's voluminous personal and public writings, correspondences between herself, her husband, friends, and family. Hers was the first study to openly discuss Roosevelt's complex intimate relationships.

ADDITIONAL BIBLIOGRAPHY

Women Face the Depression

Jacqueline Jones. *Labor of Love, Labor of Sorrow: Black Women, Work, and the Family from Slavery to the Present.* New York: Basic Books, 1985.

Jessie M. Rodrique. "The Black Community and the Birth Control Movement" in Kathy Peiss and Christina Simmons, eds., *Passion and Power: Sexuality and History.* Philadelphia: Temple University Press, 1989.

Rosalind Rosenberg. *Divided Lives: American Women in the Twentieth Century.* New York: Hill and Wang, 1992.

Susan Ware. *Holding Their Own: American Women in the 1930s.* Boston: Twayne Publishers, 1982.

Activism

Darlene Clark Hine. *Black Women in White: Racial Conflict and Cooperation in the Nursing Profession, 1890–1950*. Bloomington: University of Indiana Press, 1989.

Nancy Cott. *The Grounding of Modern Feminism*. New Haven: Yale University Press, 1987.

Jacquelyn Dowd et al. Hall. *Like a Family: The Making of a Southern Cotton Mill World*. Chapel Hill: University of North Carolina Press, 1987.

Dolores Janiewski. *Sisterhood Denied: Race, Class, and Gender in a New South Community*. Philadelphia: Temple University Press, 1985.

Lois Scharf and Joan Jensen eds. *Decades of Discontent: The Women's Movement, 1920–1940*. Westport: Greenwood Press, 1987.

Judy Yung. *Unbound Feet*. Berkeley: University of California Press, 1995.

Women and the New Deal

John D'Emilio and Estelle Freedman. *Intimate Matters: A History of Sexuality in America*. New York: Harper and Row, Publishers, 1988.

Ruth Feldstein. *Motherhood in Black and White: Race and Sex in American Liberalism, 1930–1965*. Ithaca: Cornell University Press, 2000.

Estelle Freedman. "Separatism as Strategy: Female Institution Building and American Feminism, 1870–1930," 1979, reprinted in Kathryn Kish Sklar and Thomas Dublin, *Women and Power in American History from 1870*. New Jersey: Prentice Hall, 1991.

Gwendolyn Mink. *The Wages of Motherhood: Inequality in the Welfare State, 1917–1942*. Ithaca: Cornell University Press, 1995.

Winifred Wandersee. *Women's Work and Family Values, 1920–1940*. Cambridge: Harvard University Press, 1981.

Susan Ware. *Partner and I: Molly Dewson, Feminism, and New Deal Politics*. New Haven: Yale University Press, 1987.

Cultures of the Thirties

Jeanine Basinger. *A Woman's View: How Hollywood Spoke to Women, 1930–1960*. New York: Alfred A. Knopf, 1993.

Andrew Bergman. *We're in the Money: Depression America and Its Films*. New York: New York University Press, 1971.

Michael Denning. *The Cultural Front: The Laboring of American Culture in the Twentieth Century*. New York: Verso, 1997.

Margaret T. McFadden. "America's Boyfriend Who Can't Get a Date": Gender, Race and the Cultural Work of the Jack Benny Program 1932–1946," *The Journal of American History*, Vol. 80, No. 1. June, 1993, pp. 113–134.

Emily Wortis Leider. *Becoming Mae West*. New York, Farrar, Strauss & Giroux, 1997.

Memoirs, Autobiographies, and Biographies

Blanche Wiesen Cook. *Eleanor Roosevelt, Volumes I & II*. New York: Viking, 1999.

Dorothy Rae Healey. *California Red: A Life in the American Communist Party*. New York : Oxford University Press, 1990.

Ann Marie Low. *Dust Bowl Diary*. Lincoln: University of Nebraska Press, 1984.

Milton Meltzer. *Dorothea Lange: A Photographer's Life*. Syracuse: Syracuse University Press, 2000.

Eleanor Roosevelt. The *Autobiography of Eleanor Roosevelt*. Cambridge: DeCapo Press, 2002.

Susan Ware. *Partner and I: Molly Dewson, Feminism, and New Deal Politics*. New Haven: Yale University Press.

Emily Wortis Leider. *Becoming Mae West*. New York: Farrar, Strauss & Giroux, 1997.

WORLD WAR II HOME FRONTS, 1940–1945

WOMEN AT WORK ON THE HOME FRONT
Working for Victory
For the Duration
Double V Campaign

GENDER AND WARTIME POPULAR CULTURE
Advertising the War
Hollywood's War
Wartime Fashion
All-Girl Players

WARTIME DOMESTICITY
Feeding a Family
Housing Shortages
Homemaking in the Internment Camps
Parenting During the Crisis

CREATING A WOMAN'S ARMY
The Women's Army
Gender Anxieties in the Women's Army Corps
Women's Air Force Service Pilots
Prejudice in the Women's Army
Demobilization

WHAT EFFECTS did World War II have on American women's work lives?

HOW DID the war change American family life?

HOW DID minority women experience the war and what were their experiences?

HOW DID women serve in the military during the war?

CHAPTER 18

September 14, 1942

Dear Miss Breed,

We are all getting used to the weather and dust and beginning to think that it isn't such a bad place after all. Partitions have been put up in the lavatory and the wash room here is much nicer and much closer.

We have each been given a cot bed and a blanket. Now that we have caught up on our sleep, the cots feel rather uncomfortable. We will be issued either hay or steel army cots and matresses, but as yet no one seems to know when! Something should be done, though, because we need something as a mattress because it is colder at night.

It seems as though my life is going through a thorough transformation! Here I go to Sewing School, Sunday School, Church, Singsperation, and Girls' Club Meetings. No more of those swell Saturday night dances! Gee, how I miss them! . . . The young girls from Reedley, Visalia, and Fresno and thereabouts no longer go to dances cause they are afraid of the "Santa Anita yogores" (a colloquialism meaning "not the best of boys"). Due to this, the young fellows act twice as rowdy and really make us disgusted!

We, [Santa Anita] girls no longer go out to dances either! Most of us stay at home and are truly good girls. Sometimes we go to each others house and look up into the dark blue star-filled sky. I regret that I did not take astronomy in school—the sky is truly beautiful at night!

I know I'm asking a great deal of you—but I wonder if you would be so kind as to send me a dictionary. If you have one that you don't need, would you please send it to us. If you don't have an extra one I will send you the money for one in my next letter.

Gee, Christmas must fall on Friday! It certainly would be elegant if you could come to Arizona. Visitors here are allowed to enter the barracks and visit people. It doesn't feel like a prison here. Gee, but this is such a desolate place I wonder if your tires will hold out—also your gas will be rationed won't it?

Please give your mother our best regards. My mother sends you her love.

Sincerely,

Fusa

Source: A letter to Clara Breed from Fusa Tsumagari, "Letters from the Japanese American Internment" Smithsonian Education, accessed at http://www.smithsonianeducation.org.

usa Tsumagari was one of 110,000 people of Japanese descent who were sent to internment camps following the outbreak of World War II. America formally entered the war against the Axis powers of Germany, Japan, and Italy on December 8, 1941, the day after Japanese pilots attacked the U.S. Naval Base at Pearl Harbor, Hawaii. Fearing espionage and sabotage along the Pacific, the government removed American men, women, and children of Japanese descent from their homes and placed them in internment camps in the interior of the country. Two-thirds of the internees were U.S. citizens and half were women.

While the Japanese attack on Pearl Harbor formalized America's entry into World War II, the country had since the late 1930s been anxiously watching the saber rattling of Japan in its war against China and of Germany with the rise of Adolf Hitler's National Socialist Party. Americans were reluctant to get involved in another overseas conflict, but popular opinion shifted as the nation followed troubling reports coming out of Europe. By 1940, the imperial aspirations of Germany were impossible to ignore. In 1939, Germany had incorporated or conquered Austria, Czechoslovakia, and Poland; and the following year, the army of the Third Reich smashed through Denmark, Norway, the Netherlands, Belgium, and Luxembourg. With the surrender of France in 1940, Hitler moved against Britain. Throughout the 1930s, Japan was flexing its military might in the Pacific. The Japanese ambition to dominate Asia began with the Japanese invasion of the northern Chinese province of Manchuria in 1931. In 1941, while still in Manchuria, Japan had set its sights on the Dutch East Indies and the Philippines. Adding to the mounting anxiety in the United States that war was coming, Italy, Germany, and Japan entered a defensive alliance. Americans' efforts to remain isolated from the conflict ended abruptly with the attacks on Pearl Harbor.

In the wake of the attacks, civilian and military leaders rushed to secure the nation against other possible enemy attacks, beginning a massive military mobilization that would at last pull the country out of the Great Depression. Government contracts flowed to large corporations such as General Electric, Ford, and U.S. Steel, worth one hundred billion dollars in 1942 alone. During the war, the gross national product (GNP) doubled and the federal budget swelled to ten times larger than that of the New Deal. Able-bodied men became a limited resource. Sixteen million men served in the armed forces at the same time that the economy needed thousands of new workers.

As the U.S. entered the war, the number of female employees in air industry grew. The six plane factories of the Douglas Aircraft Company, including this one at Long Beach, were hailed as an "industrial melting pot" where men and women of all ethnicities worked side by side in the war effort.

As the nation mobilized for war, America faced a labor shortage, setting the conditions that would recast women—married, single, with or without children—as valuable workers. At home, women faced food and gasoline rationing, housing shortages, and other war-related restrictions, adding to the difficulty of maintaining their families during wartime. Women filled jobs left vacated by fighting men, jobs ranging from architecture to baseball, welding to doctoring. Upsetting as it was for families to send their fathers, husbands, and sons to war, the home front disruptions of the war enabled women to take measure of all they could do for themselves and the nation.

WOMEN AT WORK ON THE HOME FRONT

The speed with which the country shifted to wartime production transformed the economy. In 1940, nearly one worker in seven was still without a job and the nation's factories ran far below their productive capacity. Once America entered the war, a rush to produce military supplies transformed the economy, at last pulling the country out of the decade-long Depression. Manufacturers converted their factories from producing cars and trains to building tanks and airplanes. After straining under new production schedules, war industries reluctantly turned to women to fill the dwindling ranks of male workers. Women eagerly filled jobs vacated by men, drawn in part by the rhetoric of patriotism and duty to nation but certainly by higher wages and, for some, by the excitement of learning new skills. While ready to do their part in the war effort and eager to bring in better wages, women faced many of the same work-related obstacles they faced before the war. Employers and union leaders persisted in discriminating against women by reclassifying the work they did as "women's work" and paying them on a different pay scale. Women workers earned no seniority or job security. The phrase "last hired, first fired" and "there for the duration" characterized the roller coaster of women's work during the war years.

Working for Victory

As the economy shifted from the Depression to mobilization, women workers were poised to take advantage of new opportunities. As was the case during World War I, women found jobs in areas previously closed to them. Millions of American women left their homes to take a place on assembly lines in defense industries. Yet the labor reserves of single women, many of whom were already in the workforce, were quickly depleted. By mid-1942, economists calculated that only 29 percent of America's fifty-two million adult women had jobs. The majority of women remained at home. The **War Manpower Commission**, the government agency charged with balancing the labor needs of agriculture, industry, and the armed forces, started a campaign to recruit women. The popular press jumped in to do its part, stressing the glamour of war work. Stories abounded about women who jumped into war work: a beautician who overnight became a switch woman for six hundred Long Island Railroad trains; a wealthy designer of perfume bottles who became a precision toolmaker in Hoboken's shipyards. The radio popularized tunes like "Rosie the Riveter" who was "making history working for victory." The federal government lowered the age limit for the employment of women from eighteen to sixteen years.

By July 1944, nineteen million women were employed and 72 percent of those women were married. For the first time in American history, married women outnumbered single women in the female workforce. Yet a full three-quarters of the women who worked for wages during the war had worked before and would have worked regardless of the national crisis. The number of women who had not worked for wages previously and who responded to the mobilization by taking work for the duration was quite small. Less than five million of the nineteen million women who worked during the war had not been in the labor force before the emergency. The war gave already working women new opportunities. Postwar estimates concluded that 75 to 85 percent of women working during the war wanted to keep their jobs after the war ended and reflected the normal proportion of wage-earning women in the labor market.

The greatest change in women's wartime wage work was less in the numbers of women working than in the kind of work they did. Between 1940 and 1944, the number of women working in the historically male-dominated manufacturing sector increased 141 percent. Women worked in shipyards welding hatches, riveting gun emplacements, and binding keels. They assembled tanks in Flint and Detroit and B-29 bombers in Washington. According to the Office of War Information, war production work had "disproved the old bugaboo that women have no mechanical ability." Not all women found work in manufacturing. One million women worked for the government, an increase of 260 percent from 1941 to 1943. By the end of the war, women comprised 38 percent of all federal workers. Drawn by the lure of earning a

War Manpower Commission The federal agency charged with balancing the labor needs of agriculture, industry, and the armed forces.

FIGURE 18-1   WOMEN'S WARTIME WORK

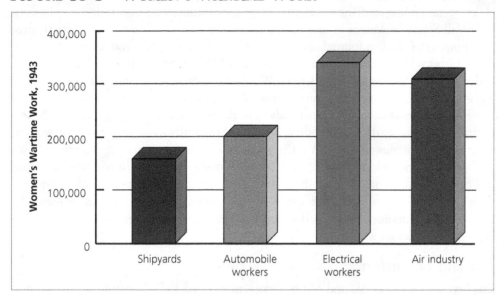

Women entered the workforce at record numbers during the war and made gains in historically male industries like shipping, automobile assembly, and shipyards.

higher wage doing "man's work" and by new working conditions, waitresses, saleswomen, and maids became riveters and welders. Women greased and repaired locomotives, serviced airplanes, took the place of lumberjacks, and worked as blacksmiths and drill-press operators. They drove taxis and public buses, drafted blueprints, and oversaw government expenditures, proving that women could fill any job.

Wartime labor shortages led to new opportunities for Latinas, particularly for those who lived in the urban areas of Southern California where the aircraft and shipbuilding industries were centered. Young Mexican American women found that their ability to take advantage of wartime jobs was greater than for other family members. Their parents, who might not be naturalized citizens, were barred from defense work, but their American-born children were not. The large number of young Hispanic men serving in the military meant that young women shouldered more economic responsibilities for their families. Many second-generation Latinas were able to move into clerical and sales work. Chinese American women found new opportunities to participate outside their ethnic enclaves. Before the war, Chinese American women worked predominantly in garment shops, laundries, canneries, and restaurants. Defense industries in San Francisco, for example, posted jobs in local Chinese newspapers, hired and trained Chinese women for skilled war work, and even went so far as to provide shuttle buses between Oakland's Chinatown and the shipyard.

Black women and professional women, accustomed to working, took advantage of the labor crisis to improve their job situations. Twenty percent of black women left domestic service for better-paying jobs. In the South, white women left jobs in laundries for factory work and black women readily took the jobs they vacated. Professional women found their services suddenly in demand. Large corporations like Montsanto, Du Pont, and Standard Oil hired women chemists for the first time. Seattle's airplane producer, Boeing, hired five women engineers; and the Puget Sound Navy Yard had eight women doing drafting work. In Washington, women lawyers found ample work and Wall Street brokerage houses scrambled to hire women analysts and statisticians. The number of women journalists covering Capitol Hill tripled from thirty to ninety-eight. Groups like the American Association of University Women and the National Federation of Business and Professional Women's Clubs met with the Women's Bureau with optimism to plan for retaining women's gains after reconversion.

For the thousands of women already at work, the war presented them with the opportunity for occupational mobility. War industries attracted thousands of women from other industries and jobs. A waitress who had earned twenty cents an hour (with no tips allowed) could earn $1.15 an hour at an assembly plant. In war-affected cities like San Francisco and Mobile, where workers were in demand, women who stayed in their jobs could command better wages. In these cities, beautician wages increased by 28 percent and domestic workers doubled their pay. Such opportunities, even if for the duration, broadened women's life chances.

For the Duration

Employers, trade unions, and the government viewed their dependence on women workers as exisiting "for the duration" of the war. They did not anticipate or plan for permanent equality between the sexes at work. The wartime labor crisis put a premium on hiring the largest number of workers in the shortest amount of time. While the press and the government stressed the satisfaction that went along with war work, such jobs were far from glamorous. With demands for war planes, tanks, and munitions high, war manufacturing required long hours from workers. The government pressured war-related industries to keep outflows high by mandating six-day, forty-eight-hour work weeks. Overtime was common. Work in shipyards was notoriously hard. In the Puget Sound Navel Yard, workers had one day off for every fourteen worked. Housing shortages added hours to the already long workday for many women. A woman in Seattle, who faced a two-hour commute each way, explained that the only "place I could find to live is so far out. I make two transfers before I get the Boeing bus." War plants resisted experiments with part-time shifts that would accommodate more women, in contrast to civilian employers who were more willing to turn to part-time workers to make up for the labor shortage.

A woman's successful entry into male-dominated factories rested in large part on the willingness of male workers and supervisors to train her. Women workers reported facing hostility from their male coworkers. Men did not like having women on their factory floors. Men whistled and catcalled as women passed by. One male Boeing mechanic said, "Every time a skirt would whip by up there, you could hear the whistles above the riveting, and I'll bet the girls could feel the focus of every eye in the place." Because many of the new workers had no previous experience in industry, they depended on male workers to train them. One woman who left her job at Boeing said to the *Seattle Times* that "I had to work with a man who had never had a woman helper before. He hated me. He was supposed to show me how to do the work, but he would sort of get around a corner where I couldn't see him, then when I had to do it, I couldn't. . . . " As the novelty of women in manufacturing plants wore off, overt hostility and harassment abated but persistent refusal to promote women to higher skill levels or to supervisory positions remained. At Boeing, for example, of the 14,435 women it employed, only 109 held skilled positions.

The struggle for equal pay continued. For years, trade unions supported equal pay for women only when jobs of male union members were threatened by women's lower wages. As women literally took men's jobs during the war, they joined unions. By 1944, they made up 22 percent of trade union membership. Yet union leaders worried that paying women the same wages men earned would erase the barriers that divided women's from men's work and would undermine men's wages once they returned from military service. Union leadership did not want management to use the presence of women workers to lower wage scales for all workers and so opted to accept women as dues-paying full members, with the wage protections that afforded, to protect the wages of their overwhelmingly male membership. Women of the International Association of Machinists (IAM) and the United Auto Workers (UAW) earned the same wages as a man earned for the same job.

While pay differentials between men and women diminished, full economic equality never materialized. One major cause for the persistence in gender-based pay differences lay in the government's willingness to go along with union contracts that insisted on maintaining job classifications such as "light" and "heavy" to keep men's wages higher. Throughout the war, the Detroit Edison Company placed women in jobs that required dexterity, concentration, and speed and placed men in heavier and more skilled positions. Likewise, women in the auto industry were assigned "women's jobs" such as assembly, inspection, drill press, punch press, sewing machines, filing, and packing—jobs

As women took industrial jobs during the war, they joined labor unions, like these women in Buffalo, New York, who were being sworn into the Rubber Workers Union in 1943. Some women had never worked outside their homes before, but most had and jumped at the prospect of higher paying and more skilled industrial jobs.

management deemed to be "suitable" for women. A 1943 government survey of Detroit's auto industry found that over one-half of the women clustered in just five of seventy-two job classifications. Justifications for job discrimination abounded. One manager asked, "Why should men, who from childhood on never so much as sewed on buttons, be expected to handle delicate instruments better than women who have plied embroidery needles, knitting needles, and darning needles all their lives?" Women, like most wartime workers, nevertheless found their wartime wages were higher. Prewar nonunion jobs in service, laundries, and department stores paid $24.50 a week, whereas wartime manufacturing jobs, even with gendered pay scales, averaged $40.35.

Another strategy used by trade unions to protect their male membership was to invalidate union women's claims to job seniority, a distinction based on the numbers of years of employment. For example, the Seattle Local 104 of the Boilermakers Union kept women on a separate seniority list from men by classifying them as temporary workers. Other unions supported systems in which an employee retained seniority in his or her job regardless of whether he did wartime work or military service. Most trade unions overlooked work-related issues of particular importance to women, such as day care and time off to care for sick children. Women war workers found that promises of equality in the IAM, the UAW, and other unions evaporated when postwar cutbacks occurred. The principle of equal pay did not protect women from an institutionalized pattern of discrimination in terms of pay or promotion. Labor unions offered benefits to women only to the extent it was necessary to ensure the pay, seniority, and labor standards their contracts guaranteed for men. As a result, as a group, women war workers earned considerably less then their male counterparts.

Women did not fare badly in every union. The competition for workers helped some unions to achieve demands they first laid out in the 1930s. Workers in the canning industry, for example, found their union's demands for better wages met with greater success during the war. To feed the troops at home and abroad, as well as the civilian and military populations of America's allies, the federal government turned to canneries and packing houses to meet its growing need for food. Food industries found themselves competing for employees against the higher-paying defense industries. As result, cannery workers were able to achieve better contracts, higher wages, and day care. The United Auto Workers (UWA) integrated women into the union administrative structure. It held rallies to encourage women to be active in the shop committees. In the spring of 1944, the UAW set up its own Women's Bureau to serve the union's three hundred thousand members. It was charged with giving special consideration to seniority, workplace safety, maternity leave practices, and "other problems relating to the employment of women." As positive as such union support was for women, trade unions faced a tricky issue in how to involve women unions while also preparing them for the inevitable postwar layoffs.

Double V Campaign

At the outbreak of the war, President Roosevelt urged the country to move past prejudice in the name of mobilization. "In some communities employers dislike to hire women. In others, they are reluctant to hire Negroes. We can no longer afford to indulge such prejudice." However, the pressure of a labor crisis only selectively broke down racial barriers in the labor market. Black Americans, hoping to take advantage of the labor crisis, found themselves barred from lucrative defense jobs. At the same time, the war against Nazi Germany and its ideology of Aryan racial supremacy confronted Americans with their own ongoing racism. Articulating the mounting frustration among black Americans, the *Pittsburg Courier*, a popular black newspaper, called for a **double V campaign**, a campaign for victory that would overcome fascism abroad and racism at home.

Black leaders mounted a political effort to open up defense industries. In 1941, A. Philip Randolph, head of the Brotherhood of Sleeping Car Porters, promised that one hundred thousand African American men and women would descend on Washington if the president did not integrate the defense industries. In June 1941, faced with mounting political pressure, President Roosevelt issued **Executive Order 8802** outlawing discrimination in hiring practices by defense contractors and established the Committee on Fair Employment Practices.

Change came slowly. Five and a half million black Americans moved from the South during the war to cities in the North and West looking for better wages. When minority women found employment, they tended to be clustered in undesirable jobs such as janitors or matrons. In Detroit and Baltimore, for example, cities where black women made up approximately 18 percent of the female labor force, employment agencies continued to refer them to service jobs in hospitals, restaurants, and private homes well into the war. Employers justified their discriminatory practices by claiming that having African American women in their factories would provoke resistance in white women. In many instances, managers proved correct in their view of how much contact with black women white women would tolerate. In Detroit, white women participated in five separate walkouts in two weeks to protest African American workers, claiming they did not want to share bathrooms and other facilities. Some industries were more covert in their refusal to hire minority women by telling applicants there were no current openings or hiring them for work that did not involve interacting with the public, such as jobs in wrapping and stock departments.

Frustration over unfair hiring practices continued to simmer. Detroit resident Louise Thomas, for example, worked without pay at the Commerce School for 120 hours in order to learn riveting. After successfully completing her training, she went to Ford's Willow Run bomber plant in 1942. On two different days, she spent money on the bus ride that took her fifteen minutes out of town only to wait in the employment office to be told they could not hire her. Thomas, however, refused to go back to her old job. She took her story to one of Detroit's major black newspapers, where she equated war jobs with racial justice. "If the defense plants in Detroit are not going to hire colored women, and if the Government's Fair Employment Practice Committee (FEPC) is not going to enforce the President's order in this matter, why don't they be frank and tell the colored woman the facts," she wrote. "I have spent long hours and sacrificed to get this defense training . . . but I have not been hired. . . . It is time for those in authority to get behind these issues and help get a square deal for Negro Women in defense industries. We, too, are Americans."

African American women workers combated unfair hiring practice by petitioning the FEPC for help in opening up defense industry jobs, writing directly to the president and to the first lady, and using the black press to draw attention to their plight. In some instances, their efforts bore fruit. After much pressure, Detroit's auto industry opened its doors in 1943 to black women. This created a small foothold on the factory floors, which in turn led to more black women being hired throughout the war.

double V campaign
Winning the fight against racial segregation, or Jim Crow, and against fascism.

Executive Order 8802
This order prohibited government contractors from engaging in employment discrimination based on race, color, or national origin.

Women at work during the war years gained footholds in unions and industries that they might never have had the opportunity to join without the labor shortage brought on by the war. At the same time, a job market shaped by gender and race placed limits on how far women could go in high-paying industrial work. Employers reluctantly let women into their factories, suspending their belief in men's superiority in heavy industry—but only for so long. Skilled industrial work remained men's domain in terms of hiring and job classification. Women workers were continually reminded that, in the words of an *Aero Mechanic* editorial, "Women who are now taking the men's jobs in the war production plants should never forget the fact that a labor union man gave up his job so that he could put on a uniform and fight the battle that may cost him his life. He expects you to be loyal to your union and his union." Despite the reality that most women at work during the war would need jobs after the war, the message that war work was temporary was hard to ignore.

GENDER AND WARTIME POPULAR CULTURE

American audiences eagerly turned to movies, music, sports, and radio for a welcomed diversion from the day's worries and fatigue. A veritable campaign to encourage women to "join" the workforce for the duration redrew the boundaries of proper femininity. Popular culture helped to create a picture of the home front that stressed both women's opportunity to do new work and their willingness to sacrifice for their country. Wartime popular culture stressed the appeal of combining masculine skill with feminine charms, a strategy that perfectly fit the wartime labor crisis. Athletic women, whose participation in organized sports had been limited to local leagues, found themselves with new opportunities to play for wages and tour nationally. Likewise, female musicians took advantage of the wartime shortage of men to promote their all-girl bands. In each arena, women forged a temporary place to show the extent of their talent and their ability to entertain amusement-starved Americans.

Advertising the War

The need to mobilize women as workers to fill jobs vacated by men and as consumers to make the sacrifices needed to support American and Allied troops abroad led the government to create a massive advertising campaign organized around patriotism and sacrifice. To do so, it launched a coordinated effort between advertising agencies, industries, and government that utilized billboards, magazine advertisements and fiction, and Hollywood's *March of Time* newsreels. In November 1941, one month before the Japanese attack on Pearl Harbor, the government created the **War Advertising Council** to enlist the power of advertising in presenting war-related issues to the public. After the United States entered the war, in 1941, the **Office of War Information (OWI)** directed a major advertising project to recruit women into war production. The OWI distributed special newspaper stories targeted for rural and African American newspapers and women's pages. The agency also circulated informational films to churches, schools, war plants, and citizens' groups on topics ranging from war work to absent fathers and delinquent children. The OWI placed billboards in any community with a population of twenty-five thousand and supplied radio stations with three daily announcements on seventy-five programs.

War Advertising Council Charged with the task of selling wartime government programs and war bonds to the American public.

Office of War Information (OWI) Created in 1942 and served as an important U.S. government propaganda agency during World War II.

Women's magazines became important tools in the government's mobilization efforts. The Magazine Bureau of the OWI, established in 1942, worked closely with magazine editors to develop stories that would encourage women to take jobs where they were needed. The *Magazine War Guide* suggested that fictional characters be shown buying war bonds, conserving sparse resources, renting rooms, planting victory gardens, and maintaining positive and patriotic attitudes. To discourage the use of telephone lines, overburdened with war-related government business, the bureau asked that characters not be shown calling loved ones long distance for trivial conversations. It suggested that mundane government regulations like conserving rubber through gas rationing and carpooling could be the premise of a romantic or adventure plotline. Special effort was directed toward pulp publications whose audiences were primarily working-class women. Suggested story lines included encouraging women into particular jobs, as in this suggestion about nurse recruitment: "A story might show a seduced and despondent girl regenerated through observation of the good done by a nurse, and her self-sacrifice." Government agencies hoped that such stories would encourage readers to take war jobs, conserve rationed goods, and support the war.

The popular culture of World War II indelibly imprinted patriotic images of women's home front service in the national consciousness. No image dominated more than Rosie the Riveter, the plucky white war worker who put down her vacuum cleaner for a welding flame. Norman Rockwell drew one of the most popular images of Rosie for the May 29, 1943, cover of the middle-class family magazine, *The Saturday Evening Post*. Rockwell's Rosie was a thirtyish-year-old white woman, eating her lunch with a large riveting tool on her lap. Under her feet lay a copy of Adolf Hitler's *Mein Kampf*, which, along with the American flag behind her, established the patriotism of her war work. The image's meaning was clear: it urged women to join the workforce for "the duration" as a way to contribute to the war effort. Yet, with its assortment of gender codes, the image reassured viewers that doing "a man's job" would not fundamentally alter women's femininity. The image of Rockwell's Rosie neatly blended masculine signs of gender (overalls, industrial tool, muscular arms) with feminine ones (rouge and lipstick on her face, necklace of merit buttons, lace hanky, and compact visible in her pocket). More significantly, Rockwell's painting did not show the work Rosie did side by side with men on a factory floor. Rosie was not shown demonstrating her skills at riveting, a task that before the war was seen as "masculine" and beyond the capacities of women like her. Rather, she sat, eyes closed, nose upturned, relaxing with a homemade sandwich. Rosie's femininity—and more generally, women's ties to nurturance and the home—appeared untouched by the industrial setting around her. The image of Rockwell's Rosie reflected the complex gender accommodations required of women for the duration. While accounts of real Rosies impressed the nation with the women's ability to do what was required to help their fighting sons, husbands, and brothers, such images masked key features of women's wartime work.

"Rosie the Riveter" by Normal Rockwell appeared on the May 29, 1943 edition of the Saturday Evening Post and captured the patriotism of the moment. (Printed by permission of the Norman Rockwell Family Agency. Copyright © 1943 the Norman Rockwell Family Entities).

WOMEN'S VOICES

LIFE ON THE HOMEFRONT

In this oral history, Helen Brown describes how her life changed as a result of the war. She describes herself as "Rosie the Riveter" for her work at the Goodyear Aircraft plant in Akron, Ohio. She describes the patriotic mood of the country that nudged her to take a war job as well as the ever-present sorrow of lost friends, neighbors, and coworkers. Helen gave her story to Harold Phillips for the Hanley Library Archives and the Winchester Frederick County Historical Society on September 4, 2002.

I'm Helen Brown, born April the 5th, 1925, at Rosedale, West Virginia, which was a little oil town in the central part of West Virginia. Then I went to elementary school in a one-room schoolhouse in a little place called Walker, West Virginia. Then I graduated from high school in 1944. World War II was deep into war with Japan and Germany. Uncle Sam was on every billboard and posed, pointing his finger at us, saying, "I need you." Of course, I thought that meant me. There was very few young men in our community. We didn't have proms or yearbooks during the year—war years; and when I was a senior in school I had two brothers in the Navy and the Army. One went in the Navy at seventeen. Of course, Rick and I were planning to be married when the war was over. Rick was in the Philippines at the time. I boarded a bus with $20.00 in my—my purse to Akron, Ohio and was hired at Goodyear Aircraft and had the privilege of joining the flying squadron, a group of ladies who would work in every department in the plant. We were also offered night classes which I took advantage of. I worked as Rosie the Riveter, any mechanics on the Corsair, office work, payroll, where we—anywhere we were needed, except the paint shop. We were paid $1.97 when the war ended August the 14th, 1945. During—during the war were the—

during the war was the saddest days of my life. Every day was filled with anxiety, not knowing—not knowing there was—not knowing if our family and friends would return. Families placed a white square in your window with a blue star; and if your loved one was killed in serve—in service, you replaced with a gold star. It was a terrible, sad day when a blue star turned to gold. During the war we needed rationing stamps for most everything—leather shoes, gasoline, nylon hose, many groceries. We lived on a farm and had most of our fruits, vegetables, and meat. If, as young people, couldn't get—could get a gallon of gas, we would get to a friend's house, listen to records, exchange books, or whatever. We had one class in school where we learned to knit sweaters for the soldiers. I was left-handed, so my sweater was always wrong side out. We sent many letters to servicemen. Of course, I wrote Rick every day. I received 500 letters from him, kept 50 and have misplaced them somehow. While at Akron we would go downtown to the USO, United Service Organization, where several military service boys would be. There were very few cars. We rode buses everywhere. Sometimes you would wait for a second and third bus, but as they were full, sitting and standing. There was very little communications during the war. We either heard a radio from some of our famous broadcasters or newspapers. But we had to get our newspapers a day behind because we got them by mail. They were not delivered in the country. That's what I had there.

Source: *Veteran's History Project, American Folklife Center, Library of Congress: http://lcweb2.loc.gov/diglib/vhp/bib/1901*

Questions

1. What shaped Helen's decision to do war work?

2. How did the war years change the ways Helen spent her leisure time?

Hollywood's War

Urged by the OWI and the Office of War Manpower, the motion picture industry undertook a concerted effort to recruit and inspire women to work and "do their part" for the war. Wartime newsreels and short Victory films chronicled women's work in the factory, the hospital, the shipyard, and the combat zone. Hollywood feature films also honored women's work on the home front in films such as *Since You Went Away* (1944), which showed Claudette Colbert managing her rationing points cheerfully, and *So Proudly We Hail!* (1943), which featured Veronica Lake struggling against lecherous Japanese.

Hollywood's wartime films managed gender anxieties about women becoming too dominating in the absence of men by recreating traditional domestic gender roles in unconventional work settings. In *Tender Comrade* (1943), Ginger Rogers plays a recently wed factory worker who learns to be a more loving and supportive wife through her wartime work experiences. In John Ford's *They Were Expendable* (1945), Donna Reed plays a Bataan nurse whose feminine ways in the surgical operating room won praise from her male peers. "That's a nice kind of gal to have around in wartime," admitted John Wayne. After a long night of hard work, the all-male squadron invited the nurse to dinner where she again inspired devotion from the sailors for her perfect balance of competency and submission. For Hollywood, women's wartime importance as workers was cast as an addition to their prime roles as sweethearts, wives, and mothers, with films rarely straying from the message that women's role in the home was always the first line of national defense.

No less than women's work, the status of manliness underwent change in wartime America. The OWI stressed that heroes were not all soldiers. Heroes were also men who demonstrated courage, duty, and sacrifice in essential home front tasks. This recalibration of courage by Hollywood cast positive light on the factory worker, the morale builder, and the air raid warden. As one *March of Time* newsreel, *Mr. and Mrs. America* (November 1942), described, "Serving their country more humbly but in the same measure as its fighting men are the American people." All were doing work that would hasten the victory. But the good factory worker at home who supported the soldier abroad was not the stuff of Hollywood feature drama. *Wings for the Eagle* (1942), billed as "the first big story of Uncle Sam's Army in overalls" failed to capture audiences. Workplaces were quickly recast as battlefronts of ordinary men against the forces of war-tinged evil as in *Joe Smith* (1942), the story of an everyman worker tortured by thugs for vital aircraft blueprints.

But not all images of women in the 1940s were focused on women as wives and mothers persevering until their men came home. Pinup art flourished during the wartime years. Pinup pictures of glamorous Hollywood starlets like Veronica Lake, Rita Hayworth, and Betty Grable appeared in calendars and posters and hung in auto shops, locker rooms, and barracks across the country. Air crews in World War II decorated their planes with pictures of pinups and pretty girls, typically modeled after the "cheesecake" art of Gil Elvgren, Alberto Vargo, and George Petty, perhaps with the hope that attaching a talisman or a good-luck charm to the aircraft would ward off evil, death, and bullets. When the ships of the Pacific Fleet anchored off Southern California, the first stop for many sailors was an amusement park in Long Beach known as "The Pike." Swabs lined up to drop a coin in an arcade machine and view short film loops of women in swimming suits, negligees, and, sometimes, nothing at all. A direct

WOMEN'S LIVES

RITA HAYWORTH

Rita Hayworth became the first Hispanic American sex goddess during Hollywood's Golden Age. Margarita Carmen Dolores Cansino was born in 1918 in Brooklyn, New York, the daughter of a Spanish flamenco dancer Edward Cansino and Ziegfeld girl Volga Haworth. From the age of six, she performed with The Cansinos, Spanish dancers working in vaudeville. While dancing with The Cansinos, she was noticed by film producers and was signed by Fox Studies in 1935. In the 1930s and 1940s, a Spanish beauty cult captured the public's imagination. Hayworth capitalized on the trend, changed her name, and underwent painful electrolysis by cosmetics giant Max Factor, which minimized her ethnic features. She signed with Columbia Pictures in 1937.

After two more years of minor roles, she gave an impressive performance in Howard Hawk's *Only Angels Have Wings* (1939) as part of an ensemble cast headed by Cary Grant. Her sensitive portrayal of a disillusioned wife sparked the interest of other studios. While on loan to Fox Studies for *Blood and Sand* (1941) starring Tyrone Power, Hayworth achieved stardom with her performance of the seductive Dona Sol des Muire. Shot in Technicolor, the film established her as one of Hollywood's most beautiful redheads. Her celebrity was solidified when she made the cover of *Time* magazine as Fred Astaire's new dancing partner in *You'll Never Get Rich* (1941). Her photograph in a 1941 issue of *Life* magazine portrayed her as a "love goddess," and it became one of the most requested wartime pinups with over five million copies of it published. Rita Hayworth became one of Columbia's biggest stars of the 1940s. She had a daughter with her husband, actor-director Orson Welles. The five-year marriage ended in 1948.

Hayworth left her film career in 1948 to marry Prince Aly Khan, the son of the Aga Khan, the leader of the Ismaili sect of Shia Islam. The couple moved to Europe and had a daughter, Yasmin Aga Khan. The couple divorced, and Hayworth returned to the United States in 1951, where she resumed her successful film career. In the 1960s and 1970s, Hayworth increasingly suffered from extremely early onset of Alzheimer's disease that went undiagnosed until 1980. She died of the disease in 1987 at the age of 68. ■

outgrowth of wartime cheesecake imagery was the burlesque film. Producers in Los Angeles who witnessed the huge business for arcade "peep shows" during the war invested in creating an improved and more theatrical product to go the theatrical route. Quality Studios, founded by Merle Connell from rural Yakima, Washington, started producing burlesque shorts in 1947, using dancers from Los Angeles houses and music from such name acts as Billy Rose and His Orchestra. In Los Angeles, the "Bur-Le-Qs" thrived and dancers like Aleene, Lotus Wing, and Evelyn West held sway. Connell was among the first to realize the economic benefits of filming these shows; shipping film around the country was far easier and more lucrative than doing the shows live. For a relatively small fee up-front, the women would do an extra performance just for the camera.

Wartime Fashion

When Nazi troops occupied Paris, the European center of high fashion, in June 1940, they unintentionally unleashed a flurry of speculation as to whether American fashion industry could survive without French leadership. Cut off from Paris designers, from whom it took its inspirations, the American fashion industry turned its sights on New York City. The major fashion magazines *Vogue* and *Harper's Bazaar*, along with newspapers and magazines that ran fashion columns, increased their coverage of the shows held in New York. They featured American designers like Claire McCardell, Jo Copeland, and Hattie Carnegie, propelling a generation of home-grown talent into the international limelight. Fashion editors like Diana Vreeland and Carmel Snow of *Vogue* and Sally Kirkland at *Life* supported American designers by showing their clothes and commissioning special designs.

Wartime designers faced a unique challenge as raw materials like cotton, brass, and leather were commandeered by the military. In 1943, the government issued L-85, restricting the amount of clothing that could be made out of materials needed for the war effort. Buttons, zippers, cotton, wool, silk, and rayon were severely limited. L-85 was intended to freeze the silhouette, or popular shape, of dresses to avoid costly changes in machinery, technique, and labor that came with changing styles. The restrictions held men to single-breasted, two-piece (rather than three-piece) suits and pants without pleats or cuffs. For the most part, men's fashion was restricted less by L-85 than by the need to produce military uniforms. The application of L-85 to women's clothing included limiting the length of wool skirts to seventy-two inches at the hem. Suit jackets were to fall to just below the hip, and pants were to be narrow. L-85 banned turned-back cuffs on shirts and blouses, double yokes, sashes, scarves, and hoods and permitted only one patch pocket. In a display of patriotism, designers pledged to use less fabric than L-85 allowed and popularized the shoestring silhouette.

The wartime silhouette was tailored and narrow. The new visual imagery reaffirmed traditional gender roles even as it embraced the era's emphasis on women's abilities to do "a man's job." Hollywood designer Adrian created the most well-known wartime look when he introduced narrow dresses with broad shoulders and graceful tailored waistlines and narrow, pleatless skirts that fell just below the knees. The padded broad shoulders lent women an air of strength and authority, traits seen as crucial to surviving the war. Most outfits were topped with a hat, making milliners such as Lily Dache and Sally Victor famous. Stylish women wore platform soled shoes, large costume jewelry, long pocketbooks, and bold red lipstick. Many women tucked a small piece of lace in the pocket or collar of these outfits as a feminine contrast to the military look that was so popular.

Designers looked for ways to provide women war workers with stylish additions to their work clothes. While doing industrial work, women typically wore the same clothing that men did—sturdy overalls or trousers, hard hats, tool belts, and thick-soled shoes. Boeing, the airplane producer, however, hired Muriel King to design uniforms for women workers. Her uniforms had slim waistlines, fitted tops, and trim trousers. *Life* magazine reported that women workers liked them because they were stylish and safe—with no extra flaps, cuffs, or skirts to get tangled up in machinery. Designer Lily Dache designed a stylish "factory bonnet" hat for women war workers that kept hair pulled back. It combined tough plastic mesh and a protective brim to protect eyes with feminine styling.

All-Girl Players

With fewer and fewer young men on the home front, women found unlikely opportunities to be Rosies on baseball diamonds and in jazz clubs. Faced with few bands to entertain and sports teams to watch, enterprising men and women capitalized on the absence of men and stepped into the limelight. In each arena, female players walked the line of playing "like a man" while dressing very much like a woman. Combining manly strength and skill with womanly softness and charm had become a popular notion, used to reconcile the temporary expansion of women into historically male entertainment arenas.

"You've got to see those girls play (baseball) to believe it. They slide, steal bases, throw overhand and pitch curves—and the fans love it. . . . Talk about crowds—why, some towns draw four times their population every season," Bill Fay told a reporter from the family magazine *Collier's*. The **All American Girls Baseball League (AAGBL)** was founded in 1943 by Chicago Cubs owner Philip Wrigley amid fears that Major League Baseball could shut down for the duration of World War II. At its peak in the late 1940s, the ten teams of the AAGBL drew approximately one million fans. In June 1943, *Time* magazine estimated there were forty thousand women's softball teams in the United States, including popular touring clubs like Barney Ross's Adorables and Slapsie Maxie's Curvaceous Cuties. The AAGBL had an unwritten policy against hiring women of color. Not until 1951, five years after the integration of men's baseball, did the league discuss hiring black women.

Wrigley wanted his players to epitomize middle-class respectability and to avoid the image of "short-haired, mannishly dressed toughies." The league handbook explained that it was "more dramatic to see a feminine-type girl throw, run and bat than to see a man or boy or masculine-type girl do the same things. The more feminine the appearance of the performer, the more dramatic the performance." Players attended mandatory charm lessons as part of spring training during the league's first three seasons. Charm instructors included beauticians from the Helena Rubinstein salon and the *Chicago Tribune* beauty editor who coached players on the application of makeup, proper manners, and "graceful social deportment at large." Many of the players resented the charm and beauty requirements for playing in the league, including their knee-high skirt uniforms, which often left their legs bruised and bleeding.

Along with all-girl baseball teams, all-girl swing bands became popular during the war. As the draft wore on and fewer and fewer male musicians were available, women

All American Girls Baseball League (AAGBL) Women's professional baseball league that began as a response to the lack of young male athletes who had joined the armed services.

Chicago Cubs owner Philip Wrigley founded the All-American Girl Baseball League in 1943 out of concerns that Major League Baseball might shut down for a lack of players. At its peak, the ten women's teams drew in nearly one million spectators.

musicians were able to fill their places. For the duration, female bands found themselves enjoying new popularity and exposure as they made bookings across the country. Musician Viola Smith, in an editorial in the industry magazine *Down Beat*, argued that the war "marks the most opportune time we girl musicians have ever had to take our right places in the big dance bands and do our bit to keep up the morale of the country" by keeping "music alive." As with the fictional Rosie the Riveter, many audiences assumed that when the boys returned from war, the girl musicians would gladly give up their instruments and return home. However, most women in all-girl bands were professional musicians and belonged to the American Federation of Musicians (AFM), which had enabled them to work in hotels, restaurants, ballrooms, and radio before the outbreak of war.

The country's desire for entertainment only seemed to grow during the war, fueling the market for women jazz bands. The sheer popularity of dance clubs compelled desperate owners to book all-girl bands. Club owners soon discovered that girl bands brought to their shows a form of visual entertainment their male peers did not. Female players dressed in stylish evening wear. According to bandleader Ada Leonard, "Because you're a girl, people look at you first, then listen to you second." For women who saw themselves as professionals, the emphasis on glamour and novelty was an obstacle. Women complained of having to wear high heels for long shows and the way their saxophone neck straps cut into their exposed necks. Others were asked to lose weight or told to put away their eyeglasses. For these musicians, their patriotism and physical appearances were intimately linked.

Like women war workers and baseball players, women musicians faced a sex-and race-segregated labor market. Few men's bands hired women musicians, and few white

WOMEN'S VOICES

JOINING THE BAND

Clora Bryant, jazz trumpeter, recalls how she found her way to jazz in the 1940s as a high school student in Denison, Texas. After graduating, she joined the Prairie View Co-Eds, a band out of Prairie View Agricultural and Mechanical University near Houston, and toured.

The reason why they stressed home economics for girls in school and shop for boys was because that's the way the education system had it down South. It wasn't because that's what the parents wanted. That's the way the supervisor of the schools in Texas had it. The educational system in Texas and in your hometown, that's the way it was. But when we had the band, the parents were behind all the kids who played. And they finally had car washes and things and bought us uniforms. It was during the war, and rubber was rationed. You had the ration stamps for meat and sugar and butter. And they'd put their stamps together and have banquets so they could raise money for us to get music and uniforms and things like that. When I got to my senior year and we were traveling around, they had what they called— What kind of rubber was that? Synthetic rubber. And we'd have blowouts. And we'd have a time trying to get tires up and down the highway, because they would say, "Niggers can't stop here." You couldn't use the restrooms, you couldn't get water, you couldn't buy things. You'd go in the back of the restaurant. You know, "Go around to the back" to get waited on. You'd go in the bus stations and you'd go in the side door. You know, all those kinds of things were prevalent then. If you rode on the train, you had your own separate segregated cars to ride in at the front of the train where all the smoke and cinders could come in the windows. You weren't allowed up in the other cars. We didn't have city buses and things when I was growing up. After I left, then they got buses that went around our city. But when I came up, you walked everywhere.

Having a lot of time on my hands, after I did my chores and stuff, that was what I did. I forgot to mention, when I was younger I had to learn how to sew. I had to learn how to can and preserve food. We canned vegetables and fruits and things like that. They'd have quilting parties. I learned how to quilt on the quilting horses. You know, I learned all the things that, down South, you learned to do. Because, see, at that time if you were black, in school your main thrust for girls was home ec[onomics]. You learned how to cook and clean up. With boys it was wood shop. You learned how to build, how to do carpentry and paint stuff, because there weren't too many other outlets that they were going to let you get into or to learn how to do.

But that was the way I got started with the music in high school. We had a teacher, Conrad Johnson . ., I would take lessons from him on Saturdays. . . . To pay for the lessons, I babysat, I'd wash dishes, I'd iron, or do whatever, run little errands. And he would teach me on Saturdays. That's the way I really got into wanting to seriously play the trumpet. He would pump me up and make me feel good about what I was doing, which was being very good. He would pump me up so he would make me want to keep doing it. Each step I made, I wanted to make the next one and the next one, so that by the time that I graduated, in 1943, I got scholarships.

Source: "Central Avenue Sounds: Clora Bryant," Online Archive of California. Accessed at http://oac.cdlib.org/

Questions

1. What conditions enabled Clora to become a musician? How much did the war affect those conditions?

2. Describe the racism that Clora faced. What enabled her and others in her band to carry on despite such obstacles?

all-girl bands hired African American women. Nevertheless, black women formed some of the era's most popular swing bands and played for both black and white audiences. Black all-girl bands that traveled had the additional difficulty imposed by Jim Crow segregation. Road trips involved searching for "colored" washrooms and restaurants that would let them take their food out. African American all-girl bands put themselves in additional danger when they hired white band members. Bands like the International Sweethearts of Rhythm, Eddie Durham's All-Star Girl Orchestra, and the Darling of Rhythm toured in the South with white band members when it would have been safer for them to have not. For those bands with white and black members, traveling together in the South was a crime, as was walking down the street together or eating together. One white woman recalled being chased out of a bus station in Shreveport, Louisiana, when someone tipped off the police that she was using the "colored" ladies room with her band. White women who chose to work in black bands explained that they did so because black bands tended to emphasize music more than "corny" or "Mickey Mouse" music that white audiences wanted from white all-girl bands. White Bobbie Morrison said she felt "we were more accepted in the black community playing [swing] music." Black women who played with white women saw integration as simply more democratic: "The white musicians and colored musicians, I don't care where we were, we had no prejudice in us. If they say gig . . . we would all get together like a family."

Popular culture provided much-needed relief from the painful realities of wartime. While Rosie is remembered as representing women's abilities and the opening of opportunity for women in work, in sports, and in music, she also functioned to mask the other message her novelty signified: women would return "home" after the war. As much as popular entertainment promoted the careers of women, the message endured that these thrilling and entertaining women would return home once the boys returned.

WARTIME DOMESTICITY

Across the country, families altered their daily patterns to adjust to wartime issues: absences of husbands and fathers, shortages in everyday goods, and food rationing. Materials found in nylon hosiery, rubber car tires, and aluminum cans, as well as meat and gasoline, all necessary for the military, were rationed. Wartime homemakers supplemented their families' diets by growing and canning their own fruits and vegetables, cleverly made do or did without consumer goods, and bought **war bonds**. Women's sacrifices were celebrated as crucial to victory in magazine advertisements and films. Yet, while American women wanted to do whatever they could for the war effort, many found themselves facing a daunting number of obstacles in their efforts to sustain home and hearth. Even as many struggled through profound wartime dislocations, long work hours, and new family disruptions, domesticity and motherhood continued to define women's identity.

war bonds Issued by the government and purchased by civilians, war bonds functioned as a loan to the government to help finance the war effort.

Feeding a Family

Wartime realities altered every aspect of running a home. Women who worked long hours found it hard to shop. Even when stores offered extended hours, women found fewer consumer goods to buy. To feed troops abroad, the government imposed rations on meat, flour, sugar, milk, and gasoline through a system of ration cards and points. Red points, the most desirable, were for meat; blue points were for the more abundant canned fruits and vegetables. Twelve weekly ration points were granted per person. Out of those twelve points, a homemaker could buy one pound of porterhouse steak or could use only seven points for a pound of ground beef. Chicken, which was not rationed, was costly. Overall, Americans were granted an average of six ounces of meat a day during the war. One white woman who lived in Washington, D.C., recalled the butcher shop after a much awaited meat delivery. "People stood on tiptoe, straining to get a glimpse of the treasured meat. Noses were pressed against the glass showcase. . . . Bets were placed as to how many customers could be served before the hamburger ran out. Pessimists were certain there would be nothing at all left by the time their number was reached."

Other staples of the American diet were in short supply. According to one homemaker, "The butter situation was chronically discouraging. . . . the value of butter grew and grew until it finally reached a maximum of twenty-four points! No longer did we call it by its proper name but now—with proper reverence—we referred to it as twenty-four-karat gold." Electricity was another area where rationing was prevalent. As an alternative to using energy, people turned to the Hay Box Cooker that used coal to supply the energy and heat to cook the meal. It was an extremely slow cooking process, usually lasting ten hours. Aluminum and metals of any sort were conserved and recycled in munitions. Nylons for screens, for hose, and for curtains and rugs virtually disappeared from the consumer market, commandeered from nylon producer Du Pont for military use.

In 1941, the Agricultural Department informed the American people that if they wanted fresh fruits or vegetables in their kitchens, they should plant a "victory garden." By 1943, over twenty million victory gardens produced an estimated eight million tons of food and nearly 50 percent of all the fresh vegetables consumed in the country. Victory gardens also freed freight cars for supplying raw materials to be used in the manufacture and transportation of munitions and helped conserve coal and steam power required in shipping fruits and vegetables.

Housing Shortages

War jobs drew thousands of Americans from their homes to booming industrial centers. Recruiters toured the South convincing whites and blacks to head North with promises of high wages in the converted factories. Newcomers strained these cities' transportation, education, and recreational facilities and caused housing shortages. Black southerners who believed they were heading away from Jim Crow found a northern bigotry every bit as pervasive and virulent as what they left behind. Facing a labor market structured by gender and race, shortages in housing, and inadequate day care, working women struggled to create and sustain homes for themselves and their families.

Women with children who moved to new cities for war jobs had few choices. Housing shortages gave landlords power to set high rents and to discriminate against families with children and minorities. Families often doubled up to meet soaring rents. Single men could find rooms in dormitories, in tents, or abandoned buildings and trailers; but it was harder for families to find decent and affordable places to live. Housing in boom cities like Detroit, the nation's largest defense producer, was segregated, often unsanitary and crowded, made worse for African Americans by defacto segregation of public housing. A 1944 study found that the number of black families living in boardinghouses and residential hotels increased by 311 percent during the war. Many black families lived in "kitchenette" apartments or small homes without indoor plumbing, yet paid rent two to three times higher than did families in white districts. Cramped living quarters heightened the possibilities of fire, made adequate garbage disposal nearly impossible, and bred rats. The rodents, "big enough to ride on" according to one black woman, invaded apartments in groups large "enough for a ball game."

Conflicts over housing broke out in many U.S. cities. In Detroit, a riot broke out when defense housing for African Americans was built in a white neighborhood. The Sojourner Truth housing project, named in memory of the nineteenth-century female African American activist, opened its doors in February 1942 to a cross burning on its lawn and a crowd of 150 angry whites. By dawn the following day, the crowd had grown to twelve hundred, many of whom were armed. The first black tenants, who had already paid their rent, signed leases, and given up whatever shelter they had in anticipation of their new homes, arrived at 9 a.m.; but crowds barred them from claiming their apartments. Days of clashes broke out. By the end of the riot, 34 people had been killed and 675 had been injured. Detroit's middle-class clubwomen joined with the city's working-class African American women to picket the Detroit Housing Commission for access to affordable and safe housing. The Delta Sigma Theta Sorority protested what it called "the unfair, undemocratic, and prejudicial" actions of the city, insisting that racial prejudice at home undermined the battle for democracy abroad. "Our national organization has just purchased $5,000 worth of defense bonds, our local chapters purchased $300 worth. We believe in America! We want America to believe in us. *Democracy, like charity, begins at home!* We urge you to bring your influence and pressure to bear in this case and see that justice is done."

Working-class women and fifty YWCA industrial clubwomen picketed City Hall for four hours a day for nearly two months. They too insisted that fair and decent housing was a right to which they were entitled and that fair housing would encourage war workers to do all they could for victory. In the words of one picketer, "When those families are in their new homes and safe from KKK terrorism they'll work better and harder in the war factories, too." Such tactics proved successful. Two hundred black families moved into the Sojourner Truth housing project in April 1942 under the protection of 1,750 police and militia. The *Sojourner Truth Daily News*, a community newsletter, urged residents to remember the "heroic work" of the women who fought in "the Battle of Sojourner Truth."

Homemaking in the Internment Camps

"My new address is now: Blk 328-11-A," wrote teenager Louise Ogawa in a letter to her friend, librarian Grace Breed, back home in San Diego, California, in November 1942. Like 110,000 other Japanese Americans relocated to internment camps, Louise faced the prospect of establishing a sense of normalcy under adverse conditions. The day after the attack on Pearl Harbor, the government froze the financial resources of the Issei, or first generation of Japanese-born immigrants, while the FBI seized community leaders they believed to be pro-Japan. Two months later, on February 19, 1942, President Roosevelt issued Executive Order 9066, ordering the forced evacuation of all Japanese Americans living on the West Coast to internment camps in Arizona, California, Washington, and Idaho. Women had less than a week to store or sell their family possessions, help husbands close businesses, and clear out of their homes, often selling their assets far below their market value. Each person was allowed to bring only as many clothes and personal items as she could carry. Shelters for one hundred thousand evacuees were constructed in three weeks. Located in isolated areas of the United States on either deserts or swampland, the camps were surrounded by barbed wire and guarded by armed sentries. Of the 110,000 evacuated, over two-thirds were native-born American citizens and half were women.

For the second generation Nisei women who grew up listening to the week's most popular songs on the *Hit Parade* and Jack Benny on the radio, talking to friends in English, and celebrating Thanksgiving and Christmas, internment brought them into contact with many more Japanese than ever before. Young Nisei women found unexpected opportunities as camp life suspended traditional family relationships. Issei women, most who had spent their adult lives in Little Tokoyos or on rural western farms, found little to redeem camp life. Their roles as housewives and their identities as wives and mothers eroded under the harsh conditions of internment.

The conditions of camp life profoundly changed Japanese American family life. Many of the daily domestic tasks a homemaker was responsible for were stripped away in the camps. Washing clothes, bathing a child, preparing food, and keeping an eye on children and teenagers were no longer done in the privacy of a home but became all-day tasks, done communally and publicly. Residents ate at large central dining halls where they waited for hours in long lines for American food. They used silverware, not chopsticks, and ate bread, not rice, with meals. Dirty dishes were washed in an assembly line and thrown on racklike shelves to drain. The loss of control a woman once exerted over meals reverberated to a loss of control over her family life. Family members gradually started to eat separately: mothers and small children, fathers with other men, and teenagers with their friends. Table manners were forgotten. "Guzzle, guzzle; hurry, hurry, hurry. Family life was lacking," recalled the Artist Mine Okubo, in her twenties when evacuated. She recorded her experience of the camps in an illustrated novel, *Citizen 13660*, published in 1946. Similarly, Jeanne Wakatsuki Houston, in *Farewell to Manzanar*, recalled that within weeks of arriving at Manzanar, "we stopped eating as a family. Mama tried to hold us together for awhile, but it was hopeless."

Women also lost control over their living spaces. Sleeping quarters were small and crowded, with thin partitions separating families. Poorly constructed buildings let in dust, bugs, and rodents. Mattresses were ticking filled with straw. Residents constructed benches, tables, and hooks from scrap and stolen wood. Camp housing was made up of barracks that were twenty feet by one hundred feet and divided by partitions into four or six rooms, each furnished with steel army cots. "Apartments" or rooms held an average of eight people. Nights were noisy, filled with the crackling of straw as bodies shifted, loud snores, the crying of babies, and hushed conversations from other stalls. Collective washrooms, showers, and latrines were large, crowded, and difficult to adjust to. Hot water ran out quickly. Flush toilets frequently did not work. Toilet paper was scarce.

While able-bodied women were expected to take jobs in the camps, older Issei women faced unexpected leisure time. Issei women who faced their first experience of enforced spare time took up flower arranging, sewing, painting, and calligraphy or spent time in Buddhist and Christian church meetings. For working women, camp jobs paid the same wage to all, regardless of sex or prior experience. Doctors and teachers, for example, earned nineteen dollars a month. Many female residents took jobs in

Japanese-American women, like the ones shown here in the Central Utah Relocation Center, Utah on April 23, 1943, left behind friends, jobs, and homes when President Roosevelt issued Executive Order 9066, ordering the forced evacuation of all Japanese Americans living in the West Coast.

camp administration offices, in the canteen, in the fields, or in the mess halls, jobs that paid eight to sixteen dollars per month for full-time work. Earning money for some women gave them a new sense of autonomy. On July 15, 1942, Louise Ogawa described receiving her first paycheck. "The distribution of our second checks began today. It was, of course, my first check. I felt so proud to receive it because I really earned it all by myself. It makes me feel so independent. We receive about 37¢ a day. For 11 days work I received $3.04." Other women developed new skill in accounting, optometry, and clerking. Residents were also released to do voluntary seasonal farm work in neighboring areas with labor shortages.

If mothers and grandmothers found that camp life painfully stripped them of their homes and their roles as homemakers, teenagers found unexpected bright spots living in close proximity to each other. Those from isolated regions discovered ideas, styles, and activities more typical of urban youth. Freed from lack of transportation and strict parental supervision, teenagers created a social world of their own made through school, work, sports, shared meals, and dances. Camp life intensified the already

WOMEN'S LIVES

MINE OKUBO

Mine Okubo was born on June 27, 1912, in Riverside, California, to Japanese immigrant parents. Her gift for sketching was recognized early. She received an undergraduate degree from Riverside College (now U.C. Riverside) and a master's degree in fine arts from U.C. Berkeley in 1938. Okubo worked for the federally sponsored Work Projects Administration (WPA) during the Depression. Like other promising artists of her day (most of them men), she traveled in Europe on an art fellowship from the University of California. In Paris, Okubo studied with the famous twentieth-century avant-garde painter Fernand Leger.

The outbreak of war ended Okubo's European art studies. With the death of her mother, Okubo and her younger brother settled in the San Francisco area. During these years, Okubo continued her affiliation with important modernist painters. She worked with Mexican muralist Diego Rivera for the Golden Gate International Exposition on Treasure Island in the San Francisco Bay. The Japanese attack on Pearl Harbor, Hawaii, in December 1941 profoundly and abruptly changed Okubo's life. In May 1942, she and her brother were among the 110,000 Japanese Americans evacuated from the West Coast by Executive Order 9066. They were separated from the rest of their family, who were interned in Montana and Wyoming. Okubo did not let her forced confinement in Tanforan Assembly Center and Topaz "Relocation Center" (in west-central Utah) keep her from producing art. She sketched daily life in the camps, taught art classes for children, and was one of the cofounders of *Trek*, one of the few literary magazines started in

the camps. *Fortune* magazine saw her illustrations and recruited her in 1944 to work on a special issue on Japan.

Okubo published *Citizen 13660* in 1946, the first book on the Japanese American internment. Without fiery rhetoric, Okubo describes the daily indignity of being forced to use smelly public latrines or the difficulties of raising children in a place encircled by barbed wire. *Citizen 13660* won the 1984 American Book Award, and Okubo received a Lifetime Achievement Award in 1991 from the Women's Caucus for Art. Okubo died in 2001 at the age of 88 in New York City. ∎

existing generational divide between Issei mothers and Nisei daughters, as the daughters actively constructed lives more modeled on their own peer group standards and less on those of their parents. Teenagers maintained connections to the world outside the barbed wire fences through listening to the radio, watching movies brought in on the weekends, and reading magazines sent by friends. Such consumption confirmed their sense of themselves as Americans. When the evacuation was lifted, the second generation of Japanese Americans no longer felt as tied to the little Tokyos of their youth. For these women, the evacuation had opened doors and suggested new ways to live, despite the hardships of camp life.

Parenting During the Crisis

With changes in family life brought about by the war, discussion about women's domestic responsibilities intensified. But as the war went on, family life itself seemed to have become a casualty. The family, a focal point of the country's understanding of its health and well-being since the Depression, again seemed to stand in for the the state of the nation. While some commentators celebrated the family as the central institution of American life, others feared for its future, worried about its delinquent youth, and wondered why the divorce rate was so high. Experts who sought to explain such changes lay the responsibility for juvenile delinquency on working mothers. Increasingly, experts and the press that popularized their findings relied on a psychological framework to explain children's problems as the fruits of parental neglect.

Faced with improving job prospects and departing boyfriends, Americans rushed into family making. Between 1940 and 1943, 1,118,000 more couples married than would have been expected at national prewar rates, and those that did so were younger. Quick romances and marriages, followed by a husband's lengthy absence, left many new wives dissatisfied. A Women's Bureau reported that a surprisingly high number of servicemen's wives were planning on divorcing their husbands after the war, explaining that their marriages had been rocky before their husbands were called up. Separations were no easier for those women whose husbands left to find higher-paying war work in a new city. Housing shortages made it difficult for wives and children to join men who found work in the defense industries. Once they did move, women found themselves living in crowded housing projects. Marriages also frayed and broke over women's wartime work. Working in mixed-sex settings increased the opportunity for women to socialize with other men. Sex researcher Alfred Kinsey reported that infidelity among very young married women increased during the 1940s, making them the only group to experience such a change.

Work- and war-related stresses on the family, however, did not dominate popular accounts of America's growing divorce rates or explain the country's "family crisis." Rather, the working mother, who "neglected" her children to work, was identified as the culprit. Ironically, the same magazines that celebrated the patriotism of working women just as often railed against those whom they accused of letting their wage work get in the way of their parenting. In an article in *Survey Midmonthly*, Josephine Abbott wrote that women who worked were "repudiating their children in their newly found freedom" and that "many of them are rejecting their feminine roles. They wish to control their own fertility in marriage and say they never wanted the children they had." Hand-wringing stories about "latchkey children" and "eight-hour orphans" overshadowed most surveys of working women that reported the vast majority made arrangements for the care of their children before they took jobs. Rather than addressing the difficulties of balancing work and family, the popular press focused on whether or not working women had healthy "maternal instincts." Magazines were not the only voices that blamed working mothers for a host of social problems. For example, one woman who took a job at Boeing found herself facing a judge in divorce court who laid the responsibility for an unhappy family life squarely on her shoulders. The judge refused her petition for divorce saying, "I can't order a reconciliation, but I can deny the divorce with the provision that this woman quit her job and undertake to rear her family properly. . . . It is not her privilege to work when her husband objects and when her duty is toward her children. It will be too bad for Boeing, but this temporary war expediency is ruining too many families."

The reality of the home front did weaken the traditional family structure. Children spent more time with grandparents or babysitters, and parents were less able to supervise older children. Parents worked long shifts, with changing schedules, further straining parents' ability to keep track of teenagers. Few factories offered help to working mothers who, as *Fortune* reminded its readers, had "marketing, cooking, laundering and cleaning to attend to" after a twelve- or fourteen-hour day. Communal kitchens, cleaning services, and hot meals were rare, a far cry from the British experience of factory-delivered laundry services, packaged ready-to-eat foods, and special shops for workers. Community officials who had become well versed in the dangers of poverty during the Great Depression now worried that wartime prosperity posed its own threat to children. Teenagers spent more time away from their families participating in voluntary activities or working. One million teenagers dropped out of high school during the war.

juvenile delinquency
Antisocial or criminal acts performed by juveniles.

While rising divorce rates seemed to foretell the demise of the family, **juvenile delinquency**, particularly that of teenage girls, symbolized a frightening moral crisis. Working mothers were accused of doing the most damage to teenage girls who, without the firm hand of mothers to socialize and protect them, either ran amok or impulsively left home under the influence of a man in a uniform. "Mothers, proudly winning the war on the production line, are losing it on the home front," became a persistent refrain. Cities began to regulate young women who represented the problem of sexual promiscuity and fraying parental oversight. In Seattle, campaigns ostensibly mobilized to stop the spread of venereal disease targeted sexually active women for medical and psychological treatment. Police arrested women who were accused of promiscuous behavior, drunkenness, or patronizing bars too much or without a male escort. Throughout, city experts relied on a language provided by psychologists to explain and contain female sexuality. Experts explained that delinquent girls were motivated by a need for love and attention, caused by inadequate mothering, while their male partners merely sought relief from their immutable biological urges.

CREATING A WOMAN'S ARMY

As the country mobilized for the war, many women wanted the opportunity to enlist in the military. They wanted to serve the country in a time of national crisis as well as to lay claim to the symbolic meaning of the soldier. Like the skilled industrial work Rosie the Riveter did for the duration, military service was understood as men's work. While only 12 percent of male soldiers faced combat and 25 percent remained state-

FIGURE 18-2   WOMEN SERVING IN THE AMERICAN MILITARY

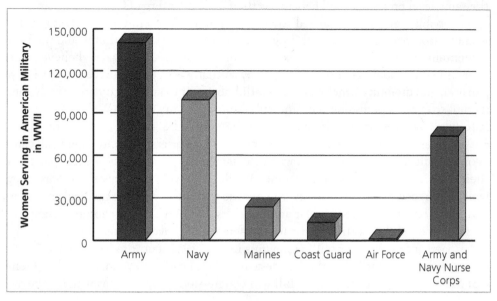

Women jumped at the opportunity to enlist. 350,000 women served in all branches of the U.S. military during World War II

side doing support work, the ideological underpinnings of "the soldier" forged a strong congruence between men and soldiering that made women's entry into the armed services uniquely challenging. In the cultural imagination, the "soldier" was a white man, whether or not he faced a combat situation. For the approximately 350,000 women who served in all branches of the U.S. military during World War II, wartime service offered new opportunities as well as familiar restrictions.

The Women's Army

More than 150,000 American women served in the Women's Army Auxiliary Corps (WAAC) during World War II. Members of the WAAC were the first women other than nurses to serve within the ranks of the U.S. Army. Both the army and the American public initially had difficulty accepting the concept of women in uniform. However, political and military leaders, faced with fighting a two-front war while continuing to send material support to the Allies, realized that women could supply the additional resources so desperately needed in the military and industrial sectors. Given the opportunity to make a major contribution to the national war effort, women seized it.

Early in 1941, Congresswoman Edith Nourse Rogers of Massachusetts announced to General George C. Marshall, the army's chief of staff, that she intended to introduce a bill to establish an army women's corps, separate and distinct from the existing Army Nurse Corps. Rogers was motivated by the memory of the women who had worked overseas with the army as volunteers during World War I as communications specialists and dietitians. Serving the army without an official status meant that they received no legal protection and no medical care and were not entitled to the disability benefits or pensions available to U.S. military veterans. Rogers was determined that if women were to serve again with the army in a wartime theater they would receive the same legal protection and benefits as their male counterparts.

As public sentiment changed to accept some form of military involvement for women, army leaders worked with Rogers to form an organization that would not fundamentally unsettle the army's existing culture. Although Rogers believed the women's corps should be a part of the army so that women would receive equal pay, pension, and disability benefits, the army did not want to accept women directly into its ranks. The bill proposing the Women's Army Auxiliary Corps (WAAC) intended it to work *with* the army, not be a part of the army. The army would provide up to 150,000 "auxiliaries" with food, uniforms, living quarters, pay, and medical care. Women officers would not be allowed to command men and received less pay than their male counterparts of similar rank. While WAACs could serve overseas, they would not receive overseas pay, government life insurance, veterans medical coverage, and death benefits granted regular army soldiers. If WAACs were captured, they had no protection under existing international agreements covering prisoners of war.

Rogers introduced her bill in Congress in May 1941, but it failed to receive serious consideration until after the Japanese attack on Pearl Harbor in December. General Marshall's support helped the bill win congressional approval. Marshall believed

Wartime designers faced a unique challenge as raw materials like cotton, brass, and leather were commandeered by the military. In 1943, the government issued L-85, restricting the amount of clothing that could be made out of materials needed for the war effort and froze the silhouette for the duration. At the same time, American designers molded women's civilian clothes on the women's military uniforms, shown here.

that the two-front war in which the United States was engaged would cause an eventual manpower shortage. The army could not afford to spend the time and money necessary to train men in essential service skills such as typing and switchboard operations when highly skilled women were already available. Marshall and others felt that women were inherently suited to certain critical communications jobs that, while repetitious, demanded high levels of manual dexterity. The bill passed on May 14, 1942.

The day the bill became law, Secretary of War Henry L. Stimson appointed Oveta Culp Hobby to be director of the WAAC. She had impressed both the media and the public when she testified in favor of the WAAC bill in January. In the words of the Washington *Times Herald,* "Mrs. Hobby has proved that a competent, efficient woman who works longer days than the sun does not need to *look* like the popular idea of a competent, efficient woman." Major Hobby and the WAAC captured the fancy of press and public alike. Her husband William Hobby was quoted often when he joked, "My wife has so many ideas, some of them have got to be good!" Although she was bombarded with questions as whether the WAACs would be allowed to wear makeup and date officers, Hobby handled the press with aplomb. In frequent public speeches, she explained, "The gaps our women will fill are in those noncombatant jobs where women's hands and women's hearts fit naturally. WAACs will do the same type of work which women do in civilian life. They will bear the same relation to men of the Army that they bear to the men of the civilian organizations in which they work." Both WAAC officers and auxiliaries accepted this philosophy. A WAAC recruit at Fort Oglethorpe, Georgia, wrote her friend that "The WAAC mission is the same old women's mission, to hold the home front steadfast, and send men to battle warmed and fed and comforted; to stand by and do dull routine work while the men are gone." In 1943, the WAAC was converted to a full branch of the army and renamed the Women's Army Corps (WAC).

"WACs" (Women's Army Corps members) were assigned to every department of the military and did a wide range of work. They worked as draftsmen, mechanics, and electricians, and some received training in ordinance engineering. Some women were trained as glass blowers and made test tubes for the army's chemical laboratories. Other work included field testing equipment such as walkie-talkies and surveying and meteorology instruments; managing tracking of stockpiles of supplies scattered in depots across the country; and working as laboratory, surgical, X-ray, and dental technicians as well as medical secretaries and ward clerks, freeing army nurses for other duties. Women's Army Corps members also served worldwide—in North Africa, the Mediterranean, Europe, the Southwest Pacific, China, India, Burma, and the Middle East.

Gender Anxieties in the Women's Army Corps

Critics of women's armed service saw the military and women as fundamentally incompatible. The military was a masculine institution in which women could never function successfully. In such an environment, the woman soldier could succeed only if she put aside her femininity and performed "like a man," that is, became authoritative, strong, and well-disciplined. For many in the public, these traits were those of white men, leading to labeling women who demonstrated such traits as mannish. Members of the Women's Army Corps faced a stream of ridicule for their soldiering and rumors about their sexual orientation.

Nationally syndicated cartoons lampooned the female Wac, showcasing the ways that femininity and soldiering were fundamentally incompatible. In one series, a Wac dumped her purse all over a general's desk to find a message for him and reported to reveille with her hair in curlers and dressed in a bathrobe. The counterpart to the featherbrain Wac was the mannish Wac. The mannish Wac expressed the belief that only mannish women would want to be soldiers. In cartoons, the mannish Wac drilled soldiers, towering over smaller servicemen of lesser rank or marching a soldier into the justice of peace. Another showed a man at home knitting a sweater for his Wac wife. All this underscored the ways that women in the army had the potential to emasculate men and the conviction that the army was no place for a women.

The ambivalence over what kind of woman would join the army reflected the concerns over women's sexual morality. Some worried that in establishing a women's corps the army was creating a pool of prostitutes. To address such concerns, WAC officials imposed a system of protection on female enlistees that regulated their sexuality to a greater extent than the army regulated men's. While the military encouraged men's heterosexual activity, the need for manpower meant that the male soldier was not punished for behavior resulting in pregnancy or venereal disease. Instead, the women with whom the soldiers were involved were held responsible for the consequences of heterosexual behavior. At the other end of the spectrum, others worried that military service would encourage not heterosexual promiscuity but lesbianism. Colonel Oveta Hobby dismissed such concerns by comparing the resistance to women's suffrage to that of women entering the army: "Just as a startled public was once sure that that women's suffrage would make women unwomanly, so the thought of 'woman soldiers' caused some people to assume that WAC units would be hotbeds of perversion." Others assumed that the army was an ideal breeding ground for lesbianism because of the long-standing association between masculine dress and homosexuality.

Worries about lesbianism in the WAC were not only symbolic. Military service provided women with economic autonomy and a social space away from their families and communities that enabled some to experiment with and express a wider range of their sexual desires. Lesbian WACs faced a homophobic discourse that pathologized any trait deemed "masculine" that a Wac could demonstrate. At the same time, lesbians in the armed services found each other through the visibility of butch or masculine women. One Wac explained that she knew her commanding officer was a lesbian because she had a man's haircut and demeanor. Double talk, or speaking in coded phrases that presumably only other lesbians would understand, helped women determine who was or was not gay. Signals included whistling "the Hawaiian War Chant," talking about parties as "gay times," and referring to friends as "dykes" or "queers." On one army base, the lesbian WACs claimed the service club as their own, going so far as to dance with each other. Other clubs held "girls' nights," when the men on base were barred from attending. Going off the base to bars and clubs that made up the growing gay nightlife in larger cities enabled women to meet

Oveta Culp Hobby served as director of the newly formed Women's Army Corps from 1942 to 1945. Known for her competency and efficiency, Hobby faced down critics of women's military service throughout the war. WACs were assigned to every department of the military and did a wide range of work that freed male soldiers and Army nurses for other duties.

up and relax away from army officials who could discharge a woman for "sex perversion." Black and white lesbians at bars and service clubs enjoyed such settings as temporary refuges during the war, settings made all the more special by the strict scrutiny the army focused on any "mannish" behavior.

Women in the armed services were perceived by other soldiers, by commanders, and by the public as being a threat to the gender order in which women served men, not served alongside men. Combat, preserved for male soldiers alone, remained a line no woman in the armed services was permitted to cross. Maintaining lines between male and female, through ridicule, separate auxiliaries, pay and benefit scales, and combat contained the worrisome potential that women could claim too many of the rights and privileges derived from military service.

Women's Air Force Service Pilots

Women's entry into the armed services offered some women the chance to do work not only historically reserved for men but work perceived as the pinnacle of masculine skill and bravery. The Women's Air Force Service Pilots (WASPs) became the nation's first women to fly planes for the military. While short-lived, operating only from 1942 to 1944, the WASPs trained 1,074 women to fly. As with civilian women, their primary mission was to free up men for combat duty, yet the government also used the program to take the measure of women pilots if the U.S. mainland came under attack. Wasps flew the entire air force arsenal over the American mainland, piloting multiengine bombers, as well as fighter, cargo, and jet planes in a range of tasks, including ferrying aircraft from factories to bases, towing targets for gunnery practice, test piloting new and refurbished planes, and flying military personnel. Most important, Wasps trained male pilots and simulated combat situations for troops. The work, while exciting, was also dangerous. Thirty-eight Wasps died during the war, twenty-seven in active service and eleven in training exercises. Despite their service, the air force classified Wasps as civilians, making them ineligible for insurance, military benefits, or, after their service, veteran benefits. Wasps also paid for their own board and bought their own uniforms out of their monthly pay of $250. Madge Rutherford Minton described just how unsupported Wasps felt by their government. "If we got killed in action our friends passed the hat to get enough money to send our personal effects home to the family. We couldn't have a military internment; we didn't get a flag for the coffin; and we got no burial expenses." Wartime service included moments of exhilaration and disappointment for women as they tested their new roles and new skills. Wasp Adaline Blank wrote her sister about her first solo cross-country flight: "It was a real thrill to set out in a BT entirely on my own for a long flight. . . . There really isn't anything in this world that compares with the contentment that comes with flying . . . The best fun out of a cross country is landing. . . . at some strange air field and seeing the surprised expressions on the officers' faces when a mere girl climbs out of that plane." Yet, at the same time, the coda

British women, like the one shown here, joined the military in record numbers, as did their American counterparts. The primary mission of Women Air Service Pilots (WASPs) and WAAF was to free up men for combat duty, but they also taught male air force pilots to fly, piloted aircraft from factories to bases, and towed targets for gunnery practice.

of masculinity attached to the armed services made women's presence difficult for many men. Women faced constant harassment. Mary Amanda Sabourin said of her years in the military that "some of the men resented us because we took their place and they had to go fight." Civilians also resented women in the service. One woman described a situation in which a woman on a bus began hitting her with her umbrella and screaming, "It's your fault that my son is now at sea. If he's killed, it's your fault!" Laying claim to the status of soldier brought with it far more than appreciation for the women's hard work and their service to the country. Many who served faced accusations of being selfish, accused of wanting to serve merely as a way to claim male privilege and power.

Prejudice in the Women's Army

Women who served in the military entered an institution that represented the duty and rights of male citizenship. As such, men of all races saw military service as crucial to their claim for equality at home. Both African American and Japanese American servicemen saw military service as advancing their political aims for wider social acceptance. Black leaders framed African American women's service in the larger struggle for racial equality or the "double V": victory abroad in the war against fascism as well as victory at home against racial injustice. Japanese Americans saw military service as compelling proof that their loyalties as a community fell squarely with the United States.

African American women who entered the military shared with their male peers a racially segregated institution characterized by hostility, racial quotas, and Jim Crow segregation. The NAACP, editorial writers for the black press, and political leaders like Mary McLeod Bethune called for inserting a nondiscrimination clause into the law creating the WAC but the War Department refused, claiming such a clause was unnecessary. Yet, the WAC imposed a 10 percent quota on the number of African American women it would accept. Of the 440 women selected for officer training in 1942, forty were African American. The WAC also rigidly enforced the military's policy of racial segregation. Like their counterparts in industry, many white women refused to live or work near African American women and demanded segregated bunks and cafeterias. Black women were segregated into all-black platoons in which they trained, dined, socialized, and slept in separate areas. Women with professional skills were too often assigned to menial work due to the stigma placed on their race.

Prejudice left black WACs vulnerable to a host of humiliating and potentially dangerous situations. In 1945, four African American WACs were court-martialed and dishonorably discharged for refusing to obey a direct order. According to the *Washington Post*, "a colonel had refused to let them perform more advanced duties to which white WACs were assigned because 'I don't want black WACs as medical technicians in this hospital. I want them to scrub and do the dirty work,' The women, and nearly fifty others, refused to carry out their menial duties, even after a general personally ordered them to do so. The four were sentenced to a year at hard labor. The court-martial was voided only after three congressmen launched an investigation into the incident claiming that such blatant discrimination undermined the morale in the Women's Army Corps. In the spirit of racial equality that many women in the army found illusive, the congressmen stated, "There is no room for racial discrimination among the men and women who wear the uniform of the United States."

*African American women who entered the military shared with their male peers a racially segregated institu-
tion. WAC imposed a ten percent quota on the number of African American women it would accept and appointed very few women to the rank of officer. They were segregated into all-black platoons where they
trained, dined, socialized, and slept in separate areas.*

African Americans found the army's treatment disheartening. Upon arriving at
Fort Des Moines, Iowa, for training, New Jersey resident Marjorie Randolph realized
that she would be living and working in separate and unequal worlds: "I began to take
notice. . . . They had two of everything, two service clubs and two theatres. . . . Everything was separate, different but not equal." Randolph came to see that she was fighting not only Hitler and the Japanese emperor but also discrimination at home: "Of
course, you fought the war between the men and the women. . . . Then you had the
racial thing that you were facing. Then you had the war that you were fighting between the overseas and the United States. So you were fighting these three wars at the
same time and that was very difficult."

Japanese women who joined the WAC faced little of the personal animosity and
institutional prejudice that African American WACs encountered. Some of their better treatment was due to the Japanese American WACs being assigned to units based
on skill and training, not segregated on the basis of race. In January 1943, the War Department began a special effort to recruit Japanese linguists for the WAC whose primary responsibility would be in cryptography and communications. Recruiters turned
to second-generation or Nisei women from internment camps. For potential Nisei
WACs, their loyalty to the United States was the issue: each woman was interviewed
by at least two sergeants of the loyalty investigative branch of the combined service
commands and one American male soldier of Japanese ancestry to determine if she
supported the United States in the war.

Military service for a Japanese American women also involved laying claim to the promise of American democracy. For a Japanese American woman, military service would help her be considered as much of an American citizen as a person of Japanese descent. Applicants stressed that they saw themselves as "modern American women" who had outgrown "oriental ideas." One woman from Manzanar explained that she wanted to join the WAC because "I wanted to serve my country. I also thought that all Japanese Americans might find it easier to return to a normal way of life after the war if we did our share during the war." Japanese WACs were assigned to work as clerical or administrative personnel, mechanics, radio operators, intelligence analysts, photographers, carpenters, painters, parachute riggers, and postal workers. Like the few Chinese, Korean, and Filipino WACs, most Nisei WACs were encouraged to enlist in the clerical positions so that Military Intelligence could utilize their language skills. Nisei WACs were not forced to live, socialize, and eat separated from white women and tended to emphasize the equality they felt within the army.

Demobilization

Germany surrendered in early May 1945, bringing a formal end to the war in Europe. By 1945, the war was fast reaching a conclusion. In April, Germany Chancellor Adolf Hitler committed suicide and a week later, Germany surrendered. In August, American bombers dropped atomic bombs on the Japanese cities of Hiroshima and Nagasaki, leading to the Japanese surrender on August 14, 1945. American families eagerly awaited the return of their fighting men and women.

The Women's Army Corps was demobilized along with the rest of the army. Not all the women were allowed to return home immediately, however. In order to accomplish its occupation mission, the army granted its commanders the authority to retain some specialists, including WACs, in place as long as they were needed. Within six months, the army bowed to public and political pressure and sent most of its soldiers home. On December 31, 1946, the WAC strength was under ten thousand, the majority of whom held stateside duty and hoped to be allowed to stay in the army. Earlier in 1946, the army asked Congress for the authority to establish the Women's Army Corps as a permanent part of the regular army. The army acknowledged a need for the skills society believed women could provide. Although the bill was delayed in Congress for two years by political conservatives, it finally became law on June 12, 1948. With the passage of this bill, the Women's Army Corps became a separate corps of the regular army. It remained part of the U.S. Army organization until 1978, when its existence as a separate corps was abolished and women were fully assimilated into all but the combat branches of the army.

Most women felt their service had changed them for the better. Ex-WACs took advantage of the readjustment allowances of twenty dollars a week for one year after discharge; one-third began college or made plans to go to school after the war. Fifty percent of ex-WACs returned to the workforce upon discharge, many of whom opted to try their chances at new jobs for which the skills they learned in the military had prepared them. A handful took advantage of the **GI Bill or the Servicemen's Readjustment Act of 1944**, which provided college or vocational education for returning veterans or GIs as well as one year of unemployment compensation. It also provided loans for returning veterans to buy homes and start businesses. Former WACs used the low-interest business loans to open cafés, beauty shops, and bookstores. Loretta Howard summed up the war's legacy when she wrote: "I have gotten so much as a di-

GI Bill or the Servicemen's Readjustment Act of 1944 Provided college or vocational education, one year of unemployment compensation, and loans for returning veterans.

rect result of my service, my degree which gave me a better job and consequently better pay, which of course, resulted in a better standard of living. I have always been so thankful I did enter the WAC."

Other women found the home they returned to was not as happy as it had been before the war. For Doris Samford, the war's end brought an end to the sense of camaraderie and adventure that now made home life seem dull and lonely by comparison. "The war was over. I was out of the army. There were no wartime buddies, no strict regulations, no practical jokes, no uniform of the day, no long working hours. . . . I hung my uniform on a hook on the back of the bathroom door. . . . I was, and felt, stripped and exposed. I stepped into the tub. . . . I held the washcloth in trembling hands and pressed it to my face. I would have to figure out later why I was crying, when I knew that I must be so very happy."

CONCLUSION

Months before peace broke out, American industries that had been converted to military production began preparing for reconversion to domestic and civilian production. Labor leaders optimistically assumed women workers would voluntarily leave their jobs. Women's exit from industrial work, however, was far too important to be left to the individual worker. Federal law required employers to rehire veterans to their former or similar positions even when this meant letting go workers with more seniority. Women's low seniority combined with employers' preferences toward hiring men resulted in a nearly universal replacement of women workers with men.

"Mother blaming" proved a useful tool in the efforts to ease women out of the workforce to make room for returning veterans. In the midst of the wartime celebration of women's abilities to do a man's job for the duration, journalist Philip Wylie published *Generation of Vipers* (1942) and introduced the term "momism" to explain the myriad ways mothers undermined their sons' confidence and independence. Wylie's wartime definition of dangerous mothers joined gender anxieties of the 1930s to those of the postwar years. Psychological care of children, which now demanded mothers to be neither overinvolved nor rejecting of children's budding development, became a science that required full-time devotion from mothers. With its stress on maternal failure, Wylie set the stage for the high-stakes domesticity that came to characterize America in the 1950s.

REVIEW QUESTIONS

1. Why did women enter the industrial workforce in unprecedented numbers during the war?

2. How did the government mobilize the country for war? In what ways did it target women?

3. How did the representation of women change during the war years?

4. Did minority women experience greater freedom and opportunity during the war?

5. How was the home front different in World War II than in other eras?

6. Did Japanese American women gain anything from the war?

WOMEN'S EVENTS	GLOBAL EVENTS
	1930
	1937 Japan invades China
	1939 Britain and France declare war on Germany
	1940
	1940 Germany, Italy, and Japan sign Tri-Partite Pact
1941 President Roosevelt issues Executive Order 8802 outlawing discrimination in hiring practices by defense contractors Formation of Women's Army Corps	**1941** Germany invades the Soviet Union U.S. passes Lend Lease Act to supply Allies with needed war materials Japanese air force bombs the American Navy fleet stationed in Pearl Harbor, Hawaii America declares war on Japan Germany declares war on America Formation of Women's Army Corps
1942 Creation of the Office of War Information Creation of the Women's Air Force Service Pilots (WASPs)	**1942** Congress for Racial Equality forms Sojourner Truth Project housing riots take place in Detroit, Michigan President Roosevelt issued Executive Order 9066, ordering the forced evacuation of all Japanese Americans
1943 The All-American Girl Baseball League (AAGBL) was founded	**1943** Racial violence peaks with 250 incidents in 47 cities
1944 Nineteen million women working	**1944** D-Day as Allied troops land in France GI Bill of Rights passed
	1945 Germany surrenders Atomic bombs dropped on Hiroshima and Nagasaki Japan surrenders United Nations forms

RECOMMENDED READING

Karen Anderson. *Wartime Women: Sex Roles, Family Relations, and the Status of Women During World War II*. Westport: Greenwood Press, 1981. Compares the war's effect on women's consciousness of themselves as women and as workers in Detroit, Baltimore, and Seattle.

Susan Hartmann. *The Home Front and Beyond: American Women in the 1940s*. Boston: Twayne Publishers, 1982. Hartmann offers a general overview of American women's wartime experiences.

Maureen Honey. *Creating Rosie the Riveter: Class, Gender, and Propaganda during World War II*. Amherst: University of Massachusetts Press, 1984. Honey examines the tension between traditional views of womanhood and women's entry into nontraditional occupations during the war.

Leisa Meyer. *Creating GI Jane: Sexuality and Power in the Women's Army Corps During World War II*. New York: Columbia University Press, 1996. Detailed and engaging study of gender anxieties in and around the Women's Army Corps.

Vicki Ruiz. *Cannery Women, Cannery Lives: Mexican Women, Unionization, and the California Food Processing Industry, 1930–1950*. Albuquerque: University of New Mexico Press, 1987. An examination of Mexican women's work and union activism in California's cannery industry.

Megan Taylor Shockley. *"We, Too, Are Americans": African American Women in Detroit and Richmond, 1940–1954*. Urbana: University of Illinois Press, 2004. A detailed and engaging study of the work, activism and race consciousness of African American women in two very different cities.

Sherrie Tucker. *Swing Shift: "All-Girl" Bands of the 1940s*. Durham: Duke University Press, 2000. A fascinating examination of white and black female jazz musicians during the war.

ADDITIONAL BIBLIOGRAPHY

Women and Work

William Chafe. *The Paradox of Change: American Women in the 20th Century.* New York: Oxford University Press, 1991.

Claudia Goldin. *Understanding the Gender Gap: An Economic History of American Women.* New York: Oxford University Press, 1990.

Alice Kessler-Harris. *Out to Work: A History of Wage-Earning Women in the United States.* New York: Oxford University Press, 1982.

Amy Kesselman. *Fleeting Opportunities: Women Shipyard Workers in Portland and Vancouver During World War II.* Albany: State University of New York Press, 1990.

Ruth Milkman. *Gender at Work: The Dynamics of Job Segregation by Sex During World War II.* Urbana: University of Illinois Press, 1987.

Nancy Baker Wise and Christy Wise. *A Mouthful of Rivets: Women at Work in World War II.* San Francisco: Josey-Bass Publishers, 1994.

Xiaojian Zhao. *Remaking Chinese America: Immigration, Family, and Community, 1940–1965.* New Brunswick: Rutgers University Press, 2002.

Gender and Wartime Popular Culture

Caroline Rennolds Milbank. *New York Fashion: The Evolution of American Style.* New York: Harry N. Abrams Publishers, 1989.

Thomas Doherty. *Projections of War: Hollywood, American Culture, and World War II.* New York: Columbia University Press, 1993.

Melissa Dabakis. "Gendered Labor: Norman Rockwell's *Rosie the Riveter* and the Discourses of Wartime Womanhood." Barbara Melosh, *Gender and American Women since 1890.* New York: Routledge, 1992.

Susan Cahn. *Coming on Strong: Gender and Sexuality in Twentieth-Century Women's Sport.* New York: The Free Press, 1994.

Maureen Honey ed. *Bitter Fruit: African American Women in World War II.* Columbia: University of Missouri Press, 1999.

Leila Rupp. *Mobilizing Women for War: German and American Propaganda, 1939–1945.* Princeton: Princeton University Press, 1978.

Wartime Domesticity

Beth Bailey and David Farber. *The First Strange Place: The Alchemy of Race and Sex in World War II Hawaii.* New York: The Free Press, 1992.

Amy Bently. *Eating for Victory: Food Rationing and the Politics of Domesticity.* Urbana: University of Illinois Press, 1998.

D'Ann Campbell. *Women at War with America: Private Lives in a Patriotic Era.* Cambridge: Harvard University Press, 1984.

Philip Foner. *Women and the American Labor Movement: From World War I to the Present.* New York: Free Press, 1980.

Valerie Matsumoto. *Farming the Home Place: A Japanese American Community in California, 1919–1982.* Ithaca: Cornell University Press, 1993.

Sonya Michel. *Children's Interests/Mother's Rights: A History of Child Care in the United States.* New Haven: Yale University Press, 1998.

Evelyn Nakanno Glenn. *Issei, Nisei, War Bride: Three Generations of Japanese American Women in Domestic Service.* Philadelphia: Temple University Press, 1986.

Emily Yellin. *Our Mothers' War: American Women at Home and at the Front During World War II.* New York: Free Press, 2004.

Winifred Wandersee. *Women's Work and Family Values, 1920–1940.* Cambridge: Harvard University Press, 1981.

Creating a Woman's Army

Allan Berube. *Coming Out Under Fire: The History of Gay Men and Women in World War II.* New York: Free Press, 1990.

Margaret Randolf Higgonet, Jane Jenseon, Sonya Michel, and Margaret Collins Weitz, eds. *Behind the Lines: Gender and the Two World Wars.* New Haven: Yale University Press, 1987.

Brenda Moore. *Serving Our Country: Japanese American Women in the Military During World War II.* New Brunswick: Rutgers University Press, 2003.

Molly Merryman. *Clipped Wings: The Rise and Fall of the Women's Airforce Service Pilots WASPs of World War II.* New York: New York University Press, 1998.

Martha Puttney. *When the Nation Was in Need: Blacks in the Women's Army Corps during World War II*. Metuchen: The Scarecrow Press, Inc. 1992.

Memoirs, Biographies, Autobiographies

Jeanne Wakatsuki Houston. *Farewell to Manzanar*. New York: Houghton Mifflin, 1973.

Mary Matsuda Gruenewald. *Looking Like the Enemy: My Story of Imprisonment in Japanese American Internment Camps*. Troutdale: New Sage Press, 2000.

Ralph G. Martin. *Henry and Clare: An Intimate Portrait of the Luces*. New York: Putnam, 1997.

Mine Okubo. *Citizen 13660*. Seattle: University of Washington Press, 1946.

Ingrid Winther Scobie. *Center Stage: Helen Gahagan Douglas, A Life*. New York: Oxford University Press, 1992.

Susan Ware. *It's One O'Clock and Here is Mary Margaret McBride: A Radio Biography*. New York: New York University Press, 2005.

THE FEMININE MYSTIQUE, 1945–1965

BEYOND DOMESTICITY
Rosie Does Not Go Home
Working Mothers
Challenging Segregation at Work

COLD WAR MOTHERING
Bringing Up Baby
Momism
The Black Mother and Racism

REMAKING THE AMERICAN HOME
The Suburb
Chinatown
The Barrio

THE HETEROSEXUAL IMPERATIVE
Beauty Icons
Sexual Brinkmanship
Beats and Bohemians
Writing Womanhood

SEXUAL DANGERS
Back-Alley Abortion
The Homosexual Menace
Lesbian Subcultures

HOW DID women's paid work change during the 1950s?

HOW DID the cold war affect domestic life?

HOW DID families change in the 1950s?

HOW DID the experiences of teenage women differ from those of teenage men?

WHAT MEANINGS did sexuality have in these years?

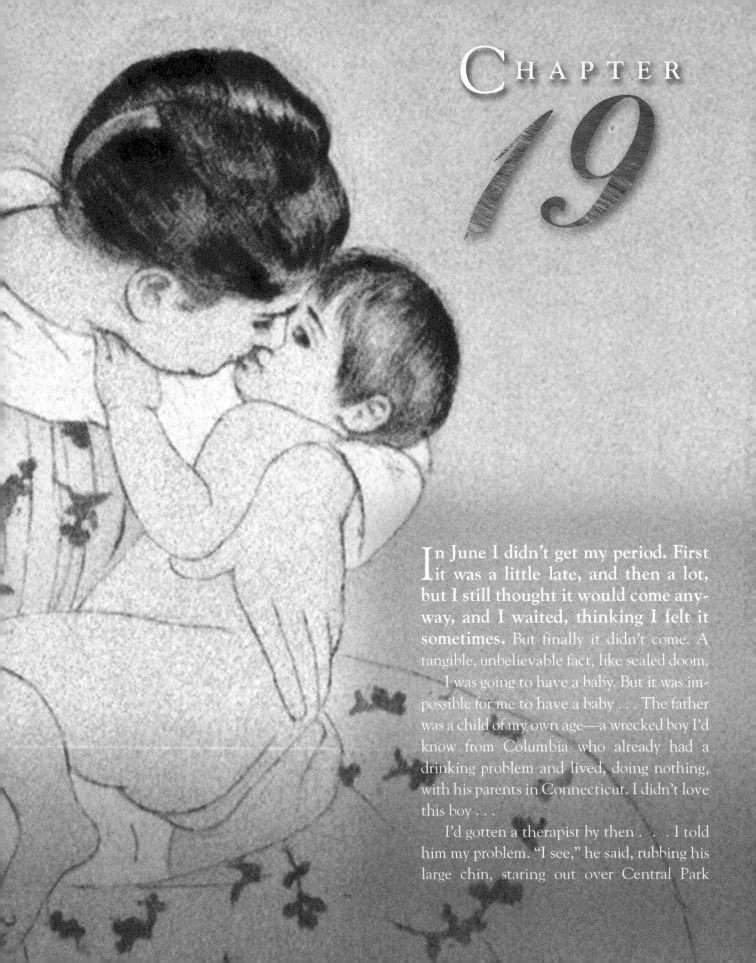

CHAPTER 19

In June I didn't get my period. First it was a little late, and then a lot, but I still thought it would come anyway, and I waited, thinking I felt it sometimes. But finally it didn't come. A tangible, unbelievable fact, like sealed doom.

I was going to have a baby. But it was impossible for me to have a baby . . . The father was a child of my own age—a wrecked boy I'd know from Columbia who already had a drinking problem and lived, doing nothing, with his parents in Connecticut. I didn't love this boy . . .

I'd gotten a therapist by then . . . . I told him my problem. "I see," he said, rubbing his large chin, staring out over Central Park

West . . . I explained to this therapist why I didn't see how I could become a mother. Aside from being twenty years old, I lived on fifty dollars a week and had cut myself off from my family. I said I would rather die. And then I asked him what Elise had told me to: "Could you get me a therapeutic abortion?" (I"d never heard the term before she explained what it meant.)

"Oh, I wouldn't even try," he said.

I hadn't thought he wouldn't try.

Source: Joyce Johnson, Minor Characters: A Beat Memoir *(New York: Houghton Mifflin, 1983), 107.*

Young women like Joyce Johnson found themselves plagued by multiple contradictions. As more young women reaped the benefits of higher education, they were taught that their primary destiny lay in motherhood. Hollywood movies and popular music, as well as parents, teachers, and doctors, stressed the importance of sexual appeal and a submissive demeanor to a woman's ability to find and hold a man. Yet, young women, far more than young men, paid the price for too much sexual expressiveness. The double standard, still intact, granted young men permission to experiment with nonmarital sexual behaviors yet denounced young women who went "all the way." Women like Johnson, who fell outside the parameters of good girlhood, faced social alienation as well as physical danger in seeking out illegal abortions. Putting their health on the line to salvage their reputations, unmarried pregnant women experienced firsthand the paradoxes of the postwar celebration of motherhood.

The women who came to age between 1945 and 1965 were shaped by a society driven by a desire for security as well as by a pervasive anxiety. After the roller-coaster uncertainty of the Great Depression and World War II, most people in the United States were eager for stability and they sighed a breath of relief after the troops came home and factories returned to producing consumer goods. Wartime shortages disappeared. After years of putting off buying a new dining room set, a washing machine, a car, or a home, U.S. consumers in the 1950s spent freely, spurring one of the longest periods of economic growth in U.S. history. In turn, the rapidly expanding economy drew more women into the workforce so that their families could buy yet more consumer goods and services. Two-income families, in which both women and men earned wages by working outside the home, became a linchpin in the postwar economic growth that kept at bay the prospect of another depression.

Paradoxically, at the same time that more women entered the workforce, the craving for security led U.S. citizens to create a new "traditionalism" that centered on the nuclear family with the stay-at-home mother. This idealized family, maintained by husbands who earned the bread and by mothers who cared for the home and raised the children, seemed to many to promise a stability that the Great Depression and World War II had disrupted. At the same time, this ideal appeared to be the best buffer against a new threat—Communism.

As the "hot" war against Fascism in World War II ended, U.S. foreign policy shifted to one of strategic containment of the military and economic power of the Soviet Union. Adding to the sense of political insecurity, the atomic age that began in the wake of the bombing of the Japanese cities of Nagasaki and Hiroshima in 1945 produced a nuclear arms race, with both the United States and the Soviet Union building arsenals that made the threat of nuclear war all the more pressing. The two superpowers avoided direct conflict by mapping the globe through their zones of influence and waging proxy wars in Korea, Cuba, and Vietnam. Not incidentally, the development of new military technologies fueled defense spending, the second linchpin in the postwar economy.

The "age of anxiety" furthered by the cold war recast the U.S. home as the primary defense against Communism and elevated motherhood into a national symbol of U.S. freedoms. Could U.S. mothers raise children who would grow into strong citizens, able to resist the dangers of Communism, homosexuality, and, by decade's end, racism? Not since the American Revolution had motherhood seemed so important.

Beyond Domesticity

People in the United States embraced and celebrated motherhood and homemaking in the 1950s as expressions of U.S. values of home, family, and freedom. Yet, the celebration of domesticity in the 1950s covered over the ongoing reality that more and more women worked outside the home for wages. In no other era were women's roles in the wage economy so hidden by the image of a stay-at-home mom and primary consumer of the family's food, clothes, and other domestic necessities. Yet, in reality, women's economic contribution came not solely through **consumption.** Women's workforce participation increased during the 1950s. And no group increased its presence more than married mothers.

consumption The purchasing of consumer goods.

Rosie Does Not Go Home

With the end of World War II, the four-year heightened schedule of military production cooled off, resulting in widespread layoffs. Women were laid off from factory jobs at nearly double the rate of men, and layoffs were greatest in the higher-paying industries that were historically male dominated. Women's share of jobs at Detroit's automobile manufacturing jobs fell from a wartime high of 25 to 7.5 percent. By 1947, women had lost one million factory jobs.

Women who wanted to work for wages soon discovered that the war had little long-term impact on the historic division of work along gender lines. The persistence of the sex-segregated labor market meant that most women in the postwar period worked mainly in nonunionized and lower-paying "female" or pink-collar occupations. Clerical work expanded, helping to further widen the wage gap between men and women. In 1939, women earned 62 percent of what men earned; but in 1950, they earned only 53 percent. For example, a married woman who had earned $40 a week in an aircraft plant earned $29 in a hat factory; an electrical apprentice who earned $48 saw her wages cut nearly in half as a salesclerk, earning $28 a week. Two-thirds of women in retail and service reported wanting other kinds of work. Sensitive to the climate of opinion, women were unwilling to talk about preferring their wartime jobs. One woman explained, "I'd stay if they want me without taking a man's place away from him."

By 1948 most of the gains that African Americans had achieved during the war had been wiped out. Without a shortage of workers, the peacetime economy shut its doors to black women and forced many to return to domestic service. During the postwar years, nearly forty-one percent of black wage-earning women lacked minimum wage or maximum hours standards, unemployment compensation, and social security.

Black women workers felt the impact of demobilization before white women workers. A government researcher noted unemployment rates for African Americans were double that of whites in the immediate postwar years. By 1948, most of the gains that African Americans had achieved during the war had been wiped out. Without a shortage of workers, the peacetime economy shut its doors to black women and forced many to return to domestic service. The chances were greater in 1950 than in 1940 that a black female wageworker was a domestic. Bernice Mc-Cannon, a thirty-year-old black woman, told a *Washington Post* reporter, "I have always done domestic work for families. When war came, I made the same move many domestics did. I took a higher paying job in a government cafeteria as a junior baker." McCannon lost her job after the war and returned to domestic work. "If domestic work offers a good living, I see no reason why most of us will not return to our old jobs . . . we will have no alternative." Leaving war jobs meant returning to working conditions unregulated by federal labor legislation. Forty-one percent of black, wage-earning women lacked minimum wage or maximum hours standards, unemployment compensation, and Social Security. Restricted work choices, unregulated wage standards, a reliance on tips rather than wages, and a heightened expectation of personal loyalty lent service work more of the characteristics of bound labor than did the jobs held by white women. Despite such setbacks, women continued to enter the workforce. By 1950, nearly 29 percent of all adult women, approximately 18.5 million, worked for wages.

Working Mothers

The National Manpower Council reported in 1954 that married women's work had become an integral element in the lives of many middle-class families. Married women made up half of all women workers, and by 1960 the numbers of mothers who worked had increased by 400 percent to 6.6 million. Over a third of these married women had children between the ages of six and seventeen. The greatest growth in the female labor force was among the well-educated married women from families of moderate income. Before World War II, predominantly working-class married women worked for wages. By 1960, middle- and working-class married women were equally likely to be in the labor market. Women with a college education were more likely to work than their high-school-educated peers. Seventy percent of women with more than five years of higher education worked.

The rapid growth of the consumer market as well as changing standards of economic need motivated women to work outside the home. Women worked not only to secure their survival but to have things that had been out of many Americans' reach for more than a decade: their own homes, a new car, and newly available and affordable products like washing and drying machines. One survey of nine thousand women trade unionists in 1952 found that 66 percent of working women were saving for a home and that between 14 and 26 percent worked to educate their children, pay medical bills, or buy new furniture. An Illinois survey showed that families in which both the husband and wife worked spent 45 percent more on gifts and recreation, 95 percent more on restaurant meals, and 23 percent more on household equipment than did single-wage families. Women's wages provided U.S. families with the means by which a family could buy more than the bare necessities that had defined the Depression-era household. A quest for a higher standard of living remained the primary factor in women's decision to work outside the home.

But more women also appeared to value a job for its own sake, reporting that they liked their jobs not only for the wages but also for the sociability and sense of independence a job conferred. One study by the University of Michigan in 1955 found that while 48 percent of respondents said that their families required their wages, 21 percent of the women surveyed said they worked for a sense of accomplishment. Sociologist Mirra Komarovsky studied working-class families in particular and also found that wage work enhanced some women's sense of power within their marriages. "If I tell my husband that I'm running short of food money he says, 'Well, don't entertain so much,' or he may tell me that I don't need to give somebody a gift. When I work and have my own money, I do as I please." The women who worked reported that they enjoyed the "self-esteem" that an independent income brought, as well as the opportunity "to get out of the house." In one survey, a large number of women appeared to derive a deeper sense of satisfaction from their occupational roles than from their domestic ones. Almost two-thirds of married women workers referred to their jobs as giving them a basis for feeling "important" or "useful," while only one-third described housework as giving those feelings.

While wage work increased fastest among women whose children were school-aged, married women made gains mainly in the pink-collar category, that is, in sex-segregated jobs that did not place women in competition with men. At the same time, service, clerical, and sales jobs resembled the helpful role women were expected to play at home. For middle-class women, a second paycheck helped their families enjoy more affluent lifestyles. In this way, the needs of businesses for relatively inexpensive secretarial and sales help and for more free-spending customers dovetailed neatly. But for working-class women, whose wages kept food on the table, the sex-segregated marketplace and lower wages associated with pink-collar work were hardly avenues to buying extras. They were their family's bread and butter.

Challenging Segregation at Work

The legality of job segregation by race and sex came under scrutiny in the postwar era, thanks in part to women active in the labor movement. Much like the Progressive-Era reformers Florence Kelley, Rose Schneiderman, and Jane Addams, postwar women trade unionists believed that women's disadvantage in the workplace had multiple sources and required multiple reforms to eliminate (see chapter 15). Their efforts to break down sex-segregated job classifications proved important to the larger goal of eliminating job segregation by race.

In the immediate postwar period, the number of women in industrial unions dropped sharply as returning veterans reclaimed blue-collar jobs. But by mid-decade, women had regained their numbers. By 1956, 3.5 million women belonged to various unions and represented 18 percent of the total membership, double the 1940 rate. The sizable influx of women into the labor movement reflected the tremendous growth of trade unions across industries, with membership reaching fifteen million and including nearly 40 percent of all wage earners.

sex-segregated labor market The division of job classification along gender lines.

United Packinghouse Workers of America A union was committed to organize all workers in the meatpacking industry, regardless of skill or trade.

Two unions played important roles in challenging the race- and **sex-segregated labor market.** Both had strong alliances with the Communist Party, one of the few groups that actively fought against racism and for the rights of black workers. The first was the **United Packinghouse Workers of America** (UPWA). African Americans comprised 30 percent of the membership, one of the largest groups of organized black workers after the Brotherhood of Sleeping Car Porters. Women made up 20 percent of the UPWA, one-third of whom were black. In the flagship meatpacking plants of Armour and Swift in Chicago, for example, women were the majority in the workforce and the union. However, black women and white women did not do the same work in the factories. White women trimmed meat or weighed, sliced, packed, and wrapped it after it had been cut into sections. Black women were restricted to the dirty task of flushing the intestines of slaughtered animals. Yet, within the union, a sense of solidarity across race existed. According to African American labor activist Addie Wyatt, "I saw a picture I have never been able to forget. It was a room full of black [and] white workers, Hispanic workers, young and old, middle-aged workers, male and female. And they were talking about problems of decent wages and working conditions. But in addition they were talking about the struggle of black people and women."

Women in the black-led Chicago UPWA Local 28 set up a separate women's committee to encourage women to talk about their work grievances more freely. In 1950, the women's committee began a campaign to document discrimination in the hiring practices of Swift and Company by sending black women to apply for jobs in the all-white pork trim unit, all of whom were denied. The newly established UPWA Anti-Discrimination Department joined in by sending white women to the same jobs and documenting their subsequent hiring. To protest, unionists organized factory slow-downs and stoppages. In 1951, a government arbitrator ruled in favor of the union and required Swift to hire thirteen black women.

The success of Local 28, publicized through the pamphlet "Action Against Jim Crow," inspired other locals to fight discriminatory practices and win new contracts prohibiting racial segregation inside plants. While many white women supported the union, not all supported desegregation in the plants. For example, at the Cudahy plant in Kansas City, black and white women worked in the same room but at different tables: the black women worked on hog casings and the white women worked on sheep casings, work that all the women preferred. When African American Marian Simmons was elected steward for the entire casing department, she Argued that seniority, not race, ought to determine work. According to her, "all women were given the privilege, regardless of color, of working on sheep casing."

Together, the UPWA Women's Committee and the Anti-Discrimination Department worked for full integration of nonwhite women into the industry. Their efforts

Women made up 18 percent of union membership in the 1950s. Women in leadership, like Mary Petillo, vice president of her local United Electrical Radio and Machine Workers of America, worked to make unions more responsive to the needs of women. The sizable influx of women into the labor movement reflected the tremendous growth of trade unions across industries, with membership reaching 15 million.

bore fruit. In many plants, white and black women worked together in the same departments, used the same restrooms and locker rooms, ate in the same cafeteria, and were entitled to the same union rights and benefits.

United Electrical, Radio and Machine Workers of America
One of the first unions to affiliate with the Congress of Industrial Organization in 1936.

Other unions used fair wage standards as a way to combat race and sex discrimination. The **United Electrical, Radio and Machine Workers of America** (UE), one of the most radical postwar labor unions, had a membership that was approximately 40 percent female. In 1946, two hundred thousand UE women strikers helped shut down seventy-eight plants nationwide in demanding equal pay at General Electric and Westinghouse. In 1949 and 1950, union activists, following the recommendations of the Communist Party, advocated the automatic granting of seniority to all African Americans as compensation for years of discrimination in the electrical industry. Against great odds, the UE also worked to improve the seniority system for women. A young labor journalist, Betty Goldstein, soon to be Betty Friedan, wrote articles for *UE News* on the economic origins of women's oppression, discrimination against African American women, and women's secondary status in a variety of institutions, including the family. She challenged stereotypes of women as physically weaker, as temporary or pin-money workers, or as workers free of family obligations. In 1953 in New York, the UE held its first national women's conference, which became an annual event.

The racial integration of women's service and semiprofessional jobs proved harder to accomplish. Many pink- and white-collar occupations were not integrated until the 1960s. Women of color held a larger proportion of low-paying service jobs; but outside the South, few were hired into "interactive service jobs," or jobs that entailed sustained personal contact with white women. In the hotel industry, for example, white women worked the "front of the house" as desk clerks, hostesses, or waitresses, and women of color worked in "back-of-the-house" positions in housekeeping or in the kitchen. Even as waitress work doubled between 1940 and 1960, employers refused to hire nonwhite women. Some employers justified their racism by arguing that only white women could achieve the desirable femininity, beauty, and professionalism. Others believed that white patrons would reject nonwhite servers. Such prejudices extended to voice-to-voice contact and the airline industry as well. By 1960, less than 3 percent of the female telephone workforce was black and almost all were concentrated in large northern cities. Airline officials defended their discriminatory hiring policy as a strategy to maintain high standards. "The ranks of white stewardesses would dwindle fast if the glamour of the job were downgraded by employment of Negro girls," one company executive explained.

COLD WAR MOTHERING

cold war The foreign policy of containment directed at Communist Soviet Union and includes the alignments between foreign policy abroad and the expression of anti-Communism throughout U.S. culture.

The **cold war** played out in multiple arenas, not all of them military. Anti-Communism in the United States targeted not only threats it posed abroad in places like China and Africa but also the infiltration of Communism beliefs at home. The postwar Red scare from the late 1940s to the late 1950s expressed fears that Communists had taken over key U.S. institutions like the State Department and the film industry. In this context, where the enemy was battled on the terrain of ideology and influence as well as nuclear and military might, family life took on added significance. Mothers who nurtured independent judgment in their children made citizens who could resist what critics of Communism saw as the Soviet's blind obedience to centralized authority. In the symbolism of the cold war, families headed by strong husbands and tended to by loving mothers acted as bulwarks against the threat of Communism.

Bringing Up Baby

With soldiers returning from Europe and the Pacific and the nation eager to reestablish a sense of normalcy, people in the United States jumped into family making and began what would be the largest generational cohort of the twentieth century. The **baby boom,** the upsurge in babies born between 1946 and 1963, changed what people in the United States understood as family life. The baby boom was caused by a number of factors. Americans in the 1950s married at younger ages than had their parents. The median age at first marriage for women in 1930 was 21.3; in 1950, it had dropped to 20.3. A similar pattern happened with men. A first marriage for men at the turn of the century was 26.7; in 1950, it was 22.8. Couples also stayed married longer. The divorce rate dropped in the 1950s, reaching the lowest point in the twentieth century in 1958 when there were only 368,000 divorces.

baby boom The cohort of babies born in the United States between 1946–1964.

In addition to marrying at younger ages, young newlyweds rushed to establish their families and had children in close succession. By the end of the decade, about thirty-two million babies had been born, eight million more than in the 1930s. In 1954, annual births first topped four million and did not drop below that figure until 1965. Many European countries, as well as Australia and New Zealand, also experienced a baby boom. In some cases, the total fertility rate almost doubled. In the United States alone, approximately seventy-nine million babies were born during the baby boom. In this context, motherhood returned as the dominant meaning of womanhood.

With the rise of psychology to explain parenting and child development, mothers faced a daunting array of advice about how much they could help—or harm—their young charges. Since the days of the early republic, family making had been seen as a civic value; but during the 1950s, concern about raising citizens ready to meet the challenges of an ever more dangerous and complex world lent a specific cast to motherhood. Experts in the 1950s warned that overly dominant or overly indulgent mothers ran the risk of emasculating their sons, creating a generation of sissy boys and homosexuals who would be vulnerable to blackmail or Communist manipulation. The best mothers were those who knew their place as helpmates to their husbands, who did not overreach their proper spheres of influence by challenging the principle of "father knows best," and who applied gentle but firm discipline to their children. Love brought security to children, but too much discipline made nervous children who became anxious and uncertain adults.

Experts whose writing appeared in newspapers and magazine columns and mass-marketed paperbacks helped mothers to strike the proper balance in parenting matters. In 1946, a young pediatrician, Dr. Benjamin Spock, published *Baby and Child Care*, which became one of the most-read parenting manuals of all time. Spock revolutionized child-rearing when he rejected the strict "scientific" child-rearing style that had stressed that children needed to sleep on a regular schedule and that picking them up when they cried would not prepare them to be strong and independent individuals in a harsh world. In contrast, Spock initiated a child-centered approach to parenting. Spock spoke to mothers directly, encouraging them to see their children as individuals and to trust their own instincts, telling them that "you know more than you think you do." Popularizing the work of child psychologist Arnold Gesell, Spock urged mothers to have fewer rules so as not

The Baby Boom created a need for parenting advice that was updated for the nuclear age. Pediatrician Benjamin Spock advocated a child-centered approach to parenting and spoke to mothers directly, encouraging them to see their children as individuals and to trust their own instincts.

to restrict the child's development. The mother was urged to closely watch and respond to the child's moods and needs rather than imposing her own rules on the child. Concern with the developing psyche of the child altered the terms on which successful parenting happened.

Momism

Throughout the 1950s, U.S. culture celebrated mothers for the love and devotion they gave to their families. But concern with women having too much influence over children and family life also grew during the 1950s. While Spock urged mothers to be attentive to their babies needs, other postwar experts warned of the dangers posed by mothers who dominated their children or who lived vicariously through them. In 1942, Philip Wylie launched one of the most extreme attacks on U.S. motherhood ever penned in his best-selling book *Generation of Vipers*. According to Wylie, **momism** was the condition created by neurotic women who reigned unchallenged at home and who lived vicariously through their children. The American mom, Wylie wrote, had created a generation of weak, dependent men who were not up to the complex pressures of modern society. Five years later, Freudian psychiatrist Marynia Farnham and sociologist Ferdinand Lundberg made a similar argument in *Modern Woman: The Lost Sex*. They argued that modern women had become neurotic from striving for social and economic equality with men and rejecting their true destinies as mothers. Mother, the symbol of childhood security, had also become a source of profound anxiety.

momism The tendency in the 1950s to blame all social ails and psychological problems on bad mothers and failed mothering.

The seeds of momism had been planted during the war when experts blamed women for raising sons who were unfit for soldiering. After the war, experts worried that women would cling to their wartime jobs and make it hard for veterans to reclaim their rightful roles in civilian life and their roles as heads of households. The discourse of momism gained particular virulence under escalating anti-Communism. According to psychological experts, dysfunctional mothers ran the risk of raising men whose dependence on their mothers left them vulnerable to Communist influence or homosexuality. The director of the Federal Bureau of Investigation, J. Edgar Hoover, in a speech to the National Council of Catholic Women in 1956, underscored the social significance of healthy mothering to the success in the fight against "the twin enemies of freedom—crime and Communism." While mothering took place in the privacy of the home, motherhood should not be dismissed as a purely personal or private activity. "I feel there are no careers so important as those of homemaker and mother," he insisted.

To balance the power of the mother, the new child-rearing literature stressed the importance of father on the growing child. Some experts publicly worried that without a strong father children would view mothers as the authority in the family and emphasized that fathers were central for children to learn appropriate sex roles. Rejecting the distant father of earlier generations, experts encouraged fathers to get involved. "We know that the father's closeness and friendliness to his children will have a vital effect on their spirits and characters for the rest of their lives. So the time for him to begin being a real father is right at the start." (Weiss, p. 89) Fathers enjoyed special influence over young daughters. One psychiatrist explained, "For it is only as he becomes her first boyfriend that she can experience the *feel* of being feminine and later make a happy marriage herself." But a father also had a role to play in helping his young son's transition into adulthood. If the father could keep his own jealousy in check when "the boy seems to prefer his mother as he is bound to at this age," the father could help his son achieve healthy masculinity. Experts agreed that men contributed psychological character to their children that women could not. However, because men worked outside the home, they had to make special efforts to participate and shape what happened in the home. This meant that the new conception of fatherhood centered on friendship, fun, and leisure. Hobbies, sports activities, and vacation were arenas in which fathers could do the work of parenting without being sullied by the gendered connotation of home life.

Mother blaming and the celebration of motherhood went hand in hand. Momism did not simply mark the new imperative to get women back to the kitchen. It represented the importance of mothers—in the words of anthropologist Ashley Montagu in his book *The Natural Superiority of Women,* the role of women in "teaching men how to be human." Images of good mothers, mothers who found fulfillment by taking care of husbands and children, were central not only to the health of families but to the health of the nation. Conversely, failing moms posed threats that appeared to have frightening consequences.

The Black Mother and Racism

During the 1950s, the black family and, specifically, the black mother came under new scrutiny. Part of the renewed attention stemmed from the cold war. In the scramble for postwar international influence, Jim Crow segregation at home undermined U.S. policy initiatives in Africa where the Soviet Union supported African nations in their struggles for independence against their former colonial rulers. At the same time, black mothers were not immune from the domestic climate in the United States, which warned mothers against neurotic overinvolvement with their children. The idea of the "black matriarch," the domineering and powerful black mother who emasculated her sons, built on and amplified the anxious rhetoric of momism.

Since the 1930s, experts studying the black family had found a high degree of "disorganization" that they believed stemmed from the high proportion of working mothers and female-headed households. According to these studies, black women's wage earning tilted the balance in power dynamics within the black family, giving women too much authority over men. Experts suggested that black families would have healthier children when fathers were restored to their rightful place at the head of the household. But the problem of strong mothers was not only economical. Horace Cayton and St. Clair Drake, authors of *Black Metropolis*, explained that black women undermined black men by women being too critical of their husbands and too indulgent of their sons, leaving both weak and dependent. Others explained that too many black men retained an infantile dependence on their dominant mothers that left them without the necessary discipline and self-reliance to overcome racial prejudice. The discourse of the black matriarch stressed that women would have to learn to subordinate themselves to men and to allow properly gendered family roles to flourish if their communities were to overcome generations of racial prejudice.

At the same time that black mothers were criticized for the ways their parenting created weak men, other experts harnessed the language of psychology to fight against segregation. In 1946, African American psychologists Kenneth and Mamie Phipps Clark founded the Northside Center for Child Development in Harlem, where they conducted experiments on racial biases in education. They designed experiments to show that racial prejudice—not family disorganization or bad mothering—damaged

WOMEN'S LIVES

MAMIE PHIPPS CLARK

Mamie Phipps Clark is best known for her work with her husband Kenneth on the effects of segregation on the self-esteem of African American children. Together they established the ground research used in the *Brown v. Board of Education* segregation case in 1954. Phipps was born in Hot Springs, Arkansas. She graduated from high school in 1934 and began her college career at Howard University as a physics and math major She met her husband Kenneth at Howard. He was a psychology major and persuaded her to switch majors. Phipps graduated in 1938 magna cum laude. That summer she took a job in the law office of William Houston. Houston was instrumental in the early planning of civil rights cases. This job helped Phipps learn more about the psychological effects of segregation in the South. Phipps continued her work at Columbia where, in 1943, she became the first African American woman and the second African American (after her husband) in the university's history to receive a psychology doctorate. The Clarks had two children.

In 1946, Mamie Phipps Clark established the Northside Center for Child Development in a Harlem apartment basement. The center provided a homelike environment for children. Services were provided by social workers, psychologists, psychiatrists, and physicians. Due to the stigma of being mentally ill, most parents did not seek help for their children. Clark had long suspected that many of the African American children who were tested and told they were retarded or had some other learning disability were in fact not retarded. The IQ tests were racially and economically biased toward white children.

Clark's research involved a coloring test and a doll test. In the coloring test, three-year-old African American children were given a sheet of paper with the drawings of an apple, a leaf, an orange, a mouse, and a boy and a girl. They were also given a box of twenty-four crayons with the colors brown, black, yellow, white, pink, and tan. Clark would then ask them to color the picture of either the girl or boy the same color they were. After the children responded, Clark would ask the children to color the opposite-gendered picture the color they wanted it to be. Her research showed that children with very light skin colored the picture correctly. Most of the darker-skinned African American children colored the picture with yellow or white crayons. Clark concluded that the children's choice of inappropriate colors indicated emotional anxiety in terms of the color of their own skin; that because they wanted to be white, they pretended to be. In the doll test, children were shown a white doll and a black doll. They were asked simply which doll they preferred to play with. Over half of the children rejected the black doll and preferred the white doll. It was Clark's work on the way black children seemed to prefer white dolls to black ones that particularly impressed the Supreme Court justices. Mamie Phipps Clark died on August 11, 1983. ∎

the psychology of black children. One famous experiment involved showing groups of black and white children two black and two white dolls purchased from Woolworth's for fifty cents, then asking the children to choose which doll was nice, pretty, or bad. The results showed that both groups of children associated the white dolls with positive characteristics. The Clarks concluded that "the Negro child, by the age of five is aware of the fact that to be colored in contemporary American society is a mark of inferior status." They presented their findings at school desegregation trials in Virginia, South Carolina, and Delaware. Their research also appeared in the 1954 *Brown v. Board of Education of Topeka*, the landmark Supreme Court decision that ruled public-school segregation unconstitutional (see chapter 20).

Cold war culture invested mothers in 1950 with the power to raise future citizens who could overcome national and international threats to peace and security. Healthy citizens, psychologically disciplined and responsible to work and family, could end racism at home and resist Fascism abroad. Conversely, pathological mothers could undermine national strength if they failed in their role as primary parent. Motherhood, done in the privacy of the home, enacted in miniature the drama playing out on the world stage between democracy and Communism. Nothing short of world peace rested on the shoulders of U.S. mothers.

REMAKING THE AMERICAN HOME

After years of housing shortages, rationed foods, and few consumer goods, people in the United States entered the postwar years eager to establish a new sense of family life. At the top of the list of priorities was decent housing. Consumers bought previously hard-to-get household appliances such as vacuum cleaners, refrigerators, electric ranges, and freezers. New car sales in 1945 totaled 69,500; ten years later, the number rose to 7.9 million. A seemingly endless demand for housing propelled massive increases in building, resulting in some fifteen million housing units being built in the United States from 1945 to 1955. By 1960, 60 percent of U.S. families owned their own homes. The government subsidized much of this housing boom. The Federal Housing Administration provided home loans for which buyers put up 10 percent of the costs, with low interest rates and thirty-year terms for repayment. The Veterans Administration enabled many returning soldiers to buy homes with virtually no down payment as part of the GI Bill (see chapter 18). However, U.S. family life was far from uniform. New immigrants, legal and illegal, changed rural and urban enclaves. Immigrant women and their daughters adapted traditional homemaking to new circumstances and created celebrations and rituals to reflect their dual identities. Suburban living, represented by the media as new and modern, was only one way U.S. women in the 1950s remade family life.

The Suburb

The suburb captured, like few other neighborhoods, the spatial and gender separation of public and private life. Wageworkers, predominantly men, left suburban neighborhoods to work; while homemakers stayed put, tending to the daily round of domestic work and child care. The growth of suburbs went hand in hand with the growth in the automobile industry. The popularity of cars remapped the landscape, fueling construction of suburban housing developments and shopping centers and signaling the decline of downtowns with their blocks of apartments and lack of parking spaces. Cities on the West Coast, where millions of workers settled to take advantage of the aerospace and defense industries, saw the most dramatic growth. Single-family housing suburbs ringed West Coast cities like Los Angeles, Sacramento, and San Francisco.

The suburbs, with their highly scripted gender roles, were a distinctive product of the postwar years. The most famous of suburbs were those built by William and Alfred Levitt who innovated both the plan and production of suburban housing by applying assembly-line techniques to track housing. At its peak, a Levitt team of builders could put up a house using preassembled materials in sixteen minutes, including plumbing. The first "Levittown" was built in 1958 thirty miles outside of New York City near Hempstead, New York, on Long Island. It had seventeen thousand homes with eighty thousand residents, and had amenities that stay-at-home mothers needed. It had seven village greens and shopping centers, fourteen playgrounds, nine swimming pools, two bowling alleys, and a town hall. The two-story Levitt house, organized to reflect the postwar nuclear family, was comprised of a kitchen, a living room, two bedrooms, a bathroom, an expandable attic, and, in later models, a carport. A house included central heating; built-in bookcases and closets; a refrigerator, stove, and washing machine; and an eight-inch Bendix television set. Houses cost $7,990, approximately two and a half times the median family income and $1,500 less than other comparable houses. Average mortgages were fifty-eitht dollars per month for twenty-five years. Eager buyers lined up the night before houses came up for sale.

A seemingly endless demand for housing propelled massive increases in building, resulting in the construction of 15 million housing units from 1945 to 1960. By 1960, 60 percent of American families owned their own homes, many in massive developments like this one, built by William and Alfred Levitt.

Many women embraced the gender roles the suburbs embodied. Sociologist Herbert Gans reported that for Levittowners, suburban life was very satisfying. "Most Levittowners grew up in the Depression and remembering the hard times of their childhood, they wanted to protect themselves and their children from stress." Children and husbands enjoyed the home as a stress-free haven, but for women, it was a place of labor. Homemakers threw themselves into a daily round of housekeeping, cooking, and child care. Women's role as primary consumer took more and more time. Shopping, driving, and selecting goods from the supermarket became major tasks. All together, full-time homemakers put in fifty-five-hour workweeks. In addition to the round of housework, suburban women joined a range of community activities organized by church groups, parent-teacher associations, the YMCA, local branches of the League of Women Voters, and women's leisure and religious clubs.

Other women found the gender imperatives of the suburbs to be confining. Betty (Goldstein) Friedan captured the confining aspects of suburbia for women in her groundbreaking work *The Feminine Mystique*, published in 1963. Friedan sent a

1950s Home Economics Textbook

1. **Have dinner ready:** Plan ahead, even the night before, to have a delicious meal—on time. This is a way of letting him know that you have been thinking about him, and are concerned about his needs. Most men are hungry when they come home and the prospects of a good meal are part of the warm welcome needed.

2. **Prepare yourself:** Take 15 minutes to rest so you will be refreshed when he arrives. Touch up your makeup, put a ribbon in your hair, and be fresh looking. He has just been with a lot of work-weary people. Be a little gay and a little more interesting. His boring day may need a lift.

3. **Clear away the clutter:** Make one last trip through the main part of the house just before your husband arrives, gathering up school books, toys, paper, etc. Then run a dust cloth over the tables. Your husband will feel he has reached a haven of rest and order, and it will give you a lift, too.

4. **Prepare the children:** Take a few minutes to wash the children's hands and faces if they are small, comb their hair, and if necessary, change their clothes. They are little treasures and he would like to see them playing the part.

5. **Minimize the noise:** At the time of his arrival, eliminate all noise of washer, dryer, dishwasher or vacuum. Try to encourage the children to be quiet. Be happy to see him. Greet him with a warm smile and be glad to see him.

6. **Some don'ts:** Don't greet him with problems or complaints. Don't complain if he's late for dinner. Count this as minor compared with what he might have gone through that day.

7. **Make him comfortable:** Have him lean back in a comfortable chair or suggest he lie down in the bedroom. Have a cool or warm drink ready for him. Arrange his pillow and offer to take off his shoes. Speak in a low, soft, soothing, and pleasant voice. Allow him to relax and unwind.

8. **Listen to him:** You may have a dozen things to tell him, but the moment of his arrival is not the time. Let him talk first.

9. **Make the evening his:** Never complain if he does not take you out to dinner or to other places of entertainment; instead, try to understand his world of strain and pressure, his need to be home and relax.

10. **The goal:** Try to make your home a place of peace and order where your husband can relax.

(Source: From http://www.history.ilstu.edu/nhp/civilization/site/suburbia_guide.html)

questionnaire to other women in her 1942 Smith College graduating class and discovered that her classmates indicated a general dissatisfaction with their lives. This led Friedan to conduct more detailed research into what she called "the problem that has no name." She defined this "mystique" as women's feeling of worthlessness that came with being financially, intellectually, and emotionally dependent upon their husbands. Through her findings, which subsequent historians have challenged, Friedan hypothesized that women were victims of a false belief system that required them to find identity and meaning in their lives through their husbands and children. According to Friedan, "It was a strange stirring, a sense of dissatisfaction, a yearning that women suffered in the middle of the twentieth century in the United States. Each suburban wife struggled with it alone. As she made the beds, shopped for groceries, matched slipcover material, ate peanut butter sandwiches with her children, chauffeured Cub Scouts and Brownies, lay beside her husband at night, she was afraid to ask even of herself the silent question, "Is this all?" Suburbia, cast as the pinnacle of middle-class accomplishment, was a location of boredom and despair for some women. Friedan criticized the hoards of experts who told women that "all they had to do was devote their lives from earliest girlhood to finding a husband and bearing children." For many a generation of women who attended high school and college, the role of the homemaker, so celebrated in popular culture and by experts, was too narrowly drawn to satisfy all their aspirations.

Chinatown

While symbolically the suburbs represented 1950s America, not all Americans lived there. Women in urban neighborhoods, long a stronghold for ethnic communities, continued to create homes for themselves and their families. Such was the case with Chinese American women, many of whom were newcomers, aided by changes in immigration law. In 1943, Congress had repealed all Chinese exclusion laws, a shift that granted Chinese living in the United States the right to naturalize into U.S. citizens and established a very small immigration quota. The 1945 **War Brides Act** allowed Chinese American veterans to bring brides into the United States. The following year, Congress granted the rights of wives and children of Chinese American citizens to enter as nonquota immigrants. As the cold war intensified with the establishment of the Communist People's Republic of China in 1949 and the Korean War (1950–1953), the United States allowed a trickle of educated Chinese to enter the country as political refugees. With many obstacles to immigration removed, Chinatowns on the East and West coasts welcomed an influx of women to their neighborhoods.

New Chinese immigrants to New York City tended to be from wealthier families and to have come from larger cities than their counterparts earlier in the century. Many had attended colleges or universities in China and had been exposed to Western culture before they arrived in the United States. Importantly, more women immigrated, bringing the sex ratio into a near balance.

With the arrival of more women, traditional Chinese family values and paternal authority were reestablished. In groceries, restaurants, and laundries, women worked alongside their husbands, sharing in the daily round of work that kept the businesses running. All family members, including older children, were expected to help. Chinese women in the United States found relief from the traditional authority wielded by their mothers-in-law in these nuclear households, yet they also complained of feeling cut off from female relatives and of shouldering the entire burden of child-care and

War Brides Act The 1945 Act that allowed Chinese American veterans to bring brides into the United States.

Changes in the post war period allowed more Chinese women to immigrate. Most settled in cities on the west and east coasts, like these women in San Francisco. Ethnic enclaves in large cities enabled women to blend traditional Chinese and modern American practices in new ways.

household duties. Some husbands barred their wives from moving about the city and learning about their new country. One woman told a Chinese press reporter that her life was like "being in jail." The long hours of work, coupled with the dismantling of traditional networks of female relatives, left many Chinese women isolated.

Marriage difficulties were common among new or reunited families. Most Chinese women who came to the United States in the immediate postwar period came as war brides, never having met their husbands or having been separated from them for years. In both cases, women found themselves adapting to a new country and to new marital circumstances. The reunited wives who had experienced long periods of separation from their husbands had often developed their own survival strategies. The younger war brides faced greater pressure from their more assimilated husbands to adapt to their lives in the United States. As the press reported, women were frequently battered, abused, and even forced to divorce their husbands. High suicide rates and high divorce rates among newly united families were recognized as major problems.

Community activities fostered new friendships and social networks among women that helped new brides and wives transition into their new lives. Women's clubs and close friends frequently gathered to play mah-jong, eat Chinese food, and talk. Chinese women devoted much time and energy into parenting. Traditional Chinese teachings reminded women to devote their entire lives to cultivating their children's success: "Hoping your sons become dragons" (symbolizing ruling powers and authority), "parents should be blamed for the evildoing of their children," "raising children for one's future happiness," and "a mother's honor and well-being depend on her children."

Younger and more affluent Chinese women assimilated with relative ease. Many urban women with formal educations moved around the city in Western clothes, shopped, and made friends with their white neighbors. The assimilation of the U.S-born Chinese both frightened and excited the older generations. They wanted the younger generation to succeed in the United States, yet they did not want them to lose their Chinese heritage. Like most second-generation immigrants, the Chinese youths quickly adopted the dominant culture's language and customs. To help their children retain their Chinese heritage, the Chinese community established language schools and participated in ethnic events, such as the Chinese New Year celebration. China-towns adopted U.S. rituals and made them their own. Young women competed in the first Miss Chinatown USA beauty pageant in 1958. While the pageant required all participants to speak English, winners traveled the country acting as ambassadors of Chinese culture. Yet, even assimilated Chinese women reported incidences of discrimination. Mrs. Yu, writing in the *China Daily News*, described the difficult time she and her husband had trying to rent a home because of the racial bias of white home owners. "I knew people had different feelings, but I did not expect I would be discriminated just because of the color of my skin."

The Barrio

In the Southwest, Mexican migration increased dramatically in the postwar period. Mexican men and women were drawn to the United States during the war by labor shortages, particularly in agriculture. Long-standing Mexican enclaves grew in San Antonio, Los Angeles, El Paso, and Denver. As important as Mexican workers were to ensuring that crops were harvested during the labor shortages of the 1940s, by the 1950s, the attitude toward illegal aliens had changed. President Dwight D. Eisenhower became worried that profits from illegal labor led to corruption. An on-and-off guest-worker program for Mexicans operating at the time had allowed farmers and ranchers in the Southwest to become dependent on low-cost labor of illegal aliens. As illegal immigration from Mexico continued in the 1950s, the federal government moved to close the porous border in Texas, California, and Arizona. The Immigration and Naturalization Service (INS) removed eighty thousand illegal immigrants in its 1954 **Operation Wetback,** many of whom were women and their U.S. born children, who by law were U.S. citizens.

Operation Wetback A 1954 federal program to close the border between Mexico and Texas, California, and Arizona.

Throughout the 1950s, conditions in many rural barrios were difficult. One study published in 1947 described Mexican Americans as the nation's "stepchildren" for the stark poverty most faced. In San Antonio, the number of infant deaths among Mexican Americans was three times that of Anglos. Of seventy thousand migrant agricultural workers in Colorado, Montana, and Wyoming, sixty thousand had no toilets, ten thousand used ditch water for drinking, and thirty-three thousand had no bathing facilities. Yet, despite such conditions, Mexican American women found ways to raise children and keep their families intact. Hispanic writer Frances Esquibel Tywoniak recalled her life in a barrio in Visalia, California, in the 1940s and 1950s. Tywoniak's family lived in a two-room house with electricity but no indoor plumbing. The town was divided into Mexican and Anglo sections. Houses on the Anglo side were connected to the sewer system, had paved sidewalks and streets, and communicated a sense of cohesive neighborhoods. The Mexican section was comprised of frame houses, each build differently. Instead of lawns, most Mexicans used their front yards to grow flowers or vegetables or to park their cars. There were no sidewalks, and only a few streets were paved.

Despite its lack of amenities, the barrio fostered a sense of community. Regular school and church attendance were important. Tywoniak recalled that her parents conveyed to their children a faith in the educational process just as they conveyed their faith in the Catholic Church. "I don't care what people say," she recalled her mother saying to her father. "It isn't true that a child's only obligation is to add to the family income while she lives at home. A person needs an education to improve her lot, *para ver si un dia cambia* [to see if one day changes]." Mexican American students, however, were routinely placed in less academically oriented classes. Tracking and segregation limited Mexican American teenage women to vocational classes in homemaking and sewing, skills they already had. Attending school did, however, immerse young Mexicanas in U.S. culture, changing their clothing and food preferences and social behaviors.

Produced in 1954, "Salt of the Earth" told the story of a long and difficult strike led by Mexican American and Anglo miners. With its heroic portrayal of the union men and their wives, the film became a Hollywood classic.

In migrant communities, women cared for their homes and families while also looking for ways to bring much needed cash into their families. In rural areas, women raised cows or chickens and sold eggs and milk, while others took in laundry and sewing. To make ends meet, women like union activist Jessie de la Cruz worked alongside the men during weekends and holidays, picking grapes, apricots, peaches, walnuts, tomatoes, and cotton at nearby farms, often bringing along their infants and young children. Women's responsibilities for home life included spiritual as well as material help. Women nurtured their children's religious identifications to the Catholic Church, insisting on attendance, daily prayers, and proper behaviors from children. Through food and religion, Mexican American women were central in maintaining their cultural heritage.

Women at home managed their roles as primary consumer, homemaker, mother, and wife by drawing on both traditional and contemporary resources. For some, this meant drawing on communities of women who shared similar circumstances in ways that were similar to what their mothers did in ethnic enclaves. For others, it meant starting life by moving beyond traditional networks of communal ties in new housing developments or in new countries. Caring for children and home, materially and psychologically, remained the anchor of most women's daily life.

THE HETEROSEXUAL IMPERATIVE

For many young women coming of age in the 1950s, the search for a boyfriend, a fiancé, and eventually a husband constituted the highest priority of life and a major social, sexual, and economic activity. Marriage was viewed as the ultimate goal for women, yet part of winning that prize involved navigating the fraught terrain of dating, a social ritual that by the 1950s had been stripped of adult supervision. With the anxiety and dislocation of

WOMEN'S VOICES

WOMEN CAN NO LONGER BE TAKEN FOR GRANTED

Jessie Lopez de la Cruz worked as a union organizer for migrant workers in California in the early 1960s. In this excerpt, she retells how she became active in the union and how she reached out specifically to Mexican American women.

One night in 1962 there was a knock at the door and there were three men. One of them was Cesar Chavez. And the next thing I knew, they were sitting around our table talking about a union. I made coffee. Arnold had already told me about a union for the farmworkers. He was attending their meetings in Fresno, but I didn't. I'd either stay home or stay outside in the car. But then Cesar said, "The women have to be involved. They're the ones working out in the fields with their husbands. If you can take the women out to the fields, you can certainly take them to meetings." So I sat up straight and said to myself, "*That's* what I want."

When I became involved with the union, I felt I had to get other women involved. Women have been behind men all the time, always. In my sister-in-law and brother-in-law's families the women do a lot of shouting and cussing and they get slapped around. But that's not standing up for what you believe in. It's just trying to boss and not knowing how. I'd hear them scolding their kids and fighting their husbands and I'd say, "Gosh! Why don't you go after the people that have you living like this? Why don't you go after the growers that have you tired from working out in the fields at low wages and keep us poor all the time? . . . Then I would say we had to take a part in the things going on around us. "Women can no longer be taken for granted—that we're just going to stay home and do

the cooking and cleaning. It's way past the time when our husbands could say, "You stay home! You have to take care of the children. You have to do as I say."

Then some women I spoke to started attending the union meetings, and later they were out on the picket lines.

I was well known in the small towns around Fresno. Whenever I went to speak to them, they listened. I told them about how we were excluded from the National Labor Relations Board in 1935, how we had no benefits, no minimum wage, nothing out in the fields—no restrooms, nothing . . . I said, "Well! Do you think we should be putting up with this in this modern age? You know, we're not back in the 20s. We can stand up! We can talk back! It's not like when I was a little kid and my grandmother used to say, 'You have to especially respect the Anglos', 'Yessir,' 'Yes, Ma'am!' That's over. This country is very rich, and we want a share of the money those growers make of our sweat and our work by exploiting us and our children!" I'd have my sign-up book and I'd say, "If anyone wants to become a member of the union, I can make you a member right now." And they'd agree!

Source: *Ellen Cantarow, ed.,* Moving the Mountain: Women Working for Social Change *(Old Westbury, NY: Feminist Press, 1980).*

Questions

1. How did de la Cruz understand the relationship between home and work, between the private and public spheres, in her own life?

2. What enabled de la Cruz to be an effective union organizer?

3. Why had the time come to no longer "take the women for granted"?

the Depression and war firmly in the past, a new cohort of young women lived their teenage years in ways that would have been unthinkable to all but the most wealthy in previous generations. They stayed in school longer, and more of them completed high school and planned to attend college. As a group, they had far fewer responsibilities, held only part-time jobs, and crucially, had far more money at their disposal than had their parents during their teenage years. Cars allowed girls and boys private time away from friends and families; radio stations offered romantic and sexual ballads designed for teenagers; and beauty products emphasized sex appeal—all of which were used by teenagers to forge their own standards of behavior and sexual subculture in the 1950s.

Beauty Icons

The message directed at young women in the 1950s obsessively focused on the pleasures and dangers of the female body. Young women actively constructed themselves with the purpose of being seen. In the words of novelist Lynn Lauber, "She had entered the world of boys and men, and there didn't seem to be a moment, from when she rose each morning, her skull a complex arrangement of split curlers and spike rollers, that appealing wasn't on her mind." Advertising agencies, armed with an array of new strategies, targeted the lucrative teen market. Magazines directed at young women appeared, including *Seventeen* and *Modern Teen*, and were filled with advertisements for products especially designed for teenage women. The teenage body became a location for new products. "Halitosis" or bad breath, sweat, menstrual odors, and pimples became social perils that required scrubbing, bathing, and a range of new products. Controlling the body was one way to contain postwar fears of changing teenage morality.

Young women sculpted their bodies through undergarments and form-fitted outfits. They wore clothes that drew inspiration from designer Dior's "New Look"—full skirts, narrow waists, form-fitting tops. Skirts came to mid calf and were held out with stiff petticoats. Breasts were formed through padding and underwiring to be large, high, and pointy. Manufacturers invented the "training bra" to introduce their product to younger and younger girls. Hollywood film star Jane Russell, a "bombshell," became famous in one of the era's most seen advertising campaigns that showed women doing ordinary activities dressed only in their Maidenform bras. Girdles, which had all but disappeared during the war, came rushing back into popularity. Tight, with slender bones and rigid elastic casing, the girdle gave women a look that was at once curvy and armored. Young white women wore larger curlers to bed and upon waking, relied on cans of hairspray to achieve styles that were big and stiff. African American women ironed and curled their hair to achieve the smooth full look that dominated.

Fashion icons delivered the message that beauty was central to young women. Barbie made her debut in 1959 and became a dominant icon of femininity. Barbie came from a

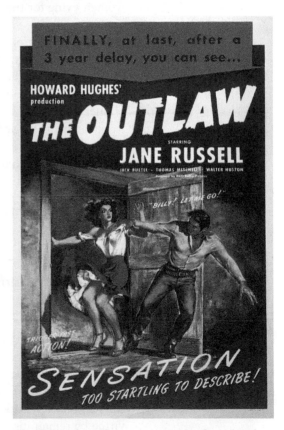

The message directed at young women in the 1950s obsessively focused on the pleasures and dangers of the female body. Hollywood film star Jane Russell, a "bombshell," shown here in a poster for The Outlaw, released in 1950 after years of delays from censors, was known for her missile-shaped form.

German fashion doll for adults named Lilli. Ruth Handler, Barbie's designer, came across Lilli in Switzerland and bought one for her daughter Barbara. Lilli's fashion sensibility and adult body were parts of exactly the kind of doll Handler had wanted to make for the U.S. market, which had nothing for older girls to play with. Girls loved the doll. Part of Barbie's appeal was the fact that she was different from any other doll on the market; Betsy Wetsy, who required regular diaper changes, and Chatty Cathy, who asked an endless stream of questions, were designed to teach the skills required for being a mother. Barbie made her first television appearance on the *Mickey Mouse Club*. Such advertising as this and other marketing techniques helped to sell 351,000 Barbies in her first year, a new sales record.

Another famous beauty icon was Miss America, the winner of a pageant that was broadcast on television for the first time in 1954. The annual program provided a kind of entertainment never before experienced. The first broadcast broke viewing records from coast to coast. Twenty-seven million Americans watched the crowning of their new Miss America. By the end of the 1950s, Miss America had become an international symbol of the ideal young woman. For many, their earliest memories of television were of Bert Parks surrounded by intelligent, talented, and beautiful young women vying for the crown. Miss World (1951) and Miss Universe (1952), founded by California clothing company Pacific Mills to showcase its swimwear, brought pageantry to international heights.

In another vein, magazine editor Hugh Hefner introduced a decidedly sexy icon of female beauty, the *Playboy* playmate. Hefner began publishing his monthly men's magazine, *Playboy*, in 1953 with Hollywood star Marilyn Monroe as the first playmate. Hefner's vision of women combined sex appeal with Americanism, and he sought out women for his magazine that were like the "girl next door." Playmates were everywhere, explained Hefner, "the new secretary at your office, the doe-eyed beauty who sat opposite you at lunch yesterday, the girl who sells you shirts and ties at your favorite store. We found Miss July in our circulation department . . ." *Playboy* cast an air of glamour on the bachelor and encouraged its readers to resist the era's message of early marriage and family togetherness. Hefner's playboy bunny, sexy and available, joined Barbie and Miss America to offer U.S. teenage women a confusing message about sexual allure.

Sexual Brinkmanship

Dating became a central activity for teenage girls in the 1950s. Whereas in the 1920s, flappers stood at the edge of changing sexual behaviors, in the 1950s, high-school-aged women experimented with premarital sexual behaviors (see chapter 16). The continued growth in high-school attendance made school the single most important institution for establishing peer group dating standards. Once the last dance ended or the movie credits rolled, teenage women began their weekly struggle to enjoy and control their sexuality. The double standard put these women in the position of guarding their virtue by remaining chaste, despite the ardor of their boyfriends. A woman's reputation was tied to her sexual behavior and her ability to say no at the right moment. One sociologist commented on the contradictory values teenage women faced. "It seems that half the time of our adolescent girls is spent trying to meet their new responsibilities to be sexy, glamorous and attractive, while the other half is spent meeting their old responsibilities to be virtuous by holding off the advances which testify to their success." Girls were expected to be virgins until marriage. They were overwhelmed with advice about not "going all the way" without being prudish and unpopular. "Virginal" had racial meanings as well. Many men expected white girls to be virgins and viewed minority women as always available.

When Alfred Kinsey published *Sexual Behavior of the Human Female* in 1953, the country discovered that many men and women alike violated enshrined ideas about proper sexual behavior. One of the most notorious findings was that approximately 50 percent of the women in Kinsey's study had engaged in premarital intercourse. Kinsey first became interested in sex research when he taught a class on marriage at Indiana University in 1938. Amazed at the paucity of sources, he began a massive study of human sexual behavior that, by its end, involved interviews with 17,500 women and men. Much to the surprise of the country, Kinsey discovered that what Americans said about sexual morality and their actual behavior differed significantly. In *Sexual Behavior of the Human Male* (1948), Kinsey found the sexual double standard firmly in place. Sixty-eight percent of college-educated men in his sample had had premarital intercourse, often with women of a lower social class than themselves. Yet, he also found that half of the men surveyed wanted to marry a virgin.

As a young woman decided whether to "go all the way," she was informed both by her peers and by popular culture that sexual intercourse would be the most important and the ultimate romantic experience in a girl's life. Yet, for many women, sexual intercourse with their boyfriends did not live up to their high expectations of a life-changing event. In novels and memoirs of the 1950s, women often asked, "Was this all there was? Was this IT?" "Going all the way," the experience that was to be effortless and perfect, in reality, too often fell short. Actor and singer Cher recalled that when she was fourteen, her girlfriends told her "how much fun sex was, that I could get away with it and that boys would respect me—as long as I didn't go all the way. But I thought stopping short was ridiculous. I wanted to find out what it was all about so I just did it, all at once, with the little Italian guy next door I was madly in love with. When we'd finished, I said, 'Is this it?' He said, 'Yeah,' and I said, 'Well, you can go home.'"

Hanging over the head of young women was the ever-present threat of exposure and pregnancy. Birth control, which was not readily available to unmarried women, was very difficult for teenage women to obtain. Some women opted to marry their sexual partner as a way to protect themselves from becoming a woman with a reputation. The preoccupation with virginity and sexual intercourse created an extreme double standard in which women bore the responsibility and punishment for

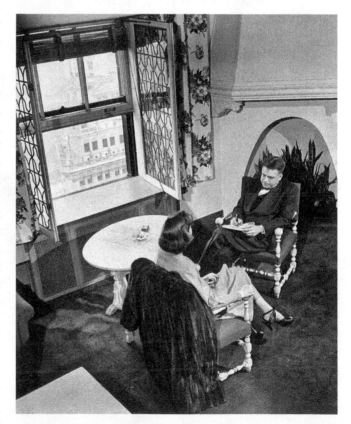

Alfred Kinsey shocked the country with his two-volume report Sexual Behavior of the Human Male *(1948)* and Sexual Behavior of the Human Female *(1953)* which documented the various ways men and women violated enshrined ideas about proper sexual behavior. One of the most notorious findings was that approximately 50 percent of the women in Kinsey's study had engaged in premarital intercourse.

WOMEN'S LIVES

MARY STEICHEN CALDERONE

Mary Calderone was a physician and public health advocate, known for her work in the advancement of sexual education. She served as president and co-founder of the Sexuality Information and Education Council of the United States (SIECUS) from 1954 to 1982. She was also the medical director for Planned Parenthood and helped overturn the American Medical Association's policy against the dissemination of birth control information to patients.

Mary Steichen was born in Paris but came to the United States for her education. She graduated in 1925 from Vassar College and went on to study theater, where she met and married her first husband. The death of her eight-year-old daughter, along with dashed acting dreams and a divorce, plunged Steichen into depression. After a series of psychoanalytic tests, she decided to return to school and study medicine. She graduated from the University of Rochester medical school in 1939 and received her Master of Public Health (MPH) from Columbia University in 1942. During her many internships, she met and married Dr. Frank Calderone, who worked as a physician in the New York public school system. He eventually became the chief officer of the World Health Organization.

In 1953, Mary Calderone joined the staff of Planned Parenthood Federation of America. In 1958, she organized a national conference that launched the movement to legalize abortion. In 1964, she helped overturn the American Medical Association policy against doctors giving out contraception information to patients. Through letters, she came to see that people in the United States had questions not just about sex but about sexuality and that sex education in the United States was sorely deficient. Determined to expand the discussion of sexuality from a simple focus on contraception, Calderone left Planned Parenthood in 1964 and formed SIECUS. Its mission statement announced its ambitious goal "to establish man's sexuality as a health entity." The organization became an essential umbrella group for school administrators, sex educators, physicians, social activists, and parents seeking to access information about teaching sexuality education. She died in 1998 at the age of 94. ∎

breaking sexual and social norms. The fear of being known as a "bad girl" was ever present. A woman remembered a sex education lesson in the sixth grade: "Lessons, lectures, what one must do. You must be careful with your reputation. . . . I feel eyes on me, expectant. They are waiting to see what kind of girl you will turn into once your period starts. Good girl or bad?"

Beats and Bohemians

Not every girl could or would try so hard to adhere to the rigid strictures of the double standard. Not every girl felt a part of her high-school social scene. Sociologist Jessie Bernard reported that many high-school students felt like outsiders. Twenty-two percent felt marginal, 11 percent felt different, 44 percent seldom had dates, and 20 percent felt lonesome. Some teens were repelled by the frivolity and anti-intellectuality of 1950s youth culture. They found its attention to dating, appearance, and peer approval deadening. For girls who felt alienated, the vision of a suburban life with children and a husband was not the life they wanted for themselves. One woman recalled that she knew "no white, middle-class woman with children who had a job or any major activities beyond the family. . . . The idea that this was all made me frantic."

Some disaffected young women adopted a bohemian lifestyle made infamous by the **Beats,** a group of mostly male writers and poets centered in Greenwich Village, New York, and North Beach, San Francisco. Allen Ginsberg and Jack Kerouac were the best-known Beats. As a group, the Beats exposed their sexual fantasies and prioritized authenticity over conformity and experience over materialism. Beats, bohemians, and other disaffected youths rejected the foundations of postwar domesticity: making money, maintaining a home, having children, and planning for the future. Joyce Johnson, Jan Clausen, Janis Joplin, Hettie Jones, and Diane di Prima each recalled the restrictions placed on women in the 1950s as unbearable. Johnson, who lived with Kerouac, wrote that "The 'looking for something' Jack [Kerouac] had seen in me was the psychic hunger of my generation. Thousands were waiting for a prophet to liberate them from the cautious middle-class lives they had been reared to inherit." Rebellious girls ran away from home and adopted lifestyles more akin to men than to women: they experimented with sex, drugs, and alcohol, explored their creativity, and decided to avoid domesticity at all costs. Joplin wrote of her adolescence, "I was raised in Texas, man, and I was an artist and I had all these ideas and feelings that I'd pick up in books and my father would talk to me about it, and I'd make up poems and things. And, man, I was the only one I'd ever met. There weren't any others." African American jazz and rhythm and blues artists influenced the Beats and bohemians as did an exoticized view of black culture as being outside of and oppositional to mainstream U.S. society. Di Prima wrote, "Jazz was for us the most important, happening art . . . Miles [Davis] at the Café Bohemia, slick and smart as they come, exchanging sets with Charlie Mingus, cool then and cool now."

Beat women's experience of bohemia was complicated by the sexism of their male companions. Johnson described a woman's place in the Beat scene: "As a female, she's not quite part of this convergence. A fact she ignores, sitting by in her excitement as the voices of the men, always the men, passionately rise and fall and their beer glasses collect and the smoke of their cigarettes rises toward the ceiling and the dead culture is surely being wakened. Merely being here, she tells herself, is enough." Female Beats also faced the vulnerability that came with sexuality in an age of restricted birth control and illegal abortions. Beat men preached a credo of no responsibilities, no commitments, and the value of male friendship or "Beat brotherhood." They defined themselves in opposition to the domesticated masculinity of mainstream white society, thereby placing their girlfriends in the position of bearing full responsibility for pregnancies with no promises of support or marriage. Beat women, like their mainstream counterparts, struggled alone to manage the contradictions of liberating sexuality without more available birth control.

Beats A group of mostly male writers and poets centered in Greenwich, who rebelled against 1950s social and sexual conventions.

Writing Womanhood

Women writers represent the paradoxes of growing up female in the 1950s, fictionalizing the sexual dramas and gender scripts they and their cohorts internalized and often rebelled against. Grace Metalious's *Peyton Place* (1954); Mary McCarthy's *The Group* (1963); and Marilyn French's, *The Women's Room* (1977) were best sellers that explored the paradoxes of femininity in the postwar years. Erica Jong, looking back on her coming of age in the 1950s in *Fear of Flying* (1973), explored the ways girls learned to replace larger life goals with the empty pursuit of beauty. Jong's heroine, Isadora Wing, recalled her growing up as intimately bound up with advertisements that implored girls to "be kind to your behind!" and "That shine on your face should come from him, not from your skin." "What all the ads . . . seemed to imply," wrote Jong, "was that if only you . . . took proper care of your smells, your hair, your eyelashes, your armpits . . . you would meet a beautiful, powerful, potent, and rich man who would satisfy every longing."

Authors recounted the wrestling matches in the backseat of cars on Saturday nights, as their boyfriends pushed them to go farther, without understanding the terrible cost it might entail for the women. Sasha, the heroine of Alix Kates Shulman's *Memoirs of an Ex-Prom Queen* (1969), described the evolution toward "going all the way" with her boyfriend Joey: "The kissing and petting I had so enjoyed had been reduced to a five-minute warm up before the struggle, and I had been forced to trade abandon for vigilance." Sasha's anxiety over protecting her reputation made any encounter with her own sexual desire frightening. "Passionate as I was, I looked for excuses to go straight home from a date." Under pressure from her boyfriend, Sasha reluctantly decided to give in to Joey. "This is it! I said to myself. This is love! Enjoy it. I tried to enjoy it, at least to attend to this celebrated moment in the most touted of acts," yet "I wondered: is this all there is to it?"

Poet and novelist Sylvia Plath was one of a generation of women writers that explored cracks in the gendered world of 1950s America. Like Plath herself, the heroine of The Bell Jar *struggled to reconcile the competing demands of being a woman and a writer at a time when motherhood was viewed as a woman's highest calling.*

Novelist and poet Sylvia Plath captured the psychological pressures to conform to the gender scripts of the 1950s in her semiautobiographical novel *The Bell Jar*. The book is often regarded as a roman à clef, with the protagonist's descent into madness paralleling Plath's own experiences with depression. *The Bell Jar* was originally published under a pseudonym, but after Plath's suicide in 1963, it appeared under her real name. The protagonist, Esther Greenwood, gains a scholarship in New York City to work at a prominent magazine. Esther is exhilarated by the rush of Manhattan, but her experiences also frighten her. She struggles to cope with life in New York City and returns to her home in Boston in low spirits. She has no idea what to make of her life once she leaves school, and the choices presented to her (motherhood or stereotypical female careers such as stenographer) are less than appealing to her. Esther becomes increasingly depressed. She sees a psychiatrist who diagnoses her with a mental illness and administers electroconvulsive therapy. She describes her depression as a feeling of being trapped under a bell jar, struggling for breath. She makes several attempts at suicide. At one point, true to Plath's actual suicide attempt, Esther leaves a note saying she is taking a long walk, crawls into a cellar, and swallows almost fifty sleeping pills, part of her medication for insomnia. She survives; is sent to a different mental hospital; and meets Dr. Nolan, her therapist, who prescribes electroshock therapy. Esther describes the electroconvulsive therapy as beneficial in that it at last lifts the metaphorical bell jar in which she's felt trapped and stifled.

Many of the novelists explored in rich detail the problems of marriage for women. Marilyn French's *The Women's Room* described the boredom of suburban marriage, with its round of coffee klatches with women in the daytime and cocktail parties with women and their husbands flirting in the evening. In between, French's heroine struggled to find meaning in the piles of laundry, the shuttling of her two sons to baseball practice and music lessons, and the endless meals. Exploring the psychological experience of discontent, these novels narrated the deep contradictions of the 1950s celebration of motherhood and domesticity.

SEXUAL DANGERS

Sexuality fascinated people in the United States in the 1950s. The blonde bombshells and curvaceous pinup girls vied with images of sexual danger that also abounded in the 1950s. The abortionist and the homosexual stepped into public debates as immoral, potentially left-leaning Communists who preyed on innocent victims. Abortion was seen as dangerous and shameful; and a crackdown on abortionists made getting the procedure dangerous and difficult. Gay and lesbian people in the United States faced growing persecution at the same time neighborhoods and enclaves encouraged more sociability and nurtured community. The pleasures of sexual expressiveness at mid-century came at a cost for many women.

Back-Alley Abortion

The 1950s ushered in new anxiety about abortion. During the crisis of the Great Depression, when U.S. families had limited their families, and World War II, when employers immediately dismissed women known to be pregnant, abortion became an open secret. It also became more visible after hospitals and clinics took up the procedure. Medical advances, such as safer blood transfusions, penicillin, and other antibiotics, improved women's chances of surviving infections and injuries from abortion. But as the country returned to peacetime and celebrated family life, critics of abortion moved to limit its availability. At the same time, critics linked their efforts to suppress abortion to the cold war, citing the legal abortion Soviet women enjoyed as a sign of the country's "godlessness." The renewed suppression of abortion became another front in the cold war battle for strong U.S. families and against the immorality of Soviet Communism.

Raids of abortionist offices rose in the postwar period, in an adaptation of a technique used by police to crack down on gambling, prostitution, and other illegal activities to medical clinics and practitioners. In 1945, police arrested a San Francisco abortionist who was known as "a careful and clean operator" and who functioned so openly that a city official described her business as a public utility. The number of raids rose in the postwar period and included the offices of longtime abortionists in Akron, Ohio; Detroit, Michigan; Baltimore, Maryland; and Portland, Oregon. The Los Angeles police department devoted a six-member team solely to pursuing abortion cases. Corrupt officers often cashed in by conducting fake raids and extorting abortionists.

The crackdowns resulted in the arrest of the abortionists as well as the women who had had abortions. Newspaper accounts of police kicking down doors and arresting dangerous abortionists spread the message that seeking out an illegal abortion was very risky. The *Chicago Daily Tribune* reported that during one raid the police had gathered thousands of patient records with the names of doctors, nurses, and druggists who were involved. Some papers printed photos of the women caught in the raids. Such tactics relied on fear, shame, and exposure to discourage women from seeking an abortion.

Abortions became harder to obtain, more expensive, and more dangerous in the 1950s and 1960s. Women with access to medical doctors and psychiatrists could be approved for "therapeutic" abortions, granted to save the life of the woman. Hospitals voluntarily took on a new role in enforcing abortion laws and acting as an arm of the state. Hospital abortion committees defined when an abortion was therapeutic and legal and regulated which doctors could perform the procedure. The majority of therapeutic abortions were performed on white women. One study showed that white women received over 90 percent of all therapeutic abortions in New York City between 1943 and 1962. When poor women won board approval for abortion from their municipal hospital boards, they ran the risk of being sterilized. Some physicians routinely sterilized black women without their consent. One doctor critical of forced sterilization explained that a staff member at his hospital in the Southwest "would lie to the patient if he felt she had too many kids and tell her her uterus needed to come out when it didn't." In New York City, Puerto Rican women were sterilized six times more often than white women. Black, Hispanic, Native American, and poor white women were targeted by covert and overt eugenic efforts.

Women looking for abortions without the bureaucratic obstacles or who wanted their pregnancies to be kept secret relied on an underground network of abortionists for their **"back-alley" abortions.** The service was expensive, dangerous, and secretive. In Chicago, the average fee for abortion had more than quadrupled, from $68 in the early 1940s to $325 in the 1950s. Finding the money needed to pay for an abortion was often difficult. One woman reported that she had dropped out of school in order to earn the $500 needed for an illegal abortion. When she was six months pregnant, she had an abortion in "an apartment with no medical backup services." Locating an abortionist had to be done secretively. One woman explained that "you had to ask around. You asked friends and they asked friends, and the ripples of asking people widened until some person whose face you might never see gave over the secret information that could save you." Once an appointment was made, women were continually made aware of the clandestine nature of illegal abortions. When one woman met her contact man in Baltimore, he blindfolded her and walked her through hallways in an effort to confuse her before taking her to the designated apartment.

Some women turned to self-induced abortions, douching with soap or bleach. Desperate and low-income women used many of the same methods used by previous generations. Some aborted themselves with instruments found at home; others ingested alcohol or castor oil. Thousands of women poured into emergency rooms needing urgent care for botched abortions. The number of women who died because of abortion increased. Between 1951 and 1962, the number of abortion-related deaths nearly doubled, from twenty-seven deaths per year to fifty-one. The risk of dying from an abortion was closely linked to race and class. Nearly four times as many women of color as white women died as a result of back-alley abortions.

"back-alley" abortions
Illegal abortions, done in unsanitary and often dangerous nonmedical settings.

The Homosexual Menace

Cold war anti-Communism, with its attention to creating citizens able to resist Communist influence, set the stage for a new wave of hostility against homosexuals. Senator Joseph McCarthy, a Republican from Wisconsin who became prominent nationally in 1950 when he asserted that he had a list of State Department employees who were spies and members of the Communist Party, joined the sexual threat of homosexuality to the threat of Soviet Communism. He accused the State Department with knowingly harboring homosexuals and thus placing the nation's security at risk. Homosexuals, he asserted, were vulnerable to blackmail as they furtively struggled to keep their desires hidden. Further, homosexuals demonstrated "a lack of emotional stability" and a "weakness in their moral fiber." McCarthy's voice was not the only one raised against homosexuals. Republican National Committee Chairman Guy George Gabrielson wrote in the official party newsletter in 1950 that "perhaps as dangerous as the actual Communists are the sexual perverts who have infiltrated our government in recent years."

Despite figures that Alfred Kinsey gathered in the postwar period, which showed that 50 percent of U.S. men and 28 percent of U.S. women had what could be considered "homosexual tendencies," homosexuals became targets of persecution. Unlike earlier critics who viewed homosexuality as a problematic behavior of a small number of people, critics in the 1950s cast homosexuality as a neurotic symptom. According to a leading expert, Doctor Frank Caprio, lesbians were unable to experience personal happiness, and if they said they did they were lying to themselves. "Theirs is only a surface or pseudo happiness. Basically, they are lonely and unhappy and afraid to admit it." Unlike earlier conceptions of middle-class Boston marriages between two women, experts crafted a new version of same-sex relationships, one that cast off middle-class refinement and emphasized a more assertive and working-class woman. The "dyke," the lesbian whose dress and demeanor set her apart from "normal" heterosexual and feminine women, received most expert attention. She claimed masculine prerogatives in the sexual arena, was pathologically jealous, and was so dominant as to pull unsuspecting women into her clutches. Unlike earlier constructions of the masculine lesbian in the 1950s, experts emphasized her sexual desires as compulsive, aggressive, and pathological (see chapter 16).

The medical establishment and the government fell into lockstep around their accounts of the nature of sexual deviance. Between 1947 and 1950, the military and civilian agencies dismissed 4,954 men and women for being homosexual. By April 1950, ninety-one homosexuals were fired from the State Department alone. It became national policy to persecute "outcasts" by dismissing them not only from the State Department, the military, and Congress but from any government job. While homosexual men bore the brunt of government dismissals, lesbians too faced discrimination for their lifestyles. Fewer women held government positions than did men, but they understood that they were as vulnerable to persecution as their male counterparts. By 1951, federal agencies routinely used lie detectors in loyalty investigations of men and women in "sensitive" government jobs to determine if they were either Communist or homosexual. The head of the Washington, D.C., Vice Squad requested new funding to establish a "lesbian squad" to "rout out the females." One female civil service employee in Albany, New York, was summoned to New York City in 1954 and put through four days of interrogation for her homosexual and Communist leanings. Evidence of her

Communism included dancing with a Soviet male officer in Seoul, Korea, after the war and of her homosexuality was having traveled overseas with a woman. She was barred from the federal government for "security reasons, on the grounds of moral turpitude."

Lesbian Subcultures

At the same time that the State Department dismissed homosexuals, gay and lesbian people in the United States continued to build visible subcultures. According to one historian, the war had been one big "coming out party." Homefront dislocations such as moving to a new city for war work or joining the military enabled many gay and lesbian people to forge new, if temporary, communities. Demobilization did not signal the return to their hometowns where many had felt isolated. In cities like New York and San Francisco, neighborhoods, cafés, drive in theaters, and bars where gay men and lesbian women could mingle became important and for the first-time. Thanks to the affluence of the 1950s, for the first time a number of bars could survive catering exclusively to lesbians. "Lisa Ben," a pseudonym that is an anagram for lesbian, produced the first-known lesbian newsletter in 1947. She linked women's economic autonomy to a new sense of women's freedom. "In these days of frozen food, motion picture palaces, compact apartments, modern innovations and female independence, there is no reason why a woman should have to look to a man for food and shelter in return for raising his children and keeping his house unless she really wants to. . . ."

Facing intense social disapproval, lesbian women had to seek out safe spaces for themselves where they could socialize. For working-class urban women, the bar became an important community hub, working as an entry point for newcomers and as a welcoming harbor to old-timers. Writers like Ann Bannon fictionalized lesbian bars as meeting places, and memoirists like Joan Nestle and Leslie Feinberg testified to the lesbian bar's importance to their survival. In the bar, "butch" women in particular felt comfortable and temporarily safe. Butch women rejected the mandatory workday skirts and dresses for slacks or blue jeans, collared shirts or jackets, and hair cut short over their ears. More femininely attired lesbians, "femmes," and butches danced openly in the bars. Butch women made lesbianism visible and as such were the target of hostility. It was illegal to "impersonate" the other sex, so even masculine women had to be sure to have three pieces of women's clothing on them. One woman from New Orleans described being "street smart" in the 1950s: "You learned to avoid the police by walking on the side of the street where the cars were parked, or in the opposite direction on a one-way street so they would have to back up to get you. It was always in the backs of our minds that we could be arrested. Any woman wearing pants was suspect."

Police regularly raided lesbian bars, making them treacherous places for women who did not want their names published in the arrest lists. Class and race divided lesbians, despite the force of a mainstream society that deemed all lesbians deviant. Middle-class lesbians did not want their sexual orientation to be known. Fearing they would lose their jobs, middle-class women socialized privately in their own homes or apartments. Many were critical of butch-femme couples and avoided the bars. Playwright Lorianne Hansberry felt strongly that social acceptance for lesbians required conformity to middle class decorum, including proper feminine dress and proper public behavior. Hansberry criticized masculine women who announced their sexual preference by wearing slacks and cutting their hair short. "Someday I expect the 'discrete'

WOMEN'S VOICES

BUTCH IN THE 1950S

Leslie Feinberg's memoir of growing up as a butch lesbian in the 1950s and 1960s captures both the sense of isolation and pleasure that being closeted caused her. On the one hand, she suffered from feeling like she was "the only one." Yet the homophobia of the postwar period also fostered alternative social spaces, like the gay bar she describes in this passage.

I was fourteen years old. I'd finally heard a coworker at my after-school job talk about a gay bar her brother went to in nearby Niagara Falls. I memorized the name, "Tifka's," and called Information for the address.

Now I was standing in front of Tifka's, afraid, thinking, "This is the last place I could possibly fit. What if I don't?"

I wore a blue-and-red-striped dress shirt, navy blue jacket to hide my breasts, black pressed chinos, and sneakers, because I had no dress shoes. I stepped inside the bar, and it was just a bar. The patrons turned to look at me: male and female "working girls," drag queens, a couple of fierce-looking butches, and some straight male drunks. There was no turning back.

And I didn't want to. These were my people. I just didn't know how to penetrate this society.

I bellied up to the bar and ordered a Jenny.

"How old are you?" the bartender asked.

"Old enough," I countered and put my money down on the bar.

A round of smirks rolled around the bar.

I sipped beer and tried to act however fourteen-year-olds think is cool. An older drag queen studied me carefully. I picked up my beer and walked toward the back room. That's when I saw women dancing together, butch and femme. I almost started to cry, that's how much I wanted to believe that it could be possible, that it could happen to me.

"You ever been in a bar like this before?" the drag queen asked me.

"Sure, lots of times," I answered quickly. She smiled.

Then I wanted to ask her something so badly that I forgot to keep up my lie. "Can I really buy a woman a drink or ask her to dance?"

"Sure, honey," she said. "but only the femmes."

Source: *Leslie Feinberg,* Stone Butch Blues *(New York: Fivebrand Books, 1993).*

Questions

1. Feinberg describes the bar as "a society" and its patrons as "my people." What does she mean by these terms?

2. How does Feinberg adapt postwar gender codes to fit her identity?

---

lesbian will not turn her head on the streets at the sight of the 'butch' strolling hand in hand with her friend in trousers and definitive haircuts. But for the moment it still disturbs. It creates an impossible area for discussion with one's most enlightened (to use a hopeful term) heterosexual friends." Because of the consequences, lesbians often felt reluctance to trust even close acquaintances with knowledge of their personal life.

Forming institutions in such a climate was difficult and dangerous. The first such effort was the **Daughters of Bilitis** (DOB), which was originally founded in 1955 as a private social group for middle-class lesbians looking for an alternative to the gay bar.

Daughters of Bilitis A political group formed by lesbians to promote greater tolerance of homosexuality.

It soon became active in "improving" the image of lesbians and lesbianism and demanding rights (see chapter 21). The DOB insured privacy for its members by having a greeter at meetings who would allow only members to pass through. Its official magazine, *The Ladder*, arrived covered in brown paper with no return address. Despite promises to keep members safe, police informants infiltrated several DOB chapters.

CONCLUSION

In the summer of 1947, *Life* magazine ran a thirteen-page essay, "The American Woman's Dilemma," that introduced readers to what would become a dominant motif of the post–World War II years—the centrality of motherhood to the health of the family and the nation. Eleven years later, *Look* magazine articulated a new problem of adjustment when it asked "The American Male: Why Is He Afraid to Be Different?" The writer described the problem starkly: "One dark morning this winter, Gary Gray awakened and realized he had forgotten how to say the word 'I' . . . He had lost his individuality." As the decade came to a close, the gendered pillars of the cold war came under question, foremost, the construction of femininity through motherhood and homemaking and masculinity through conformity and work. It led many to wonder if a generation of men had lost its ability to be bold, to act independently, and to break away from the "gray flannel" pack mentality and if a generation of women suffered from "the feminine mystique."

The consensus about gender roles that had created a baby boom, a new national family life, and protection from Communism frayed and collapsed by the mid-1960s. No longer able to contain the fears of a rapidly changing world, traditional definitions of men, women, and family would become the focal point for liberal reform and radical social protest movements. Women's roles in both social change and as bearers of tradition and continuity became the grounds on which a new style of politics emerged.

REVIEW QUESTIONS

1. In what ways were motherhood and domesticity different in the 1950s from other periods of U.S. history?
2. What role did psychology play in U.S. cold war family life?
3. How did the era's emphasis on teenagers affect women? Was it a hard time to be a teenager?
4. How did people in the United States discuss sexuality in the 1950s?

● 1940 ●

WOMEN'S EVENTS	GLOBAL EVENTS
1942 Philip Wylie coins "momism" in *Generation of Vipers* Planned Parenthood Federation founded	1943 Congress repeals Chinese exclusion acts
1945 The War Brides Act	
1946 Benjamin Spock publishes *Baby and Child Care* The baby boom begins	
1947 One million women laid off from war-related factory work	1947 The Marshall Plan helps reconstruct war-torn Europe
1949 Marynia Farnham and Ferdinand Lundberg publish *Modern Woman: The Lost Sex*	1949 Truman passes a public housing bill Chinese dictator Chiang Kai-sheck is overthrown The North Atlantic Treaty Organization (NATO) forms

● 1950 ●

WOMEN'S EVENTS	GLOBAL EVENTS
	1950 Korean War begins Joseph McCarthy's list of communists in the government Julius and Ethel Rosenberg executed
1953 The United Electrical, Radio and Machine Workers of America holds its first women's conference Alfred Kinsey publishes *Sexual Behavior in the Human Female*	1953 Labor union membership peaks at 32.5 percent of the labor force
1954 The *Miss America* contest airs on television for the first time	1954 The Senate censures Joseph McCarthy
1955 Daughters of Bilitis begins in San Francisco	1955 The AFL and CIO merge
1958 Nation's divorce rate hits all-time low	1958 Levittown completed in Bucks County, Pennsylvania
1959 Barbie, the fashion doll, debuts	1959 Fidel Castro leads a revolution in Cuba

● 1960 ●

WOMEN'S EVENTS	GLOBAL EVENTS
	1960 John F. Kennedy is elected president
	1961 Cuban missile crisis
1963 Betty Friedan publishes *The Feminine Mystique*	1963 President Kennedy is assassinated

RECOMMENDED READINGS

Dorothy Sue Cobble. *The Other Women's Movement: Workplace Justice and Social Rights in Modern America.* Princeton: Princeton University Press, 2004. Cobble reframes the history of modern feminism by placing in squarely in the history of women's labor activism from the 1930s to the 1980s.

Lizabeth Cohen. *A Consumers' Republic: The Politics of Mass Consumption in Postwar America.* New York: Vintage, 2003. Cohen argues that between the 1930s to the 1960s, good citizenship and good consumption became joined in the post WWII era, with mixed results, particularly for women and minorities.

Daniel Horowitz. *Betty Friedan and the Making of the Feminine Mystique: The American Left, The Cold War, and Modern Feminism.* Amherst: University of Massachusetts Press, 1998. Horowitz connects the Left of the 1940s to the feminist movement of the 1960s through his biography of Betty Friedan.

Her years as a labor journalist during the Cold War forces a new interpretation of the origins of modern feminism.

Elaine Tyler May. *Homeward Bound: American Families in the Cold War Era.* New York: Basic Books, 1988. May's classic study of post WWII American family life links atomic anxieties to gender and sexuality through the trope of domestic containment.

Elizabeth L. Kennedy, and Madeline Davis. *Boots of Leather, Slippers of Gold: The History of a Lesbian Community.* New York: Penguin Books, 1993. This ground-breaking book traces the emergence and growth of a lesbian community in Buffalo, New York from the mid 1930s to the 1960s.

Leslie Reagan. *When Abortion was a Crime: Women, Medicine, and Law in the United States, 1867–1973.* Berkeley: University of California Press, 1998. An important study of medicine, law and women's experiences of abortion before Roe v. Wade.

ADDITIONAL BIBLIOGRAPHY

Beyond Domesticity

Susan Hartmann. "Women's Employment and the Domestic Ideal in the Early Cold War Years," in Meyerowitz, Joanne ed., *Not June Cleaver: Women and Gender in Postwar America, 1945–1960.* Philadelphia: Temple University Press, 1994, pp. 84–102.

William Chafe. *The Paradox of Change: American Women in the 20th Century.* New York: Oxford University Press, 1991.

Jacqueline Jones. *American Work: Four Centuries of Black and White Labor.* New York: Norton, 1999.

Cold War Mothering

Ruth Feldstein. *Motherhood in Black and White: Race and Sex in American Liberalism, 1930–1965.* Ithaca: Cornell University Press, 2000.

Deborah Gerson. "Is Family Devotion Now Subversive?": Familialism against McCarthyism," in Meyerowitz, Joanne ed., *Not June Cleaver: Women and Gender in Postwar America, 1945–1960.* Philadelphia: Temple University Press, 1994, pp. 151–176.

Ellen Herman. *The Romance of American Psychology: Political Culture in the Age of Expert.* Berkeley: University of California Press, 1995.

Regina Kunzel. *Fallen Women, Problem Girls: Unmarried Mothers and the Professionalization of Social Work, 1890–1945.* New Haven: Yale University Press, 1993.

Gerald Markowitz and David Rosner. *Children, Race, and Power: Kenneth and Mamie Clark's Northside Center.* Charlottesville: University of Virginia Press, 1996.

Remaking the American Home

Xiaolan Bao. *Holding Up More than Half the Sky: Chinese Women Garment Workers in New York City, 1948–1992.* Urbana: University of Illinois Press, 2001.

Rosalyn Baxandall and Elizabeth Ewen. *Picture Windows: How the Suburbs Happened.* New York: Basic Books, 2001.

Dolores Hayden. *Building Suburbia: Green Fields and Urban Growth, 1820–2000.* New York: Vintage, 2004.

Kenneth Jackson. *Crabgrass Frontier: The Suburbanization of the United States*. New York: Oxford University Press, 1987.

Huping Ling. *Surviving on the Gold Mountain: A History of Chinese American Women and their Lives*. Albany: State University of New York, 1998.

James Patterson. *Grand Expectations: The United States, 1945–1974*. New York: Oxford University Press, 1996.

Margaret Rose. "Gender and Civic Activism in Mexican American Barrios in California: *The Community Service Organization, 1947–1962*" in Joanne Meyerowitz, ed., *Not June Cleaver: Women and Gender in Postwar America, 1945–1960*. Philadelphia: Temple University Press, 1994, pp. 177–200.

Frances Esquibel Tywoniak and Mario T. Garcia. *Migrant Daughter: Coming of Age as a Mexican American Women*. Berkeley: University of California Press, 2000.

Jessica Weiss. *To Have and to Hold: Marriage, the Baby Boom and Social Change*. Chicago: University of Chicago Press, 2000.

The Heterosexual Imperative

Wini Breines. *Young, White, and Miserable: Growing Up Female in the Fifties*. Boston: Beacon Press, 1992.

Rachel Devlin. *Relative Intimacy: Fathers, Adolescent Daughters, and Postwar American Culture*. Chapel Hill: University of North Carolina Press, 2005.

Barbara Ehrenreich. *The Hearts of Men: American Dreams and the Flight From Commitment*. New York: Anchor Books, 1983.

Brenda Knight. *Women of the Beat Generation: The Writers, Artists and Muses at the Heart of a Revolution*. Newburyport: Conari Press, 1998.

M. G. Lord. *Forever Barbie: The Unauthorized Biography of a Real Doll*. New York: Avon, 1994.

Teresa Riordan. *Inventing Beauty*. New York: Broadway, 2004.

P. Scranton. Beauty *and Business: Commerce, Gender, and Culture*. New York: Routledge, 2003.

Sexual Dangers

Nan Boyd. *Wide Open Town: A History of Queer San Francisco to 1965*. Berkeley: University of California Press, 2003.

Joh D'Emilio. *Sexual Politics, Sexual Communities: The Making of a Homosexual Minority in the United States 1940–1970*. Chicago: University of Chicago Press, 1983.

Esther Newton. *Cherry Grove, Fire Island*. Boston: Beacon Press, 1995.

Donna Penn. "The Sexualized Woman: The Lesbian, the Prostitute, and the Containment of Female Sexuality in Postwar America," in Meyerowitz, Joanne ed., *Not June Cleaver: Women and Gender in Postwar America, 1945–1960*. Philadelphia: Temple University Press, 1994, pp. 358–382.

Steven Seidman. *Beyond the Closet: The Transformation of Gay and Lesbian Life*. New York: Routledge, 2003.

Ricki Solinger. *Wake Up Little Susie: Single Pregnancy and Race before Roe v. Wade*. New York: Routledge, 1992.

Memoirs, Autobiographies, Biographies

Leslie Feinberg. *Stone Butch Blues*. New York: Firebrand, 1993.

Betty Friedan. *Life So Far*. New York: Simon & Schuster, 2000.

Judith Hennessee. *Betty Friedan: Her Life*. New York: Random House, 1999.

Jones, Hettie. *How I Became Hettie Jones*. New York: E.P. Dutton, 1990.

Joyce Johnson. *Minor Characters: A Beat Memoir*. New York: Houghton Mifflin Company, 1987.

James H. Jones. *Alfred C. Kinsey: A Public/Private Life*. New York: Norton, 1997.

Sylvia Plath. *The Unabridged Journals of Sylvia Plath*. New York: Anchor Books, 2000.

CIVIL RIGHTS AND LIBERAL ACTIVISM, 1945–1975

THE CIVIL RIGHTS MOVEMENT

Challenging Segregation

Freedom Struggles

Coming of Age in Mississippi

A MOVEMENT TAKES SHAPE

Labor Activism

The President's Commission on the Status of Women

Building a Movement

The National Welfare Rights Organization

AGENDA FOR REFORM

Legislating Equality

Education and Athletics

Reproductive Freedom

Media and the Movement

WHAT ROLE did women play in the civil rights movement?

HOW DID women's role in the civil rights movement change?

HOW DID women use the government to promote equality for women?

As a teenager, I think I really started emerging into being a real person and I was very much aware of it and I was looking forward to college to really expanding myself and growing. I was taking those kinds of issues very seriously. And that played quite a part, when I got to Nashville, and why I so keenly resented segregation, and not being allowed to do basic kinds of things like eating at restaurants, in the ten-cent stores. So I really felt stifled . . . .

I heard about the Little Rock story, on the radio . . . I remember the Emmett Till situation really keenly. In fact, even now I can,

I have a good image of that picture that appeared in *Jet Magazine*, of him. And they made an impression. However, I had never traveled to the South at that time. And I didn't have an emotional relationship to segregation. I had—I understood the facts, and the stories, but there was not an emotional relationship. When I actually went south, and actually saw signs that said "white" and "colored" and I actually could not drink out of that water fountain, or go to that ladies' room, I had a real emotional reaction. I remember the first time it happened, was at the Tennessee State Fair. And I had a date with this, this young man. And I started to go to the ladies' room. And it said "white and colored" and I really resented that. I was outraged. So, it, it had a really emotional effect. . . . My response was, who's trying to change it, change these things. And I recall talking to a number of people in the dormitories at school and on campus, and asking them if they knew any people who were trying to—to bring about some type of change. And I remember being, getting almost depressed, because I encountered what I thought was so much apathy. At first I couldn't find anyone, and many of the students were saying, why are you concerned about that?

Source: Diane Nash, Interview at http://www.teachersdomain.org/resources.

iane Nash grew up in Chicago, Illinois, where she had only heard of the segregation in the South. Nash enrolled at Fisk University in Nashville, Tennessee, in the late 1950s, and for the first time she was forced to follow Jim Crow customs. The separate but equal doctrine, established in 1896 with the Supreme Court case *Plessy v. Ferguson,* upheld the racial segregation of public facilities such as schools, hospitals, libraries, and drinking fountains as well as the rights of restaurant and store owners to serve whites and "colored" customers separately. Frustrated by the legalized segregation she encountered and looking for ways to change it, Nash attended workshops on nonviolent protest. There, she and other participants took turns role-playing and testing each other to learn how to withstand white attacks without fighting back. In February 1960, Nash helped organize the city's first sit-in. Inspired by a similar demonstration in North Carolina, she and a group of black and white students sat down together at an all-white lunch counter, asked for food, and refused to leave when they were denied service. Within a few months, the sit-ins had forced the desegregation of Nashville's lunch counters and started the process of desegregating other public facilities.

Diane Nash's experience of segregation, while painful, was powerfully motivating. African American women like Nash moved to the forefront of civil rights activism, and their bravery inspired a generation of women to join a range of liberal reform movements in the 1960s and 1970s. This tide of women's social activism brought about significant legislation that outlawed discrimination based on race and sex. The first impetus to liberal reform had come from the civil rights movement, which developed in the wake of World War II. The Double V campaign had joined the United

States' fight against Fascism in Europe to ending racism at home. The movement grew and diversified in the 1950s and 1960s as a generation of African Americans demanded full equality. The second impetus came from the institutions and networks built by women activists during the New Deal and World War II. Women in the labor movement and in the Democratic Party urged newly elected President Kennedy to establish the President's Commission on the Status of Women, chaired by former First Lady Eleanor Roosevelt. The Commission connected a generation of seasoned women reformers to the new movements of the 1960s. Together, reformers trained in the labor and civil rights movements and young women, black and white, who were willing to put themselves in harm's way for what they believed in, helped bring the promise of equality for all closer to a reality.

de jure segregation
Racial segregation based on law.

THE CIVIL RIGHTS MOVEMENT

de facto segregation
Racial segregation based on social practice, not enforced by law.

African American women participated in the new wave of social activism that emerged with the civil rights movement. Long-standing resentment and frustration at the country's reluctance to end racial discrimination reached a critical point in the years following World War II. The war raised expectations of many African Americans who had migrated to cities in the North and West for higher-paying war work or who had joined the armed services and experienced, firsthand, less racially segregated societies. Yet when peace did not bring about the political will to solve the race problem in the United States, African American activists determined the time had come to put pressure on the government to ensure equality for all its citizens. In the first push to challenge Jim Crow segregation, church-based and female-dominated community networks nurtured the civil rights movement. As the movement grew and diversified, these women were joined by a new generation of younger women, many of whom were college educated and from the North. Old and young, church-based and university-trained women influenced each other and the direction of the movement from its inception.

Challenging Segregation

Women in the civil rights movement saw that their best hopes for ending segregation lay in the law. Jim Crow state and local laws, written in 1876 and centered in the South, enforced the legal or **de jure segregation** of the races in everyday life. Such laws supported unequal and poorly funded public facilities for African Americans in the South (see chapter 14). In this way, legal segregation lent support for a range of extralegal and nonlegal or **de facto segregation** practices. These two forms of segregation merged to create a system of racial apartheid in all arenas

In May 1954, the Supreme Court ruled in Brown v. Board of Education of Topeka *that the longstanding principle of separate but equal had no place in public education. For a generation of young African American children, like Linda Brown shown here, the ruling began to dismantle the two-tiered public education system that left them with few supplies, delapidated buildings, and little choice.*

of Southern life, ranging from politics and work to housing and schools. Education had become one of the most glaring examples of the inequalities suffered by Southern blacks. Racially segregated schools had left generations of African Americans poorly educated, taught in run-down schoolhouses heated by wood stoves and lit by kerosene lamps, with out-of-date books and few resources. Civil rights activists targeted separate and unequal education as their opening battle in the struggle for racial equality.

In the fall of 1951, the NAACP asked the parents of a Topeka, Kansas, elementary school student Linda Brown and twelve families to try to enroll their children in their neighborhood white schools. Linda Brown, a seven year old, had to cross a railroad yard and busy boulevard to wait for a bus that would take her twenty blocks to all-black Monroe Elementary in East Topeka. Her father wanted her in the nearest public school just four blocks away. The NAACP filed suit, but in August 1951, a three-judge federal panel threw out the case, ruling that although segregation might be detrimental to Topeka's black children, it was not illegal, because all Topeka schools had equal facilities and programs. The NAACP then filed a lawsuit against the Board of Education, written by the African American lawyer Constance Baker Motley, that was heard by the Supreme Court. That lawsuit and others brought on behalf of plaintiffs in Virginia, South Carolina, Delaware, and Washington, D.C., resulted in a historic victory against legal segregation. In May 1954, the Supreme Court ruled in **Brown v. Board of Education of Topeka** that the long-standing principle of separate but equal had no place in public education.

Brown v. Board of Education of Topeka
The 1954 Supreme Court case overturning the "separate but equal" doctrine established in *Plessy v. Ferguson.*

However, while the Court declared that "separate but equal facilities are inherently unequal," it did not specify the pace and process by which schools were to desegregate. The decision was followed by a second ruling, known as *Brown II* (1955), which called for the dismantling of separate school systems for blacks and whites to proceed with "all deliberate speed." Many white Southerners interpreted the ruling to mean desegregation would take place in the distant future, whereas black Southerners understood it to mean an immediate end to segregation. In 1955 and 1956, desegregation began successfully in the states of Maryland, Kentucky, Delaware, Oklahoma, and Missouri but was slow to come to the deep South.

Black female students figured centrally in one of the civil rights movement's most dramatic confrontations involving education. Three years after the *Brown* ruling, a federal court issued an order mandating Little Rock, Arkansas, to desegregate the city's schools. The order met stiff resistance from local residents and from the governor of Arkansas, Orval Faubus. On September 4, 1957, Faubus refused the order to desegregate and called the Arkansas National Guard to prevent the African American teenagers, six women and three men, from enrolling. President Eisenhower believed that he had convinced the governor to use the guard to protect the black students from white crowds; but when Faubus returned to Little Rock, he dismissed the troops and left the black students exposed to the angry white mob. Photographers and journalists captured the violent responses of whites, making visible the ugly reality of U.S. racism. Within hours, the jeering mob had beaten several reporters and the local police rescued the nine students from the high school. President Eisenhower sent armed troops to the city to restore order. Under federal protection, the "Little Rock Nine" finished out the school year. Yet, they faced daily confrontations with white students. One student, Minnijean Brown, recalled a lunch period when a group of angry white male students surrounded her. She dropped a bowl of chili on the head of one of the white students and was suspended. The white students faced no punishment. Progress was slow. By 1960, only seventeen school systems had been desegregated.

As race relations strained under new scrutiny, long-standing justifications for segregation took on new life, foremost, white Southerners' concern with protecting white women from black men. The murder of Emmett Till in Money, Mississippi, in 1955 made the gender underpinnings of Jim Crow segregation impossible to ignore. As a Northerner, Till was not aware of Southern racial code of behavior and had casually said good-bye to the white shop owner's wife, Carolyn Bryant, on his way out of a grocery store. Two days later, Bryant's husband and brother-in-law kidnapped the boy out of his uncle's home at gunpoint and murdered him. An all-white jury later acquitted the two men under the glare of national press. The acquittal triggered protest rallies around the country. "Not since Pearl Harbor has the country been so outraged as by the . . . [Till] lynching," announced the NAACP's journal *The Crisis* in November 1955. Mamie Till Bradley, his mother, insisted her son's casket be open "to let the people see what they have done to my boy!" Till's violent death and his mother's efforts to bring national attention to the ongoing practice of lynching helped U.S. citizens across the country to see the need for concerted political action to combat racism. For the first time, many Northern blacks understood that racial violence in the South had the potential to touch them. Mamie Bradley explained that before the death of her son, "when something happened to the Negroes in the South I said, 'That's their business, not mine.' Now I know how wrong I was. The murder of my son has shown me that what happens to any of us, anywhere in the world, had better be the business of us all."

The growing consensus that change had to come to the South infused local communities of black women who, in conjunction with national organizations like the NAACP, formed the core of the civil rights movement in the 1950s. A month after Emmett Till's murder, Rosa Parks, a 43-year-old department store seamstress and civil rights activist, refused to give up her seat to a white bus rider in Montgomery, Alabama. Parks had just attended a summer program at the Highlander School in Tennessee where she learned protest tactics. When Parks did not vacate her seat to a white man on a crowded bus, she was arrested for violating Montgomery's transportation laws. Her arrest set in motion a citywide bus boycott.

The Women's Political Council (WPC) in Montgomery had been planning such a boycott since the 1954 *Brown* decision. A group of activists had formed the WPC in 1946 when the all-white League of Women Voters refused to admit black women as members. Along with the NAACP, the WPC had been waiting for a test case to challenge the city's segregated busing. When word of Parks' arrest spread, Professor Jo Ann Robinson at Alabama State College set in motion the existing plan for a one-day boycott of all city buses. To coordinate the protest, they formed the Montgomery Improvement Association (MIA), headed by the young and charismatic minister, Martin Luther King Jr. The boycott, planned as a day-long event to show the city the economic power of African Americans, lasted more than a year. For the working women who depended on the bus, the boycott required commitment and sacrifice. To get to work or to do errands once done quickly with the help of buses now took hours. Women walked, taxied, or organized car pools. The boycott took 65 percent of the bus company's business and hurt white businesses, but the city did not give in until the Supreme Court ordered an end to Montgomery's bus segregation policy in *Browder v.*

Rosa Parks is fingerprinted by Deputy Sheriff D.H. Lackey in Montgomery, AL during her Febrary 22, 1956 indictment for organizing a boycott. Mrs. Parks's refusal to give up her seat for a white passenger and move to the back of a bus the previous December led to a black boycott of buses.

Southern Christian Leadership Conference (SCLC) A principal organization of the civil rights movement that formed out of the Montgomery bus boycott of 1955–1956; led by Martin Luther King Jr.

Gayle in 1956. Eager to keep political momentum nurtured by the boycott, black ministers formed the **Southern Christian Leadership Conference (SCLC)** in 1957 and appointed Martin Luther King Jr. as its first president.

Women's longtime custom of informal leadership in Southern black communities, rooted in their majorities in Baptist and Methodist congregations, made them important participants in the growing movement. While King and other male ministers took formal leadership positions, seasoned female activists continued to provide important guidance. Ella Baker joined the SCLC in hopes of creating a grassroots organization that would be welcoming to young people and women. But she soon felt constrained by the SCLC's top-down organizational style. Baker, the granddaughter of slaves, graduated from Shaw University in 1927 and moved to New York City where she worked for the federal Works Progress Administration (see chapter 17). Her political education began in earnest during World War II, when she directed the New York City branch of the NAACP. After joining the SCLC, Baker met Fannie Lou Hamer, a former sharecropper who headed the SCLC office in Atlanta. Hamer shared Baker's interest in keeping the civil rights movement tied closely to the concerns of ordinary men and women and committed to empowering those people in the United States who had been politically disenfranchised for generations. Together, the two women helped to bring about a new generation of leaders and a new style of activism.

WOMEN'S LIVES

FANNIE LOU HAMER

Fannie Lou Hamer was forty-four years old in 1962 when she saw Student Nonviolent Coordinating Committee (SNCC) workers registering voters in Ruleville, Mississippi. She had no idea that black people had the right to register to vote. Her world changed with this. The youngest of twenty children, Hamer, born October 6, 1917, grew up in a sharecropping family. By the time she was thirteen, she could pick between two and three hundred pounds of cotton a day. Her mother instilled a sense of pride about black womanhood in her daughter. Hamer recalled her mother telling her, "When you get grown, if I'm dead and gone, you respect yourself as a black woman; and other people will respect you." Watching her mother work land she did not

own and mend clothes that should have been thrown out shaped Hamer's political consciousness. Hamer was determine to register to vote. "The only thing they could do was kill me, and it seemed like they'd been trying to do that a little bit at a time ever since I could remember." When Hamer and others went to the courthouse, they were jailed and beaten by the police. On her return, she was thrown off the plantation where she was a sharecropper. She also began to receive constant death threats. Still, Hamer would not be discouraged. She became an SNCC field secretary and traveled around the country speaking and registering people to vote. Hamer cofounded the Mississippi Freedom Democratic Party (MFDP). In 1964, the MFDP challenged the all-white Mississippi delegation to

(continued)

the Democratic National Convention. Hamer spoke in front of the Credentials Committee in a televised proceeding that reached millions of viewers. She told the committee how African Americans in many states across the country were prevented from voting through illegal tests, taxes, and intimidation. "If the Freedom Democratic Party is not seated now, I question America," she said. "Is this America? The land of the free and the home of the brave? Where we have to sleep with our telephones off the hook, because our lives be threatened daily." As a result of her speech, two delegates of the MFDP were given speaking rights at the convention and the other members were seated as honorable guests.

Hamer helped to develop a number of programs to aid the poor in her community, including the Delta Ministry, an extensive community development program, and the Freedom Farms Corporation in 1969, a nonprofit operation designed to help needy families raise food and livestock, provide social services, encourage minority business opportunities, and offer educational assistance. In 1970, Hamer became chair of the board of Fannie Lou Hamer Day Care Center, an organization established by the National Council of Negro Women. She became a member of the policy council of the National Women's Political Caucus in 1971, and from 1974 to 1977 was a member of the board of trustees of the Martin Luther King Center for Nonviolent Social Change. Hamer died on March 14, 1977, at the age of 59. ■

Over the next decade, the women whose church and community networks proved so instrumental to the success of the early movement saw their efforts contribute to the growth of a more national and diverse movement. It drew thousands of new supporters as it spread to high schools and college campuses in the North and the South. The movement of the 1950s and 1960s that had been "carried out largely by women," according to Ella Baker, was now in the hands of a new generation of activists.

Freedom Struggles

As the civil rights movement became national and more Northern, its leadership grew younger and more confrontational. College students adopted new tactics to challenge the deeply entrenched social patterns of racial segregation such as the sit-in and freedom rides, both of which triggered crowds of angry white protesters.

On February 1, 1960, four black male students, active in their college NAACP group in Greensboro, North Carolina, took seats at the lunch counter of a Woolworth's five-and-dime store. The waitresses refused to serve them, yet the students stayed at the counter, doing their homework, until the store closed. Inspired by the men's determination, black women students from Bennett College and a few white women from the University of North Carolina Women's College joined the men at the counter. Soon, hundreds of well-dressed African American students filled the downtown store. Sympathetic blacks and whites across the country supported the sit-in by picketing local stores of national chains that supported segregation in their Southern stores.

As news of the sit-ins spread, more and more students determined to use them to challenge segregation. Diane Nash of Fisk University in Nashville, Tennessee, was among a group of students who had begun planning for nonviolent confrontation be-

Angry white locals surround protestors John Slater, Joan Trunpauer, and Annie Moody during a sit-in at a lunch counter in Jackson, Mississippi, 1963. Through these forms of direct and non-violent confrontations, civil rights activists succeeded in showing the need for change in the segregated South.

fore the Greensboro sit-in. When they organized a sit-in in Nashville, hundreds faced down angry white mobs before they were beaten and arrested. In Atlanta, Spelman College freshman Ruby Doris Smith convinced her friends to join with Atlanta University students to launch a series of sit-ins in Atlanta on March 15, 1960. The Atlanta sit-ins' students broadened their calls for desegregation to include all public facilities, voting rights, and equal work and educational rights. Sit-ins proved effective. In Atlanta, businessmen and political leaders set up community organizations to respond to black residents' demands and many major restaurant chains desegregated.

Organizer Ella Baker quickly recognized the untapped leadership of high-school and college students now eager to join the movement. To capitalize on their energy, Baker organized a conference for 150 high-school and college students at Shaw University in Raleigh, North Carolina, to discuss the future of the movement. The meeting led to the creation of the nationwide **Student Nonviolent Coordinating Committee (SNCC)**, which gave younger African Americans, including women and the poor, more opportunity to set a political course for the movement. These young activists, the "shock troops" of the movement, as they were called, again used the idea of nonviolent confrontation to test the government's willingness to support racial equality.

The idea of the "freedom rides" extended the principle of the nonviolent sit-in, in which women took primary roles, to interstate travel. To mark the seven years that had passed since the *Brown v. Board of Education of Topeka* ruling with little tangible progress achieved, the Congress of Racial Equality (CORE), with the support of the SNCC, initiated "freedom rides" in the summer of 1961. The CORE leaders hoped to pressure the federal government to enforce the desegregation of interstate travel,

Student Nonviolent Coordinating Committee (SNCC) A principal organization of the civil rights movement that formed in 1960 from student meetings led by Ella Baker.

mandated when the Supreme Court ruled in *Boynton v. Virginia* that segregation on interstate travel was unconstitutional. A freedom ride left Washington, D.C., on May 4, 1961, with two buses. White riders took seats in the back of the bus and black riders in the front. At rest stops, whites entered colored-only areas, and black riders entered white-only areas. On Mother's Day, May 14, the freedom riders split up into two groups to travel through Alabama. The first group was met by a mob of two hundred in Anniston who stoned the bus and slashed the tires. The bus managed to get away, but when it stopped about six miles out of town to change the tires, it was firebombed. The other group fared no better. It was greeted by a mob in Birmingham, and the riders were severely beaten. No arrests were made.

Diane Nash of the SNCC and students from Nashville were determined to continue, despite the violence. She explained, "If the freedom riders had been stopped as a result of violence, I strongly felt that the future of the movement was going to be cut short. The impression would have been that whenever a movement starts, all [you have to do] is attack it with massive violence and the blacks [will] stop." Attorney General Robert Kennedy, who was determined to enforce law, pressured the bus company to carry the freedom riders and the Birmingham police to protect them. The freedom riders left Birmingham for Montgomery on Saturday, May 20, with police protection until the buses entered the city limits, when the police disappeared. The quiet bus terminal erupted, Susan Wilbur and Susan Hermann recalled, when the riders disembarked. Over one thousand white men, women, and children attacked the riders with bricks, chains, and baseball bats. Newspapers and television cameras circulated the images of racial violence across the country and the world. Martin Luther King Jr. flew to Montgomery and held a mass meeting in support of the freedom riders. Freedom riders continued on to Jackson, Mississippi. Under mounting pressure to resolve the crisis, the Interstate Commerce Commission outlawed segregation in interstate bus travel in 1961.

Coming of Age in Mississippi

Writer and activist Anne Moody's account of her experiences of growing up in Mississippi and her political transformation through the civil rights movement captures the unique experiences of women during these years. Her story of political coming of age charts her growing awareness of herself as a person shaped by both sexism and racism. Her memoir is among the most widely read of the memoirs of the civil rights movement.

Born Essie Mae Moody, she was the eldest of nine children of Fred and Elmira Moody. She lived with her mother in Centreville, Mississippi after her parents separated. As a young girl, she began working for whites in the area, cleaning their houses and helping their children with homework for only a few dollars a week. These experiences, coupled with her family's ongoing economic insecurities, left the young Anne with a keen sense of economic injustice. She watched as men and women in her community were patronized, ridiculed, and threatened by whites. After Anne graduated from her segregated, all-black high school, she attended Natchez Mississippi Junior College in 1961 and, two years later, the historically black Tougaloo College.

Anne's political education began in earnest at Tougaloo where she became involved with the CORE, the NAACP, and the SNCC. She participated in desegregating a lunch counter at Woolworth's in Jackson, where she faced a violent crowd as she and her friends sat at the whites-only section of the counter and waited to be served. The waitress informed the women she would serve them only when they sat at the

WOMEN'S VOICES

FIGHTING SEGREGATION: AN ORAL HISTORY

Hattye Gatson was born in Pickens, Mississippi, in 1942 and grew up on a farm with her father in the community of Durant, Mississippi. All of the schools she attended were segregated. In her junior year of high school, Ms. Gatson began working in private homes and babysitting where she saw the television coverage of civil rights actions in Selma, Alabama. She knew immediately she wanted to play a part. In this section of her oral history, Gatson discusses the boycott in the mid-1960s that ended Jim Crow segregation in her town.

Well, when I was a teenager here, [it] was very segregated, and black people was not allowed into white, what they called, predominantly white cafe's and white restaurants. And everything, schools, everything here was segregated. And we just had—. Everybody had his own place, as they call it. Black people attended black schools, black churches, black restaurants. Everything. And white did the same. They attended their own. And, well, we had, except the train station, I believe, everything else was white and black. Signs in the windows saying, "Colored people" on one side; "white" on the other side. . . .

Up until sixty-five [1965], everybody went to the colored side, like the sign said, and everybody white went to the white side, like the sign said. But, it was finally integrated. It started getting integrated in 1965. . . .

I was out of high school. I got out of high school in sixty-three [1963]. And, but, what really got me interested: I was watching the television and seeing how people were being treated in Alabama. You know. And I was working at a private home during the time, and would turn on the TV and see all of the riots and how they were doing, and I just couldn't wait to get involved. And I was glad when they came through, because that's what I wanted to do. And at that time, they was called freedom riders. And that's what I said I wanted to be: a freedom rider. . . . When they was saying civil rights and

freedom riders coming through, well, I was just at that age to want to get in it. And, so I did.

. . . I always thought that people was people. You know. And it shouldn't have been, like, colored here and white there. And everybody living in the same town, only white was making decisions because they was the ones that was voting. And I always felt that everybody was important and everybody need to have voted on issues. And that's what got me started to want to get registered and try and help other people to get registered. . . . I don't remember anybody getting fired or anything for trying to register. I don't think. The only time they was getting fired was when the marches, you know, took place, and the boycott. And then, that's what year, in sixty-five [1965], boycotting the towns in order to get signs removed. You know. Now, that's when some people lost their jobs.

. . . The boycott took place in order to really get the businesses who had the signs in the windows saying, "Colored" and "White" to remove those signs, and then allow the black people to go into such restaurants at the time, they wasn't allowed. . . . They had a window, that you went to the window, and you got served through the window, but you couldn't go in and sit. . . . [The boycott] grew, and everybody cooperated here so nicely. And they caused businesses to go out, you know. . . . It really did hurt the town when the boycott took place, but through it all, they removed the signs and removed the partitions, and they got integrated.

Source: From the Civil Rights Documentation Project at http://www. usm.edu/crdp/html/transcripts/manuscript-gatson_hattye.shtml.

Questions

1. What motivated Gatson to get involved in civil rights activism?

2. How does Gatson understand the connection between segregation and racism?

3. How did Gatson's identity as a woman shape the way she entered the civil rights movement?

663

back counter. "We would like to be served here," Anne said. The waitress started to repeat what she had said, then stopped in the middle of the sentence. She turned the lights out behind the counter, and she and the other waitresses almost ran to the back of the store, deserting all their white customers. "I guess they thought that violence would start immediately after the whites at the counter realized what was going on. . . ." When local white high-school students arrived at the store, the crowd turned violent. Suddenly Anne found herself being attacked. "I was snatched from my stool by two high-school students. I was dragged about thirty feet towards the door by my hair when someone made them turn me loose. As I was getting up off the floor, I saw Joan coming back inside. We started back to the counter to join Pearlena. Lois Chaffee, a white Tougaloo faculty member, was now sitting next to her. So Joan and I just climbed across the rope at the front end of the counter and sat down. There were now four of us, two whites and two Negroes, all women. The mob started smearing us with ketchup, mustard, sugar, pies, and everything on the counter."

Despite her fear, Anne withstood the attack and committed herself to the cause. In 1961, she participated in voter registration drives in Hinds County and in the Mississippi Delta. The Delta campaign was difficult, Moody noted. "Most of these old plantation Negroes had been brainwashed so by the whites, they really thought that only whites were supposed to vote." But as the campaign continued and gained momentum, Moody wrote, "That summer I could feel myself beginning to change. I knew I was going to be a part of whatever happened." When she returned to finish college in 1962, Moody was pulled into the many actions taking place in Jackson. She taught at workshops for student demonstrators, showing them nonviolent responses to attacks from crowds or the police.

In 1963, Moody became a full-time worker in the movement, taking a job with the CORE where she worked in the voter registration campaign in Mississippi called "Freedom Summer." Registering voters in Mississippi proved dangerous. During the summer, thirty homes and thirty-seven churches were bombed, thirty-five civil rights workers were shot at, and over one thousand were arrested. Women who participated faced particular difficulties, both from male peers who wanted to keep them safe and from the threat of sexual violence from white opponents of the freedom struggle. Despite such conditions, women made up approximately 40 percent of the group of volunteers for Mississippi Freedom Summer. Anne worked in the volatile town of Canton, Mississippi. The Canton campaign proved very difficult. Older blacks avoided field workers and refused to register. Female CORE workers were kept from any activity that might turn violent. She saw her picture on a Mississippi Klan leaflet along with other civil rights leaders. Her reputation as an agitator reached Centreville and her family, barring her from returning home. Feeling more and more exhausted by the endless round of activism, she returned to Tougaloo to finish her degree and graduated in 1964. She was the first member of her family to graduate from college.

Although she was thoroughly involved in the civil rights movement, she broke away because she had doubts about the direction of black power. Racism and discrimination were not social illnesses restricted to blacks. Moody later said, "I realized that the universal fight for human rights, dignity, justice, equality and freedom is . . . the fight of every ethnic and racial minority, every suppressed and exploited person, everyone of the millions who daily suffer one or another of the indignities of the powerless and voiceless masses."

Anne Moody and other leaders in the civil rights movement—like Diane Nash, Ella Baker, and Rosa Parks, and the thousands of ordinary women who participated in formal and informal political networks—helped bring about fundamental change to the meaning of citizenship in the United States. Their activism led to the desegregation rulings that dismantled separate and unequal schools; changes in the federal government's role in ensuring equality for all its citizens by insisting that the government back up the equality under the Fourteenth Amendment; and, ultimately, the historic Civil Rights Act of 1964. The Civil Rights Act of 1964 banned all discrimination in places of public accommodation, including restaurants, hotels, gas stations, schools, parks, libraries, and swimming pools. It also banned discrimination by employers and labor unions on the basis of race, color, religion, national origin, and sex. Women of all colors would benefit from the equalities the Civil Rights Act of 1964 guaranteed.

A MOVEMENT TAKES SHAPE

The civil rights movement and the passage of the Civil Rights Act of 1964 played central roles in the revival of feminism in the 1960s and 1970s. This **second-wave feminism**, named to underscore its connections to the battle for suffrage in the early decades of the century, utilized civil rights victories to bring about new challenges to women's secondary status. The origins of feminism also lay in the labor movement and the efforts by reformers to end workplace discrimination. These reformers shared with civil rights activists the belief that the government held the answer to the problem of inequality. Pressuring the government to write and enforce new laws establishing women's equality at work, in politics, and in education became the focus of liberal feminist activism.

second-wave feminism The surge of feminist activism that took place in the late 1960s and early 1970s.

Labor Activism

Women in the 1960s lived with a growing awareness about the importance of their paid work to the economic well-being of their families. The majority of U.S. women in the labor market in the 1960s and 1970s worked out of economic necessity, not for extra "pin money" or for personal satisfaction alone. Trends that began at midcentury strengthened in the postwar years. During World War II, only one-fourth of all women worked and the majority of those who did were married women over thirty-five with no children at home. By the 1950s and 1960s, more mothers with school-age children entered the workforce. In the 1970s, women of all ages, including mothers of young children, did full-time wage work. For the first time in U.S. history, there were more women in the labor force than out of it. Yet working women often felt they had few allies among labor leaders.

Women labor leaders hoped the 1955 merger of the AFL and the CIO would bring about a change in the treatment of working women's issues by the union movement. As a result of the merger and of the growing power of labor in the wake of World War II, union membership reached fourteen million in 1950 and increased to nineteen million by 1970. The merger brought the CIO's more progressive perspectives—such as its commitment to Social Security Disability Insurance (SSDI) that provided income to people unable to work due to injury and equal pay for equal work—into the AFL-CIO. Yet, even as the labor movement adopted a more progressive political agenda, many female labor activists wanted the AFL-CIO to offer a more substantial program to address the needs of working women.

In 1958, Esther Peterson, a lobbyist for the AFL-CIO, brought together a group of women labor leaders to "take a fresh look at women's protective legislation"—specifically, the eight-hour maximum placed on women and restrictions on night work—that was used to justify discrimination against women workers. The group also examined the possibility of implementing unemployment compensation for pregnant women, creating maternity leaves, enhancing training programs, and expanding the number of jobs covered by minimum wage. To advance their ambitious agenda, labor feminists threw their support behind the Democratic Party in the elections of 1960. They began through the women's division of the Committee on Political Education (COPE), the recently formed political arm of the AFL-CIO. The COPE sponsored a national voter registration drive that focused not only on women and union members but on all registered voters. They signed up more than 1.5 million new voters and coordinated a massive election-day voter drive. Women took the lead in telephone brigades, neighborhood canvassing, and local get-out-the-vote campaigns. Complementing the efforts of COPE, Esther Peterson and other women labor leaders organized the "Committee of Labor Women for Kennedy and Johnson," creating a powerful new national organization with ties to labor's volunteer army of women in communities across the country. When Democrat John F. Kennedy narrowly won the presidency in 1960, he did not forget his labor allies. He appointed Peterson to head up the Women's Bureau.

Like Frances Perkins, secretary of labor under President Roosevelt (see chapter 17), Peterson brought to her job a close-knit network of labor women and ties to millions of women in trade unions and auxiliaries to her work. At the same time, she also brought a new perspective to the Women's Bureau, one that renewed the agency's focus on working women. "We wanted equality for women," she wrote in her memoir, "but we wanted bread for our low-income sisters first." Peterson's labor movement peers valued the union as an important way to improve working women's lives. Yet, by the 1960s, they had grown frustrated with its male-dominated leadership. Peterson convened a meeting in 1961 of 175 labor women from twenty-one international unions in Washington, D.C. The group met for three days and laid out the pressing issues confronting women workers and the labor feminists' growing alienation from their male-dominated unions. The group called for a federal law guaranteeing equal pay for equal work; prohibition of sex discrimination in federal contracts; and the extension of minimum wage to millions of women in service occupations such as restaurant, laundry, hotel, agricultural, and domestic work. The group also recommended increased funding for child-care centers and after-school activities at public schools, as well as maternity leave guarantees. In her keynote address, journalist Agnes Meyer pointed out the sexism within unions that had left the plight of women workers long ignored. "It weakens our democracy not only economically but morally when we make distinctions in our treatment of labor either on the basis of sex or color. . . . Grateful as I am to our labor leaders for the magnificent contributions to the nation's progress and welfare, I feel that theirs is the most exclusive masculine world left on the American scene." The agenda set out by Meyer, Peterson, and other labor feminists called for the federal government to play a role to ensure equality for women workers. Like their peers in the civil rights movement, labor reform women hoped to use laws guaranteeing women's equality as primary tools to bring about social change.

The President's Commission on the Status of Women

Women active in the labor movement and in the presidential campaign of John F. Kennedy wanted to see the federal government do more to level the economic field for women. In December 1961, at Peterson's suggestion, Kennedy issued Executive Order 10980 creating the **President's Commission on the Status of Women (PCSW)**. The PCSW was chaired by former First Lady Eleanor Roosevelt until her death in November 1962 and staffed by notables like historian Caroline Ware; Dorothy Height, president of the National Council of Negro Women; and Dr. Mary Bunting, president of Radcliffe College. The Commission had twenty-six members who staffed subcommittees focused on specific issues pertaining to women, such as inequities in pay, the problems facing poor women, and civil rights. In October 1963, Peterson presented the commission's report, *American Women*, to the president, noting that the report offered no "avant-garde recommendations," only "the art of the possible." *American Women* became a best seller, with sixty-four thousand copies distributed in the first year.

> **President's Commission on the Status of Women (PCSW)** A committee established by President John F. Kennedy to advise him on pending legislative issues concerning women.

The report accomplished a great deal. Foremost, it documented discrimination against women, including the disparity between men's and women's earnings. In 1960, women with full-time, year-round jobs earned 60 percent of what men earned and black women just 42 percent. The report showed that women college graduates gained little wage advantage from their degrees. On the average, they earned less than men with high-school diplomas. The report made twenty-four specific recommendations—including that marriage should be seen as an economic partnership, that any property acquired during the marriage should belong to both spouses, and that child care should be available to families of all income levels—and supported paid maternity leaves and the principle of equal pay for equal work. Although the report ended up concluding that Constitutional changes like the Equal Rights Amendment (ERA) "need not be sought," it set out concrete recommendations for achieving gender equality. Equally important, the experience of working for the Commission galvanized participants into liberal feminism. African American lawyer, Pauli Murray described the experience as "intensive consciousness-raising." *American Women*, shaped by the concerns of Peterson and other labor feminists, asserted that the problems women faced were not private or individual but social and institutional and thus were able to be addressed by sustained government attention.

The Commission directly and indirectly acted as a catalyst for a number of liberal reforms. In July 1962, before the Commission issued its final report, Kennedy directed all federal agencies to hire, train, and promote employees regardless of sex. A year later, Congress passed the **Equal Pay Act of 1963,** the first federal law forbidding sex discrimination by private businesses, extending what had previously been a ban on discrimination in hiring practices by defense contractors established in 1941 (see chapter 18). By 1967, all fifty states had State Commission on the Status of Women in operation, establishing an important network for liberal activists.

> **Equal Pay Act of 1963** Federal legislation that prohibited pay differentials based on sex.

Building a Movement

In 1964, and as Congress readied itself to pass the landmark Civil Rights Act, liberal women lobbied for the inclusion of women into the section of the law called Title VII that prohibited employment discrimination. More sweeping than the Equal Pay Act, Title VII, which included sex in its list of prohibited forms of discrimination, applied to jobs, pub-

Equal Employment Opportunity Commission (EEOC) The federal agency charged with enforcing employment antidiscrimination laws.

National Organization for Women (NOW) The feminist organization founded in 1966 to promote women's equality.

lic education, and all federally funded programs. It marked a historic turning point for labor feminists' efforts to dismantle protective labor laws that limited the number of hours women could work and the types of jobs they could perform. With the passage of Title VII, protective legislation, found to discriminate against women, once the crowning accomplishment of labor women in the Progressive Era, had been swept away with full support of labor feminists. In addition, Title VII established a government agency to investigate employment discrimination complaints, the **Equal Employment Opportunity Commission (EEOC)**. President Lyndon Johnson appointed Aileen Hernandez to the five-person commission. Hernandez brought years of experience to her position. The daughter of Jamaican immigrants, Hernandez was educated at Howard University before taking a position as a labor organizer for the International Ladies' Garment Workers Union. She later worked as deputy chief of California's Division of Fair Employment Practices where she learned firsthand about the range and extent of work-related discrimination. While the EEOC established a set of guidelines that spelled out the parameters of what constituted "discrimination," the agency tended to focus on racial discrimination more than sex discrimination. Michigan Congresswoman Martha Griffiths, who had been actively involved in Title VII debates, denounced the EEOC on the floor of the House in June 1965: "I charge that the officials of the Equal Employment Opportunity Commission have displayed a wholly negative attitude toward the sex provision of Title VII. . . . What is this sickness that causes an official to ridicule the law he has sworn to uphold and enforce? . . . What kind of mentality is it that can ignore the fact that women's wages are much less than men's and that Negro women's wages are least of all?"

In October 1965, civil rights lawyer Pauli Murray called for an outside pressure group—"an NAACP for women"—to ensure that the EEOC would enforce the law. Betty Friedan, author of the best-selling *The Feminine Mystique* (1963), had the visibility to head up such an organization. At the Third Annual Conference on the Status of Women in June 1966, Friedan, Murray, and a small group of other attendees initiated the concept of the **National Organization for Women (NOW)** and began plans for a Founding Convention in the fall. Hernandez later noted that the EEOC became "the disinterested parent of NOW and many other feminist groups that sprang up in the decade between 1965 and 1975."

The founders of the NOW intended it to bring together a small group of women who could work quickly on the enforcement of Title VII, but the group mushroomed into a wide-ranging organization devoted to promoting women's rights in all aspects of their lives, not only employment discrimination. But it quickly mushroomed into a wide-ranging organization devoted to promoting women's rights. The National Organization for Women encouraged local chapters to take on issues of relevance in their communities and not to follow in lockstep with the agenda and priorities of the national organization. Much like the "Do Everything" policy of the nineteenth-century Woman's Christian Temperance Union, the NOW "wanted [members] to move in their own style, according to their own priorities" (see chapter 13). Jennifer Macleod, first president of the Central New Jersey chapter of NOW, explained to new members that "they were not buying into a whole package. They could devote their efforts to something they believed in."

With the formation of the NOW, liberal feminism grew in force and reach, drawing a diverse group of women to participate in its sweeping reform

In 1964, *President Lyndon Johnson appointed Aileen Hernandez to the newly formed Equal Employment Opportunity Commission, the government agency charged with investigating employment discrimination complaints. Hernandez was among the group that formed the National Organization for Women.*

WOMEN'S LIVES

SHIRLEY CHISHOLM

Known for her dynamic public speaking, Shirley Chisholm became the first African American woman to run for president. She was born on November 30, 1924, in Brooklyn, New York, and was the oldest of four girls born to parents who had immigrated from the West Indies. The family barely subsisted on the wages the parents earned from factory work and housecleaning. When Shirley was three years old, she and her sisters were sent by their parents to Barbados to be reared by their maternal grandmother. Shirley attributed her academic successes to the British school system in Barbados. In 1934, ten-year-old Shirley returned to Brooklyn and attended the Girls High School, from which she graduated in 1942. Later, at Brooklyn College, Shirley's skill at political organizing first emerged. When the black students at Brooklyn College were denied admittance to a social club, Shirley formed an alternative one. She graduated in 1946 with honors. Like other talented and educated African Americans, Shirley found it hard to break into the white-dominated professions. After being rejected by many companies, she obtained a job at the Mt. Calvary Child Care Center in Harlem where she became supervisor of the largest nursery school network in New York administering to hundreds of children, the majority of them African American and Puerto Rican. Shirley's activism continued, and she served as a volunteer in the Brooklyn chapter of the National Urban League and in the National Association for the Advancement of Colored People (NAACP). In 1949, Shirley married Conrad Chisholm, a Jamaican who worked as a private investigator and who shared her interest in local politics. She started the Unity Democratic Club that became instrumental in mobilizing black and Hispanic voters in 1960. Shirley's political reputation for social justice began formally in 1964

when she was elected to the New York State Assembly; she served to 1968. During her tenure there, she proposed a bill to provide state aid to day-care centers and voted to increase funding for schools on a per-pupil basis. After finishing her term in the legislature, Chisholm campaigned to represent New York's Twelfth Congressional District. Her campaign slogan was "Fighting Shirley Chisholm—Unbought and Unbossed." She won the election and became the first African American woman elected to Congress.

During her first term in Congress, Chisholm hired an all-female staff and spoke out for civil rights, women's rights, and the poor and against the Vietnam War. In 1970, she was elected to a second term. She was a sought-after public speaker and cofounder of the National Organization for

(continued)

Women (NOW). She remarked that "Women in this country must become revolutionaries. We must refuse to accept the old, the traditional roles and stereotypes."

On January 25, 1972, Chisholm announced her candidacy for president. She stood before the cameras, and in the beginning of her speech, she said,

I stand before you today as a candidate for the Democratic nomination for the presidency of the United States. I am not the candidate of black America, although I am black and proud. I am not the candidate of the women's movement of this country, although I am a woman, and I am equally proud of that. I am not the candidate of any political bosses or special interests. I am the candidate of the people.

The 1972 Democratic National Convention in Miami was the first major convention in which any woman was considered for the presidential nomination. Although she did not win the nomination, she received 151 of the delegates' votes. She continued to serve in the House of Representatives until 1982. She retired from politics after her last term in office. Shirley Chisholm died on January 1, 2005. ∎

agenda. Women of color played central roles in liberal feminist groups. Black women such as Texas Congresswoman Barbara Jordan, activists Shirley Chisholm and Fannie Lou Hamer, and Hispanic women from the group La Raza Unida Party took leadership positions.

National Women's Political Caucus Founded as a bipartisan organization whose goal was to increase the number of women in politics.

The goal of many liberal feminist activists was to get more women into politics. Chisholm, Friedan, and other leaders formed the **National Women's Political Caucus** (NWPC) in 1971 with the goal of increasing the number of women in politics by recruiting, training, and supporting women who sought elected and appointed offices. The NWPC formed permanent caucuses for African Americans, Chicanas, Puerto Ricans, and Native Americans. In later years, permanent caucuses emerged for Asian Americans, lesbians, and Capitol Hill staff members. The NWPC was uniquely diverse. One member described a meeting: "a vast room crammed to the corners with every description of female persons: worried blue permanent waves, smart Afros, long black braids; silk print dresses with pearls, blue jeans, pants suits, who-cares-which-dress and a delegate from California in muu-muu and lavender head scarf. And no less varied and diverse were the political hues of that rainbow. . . ." The creation of permanent caucuses helped tailor liberal feminism to the needs of all women and gave women space from the concerns of white middle-class women. The caucuses functioned as an important political network for minority women who wanted to participate in organizations that articulated their needs.

Not all minority women felt their voices were heard. The black caucuses of the NOW and the NWPC joined to form the National Black Feminist Organization (NBFO) in 1973, realizing that the predominantly white feminist organizations often failed to adequately address the concerns of black women and that the only way to encourage more black women to join was to form black feminist groups. One member, Carolyn Handy, explained why the movement needed the NBFO: "It's time that minority women stand up and say, 'Listen, it's our movement, too, and we're supportive of our white sisters and if you have any questions about our commitment, here we are. Ask us.'" Within four months, the NBFO had a mailing list of one thousand. Puerto Rican feminists, motivated by the same liberal impulses, began meeting in 1970 but found that lines between Mexican, Chicana, Puerto Rican, and Cuban women were less easy to shed. One Puerto Rican feminist explained that in 1970 "Latinas were not ready to have that kind of unity for each group needed first to develop by itself." But Latina feminists continued to organize their own groups. In 1972, the National Conference of Puerto Rican Women (NCPRW) formed and grew to more than twenty local chapters.

Liberal women focused on institutional discrimination against women and formed organizations intended to work within existing systems to bring about more equality for all women. Workplace issues and political representation were important focuses for all feminists, no matter their country of origin or their race. But as the movement expanded and diversified, activists found that the number of differences between women also multiplied. Differences in education, contrasting experiences of wealth and poverty, and ongoing political debates over the agenda for feminism emerged and made the dream of a united movement elusive.

The National Welfare Rights Organization

Working-class and poor women directed their political energies in the 1960s and 1970s to reforming welfare. Inspired by the surge in activism and unwilling to wait until middle-class feminists took up the issue of poverty, women on welfare formed their own feminist groups. Welfare rights groups from Boston to Los Angeles confederated

FIGURE 20-1   PERCENTAGE OF WOMEN IN POVERTY BY RACE, 1960–1990

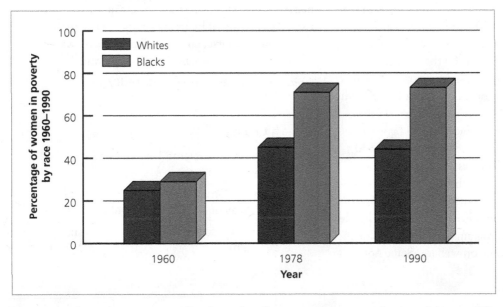

Despite growths in the economy and in the pink-collar sectors that women dominated, women fell into poverty at higher rates than did their male counterparts, a situation that only worsened as the century wore on.

WOMEN'S VOICES

"WELFARE IS LIKE A SUPERSEXIST MARRIAGE"

Johnnie Tillmon, a founding chairperson (and, in 1972, the director) of the National Welfare Rights Organization, described her life as a welfare mother. She describes the difficulties that poverty and racism bring to mothers and the misconceptions of welfare mothers that only heap shame on welfare recipients. Tillmon is particularly critical of the ways that welfare programs promote a cycle of dependency that she says is akin to a "supersexist marriage."

I'm a woman. I'm a black woman. I'm a poor woman. I'm a fat woman. I'm a middle-aged woman. And I'm on welfare. In this country, if you're any one of those things—poor, black, fat, female, middle-aged, on welfare—you count less as a human being. If you're all those things, you don't count at all. Except as a statistic. I am a statistic. I am forty-five years old. I have raised six children. I grew up in Arkansas, and I worked there for fifteen years in a laundry, making about $20 or $30 a week, picking cotton on the side for carfare. I moved to California in 1959 and worked in a laundry there for nearly four years. In 1963, I got too sick to work anymore. Friends helped me to go on welfare. They didn't call it welfare. They called it AFDC—Aid to Families with Dependent Children. Each month I got $363 for my kids and me. I pay $128 a month rent; $30 for utilities, which include gas, electricity, and water; $120 for food and nonedible household essentials; $50 for school lunches for the three children in junior and senior high school who are not eligible for reduced-cost meal programs. There are millions of statistics like me. Some on welfare. Some not.

And some, really poor, who don't even know they're entitled to welfare. Not all of them are black. Not at all. In fact, the majority—about two-thirds—of all the poor families in the country are white.

Welfare's like a traffic accident. It can happen to anybody, but especially it happens to women. And that is why welfare is a women's issue. For a lot of middle-class women in this country, Women's Liberation is a matter of concern. For women on welfare it's a matter of survival. Forty-four percent of all poor families are headed by women. That's bad enough. But the *families* on AFDC aren't really families. Because 99 percent of them are headed by women. That means there is no man around. In half the states there really can't be men around because AFDC says if there is an "able-bodied" man around, then you can't be on welfare. If the kids are going to eat, and the man can't get a job, then he's got to go. So his kids can eat.

The truth is that AFDC is like a supersexist marriage. You trade in a man for *the* man. But you can't divorce him if he treats you bad. He can divorce you, of course, cut you off anytime he wants. But in that case, *he* keeps the kids, not you.

Source: From http://us.history.wisc.edu/hist102/pdocs/ tillmon_welfare.pdf

Questions

1. What are the problems Tillmon identifies that make welfare a woman's issue?

2. How does Tillmon understand the place of men and of ideas of masculinity in welfare debates?

3. What are the connections between "a man" and "*the* man"?

into the National Welfare Rights Organization (NWRO) in 1967. Voting members were poor—most were mothers receiving Aid to Families with Dependent Children (AFDC). The multiracial organization drew heavily from urban areas, so although white women constituted more than half the nation's AFDC population, the majority of NWRO leaders and members were African American. Johnnie Tillmon, a welfare mother from Los Angeles, was elected chair. Former college professor and civil rights leader George Wiley, who had raised the money for the founding convention, became executive director. At its peak in 1969, the NWRO membership was estimated at twenty-two thousand families nationwide, mostly black, with local chapters in nearly every state and major city.

The organization worked to bring tangible improvements in the welfare system. Largely as a result of the NWRO "minimum standards" campaigns that gave grants to welfare recipients for necessities like furniture and clothing, welfare payments in New York City alone increased over thirty-fold from $1.2 million in 1963 to $40 million in 1968, an income transfer that went directly into the pockets of the poor. By 1968, militant action taken by welfare recipients across the country had resulted in a changed atmosphere inside welfare offices, as these agencies established community relations departments, provided access to state welfare manuals, and began to treat recipients as clients rather than supplicants. For the first time, organized recipients negotiated with agency directors as peers.

The NWRO reframed the right of welfare to be a civil right, not a handout. By claiming that women and poor people deserve to be treated with dignity and respect, the NWRO was the first organization to create a distinct political identity among poor black women, who comprised 90 percent of its membership. In her essay "Welfare Is a Woman's Issue," published in Ms. magazine, NWRO President Johnnie Tillmon emphasized a woman's right to adequate income, regardless of whether the woman worked in a factory or stayed at home raising children. Tillmon explained that being on welfare was a necessity created by the economic system—not the fault of individual women—and that surviving on welfare was a badge of honor, not a symbol of shame.

Reform-minded women in the 1960s, like their counterparts in the civil rights movement, viewed the federal government as a crucial part of the solution to social problems. The networks of activists in the Democratic Party, in labor organizations, and in welfare rights groups organized to help women improve their lives and the lives of their children. Liberal women's groups sought to work politically within existing social and economic institutions to secure reforms for women and to promote equality of opportunity between the sexes. Ultimately, the goal of liberal feminists was assimilation, not separatism—to end separate spheres and to see women as individuals without regard to their sex (see chapter 21).

AGENDA FOR REFORM

Liberal feminists adopted the civil rights movement's demand for equality and its use of the government to ensure rights to their own ends. Through new networks, political organizations, and key legal victories, many formal aspects of economic, political, and educational sex discrimination ended. The strength of those gains could be seen in the growing number of women in politics, professional training schools, and in previously male-dominated arenas like business, law, and athletics. Yet, at the same time that these victories opened new opportunities for women, pressing issues continued to divide women. No consensus emerged among women over divisive issues like the proposed Equal Rights Amendment and a woman's right to abortion. Women's growing presence in the mainstream of U.S. life in the 1960s and 1970s showcased their differences as well as their similarities.

Legislating Equality

Liberal activists in the late 1960s and early 1970s enjoyed a rising tide of influence and witnessed historic victories in their efforts to establish legal equality for women. A number of important laws were passed, making the 1970s the high-water mark of liberal feminist reform. Ironically, these years also marked the failure to achieve the Equal Rights Amendment as conservative women mobilized to block its passage.

A movement to pass the Equal Rights Amendment reemerged in 1946 in recognition of the work women did during World War II. Yet, the tension between the ERA supporters and those who favored protective legislation for women that had emerged during the 1920s when the ERA was first introduced into Congress had not disappeared (see chapter 16). Despite the high hopes of its supporters, political support for the Amendment did not materialize and it fell short of the two-thirds majority required for passage. Throughout the 1950s, the majority of women's organizations continued to line up against the ERA, supporting the notion that women's difference from men demanded different treatment in the workplace. The National Woman's Party, the main organization supporting the ERA, saw its influence decline and its membership dwindle.

On March 22, 1972, both houses of Congress approved the Equal Rights Amendment and within the year, 22 states had ratified it. As support for the ERA grew, opponents began to mobilize against its passage. In 1972, Republican activist Phyllis Schlafly organized a grassroots the STOP ERA campaign and held protests like this one in front of the White House. To the surprise of its supporters, the ERA was narrowly defeated in 1982.

The surge of liberal reform changed the prospects of passing the ERA. By 1970, the proposed Amendment enjoyed wide support among women's organizations, many of which had previously opposed it: the League of Women Voters, the YWCA, and the American Association of University Women. The goal of equality for all citizens and the discrediting of the separate but equal doctrine had effectively undermined the rationale for protective legislation. The ERA, which stated that "Equality of rights under the law shall not be denied or abridged by the United States or by any state on account of sex" now seemed possible. In 1970, President Richard Nixon endorsed the ERA in a report on the status of women; and on March 22, 1972, both houses of Congress approved the Amendment. Within the year, twenty-two states had ratified it, bringing the Amendment close to the thirty-five states needed for passage.

Yet, as the ERA gained supporters, opponents began to mobilize against its passage. In 1972, Republican activist Phyllis Schlafly organized a grassroots campaign to stop more states from ratifying the ERA. Her strategy emphasized to all that the ERA would take away from women, arguing that "the ERA would lead to women being drafted into the military and to public unisex bathrooms." Under her charismatic leadership, the STOP ERA campaign took off. To the surprise of its supporters, the ERA was narrowly defeated in 1982 (see chapter 22).

Despite the defeat of the ERA, the movement to establish legal equality for women reached new heights in the mid-1970s. Liberal feminists concentrated on a series of pragmatic reforms that emphasized compliance with equal opportunity legislation and the passage of laws to guarantee the equal treatment of men and women. New York Congressional Representative Bella Abzug described 1972 as "a watershed year. We put sex discrimination provisions into everything. There was no opposition. Who'd be against equal rights for women? So we just kept passing women's rights legislation." The legislative push was wide-ranging, covering consumer credit and mortgages, wages and hours, and greater access to sports. Congress passed the **Equal Opportunity Act** (1972) to give the EEOC a broader jurisdiction and strengthening its ability to enforce its rulings. Congress passed the Equal Credit Opportunity Act (ECOA), which banned credit discrimination on the basis of an applicant's sex, marital status, or age. Previously, women could not open a credit card account or take a home mortgage out without permission from her husband. The law applied to retail stores, credit card companies, banks, and home finance and home mortgage lenders for which a broad pattern of discrimination against extending credit to women had long existed.

Equal Opportunity Act
This act legislated a broader jurisdiction for the EEOC and strengthened its ability to enforce its rulings.

Liberal feminists also lay the foundations for ending discrimination in education. In the late 1960s, the Women's Equity Action League (WEAL) began legal action against sex discrimination in all levels of U.S. education. On January 31, 1970, the WEAL filed a class action suit with the U.S. Department of Labor against all the colleges and universities in the country, claiming illegal admission quotas and discrimination in financial assistance, hiring and promotion practices, and salary differentials. In October, the WEAL filed a class action suit against all the medical schools. The following year, the Professional Women's Caucus filed a suit against all the nation's law schools. The materials gathered for these cases yielded ample proof of sex discrimination in education. The congressional hearings on discrimination in education contributed to the passage of **Title IX of the Education Amendments of 1972**. The preamble to Title IX stated, "No person in the United States shall, on the basis of sex, be excluded from participation in, be denied the benefits of, or be subject to discrimination under any educational programs or activity receiving federal financial assistance." Two years later (1974), the Women's

Title IX of the Education Amendments of 1972 Passed on June 23, 1972, the law forbid sex discrimination in any educational program or activity funded by the federal government, including athletics.

OVERVIEW

Major Legislation

Equal Pay Act of 1963	Made it illegal to pay women less than men for the same job
Title VII of the Civil Rights Act of 1964	Added sex to race, religion, and national origin as categories protected by federal law from employment discrimination
Title IX of the Education Amendments of 1972	Banned discrimination under any education program or activity receiving federal financial assistance
Equal Rights Amendment (1972)	Ending discrimination on the account of sex
Equal Opportunity Act (1972)	Broadened jurisdiction of the EEOC and strengthened its enforcement capacity
Title IX of the Higher Education Act of 1972	Banned discrimination on the basis of sex in any educational program or activity that received federal funding.
Equal Credit Opportunity Act (1974)	Prohibited discrimination on the basis of sex or marital status during credit transactions and applied to retail stores, credit card companies, banks, and home finance and home mortgage lenders
Women's Educational Equity Act (1974)	Provided federal funds for educationnal programs designed to promote women's equality in education including revising sexist textbooks to teacher training seminars

Educational Equity Act was passed, which focused on gender bias in all levels of educational curriculum and included funding for women's studies programs, seminars for teachers, and the creation of nonsexist textbooks. Liberal feminist groups like the NOW, the Women's Equity Action League, the National Women's Political Caucus (NWPC), and the Center for Women's Policy Studies (CWPS) had succeeded in strengthening their influence over the legislative process and winning a place at the table of U.S. politics.

The number of women delegates to party conventions grew impressively up from 17 percent to 30 percent among Republicans and from 13 percent to 40 percent among Democrats. Women who had been active in local and state political campaigns and had years of experience in civic affairs now ran for public office. The number of women candidates for state legislatures increased 300 percent in the early 1970s. The combined efforts of policy-oriented feminists, savvy political insiders, union activists, civil rights leaders, and ordinary women newly aware of their political clout transformed the political landscape of the country.

Education and Athletics

Women active in politics placed educational reform high on their agendas. Throughout the 1940s and 1950s, educational texts routinely confirmed deeply held gender convictions that girls ought to be trained for their roles at home, not trained for professions. Mathematics and science classes were often closed to female students, and teachers and guidance counselors discouraged young women from studying traditionally "male" occupations. Women applying to college had to score much better than men typically did, and graduate and professional schools set quotas on the number of female applicants they accepted.

FIGURE 20-2   WOMEN AND THE PROFESSIONS

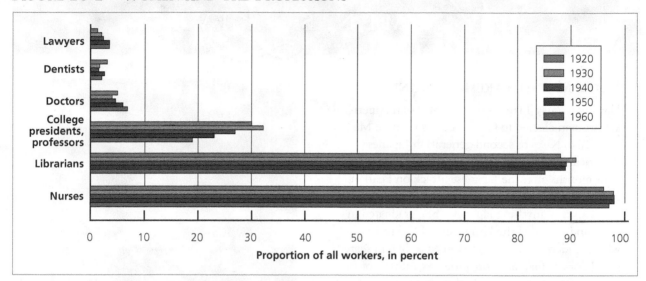

Women's entrance to the professions, in the doldrums through much of the century, surged in the wake of feminism in the 1970s. (From The Routledge Historical Atlas of Women in America, edited by Sandra Opdycke (New York: Routledge, 2000), page 112)

Title IX became one of the most important vehicles to combat discrimination against women in education. In June 1972, Congressional Representative Patsy Mink from Hawaii—and the first Asian American woman elected to Congress—drafted and helped build the coalition that supported Title IX. Because virtually all public schools and colleges, as well as many private colleges, received federal assistance, the bill cast a wide net. At the time of its passage, few people realized Title IX would affect such things as athletics, classes that did not admit women, policies on maternity leave, and the question of whether schools could expel pregnant students. Once the full extent of the bill was known, it became the focal point of controversy, most often centered on athletics.

Critics opposed the mandatory redistribution of resources required by Title IX. Bias against girls in sports had gone without notice for most of the twentieth century. School districts regularly allotted far more funds to boys' teams than they did to girls' teams. One district in Texas in the 1970s budgeted $250,000 for athletics, but the only sport women were permitted to play was tennis, which received a mere $970. Such poor funding continued all the way to college. College and university women's sports teams typically received 1 or 2 percent of what was budgeted for men. With the passage of Title IX, high-school and college sports administrators complained that making women's teams equitable to men's would take too much money from men's teams. One coach at a Wisconsin high school captured the feeling of many of those opposed to Title IX in 1973 when he said, "I think girls have a right to participate but to a lesser degree than boys. If they go too far with the competitive stuff, they lose their femininity."

It took Congress nearly two years to develop regulations for Title IX and then another year until the regulations went into effect. The agency that was granted powers to enforce compliance, the Office of Civil Rights, however, had few funds and, according to the National Women's Law Center's Attorney Marcia Greenberger, was recalcitrant and had "no will to enforce" the regulation. By 1976, only 20 percent of its

WOMEN'S LIVES

PATSY MATSU TAKEMOTO MINK

Hawaiian Patsy Takemoto, the first Asian American woman elected to Congress, was born on Maui in 1927 to Nises or second-generation Japanese American parents. She became student body president months after the Japanese attack on Pearl Harbor, Hawaii, despite the great anger of the students against anything Japanese. She graduated in 1944 and attended the University of Nebraska where students of color were forced to live in segregated dorms. Takemoto organized a coalition of students, parents, administrators, employees, alumni, sponsoring businesses, and corporations and ended the university's segregation policies. In 1948, Takemoto was appalled to learn that none of the twenty medical schools to which she had applied accepted women. She decided the best way to force medical schools to accept women would be through the judicial process. Takemoto was one of a handful of women to graduate from the University of Chicago Law School in 1951. Newly married, Mink returned to Hawaii where she became active in the territorial and, after 1959, the state legislature. In 1965, she was elected to the House of Representatives.

There, Mink's savvy ability to build coalitions served her well. She drafted Title IX of the Education Amendments of the Higher Education Act and proved instrumental in creating a political coalition to ensure its passage. She also introduced the Early Childhood Education Act, which gave funding for childhood education from preschool through kindergarten, and the Women's Educational Equity Act.

In 1977, President Jimmy Carter appointed Mink to his cabinet as assistant secretary of state. In 1990, she returned to Congress where she served until her death in 2002. ■

caseload for elementary and secondary schools had been resolved; and by 1978, only 13 percent of what was spent on men's sports was spent on women's intercollegiate athletics, an improvement from the 2 percent in 1974.

Despite poor enforcement, sex discrimination in athletics diminished in the 1970s. Studies found that women who were under age ten when Title IX passed had higher sports participation rates than women who grew up before Title IX. Title IX increased the number of women who received athletic scholarships and improved the salaries of female coaches. At the Olympics of 1984, three-fourths of the U.S. women who competed said they would not have participated if not for Title IX.

Reproductive Freedom

Under the climate of reform, the movement to relegalize abortion gained strength. But despite the support it enjoyed from many feminists, a woman's right to abortion was a divisive issue. The movement for relegalization began in 1967 when the NOW came out in support of lifting restrictions on women's right to the procedure. They were joined by radical feminists who staged a wave of sit-ins, speakouts, and other demonstrations to highlight the dangers and trauma of illegal abortion (see chapter 21). Both liberal and radical feminist groups asserted that abortion was a decision only a woman could make for herself in consultation with partners and doctors. Even feminists who focused on workplace issues saw the right to abortion as essential. As one California woman stated, "We can get all the rights in the world . . . and none of them means a doggone thing if we don't own the flesh we stand in."

By 1967, Colorado, North Carolina, and California passed new laws liberalizing restrictions on obtaining an abortion. Efforts to repeal state laws met with opposition from antiabortion advocates like the Catholic Church, which mobilized a counteroffensive to block abortion reform efforts. Despite its critics, the abortion rights movement grew more radical. In February 1968, 350 abortion activists from twenty-one state organizations met in Chicago to garner support for the repeal of all laws restricting women's right to abortion. Out of the meeting, the National Association for the Repeal of Abortion Laws (NARAL) formed. In 1970, the NARAL spearheaded a campaign in New York to decriminalize abortion in the first six months of pregnancy. It succeeded, establishing New York as having the most liberal abortion law in the country. Critics of the law mobilized immediately. In 1971, the New York Commissioner of Social Services announced that Medicaid, a medical insurance program for the poor, would not cover "elective" abortions, effectively restricting women's access to the procedure.

The debate over the legal status of abortion headed to the Supreme Court. The Court's historic decision to legalize most abortions involved two cases, *Roe v. Wade* and *Doe v. Bolton*. The decisions were issued on January 22, 1973. The more famous *Roe* case challenged a Texas law that permitted an abortion only if the life of the woman was at risk. The *Doe* case challenged the complex and forbidding process by which a woman could gain an abortion in Georgia, which permitted abortion only in cases of rape, severe fetal deformity, or severe danger to the life of the mother. The Supreme Court struck down both states' abortion laws, arguing that the laws invaded a woman's right to privacy. In the place of state laws, a new formula was created that allowed abortion before the end of the first trimester, after which the state could regulate abor-

Norma McCovery, the Dallas mother whose desire to have an abortion, was the basis for the landmark Supreme Court decision of Roe v. Wade *in 1973.*

tion procedures to protect a woman's health. Once the fetus was viable, or capable of surviving outside the womb, the state could regulate and even prohibit abortion in the interest of preserving potential life. This aspect of the ruling gave states with more liberal statutes the authority to rewrite their abortion laws and make them narrower. At the same time, the use of fetal viability as the time after which an abortion became illegal lay the groundwork for the idea of fetal rights, which became a rallying point of pro-life groups who opposed abortion (see chapter 22). The ruling established a woman's control over her body when the court struck down state laws that required a woman to get approval of a hospital committee or independent doctors before being allowed to have the procedure. With this, the Supreme Court reinstated abortion guidelines that prevailed throughout the nineteenth century when abortions before "quickening" took place were legal.

Media and the Movement

The 1970s brought important changes in women's legal status and new opportunites for women in formerly male-dominated political, economic, and educational institutions. Yet, the impact of the women's movement in the 1970s was also felt more broadly. The concept of sexism and the need for greater equality between the sexes were packaged and sold through the court of popular opinion as much as they were through the courts and Congress. Feminists focused on the pernicious impact negative representations of women in the media had on women of all ages. Prominent feminists, like writer and activist Kate Millett and magazine editor Gloria Steinem, argued persuasively that images of women as sexual objects undermined their effort to establish full equality at home and at work.

Images of women in magazines before the women's movement centered on women's roles as wife, mother, housewife, and primary consumer, with regular inspirational pieces on extraordinary women or women active in politics. In the pages of the nation's magazines, women's primary interests in life appeared to be shiny kitchen floors, wholesome and home-cooked family meals, and their appearance, images that seemed mired in female fantasies of the 1950s. Feminists challenged the image of woman as mother and helpmate-playmate to her husband, arguing for representations of women that showed their diversity, their complexity, and their autonomy. However, from the beginning of the women's movement, the print media had been actively covering feminist activism with a mixture of dismissive humor and appreciation. Politically oriented magazines such as *Newsweek*, *Time*, and the *Atlantic Monthly*, as well as women's magazines like *Ladies Home Journal*, *Mademoiselle*, and *Seventeen*, covered the movement, spreading its ideas to thousands of readers otherwise untouched by feminist ideas. Feminists were quick to take advantage of the media coverage and tried with mixed results to communicate their vision of women. New York radical women capitalized on the huge amount of media outlets centered in the city by staging protests and other attention-garnering activities designed explicitly to win media coverage. The most famous of these was the March 1971 takeover of the *Ladies Home Journal* by over one hundred feminists. The eleven-hour takeover resulted in the publication of an eight-page supplement titled "The New Feminism" in the August edition that went out to the *Journal's* sizable readership.

At the same time that they called for less sexist and sexualized images of women in the media, feminists looked for ways to improve the institutional status of women in journalism. They called for the end of sex discrimination in hiring and promotion in news and magazine organizations. In the 1970s, women filed complaints of sex discrimination against *Newsweek* and *Time*. Feminists also tried to support women journalists by seeing them as "natural" allies in their struggle for equality. Radical feminists protesting the Miss America pageant in 1968 refused to talk to any male reporters (see chapter 21).

Finding themselves riding a wave of media interests in the new movement, feminists had a hard time controlling the ways they and their ideas were represented. Media coverage tended to legitimate feminist complaints of economic discrimination because of the statistical strength of the assertion and because the message fit neatly with the view of the United States as a society based on equality. Yet, at the same time, media coverage of individual feminists, particularly young and more radical women, cast them as angry, man hating, and ugly. The media coverage of the women's movement moved between casting it as a joke and taking it seriously. Whether feminism was a joke or not played itself out throughout the late 1960s and 1970s in a wide venue of ways, from athletics to politics. The 1973 tennis match between Billie Jean King and the aging playboy Bobby Riggs was deemed in the media as "the battle of the sexes." King, who many considered to be the finest female player of her generation, worked tirelessly to equalize the sex-segregated tennis circuits, where historically women earned a fraction of what men earned in prize money and endorsements. Her talent and her visibility as an activist for women's tennis made her a media symbol of the movement and a target for Riggs and his efforts to be the nation's "number one chauvinist pig." Riggs took the court wearing a "Men's Liberation" T-shirt, to the delight of the fifty million television viewers. When King defeated him, he conceded she was simply "too good, too fast" to beat. The match, despite its comic elements, helped bring about greater recognition and respect for women's tennis.

In an effort to combat the discriminatory representation of women, activist and journalist Gloria Steinem in 1972 founded the first glossy women's magazine run by women and committed to feminist goals, *Ms.* magazine. Steinem had worked as a journalist in New York in the 1960s and had been active in liberal causes and in the Democratic Party. Steinem's feminist concerns were first sparked when she went to a meeting of the Redstockings, a New York women's liberation group. Although she went as a journalist with the intention of writing a story about the group, she found herself deeply moved by the stories the women told, particularly of the dangers of illegal abortions. In 1971, she joined Bella Abzug, Shirley Chisholm, and Betty Friedan to form the National Women's Political Caucus, encouraging women's participation in the 1972 election. Steinem herself was active in the National Democratic Party Convention in Miami that year, fighting for an abortion

In an effort to combat the discriminatory representation of women in the media, activist and journalist Gloria Steinem founded the first glossy women's magazine committed to feminist goals, Ms. Magazine *in 1972.*

Gloria Steinem was regularly selected by mainstream media to represent feminism. Her good looks and quick wit made her an effective advocate for feminism, but she and others rejected the notion that the feminist movement could speak through one or two spokespersons.

plank in the party platform and challenging the seating of delegations that included mostly white males. Those efforts drew attention to the issue of underrepresentation of women in politics and the centrality of political issues for women's lives. In 1972, Steinem, as part of the Women's Action Alliance, gained funding for *Ms.* The preview issue sold out, and within five years *Ms.* had a circulation of five hundred thousand. As editor of the magazine, Steinem gained national attention as a feminist leader and became an influential spokesperson for women's rights issues.

Television also covered the women's movement, as well as the other social protest movements of the 1960s, through situation comedies and family dramas. The first situation comedies centered around ethnic and working-class families in the early 1950s and white suburban families in the 1960s. Television in the early 1970s had retooled itself to meet the changing times. Striving to be "relevant," the 1970s sitcoms humorously addressed contemporary social issues. In January 1971, *All in the Family* aired, a sitcom about the trials and tribulations of Archie Bunker and his white, blue-collar family living in Queens, New York, as they faced "the generation gap." The sentiment of the antiwar movement informed *M*A*S*H*, which debuted in 1973, and the struggles of working-class and middle-class African Americans in *Good Times* (1974) and *The Jeffersons* (1975).

The first television show that dealt with feminism was the enormously popular Mary Tyler Moore Show (MTM), which debuted in September 1970. In the show, Mary Richards, a single woman, negotiated her work life through the very same skills most women applied to their families: caretaking and listening. Maude debuted in 1972 and addressed such once-taboo issues as abortion, menopause, and bankruptcy. The first divorced woman to star in a sitcom appeared in *One Day at a Time* (1975), a sitcom that followed the newly divorced Ann Romano as she began a new life with her two teenage daughters. These shows introduced the ideas of women's liberation without demanding fundamental change to U.S. gender roles. At the same time, the characters represented a new kind of television heroine who assumed she would work, as well as parent, and for whom marriage did not represent a lifetime of security.

CONCLUSION

Women's activism in the years following World War II profoundly changed U.S. society. The civil rights movement challenged the long-standing view that segregation could exist in a democratic society. Civil rights activists argued that segregation, be it based on race or gender, created inequality; and they called on the federal government to use its force to uphold basic rights and equal opportunity for all Americans. The generation of activists who directly confronted Jim Crow segregation at schools, at lunch counters, and on buses discredited, at last, the legal doctrine of separate but equal.

WOMEN'S EVENTS	GLOBAL EVENTS

1950

1954 Women's Political Council forms	1954 Supreme Court rules in *Brown v. Board of Education of Topeka*
1955 Rosa Parks arrested	1955 Montgomery bus boycott begins Emmett Till is lynched
	1956 *Browder v. Gayle* ends Montgomery bus segregation policy
	1957 Southern Christian Leadership Conference is founded Little Rock Central High School is desegregated

1960

	1960 Student Nonviolent Coordination Committee is founded Greensboro sit-ins begin *Boynton v. Virginia*
1961 Eleanor Roosevelt chairs the President's Commission on the Status of Women	1961 Peace Corps established Freedom rides begin
	1962 Cesar Chaves and Dolores Huerta found the United Farm Workers
1963 Passage of the Equal Pay Act of 1963	1963 NAACP leader, Medgar Evers is assassinated Martin Luther King, Jr. delivers "I have a dream" speech
	1964 The Beatles tour the U.S. Congress passes the Gulf of Tonkin Resolution President Johnson declares a War on Poverty Freedom Summer takes place in Mississippi
1966 The founding of the National Organization for Women (NOW)	Passage of the Civil Rights Act of 1964
1967 The National Welfare Rights Organization is founded	1965 Congress enacts Medicare New Immigration Act eliminates quota system
1968 The formation of the Women's Equity Action League	1968 Martin Luther King, Jr. is assassinated Robert Kennedy is assassinated

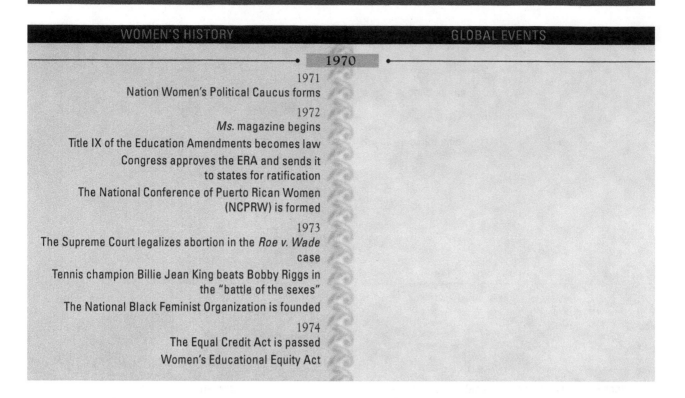

WOMEN'S HISTORY   GLOBAL EVENTS

1970

1971
Nation Women's Political Caucus forms

1972
Ms. magazine begins
Title IX of the Education Amendments becomes law
Congress approves the ERA and sends it
to states for ratification
The National Conference of Puerto Rican Women
(NCPRW) is formed

1973
The Supreme Court legalizes abortion in the *Roe v. Wade*
case
Tennis champion Billie Jean King beats Bobby Riggs in
the "battle of the sexes"
The National Black Feminist Organization is founded

1974
The Equal Credit Act is passed
Women's Educational Equity Act

The movement to end racial discrimination started a wave of reform movements, including liberal feminism, that reinvigorated debates about equality, opportunity, and democracy for all citizens. Liberal feminists forged political organizations that pressured the government to outlaw gender discrimination, while a generation of women entered state, local, and federal government and the political parties themselves to ensure that change would come. The movement for women's equality spread out from its activist and reformist roots to reshape all aspects of U.S. life, from work and politics to television shows and athletics. Liberal women, from the civil rights, labor, and women's movements watched as a new cohort of activists took the ideas of equality and citizenship they had so effectively promoted to a new moment of political engagement and conflict.

REVIEW QUESTIONS

1. What motivated women to participate in the civil rights movement? What did they do to bring about social change in their communities? In their cities? Nationally?

2. How did women petition the federal government to promote gender equality? What groups and organizations did women create?

3. How did women embrace liberal reform in these years? What did liberal women accomplish? What role did the federal government play?

4. Why are reproductive rights important for women's equality? How did women mobilize around this issue?

RECOMMENDED READING

Raymond Arsenault. *Freedom Riders: 1961 and the Struggle for Racial Justice*. New York: Oxford University Press, 2007. A detailed account of the freedom rides of 1961 and the dramatic events that surrounded them.

Vickie Crawford, Jacqueline Rouse, and Barbara Woods, eds. *Women in the Civil Rights Movement: Trailblazers and Torchbearers*. Orlando, FL: Carlson, 1990. An important anthology on the often overlooked or neglected contributions of women to the civil rights movement.

Sara Evans. *Tidal Wave: How Women Changed America at Century's End*. New York: Free Press, 2003. An important examination of liberal, radical, and multicultural feminist activism from the 1960s to the present. Evans is very strong on showing the involvement of feminists of color in liberal reform.

Cynthia Harrison. *On Account of Sex: The Politics of Women's Issues, 1945–1968*. Berkeley: University of California Press, 1988. An examination of women's activism in political parties and reform, particularly the history of the Equal Rights Amendment.

Annelise Orleck. *Storming Caesar's Palace: How Black Mothers Fought Their Own War on Poverty*. Boston: Beacon Press, 2005. Orleck examines the political activism of poor women and their efforts to remake welfare in the 1960s, 1970s, and 1980s.

Jo Ann Robinson. *The Montgomery Bus Boycott and the Women Who Started It: The Memoir of Jo Ann Gibson Robinson*. Knoxville: University of Tennessee Press, 1987. An account of the role of African American working women in the civil rights movement.

ADDITIONAL BIBLIOGRAPHY

Civil Rights

Taylor Branch. *Parting the Waters: America in the King Years 1950–63*. New York: Simon & Schuster, 1988.

Steward Burns. *Daybreak of Freedom: The Montgomery Bus Boycott*. Chapel Hill: University of North Carolina Press, 1984.

Carolyn Calloway-Thomas and Thurmon Garner. "Daisy Bates and the Little Rock School Crisis: Forging the Way." *Journal of Black Studies* 26 (1996): 616–28.

Carson Clayborne. *In Struggle: SNCC and the Black Awakening of the 1960s*. Cambridge, MA: Harvard University Press, 1981.

Aprele Elliott. "Ella Baker: Free Agent in the Civil Rights Movement." *Journal of Black Studies* 26 (1996): 593–603.

Cynthia Griggs Fleming. "'More than a Lady': Ruby Doris Smith Robinson and Black Women's Leadership in the Student Nonviolent Coordinating Committee." *Journal of Women's History* 4 (1993): 64–82.

Henry Hampton and Steve Fayer, eds. *The Voices of Freedom: An Oral History of the Civil Rights Movement from the 1950s to the 1980s*. New York: Bantam Books, 1990.

Steven Lawson. *Running for Freedom: Civil Rights and Black Politics in America since 1941*. Philadelphia: Temple University Press, 1991.

Aldon D. Morris. *The Origins of the Modern Civil Rights Movement: Black Communities Organizing for Change*. New York: Free Press, 1984.

Charles M. Payne. *I've Got the Light of Freedom: The Organizing Tradition and the Mississippi Freedom Struggle*. Berkeley: University of California Press, 1995.

A Movement Takes Shape

Steven Buechler. *Women's Movements in the United States: Woman Suffrage, Equal Rights and Beyond*. New Brunswick, NJ: Rutgers University Press, 1990.

Flora Davis. *Moving the Mountain: The Women's Movement in America since 1960*. Urbana: University of Illinois Press, 1991.

Marth Davis. "Welfare Rights and Women's Rights in the 1960s." *Journal of Public History* 8 (1996): 144–165.

Nancy Gabin. *Feminism in the Labor Movement: Women and the United Auto Workers, 1935–1975*. Ithaca, NY: Cornell University Press, 1990.

Susan Hartmann. *From Margins to Mainstream: American Women and Politics since 1960*. New York: Alfred A. Knopf, 1989.

_____. *The Other Feminists: Activists in the Liberal Establishment*. New Haven, CT: Yale University Press, 1998.

Susan Lynn. *Progressive Women in Conservative Times: Racial Justice, Peace and Feminism, 1945 to the 1960s*. New Brunswick, NJ: Rutgers University Press, 1992.

Gwendolyn Mink. *Welfare's End*. Ithaca, NY: Cornell University Press, 2002.

Annelise Orleck. *Common Sense and a Little Fire: Women and Working-Class Politics in the United States, 1900–1965*. Chapel Hill: University of North Carolina Press, 1995.

Leila J. Rupp and Verta Taylor. *Survival in the Doldrums: The American Women's Rights Movement, 1945 to the 1960s*. Columbus: Ohio State University Press, 1990.

Winifred Wandersee. *On the Move: American Women in the 1970s*. Boston: Twayne, 1988.

Agenda for Reform

Mary Frances Berry. *Why the ERA Failed*. Bloomington: Indiana University Press, 1986.

Susan Cahn. *Coming On Strong: Gender and Sexuality in Twentieth-Century Women's Sport*. New York: Free Press, 1994.

Jane DeHart-Matthews and Donald Matthews. *The Equal Rights Amendment and the Politics of Cultural Conflict*, 1998.

Susan Douglas. *Where the Girls Are: Growing up Female with the Mass Media*. New York: Random House, 1994.

Bonnie Dow. *Primetime Feminism: Television, Media Culture and the Women's Movement since 1970*.

Philadelphia: University of Pennsylvania Press, 1996.

Blanche Linden-Ward, and Carol Hurd Green. *American Women in the 1960s: Changing the Future*. New York: Twayne, 1993.

Rosalind Pollack Petchesky. *Abortion and Women's Choice*. Boston, MA: Northeastern University Press, 1990.

Deborah Gray White. *Too Heavy a Load: Black Women in Defense of Themselves, 1894–1994*. New York: Norton, 1999.

Memoirs, Autobiographies, Biographies

Douglas Brinkley. *Rosa Parks*. New York: Viking, 2000.

Shirley Chisholm. *Unbought and Unbossed*. Boston: Houghton Mifflin, 1970.

Betty Friedan. *Life So Far: A Memoir*. New York: Touchstone, 2000.

Joanne Grant. *Ella Baker: Freedom Bound*. New York: John Wiley, 1998.

Carolyn Heilbrun. *The Education of a Woman: The Life of Gloria Steinem*. New York: Dial Press, 1995.

Daniel Horowitz. *Betty Friedan and the Making of* The Feminine Mystique. Amherst: University of Massachusetts Press, 2000.

Chan Kai Lee. *For Freedom's Sake: The Life of Fannie Lou Hamer*. Urbana: University of Illinois Press, 1999.

Pauli Murray. *Pauli Murray: The Autobiography of a Black Activist, Feminist, Lawyer, Priest and Poet*. Knoxville: University of Tennessee Press, 1989.

THE PERSONAL IS POLITICAL, 1960–1980

SEXUAL REVOLUTIONS
Liberation for All
Obscenity Redefined
Gay Liberation

WOMEN'S LIBERATION
Women of the New Left
Black Feminism
"We Called Ourselves 'Feministas'"
The Woman Warrior

PERSONAL POLITICS
Rethinking Heterosexuality
Lesbian Feminism
The Feminist Art Movement
The Women's Health Movement
Abortion Activism

FAMILY LIFE, ONE DAY AT A TIME
Women at Work
The Second Shift
Marriage and Divorce
The Feminization of Poverty

WHAT ASPECTS of women's lives did the sexual revolution change?

WHAT MOTIVATED young women into feminism?

WHAT SET radical feminism apart from other social movements?

HOW DID women's work change in these years?

I became aware of feminism and the Women's Liberation Movement in high school. We formed a group and became a recognized school club. When I began to notice subtle discriminations by teachers and "deferential" treatment by the boys in my class, which lowered my self-esteem as a student and person—I was elated! Of course there was pain in the realization, but suddenly so much incoherent hurt and anger became focused and articulated. From the women in the group, I gained a lot of strength and courage which I needed to take myself and my career aspirations seriously. Together, we built a protective shield for each other, reinforcing our hopes, and reassuring one another that we were not "tomboys," or "crazy

Women's Libbers." I got a sense of power from the growth of the Movement, and I felt everything was possible.

However, as I grow older I find myself dealing with realities, not ideological conflicts. The pressures to choose a career or a mate have become greater. It is hard to be a woman. It is even harder to be a woman who is assuming new roles and questioning old expectations. Each one of us does battle with our upbringing, the opinions of our parents and peers, and, most difficult of all, our own grave self-doubts.

We are beautiful in our conviction, our sisterhood, and our struggle. Each of us must remember that we are not alone. We can seek and find each other. Only if we are true to ourselves, our aspirations and dreams, can our lives have meaning.

Source: From Harriet Sigerman, ed., The Columbia Documentary History of American Women since 1941 *(New York: Columbia University Press, 2003), 293.*

The anonymous letter, published in 1974 in Ms. magazine, was one of many written by high-school and college-age women about their experiences of living as feminists. Their stories captured the highs of personal empowerment and the lows of self-doubt that were part of how ordinary women experienced second-wave feminism. One of the most lasting effects of feminism was on private life, specifically on sexuality and family life.

As in the 1920s, U.S. women in the 1960s and 1970s found themselves facing a revolution in morals and manners. A new casualness in matters of sexuality emerged. Heterosexual couples opted to "live together" before getting married. The double standard that endorsed sexual experimentation for men but not for women faded, helped along by the birth control pill that became available in 1960. Changes in divorce laws made it easier to end marriage. First young people but soon middle-aged Americans adopted a spirit of experimentation and embraced personal growth in the quest for relevance and vitality in their lives. Cold war gender conformity, once seen as markers of health and maturity, was now seen as "square" and "uptight," no longer in the spirit of the times.

The turn toward self-discovery in what some commentators called the "me generation" took place against a backdrop of social protest and the escalating war in Southeast Asia, a war justified by presidents Kennedy, Johnson, and Nixon as crucial in the U.S. battle against the spread of Communism. The civil rights movement of the 1950s and 1960s, which had confronted people in the United States with the ongoing reality of racism and inequality, entered a more militant Black Power phase, changing the role of young black women in the movement. The liberal feminist movement that built on the political accomplishments of the civil rights movement brought awareness to the restrictions on women's equality based on gender, and its successes inspired a younger generation of women of all races to embrace a more "radical" style of feminism. Adding to the ferment of social protest was the growth of the New Left, the student-led protest movement against U.S. involvement in the Vietnam War that helped end it in 1975. Young women, protesting the war and the military draft alongside male peers, still found themselves marginalized by the New Left's focus on men and the draft. The social protest movements and the lifestyle revolutions or countercultures they nurtured profoundly altered the life expectations and aspirations of the baby boom generation.

At the same time, broad economic forces also shaped changes in family and had profound consequences for working women. The affluence that had characterized the post–World War II period came to an end as high inflation and ongoing recession stalled the nation's economic machine. An oil crisis in 1973, triggered by deteriorating political conditions in the Middle East, only worsened the economic picture and added pressure to U.S. families already rocked by generational and gender conflicts. By decade's end, working-class and poor women found that the dreams of equality nurtured by a decade of civil rights activism and feminism did little to help lift them out of the poverty or help combat economic insecurity. With more single mothers and female-headed households, family life itself seemed imperiled. The spirit of experimentation and political engagement of the late 1960s appeared to have disappeared into what President Jimmy Carter described in 1979 as the "malaise" that had settled over the nation.

SEXUAL REVOLUTIONS

Family life in the 1950s had been celebrated as the bulwark against Communism and the source of U.S. values. But by the mid-1960s, a renewed celebration of youth, individualism, and autonomy swept over the country and pushed family life out of the rhetorical center it had enjoyed. Sexual expressiveness and experimentation became central values of the new revolution of morals and manners. By the 1960s, the belief that sex was an important part of identity and a source of personal meaning was no longer a view held just by radicals. The Supreme Court advanced the liberalizing of sexuality by further narrowing the definition of obscenity, which resulted in the rapid growth of sex-related businesses and more sexualized images of women to adorn advertisements, movie posters, and magazine covers. At the same time, gay men and lesbians launched a movement for equal rights and against discrimination based on sexual preference. Changing standards of heterosexual behavior and new tolerance for homosexuality combined to create a sexual revolution.

Liberation for All

If the United States' favorite bachelor in the 1950s was *Playboy* magazine founder Hugh Hefner, its favorite single woman in the 1960s was Helen Gurley Brown. In her 1961 best-selling book *Sex and the Single Girl*, Brown spoke for the single working woman, who like Hefner's playboys had little use for marriage. She took her message to a larger audience when she became editor of *Cosmopolitan* and made it into a new kind of woman's magazine. Echoing a message similar to the one found in *Playboy*, she told her readers to enjoy all the pleasures being free and single could give them, without becoming ensnared in romance and marriage. Brown tutored her readers in how to dress for sexual success, how to enjoy restaurants and nightclubs without paying a cent, and how to manage "the affair" with a married man. Brown made actions once viewed as acceptable for bachelors only, such as dating many people, staying out late, and casting off family life, as signs of sophistication and glamour for single women.

Author and magazine editor, Helen Gurley Brown made a name for herself when she her book, Sex and the Single Girl, *became a publishing sensation. Emphasizing financial autonomy for women and the glamour of staying single, Brown captured one element of the sexual revolution for women.*

counterculture The youth culture of the mid-1960s that grew out of the student protest movements, with a focus on lifestyle liberation.

Prosperous urban Americans in the 1960s created a new kind of singles scene. Once informally structured through friends, single life became organized through commercial venues like restaurants, singles bars, and parties that were advertised in city newspapers. For a modest fee, single men and women could meet someone outside their circle of friends. Guidebooks and "computer dating services" serviced the same desire, to date and mate, but not necessarily to find "Mr. Right." Unlike the young working-class women in the turn of the century whose appearance at commercial dance halls shocked respectable onlookers, the young women who went to singles bars and used dating services were not pitied. They very quickly became, according to one commentator, "a new, privileged, spotlighted, envied group." These young urban women adorned themselves with the symbols of single life—clingy blouses, miniskirts, and boots or shoes that set off bare legs. As Mary Quant, the designer of the miniskirt, explained the appeal of modern fashions: "Am I the only woman who has ever wanted to go to bed with a man in the afternoon? Any law-abiding female, it used to be thought, waits until dark. Well, there are lots of girls who don't want to wait. Mini-clothes are symbolic of them."

While some young singles embraced consumerism in their quest for sexual liberation, others broke from the materialism of the postwar period. Hippies, or flower children as the press called them, found countercultural ways to reach ecstasy, mainly through music, drugs, and an ethos of "free love." "Turn on, tune in, drop out," preached psychologist Timothy Leary, a leader of the hippy rebellion who argued for the spiritual and therapeutic benefits of LSD. Young women experimented with alternative group living situations and explored open relationships in an attempt to "smash monogamy." Living in communes in western cities like San Francisco and in rural areas such as northern Vermont, hippies abandoned sexual restraint and their allegiance to the nuclear family. They made their own rituals, like the 1967 "human be-in," modeled on civil rights' sit-ins, and focused on changing consciousness through drugs and intimacy. Twenty thousand people attended the be-in, making San Francisco the epicenter of the **counterculture**. Many of the participants stayed, creating the Summer of Love and catapulting hippies and "flower power" into national attention. But no rituals were as historic as the concert that took place in August 1969 when 500,000 young people converged on Woodstock, New York, for a three-day rock festival that included drugs, nudity, and open sexual encounters. Female singers Joan Baez and Janis Joplin were among the performers, as well as countercultural leaders like Leary, Beat poet Allen Ginsberg, and Youth International Party leader Jerry Rubin.

Both the fevered lifestyle revolution of the hippies and the burst of the mainstream single scene were aided by the introduction of the birth-control pill in 1960. Young women who came of age during the sexual revolution found the pill was part of a larger change in their path to sexual maturity. In the 1920s, young women shocked their elders when they kissed men they might not marry, but strict guidelines remained that kept female sexuality firmly in marriage. In the 1950s, teenage women struggled to keep the more tolerated premarital sexual behavior within the bounds of respectability. Premarital petting was permissible with a partner one promised to marry. By the 1960s, the commitment to marriage was no longer the gateway to sexuality. Young Americans "lived together" with their boy or girl friends, often for years or with consecutive people, before they married. The decision to live together without marriage was one of the sharpest parts of what social commentators called the "generation gap." Young Americans expressed their sexual liberation by separating sexuality from romantic commitment and from the responsibilities of reproduction.

Married couples were not impervious to the new attention placed on "liberating" sexuality. As in the 1920s, experts cast sexual satisfaction as a crucial ingredient to marital happiness. The most famous team of sex experts in the 1960s was that of William Masters and Virginia Johnson, direct heirs of sex researcher Alfred Kinsey, who authored the pathbreaking studies of U.S. sexual behavior in the 1940s and 1950s (see chapter 19). Masters and Johnson began their research in the sexually conservative 1950s, but by the time they published *Human Sexual Response* in 1966, the resistance to discussing sexual matters was fast evaporating. While one of their goals was to help define sexuality as a healthy human trait and the experience of sexual pleasure and intimacy as socially acceptable, they also provided new information about female sexual response. Through physiological measurements, they demonstrated the strength of female orgasm and did away with the notion of the asexual woman. Masters and Johnson were quickly catapulted to celebrity status when their book became

William Masters and Virginia Johnson, direct heirs of sex researcher Alfred Kinsey, published Human Sexual Response *in 1966 to a public with far less resistance to discussing sexual matters than the one Kinsey faced. They provided new information on female sexual response and brought sex therapy into the mainstream with their attention to married couples.*

a best seller. In 1970, they published *Human Sexual Inadequacy*, which was concerned with the treatment of impotence, premature ejaculation, frigidity, and other sexual problems. In the wake of these two publications, the field of sex therapy—the clinical treatment of sexual problems—was born. Other sex experts soon followed, opening treatment programs, sponsoring couples weekends, and publishing self-help manuals. *The Joy of Sex* by Alex Comfort and *All You Ever Wanted to Know about Sex* But Were Afraid to Ask* by David Reuben became best sellers, at last replacing Theodore Van de Velde's 1926 *Ideal Marriage* on night tables across the country (see chapter 16).

Obscenity Redefined

The rediscovery that sexual pleasure mattered to the health of marriage worked in tandem with the growing commodification of sexuality and sexual imagery. The Supreme Court set the stage for the explosion of the business of selling sex through a series of rulings that narrowed the definition of obscenity. Between 1957 and 1967, a number of obscenity cases came before the court, which responded by affirming the right for adults to consume and use sexual materials and images. In the 1957 *Roth v. United States* decision, the Court stated that "sex and obscenity are not synonymous" and only materials that appealed to "prurient interest" could be prosecuted. In rulings like these, the court did away with the remnants of Comstockery (see chapter 10).

In response to these rulings, more sexualized imagery became a part of daily life. The growing pornography industry became more visible and accessible. Thousands of movie houses featured X- and triple-X-rated films. Adult bookstores displayed hardcore sex magazines and paperbacks without fear. New men's magazines challenged the dominance of *Playboy*. Larry Flint's *Hustler*, started in 1974, offered readers full frontal nudity. The introduction of the videocassette recorder, or VCR, in the late 1970s opened a booming business of sex films for home use. But the effect could be felt in mainstream popular culture as well. In 1967, Hollywood dropped the Production Code that had been in place since 1934 and instituted a film rating system that specified the suitability of a movie for younger audiences. The number of films released with "R" ratings, suitable for audiences over the age of 17, skyrocketed from 25 in 1968 to 276 in 1973. Sexually explicit novels like William Burroughs' *Naked Lunch* (1962) and poems like Allen Ginsberg's *Howl* (1957) became best sellers.

To assess the effects of the mainstreaming of pornography, President Johnson appointed the Commission on Obscenity and Pornography in 1967. Its final report, issued in 1970, concluded that "interest in sex is normal, healthy [and] good." The report went so far as to describe obscenity legislation as a menace to freedom of expression. It called for the repeal of all federal, state, and local laws against the showing and selling of pornographic films, books, and other materials to adults while also acknowledging the need to shield pornography from minors. Not all people in the United States agreed with the report's findings. President Nixon, elected in 1968, denounced the report as "morally bankrupt" and pledged, "as along as I am in the White House, there will be no relaxation of the national effort to control and eliminate smut from our national life." Yet, by the 1980s, economists regarded the "sex industry" as a multibillion-dollar business.

The growing tolerance for sexual imagery in public had mixed consequences for women. The women who worked in the pornography industry as actors in films or dancers in strip clubs and bars reaped little of the profits. Women rarely owned or managed sex-related businesses but remained poorly paid employees of an industry that depended on the display of their bodies. Yet, the influence of the growing pornography industry could be seen beyond the red light districts. Scantily clad women appeared in more advertisements selling cigarettes, liquor, and cars. These images appeared in magazines and on huge billboards across cities. It became more fashionable for women to show more skin. However, many critics, both feminist and conservative, complained that these sexualized images taught girls and women that their value lay in their sex appeal. Others viewed sexually explicit images as expressions of women's greater freedom to be as sexually expressive as they wanted. Obscenity and pornography became political flashpoints.

Gay Liberation

The sexual revolution also reshaped the experiences of gay, lesbian, bisexual, and transgendered Americans in intimate and public ways. For much of the century, homosexual men and women had chosen to remain "in the closet," hiding their true sexual identities from almost everyone, often including their parents, siblings, and coworkers. In the social activism of the 1960s, gays and lesbians began to speak out for their own rights to live their lives as they wanted, without risking harassment or arrest.

The first major protest took place on a hot summer night in 1966 in San Francisco's Tenderloin district, when a group of transgender women and gay street hustlers who socialized at Gene Compton's Cafeteria fought back against the police harassment they regularly faced. Transgender patrons threw bottles, tables, and chairs against windows and set a police car on fire. This act of resistance was a turning point for the transgender community and the beginning of a new political movement to win the basic right for sexual minorities to congregate in public without harassment.

A second and more widely publicized riot took place three years later on June 28, 1969, when police raided the Stonewall Inn in New York City's Greenwich Village neighborhood. Rather than enduring the harassment as they had in the past, the two thousand patrons hurled insults and debris at the police. Announcing the birth of a new politics of sexuality, the slogan "Gay Power" appeared in graffiti on buildings and sidewalks across Greenwich Village.

By 1970, more than 150 gay activist groups had organized. College students in the United States and Canada formed local Gay Liberation Fronts and Gay Activists Alliances. They created new magazines such as the *Advocate* and *Out* to serve the homosexual community. Gay-pride parades became yearly events commemorating the events of Stonewall. Thanks to a persistent campaign of gay and lesbian activists, the American Psychological Association removed homosexuality from its list of psychological disorders in 1973. Prominent lesbian feminists Ti-Grace Atkinson, Rita Mae Brown, and Karla Jay experienced their political awakening at this time, and even the confrontational Daughters of Bilitis, a homophile organization founded in the 1950s, found itself radicalized by the surge in gay activism.

The **sexual revolution** of the 1960s and 1970s changed understandings of both homosexuality and heterosexuality for women. For lesbians, the new wave of protesting their second-class status was empowering. For heterosexual women, the new emphasis on sexual pleasure rewrote traditional gender scripts in which men pushed and women resisted sexual intercourse. For gay and straight women, sexual experimentation became an important expression of their generational identities. They were no longer willing to live in the closet or suffer sexually unfulfilling marriages as their mothers had been taught to. However, new freedoms did not do away with old patterns

sexual revolution The liberalization of U.S. attitudes toward sexuality that took place in the 1960s and 1970s.

WOMEN'S VOICES

LESBIANS IN THE CIVIL RIGHTS MOVEMENT

Joan Nestle recalls participating in the civil rights movement as a white Northern woman, and the inspiration she drew from the bravery of ordinary men and women who put their bodies on the line to vote. Yet, as she describes in her memoir, Nestle felt compelled to keep her homosexuality hidden from her activist peers.

. . . I had not seen the images of hatred that were pouring out of Alabama that March: the black men, women, and children beaten with the flailing clubs of (sheriff of Dallas County) Jim Clark's men; the hoses turned full force on the peaceful marchers, washing away the grip of held hands, pushing slamming people against the earth, the trees, each other, the dogs teeth bared in never ending snarls—all these forces marshaled against a band of would-be voters.

But I had ridden freedom buses into Philadelphia and Baltimore, had hidden from thrown rocks, had washed spit from my face and hair, had sat with CORE (Congress of Racial Equality) comrades at soda fountains while no-trespassing laws were read to us, and had been dragged out of restaurants that black CORE members could not even enter. . . .

I wore a double mask in these early sixties years, in those white restaurants. My first deception was to the enemy: the pose of a nice white person who could be let in and would sit down and eat in quiet tones, ignoring the battle for human dignity that was happening outside the windows. The second was to my friends: the pose of straightness, the invisibility of my queerness. They did not know that when the police entered, with their sneers and itchy fingers, I was meeting old antagonists. Perhaps their uniforms were a different color, but in the Lesbian bars of my other world I had met these forces of the state. I never told my comrades that I was different because a secret seemed a little thing in such a time in history.

Source: *From Joan Nestle,* A Restricted Country *(New York: Firebrand Books, 1987), 51–53.*

Questions

1. Does Nestle suggest commonalities between the struggle for equality between African Americans and gay and lesbian Americans?

2. What is the "double mask" Nestle feels she donned in the early 1960s? In what ways does her identity as a white woman mask her lesbianism?

3. Why does Nestle refer to her lesbianism as seeming like "a little thing"?

---

of gender discrimination. Women's experiences of the sexual liberation of the 1960s were not all positive, a discovery that led many young women to feminism.

WOMEN'S LIBERATION

Second-wave feminism, which emerged out of the civil rights movement, the labor movement, and liberal reform, also had roots in the student New Left and Black Power (see chapter 20). For younger women coming into new consciousness about the role of gender in their lives, politics and private life, however, were difficult to separate.

This cohort of college-age women shared with liberal women the difficulty of promoting new ideas about women's rights within movements dominated by men. Yet, unlike liberal women, this group of feminists rejected government reform as a tactic for creating equality between the sexes. They developed a distinctive analysis of sexism that distinguished it from liberal reform in its emphasis on sexuality and private life.

Women of the New Left

Angered by U.S. involvement in an escalating war in Vietnam and inspired by the civil rights movement, college-age students formed a student antiwar movement called the **New Left**. The New Left was a loosely connected network of campus groups that sought not only an immediate end to the war but also broad and wide-reaching reforms of U.S. society. New Left radicals, male and female, opposed racism at home and imperialism abroad and called for a more just distribution of wealth among all Americans.

New Left A loosely connected network of campus groups that sought an immediate end to the Vietnam War and broad and wide-reaching reforms of U.S. society.

Through their participation in the New Left, women "began to identify a whole new world of meaningful concerns and actions," recalled a college-age activist. The main organization of the New Left, **Students for a Democratic Society(SDS)**, held its first meeting in 1960 in Ann Arbor, Michigan. Its political manifesto, the Port Huron Statement, written in 1962 by SDS founder Tom Hayden, criticized U.S. society for failing to address social ills and advocated for civil disobedience as the means by which students could bring about a "participatory democracy." The escalation of troop levels

Students for a Democratic Society (SDS) The main organization of the New Left.

Members of "Women's Strike for Peace" march on Washington D.C. in 1967. As the war dragged on, more mothers, sisters, and girlfriends of soldiers joined the anti-war movement. Even family members of prisoners of war (POW) began demanding immediate withdrawal of US troops. For soldiers, and the 10,000 nurses serving in the military, such calls were often painful.

in Vietnam and the military draft tested their vision of activism. President Johnson increased the number of U.S. troops in 1965, which translated into a jump in the number of men drafted each month from seventeen thousand to thirty-five thousand. Protests against the draft began in 1965 with the first draft card being burned at a Berkeley protest that summer.

Women were drawn into the New Left for the same reasons as their male counterparts, particularly by concerns over the war in Vietnam and the powerful combination of military and industrial interests that supported it. Even if they could not be drafted, many women felt keenly that their generation was being sent to fight in a war they did not support. In April 1965, the SDS organized twenty thousand protesters to converge on Washington, D.C., to demonstrate against the war. Thousands of men and women joined campus protests against Reserve Officers' Training Corps (ROTC), CIA recruiters, and university research for the Department of Defense. By 1969, nearly two million Americans protested the war through demonstrations, marches, and antiwar events. By 1970, the antiwar movement shut down college campuses in what *Time* magazine called "a nationwide student strike."

As the war dragged on, more mothers, sisters, and girlfriends of soldiers joined the antiwar movement. Even family members of prisoners of war (POWs) began demanding immediate withdrawal of U.S. troops. For soldiers and the ten thousand nurses serving in the military, such calls were often painful. On the opening day of Congress on January 15, 1968, a coalition of women's peace groups called the Jeannette Rankin Brigade staged a protest in Washington, D.C., to show women's opposition to the war. Five thousand women attended, the largest gathering of women for a political purpose in decades. The Brigade, named in honor of the first woman elected to the U.S. Congress and who had cast her vote against both World War I and World War II, was the brainchild of **Women Strike for Peace (WSP)**, a group formed in the 1950s to protest nuclear weapons that had evolved into an antiwar network for liberal women. Older and younger women, both liberal and radical in their politics, participated in the demonstration. However, a group of more radical women disliked the link WSP activists drew between motherhood and antiwar activism, finding it too traditional for their liking. Over thirty women staged a counter demonstration over the following two days, urging women to stop "acquiescing to an order/that indulges peaceful pleas/And writes them off as female logic/Saying peace is womanly." The protest was the first time that the slogan "sisterhood is powerful" was used. For many participants, including student activist Shulamith Firestone, it became an important event in their growing feminism.

Many women found that as the antiwar movement grew, their position in the New Left worsened. Women activists complained that they were marginalized, assigned to do the tedious movement work of stuffing envelopes, making coffee, and typing instead of participating in decision making. In 1965, SDS activists Mary King and Casey Hayden, wife of Tom Hayden, mailed a long memo to forty women protesting what they saw as the existence of a "sex caste" system in a movement supposedly committed to equality and democracy. When activist women raised the issue of women's equality, they were frequently met by indifference, ridicule, and anger. Sexism and machismo were in evidence everywhere. At a New Left conference in 1967, Shulamith Firestone, a central figure in the development of radical feminism, stood at the microphone demanding to present a set of woman's rights resolutions. The chair patted Firestone on the head and said, "Move on little girl; we have more important issues to talk about here than women's

Women Strike for Peace (WSP) A group formed in the 1950s to protest nuclear weapons.

WOMEN'S VOICES

A VIETNAM WAR NURSE WRITES HOME

Lynda Van Devanter (1947–2002) served as a U.S. Army nurse at the 71st Evacuation Hospital in Pleiku, Vietnam, from 1969 to 1970. In 1979, a year after the founding of Vietnam Veterans of America, she helped launch and became the head of Vietnam Veterans of America Women's Project. In this letter written in 1969 from Pleiku Air Force Base to her parents, Lynda explains her feelings of patriotism and her ambivalence over the antiwar movement at home.

Dear Mom and Dad,

Things go fairly well here. Monsoon is very heavy right now—have barely seen the sun in a couple of weeks. But this makes the sky that much prettier at night when flares go off. [. . .]

At 4:16 a.m. our time the other day, two of our fellow Americans landed on the moon. At that precise moment, Pleiku Air Force Base, in the sheer joy and wonder of it, sent up a whole skyful of flares—white, red, and green. It was as if they were daring the surrounding North Vietnamese Army to try and tackle such a great nation. As we watched it, we couldn't speak at all. The pride in our country filled us to the point that many of us had tears in their eyes.

It hurts so much sometimes to see the paper full of demonstrators, especially people burning the flag. Fight fire with fire, we ask here. Display the flag, Mom and Dad, please, everyday. And tell your friends to do the same. It means so much to us to know we're supported, to know not everyone feels we're making a mistake being here. [. . .]

Here in the emergency room, doctors and nurses hustle about fixing up a little girl. There stands her shy little (and I mean little—like four feet tall) Papa-san, face looking down at the floor, in his loin cloth, smoking his long marijuana pipe. He has probably never seen an electric light before, and the ride here in that great noisy bird (helicopter) was too much for him to comprehend. . . . One comes to the hospital and the whole family camps out in the hall or on the ramp and watches over the patient. No, nobody can tell me we don't belong here.

Love,
Lynda

Source: *From Lynda Van Devanter,* Home Before Morning *(New York: Warner Books, 1983) pp. 126–28.*

Questions

1. What makes the antiwar movement painful for Lynda?

2. What gives Lynda the conviction that "nobody can tell me we don't belong here"?

3. What does Lynda mean when she says "fight fire with fire"?

liberation." At an antiwar event the following year, a representative of women's groups was greeted with shouts of "take it off." Such disrespect from male political allies motivated radical women to form a separate movement for women's liberation.

As common as the experience of sexism was, radical women found that there was much that divided them. The radical women's groups that formed in the late 1960s, referred to as the **women's liberation movement**, differed from each other in orientation, in political analysis, and in strategy. "Politicos" or socialist feminist groups such as Bread

women's liberation movement The burst of radical feminist groups that formed in the mid- to late 1960s that pioneered an analysis of sexuality and private life.

and Roses in Boston, the Chicago Women's Liberation Union, and New York's WITCH analyzed women's condition through economics. These groups maintained close ties with the New Left while calling for an end to sexism within it. Another faction was called simply "feminists." Feminists pioneered an analysis of sexuality and private life. Groups like the New York Radical Feminists, Redstockings, and Cell 16 argued that women's oppression predated economic systems like capitalism and that sexism and control over women were embedded in all political systems. Radical feminism, as it came to be known, was never a coherent and centralized movement but rather a ground swelling of various politically active women who organized themselves, built temporary coalitions among groups, and articulated new theories of women's oppression.

Black Feminism

Black Power movement A younger and more militant phase of the civil rights movement that highlighted the importance of black masculinity.

Feminists within the **Black Power movement** also reacted to the sexism of their male peers. They rejected the assumption that men experienced racism more keenly than women and the movement's new ideological program of advocating middle-class, traditional gender roles as a means of remaking a more empowered black family. According to Black Power leaders, the truly "revolutionary" woman kept house while the black man waged revolution. The gender traditionalism of the Black Power movement was a response to Assistant Secretary of Labor Patrick Moynihan's 1965 *The Negro Family: The Case for Action*, which unleashed a storm of controversy over its assertion that the strong "matriarch" had "emasculated" her husband and thereby contributed to male underachievement and ultimately to black poverty. While Black Power leaders condemned the report as racist, many nevertheless believed that the patriarchal family had to be restored if the black community was going to prosper. Black feminists, however sympathetic to their male peers, could not support a political program that glorified a style of motherhood and domesticity modeled on the white family.

By 1968, black feminists publicly responded to the Black Power endorsement of traditional gender roles. The Black Women's Liberation Group of Mount Vernon/New Rochelle, New York, challenged the directive to women to stop using birth control. The group countered the Black Power leadership by arguing that using birth control did not make black women agents of racial genocide. Rather, birth control gave "poor black sisters" the ability to combat racism by limiting the number of children they supported and giving them control over their bodies. They charged their male leaders with wanting "to use poor black women's children to gain power for yourself. You'll ruin the black community with your kind of black power!"

Black feminists felt the need for their own liberation movement. As they broke away from their male peers and formed their own groups, they pioneered an analysis of power that drew on an appreciation of multiple sources of oppression of black women. The black feminist movement began when Frances Beal and others formed a women's liberation group within the Student Nonviolent Coordinating Committee (SNCC) but broke away to form the Third World Women's Alliance (TWWA) in 1968 when they could no longer support the SNCC's calls for women to "step back" from leadership positions. The TWWA accused black militant men of "being white" and middle class when they expected black women to be "breeders" for the revolution. By November 1970, the TWWA had grown to two hundred members, including Puerto Rican and Asian American women, and had established connections to white radical feminist groups.

Black feminists found themselves navigating ties to both Black Power and women's liberation movements. Many black women hesitated working with white feminist groups that did not recognize race and class as feminist issues and were wary of alliances with white women who had not educated themselves enough to understand other women's experiences and political priorities. As the Moynihan report demonstrated, issues of family life, including birth control and abortion, had different meanings for white and black feminists. At the same time, many in the Black Power movement saw feminism as a "white" movement and viewed black women who embraced it as traitors to the cause of black liberation. The Combahee River Collective, formed in 1974, articulated the tensions many women felt as they moved between the two movements. In their mission statement, the collective provided a framework for thinking past the universal understandings of women's experience through what they called "identity politics." Black women—but not *just* black women—could organize based on their own experiences of the multiple forms of oppression they faced. By acknowledging differences among women, feminists could form coalitions among diverse groups of women, each using feminism in their own community-specific way. Lesbian feminist Audre Lorde, along with others, called for feminism to embrace difference and for white feminists not to base their understanding of gender oppression solely on their own, relatively privileged position as white women. **Identity politics** became an important means for women to reconcile their alliances within their own communities and with other feminist groups.

identity politics
Political action to advance the interests of members of groups that share a marginalized identity, such as race or gender.

"We Called Ourselves 'Feministas'"

Like their white and black peers, Latina and Chicana women in the 1960s also discovered their men were slow to support their feminist aspirations. The first Chicana organizations grew out of women's experiences in the Chicano movement of the 1960s, a movement in the Southwest and California that embraced gender traditionalism as part of its revolutionary future. The younger generation criticized their parents' strategy of assimilation and integration into white middle-class society, arguing instead that they ought to maintain their ethnic communities and traditions. Male and female students emphasized a generational "pride in our heritage, our language, and the humanistic values governing our personal relationships," all seen as distinct from Anglo society. On university and college campuses, Chincano/a student organizations such as the United Mexican American Students (UMAS) mobilized to secure greater coverage of Chicano history and literature in their courses. The UMAS had ten chapters in the Los Angeles area alone. Unlike African American college students, Chicano/a students felt especially isolated, as they were a small minority on most campuses. Anna Nieto-Gomez, founder of one of the first Chicana feminist groups, Las Hijas de Cuauhtemoc, recalled attending her first UMAS meeting and feeling a terrible sense of isolation lift. Women played active roles in student organizations, yet the leadership of these groups were male.

Chicanas found parallels between how men treated women at home and how they treated them in political settings. The philosophy of Chicanismo and *carnalism* (brotherhood) linked cultural preservation to a strong masculinity. Machismo kept women subordinate to men and confined to the family. Elma Barrera explained to the *Houston*

WOMEN'S LIVES

AUDRE LORDE

Audre Lorde was born on February 18, 1934, in New York City. Her parents were immigrants from Grenada. The youngest of three sisters, she was raised in Manhattan and attended Catholic school. While she was still in high school, her first poem appeared in *Seventeen* magazine. Her first lesbian affair was with a coworker in Bridgeport, Connecticut. She attended the National Universtiy of Mexico for a year starting in 1954. When she returned, she entered the "gay girl" scene in Greenwich Village but was often the only black woman in the bars. She recalled in her memoir that she did not try to build ties to the other three or four black women in the scene because it seemed to threaten their status as "exotic outsiders." She entered Hunter College, worked as a librarian, and wrote poetry. She tried to join the Harlem Writers guild, but homophobia made it uncomfortable for her. In 1959 and the following year, she completed her masters in library science at Columbia University. She served as a librarian in New York public schools from 1961 through 1968. In 1962, Lorde married Edward Rollins. They had two children, Elizabeth and Jonathan, before divorcing in 1970. Her first volume of poems, *The First Cities*, was published in 1968. In 1968, she also became the writer-in-residence at Tougaloo College in Mississippi, where she discovered a love of teaching. In Tougaloo, she also met her long-term partner, Frances Clayton. *The First Cities* was quickly followed with *Cables to Rage* (1970) and *From a Land Where Other People Live* (1972), which was nominated for a National Book Award. Lorde was diagnosed with cancer and chronicled her struggles in her first prose collection, *The Cancer Journals*, which won the Gay

Caucus Book of the Year award for 1981. Her other prose volumes include *Zami: A New Spelling of My Name* (1982); *Sister Outsider: Essays and Speeches* (1984); and *A Burst of Light* (1988), which won a National Book Award.

Lorde was active in the feminist movement. In the 1980s, Lorde and writer Barbara Smith founded Kitchen Table: Women of Color Press. She was also a founding member of Sisters in Support of Sisters in South Africa, an organization that worked to raise concerns about women under apartheid. Lorde was professor of English at John Jay College of Criminal Justice and Hunter College. She was the poet laureate of New York from 1991 to 1992. She died of breast cancer in 1992. ■

Post in May 1971 that "The woman still waits on the man. . . . She often eats after the man has eaten. And she's so dependent on his whims that he can walk into the room while she is watching a TV show and switch the channel to another station without asking her."

Like black feminists, Chicana feminists faced the view that they ought to return to domestic roles as wife and mother to protect their unique cultural heritage—and resist Anglo society. By doing so, they could restore a strong sense of masculinity in their men whose experience of racism undermined their authority and status. Chicanas in the movement found themselves increasingly marginalized, ignored at political meetings, given clerical tasks, and shut out from decision making. Chicana feminists fought against the sense that many in Chicano movements and in the broader communities had of feminism as "Anglo" and thus not relevant to their communities or to their political struggle. With considerable frustration, one feminist recalled insisting at meetings that "we [women] don't want to take over and we don't want to wear the pants . . . , we just want to help you, we want to be side by side, and be equal partners."

Chicana feminists, like Leticia Hernandez, framed feminism as central to their anti-racist activism.

In 1969, Chicana feminists formed Las Hijas de Cuauhtemoc at Long Beach State University in California and, in 1970, Concilio Mujeres at San Francisco State College. Groups did campus work to recruit and support Chicano/a students, participated in the underground abortion movement, and worked on community welfare rights issues. In 1973, Las Hijas's newspaper became a national Chicana studies journal, *Encuentro Feminil* (Women's Encounter/Meeting). Despite their community efforts, Leticia Hernandez, a founding member of Las Hijas, recalled that activist women faced ridicule from their male peers: "'Oh here come the feminists, they're trying to be white women.'" Chicana feminist refused to make a choice between two unacceptable options: organize with men to improve the status of Mexican Americans but not include an analysis of gender or sexism, or organize with outsiders around gender and sexism and not include an analysis of ethnicity and race.

While many Chicana feminists were sympathetic with what they called Anglo and black feminism, they remained wary of building alliances. Reluctant to bring on more conflict with their movement brothers, yet fed up with dealing with unchecked machismo, Chicanas cultivated their feminism within the larger Chicano movement. Black feminism provided useful models for producing culturally specific ideas about gender, and they applied them to strengthen, not sever, connections to their male peers. Most activism in the 1970s took place within women's caucuses of larger groups and within community organizations.

The Woman Warrior

The involvement of Asian Americans in the civil rights movement, the antiwar movement, and campus activism for ethnic studies and curricular changes created a new generation of women activists concerned with sexism and restrictive gender roles in their communities. The Asians who immigrated to the United States after 1965, when the Immigration and Nationality Act of 1965 allowed more Asians to enter the country, were well educated, affluent, and willing to organize to ensure equal opportunity for themselves. Most settled in East and West Coast cities. As the myth of the high-achieving Asian immigrant—the "model minority"—took hold, Asian American women found themselves in an uneasy relationship with Latinas and African American women, many of whom struggled against poverty, making feminist alliances around racial discrimination difficult. Coastal communities of Asian American feminists emerged in the 1970s, like Unbound Feet in San Francisco and the Basement Workshop in New York City, which published writings by and about Asian American women. Asian Pacific women's conferences took place in New York, Hawaii, and California in the late 1970s, helping to consolidate networks of activist women.

Leaders of the Asian American women's movement such as poet Mitsuye Yamada provided crucial connections between earlier generations of Asian American women who prioritized assimilation into U.S. society and a younger generation of women eager to preserve their cultural distinctiveness. Yamada was born in Japan in 1923 and immigrated to Seattle in 1926. At the outbreak of World War II, Yamada was interned with her family in Camp Minidoka, Idaho, although she and her brother were allowed to leave the camp to work and attend college. When people of Asian origin were granted the right to become U.S. citizens with the passage of the Walter-McCarran Immigration and Naturalization Act of 1952, Yamada became a naturalized citizen of the United States. She became a writer to encouraged other Asian American women to speak out and defy the cultural codes that encouraged them to be silent.

A burst of Asian American women's writing followed, capturing the unique experiences of growing up Asian and female in the United States. One important voice was that of novelist Maxine Hong Kingston, whose *The Woman Warrior, Memoirs of a Girlhood among Ghosts* was published in 1976 to critical acclaim for its blend of Chinese mythology, personal history, and Asian American feminism. Maxine Hong was born in 1940 in Stockton, California, where her parents, Tom and Ying Lan Hong, operated a laundry. After graduating from Berkeley in 1962, Kingston became active in the antiwar movement. That same year, she moved to Hawaii, where she taught English and wrote *The Woman Warrior*, which won the National Book Critics Circle Award for nonfiction.

Novelist Maxine Hong Kingston, whose novel, The Woman Warrior, Memoirs of a Girlhood Among Ghosts, *was published in 1976 to critical acclaim, blended Chinese mythology, personal history, and Asian American feminism.*

The Woman Warrior told the stories of five women; "No-Name Woman"; a mythical female warrior Mu Lan; Brave Orchid; Kingston's aunt; and, finally, Kingston herself. The chapters integrated Kingston's personal experiences with a series of talk-stories—spoken stories that combined Chinese history, myths, and beliefs—that her mother told her. One of the most inspirational stories, "White Tigers," followed the mythical female warrior Fa Mu Lan as she trained to become a warrior. Fa Mu Lan led an army of men—even pretending to be a man herself—against the forces of a corrupt baron and emperor. After her battles ended, she returned to a life of a wife and mother. The story of Fa Mu Lan contrasted sharply with Kingston's own life in the United States, in which she could barely stand up to her racist bosses. Kingston realized, however, that her weapons were her words.

The final chapter of the memoir, "A Song for a Barbarian Reed Pipe," focused mainly on Kingston's childhood and teenage years as she grew more and more frustrated in trying to express herself and in attempting to please an unappreciative mother. There were a number of characters whose personalities highlighted many of Kingston's own struggles, among them a shy girl whom Kingston torments as a little girl and her critical mother who could not appreciate Kingston's feelings. Later in her life, Kingston came to appreciate her mother's talk-stories and, at the end of the chapter, retold one herself through a warrior poetess captured by barbarians who returned to the Chinese with songs from another land, an apt allegory of her experience of growing up Asian American.

The young women—white, black, Chicana, and Asian—who embraced feminism cultivated a new definition of politics. Radical feminists understood power as a relationship enacted between differently situated people, not only as decisions made in Washington, D.C., by elected officials. This expansive definition of politics and power enabled feminists to connect intimate relationships lived outside the public eye to larger structures of power. For these young feminists, neither racism nor sexism could be eradicated by laws alone and demanded changes in consciousness. By focusing on the intersections of race, gender, and sexuality, this generation of activists challenged liberal strategies of reform.

PERSONAL POLITICS

One of the most famous slogans to emerge from the radical feminism in the 1970s was **"the personal is political."** The phrase captured feminists' attention to the psychological, sexual, and privately experienced aspects of women's oppression. While changes in laws and legislation were important, legal, political, and economic transformation could not be achieved and, indeed, were not possible without the full liberation of women from the internalized confines of femininity. Laws alone could not wipe out generations of gender socialization that taught women to curb their intelligence, their assertiveness, and their sexuality. As women met in small and large groups to understand their status as women in a patriarchal society, that is, a society dominated by men, the female body and sexuality became focal points for feminist thought and revolution.

"The personal is political" One of the founding principles of second-wave feminism; the phrase captured feminists' attention to the psychological, sexual, and privately experienced aspects of women's oppression.

Rethinking Heterosexuality

Called "radical" for its critique of men, heterosexuality, and the nuclear family, feminists pioneered an analysis of sexuality that insisted that the personal sphere had political significance. To explore this dynamic, radical feminists promoted the practice of **consciousness raising**, modeled on the Chinese practice called "speaking bitterness." Between 1967 and 1975, thousands of small groups formed to raise their consciousness about sexism by voicing their private fears, discussing their intimate relationships, and sharing their experiences as women. As one woman explained, "If we were truly to understand the situation of women in our society, we had to base our analysis on information we could trust, information that was not suspect, and for this we had to gather it ourselves. We had to question all the generalizations that had been made in the past about women, and question the interest they served. . . ." Sitting in living rooms, kitchens, and church and community center basements, women began to regard their individual frustrations within a larger framework of oppression. Women claimed authority and became their own experts. The interrogation of private life for

consciousness raising A popular practice of groups of women sharing intimate details of their lives to study them for the effects of sexism and gender oppression.

the symptoms of male dominance was the vehicle through which radical feminism politicized "the personal."

To dramatize the confining aspects of sex roles, radical feminists turned to street theater and other media-oriented "events." One of the more outrageous protests came in 1968 when a group of feminists picketed the Miss America pageant in Atlantic City to show how women are degraded and judged as sex objects. Inside the convention hall where the contest was taking place, an undercover group of feminists unfurled a huge banner that read "Women's Liberation," surprising those gathered inside. Using the confrontational style of civil rights and other protest movements, demonstrators outside the hall drew attention to the sexual objectification of women by ridiculing the beloved pageant. They crowned a live sheep "Miss America" and filled a "freedom trash can" with items of "female torture" like curlers, bras, girdles, and high-heeled shoes. Protesters linked standards of female beauty to women's political oppression, explaining that all women, not just Miss America contestants, were "forced daily to compete for male approval, enslaved by ludicrous 'beauty' standards we ourselves are conditioned to take seriously." Miss America, as an icon of white womanhood, "represents what women are supposed to be: inoffensive, bland, apolitical." As one participant later recalled: "Many onlookers and reporters were incensed . . . So acceptable was the practice of valuing women for their sexual attractiveness that many people genuinely believed the demonstrators must be ugly women, motivated by simple jealousy of the contestants, proclaiming the politics of sour grapes."

In the wake of the protest, which drew the attention of the national media, radical feminist groups decided to stage more "events." The New York group WITCH (Women's International Terrorist Conspiracy from Hell) staged one of the more dramatic examples of feminists' public consciousness-raising events. Dressed as witches, the group stormed a bridal show held in New York's Madison Square Garden in 1969, warning brides against marriage by singing "Here come the slaves/off to their graves" and then releasing live white mice into the hall. Other actions included a "whistle-in," which involved groups of women whistling and cat-calling to men walking on the street and defacing billboards that represented women as sex objects. In actions like these, feminists pioneered a political analysis of private life, exposing the pervasiveness of male dominance and privilege.

The ideology, "the personal is political," challenged the distinction between public and private life that had historically defined sexuality and women's unpaid work in the domestic sphere as private and unconnected to the public realm of politics. Radical feminists argued that the intimate and domestic spheres were the arenas where power relationships between men and women were played out. As such, what took place in private between couples and within families must be analyzed as part of the larger system of male dominance. From this insight, feminists produced a range of political writings that challenged traditional understandings of femininity. Radical feminists focused on the family, the institution of marriage, the division of labor within the home, and sexual relationships between men and women, pointing out that all were areas that were organized so that males could dominate females. The insights of radical feminism brought thousands of new recruits into the movement.

Radical feminists argued that growing up female, women were in effect trained for the job of being a submissive wife. Women were taught to feel subservient to their husbands in all arenas of life, including the sexual. Since the 1910s and 1920s, married women were advised that their pleasure lay in surrender to their husbands' sexual desires and that their deepest fulfillment came not from orgasm but from having babies. In her article "The Myth of the Vaginal Orgasm" (1969), Anne Koedt argued that the legions of marriage counselors constructed "the myth" of the vaginal orgasm and the myth that women did not enjoy sex as a way to justify male power in heterosexual re-lationships. Women, according to Koedt, could enjoy sex as much as men, but only if their male partners understood that women might want more than missionary-style in-tercourse. By questioning the view that heterosexuality was the only healthy way for women to be sexual, Koedt formulated a radical challenge to the sexism of the sexual revolution. Critiques of heterosexuality like those by Koedt attempted to give women more power in their relationships with men. Kate Millett, author of the best-selling *Sexual Politics* (1970), argued that a long history of patriarchy and sexism had undercut the promise of sexual liberation for women. While the sexual revolution granted women the right to say yes to sex, radical feminists insisted that sexual freedom also de-pended on the right to say no. Roxanne Dunbar of Boston's Cell 16 spoke for many women when she wrote that sexual liberation had come to mean the "freedom to make it with anyone, anytime." More sex with more partners did not fundamentally make the experience of sex for women positive. Feminists demanded that men be more at-tentive to women's desires. According to Dana Densmore, the sexual revolution offered little that women needed to be truly free. "Our 'right' to enjoy our own bodies has not only been bestowed upon us, it is almost a duty." Sexual self-determination became a feminist goal in the late 1960s, intended to empower every woman to claim more rights over her own body and desires. For some women, this meant withdrawing from men temporarily, experimenting with lesbianism, and questioning the authority of male ex-perts who had for decades defined women as less sexual than men or as hypersexual and disordered. Radical feminists applied their analysis of sexuality to violence against women, both at home and in public. They created networks of women's shelters to give women and children a place to stay as they left abusive husbands and boyfriends. They held speak-outs on rape and raised awareness of the legal obstacles women faced when they pressed charges against their attackers. Radical feminists spoke out on the dangers of illegal abortion and the difficulty in getting effective contraception that they them-selves could control. They brought new attention to sexual harassment at the work-place, where generations of women had had little recourse against bosses, supervisors, or male peers who sexualized the workplace. Radical feminists pioneered the politics of sexuality, whether it was in the arena of personal relationships and pleasure or in the public world of work, medical care, law, and the courts.

Lesbian Feminism

One of the most important aspects of second-wave feminism was the development of lesbian feminism. An outgrowth of radical feminism, lesbian feminists extended the critique of heterosexuality to include a new understanding of lesbianism as a political and sexual alternative to heterosexuality and a way to fight patriarchal oppression.

One of the most important lesbian feminist groups was the Furies. Formed in 1971 in Washington, D.C., by Charlotte Bunch and Rita Mae Brown, they published a newspaper—*The Furies*—that disseminated their views broadly. In the premier issue in January 1972, Ginny Berson declared that lesbianism was the best tool against male domination: "Lesbianism is not a matter of sexual preference, but rather one of polit-ical choice which every woman must make if she is to become woman-identified and

WOMEN'S LIVES

KATE MILLETT

Kate Millett's 1970 best seller *Sexual Politics: The Classic Analysis of the Interplay between Men, Women, and Culture* put radical feminism on the national map. Millett's book was a mix of literary criticism and feminist theory, a combination that highlighted the connections between literary and social values. She argued that generations of women had learned about female sexuality from novels written by men who viewed them as sexual objects. Her analysis of patriarchy, what she explained as the unacknowledged yet pervasive "birthright priority whereby males rule females," cast it as the oldest and most enduring form of oppression and the one most intimately experienced.

Millett was born in 1934 in St. Paul, Minnesota. She graduated from the University of Minnesota in 1956 with a degree in English and went on for postgraduate work at St. Hilda's College, Oxford, in 1958. She moved to New York City in 1959, where she taught and continued to study art, and in 1961, to Japan. There she met sculptor Fumio Yoshimura. The two returned to New York City in 1963 and married in 1965. Millett completed her doctorate in Comparative Literature in 1970, and her doctoral dissertation was published in July of that year as "Sexual Politics."

Published as the women's liberation movement burst on the national scene, "Sexual Politics" caused a sensation and catapulted Millett into celebrity. The media crowned her a leader of the feminist movement. *Time* magazine featured her on the cover of its August 31, 1970, issue. The accompanying article on "Women's Lib" labeled Millett the "Mao Tse-Tung of Women's Liberation." Active in New York radical feminist groups like New York Radical Women, Millett was considered to be an intellectual leader of the burgeoning movement, along with

Ti-Grace Atkinson, Shulamith Firestone, and Anne Koedt. And like her peers, Millett approached the mainstream media with suspicion, particularly its attempts to identify "leaders" where there were none. Millett's celebrity brought her criticism from those within the movement who saw strong leaders or "stars" as chauvinistic and male-identified.

The controversy swirling around Millett was only amplified by her announcement, later published by *Time* magazine in a follow-up piece, that she was a bisexual. Her announcement added to the media frenzy over her but caused some feminist activists to complain that Millett's bisexuality only confirmed the popular assumption that all feminists were lesbians, a view they said limited the movement. Lesbian feminists supported Millett and expressed deep concern that heterosexual feminists could imagine lesbianism as a diversion from the true work of a feminist movement.

Determined to find peace within the chaos of her life, Millett founded a women's art colony near Poughkeepsie, New York, in 1971. She also separated from her husband, whom she divorced in 1985. Millet continued to write. She published *Flying* in 1974 about her life after "Sexual Politics," *Sita* in 1977, and *A.D.: A Memoir* in 1995—the latter two both about her lesbianism. Millett continues to produce art and write books on women's issues. ■

thereby end male supremacy." Furies members lived collectively, engaged in rigorous consciousness-raising sessions, and were active in D.C. feminist politics. The New York City group, Radicalesbians, coined the phrase "the woman-identified woman" to reformulate lesbianism as a political, as well as sexual, commitment to women. All feminists, they argued, should be "woman-identified," should put women first in every aspect of their lives, a conception that expanded the meaning of lesbianism to include feminism. "A lesbian is the rage of all women condensed to the point of explosion. She is a woman who . . . acts in accordance with her inner compulsion to be a more complete and free human being . . . she has not been able to accept the limitations and oppressions laid on her by the most basic role of her society—the female role."

In their radicalism, lesbian feminists played a role in the women's movement that was larger than their actual numbers. Some radical feminists experimented for a few

Representatives of the Lesbian Herstory Archives march with a banner beneath portraits of various famous lesbians in a street in New York. An outgrowth of radical feminism, lesbian feminism extended the feminist critique of heterosexuality to include a new understanding of lesbianism as a political and sexual alternative to heterosexuality and a way to fight patriarchal oppression.

months or years with lesbianism, feeling that to not adopt a woman-identified life compromised their politics. Called "political" lesbians, these feminists adopted lesbianism as a political lifestyle. However, not all lesbians or straight feminists accepted "political lesbianism." For some lesbians who felt that homosexuality was not a matter of choice, straight women experimenting with a gay lifestyle led only to confusion and resentment. Some straight feminists resented the idea that the only way to be a feminist was to be a lesbian and felt as if the lesbian-feminist agenda was taking over the movement. The split between straight and gay feminists widened in the mid-1970s, with each group staying within its own political networks.

Lesbian feminists helped to create a thriving feminist counterculture comprised of bookstores, music festivals, and dances, all of which became important sources of community formation. Women's music festivals and concerts attracted huge crowds. The first musician to perform as an out lesbian was Maxine Feldman, quickly followed by Alix Dobkin, Holly Near, Meg Christian, and others. In 1973, the first lesbian-feminist record company formed, Olivia Records, and it soon became a leader in women's music. With the growing number of artists and songs, women's music festivals became weekend-long events that combined music and dance with political workshops and shopping. The festival producers were careful to make feminist politics foundational to how the weekends were managed. They provided day care, access for the disabled, sign interpreters for the deaf, sliding scale entrance fees, and vegetarian meals. Similarly, women's bookstores and publishing houses grew in the 1970s. Run collectively and careful to enact feminist values in such things as pay and decision making, the women's publishing industry flourished for a number of years and produced a new and much more positive literature on lesbianism. The synergy between readers and publishers in the lesbian publishing world was impressive enough to attract mainstream attention. Established presses began to bid on books that dealt with lesbian issues. By the end of the 1970s, every major publishing house in New York had published at least one novel or nonfiction book that represented lesbianism in a positive light.

The Feminist Art Movement

Contemporary feminist art originated in the early 1970s, inspired by the women's liberation movement. Although women had increasingly swelled the enrollments of art schools in the middle of the century, very few had been successful in the transition from amateur to professional. Georgia O'Keeffe was the most well-known exception (see chapter 16). Throughout the 1940s and 1950s, only a few female artists made a name for themselves in the all-male world of fine art in which galleries would only carry one or two works by women. Painter Joan Mitchell described the isolation many of the women felt. "The men helped me more than the women. It's still a small world for women and they're cutthroat with each other." Women artists in the 1950s and 1960s suffered professional isolation from each other and from their own history. Influential art history textbooks routinely had neither the name nor the work of a single woman artist. The predominant attitude in the art world was that no female artist could make a piece that was worthy of inclusion in the art cannon. Women of color were doubly discriminated against, with artists like Faith Ringgold told they could only exhibit in museums devoted to African American art. Adding to women's invisibility in the art world, few women taught on the faculties of art schools.

By the early 1970s, the women's liberation movement inspired women artists, art educators, and activists to protest their marginalization at museums, galleries, and art schools. In terms of content, they also challenged what counted as "art." Women visual artists, art educators, and art historians formed consciousness-raising groups, woman-centered art education programs, women's art organizations, and cooperative galleries to provide women artists greater visibility. Feminist art in the 1970s combined politics and art in a new way.

In 1969, Women Artist in Revolution (WAR) was formed within the male-dominated Art Workers Coalition, a group of radical artists. WAR was triggered by the Whitney Museum's 1969 Annual, which included only eight women among the 143 artists shown. WAR demanded that the museum change its policies to include more women. In 1970, Women, Students, and Artists for Black Art Liberation, led by artist Faith Ringgold, mobilized to bring more attention to the reality of gender and race discrimination in the art world. Together with the Ad Hoc Women Artists Group, such pressure proved effective. The percentage of women in the Whitney Sculpture Annual of 1970 rose to 22 percent, a big jump from the 5 to 10 percent of previous years. Feminist artists on the West Coast organized the Los Angeles Council

Artist Judy Chicago's The Dinner Party *(1976) became one of the most well known works from the Feminist Art Movement of the 1970s. The Women's Liberation Movement inspired women artists, art educators, and activists to protest the lack of representation at museums and galleries, and their marginalization at art schools.* The Dinner Party *challenged what counted as "art" with its use of handwork, needlework, and forgotten techniques of women's crafts. (© 2008 Judy Chicago/Artists Rights Society (ARS), New York)*

of Women Artists to pressure the Los Angeles County Museum of Art to show more women's work. It also served as an important network for women artists, where artists shared their stories of discrimination and compiled statistics about sex discrimination.

The first program in feminist art was started by Judy Chicago and Miriam Schapiro at Fresno State College in 1970 and moved to California Institute of Arts in 1971. Using techniques like consciousness raising, students in the Feminist Art Program explored how "growing up female" had shaped and often limited women's artistic horizons. Feminist workshops explored the expression of "femaleness" in art in terms of shape, pattern, decoration, color, and texture. Students incorporated "female" materials like lipstick, sequins, pins, lace, and paper dolls into their paintings and constructions and emphasized the female body through work on menstruation, rape, sexual pleasure, and childbirth.

feminist art movement A movement in the 1970s to redefine women's art and women's place in the art world.

The **feminist art movement** was diverse in its goals. Some artists wanted to transform traditional fine art with feminist awareness. Other artists sought to introduce aesthetics and values from non-European traditions or abandon object making in favor of performance art and video, questioning the division between craft and fine art. Many women artists sought to reclaim the female body from the sexualized and idealized representations that dominated the images of women created by men. Judy Chicago's well-known and controversial *The Dinner Party* installation (1979) was created collaboratively and celebrated women's traditional needlework. It also visualized a new women's history with each of its ornate settings devoted to a famous woman in history, including Sacajawea, Sojourner Truth, and Susan B. Anthony. The piece showed to sold-out crowds for several years.

By the late 1970s, the feminist art movement shifted from activism to consolidation. Groups and networks that came together to protest museums, galleries, and art programs now devoted themselves to long-term institutional change, including pressuring the National Endowment for the Arts to include more women on its panels. The founding of the *Feminist Art Journal* in 1972 gave feminist art historians and critics a national readership. Throughout the 1970s and 1980s, the Women's Caucus for Art (WCA), created in 1972, held a series of conferences in which feminist artists debated if significant differences between the art of men and women existed and the value of separatist art training for women. In 1979, the WCA inaugurated the first Honor Awards for Lifetime Achievement by women artists at the White House. The Awards given included African American artist Selma Burke and Georgia O'Keeffe.

The Women's Health Movement

Another way radical feminists addressed female sexuality was by questioning medical experts. In the spring of 1969, a small group of women met at a workshop on "women and their bodies" at Emmanuel College in Boston, and several decided to continue meeting as a group, do research into specific areas of women's health, and put together a course on women's health. Out of this, the Boston Women's Health Book Collective (BWHBC) formed and in 1970 published *Our Bodies, Ourselves*. Through the processes of research and discussion, the collective established themselves and, by extension, individual women as experts in their own right. Since 1970, 3.5 million copies of the book have sold in twelve languages. Throughout *Our Bodies, Ourselves*, the collective stressed that medical experts had rendered natural events like menstruation, childbirth, and menopause into medical conditions, alienating women from their bodies and their health care.

Our Bodies, Ourselves was a part of a growing grassroots **women's health movement (WHM)** sweeping across the country in the 1970s, fueled by social protest movements, struggles for reproductive rights, and consumer action groups. The feminist practice of "consciousness-raising" and "know-your-body" group experiences altered participants' outlooks on their bodies and their medical experiences and gradually helped them to see these "private" events for the first time in political terms. In women's groups across the country, activists advocated gynecological self-examination, alternative remedies, fertility awareness, and basic body knowledge and sparked the formation of self-help groups across the country. Natural childbirth and midwifery also returned as options to hospital births.

As with radical feminist groups, no single individual or group founded or fully represented the WHM. Women of various ages, races, and classes participated in their own groups. Latinas, black women, and Native American women knew firsthand about clinic care, illegal abortions, infant mortality, sterilization abuse, and population control and organized in response to issues most pressing to themselves and their communities. Feminist women's health centers in several U.S. cities provided women-controlled settings for self-help programs and, once abortion became legal in 1973, abortion services. Simultaneously, other women's communities across the country launched their own well-woman health and abortion centers as "alternatives" to conventional care.

The WHM focused on harmful drugs—specifically, the birth control pill that in its early days delivered unhealthy amounts of hormones. Activists also focused on unnecessary hysterectomies, ovariectomies, mastectomies, and sterilization. Reproductive rights activists in groups like the Coalition to End Sterilization Abuse in New York and the Coalition for Abortion Rights and against Sterilization Abuse in California brought the racist pattern of forced sterilization against poor and minority women to national attention. Congressional hearings in 1972 revealed that sixteen thousand women and eight thousand men had been sterilized with federal government funds, and more than three hundred of these patients had been under the age of twenty-one. In 1977, ten Mexican American women tried unsuccessfully to sue the Los Angeles County Hospital for obtaining their consent to be sterilized while they were in labor—and in English, when they spoke only Spanish. Bureau of Indian Affairs hospitals were particularly aggressive in their sterilization practices, with over three thousand women being sterilized between 1973 and 1976.

Outraged by the forced sterilization of poor women—mostly women of color—activists quickly took up the issue of population-control practices. In the 1970s, the policies of the U.S. Agency on International Development (USAID) made aggressive, high-technology birth-control programs a precondition for loans and economic aid to Third World countries. When U.S. WHM activists realized their efforts were effective in protecting U.S. women by keeping dangerous or questionable drugs and devices off the U.S. market such as the "high-dose" pill, the Dalkon Shield IUD, and the birth-control pill Depo-Provera, they saw these products simply "dumped" on Third World women who ran the risk of being harmed by these rejected products. By 1975, the National Women's Health Network (NWHN) was formed, the nation's first and only public-interest membership organization devoted exclusively to all women's health issues, especially those related to federal policy.

women's health movement (WHM) A movement in the 1970s to bring women greater knowledge of and control over their own health.

Abortion Activism

No issue defined the feminist politics of sexuality more than did abortion. The ongoing reality of illegal abortions and the dangers they posed to women mobilized a new wave of abortion activism in the mid-1960s. Abortion rights activists responded in two ways. One was to directly challenge abortion laws (see chapter 20); the other was the creation of their own networks of underground abortion services. In Chicago, a group of women formed "Jane," a feminist network that helped women get abortions under more healthy conditions. Heather Booth, a student at University of Chicago who had participated in sit-ins at Woolworth lunch counters in New York and in Freedom Summer in Mississippi, organized "the Service" in 1967, which provided abortions to women without questioning the validity of their requests. In the beginning, Jane members transported women to doctors who would perform the operation. Yet, seeing that these "doctors" were not certified physicians, they decided to learn to perform abortions themselves. The Chicago Women's Liberation Union, a city coalition of women's liberation groups, advertised the Service through underground newspapers and by word of mouth. When a woman called the union about an abortion, she was given a phone number and told to ask for "Jane." Between 1969 and 1973, Jane provided over eleven thousand abortions. The women who went to the Service represented every age, racial, and ethnic group and every class.

Roe v. Wade The 1973 Supreme Court case that established women's right to have an abortion.

On the eve of the Supreme Court case **Roe v. Wade** (1973), abortion law was a patchwork of different state laws. One-third of the states had liberalized abortion restrictions, and four had repealed them. Women with enough money could travel out of state to obtain an abortion if they so wished. Women with fewer resources still turned to illegal abortionists. More than one million illegal abortions were done every year during the 1960s. Of these, more than 350,000 women suffered complications serious enough to be hospitalized and between five hundred and one thousand died. In the court of public opinion, support for abortion rights had grown. In 1965, 91 percent of those polled opposed changing laws. In 1972, a Gallop poll reported that 64 percent of respondents said the abortion decision should be made by a woman and her doctor and not by legislators. The strategy to use the courts to establish abortion as a woman's right culminated in the Supreme Court's historic 1973 decision in *Roe v. Wade*. Justice Harry Blackmun, writing for the Court, maintained that the Fourteenth Amendment's definition of personal liberty included a woman's right to determine when or if to carry a pregnancy to term.

While *Roe*'s rights-based strategy triumphed, it had the paradoxical effect of weakening the political coalitions and institutions needed to sustain abortion as a matter of women's health. Opponents of abortion, unable to directly challenge *Roe* without a Constitutional amendment, used the language of rights established by *Roe* to chip away at federal health programs and the financial support and political shelter abortion received through them. In the years following *Roe*, opponents of legal abortion amended a wide variety of bills to restrict federal funding of abortion, in addition to monies for family planning and contraception services abroad. Medicaid funding became the central battleground. As one of the largest federal health programs and the one that provided health care primarily to young women, Medicaid provided between forty-five and fifty million dollars' worth of abortion funding in 1973. It was an easy target for conservatives because it was funded through annual appropriations processes. In 1976, Congress passed the Hyde Amendment, which excluded abortion from the comprehensive health care services provided to low-income people by the federal government through Medicaid. In 1980, the Supreme Court upheld the Hyde Amendment in *Harris v. MacRae* by declaring that the rights of women to obtain an abortion established in *Roe* did not require the federal government to fund abortion. Writing for the majority, Justice Potter Stewart stated, '[I]t simply does not follow that a woman's freedom of choice carries with it a constitutional entitlement to the financial resources to avail herself of the full range of protected choices." Without a firm basis in federal health policy, the right to abortion conferred through *Roe* carried with it none of the institutional and political support needed to protect women's access to the procedure.

The feminist politics of sexuality was far-reaching in its effects. From the women's health movement to abortion rights, women claimed the right to control their bodies and their medical treatment. From radical feminists reformulating the terms of heterosexuality to lesbian feminists who pioneered a positive view of lesbianism, women claimed their rights to sexual self-determination. Feminists politicized issues of sexuality and mapped them onto the political life of the United States.

FAMILY LIFE, ONE DAY AT A TIME

The politics of private life were shaped by economic transformations that, in turn, profoundly altered the formation of U.S. family life in the 1970s. Trends in married women's work that had begun at midcentury strengthened. In the beginning of World War II, only one-quarter of all women worked and the majority of those who did were married women over age thirty-five with no children at home. By the 1970s, working women and working mothers had become the new norm and they were motivated to work not by a feminist goal of equality but because of broad economic downturn that brought the post–World War II affluence to an end. Women worked to support their families, be they middle or working class. However, the combination of low wages and changes in divorce law meant that women fell into poverty at higher rates than did men. During the 1970s, the number of poor families headed by women increased by nearly 70 percent.

Women at Work

While Betty Friedan suggested in 1963 that middle-class women could find personal fulfillment in careers, the majority of U.S. women who worked in the 1960s wanted to have two paychecks in the family so that they could buy more consumer goods. By the 1970s, women's wage work had become an economic necessity for most families. Middle-class families experienced a drop in their standard of living, driven by falling wages and the higher cost of living. The 1973 oil crisis, triggered when the Organization of Petroleum Exporting Countries (OPEC) placed an embargo on shipments of oil to the West, left the United States with skyrocketing fuel costs and the first gas shortage since World War II. The oil crisis set off economic recessions and high inflation. To make ends meet, Americans tightened their belts and more women took paid jobs. For the first time in U.S. history, there were more women in the labor force than out of it. As the Carnegie Council on Children observed in 1977, "We have passed a genuine watershed: this is the first time in our history that the typical school age child has a mother who works outside the home." The growing presence of married women and mothers in the workforce was accompanied by a declining birthrate. A study conducted by the Census Bureau found that while 26 percent of young wives had expected to have four children or more in 1967, the average family in 1972 now had only 2.3 children.

Two trends in women's work converged in the 1970s. The first was the impressive gain women made in the professions, caused by the expansion of women's postgraduate education. In the 1940s, 1950s, and 1960s, women entering medical, law, and business schools constituted 5 to 8 percent of their classes. With the legal gains of the 1970s, that percentage rose dramatically. By the mid-1980s, women made up more than 40 percent of all students entering traditional professional schools. Women who might have been secondary school teachers, nurses, or social workers were now able to command competitive salaries in law firms and in business. Such gains did not mean that significant barriers to women's professional advancement had disappeared. Most professional women earned 73 percent of what men did.

Despite gains and advancements by professional women, the second and more persistent trend in women's work continued and made women workers more economically vulnerable. Sex segregation of the labor market, a feature of women's work throughout the century, continued to cap women's earnings. Furthermore, many of the new jobs created after 1950 were in the service sector, part of the gradual shift in the U.S. economy away from heavy industries and toward service work. Women were perceived as particularly suitable for work in the service sector. Women stayed clustered in these sex-segregated "female" job classifications that paid less and had less opportunity for advancement. Eighty percent of all women workers worked in 5 percent of all jobs, the five lowest-paying jobs. For example, in 1970, American Telephone and Telegraph hired five times as many black women as it had in 1960, yet the jobs they held—clerical workers and telephone operators—were the lowest rung of the occupational ladder. Between 1955 and 1981, women saw their actual earnings fall from 64 percent of what men earned to 59 percent, meaning that women's earnings were barely sufficient to keep her family above the poverty level. Saleswomen earned only 50 percent of what salesmen earned, waitresses 72 percent of waiters. The higher-paying jobs remained male controlled. Women made up only 6 percent of engineers, 3 percent of mechanics, and 1 percent of plumbers.

Long-term trends in the economy—specifically, the growth of clerical and service jobs—locked most women into low-paying jobs at the same time the impact of the women's movement opened new avenues for advancement in the professions. This set the stage for a widening wage gap between those women who had gotten out of the pink-collar ghetto and those who had not.

The "Second Shift"

"second shift" The full-time and unpaid domestic work women did when they came home from work.

With pressure from the women's movement still fresh, more women were more vocal about the pressures of the **"second shift,"** the full-time domestic work women did when they came home. As one woman put it, "You're on duty at work. You come home, and you're on duty. Then you go back to work and you're on duty." While time studies in the 1970s found that men spent more time with their children, household work like cleaning and cooking remained women's domain. In a parallel to the wage gap working women faced, a leisure gap opened between husbands and wives.

Studies on time management in the 1970s showed that for the first time in fifty years, the average number of hours spent doing housework had declined—and for women in general, not only for working women. Whereas the cold war media directed at women had expanded the duties of household management, in the 1970s, women's magazines stressed time-saving devices and a lowering of the high standards of bygone days. Between the mid-1960s and the mid-1970s, the amount of time spent on household work went from forty-four hours to thirty hours a week for full-time housewives and to twenty-one hours a week for employed women. Some of the change came from more efficiency and the setting of more realistic standards, but some came from the new idea that housework was the responsibility of all family members. However, while the survey reported that men increased the time they spent on domestic work from nine hours in 1965 to ten hours in 1975, women, who had done 80 percent of the housework in 1965, ten years later still did the lion's share of the work of maintaining the house—some, as much as 75 percent of it. While time spent on housework had declined since the 1950s, the length of a woman's workweek expanded. Major time studies from the 1960s and 1970s documented that women worked fifteen hours longer each week than men.

By the 1970s, working mothers had become the new norm. While women worked out of financial necessity, they found juggling competing demands of family and work difficult. The second shift meant that most women put in additional hours doing household work once they returned home.

While men did not do much more housework than their fathers, they did spend more time with their children. Studies found that men were psychologically more invested in their families than their jobs and that both parents spent more time with their children than they had earlier in the century. Fathering itself increasingly mattered for those men interested in liberating themselves from work to be more involved with their families. Fathers more regularly attended their children's births, and new attention was paid to the "fathering instinct."

In many respects, the situation of white, middle-class U.S. women in the 1970s became more like African American women for whom juggling work and family had long been familiar. Married black women were the original super-women who managed the competing demands of being mothers and full-time wageworkers who suffered from both the wage and leisure gap. Middle-class women in the 1970s discovered the limits to the "superwoman" ideal. As married working women struggled with their multiple roles, more and more discovered how much harder it could be to be without a husband, no matter how little he helped around the house.

Marriage and Divorce

In *The Inner American*, three sociologists compared U.S. attitudes toward marriage and divorce in 1957 and 1976 and found a sea change had taken place. Only 33 percent of the public held negative views of the unmarried. Divorce had been upgraded from a sign of mental instability to "a viable alternative." The divorce rate that had slowly grown over the course of the twentieth century doubled between 1965 and 1975. California first adopted the "no-fault" divorce in 1969, virtually eliminating the adversary principle in divorce. Within four years, thirty-six states had made it an option. New divorce laws viewed both mothers and fathers as potential earners and caretakers, requiring that material assets be divided equitably and that alimony and child support be gender neutral and reciprocal. Women typically won custody. According to the National Children's Survey conducted in 1976 and 1981, two-thirds of divorced fathers had had no contact with their children for ten years. The number of U.S. families with a mother and father living together declined. In 1950, almost 80 percent of U.S. households contained husband-wife couples. By 1980, this had dropped to just over 60 percent.

While feminists had supported liberalizing divorce laws, many recognized women's vulnerability in an unequal socioeconomic system. The National Organization for Women (NOW) opposed the unilateral no-fault divorce statutes because such laws made it easy for men to legally abandon their families. While women found it easier to leave bad marriages in the 1970s, it did not improve their economic situations; in fact, men initiated divorce more frequently than did women. Divorced men experienced a 42 percent rise in their standard of living, whereas divorced women and their children experienced a 73 percent decline. The connection between divorce and poverty for women in the 1970s translated into poor housing, few funds for recreation and education, and intense pressures on women's time and money. The unequal earning capacity of men and women and the unequal focus on the man's career during marriage meant that most divorced women in the 1970s found their economic situation far worse after divorce than that of their ex-husbands.

The Feminization of Poverty

The combination of divorce, which left women heading their own households; women's labor segregation in lower-paying service industries; and the ongoing slow-down of the U.S. economy left more women vulnerable to falling into poverty. In 1978, Diana Pearce, a visiting researcher at the University of Wisconsin, issued the first warning that poverty was becoming "feminized" in the United States. According to Pearce, almost two-thirds of the poor over age sixteen were women. Women's economic status had declined from 1950 to the mid-1970s, Pearce claimed, even though more women had entered the labor force in those years. Pearce blamed the **feminization of poverty** on the lack of government support for divorced and single women. She argued that, "for many the price of that independence has been their pauperization and dependence on welfare." Following Pearce's study, other population researchers blamed the feminization of poverty on changes in the family that had uncovered women's latent economic vulnerability. Among working-age adults, the growth of single-parent families was the crucial factor. The increase in divorce, coupled with the decline in marriage and marriage age overall, meant that an increasing proportion of adult women were living separately from men and relying on themselves for economic support. Because women generally earn less than men, single women have a higher risk of being poor than single men.

The government had targeted poverty as a national problem in the 1960s. President Johnson's "War on Poverty" (1964–1968), part of the federal attempts to bring about greater equality among U.S. citizens, created a range of federal programs designed to end poverty in the United States. The Medicare program, which Congress approved in 1965, was a first step toward creating the system of national health insurance that liberals had been advocating since World War II. It provided federal funding for many of the medical costs of older Americans; and it overcame resistance to the idea of "socialized medicine" by making its benefits available to everyone at or over age sixty-five, regardless of need, and by linking payments to the existing private insurance system. A year later, the government extended the system to welfare recipients of all ages through the Medicaid program. These programs, like those of the New Deal, distributed federal funds through Aid to Families with Dependent Children (AFDC) and Social Security insurance. After 1970, the trends in AFDC and social insurance diverged sharply. Social Security pensions were raised and indexed to inflation in the early 1970s, and the value of these benefits continued to rise throughout the

feminization of poverty The gradual and proportionate increase of women living in poverty in the 1970s.

1970s. In contrast, welfare benefits, which were not linked to inflation, peaked in the mid-1970s and then began to fall, due in part to high inflation in the later 1970s, leaving mothers with shrinking support. Elderly women fell into poverty more frequently than did men, given that Social Security pensions for never-married women were lower, on average, than pensions for never-married men because women earn less than men while they are working and women live longer and live alone more than men.

Poverty rates reflected the particular economic vulnerability of minority women. Working-class black women fell into poverty at higher rates than white women and were less able to use new programs to help pull themselves out of poverty. The percentage of female-headed households for African Americans was double that for white households and rose from 17.6 percent in 1950 to 40.2 percent in 1980. Black women who headed households were more likely to be young and separated rather than divorced, mothers of children under the age of eighteen, and unemployed—all which conspired to keep their earnings very low. Wives in two-parent black families had household incomes in 1981 of $19,620, whereas single women earned less than half that—$7,510 on average.

AFDC caseloads swelled as the tide of poverty rose, growing from 3 million in 1960 to 11.4 million by 1975. As President Jimmy Carter prepared to take office in 1976, he struggled to respond to the growing ranks of the poor. Sixty percent of wage earners and 94 percent of AFDC recipients still fell below the poverty line. A government report explained that only one-tenth of AFDC mothers were chronically unemployed, with 40 percent moving "back and forth between low-income employment and welfare," and 50 percent were on welfare temporarily.

The examination of the nation's growing poverty rates exposed the forces that uniquely conspired to push more women into poverty and onto welfare in the 1970s. Low wages paid to women, changes in divorce law that left women without financial support from ex-husbands, and more female-headed households pushed working and poor women into poverty. At the same time that middle-class women enjoyed the fruits of expanding opportunities for work, working-class and poor women struggled to keep their families fed and intact. Women with husbands and jobs, those of the middle and upper classes, found that their duties and responsibilities at home had not changed along with their work prospects. The second shift remained burdensome to a new generation of "superwomen" who "had it all."

CONCLUSION

The 1960s and 1970s brought a consolidation of gains made by women since World War II and were particularly visible in the realms of politics and education. The age of liberal reform and social protest came to an end by the 1970s, having achieved historic legislation, including the Civil Rights Act of 1964, the legalization of abortion in the Supreme Court case *Roe v. Wade*, and Title IX. A generation of young Americans rewrote the rules of political engagement. The antiwar movement helped to end the United States' unpopular involvement in Vietnam in 1975, and the women's movement had made sexism part of the vernacular. A new analysis of the connections between public power and private life created a radical feminism. A second "revolution" in morals and manners brought greater tolerance about issues of sexuality and sexual identity. Yet the same years marked the first stirring of changes that would threaten the very gains women achieved. Women's economic vulnerability, masked by post–World War II affluence, was laid bare by the end of the 1970s.

WOMEN'S HISTORY	GLOBAL EVENTS

1950

1957
Roth v. United States rules on sex and obscenity

1959
The United States enters the Vietnam War

1960

1960
The birth-control pill becomes available

1960
Formation of Students for a Democratic Society

1961
Helen Gurley Brown publishes *Sex and the Single Girl*

1962
Tom Hayden writes the Port Huron Statement

1964
The Berkeley Free Speech movement begins
President Johnson declares a "war on poverty"
President Johnson increases the number
of U.S. soldiers in Vietnam

1965
Malcom X is assassinated
United Farm Workers organize a boycott against California grape growers
Congress establishes the Medicare program
Daniel Patrick Moynihan issues "The Negro Family: A Case for National Action"

1966
Masters and Johnson publish
Human Sexual Response
Transgender women fight San Francisco police

The SDS organizes a massive antiwar march
Women in SDS complain of sexism in the movement
The Immigration and Nationality Act allows more Asians to enter the United States

1967
Women begin meeting in small consciousness-raising groups
Jane, an underground abortion service, forms

1967
Hippies stage a "Human Be-In" in San Francisco

1968
Feminists protest the Miss America contest
Founding of the National Association for the Repeal of Abortion Laws (NARAL)
The Jeannette Rankin Brigade coins the phrase "sisterhood is powerful"
The Black Women's Liberation Group of Mount Vernon/New Rochelle forms
The Third World Women's Alliance forms

1969
California adopts no-fault divorce laws
Stonewall riots in Greenwich Village, New York
Chicana feminists form Las Hijas de Cuauhtemoc
Women Artists in Revolution formed

1969
Woodstock festival

WOMEN'S HISTORY	GLOBAL EVENTS

1970

1970
The Boston Women's Health Collective
publishes *Our Bodies, Ourselves*

Chicana feminists formed Concilio Mujeres

Founding of the Gay Liberation Front
and Gay Activists Alliances

1970
The Presidential Commission on Obscenity
and Pornography redefines obscenity

1971
The first feminist art program begins
at Fresno State College

The lesbian feminist group the Furies forms

1972
The *Feminist Art Journal* begins publication

The Women's Caucus for Art has its first conference

1972
President Nixon visits China

Watergate scandal begins

1973
The Supreme Court legalizes abortion in *Roe v. Wade*

Olivia Records begins publishing women's music

The American Psychological Association removes
homosexuality from its list of psychological disorders

First Chicana feminist journal, *Encuentro Feminil,* begins
publication

1973
Oil crisis in the US

1974
Combahee River Collective forms

1974
Richard Nixon resigns as president and Gerald Ford issues a pardon

Larry Flint publishes *Hustler*

1975
Founding of the National Women's Health Network

1975
Unemployment rate reaches nearly 9 percent

Vietnam War ends

1976
Maxine Hong Kingston publishes *Woman Warrior*

1977
The divorce rate reaches historic highs

1978
The first report on the "feminization of poverty"

1979
Judy Chicago's *The Dinner Party* opens

REVIEW QUESTIONS

1. Where did women come across changing ideas of sexuality? How did women's sexual behavior change in these years?

2. How did younger American women become active in feminism? How were their paths to feminism different from liberal activisit women?

3. How did radical women change feminism in the U.S.? What organizations did radical women form in these years?

4. How did American women's work lives change? How did their home lives change? How much of these change can we attribute to feminism?

RECOMMENDED READING

Beth Baily. *Sex in the Heartland*. Cambridge, MA: Harvard University Press, 2002. Bailey looks at the sexual revolution as it happened in one decidedly tame city, Lawrence, Kansas.

Norma Broude and Mary D. Garrad, eds. *The Power of Feminist Art: The American Movement of the 1970s, History and Impact*. New York: Harry N. Abrams, 1994. A comprehensive look at the key players, institutions, and events of the feminist art movement.

Flora Davis. *Moving the Mountain: The Women's Movement in America since 1960*. Chicago and Urbana: University of Illinois Press, 1991. Davis documents the half-won revolution in women's struggle for equality between 1960 and 1990 through a focus on organized feminism.

Alice Echols. *Daring to Be Bad: Radical Feminism in America, 1967–1975*. Minneapolis: University of Minnesota Press, 1988. A close look at the formation, ideas, and demise of radical feminist groups.

Karla Jay. *Tales of the Lavender Menace*. New York: Basic Books, 1999. A mix of memoir and history, Jay describes the convergences of women's and gay liberation movements and what kept them at odds from the 1960s to the 1980s.

Benita Roth. *Separate Roads to Feminism: Black, Chicana, and White Feminist Movements in America's Second Wave*. New York: Cambridge University Press, 2004. Roth shows the similarities and differences among radical women's groups.

Natasha Zaretsky. *No Direction Home: The American Family and the Fear of National Decline, 1968–1980*. Chapel Hill: University of North Carolina Press, 2007. In this study of U.S. families in the 1970s, Zaretsky links gender, foreign policy, and popular culture.

ADDITIONAL BIBLIOGRAPHY

Sexual Revolutions

David Allen. *Make Love Not War: The Sexual Revolution: An Unfettered History*. New York: Routledge, 2001.

John D'Emilio and Estelle Freedman. *Intimate Matters*. New York: Harper & Row, 1988.

Susan Douglas. *Where the Girls Are: Growing Up Female with the Mass Media*. New York: Times Books, 1990.

Barbara Ehrenreich. *Re-Making Love: The Feminization of Sex*. New York: Anchor, 1987.

John Heidenry. *What Wild Ecstasy: The Rise and Fall of the Sexual Revolution*. New York: Simon & Schuster, 1997.

Janice Irvine. *Disorders of Desire: Sex and Gender in Modern American Sexology*. Philadelphia: Temple University Press, 1990.

Lynn Segal. *Straight Sex: Rethinking the Politics of Pleasure*. Berkeley: University of California Press, 1994.

Personal Politics

Patricia Hill Collins. *Black Feminist Thought*. Boston: Unwin Hyman, 1990.

Sara Evans. *Personal Politics*. New York: Vintage Books, 1978.

Amy Erdman Farrell. *Yours in Sisterhood: Ms. Magazine and the Promise of Popular Feminism*. Chapel Hill: University of North Carolina Press, 1998.

Jane Gerhard. *Desiring Revolution: Second-Wave Feminism and the Rewriting of American Sexual Thought, 1920–1985*. New York: Columbia University Press, 2001.

Barbara Ryan. *Feminism and the Women's Movement.* New York: Routledge, 1992.

Lauri Umanksy. *Motherhood Reconceived: Feminism and the Legacies of the Sixties.* New York: New York University Press, 1996.

Family Life, One Day at a Time

Beth Bailey and David Farber. *America in the 70s.* Lawrence: University of Kansas Press, 2004.

David Frum. *How We Got Here: The 70s.* New York: Basic Books, 2000.

James Patterson. *Grand Expectations: The United States, 1945–1974.* New York: Oxford University Press, 1996.

Winifred Wandersee. *On the Move: Women in the 1970s.* Boston: Twayne, 1988.

Memoirs, Biographies, Autobiographies

Judy Chicago. *Through the Flower: My Struggle as a Woman Artist.* New York: Penguin Books, 1975.

ENDINGS AND BEGINNINGS, 1980 TO 2008

THE NEW RIGHT
The STOP ERA Campaign
The Pro-Family Movement
Moral Panics and Culture Wars
Embattled Feminists
The Antiabortion Movement

WORK AND FAMILY IN THE 1990S
Work and Welfare
Gender Gaps
Caring for the Elderly

GLOBAL AMERICA
New Faces, New Families
The Gulf Wars
Terrorism at Home and Abroad
Global Feminism
Third-Wave Feminism

WHAT ROLE did women play in the conservative movement?

HOW DID anxiety about changing gender roles and sexual morality shape conservative activism?

HOW WAS immigration after 1980 similar to and different from earlier eras?

I was really worried because Joaquin I was only one, and with so much cold children can get very ill. And also, I had my other children [ages five and eight], and really all I could think about was them—they were too little. Imagine a child of five walking across the hills? No, it is not just, and I knew it was not just, but one has to eat their rage so that it does not stop you. What gave me strength was that my cousins were there with me, and they each took one of the children—and, well, I had invested so much time, and I had left my life behind, and I really had no other choice but to go forward. And so the coyote . . . there were two . . . took

Hillary Clinton arrives for a campaign rally in Concord, New Hampshire Reuters: Brian Snyder

us across and we walked a while—I don't know how long. One becomes disoriented with so much worry, but I think very soon . . . The people started shouting, because the lights [border patrol helicopter] were coming toward us. And one of the coyotes told us to get down, but obviously, everyone was scared, and I just remember that I couldn't move. Fear paralyzed me, because I was afraid that if I ran they would kill my child. And the worst part was that I couldn't immediately see the other two [cousins and children], and I just shouted out, "Francisco, don't run, they'll kill us." And thank God, he heard me. He shouted back to me, "Here I am cousin." And, I didn't hear anymore because there was a lot of shouting—I don't remember how many men [border patrol] there were, at that time it seemed a lot. I don't think I moved, but the baby's crying and everything else, I was very nervous, and I don't know, one of the agents hit me as he tried to hold someone else, and I fell, and all I could think of was to hold on to my baby. But he fell out of my hands anyway, and that's when I just could not [stand it]. I began to cry out of fear, yes, but also rage. There I was a grown woman with a child, where could I have gone? But the only thing that mattered to them was to get us. I swear to you, I am a good person, but in that moment, I wanted to do something to him [border patrol agent]. There I was like an animal, worse, a nothing. I get so angry . . . but I did nothing. I stayed there and waited for them to load us on the van.

The border patrol transported Guadalupe back to Tijuana, but that did not deter her from trying again. Two days later, she crossed again, this time without attracting the notice of the border patrol, and arrived safely at her cousin's home in Los Angeles. Since the 1980s, globalization and the growing disparity of wealth between the developed and developing worlds pulled record numbers of immigrants to the United States. Women made up nearly half of all new immigrants. Legal and illegal immigrant women alike found work in all sectors of the economy—in garment and service industries, managerial and sales, medicine, and research. Many found domestic work and child-care jobs as more middle- and upper-middle-class women worked longer hours outside the home. At the same time, U.S. immigration and welfare policy changed to reflect a growing concern with what was termed "traditional family values" and Christian morality, allowing family members to reunite with their relatives who had come before. As the country faced the largest influx of immigrants in its history, political debates intensified over immigration policy, while communities embraced or battled newcomers in their schools, hospitals, and neighborhoods.

Domestically, a new generation of conservative activists revitalized the Republican Party and challenged the liberal notion of the state as a social provider that had been in place since Franklin D. Roosevelt's New Deal. Reasserting the family as the proper caregiver against state-supported welfare and promoting self-reliance and religious morality, conservative activists reshaped politics and government. This new age of conservative activism spelled the end of the second wave of feminism. It brought women into the political process through local issues like school prayer and on national campaigns designed to undermine reproductive rights and return working women to the home through the antiabortion and pro-family movements.

Feminists and liberals clashed with conservative women over many issues, including the role of the United States in global affairs. The Middle East had replaced the Communist Soviet Union as the new center of U.S. foreign policy concerns, driven in part by an expansion of a global economy that made access to the oil-rich supplies of the region a new political priority. The Middle East stormed onto U.S. newscasts with the oil crisis of the 1970s, the takeover of the U.S. embassy, and the hostage crisis in Iran in 1979. As the new century opened, attacks on the Pentagon and the World Trade Center on September 11, 2001, sparked an ideological "war on terrorism" and ground wars in Afghanistan and Iraq. Women found a place in the all-volunteer army of the new century, deployed to militarized areas where no clear combat front existed. People in the United States grew familiar with media stories of working-class families in which both mother and father were deployed, a development that would have been unthinkable in any previous era. The growing sense of being part of a single world where national boundaries had grown porous and problems too large for a single state to tackle informed a new global feminist movement. Feminist activists joined pressing issues of women's health to larger international concerns with human rights. At home, a third wave of feminism redefined activism as a generation of women joined the ongoing battle to define equality for women.

THE NEW RIGHT

As the twentieth century drew to a close, the progressive milieu that had sustained feminism and women's activism for decades vanished. In its place, a new conservatism dug in. Disillusioned with what many deemed the lifestyle excesses of the 1960s and 1970s, particularly the sense that the sexual revolution had promoted homosexuality and heterosexual promiscuity to the detriment of marriage, U.S. voters elected Republican Ronald Reagan in 1980. Reagan ran on his accomplishments as a two-term governor of California. He promised to restore the United States' status internationally, to reign in the social activism of a federal government too focused on "special interests," and to promote what conservatives called "traditional family values." Reagan's victory was only one sign that feminists would be swimming against a conservative tide. Between 1970 and 1990, evangelical churches added more than six million new members, with the fastest growth taking place in the West rather than in the Southern Bible belt. The synergy between Republicans and conservative Evangelicals set in motion a powerful surge of social activism concerned with issues of family and morality and brought religious conservatives into school boards, town councils, and other local offices. Women played key roles in the New Right in local and national groups, bringing their organizational skills and determination to a range of issues. Along the way, these women repoliticized gender and private life in distinctively conservative ways and undermined many of the gains of second-wave feminism.

The STOP ERA Campaign

Conservative women had built strong networks in the 1970s in their successful campaign to defeat the Equal Rights Amendment. When the ERA passed in 1972, few suspected that it would become the epicenter of a political transformation. Phyllis

Schlafly, a Catholic mother of six and longtime activist in the National Federation of Republican Women (NFRW), had not paid much attention to feminism or the ERA. But with its passage, she turned away from her preoccupation with Republican Party politics and embraced issues associated with women and the family. In her widely read newsletter, *The Phyllis Schlafly Report*, begun in 1967, Schlafly launched a full force attack on the ERA and laid out the tenants of the antifeminism that would define the conservative agenda. The family, she argued, "is the basic unit of society, which is ingrained in the laws and customs of our Judeo-Christian civilization and [is] the greatest single achievement in the history of women's rights. . . . [T]he family . . . assures a woman the most precious and important right of all—the right to keep her own baby and to be supported and protected in the enjoyment of watching her baby grow and develop." According to Schlafly, feminism and, specifically, the ERA threatened women's primary role as mothers and undermined the strength of families.

A savvy organizer, Schlafly soon realized that she had in the ERA an issue that would mobilize the grassroots of the Republican Party. The national campaign against ERA began on July 7, 1972, when Schlafly and other members of the NFRW formed STOP ERA (Stop Taking Our Privileges). These women brought to the movement tremendous organizational experience. By early 1973, STOP ERA organizations existed in twenty-six states. Much like the Woman's Christian Temperance Union at the end of the nineteenth century, STOP ERA was a loosely organized group with strong local leadership (see chapter 13). Schlafly appointed state directors who then developed their own campaign tactics and raised their own funds. Other women's groups joined STOP ERA, such as Women Who Want to Be Women, the Family Preservation League, and the National Council of Catholic Women. As the campaign grew, it pulled in women previously not involved in politics, including younger Evangelical Christians, Southern Baptists, Mormons, Orthodox Jews, and Roman Catholics. Demographically, women who opposed the ERA had much in common with ERA supporters. Both were predominantly white middle-class women. Most were to be married, over thirty years of age, and college educated. The major distinction between pro- and anti-ERA supporters was church attendance. Surveys showed that 98 percent of anti-ERA activists claimed church membership.

Activist Phyllis Schlafly gives a speech against the passage of the Equal Rights Amendment on July 19, 1978 under the rotunda at the Illinois State Capitol. Other conservative women's groups joined STOP ERA, such as Women Who Want to Be Women and the Family Preservation League.

Schlafly self-consciously drew on traditional ideas of femininity to accomplish her political goals. To support the army of activists, Schlafly traveled and offered workshops on how to debate and testify at a public hearing and offered advice about what colors look good on television and how to be poised under pressure, as well as providing point-by-point rebuttals to ERA arguments. She emphasized that looking and acting feminine were political assets, and she encouraged local groups to send young and pretty women to win over state legislators. STOP ERA supporters, wearing dresses and heels, delivered homemade bread and pies to their legislators, many of whom they knew from their church and neighborhood communities. Such tactics were well suited to win over the middle-aged white male legislators who dominated the state legislatures. These were women that local politicians feared to alienate because they were not only well informed but also volunteered in political campaigns. They represented themselves as "typical" women and cast feminists as out of touch with the average U.S. woman. A letter sent to an Ohio state legislator underscored their use of traditional gender ideology: "We, the wives and working women need you, dear Senators and Representatives, to protect us. We think this is the man's responsibility, and we are dearly hoping you will vote NO on ERA."

By 1974, the STOP ERA campaign helped defeat ratification in seventeen state legislatures. Its success lay in its focus on local contests, a strategy the more nationally oriented pro-ERA movement did not share. In the key state of Illinois, STOP ERA had a coordinator in all fifty-nine districts, it passed out thousands of anti-ERA pamphlets, and supporters came to the state capital in carloads every week to lobby state legislators to vote against the Amendment. According to one local newspaper, the women came "to wage holy war against the Equal Rights Amendment. Neatly dressed teenage daughters with scrubbed faces and frilly blouses cried, "please don't draft me," while their mothers carried signs reading "Send the Libbers to Siberia. We'll Stay Home and Keep the Beds Warm." Such activism successfully defeated the ERA in Illinois.

By 1978, conservative women had demonstrated their power. Even with the endorsement of Democratic President Jimmy Carter, by 1978, a total of five states had overturned their previous votes ratifying the ERA. An intensive lobbying effort by ERA supporters resulted in a thirty-nine-month extension of the ratification deadline to June 1982, but conservatives had turned the tide against the Amendment, and it expired with three states short of the thirty-eight required for ratification.

The Pro-Family Movement

Conservative women mobilized to do more than defeat the ERA. In alliance with Evangelical ministers, Catholics, and Republican politicians, they formed a pro-family movement to challenge the liberal definitions of the family that had gained ground in the 1970s. Conservative activists defined the family as nuclear, comprising a heterosexual man and woman and their children. They dismissed other family configurations as unhealthy, particularly for children.

The pro-family movement grew out of a series of clashes between conservatives and feminists over the definition of the family. The first clash took place at the national conference for International Women's Year (IWY) held in Houston in 1977, a conference that signified just how far second-wave feminism had come and marked the start of a religious backlash against it. Twenty thousand people attended the conference, including notable feminists Bella Abzug and Barbara Jordan and three first ladies: Rosalyn Carter, Betty Ford, and Lady Bird Johnson. The IWY movement with its support of abortion rights and lesbian rights and a rejection of traditional gender roles proved to be a galvanizing event in the pro-family movement. Conservative women were so dismayed by the liberal orientation of the conference agenda that they organized a counterdemonstration, the Pro-Family Rally, in Houston for the same weekend. While it did not garner the same level of media attention as did the IWY, the Pro-Family Rally testified to the rising importance of religious values in U.S. political life. It also led to the establishment

Twenty thousand people attended the National Conference for International Women's Year, held in Houston in November 1977, including notable feminists Bella Abzug, Barbara Jordon, and three first ladies, Rosalyn Carter, Betty Ford, and Lady Bird Johnson. With the gathering's support of abortion rights, lesbian rights, and a rejection of traditional gender roles, it proved to be a galvanizing event for conservatives who staged a "Pro Family" counter demonstration.

of conservative women's political networks that monitored the impact governmental actions had on families as other political groups did for taxes and defense issues.

In 1978, President Carter organized a second conference, the White House Conference of Families, which again provided an impetus for conservative women to mobilize in defense of the traditional family. Conservatives viewed the conference's use of "families" in the plural instead of "the family" as indicating support for homosexual families. Beverly LaHaye, who founded Concerned Women for America (CWA) in 1979, explained, "Early in 1980 we saw that homosexuals were driving in, because they wanted to be part of the whole definition of the family. And we objected to that." Conservatives ultimately organized over three hundred pro-family groups into the American Family Forum to strengthen their collective voice.

Throughout the 1980s and 1990s, the pro-family movement expanded. In 1980, child psychologist James Dobson organized the Family Research Council, which became the premier pro-family research organization in Washington, D.C. The pro-family **Eagle Forum**, founded by Schlafly in 1972, boasted fifty thousand members in state chapters across the country. New organizations—including Teen-Aid, which focused on abstinence-only sex education curricula; the Liberty Counsel, which provided antiabortion legal services; and Morality in Media—brought further institutional force to the pro-family movement. The pro-family political groups and lobbies enjoyed a close relationship to President Reagan, whom they saw as sharing their social values. Their political power, nurtured through a growing infrastructure of

Eagle Forum Pro-family organization founded by Phyllis Schlafly in 1972.

think tanks and political action groups and articulated through conservative office holders, continued to grow. By 1997, the Christian Values in Action Coalition listed 1,450 organizations solely dedicated "to help individuals put into practice family building and marriage enrichment principles."

At the same time the pro-family movement grew, conservative women also began to target public education and issues of curriculum as areas for activism. Gaining seats on local school boards became a goal of organizations like the **Christian Coalition**, which held hundreds of training seminars across the country on how to win local offices. The Supreme Court's 1962 banning of officially sponsored prayer and Bible reading in public schools in *Engel v. Vitale* had earned the Court tremendous animosity from Evangelical Protestants and Catholic groups. The Court ruled on First Amendment grounds that prayer in public school violated the separation of church and state. Critics viewed the decision as a declaration of war against Christianity and complained that it put in the hands of school issues of morality that were the rightful purview of parents. Curricula also became an issue. In 1974, the first of many textbook battles began in Kanawha County, West Virginia, where Alice Moore, the wife of a fundamentalist minister, organized a group of parents against a textbook she saw as "obscene" and "anti-American." The West Virginia conflicts received national media coverage, extending their impact beyond the state. To avoid similar conflicts, many school boards and administrators refused to adopt any textbook containing any potentially controversial material. Libraries also felt pressure from religious groups who wanted books like J. D. Salinger's *The Catcher in the Rye* and Judy Blume's *Forever* banned from public libraries. The teaching of science was under attack as conservatives introduced the notion of intelligent design as an alternative account of evolution in the late 1990s.

Christian Coalition A group formed by Roman Catholic and Evangelical Protestants to influence Republican party politics.

Moral Panics and Culture Wars

Conservatives who were concerned with the health of the U.S. family and the secularism that many felt had weakened the United States' moral fiber turned to the media to spread their message. Mass media enabled key Evangelicals to reach huge audiences spread across the country. Religious broadcast stations, televangelists, and publishing houses worked with church groups and grassroots lobbyists to remake contemporary moral culture. The **culture wars** between conservatives and liberals reached a fevered pitch. *Focus on the Family*, the syndicated radio ministry headed by Dr. James Dobson, declared the 1990s "the Civil War Decade." He pointed to controversies over homosexual rights, abortion, and obscenity as the battles in which Christians would serve as "foot soldiers" in the war over values.

culture wars A set of clashes between conservative and liberal Americans over issues pertaining to private life.

Given the centrality of traditional gender roles and family strength, religious activists saw in feminism a multileveled assault on the foundation of Christian social order. Women of the religious Right understood feminism as a symptom of how far the country had fallen into the pathology of secular humanism, with its attention to individual and minority rights. Conservatives viewed changes in family life, women's workforce participation, teenage sexual promiscuity, and drug use as direct results of feminism's power to undermine families. According to Schlafly, "Women's liberationists operate as Typhoid Marys carrying a germ called lost identity. They try to persuade wives that they have missed something in life because they are known by their husband's name and play second fiddle to his career." Some of the most pointed attacks against feminism came from Beverly LaHaye's Concerned Women for America. Beverly LaHaye, the wife of one of the founders of the Moral Majority, Tim LaHaye, emphasized submission to God's plan, which, for women, included an acceptance of the authority God gave to men to lead women and families. She herself submitted to her religious calling when she formed CWA. "In January 1979, God opened the door to start Concerned Women for America. I only had plans to form this group in San Diego County where my church was, but God had other plans. He just blew His breath of blessing on it, and it grew like a prairie fire to other churches." Unlike Schlafly's Eagle Forum, CWA was more frankly evangelical, organizing prayer circles for its six hundred thousand members and calling for religious activists to become more politically involved. By the mid-1980s, CWA had a membership of five hundred thousand, far larger than that of NOW.

Homosexuality was another major source of political and moral mobilization by the Christian Right. In 1977, the antigay rights cause surged to the top of the Christian Right's political agenda when popular singer Anita Bryant led a successful fight to overturn a Miami, Florida, ordinance designed to end discrimination against homosexuals. Christian Right activists saw state ordinances like Miami's and bills passed in the 1980s to protect gay and lesbians from housing and employment discrimination as part of a growing movement to establish "special rights" for homosexuals and a strategy to force Americans to accept homosexuality as just as "natural" as heterosexuality. They launched their own local and state ballot initiatives to limit the extent of discrimination based on sexual orientation. In 1996, the Supreme Court ruled that discriminatory ballot initiatives limiting gay civil rights were unconstitutional.

The Acquired Immune Deficiency Syndrome (AIDS), first reported in 1981 and initially hitting the gay male community hardest, further intensified the conservative Right's antigay activism. In the face of the growing AIDS epidemic, Surgeon General Dr. C. Everett Koop proposed federal funding for AIDS education programs in schools. He faced stiff opposition from Senator Jesse Helms who attempted a series of unsuccessful antigay bills to ban federal funding for any sex-related public education, including for AIDS education, explaining that funding was tantamount to "promoting" homosexuality. Characterizing AIDS as a disease that only gay men contracted fueled Christian Right denunciations of homosexuality, with extremists charging homosexuals with deliberately spreading the virus.

Concern over "special rights" for homosexuals reached new heights when newly elected President Bill Clinton announced in 1992 his intention to lift the ban on openly gay military personnel. A wave of calls to the White House against lifting the ban, coupled with strong Congressional opposition, led Clinton to back off his promise. The result was a Congressional compromise of "Don't ask, don't tell" that was later amended to include "don't harass." The compromise dictated that the armed forces would no longer ask recruits about their sexual activity or orientation and self-identified homosexual servicemen and women would agree not to engage in homosexual acts or announce that they were homosexual. In 2007, the policy came under new scrutiny when twenty-eight retired generals called for a repeal of "don't ask, don't tell," citing data that showed that in 2006, sixty-five thousand gay men and lesbians served in the armed forces and that there were over one million gay veterans.

Gay marriage became another flash point. Building on networks established during years of antigay rights organizing, the New Christian Right mounted successful campaigns to limit marriage as a right for heterosexual couples only. In 1996, the National Campaign to Protect Marriage began. Its steering committee was made up of

Activists Phyllis Lyon and Del Martin, founders of the homophile group, Daughters of Bilitis, became the first same-sex couple to be married in San Francisco on February 12, 2004. In an open challenge to California law, city authorities performed at least 15 same-sex weddings and issued about a dozen more marriage licenses to gay and lesbian couples.

leaders from the American Family Association, the Family Research Council, and Concerned Women for America. Gay marriage became a centerpiece of the 1996 presidential campaign. President Clinton, whom many gay and lesbians saw as a potential ally, responded by endorsing the Defense of Marriage Act, which defined marriage as a relationship between one man and one woman and gave states the right to recognize or not recognize same-sex marriages performed in other states.

The issue of same-sex marriage, which would grant gay and lesbian couples the same rights and privileges as heterosexual couples, continued to divide the country, particularly in the wake of the 2000 election of George W. Bush. At stake were such matters as visiting a sick partner in the hospital, adoption of children, and spousal benefits. In 2004, Massachusetts recognized same-sex marriage. Connecticut, Vermont, New Jersey, California, and New Hampshire created legal unions that offered all the rights and responsibilities of marriage under state law to same-sex couples. At the same time, twenty-six states passed constitutional amendments explicitly barring the legal recognition of same-sex marriage. Forty-three states restrict marriage to two persons of the opposite sex. In 2006, Congress debated but declined to pass a proposed Federal Marriage Amendment, which would prohibit states from recognizing same-sex marriage.

Embattled Feminists

The majority of women who identified themselves as feminists found the change in the political climate of the country to be alarming. The defeat of the ERA in 1982 was seen by many as the first shot in the culture wars. On the defensive, feminists focused on the

Child Support Enforcement Amendments Act This act strengthened child support agencies' abilities to get money from the nonresidential parent of children on Aid to Families with Dependent Children (AFDC) for medical expenses and cost of living.

Retirement Equity Act Attempted to meet the needs of women in the work force and those women married to, or divorced from, working men by providing more benefits for surviving spouses, lowering the age for participation to 55, and granting the divorce spouse rights to retirement pension if stipulated in the separation papers.

worsening economic situation of working and poor women, a consequence of the growing number of single-female-headed households. The **Child Support Enforcement Amendments Act**, part of a retooling of the Social Security Act in 1975, strengthened child support agencies' abilities to get money from the nonresidential parent of children on Aid to Families with Dependent Children (AFDC) for medical expenses and cost of living. To help older women, feminists supported the **Retirement Equity Act** of 1984, which made it easier for divorced and widowed women to access their husbands' pensions and enabled more women to qualify for private retirement pensions.

Historic "firsts" for women continued throughout the 1980s despite the climate of backlash against feminism. Feminists watched with mixed feelings as Sandra Day O'Connor became the first female Supreme Court Justice in 1981. While many appreciated Reagan's commitment to appoint the Court's first female justice, many feminists worried that O'Conner had little sympathy with feminist goals and took note that her appointment came during a general decline in the number of women in high-level government positions. Her long career on the bench, however, demonstrated her commitment to upholding some of the gains women had made, particularly her defense of the controversial *Roe v. Wade*.

New York Representative Geraldine Ferraro became the first woman to run as vice president on a major political ticket in 1984 with Democratic candidate Walter Mondale. Ferraro enjoyed support of both Republican and Democratic women, many of

Historic "firsts" for women continued throughout the 1980s despite the climate of backlash against feminism. New York Representative Geraldine Ferraro became the first woman to run as vice president on a major political ticket in 1984 with Democratic candidate, Walter Mondale. Ferraro enjoyed support of both Republican and Democratic women, many of whom admired her three terms in the House of Representatives.

WOMEN'S LIVES

SANDRA DAY O'CONNOR

Sandra Day O'Connor, the first female justice to sit on the Supreme Court, served from 1981 to 2006. She was appointed by Republican President Ronald Reagan, whose commitment to appoint a woman to the Court threatened to clash with his commitment to his conservative and antiabortion supporters, many of whom felt O'Connor was too liberal on abortion. O'Connor's judicial independence won out, winning her the ire of conservatives and reluctant support from abortion supporters who, by the late 1990s, viewed her as the crucial swing vote in any case that might overturn *Roe v. Wade*. O'Connor's position on the Court made *Ladies Home Journal* select her as the most powerful woman in the United States in 2001, after Oprah Winfrey.

Sandra Day was born on a cattle ranch outside of El Paso, Texas, in 1930. The ranch was twenty-five miles from the nearest town, and she lived without running water or electricity until she was seven years old. By then, she was roping, riding, and repairing fences with the cowboys, and she knew how to shoot a gun and steer a pickup. Even though she lived on a ranch, her favorite activity was reading. Her parents sent her to live with her grandparents in the Texas city of El Paso. She skipped several grades and graduated high school at sixteen. O'Connor graduated from Stanford University in 1950 and went to the Stanford Law School where she finished at the top of her class. In 1952, she met and married fellow law school student, John Jay O'Connor III. Their first child, Scott, was born in 1957. Two more sons joined the family in 1960 and 1962. No law firm in California would hire her as a lawyer, but one firm offered her a job as a legal secretary. She turned to public service, holding a number of positions, including assistant attorney general of Arizona from 1965 to 1969. O'Connor entered politics at this point, winning

appointment to the Arizona State Senate in 1969. In 1973, she became majority leader, the first woman to serve as majority leader of a state senate. In 1975, O'Connor left politics for the bench when she was elected judge of the Maricopa County Superior Court; four years later, she was elected to the Arizona Court of Appeals.

Ronald Reagan made good on his election pledge to appoint the first woman to the Supreme Court and nominated O'Connor, whom the Congress confirmed unanimously in September 1981. In her first year on the Court, O'Connor received over sixty thousand letters from the public, more than any other justice had received.

O'Connor approached the cases she ruled on as narrowly as possible, avoiding setting precedents

(continued)

that might limit the Court in the future. In the early years of her tenure, when the Court was more liberal, she formed part of the conservative axis; but by the 1990s, she was regarded as a centrist as the Court moved to the Right.

O'Connor ruled on the significant abortion rights cases that moved through the courts during the 1980s and 1990s. In 1989, she ruled with the majority on *Webster v. Reproductive Health Services*, which allowed states more powers to regulate abortion, but wrote a concurring opinion in which she refused to explicitly overturn *Roe v. Wade*. In the 1992 *Planned Parenthood v. Casey*, O'Connor's opinion introduced a new test that reined in the unrestricted freedom from regulation during the first trimester as established in *Roe*. Whereas before the regulatory powers of the State could not intervene so early in the pregnancy, O'Connor openly allowed that a State could enact measures so long as they did not place an "undue burden" on a woman's right to an abortion.

O'Connor retired from the Court in 2005 and is currently the Chancellor of the College of William and Mary. O'Connor has written two memoirs: the first, in 2002, *Lazy B: Growing Up on a Cattle Ranch in the American Southwest*, about her childhood; and *The Majesty of the Law: Reflections of a Supreme Court Justice* in 2003. ■

whom reported admiring her for her three terms in the House of Representatives. Yet, even with such endorsement, most women voted to return Reagan and his vice president, George H. W. Bush, to office. Some conservatives found Ferraro's candidacy offensive. After a preelection vice-presidential debate, the press asked Bush's wife Barbara what she thought of Ferraro. Barbara Bush responded that the word she was thinking of rhymed with "rich." The scandal that broke out, even after Bush called Ferraro to apologize, captured the waging ideological war over the proper place of women.

Feminists had successes, despite the conservative turn of the country. Some major accomplishments were in the area of rape law, funding for battered women's shelters, and new protections against sexual harassment. In the late 1970s, feminists succeeded in changing the rules of evidence and corroboration in rape cases, making it illegal to bring up a woman's sexual past in a rape trial. Laws were rewritten to cover men who were victims of rape. By the 1980s, concern over date rape on college campuses resulted in special programs to teach men and women about coercion and violence and to combat the commonly held view that there was nothing wrong with a man using a little force to get what he wanted. "Take back the night" marches, in which young women marched at night to demand their rights to be safe from rape and from sexual violence, became yearly rituals on many college campuses. Laws on wife rape changed as well. In 1980, thirteen states had laws in which a man could not be charged with raping a woman if they were living together, even if they were not married. By 1991, only five states still had such laws. Despite feminists' success in redefining marital rape as rape, thirty-three states continue to view it as a lesser crime.

Conservatives and feminists found themselves at odds over how best to help women. On some issues, such as the antipornography movement, conservatives and feminists were allies, brought together by their concern over violent and sexual images of women. Feminist activist Andrea Dworkin and feminist legal scholar Catharine MacKinnon found support from the New Christian Right in their efforts to regulate pornography. Likewise, concern with the health of families often brought feminists into alliance with conservatives. In 1984, Congress passed the **Family Violence Prevention and Services Act,** which provided funds for shelters and family violence programs. By 1991, approximately sixteen hundred battered women's shelters, "safe" homes, hotlines, and advocacy projects existed. Despite the growth in programs, shelters were forced to turn away 40 percent of the women who contacted them. Yet, on other issues, conservatives and feminists clashed. One such conflict was the confirmation hearings in October 1991 for Clarence Thomas when one of his former employees at the Equal Employment Opportunity Commission, Anita Hill, accused him of sexual harassment. The dramatic hearings, filled with stories of ordinary and sexist behavior at work, brought this issue to national attention. Conservative supporters of Thomas viewed Hill's testimony as feminism gone awry, whereas feminists saw Hill as a victim of unwanted sexual attention and did all they could to block Thomas's appointment to the Court. Despite their efforts, Thomas took a seat on the bench in 1991.

The clash between conservatives and feminists centered on heated debates over the proper place of women. Women's professional aspirations and their needs to contribute to the financial health of their families were acknowledged by both sides of the culture war. The areas of disagreement centered on women's obligations to the family. According to conservatives, women's roles as wife and mother, as helpmate and partner to her husband and children, were sacred obligations. For feminists, women's private lives and autonomy were sacred and decisions about private life were best left to individual women to decide. No issue captured the culture wars more than abortion, with its ties to both female sexual freedom and women's role as mother.

Family Violence Prevention and Services Act The 1984 Act provided funds for shelters and family violence programs.

OVERVIEW

Abortion Rights Time Line

1973	January 22	The U.S. Supreme Court issues its ruling in *Roe v. Wade*, finding that a "right of privacy" it had earlier discovered was "broad enough to encompass" a right to abortion and adopting a trimester scheme of pregnancy. In the first trimester, a state could enact virtually no regulation. In the second trimester, the state could enact some regulation but only for the purpose of protecting maternal "health." In the third trimester, after viability, a state could ostensibly "proscribe" abortion, provided it made exceptions to preserve the life and "health" of the woman seeking abortion. Issued on the same day, *Doe v. Bolton* defines "health" to mean "all factors" that affect the woman, including physical, emotional, psychological, and familial factors and the woman's
1975	March 10	The first Human Life Amendment is introduced in the U.S. Senate by Senators James L. Buckley (Conservative, New York) and Jesse Helms (Republican, North Carolina).
1976	June 28	The first Hyde Amendment, sponsored by Representative Henry Hyde (Republican, Illinois), is approved by the U.S. House. The Amendment to the Department of Health and Human Services appropriations bill prohibits Medicaid funding of abortions with narrow exceptions.

(continued)

1977	June 20	In *Maher v. Roe*, *Beal v. Doe*, and *Poelker v. Doe*, the U.S. Supreme Court holds that federal and state governments are under no obligation to fund abortion in public assistance programs, even if childbirth expenses are paid for indigent women and even if the abortion is deemed to be "medically necessary."
1981	March 23	In *H. L. v. Matheson*, the U.S. Supreme Court approves a Utah parental-notification law. The law requires an abortionist to notify the parents of a minor girl who is still living at home as her parents' dependent when an abortion is scheduled.
1989	July 3	In *Webster v. Reproductive Health Services*, the U.S. Supreme Court, upholding portions of a Missouri law, finds that the federal Constitution does not require government to make public facilities such as hospitals available for use in performing abortions.
1990	June 25	In *Ohio v. Akron Center for Reproductive Health*, the U.S. Supreme Court upholds a one-parent-notification requirement with a judicial bypass procedure. The Court also rules, in *Hodgson v. Minnesota*, that a two-parent-notification law with a judicial bypass is Constitutional.
1991	May 23	In *Rust v. Sullivan*, the U.S. Supreme Court upholds the Bush administration's regulations that prohibit routine counseling and referral for abortion in four thousand clinics that receive federal Title X family planning funds. (In November, President Bush vetoes a $205 billion Health and Human Services appropriations bill because it includes a provision that would have blocked enforcement of the pro-life regulations; the veto is sustained by a twelve-vote margin.)
1992	June 29	In *Planned Parenthood v. Casey*, the U.S. Supreme Court reaffirms the core holdings of *Roe* but modifies it by discarding the trimester scheme, upholding certain restrictions on abortion, and adopting the "undue burden" test of abortion laws that requires opponents of an abortion regulation to prove the provision would create an "undue burden" on a woman's right to abortion in order for it to be declared unconstitutional. The vote is 6 to 3.
1994	June 30	In *Madsen v. Women's Health Center Inc.*, the U.S. Supreme Court says judges may create buffer zones to keep pro-life demonstrators away from abortion clinics.
2000	June 28	*Stenberg v. Carhart* rules that the Nebraska statute banning so-called "partial-birth abortion" is unconstitutional for two independent reasons: the statute lacks the necessary exception for preserving the health of the woman, and the definition of the targeted procedures is so broad as to prohibit abortions in the second trimester, thereby being an "undue burden" on women. This effectively invalidates twenty-nine of thirty-one similar statewide bans.
2000	September 28	Food and Drug Administration approves mifepristone (RU-486) as an option in abortion care for very early pregnancy.
2007	April 18	*Gonzales v. Carhart* and *Gonzales v. Planned Parenthood* upheld the Partial Birth Abortion Ban Act of 2003.

The Antiabortion Movement

Conservatives and many in the New Christian Right equated feminism with self-gratification and freeing women from their family obligations. Within this framework, they cast abortion as the ultimate selfish act. When the Court removed all existing legal barriers to abortion in the United States in its 1973 *Roe v. Wade* decision, the United States had the most lenient abortion laws of any non-Communist country in the Western world. While individual states and physicians could impose restrictions on late-term abortions, the Court did not. The historic ruling launched one of the most heated and controversial debates of the twentieth century.

Immediately following the *Roe* decision, conservatives drafted the Human Life Amendment defining life as beginning from the moment of fertilization. Yet, the measure met with little success. Antiabortionists adopted a new tactic in the mid-1970s to restrict abortion in any way they could, chipping away at the freedoms *Roe* established. In 1976, Congress passed the **Hyde Amendment**, which reframed the government's responsibility to offer abortion services. Although the Amendment did not directly challenge a woman's right to an abortion, the Amendment asserted that the government was under no obligation to ensure a woman's access to the procedure. The Hyde Amendment also restricted abortion from the comprehensive health care provided by Medicaid. By the early 1980s, Congress had passed similar restrictions affecting programs on which an estimated twenty million women relied for their health care or insurance. In 1984, the United States announced that it would no longer contribute to international family planning agencies that provided abortions or counseled women to have abortions.

Hyde Amendment A 1976 law that reframed the government's responsibility to offer abortion services and restricted abortion from the health care provided by Medicaid.

Right-to-life groups pressured state legislatures to write more restrictions on abortion into their laws. During the 1970s and 1980s, state laws were passed that decreed a woman must have her husband's permission to get an abortion and others mandated that she must sign a consent form twenty-four hours before getting the procedure. Some statutes said the doctor must show the woman photographs of fetuses before performing an abortion. Legislators focused on teenage women; and in more and more states, minors could not have an abortion without the consent of one or both parents. By 1991, seventeen states had some form of required parental notification or consent laws.

Antiabortion activists, emboldened by a growing alliance between Catholics and Evangelicals, become more extreme in the 1980s. The Roman Catholic Church organized the first antiabortion demonstrations after the *Roe* ruling and sponsored the formation of the National

No issue captured the culture wars more than abortion, with its ties to both female sexual freedom and women's role as mothers. The anniversary of the Supreme Court ruling, Roe v. Wade, was often a time when opposing sides met, as they did here, in front of the Supreme Court in 1993.

Right to Life Committee, which had a membership of eleven million when Reagan took office. In 1984, right-to-life extremists targeted abortion clinics and service providers as a way to limit access to abortion services, resulting in twenty-four bombings and arson attacks on abortion and birth-control facilities. Eighteen clinic directors received death threats. In 1988, militants Joe Scheidler of the Pro-Life Action League and Randy Terry started Operation Rescue (OR). They led demonstrations in which activists blockaded clinics, refusing to leave and provoking their arrest. Chaotic and frequently violent dramas took place in front of clinics. Antiabortion activists carried posters of bloody fetuses and shouted at the women entering the clinics to save their unborn children. Once arrested, they refused to give their names, forcing the city to jail them. Such civil disobedience tactics were effective. By the end of 1988, nearly 9,500 arrests had been made, involving two thousand activists. Eleven thousand people had participated in clinic "rescues." Under this assault, abortion clinics struggled to find funding or insurance and doctors willing to work under such threatening and dangerous conditions. Law enforcement officials estimated that by 1990 abortion clinics had experienced eight bombings, twenty-eight attempted bombings or arson, and 170 acts of vandalism. Pro-choice activists described the weekly target of picketing and vandalism as "terrible, just awful . . . sometimes there were as many as 150 picketers, and they would be . . . right up against the front door . . . in people's faces, screaming and yelling." By the early 1990s, criticism over OR's tactics led to a decline in clinic blockades and civil disobedience by antiabortion activists. However, attacks on abortion providers continued. In 1993, a doctor was shot to death outside a Pensacola, Florida, abortion clinic. Over the next five years, snipers shot twelve abortion providers and clinic employees, killing six, in incidents in Florida, New York, Alabama, and Massachusetts.

Creating legal restrictions on abortion, without outrightly overturning *Roe*, continued as a viable strategy for antiabortion activists. In 1989, the Supreme Court ruled in *Webster v. Reproductive Health Services* to uphold restrictions on the use of state funds in performing, assisting with, or counseling on abortion, including the use of facilities and the work of paid staff. The decision allowed states to regulate an area that had been previously thought to be forbidden under *Roe*. Abortion supporters hoped that the restrictions imposed by *Webster* might rouse the large numbers of Americans who supported a woman's right to obtain an abortion—or who found that the government had no role in deciding such matters—to action. California Representative Barbara Boxer, who led the abortion right forces in the House, warned that the Court might have gone too far and "awakened a sleeping giant." Her hope that feminist forces might gather enough strength to check the influence of the antiabortion movement were dashed when two years later, in *Planned Parenthood v. Casey*, the Court upheld the "informed consent" rule that required doctors to provide women with information about the health risks and possible complications of having an abortion before one could be performed. The Court also upheld Pennsylvania's parental consent rule for minors and its rule requiring a twenty-four-hour waiting period before obtaining an abortion, holding that none of these rules constituted an undue burden on the woman seeking the procedure. The case also overturned the strict trimester formula used in *Roe* to weigh the woman's interest in obtaining an abortion against the State's interest in the life of the fetus. Continuing advancements in medical technology meant that at the time *Casey* was decided, a fetus might be considered viable at twenty-two or twenty-three weeks rather than at the twenty-eight weeks that was more common at the time of *Roe*. The Court recognized viability as the point at which the State's interest in the life of the fetus outweighed the rights of the woman and abortion could be banned entirely. The antiabortion movement's ability to popularize a view of the fetus as a human and abortion as murder proved politically effective. In 2006, South Dakota passed a law outlawing all abortion except to save the mother's life, the most restrictive antiabortion law since the passage of *Roe*. Even supporters of a woman's right to abortion have adapted their rhetoric to deal with the moral issues raised when the fetus is granted rights as a human. Since 2005, pro-choice groups have added the new goal of bringing down the number of abortions performed annually.

Changes in the organization of families and in gender roles had multiple roots, including the growing number of women in the paid labor force and the decline in the family wage earned by the fully employed father. Economic changes, particularly the growing interdependence of the global economy, coupled with the social revolutions of feminism and gay liberation, left Christian conservatives concerned that the fabric of the nation had been torn. Morality and religious values were bulwarks against the threats that these social changes posed for such families. Women played crucial roles in the leadership of the Christian Right's social protest movements as well as in the grassroots organization that brought the conservative movement into political ascendancy and an end to second-wave feminism.

WORK AND FAMILY IN THE 1990S

At the end of the century, balancing work and family remained a pressing issue for women. The backlash against feminism culminated in the dismantling of the welfare state by both Republican and Democratic administrations. Many woman found that they had to take time away from work to care for infants or elders, and many hoped to resume work after a few years at home. However, the reality of the job market made those plans difficult to achieve for many women. They found it hard to find comparable jobs to those they left, or they returned to find themselves disqualified for promotion or for higher-level work. At the same time, the gender pay gap meant that after a decade of advancements, women faced worsening economic conditions. Throughout, working women pressed for changes in work and welfare that would enable them to reconcile work and family.

Work and Welfare

"Government is not the solution. Government is the problem," announced President Ronald Reagan in his 1981 inauguration speech. Reagan rode to office on the wave of hostility toward and dismay at the size and influence of the federal government. Reaganomics, as it was immediately dubbed, gave private entrepreneurs and investors greater incentives to take risks and start new business as a way to improve the overall economic health of the nation. Reagan passed deep budget cuts in a range of antipoverty programs and welfare benefits begun in the 1960s by President Johnson's War on Poverty, including housing subsidies, child nutrition programs, food stamps, public assistance, student loans, low-income energy assistance, and Medicaid payments to the states. Although such programs made up less than 10 percent of the total federal budget in 1980, they absorbed one-third of Reagan's budget cuts. The cuts fell on women and racial minorities especially hard. The average black family lost three times as much in cash and noncash benefits as did the average white family. Despite the impact on children of such cuts, the Reagan administration focused on the image of the bad welfare mother who abused government help to justify welfare cuts. In a speech delivered in the 1980s, Reagan cited a Chicago "Welfare Queen" who had ripped off $150,000 from the government, using eighty aliases, thirty addresses, a dozen Social Security cards, and four fictional dead husbands. The "Welfare Queen" driving her "Welfare Cadillac" came to symbolize welfare cheats and the pitfalls of public assistance. Reagan had campaigned on a promise to dismantle the New Deal welfare state and followed through by consolidating seventy-seven federal programs into nine new block grants to be distributed by states. States assumed control over distributing federal funds. Women active in the welfare rights movement complained about this new funding structure because it left poor women vulnerable to the political whims of their state governments.

The U.S. economy was in transition, driven by the intensifying forces of economic globalization and the deindustrialization of the United States. Changes in the international economy forced firms to switch from mass production to a new tactic known as *flexible specialization*. The oil crisis of 1973; increased competition from foreign markets, especially Southeast Asia, from globalization; and the end of the post–World War II affluence made the old system of mass producing identical, cheap goods no longer competitive. Companies diversified their product lines, trying to target different groups of consumers with different products. Firms established labor practices that could quickly respond to changes in the market, resulting in lay offs, plant closings, and outsourcing. Companies saved money by laying off workers. Those who kept their jobs saw that their incomes did not keep pace with the rising costs of goods and services. By the 1990s, the shift from an economy based on manufacturing to one centered around technological innovation, information management, and service was firmly in place.

The structural changes in the economy created a gap between rich and poor, and more families—particularly, female-headed families—fell into poverty. Deindustrialization shifted work away from historically higher-paying and male-dominated industrial work to service sector work. The new jobs created tended to be clustered in low-paying service sectors, in which women and minorities were overrepresented. With no job security, no benefits, and low wages, service sector work left many unable to make ends meet. The poverty rate jumped from 11 percent of the population in 1979 to 14.5 percent in 1992, with nearly 22 percent of all U.S. children under the age of eighteen living in poverty. Black and Hispanic women were particularly hard hit, intensifying the feminization of poverty that had begun earlier (see chapter 21). In 1992, 33 percent of all African Americans and 29 percent of Hispanics lived in poverty.

The mushrooming numbers of Americans in poverty took place alongside a surge in consumer spending of the upper and middle classes. Most families enjoyed VCRs, televisions, personal computers, cell phones, and the growing number of inexpensive products that filled new supersized stores. Stores like Wal-Mart thrived in the shifting winds of consumerism and poverty. Sam Walton, founder of Wal-Mart, opened his first store in 1962; twenty-five years later, in 1987, there were nearly two thousand Wal-Marts nationwide. By 1995, sales reached $93.6 billion. Women with little resources to spend on food and clothes flocked to the store, while thousands of others took low-paying jobs at the huge retailer. The low wages earned doing service work made staying off welfare difficult. Service jobs were plentiful but did not offer health insurance or child-care leave and thus provided little help for most women struggling to support their families. Forty-six percent of the jobs with the most growth since 1994 paid less than sixteen thousand dollars a year.

Cuts in welfare continued, enacted not only by conservatives critical of creating a permanent caste of people in the United States who depended on government relief but also by "new" Democrats like Bill Clinton, elected in 1992. In 1996, President Clinton signed the **Personal Responsibility and Work Opportunity Act**, ending sixty years of guaranteed federal aid to poor Americans, 80 percent of which were women and children. He also did away with the Aid to Families with Dependent Children, a program started under Franklin D. Roosevelt in 1933. In its place, a new program called Temporary Assistance to Needy Families (TANF) was established. Under the new law, poor families received aid for two consecutive years, with a total limit of five years. States received bonuses for significantly reducing their public-assistance rolls and lowering rates of illegitimacy. States could be penalized if they did not enforce the rule that mothers receiving aid work a minimum of twenty hours monthly. "Welfare reform helped to move 4.7 million Americans from welfare dependency to self-sufficiency within three years of enactment," announced a White House fact sheet in 1996. The law required that poor single mothers take any job available to them, even when most of the jobs offered them none of the benefits that welfare brought them, such as health care and housing help. To help keep families off welfare, Hillary Rodham Clinton, along with Massachusetts Senator Ted Kennedy, spearheaded the passing of the **State Children's Health Insurance Program (SCHIP)** in 1997. The program proved health insurance for families who earned too much to qualify for Medicare yet who could not afford the high cost of private health insurance. At its creation, it became the largest expansion of health insurance coverage since Medicaid began. In 2006, the program served 6.9 million children.

Getting off welfare did not translate into getting out of poverty. A 2003 report by the Congressional Budget Office found that even as TANF shrank, other federal benefit programs—like the earned income tax credit (EITC), food stamps, Medicaid, and Supplemental Security Income (SSI)—swelled. Republican George W. Bush, elected in 2000, continued to cut welfare programs as part of his tax cut programs. A new Child Support Enforcement Amendment passed in 2000 directed much of money collected from noncustodial parents to the federal and state governments to repay the costs of welfare, making it harder for single parents, many of which were women, to stay off welfare. As states moved more families off welfare to qualify for federal funds, more U.S. families struggled with homelessness, hunger, and poverty. In 2003, 12.4 percent of all people in the United States—almost thirty-five million people—lived under the federal poverty rate, which included 12.2 million children.

Personal Responsibility and Work Opportunity Act Passed in 1996, the Act ended welfare as an entitlement program.

State Children's Health Insurance Program (SCHIP) Established in 1997 to provide health insurance for families who earned too much to qualify for Medicare.

Gender Gaps

At the end of the twentieth century, women of all classes and races struggled to reconcile wage work and family. As more women entered the workforce or found that their state governments required them to work forty hours a week for welfare support, they found themselves pulled between the competing demands of family and work. Sick children, needy elders, and the rising costs of child care left women vulnerable to being fired, demoted, or passed over for advancement at work.

WOMEN'S LIVES

HILLARY RODHAM CLINTON

Few women have experienced firsthand the dramatic transformation in women's role in politics than Hillary Rodham Clinton. From her days as a young Republican at a small northeastern liberal college to those as the first First Lady to head a failed presidential health care task force and as the first woman to be a serious contender for president from a major political party, Rodham Clinton has been at the center of many culture wars. So complex have been the reactions she provoked that a *New York Times* reporter once referred to her as "a Rorschach test." However people in the United States view Hillary Rodham Clinton, she has carried throughout her long career the weight of a larger national debate about women and power.

Hillary Rodham was born on October 26, 1947, in Chicago, Illinois, and attended Wellesley College. Raised in a politically conservative home, Rodham brought her Republican loyalties to college and supported Republican Barry Goldwater in the 1964 election against Democrat Lyndon B. Johnson. Yet, as Rodham's political education continued, she grew critical of the U.S. involvement in the Vietnam War and what she saw as the Republican Party's inaction on pressing social issues like poverty and racism. In 1968, she joined the Democratic Party. After graduating from Wellesley College in 1969, Rodham entered Yale Law School. She met fellow law student Bill Clinton in 1971. In 1973, Rodham became a staff attorney for the Children's Defense Fund. A year later, she was recruited by the Impeachment Inquiry staff of the Judiciary Committee of the U.S. House of Representatives to work on the Watergate Impeachment proceedings against President Richard Nixon. She married Bill Clinton in 1975. The couple taught together on the law faculty of the University of Arkansas at Fayetteville, where Hillary Clinton was only the

second woman to serve on the law faculty. The couple had a daughter, Chelsea, in 1980. The family moved to Little Rock, Arkansas, in 1978 when Bill Clinton became governor.

During Bill Clinton's presidential bid in 1992, Rodham Clinton proved herself an effective strategist and key advisor. Hillary Rodham Clinton actively campaigned for her husband and, once he was elected, reshaped the role of First Lady into that of first advisor. Clinton engendered a national debate over the power and influence of wives in political life. In Arkansas, her involvement in her husband's administration had not been behind the scenes characteristic of political wives, but rather, she had served as a visible political partner. At the White House, she participated in cabinet appointment decisions and attended cabinet meetings. Her office was in the West Wing, near the Oval Office, rather than in the traditional office of the First Lady in the East Wing.

One of the first political tasks President Clinton assigned to his wife was to head the Health Care Task Force to come up with a comprehensive plan to provide universal health care for all Americans. The result, announced by President Clinton in an address to the U.S. Congress on September 22, 1993, was a complicated proposal that included a mandate for employers to provide health insurance coverage to all of their employees through competitive but closely regulated Health Maintenance Organizations (HMOs). The proposal proved to be controversial. Critics, many of whom were bothered both by the plan's details and by the fact that Hillary Rodham Clinton headed the task force, deemed it unworkable. The president abandoned the proposal, known as "Hillarycare" by its opponents, in 1994. Rodham Clinton turned her attention to an array of issues, including findings to

investigate the little-studied illness known as the Gulf War syndrome, helped to create the Office on Violence against Women at the Department of Justice, and worked closely with Massachusetts Senator Ted Kennedy to implement the State Children's Health Insurance Program in 1997 to provide health insurance to families who earn too much to qualify for Medicare yet who cannot afford to buy private health insurance.

In 2000, and while she was First Lady, Rodham Clinton successfully ran for the U.S. Senate from New York and easily won reelection in 2006. As a high-profile senator, Rodham Clinton moved easily between representing New York and representing the Democratic Party, particularly in the wake of the September 11, 2001, attack of the World Trade Center and as the country turned less and less supportive of the Iraq War. She announced her bid for president in 2007 and adopted "Hillary Clinton" as her title. The public and the press continue to debate her bid to be president, given the strong reaction she provokes. ∎

To ease the burden on working families, President Clinton signed the **Family and Medical Leave Act (FMLA)** in 1993. The Act provided twelve weeks of unpaid family leave for workers to care for a sick family member, bond with a new baby, or recover from their own illness without losing their jobs or health insurance. While millions of Americans took advantage of job-protected leave after the law was passed, nearly half of the nation's private-sector employees were not covered by the FMLA in 2000 because they worked part time or for businesses with fewer than fifty employees. Nearly half of all workers had no paid sick leave. For those women who qualified, the FMLA gave them one more bridge to span the gender gap at work, enabling more women to take time out without fear of losing their jobs.

While women's participation in the labor force rose from 43 percent of all women in 1970 to 60 percent by 2000, women still earned less than men. In 2000, women earned seventy-seven cents to a man's dollar, a gap that widened as women had children. When women entered the workforce, they earned almost as much as men, eighty-seven cents to a man's dollar for women between the ages of twenty-five and twenty-nine. But when they had children, women fell behind. By the time women reached their forties, they earned seventy-one cents to a man's dollar. Economists

Family and Medical Leave Act (FMLA) Passed in 1993, the Act provided twelve weeks of unpaid family leave for workers.

described this as a "motherhood penalty" that stemmed in part from discrimination and in part from interruptions in a woman's work life. Women interrupted their work lives more frequently than did men by taking time off, cutting back on hours, or taking advantage of parental-leave policies—all of which came with economic costs. Interruptions in women's careers accounted for up to a third of the gender pay gap. One study found that before childbearing, the wages of highly skilled mothers and non-mothers were not significantly different but highly skilled women experienced an 8 percent reduction in their wages during the first five years after they had a child compared to childless women. After ten years, it rose to 20 percent, even after taking into account any reduction in mothers' working hours. The motherhood penalty fell heavier on women with a high-school diploma than on women with a college degree.

Facing such difficulties, many women opted to stay home. A survey of three Harvard Business School graduating classes found that only 38 percent of women ended up in full-time careers. A broader study found that a third of white women with MBAs opted not to work. A Hunter College sociologist found in 2002 that many professional women gave work-related reasons—such as being placed on "the mommy track" with poor assignments and a lack of advancement opportunities once they became mothers—as the reasons they left work for parenting. One civil engineer in Pennsylvania was awarded three million dollars in a lawsuit because she was passed over for promotion after the birth of her son. She testified that the president of the company asked her, "Do you want to have babies or do you want a career here?" For other women, the combination of male chauvinism at work and strains on their family from two full-time working parents motivated them to leave. The director of admissions of the prestigious Wharton School of the University of Pennsylvania explained that some companies tried to stem the loss of talented women in their thirties. "It's hard to work for four years, go to business school, spend three years slaving away in an investment bank or consulting firm and then try to leave to start a family. They haven't achieved the seniority they need at that point." The so-called "opt-out" revolution of elite women who chose to stay home and parent over their careers masked a far more complex reality.

glass ceiling A term that refers to situations in which the advancement of a qualified person stops at a particular level because of some form of discrimination, most commonly sexism or racism.

For women who stayed in the professions, the ongoing reality of the **glass ceiling** kept many from reaching full equity with their male peers. Despite the increasing number of female MBAs graduating from top business schools, in 2005 only 16 percent of corporate officers at Fortune 500 companies were women. Women only fill nine, or less than 2 percent, of the chief executive jobs at those same companies. "There have been women in the pipeline for 20 to 25 years; progress has been slower than anybody thought it ever would be," said one leader of an executive search firm. The low number of female chief executive officers was often the result of women leaving work for family, a lack of networking or mentoring programs, and the tendency for women to end up in dead-end positions. According to a 2005 study by Catalyst, an organization that studies women in the workplace, women were almost two and one half times as likely to be channeled into jobs like human relations and communications than into operating roles where they would be generating revenue and managing profit and loss.

Choices made by employees rather than employers also explain promotion and pay differences. While 40 percent of medical graduates are women, many in 2006 opted to specialize in fields in which the pay is lower, such as dermatology, family medicine, and pediatrics. High-paying specialties remain dominated by men. Only 10 percent of orthopedic surgery residents and 28 percent of radiology residents in 2004 were women, according to the Association of American Medical Colleges. In 2005, the pay gap was widest among highly paid workers. In the nation's highest earners, such as in Wall Street, hedge funds, and technology, the top jobs are overwhelmingly held by men. In 2005, a woman making more than 95 percent of all other women earned the equivalent of thirty-six dollars an hour. A man making more than 95 percent of all other men, putting in the same hours, earned 28 percent more.

Caring for the Elderly

As people in the United States live longer and live with chronic illnesses longer, elder care has become a critical issue facing women. In another era, the task of caring for elderly parents often fell to the unmarried daughter who never left home and never worked for a living. With more women working outside the home, families have struggled to care for their older members. According to a recent study by the National Alliance for Caregiving and the American Association of Retired Persons (AARP), more than twenty-two million U.S. households—one in four—provided informal, unpaid care to a friend or relative over age fifty in 1996.

Women bore a disproportionate burden for elder care and often left jobs, either temporarily or permanently, when the double duty became overwhelming. The Business and Professional Women's Foundation reported in 1997 that women were out of the workforce approximately eleven years over the course of their working lives, primarily because

Cuts in welfare and Medicare in the 1980s and 1990s left many women without adequate health care. As Americans live longer and live with chronic illnesses longer, elder care became a critical issue facing women. The American Association of Retired Persons (AARP) reported that more than 22 million U.S. households—one in four—provided informal, unpaid care to a friend or relative over 50 in 1996.

of caregiving responsibilities, while men were out of the workforce only sixteen months. Despite a growing number of men helping aging relatives, women accounted for 71 percent of those devoting forty or more hours a week to the task, according to a 2004 study. "It is a safe assumption that women are more likely to put their careers on hold or end them because of caregiving responsibilities," said Carol Levine, director of the Families and Health Care Project at the United Hospital Fund and an adviser to the National Alliance for Caregiving.

Poverty among older Americans has fallen disproportionately on women. Differences between men and women in life expectancy, living arrangements, and work patterns contribute to higher rates of poverty for older women. At age 65, women can anticipate living twenty years more and men seventeen years. Women entered retirement with fewer resources then men, requiring them to spread a smaller income over a longer period of time. Changes in marriage patterns, specifically the trend away from marriage, have led to a growing number of women living alone in old age. Such circumstances have led women to be more dependent on Social Security after retirement and vulnerable to falling into poverty. In 2003, 3.4 million Americans age 65 and older lived in poverty, and 71 percent of them were women. Older minority women were more likely to be in poverty than their white peers.

The complexity of balancing women's work and family responsibilities and the conservatism of the turn of the twenty-first century led to a contentious public discussion on the meaning of motherhood. Prominent coverage of elite women who "opt out" of their professions to stay home with their young children underscored the message that what women really wanted was to return to a simpler age when women cared for children and left wage earning to the men. According to these reports, feminism misled a generation of women to think they could be superwomen. In reality, what women discovered was that they were overworked and overwhelmed. Poor women found little support for their desires to parent their children. Changes in welfare forced mothers of young children to work without first providing sufficient and adequate child care. Making all ends meet, at home and at work, continued to be a source of creativity, activism, and struggle for U.S. women.

GLOBAL AMERICA

At the beginning of the twenty-first century, U.S. women experienced a number of historic transformations. The powerful effects of economic globalization, rising rates of immigration, and the revolution in communication connected women to friends, families, and strangers around the globe. In the past, globalization had been associated with the expansion of U.S. business and culture to other countries. After 1990, U.S. women experienced globalization within their own local communities. A surge of immigration, twenty million immigrants between 1980 and 2005, remade the population. In 2006, more than one in every ten Americans was foreign-born. American women also felt the effects of globalization in the kinds of work they did and the wages they received. Educated women of all races fared better than their less-educated peers in the information-driven job market, resulting in a widening gap between rich and poor women. Terrorism, war, and ongoing violence against women at home and abroad, as well as the speed by which information traveled, fostered a global women's movement that raised women's health and safety as pressing human rights issues.

New Faces, New Families

The tightening economic connections between nations and the relative health of the U.S. economy in the 1990s drew millions of people to the United States, fundamentally changing the ethnic and racial makeup of the country. The 2000 census reported the largest population surge in U.S. history, with the population reaching a historic high of 281.4 million people. Aided by changes in the immigration law since 1965 (see chapter 20), the population growth was driven by immigration, with the majority coming from the Eastern Hemisphere and bringing specialized job skills with them. Large numbers also came from Mexico and Latin America, bringing fewer skills, often without legal status. By 2000, the number of Hispanic Americans exceeded thirty-five million. Immigration from China, Japan, Vietnam, Thailand, Cambodia, Laos, the Philippines, Korea, and India swelled the number of Asian Americans to more than twelve million in 2000, an increase of 63 percent from 1990. The Arab population rose by 41 percent in the 1980s and 38 percent in the 1990s. In 2000, 1.2 million people of Arab ancestry lived in the United States. Since the 1990s, immigrants have settled predominantly in California, Texas, Florida, New York, Hawaii, New Jersey, and New Mexico. Combined, these states added ten million voting-age Hispanics and Asians in the 1990s alone; and in 2000, Hispanics and Asians made up more than 29 percent of the voting-age population. Thriving ethnic communities have also sprung up in midwestern and northeastern cities, repopulating older ethnic enclaves. Half of all Californians are estimated to be Hispanic.

Once here, immigrant women participated in the vibrant social and economic lives of their communities. In Los Angeles, Koreans created the thriving community of "Koreatown"; in Brooklyn, Russian Jews settled in "Little Odessa"; while Latinos occupied entire sections of Chicago, Dallas, and Washington, D.C. With the number of immigrants rising, new businesses grew up, started by ethnic entrepreneurs, male and female, who catered to their community's tastes for food, clothing, newspapers, and music from their home countries. Women socialized through mosques, temples, and churches, made meals and parties for their extended family networks, and joined together to improve their collective situation. Daughters joined girl scout troops and town sports clubs. Many women worked outside their neighborhoods. Like immigrant women at the turn of the twentieth century, these newcomers worked for wages, bringing in much needed income to their families (see chapter 12). Educated Asian Indian women faired best in the new economy, often finding professional employment in management, engineering, and health fields. Immigrant women without specialized skills found jobs in the garment industry, agriculture, and domestic service. Unlike earlier waves of immigrants, more families sent their daughters to school and to college. In the past, sons often received the chance to go to college over their sisters, but that assumption seems to have disappeared. In 2006, most institutions of higher learning, from small liberal arts colleges to large public universities, had a sex ratio of sixty to forty, female to male, leading some parents and administrators to advocate affirmative action for male college applicants.

Many trends converged to change U.S. families at the end of the twentieth century, particularly the rising numbers of divorced families, single mothers, and multigenerational families. In 1950, 90 percent of all households were families related by birth, marriage, or adoption; but in 2000, fewer than 70 percent were. Forty percent of U.S. children lived with two working parents, 40 percent lived with a single working parent,

Korean girls wearing traditional dress, wave fans in a pattern during a parade in Koreatown in Los Angeles. Immigration from China, Japan, Vietnam, Thailand, Cambodia, Laos, the Philippines, Korea, and India swelled the number of Asian Americans to more than 12 million in 2000, an increase of 63 percent from 1990.

and 20 percent lived with the traditional working father and homemaker mother. Married couples with children for the first time accounted for fewer than one in four households. Families themselves became more racially diverse. Mixed-race marriages had become more commonplace since the 1970s, resulting in a large jump in the numbers of multiracial children living in the United States. In 1999, two million U.S. children had parents of different races. The number of foreign adoptions also grew in the 1990s. More foreign babies were adopted in the United States than in any other country. The number doubled in the 1990s to more than twenty thousand in 2000 (one in every two hundred births). China and Russia each supplied 25 percent of those adoptions, with most of the rest coming from Guatemala, South Korea, and the Ukraine. A survey of U.S. teenagers taken in 1998 reported that 47 percent of white teens, 60 percent of African American teens, and 90 percent of Hispanic teens had dated someone of another race.

Architects and city planners responded to the growing numbers of three-generational households, in which grandparents live with their children and grandchildren. The 2000 census showed that these "multigenerational households"—defined as those of three or more generations—were growing faster than any other type of housing arrangements. The number of multigenerational households was still relatively small: 4.2 million, or 4 percent of all types. But they had grown by 38 percent from 1990 to 2000. Sixty-two percent of multigenerational households were led by the first generation, that is, the grandparents. Multigenerational living, especially those in which grandparents cared for their grandchildren, have long been common in Asian and Hispanic countries, and the arrangement remained popular among immigrants from those nations. Immigrant families, particularly those from Latin America, used the 1965 immigration reform to join their relatives in the United States, creating large families and networks of extended relatives where children lived with relatives or moved between the homes of their parents, aunts and uncles, and grandparents. Illegal immigrants used these networks to ensure safe and familiar homes for their U.S.-born children whose status as citizens protected them from being deported.

Another important reversal in family life in the new century was the greater number of single women. In 2005, 51 percent of women said they were living without a spouse, up from 35 percent in 1950 and 49 percent in 2000. At one end of the age spectrum, women married later or lived with unmarried partners more often and for longer periods. At the other end, women lived longer as widows and, after a divorce, were more likely than men to delay remarriage. Marriage rates among black women remained low. Only about 30 percent of black women lived with a spouse in 2000 as compared with about 49 percent of Hispanic women, 55 percent of non-Hispanic white women, and more than 60 percent of Asian women. In a relatively small number of cases, the living arrangement was temporary, made because the husband worked out of town, was deployed in the military, or was institutionalized. "This is yet another of the inexorable signs that there is no going back to a world where we can assume that marriage is the main institution that organizes people's lives," said the director of the public education for the Council on Contemporary Families, a nonprofit research group.

The Gulf Wars

The Middle East erupted as the opening U.S. conflict in the post–cold war era. The first Gulf War took place after Iraqi leader Saddam Hussein invaded the bordering state of Kuwait on August 2, 1990, to expand Iraq's boundaries. When economic sanctions failed and Hussein did not withdraw the Iraqi army from oil-rich Kuwait, President George H. W. Bush launched "Operation Desert Storm" on January 16, 1991, with the support of a broad coalition of nations under the United Nations. The war was quickly won. To avoid a protracted war, President Bush did not try to occupy Iraq or remove Hussein from power. Instead, with support of the United Nations, he imposed economic sanctions against Iraq until it allowed weapons inspectors unfettered access to the country's munitions factories to ensure that no chemical, biological, or nuclear weapons were being produced.

As the nation watched the first Gulf War unfold on their nightly newscasts, audiences saw women soldiers prominently displaced in what the media called "the new American military." In some ways, women's place in the military had improved since World War II when 350,000 women served in noncombat positions in auxiliaries and, eventually, as part of the military (see chapter 18). The passage of the Women's Armed Services Integration Act of 1948 granted women permanent status in the military. A series of changes in military law enabled women to gain a foothold in the services. During the Vietnam War, President Johnson lifted the 2 percent legal cap on the number of women allowed in the military, yet most women served as combat nurses, not as soldiers. Five years later, in 1973, the military moved to an all-volunteer force and ended the draft, which gave women new opportunities for service. In 1976, women were allowed to attend the military academies like the U.S. Military Academy at West Point,

New York, and the U.S. Naval Academy in Annapolis, Maryland. Such changes led to significant increases in the number of women in the military. In 1991, on the eve of the first Gulf War, women made up 11 percent of the all-volunteer armed forces and forty-one thousand served.

Despite these important changes, women's role in the military remained restricted to noncombat positions, limiting women to support, nursing, and administrative duties. Some women found such restrictions outrightly prejudicial, designed to perpetuate the military as an all-male preserve and to protect men's career advantages. Without being soldiers, women had worked near combat and at the front lines in a variety of ways. Since World War II, women instructor pilots had been teaching men to fly the jets in combat situations. Likewise, female sailors had served on the navy oilers that followed aircraft carriers into war zones, supplying them with fuel and ammunition. Compared to its NATO allies, the United States was far behind in integrating women into the armed services. In the new U.S. military, women were excluded from 48 percent of all positions in the army, 80 percent of all positions in the marines, and 41 percent of those in the navy.

For many people in the United States, the idea of women in combat was disturbing. For social conservatives, women serving in combat duties represented a misguided and strident radical feminism. Equality with men, represented by the female soldier, harkened to a world in which protections for women had been stripped away. Conservative activist Phyllis Schlafly defeated the ERA in part by arguing that feminists wanted to send women into battle in the name of gender equality. For military leaders, the notion that a female officer may give orders to a subordinate male soldier reeked of humiliation and disorder. More frightening was the idea that a female soldier could be taken prisoner and paraded through the streets of a hostile city. "Will [such an image] cause such a public outcry that our leaders will be forced to terminate the conflict under less than desirable terms and in spite of any national goals which may not have been attained?" asked Air Force Major Wayne Dillingham a year before the Gulf War.

The question of whether the female soldier could represent the nation in times of crisis remained controversial. Many feared that the U.S. public simply could not see a woman solely through the lens of a public soldier rather than a private person. Despite such sentiment, women in the military faced dangerous situations regularly. In 1994, female soldiers in the army were no longer barred from positions that posed a substantial risk of capture. Although not assigned to ground combat units, women flew helicopters, served in bomb-disposal squads, drove trucks, handled checkpoints, and treated the wounded on battlefields, leaving them open to lethal fire. Deep bonds of trust were forged in such conditions. One female veteran described her experience of the military: "I was one of the fortunate ones who served with a group of thirty men in my platoon who respected me and bonded in a way beyond gender. . . . We shared family pictures, letters, talked about favorite things we missed. . . . It was understood that I would be there for them as they were there for me. I did everything from night guard during the ground war to driving an Abrams tank. They trusted my abilities, but more important was the fact that they trusted me."

When George W. Bush invaded Iraq on March 20, 2003, and the Second Gulf War began, restrictions on combat duty did not keep women from enlisting. In 1992, black

When George W. Bush invaded Iraq on March 20, 2003, and the Second Gulf War began, restrictions on combat duty did not keep women from enlisting. Fifteen percent—one of seven—of the U.S. troops deployed in the Iraq War in were women.

women made up the largest percentage of female soldiers (48 percent) in the army, with white women a close second (4 percent). In 2002, white women comprised 57 percent of female enlistees, black women 33 percent, and Hispanic women 5 percent. Fifteen percent—one of seven—of the U.S. troops deployed in the Iraq War in 2003 were women, meaning that women were wounded and killed in greater numbers than ever before. "Before this war, people only imagined how women would react in combat roles and thought that they couldn't handle it," said Lory Manning, a retired navy captain. "But for the first time women are shooting back and doing heavy lifting in a real war. The bullets are real, so are the roadside bombs and the blood. Now we see that women are bonding with the men and not going to pieces." According to U.S. military policy, women were not supposed to be placed in direct combat. But with no real front line in Iraq, combat had no bounds. "The war is everywhere," said retired Brigadier General Wilma Vaught, U.S. Air Force. "There's no real place that you can say for certainty that you are out of harms way."

Terrorism at Home and Abroad

Ideas about women gender continued to shaped foreign policy debates as the conflict between Islamic fundamentalism and the West intensified and conflicts in the Middle East festered. On September 11, 2001, Al-Qaeda terrorists hijacked four commercial jets and flew two of them into New York City's World Trade Center, destroying its twin towers and killing over 2,600 people. The third plane crashed into the Pentagon, killing sixty-four passengers and 125 Defense Department employees. The fourth plane, presumably headed for the White House, crashed in Pennsylvania when the passengers fought back against the hijackers, killing all forty-five passengers and crew. United States troops descended on Afghanistan to find Osama bin Laden, who masterminded the attacks and who many felt was hiding in the country's rough mountainous terrain. As the United States fought a new war against "terrorism" instead of "Communism," concern about the status of Middle Eastern women, specifically Afghan and Iraqi women, became justifications for U.S. military intervention.

The attacks of September 11 were not the first time the United States had faced attacks on civilians. Terrorism—violence and the threat of violence—entered U.S. consciousness through a series of highly publicized global strikes in which terrorists communicated their grievances. During the 1972 Olympic Games in Munich, Germany, eight men from the Palestine Liberation Organization (PLO) took nine Israeli team members and their coaches hostage in protest against Israel's takeover of the West Bank in 1967 and killed them hours later. Seven years later, in 1979, sixty-five U.S. embassy employees in Tehran were taken hostage by Iranian militants. In January 1979, a popular uprising had transformed Iran into an Islamic republic and led it to use and support terrorism as a means of propagating its ideals beyond its own border, a strategy that placed the U.S. media in the uncomfortable position of aiding the terrorists by covering the crisis. Yellow ribbons tied on trees and antennas and pinned on blouses became public symbols of concern for the hostages and made the entire country a family eager to welcome home its loved ones. For the U.S. public, the hostages were identified with the private sphere, emotionally associated with family and domesticity, not diplomacy or politics. For anxious Americans, terrorists who attacked noncombatants in nonmilitarized areas violated the line between public and private life and between public and private citizen. By attacking civilians going about their daily lives, terrorists violated the safety of the home and the community by turning any place, any person, any action into a military target.

Despite the ongoing efforts of President Jimmy Carter to resolve the crisis, the hostages were not released until January 21, 1981, the day Ronald Reagan was sworn into office. Before long, the use of such tactics had spread to places as far afield as Japan and the United States and beyond Islam to every major world religion. From the sarin gas attack on the Tokyo subway by the religious sect Aum Shinrikyo in 1995 to the Oklahoma City bombing of the Alfred P. Murrah Federal Building the same year, religion was again added to the complex mix of motivations that led to acts of terrorism. The first Al-Qaeda attack on the World Trade Center in 1993 shocked the country. An emotional Mario Cuomo, New York's state governor, told journalists: "We all have that feeling of being violated. No foreign people or force has ever done this to us. Until now we were invulnerable." The second attack on September 11, 2001, brought home to the world—and, in particular the United States—just how real the threat of terrorism had become.

In the wake of the September 11 attacks, Congress quickly granted President George W. Bush power to take whatever steps were necessary to find those responsible for what he called the "evil, despicable acts of terror." Saudi Arabian Bin Laden and the Al-Qaeda network he headed were protected by the Taliban, a radical Islamist group with influence over the Afghanistan government. The Taliban were fiercely critical of Western influences, including the education of women and what they saw as the immoral representation of women and sexuality in television, advertisements, and movies. On October 7, 2001, the United States bombed Taliban and Al-Qaeda forces in Afghanistan. A month later, First Lady Laura Bush laid out the gendered reasons for the new "war on terror": "Afghan women know, through hard experience, what the rest of the world is discovering: The brutal oppression of women is a central goal of the terrorists. . . .The poverty, poor health, and illiteracy that the terrorists and the Taliban have imposed on women in Afghanistan do not conform with the treatment of women in most of the Islamic world, where women make important contributions in their societies."

Some of the women whose loved ones were killed on September 11 organized themselves to become central political players in the aftermath. Four women who lost their husbands in the attacks on the World Trade Center—Kristen Breitweiser, Patty Casazza, Lorie Van Auken, and Mindy Kleinberg—fought for the creation of the 9/11 Commission, which led to a fuller accounting of the intelligence information leading up to the attacks and to the events of the day itself. Some women used the idea of sisterhood among women to reject a military response to terrorism. In 2006, two other women, Patti Quigley and Susan Retik, whose husbands were killed in the September 11 attacks, used the financial support they received afterward to help war widows in Afghanistan.

Global Feminism

The militarism, immigration, and globalization that shaped the beginning of the twenty-first century helped create a groundswell of international feminist organizing. Particularly in the developing world, the United Nations and its myriad conferences became a focal point for political work. Feminists and women's rights activists formed nongovernmental organizations (NGOs) to help foster social mobilization on the new transnational stage. This style of activism reached its height at the 1995 U.N. World Conference on Women in Beijing, where thirty thousand participants met at the NGO Forum outside the city. The participants were mostly women, including activists for disabilities, peasants, colonial struggles, and lesbian rights. These participants took advantage of the new media of the Internet and e-mail, as well as older devices like the newsletter, phone call, or meeting. Much of what the conference accomplished was to adopt the liberal language of human rights to women's issues.

A broad range of health concerns also mobilized feminists across the globe. By the 1980s, AIDS was spreading most quickly among women. In 2005, 17.5 million women and 2.3 million children had been infected globally. In response to the global pandemic, women's health activists organized to promote safer sex practices and provide services for infected women. The Society for Women and AIDS in Africa, founded in 1988, expanded to twenty-five countries. Its attention to grassroots education, support for infected women, and rehabilitation linked the response to HIV to women's economic and human rights. In the United States, women initially contracted HIV from drug use but were increasingly infected by high-risk heterosexual behavior. In 2005, women made up 26 percent of all new AIDS diagnoses, with the rate of African American women twenty-three times that for white women and four times the rate for Hispanic women.

AIDS was not the only international threat to women's health. Infant and maternal mortality rates remained troublingly high. At the end of the twentieth century, the risk of maternal mortality ranged from one in twenty-three in Africa to one in four thousand in North America. Ninety-eight percent of women living in developed nations received prenatal care, and only 59 percent of those living in developing countries did. Infant and child mortality disproportionately affected female children in parts of the world where food and health care were given to males. In the 1995 U.N. Conference on Women in Beijing, activists called for equal primary health care for women and encouraged countries to close the gender gap in infant and child mortality. The activists linked women's health to world economic policies that led to high rates of disease and malnutrition.

Another pressing issue in the international women's health movement was the controversy over female genital cutting (FGC), a broad classification of genital surgery to remove parts of the girl's genital tissue, often including parts of the clitoris and labia. Two million girls underwent such surgery in 2005, the majority of whom lived in Egypt, Ethiopia, Kenya, Nigeria, Somalia, Sudan, Saudi Arabia, and Iraq. Egyptian feminist and doctor, Nawal El Saadawi, criticized the practice, arguing that it limited female sexual pleasure, and characterized FGC as a "political issue rather than a religious one." Western feminists, along with some Middle East and African feminists, referred to the practice as a form of mutilation and as violence against women. Others believed the practice could not be ended without appreciating its underlying causes and its cultural significance. They noted that Western coverage of the practice played into racial and religious stereotypes of Muslims and ignored that FGC had been practiced by Christians as well as Muslims in Egypt. These feminists called for ending the practice of FGC by ending the widespread neglect of women's education and health and reforming unequal marriage and divorce laws, again framing women's health as a human rights issue.

International feminists turned their attention to the violence against women, specifically the issue of rape. Sexual and gender-based violence, including rape and sexual slavery or prostitution, are problems throughout the world, occurring in every society, country, and region. The World Health Organization's World Report on Violence and Health noted that "one of the most common forms of violence against women is that performed by a husband or male partner." This type of violence was frequently invisible because it happened behind closed doors and was seen as a "private" family matter or a normal part of life. The report gathered comparable data from over twenty-four thousand women interviewed in fifteen sites in ten countries and determined that sexual violence is a pervasive global problem with significant health consequences for victims. Yet, in many places around the world, available services do not meet the needs of survivors, the majority of whom are women. In the United States, the Rape, Abuse and Incest National Network (RAINN) re-

Violence against women and women's health became important parts of a growing international women's movement at the end of the century. The 1995 U.N. World Conference on Women in Beijing, where 30,000 participants gathered, brought together activists for a range of issues affecting women.

ported in 1999 that every ninety seconds, someone was sexually assaulted. The majority were young women. The National College Women Sexual Victimization Study estimated that between one in four and one in five college women experience completed or attempted rape during their college years.

International feminist groups, the United Nations, and other NGOs brought new attention to the use of rape and sexual violence against women during times of political conflict. In 2005, the U.N. Population Fund (UNFPA) reported that, while sexual violence in wartime was not new, there was evidence it had become more common. The trend toward more civil and regional conflicts meant that civilians were targeted more than before. Women and children were particularly vulnerable, not just during armed attacks but also in displacement camps, during aid distribution, and even after conflicts had officially ended. The report found that systematic rape was a prominent feature of the conflicts in Bosnia-Herzegovina, DR Congo, East Timor, and Haiti and was ongoing in the Darfur region of Sudan. In Rwanda, officials estimated that sixty thousand women were raped during the 1994 conflict, two-thirds of whom were infected with HIV/AIDS. In Bosnia-Herzegovina, forty thousand women were assaulted. Feminists across the globe have mobilized to end systematic rape. In 1998, U.S. activist and author of *The Vagina Monologues*, Eve Ensler brought considerable international attention and funds to her V-Day campaign to end rape around the world. V-Day created partnerships with local women's groups in the Middle East, Asia, and Africa to, in Ensler's words, "end violence against women and girls in all its forms—changing minds, changing laws, changing lives." In 2006, ten U.N. agencies came together to form the joint initiative, U.N. Action against Sexual Violence in Conflict (U.N. Action) with the goal of ending sexual violence in conflict and to better support victims of sexual violence. It too established a Stop Rape Now campaign. As national governments scale back social welfare and build up their military and businesses, feminists rely on international networks to bring about improvements for women.

Third-Wave Feminism

Women coming of age at the end of the twentieth century entered a world markedly unlike that of their mothers. They faced a nation that was deeply divided over the issue of abortion and sexuality and viewed their own struggles in an ever more global framework that argued that women's rights could not be separated from human rights. This generation of U.S. feminists called themselves the *third wave*, invoking a history of activism most were familiar with from high-school and college classes, the wave of writing about women on the Internet, in newspapers, and in the thousands of books on women published each year.

Third-wave feminism had roots in black, Chicana, and Asian American feminists who had pioneered analyses of identity politics (see chapter 21). A new generation of young women read the works of prominent second-wave feminists like Chicana Cherrie Moraga, African American Audre Lorde, and Chinese American Maxine Hong Kingston.

Thanks to such literary legacies, many young women had appreciation for the equality they enjoyed, understanding that their participation in sports teams, their nonsexist textbooks, and their right to have an abortion were products of an earlier struggle.

WOMEN'S VOICES

A THIRD-WAVE FEMINIST ANALYZES BEAUTY

In this excerpt, Jennifer Myhrem describes the evolution of her feminism from high school to college and beyond. Like many third-wave feminists, she was introduced to feminist writings in high school and at home from her parents. She points out that her real feminist revolution came as she discovered the ways that she enacted gender norms on her body each day through her beauty regimes. She explains that for her, coming into feminist consciousness meant leaving behind conventional body work done in the name of attractiveness.

I got my crew cut about a year and a half after what I call my feminist rebirth. Even as a child, I considered myself a feminist, supported the ERA (even though I knew very little about it) and was quick to react to statements from junior-high classmates that women should be barefoot and pregnant. I had a mother who was employed and a father who was as involved as my mother in raising me. In eighth grade, I wrote a paper on the history of the women's suffrage movement in the U.S. In ninth grade, I read *Against Our Will*. But for all this, when I look back now I feel that politically I've traveled light-years from where I was then.

My feminist rebirth came during my college years. One summer, I stuffed the ideas of Millett, Brownmiller, and Walker into my eager head. Some of us come to feminism because of abuse, harassment, eating disorders. I came to feminism because I hated shaving my legs. That summer I started to appreciate the amount of time, labor and money women put into their appearance in order to become "women," which in our culture is synonymous with "not-men."

Femininity isn't inherent, natural, or biological. It takes work to look like a "woman," and this is evident when one looks at female impersonators and drag queens—men, with the same work, can look just like "women." Put on a pair of high heels and some lipstick and you're halfway there. . . . So to christen my feminist rebirth, I quit shaving my legs. I threw away my high heels and my tight skirts, my makeup and my jewelry. I grew out my armpit hair, and I talked like a woman with a mission. . . . Giving up my "femininity" was my first action as a feminist. . . .

I am one of those feminists that are made so much of in the media: a hairy-legged, strident, "masculine" woman, a "manhater" (another word for women who chose to tell the truth about men and patriarchy). I am a feminist with whom even other feminists are sometimes uncomfortable: "She gives the rest of us a bad name."

Rather than shrinking from words like "masculine" and "butch," we should point out why we are called these names and how male supremacy is served if we keep silent in fear of being called these names. . . .

Source: Jennifer Reid Maxcy Myhrem, "One Bad Hair Day Too Many," in Listen Up: Voices from the Next Feminist Generation, *ed. Barbara Findlen, 133–37 (New York: Seal Press, Perseus Books Group, 1995).*

Questions

1. How does Jennifer link her ideas about "femininity" to her feminism?

2. What role do ideas about female beauty play in keeping women from feminism?

3. Why do women fear being seen as masculine?

Women coming of age at the end of the twentieth century entered a world markedly unlike that of their mothers. They faced a nation that was deeply divided over the issue of abortion and sexuality and viewed their own struggles in an ever more global framework.

Yet, third-wave feminists were also unlike their foremothers. They embraced a politics of pleasure that was unlike their second-wave foremothers. For these younger women, femininity, with its products and frills, could be embraced as fun and empowering. In the hands of young women, popular culture—music, television, the Internet—could be pushed past its habitual stereotypes of dumb blondes and sassy black chicks to become a place where third-wavers could talk back against such narrow images. Women's zines, small self-produced magazines, as part of the grrl movement, created new images of feminism and of feminists. More mainstream and glossy magazines like *Jane* and *Bust* sold the third-wave sensibility to readers across the country.

On issues such as motherhood and abortion, third-wavers differed from earlier generations. As the politics of abortion shifted in the 1980s toward recognition of the rights of the fetus, many third-wave feminists looked for a new formula to guide them through the thicket of unplanned pregnancies. Some felt that the pro-choice movement had failed to defend the value of motherhood in its attention to women's right to end pregnancies. Further, they felt that abortion rights rhetoric missed a crucial component of women's experience—that having an abortion was emotionally and psychologically, as well as physically, painful. In the words of one activist, "[T]he second wave is still focused on whether the woman can get the abortion, not what she does or how she feels after she chooses to have one." Women looked to controlling pregnancy as the solution to the problem of abortion, yet recognized that abstinence-only sex education in schools made this difficult.

ON THE TWENTY-FIFTH ANNIVERSARY OF *ROE V. WADE*

On January 18, 2002, the twenty-fifth anniversary of the Supreme Court case, Roe v. Wade, *antiabortion activist Phyllis Schlafly took questions from readers of the* Washington Post. *In the excerpt that follows, readers question Schlafly about the Supreme Court ruling that drew her into leading what became a major national movement against abortion. They ask her to reconcile what appears to many as her own feminist lifestyle with her fiery antifeminist rhetoric.*

Phyllis Schlafly: Hello. This is Phyllis Schlafly, sad about the anniversary of *Roe v. Wade*, which legalized the killing of millions of unborn babies. Glad to take your questions.

Fairfax, Virginia: What has changed regarding women and women's rights since the *Roe v. Wade* decision in 1973?

Phyllis Schlafly: A lot has changed for women. We've lost so much in regard to marriage, family, respect for wives and mothers, the suffering from abortion and VD and divorce. The liberation movement that liberated women from home, husband, family and children has been a negative for women's happiness, rights and fulfillment.

Arlington, Virginia: Mrs. Schlafly,

Thank you for your work and the joy you seem to have doing it. What can pro-life college women do to counteract feminists and their double standards?

Phyllis Schlafly: Pro-life college women can do so much. Feminism and political correctness are dominant on campuses. You need to set up an alternative. Bring pro-life and antifeminist speakers to campus. Have an event on the anniversary of *Roe v. Wade*. Stay away from women's studies courses. Join or organize a pro-life group and make your presence known.

Arlington, Virginia: Ms. Schlafly, women are always comparing themselves to men. Do you think women today have forgotten their unique gifts, especially the power of giving life?

Phyllis Schlafly: It's all in your attitude. The feminist attitude is wholly negative, i.e., that the world is in a big conspiracy against women, that God goofed in making us in two genders, that the government should try to remedy His mistake, that it is oppression of women that women get pregnant and that society expects mothers to care for their babies. Get a life. Rejoice that you can participate in the creation of human life. We are so fortunate to be women.

Washington, D.C.: Dear Ms. Schlafly,

I was hoping you could explain how traveling the country, practicing law, not staying home and cooking for your husband doesn't make you a hypocrite? You had a fabulous, successful, fulfilling career at the same time you were pushing to discourage other women from making the same career decisions.

I don't understand how you can take advantage of the benefits from the feminist movement (such as the ability to go to law school) but actively work against it.

Phyllis Schlafly: Get your facts before you make charges. The law school I went to has been accepting women since 1890. I went to college by working the night shift in a manual labor job. I sold 3 million copies of a self-published book in 1964 before the feminist movement got started. I don't owe the feminist movement anything. I spent twenty-five years as a full-time homemaker without any paid job or income. The wonderful thing about a woman's life is the length. After my children went off to college, I had time to lecture on college campuses.

Alexandria, Virginia: What is your evidence that women's liberation has been a negative in women's lives?

Phyllis Schlafly: The high rates of divorce, illigitimacy, abortion, VD, broken families, and the bitterness evident in the writings and faces of most of the feminists I debate. Most of them don't have husbands or children or both, and few of them have grandchildren, which are one of the greatest joys of life. I feel sorry for the feminists, and I feel sorry for men who are married to feminists.

Dupont Circle: Why should women be primarily responsible for raising children? Shouldn't men and women share child-raising responsibilities equally since they both shared equally in creating the child in the first place?

Phyllis Schlafly: Mothers and fathers are equally responsible, but that doesn't mean they have to do the same tasks. Life is more efficient when each does what he or she does best. One has to pay the rent and the grocery bills and one has to tend to the baby's daily needs. Experience shows that this is most efficient when the mother gives daily care and the father provides support. But you don't have to get my approval for a contrary

arrangement; you just have to find a guy who wants to reverse the roles.

Park Point: Phyllis Schafly: Since you say women's liberation has "liberated women from home husband and family," how has your "liberating career" affected your "happiness, rights and fulfillment"?

Phyllis Schlafly: The only person's approval I had to get was my husband's, not yours. Yes, I've had a wonderful life, but my husband and children always knew that they came first. I spent twenty-five years as a full-time homemaker.

Atlanta, Georgia: Do we need a Human Life Amendment to the Constitution or is the Constitution sufficient to protect life from conception?

Phyllis Schlafly: We should restore legal protection to all human life at any stage of development, very young and keep respect for the very old. The problem is that *Roe v. Wade* federalized the issue that should have been left in state jurisdiction. The best way would be if the Supreme Court itself remedied its mistake by reversing *Roe*. Failing that, yes, we need a Constitutional amendment. Meanwhile, we try to restore respect for life through every avenue we can.

Source: *From Washingtonpost.com, January 18, 2002, at http://discuss.washingtonpost.com/wp-srv/zforum/02/ nation_schlafly011802.htm.*

Questions

1. According to Schlafly, what has the impact of feminism been on U.S. families?

2. What reasons does Schlafly give for her antiabortion position?

3. What does Schlafly understand to be the role of the Supreme Court on issues related to human life?

1960

1967 The *Phyllis Schlafly Report* begins	**1962** Supreme Court bans school prayer in *Engel v. Vitale*

1970

1972
Equal Rights Amendment passed
July STOP ERA forms

1972
Palestine Liberation Organization kidnaps and kills
eight Israeli athletes at the Munich Olympic Games

1973
Roe v. Wade legalizes abortion

1974
School board of Kanawha County, West Virginia, battles
with parents over public school curriculum

1975
Congress passes the Child Support Enforcement
Amendments Act

1975
Strategic Arms Limitation Treaty caps development of
nuclear missiles

1976
Congress passes the Hyde Amendment
Women admitted to military academies

1977
International Women's Year Conference in Houston, Texas
Pro-Family Rally in Houston
Anita Bryant successfully leads campaign to overturn
antidiscrimination ordinance in Miami Beach, Florida

1977
Proposition 6 in California attempts to ban
homosexuals from teaching

1978
White House Conference on Families

1979
Beverly LaHaye forms Concerned Women for America

1979
Iranian revolutionaries take over the U.S. Embassy
and take sixty-five hostages
Jerry Falwell starts the Moral Majority

1980

1980
Ronald Reagan becomes president
Phyllis Schlafly founds the pro-family Eagle Forum

1981
The Acquired Immune Deficiency Syndrome reported
Sandra Day O'Connor becomes the first female
Supreme Court justice

1981
Iranian hostage crisis ends with the release
of all captives

1982
Ratification for ERA expires

1984
Retirement Equity Act
Geraldine Ferraro runs as vice-presidential candidate
Family Violence Prevention and Services Act

1984
Retirement Equity Act

1988
Founding of the antiabortion group, Operation Rescue
Webster v. Reproductive Health Services restricts
state funds used to provide abortion
Founding of the Society for Women and AIDS in Africa

1988
Mikhail Gorbachev introduces *perestroika* and *glasnost*
in the Soviet Union
Founding of the Christian Coalition

1989
Tiananmen Square protests in China

WOMEN'S HISTORY	GLOBAL EVENTS

1990

1990
Planned Parenthood v. Casey upholds parental consent lower court ruling

1991
Anita Hill accuses Supreme Court nominee Clarence Thomas of sexual harassment

1991
Soviet Union dissolves
First Gulf War

1992
Bill Clinton becomes president

1993
Family and Medical Leave Act

1993
Terrorists bomb World Trade Center in New York City

Congress approves the North American Free Trade, or NAFTA

1995
U.N. World Conference on Women meets in Beijing

Islamic terrorists detonated car bomb at the World Trade Center

1996
Defense of Marriage Act defines marriage

Personal Responsibility and Work Opportunity Act
Citizens for Community Values forms
Temporary Assistance to Needy Families (TANF)

1994
Nelson Mandela is elected president of South Africa

1997
State Children's Health Insurance Program (SCHIP)

1997
Kyoto Protocol rejected by U.S.

2000

2001
Terrorists attack World Trade Center and Pentagon
Homeland Security Department created

2002
Illegal Immigration Reform and Immigrant Responsibility Act

2004
Massachusetts recognizes same-sex marriage

2003
Second Gulf War

2006
U.N. Action Against Sexual Violence in Conflict (U.N. Action)

2005
Hurricane Katrina devastates parts of Mississippi and Louisiana and floods 80 percent of New Orleans

2008
Hillary Rodham Clinton runs for President
California approves same-sex marriages

2008
Barack Obama runs for president

CONCLUSION

Today's young women are quite likely to be daughters and granddaughters of baby-boomer women. Even if they are not, they are without doubt heirs to the unfinished revolution that women in the 1960s helped bring about. The lives of women are very different in 2006 than what they were several decades ago. Most women are bread-winners. Divorce and out-of-wedlock childbearing have become commonplace. Women have become largely independent of husbands and children for long parts of their days. More women finish college. Changes in the roles of women have affected every institution, from the family to the workplace to politics and the marketplace.

While such significant change has altered the experiences of women, ongoing prejudice against women continues to shape their daily lives. In the words of twenty-nine-year-old Didem Nisanci, "[W]e're expected to do it all, all at the same time." Women's second shift of domestic and child-care tasks at the end of an already long workday continues to be one of the most pressing aspects of the unfinished transfor-mation of U.S. society. Poor women as well as professional women face high expecta-tions for making their families healthy and happy, with little help by way of child care, elder care, or health care. Hostility toward immigration leaves too many women vul-nerable and with little recourse to improve their lives. Long-standing women's issues like racism and access to abortion continue. Women's activism at the start of the twenty-first century remains an important way for U.S. women to bring about the promise of equality and to enhance their place in society.

REVIEW QUESTIONS

1. What motivated conservative women into political activism in these years? What organizations and networks did they form? What were their central issues?

2. How did ideas about welfare change after the 1980s? How did ideas about the gov-ernment's role in supporting family life change?

3. How did immigration after the 1960s change? What were the effects of this wave of immigration on American neighborhoods and cities? How did women experience immigration? How was it like the wave of immigration in the 1880s and 1890s?

4. In what ways did the globalizing economy affect women? How did it affect feminism?

RECOMMENDED READING

George Chauncey. *Why Marriage?: The History Shaping Today's Debate over Gay Equality*. New York: Basic Books, Perseus Books Group, 2004. A history of gay and lesbian activism and its political accomplishments since World War II.

Donald Critchlow. *Phyllis Schlafly and Grassroots Conservatism: A Woman's Crusade*. Princeton, NJ: Princeton University Press, 2005. Critchlow's biography of Phyllis Schlafly situates her public life in the struggles against communism, the Soviet Union's nuclear power, and eventually her successful battle against the ERA. Critchlow uses Schlafly's story as a window into the history of conservatism and Republican party activism from the 1940s to 2000.

Barbara Ehrenreich and Arlie Hochschild, eds. *Global Woman: Nannies, Maids, and Sex Workers in the New Economy*. New York: Henry Holt & Company, 2002. Articles address issues relating to women and work in the age of globalization.

Estelle B. Freedman. *No Turning Back: The History of Feminism and the Future of Women*. New York: Random House, 2002. Freedman examines the historical forces that have fueled the feminist movement and explores new feminist approaches to issues of work, family, and sexuality.

Marilyn Halter. *Shopping for Identity: The Marketing of Ethnicity*. New York: Schocken Books, 2000. Halter demonstrates that as immigrant groups gain economic security, they tend to reinforce, not relinquish, their ethnic identifications.

Janice Irvine. *Talk about Sex: The Battles over Sex Education in the United States*. Berkeley: University of California Press, 2002. An examination of the debates around sex education from the 1960s to 2000, with special attention paid to the rhetoric and discursive tactics of the New Right as a social movement.

Rebecca Klatch. *Women of the New Right*. Philadelphia: Temple University Press, 1987. One of the earliest accounts of women's activism in the New Right and the role of gender and sexuality in consolidating the movement.

William Martin. *With God on Our Side: The Rise of the Religious Right in America*. New York: Random House, 1996. A good overview of the institutional basis for the New Right from World War II to the 1990s.

Sam Robert. *Who We Are Now: The Changing Face of America in the Twenty-First Century*. New York: Times Books/ Henry Holt & Company, 2004. Based on the 2000 census, Robert explores the changes in the United States between 1990 and 2000, including population growth, ethnicity and immigration, and family structure.

ADDITIONAL BIBLIOGRAPHY

Women and The New Right

Margaret Lamberts Bendroth. *Fundamentalism and Gender, 1875 to the Present.* New Haven, CT: Yale University Press, 1993.

Brenda Brasher. *Godly Women: Fundamentalism and Female Power.* New Brunswick, NJ: Rutgers University Press, 1998.

Pamela D. H. Cochran. *Evangelical Feminism: A History.* New York: New York University Press, 2005.

Flora Davis. *Moving the Mountain: The Women's Movement in America since 1960.* New York: Simon & Schuster, 1991.

Sara Diamond. *Not by Politics Alone: The Enduring Influence of the Christian Right.* New York: Guilford Press, 1998.

Lisa Duggan and Nan Hunter. *Sex Wars: Sexual Dissent and Political Culture.* New York: Routledge, 1995.

Susan Faludi. *Backlash: The Undeclared War against American Women.* New York: Crown Book Publishers, 1991.

Julie Ingersoll. *Evangelical Christian Women: War Stories in the Gender Battles.* New York: New York University Press, 2003.

Annelise Orleck. *Storming Caesars Palace: How Black Mothers Fought Their Own War on Poverty.* Boston: Beacon Press, 2005.

James Patterson. *Restless Giant: The United States from Watergate to Bush v. Gore.* New York: Oxford University Press, 2005.

Bradford W. Wilcox. *Soft Patriarchs, New Men: How Christianity Shapes Fathers and Husbands.* Chicago: University of Chicago Press, 2004.

Work and Family in the 1990s

Shellee Colen. "'Like a Mother to Them': Stratified Reproduction and West Indian Childcare Workers and Employers in New York." In *Conceiving the New World Order: The Global Politics of Reproduction,* edited by Faye Ginsburg and Rayna Rapp, 78–102. Berkeley: University of California Press, 1995.

"'With Respect and Feelings': Voices of West Indian Child Care and Domestic Workers in New York City." In *Immigrant Women,* edited by Maxine Schwartz Seller, 110–17. Philadelphia: Temple University Press, 1981.

Martha Gardner. *The Qualities of a Citizen: Women, Immigration, and Citizenship, 1870–1965.* Princeton, NJ: Princeton University Press, 2005.

Kamini Maraj Grahame. "'For the Family': Asian Immigrant Women's Triple Day." *Journal of Sociology and Social Welfare* (March 2003).

Gwendolyn Mink, ed. *Whose Welfare?* New York: Free Press, 1999.

Maria De la luz Ibarra. "La Vida: Mexican Immigrant Women's Memories of Home: Yearning, and Border Crossings." *Frontiers* (2003).

_____. "Mexican Immigrant Women and the New Domestic Labor." *Human Organization* (Winter 2000).

Helen Zia. "Reclaiming the Past, Redefining the Future: Asian American and Pacific Islander Women." In *Sisterhood Is Forever: The Women's Anthology for a New Millennium,* edited by Robin Morgan, 188–98. New York: New York University Press, 2003.

Global America

Jennifer Baumgardner and Amy Richard. *Manifesta: Young Women, Feminism, and the Future.* New York: Farrar, Straus & Giroux, 2000.

Gloria Heyung Chun. *Of Orphans and Warriors: Inventing Chinese American Culture and Identity.* Piscataway: Rutgers University Press, 2000.

Cynthia Costello et al., eds. *The American Women, 2003–2004.* New York: Palgrave Macmillan, 2003.

Francine D'Amico and Laurie Weinstein, eds. *Gender Camouflage: Women and the U.S. Military.* New York: New York University Press, 2000.

Mike Davis. *Magical Urbanism: Latinos Reinvent the U.S. City.* London and New York: Verso, 2001.

Barbara Findler, ed. *Listen Up: Voices from the Next Feminist Generation.* Seattle: Seal Press, 1995.

Linda Bird Francke. *Ground Zero: The Gender Wars in the Military.* New York: Simon & Schuster, 1997.

Karen Green and Tristan Taormino, eds. *A Girl's Guide to Taking Over the World: Writings from the Girl Zine Revolution.* New York: St. Martin's Press, 1997.

Inderpal Grewal. *Transnational America: Feminisms, Diasporas, Neoliberalisms.* Durham, NC: Duke University Press, 2005.

Jeanne Holm. *Women and the Military: An Unfinished Revolution*. Novato, CA: Presidio Press, 1982.

Memoirs, Autobiographies, Biographies

Leila Ahmed. *A Border Passage: From Cairo to America—A Woman's Journey*. New York: Penguin Books, 2000.

Susan Brownmiller. *In Our Time: Memoir of a Revolution*. New York: Dial Press, 1999.

Hillary Rodham Clinton. *Living History*. New York: Simon & Schuster, 2003.

Rhonda Cornum. *She Went to War: The Rhonda Cornum Story*. Novato, CA: Presidio Press, 1993.

Andrea Dworkin. *Heartbreak: A Political Memoir of a Feminist Militant*. New York: Basic Books, 2002.

Sandra Day O'Connor. *Lazy B*. New York: Random House, 2002.

APPENDIX

The Declaration of Independence (1776)

When in the course of human events it becomes necessary for one people to dissolve the political bands which have connected them with another and to assume, among the powers of the earth, the separate and equal station to which the laws of nature and of nature's God entitle them, a decent respect to the opinions of mankind requires that they should declare the causes which impel them to the separation.

We hold these truths to be self-evident, that all men are created equal; that they are endowed by their Creator with certain unalienable rights; that among these are life, liberty, and the pursuit of happiness. That, to secure these rights, governments are instituted among men, deriving their just powers from the consent of the governed; that, whenever any form of government becomes destructive of these ends, it is the right of the people to alter or to abolish it, and to institute a new government, laying its foundation on such principles, and organizing its powers in such form, as to them shall seem most likely to effect their safety and happiness. Prudence, indeed, will dictate that governments long established should not be changed for light and transient causes; and, accordingly, all experience hath shown that mankind are more disposed to suffer, while evils are sufferable, than to right themselves by abolishing the forms to which they are accustomed. But when a long train of abuses and usurpations, pursuing invariably the same object, evinces a design to reduce them under absolute despotism, it is their right, it is their duty, to throw off such government and to provide new guards for their future security. Such has been the patient sufferance of these colonies, and such is now the necessity which constrains them to alter their former systems of government. The history of the present King of Great Britain is a history of repeated injuries and usurpations, all having, in direct object, the establishment of an absolute tyranny over these States. To prove this, let facts be submitted to a candid world.

He has refused his assent to laws the most wholesome and necessary for the public good.

He has forbidden his governors to pass laws of immediate and pressing importance, unless suspended in their operation till his assent should be obtained; and, when so suspended, he has utterly neglected to attend to them.

He has refused to pass other laws for the accommodation of large districts of people, unless those people would relinquish the right of representation in the legislature, a right inestimable to them and formidable to tyrants only.

He has called together legislative bodies at places unusual, uncomfortable, and distant from the depository of their public records, for the sole purpose of fatiguing them into compliance with his measures.

He has dissolved representative houses, repeatedly for opposing, with manly firmness, his invasions on the rights of the people.

He has refused, for a long time after such dissolutions, to cause others to be elected; whereby the legislative powers, incapable of annihilation, have returned to the people at large for their exercise; the state remaining, in the meantime, exposed to all the danger of invasion from without and convulsions within.

He has endeavored to prevent the population of these States; for that purpose, obstructing the laws for naturalization of foreigners, refusing to pass others to encourage their migration hither, and raising the conditions of new appropriations of lands.

He has obstructed the administration of justice by refusing his assent to laws for establishing judiciary powers.

He has made judges dependent on his will alone for the tenure of their offices and the amount and payment of their salaries.

He has erected a multitude of new offices and sent hither swarms of officers to harass our people and eat out their substance.

He has kept among us, in time of peace, standing armies, without the consent of our legislatures.

He has affected to render the military independent of, and superior to, the civil power.

He has combined with others to subject us to a jurisdiction foreign to our Constitution and unacknowledged by our laws, giving his assent to their acts of pretended legislation—

For quartering large bodies of armed troops among us;

For protecting them, by mock trial, from punishment for any murders which they should commit on the inhabitants of these States;

For cutting off our trade with all parts of the world;

For imposing taxes on us without our consent;

For depriving us, in many cases, of the benefit of trial by jury;

For transporting us beyond seas to be tried for pretended offences;

For abolishing the free system of English laws in a neighboring province, establishing therein an arbitrary government, and enlarging its boundaries, so as to render it at once an example and fit instrument for introducing the same absolute rule into these colonies;

For taking away our charters, abolishing our most valuable laws, and altering, fundamentally, the powers of our governments.

For suspending our own legislatures and declaring themselves invested with power to legislate for us in all cases whatsoever.

He has abdicated government here by declaring us out of his protection and waging war against us.

He has plundered our seas, ravaged our coasts, burnt our towns, and destroyed the lives of our people.

He is, at this time, transporting large armies of foreign mercenaries to complete the works of death, desolation, and tyranny already begun with circumstances of cruelty and perfidy scarcely paralleled in the most barbarous ages, and totally unworthy the head of a civilized nation.

He has constrained our fellow citizens, taken captive on the high seas, to bear arms against their country, to become the executioners of their friends and brethren, or to fall themselves by their hands.

He has excited domestic insurrections amongst us and has endeavored to bring on the inhabitants of our frontiers, the merciless Indian savages, whose known rule of warfare is an undistinguished destruction of all ages, sexes, and conditions.

In every stage of these oppressions, we have petitioned for redress in the most humble terms; our repeated petitions have been answered only by repeated injury. A prince whose character is thus marked by every act which may define a tyrant is unfit to be the ruler of a free people.

Nor have we been wanting in attention to our British brethren. We have warned them, from time to time, of attempts made by their legislature to extend an unwarrantable jurisdiction over us. We have reminded them of the circumstances of our emigration and settlement here. We have appealed to their native justice and magnanimity, and we have conjured them, by the ties of our common kindred, to disavow these usurpations, which would inevitably interrupt our connections and correspondence. They, too, have been deaf to the voice of justice and consanguinity. We must, therefore, acquiesce in the necessity which denounces our separation, and hold them, as we hold the rest of mankind, enemies in war, in peace, friends.

We, therefore, the representatives of the United States of America, in general Congress assembled, appealing to the Supreme Judge of the world for the rectitude of our intentions, do, in the name and by the authority of the good people of these colonies, solemnly publish and declare, that these united colonies are, and of right ought to be, free and independent states: that they are absolved from all allegiance to the British Crown, and that all political connection between them and the state of Great Britain is, and ought to be, totally dissolved; and that, as free and independent states, they have full power to levy war, conclude peace, contract alliances, establish commerce, and to do all other acts and things which independent states may of right do. And, for the support of this declaration, with a firm reliance on the protection of Divine Providence, we mutually pledge to each other our lives, our fortunes, and our sacred honor.

Declaration of Sentiments and Resolutions Woman's Rights Convention, Seneca Falls, New York (1848)

We hold these truths to be self-evident: that all men and women are created equal; that they are endowed by their Creator with certain inalienable rights; that among these are life, liberty, and the pursuit of happiness; that to secure these rights governments are instituted, deriving their just powers from the consent of the governed . . . But when a long train of abuses and usurpations, pursuing invariably the same object evinces a design to reduce them under absolute despotism, it is their duty to throw off such government, and to provide new guards for their future security. Such has been the patient sufferance of the women under this government, and such is now the necessity which constrains them to demand the equal station to which they are entitled.

The history of mankind is a history of repeated injuries and usurpations on the part of man toward woman, having in direct object the establishment of an absolute tyranny over her. To prove this, let facts be submitted to a candid world.

He has never permitted her to exercise her inalienable right to the elective franchise.

He has compelled her to submit to laws, in the formation of which she had no voice.

He has withheld from her rights which are given to the most ignorant and degraded men—both natives and foreigners.

Having deprived her of this first right of a citizen, the elective franchise, thereby leaving her without representation in the halls of legislation, he has oppressed her on all sides.

He has made her, if married, in the eye of the law, civilly dead.

He has taken from her all right in property, even to the wages she earns.

He has made her, morally, an irresponsible being, as she can commit many crimes with impunity, provided they be done in the presence of her husband. In the covenant of marriage, she is compelled to promise obedience to her husband, he becoming, to all intents and purposes, her master—the law giving him power to deprive her of her liberty, and to administer chastisement.

He has so framed the laws of divorce, as to what shall be the proper causes, and in case of separation, to whom the guardianship of the children shall be given, as to be wholly regardless of the happiness of women—the law, in all cases, going upon a false supposition of the supremacy of man, and giving all power into his hands.

After depriving her of all rights as a married woman, if single, and the owner of property, he has taxed her to support a government which recognizes her only when her property can be made profitable to it.

He has monopolized nearly all the profitable employments, and from those she is permitted to follow, she receives but a scanty remuneration. He closes against her all the avenues to wealth and distinction which he considers most honorable to himself. As a teacher of theology, medicine, or law, she is not known.

He has denied her the facilities for obtaining a thorough education, all colleges being closed against her.

He allows her in Church, as well as State, but a subordinate position, claiming Apostolic authority for her exclusion from the ministry, and, with some exceptions, from any public participation in the affairs of the Church.

He has created a false public sentiment by giving to the world a different code of morals for men and women, by which moral delinquencies which exclude women from society, are not only tolerated, but deemed of little account in man.

He has usurped the prerogative of Jehovah himself, claiming it as his right to assign for her a sphere of action, when that belongs to her conscience and to her God.

He has endeavored, in every way that he could, to destroy her confidence in her own powers, to lessen her self respect, and to make her willing to lead a dependent and abject life.

Now, in view of this entire disfranchisement of one-half the people of this country, their social and religious degradation—in view of the unjust laws above mentioned, and because women do feel themselves aggrieved, oppressed, and fraudulently deprived of their most sacred rights, we insist that they have immediate admission to all the rights and privileges which belong to them as citizens of the United States.

In entering upon the great work before us, we anticipate no small amount of misconception, misrepresentation, and ridicule; but we shall use every instrumentality within our power to effect our object. We shall employ agents, circulate tracts, petition the State and National legislatures, and endeavor to enlist the pulpit and the press in our behalf. We hope this Convention will be followed by a series of Conventions embracing every part of the country.

The following resolutions were adopted:

Resolved, That such laws as conflict, in any way, with the true and substantial happiness of woman, are contrary to the great precept of nature and of no validity, for this is "superior in obligation to any other."

Resolved, That all laws which prevent woman from occupying such a station in society as her conscience shall dictate, or which place her in a position inferior to that of man, are contrary to the great precept of nature, and therefore of no force or authority.

Resolved, That woman is man's equal—was intended to be so by the Creator, and the highest good of the race demands that she should be recognized as such.

Resolved, That the women of this country ought to be enlightened in regard to the laws under which they live, that they may no longer publish their degradation by declaring themselves satisfied with their present position, nor their ignorance, by asserting that they have all the rights they want.

Resolved, That inasmuch as man, while claiming for himself intellectual superiority, does accord to woman moral superiority, it is pre-eminently his duty to encourage her to speak and teach, as she has an opportunity, in all religious assemblies.

Resolved, That the same amount of virtue, delicacy, and refinement of behavior that is required of woman in the social state, should also be required of man, and the same transgressions should be visited with equal severity on both man and woman.

Resolved, That the objection of indelicacy and impropriety, which is so often brought against woman when she addresses a public audience, comes with a very ill-grace from those who encourage, by their attendance, her appearance on the stage, in the concert, or in feats of the circus.

Resolved, That woman has too long rested satisfied in the circumscribed limits which corrupt customs and a perverted application of the Scriptures have marked out for her, and that it is time she should move in the enlarged sphere which her great Creator has assigned her.

Resolved, That it is the duty of the women of this country to secure to themselves their sacred right to the elective franchise.

Resolved, That the equality of human rights results necessarily from the fact of the identity of the race in capabilities and responsibilities.

Resolved, therefore, That, being invested by the Creator with the same capabilities, and the same consciousness of responsibility for their exercise, it is demonstrably the right and duty of woman, equally with man, to promote every righteous cause by every righteous means; and especially in regard to the great subjects of morals and religion, it is self-evidently her right to participate with her brother in teaching them, both in private and in public, by writing and by speaking, by any instrumentalities proper to be used, and in any assemblies proper to be held; and this being a self-evident truth growing out of the divinely implanted principles of human nature, any custom or authority adverse to it, whether modern or wearing the hoary sanction of antiquity, is to be regarded as a self-evident falsehood, and at war with mankind.

Resolved, That the speedy success of our cause depends upon the zealous and untiring efforts of both men and women, for the overthrow of the monopoly of the pulpit, and for the securing to woman an equal participation with men in the various trades, professions, and commerce.

Constitution of the Woman's National Council of the United States (1888)

Preamble

We, women of the United States, sincerely believing that the best good of our homes and nation will be advanced by our own greater unity of thought, sympathy and purpose, and that an organized movement of women will best conserve the highest good of the family and the State, do hereby band ourselves together in a confederation of workers committed to the overthrow of all forms of ignorance and injustice, and to the application of the Golden Rule to society, custom and law.

That we may more successfully prosecute the work, we adopt the following

CONSTITUTION.

Article I.

Name.

This federation shall be called the Woman's National Council of the United States.

Article II.

General Policy.

This Council is organized in the interest of no one propaganda, and has no power over its auxiliaries beyond that of suggestion and sympathy; therefore, no society voting to become auxiliary to this Council, shall thereby render itself liable to be interfered with in respect to its complete organic unity, independence or methods of work, or be committed to any principle or method of any other society or to any utterance or act of the Council itself, beyond compliance with the terms of this Constitution.

Article III.

Officers.

The officers shall be a President, Vice-President at Large, Corresponding Secretary, Recording Secretary and Treasurer. Each president of an auxiliary society shall be *ex officio* Vice-President of the National Council and the President of the National Council shall be *ex officio* Vice-President of the International Council.

The five general officers, with the Vice-Presidents, shall constitute an Executive Committee, of which seven members shall make a quorum, to control and provide for the general interests of the Council.

Article IV.

Auxiliaries.

Any society of women, the nature of whose work is satisfactory to the Executive Committee, either as to its undoubtedly national character or national value, may become auxiliary to this Council by its own vote and by the payment of a sum amounting to half a cent yearly per member, in addition to a payment of twenty-five dollars, into the treasury of the National Council not later than three months prior to its triennial meetings.

Article V.

Meetings.

The National Council shall hold triennial meetings. The Committee of Arrangements shall be composed of the Executive Committee and one delegate chosen by each auxiliary society as its representative.

Article VI.

This Constitution may be altered or amended by a majority vote of the Council at any triennial meeting, printed notice thereof having been sent to each member of the Executive Committee at least three months prior to such meeting.

Nineteenth Amendment to the Constitution of the United States of America (August 26, 1920)

SECTION 1. The right of citizens of the United States to vote shall not be denied or abridged by the United States or by any State on account of sex.

SECTION 2. Congress shall have the power to enforce this article by appropriate legislation.

The National Organization for Women's 1966 Statement of Purpose

This Statement of Purpose was written by Betty Friedan, author of "The Feminine Mystique."

We, men and women who hereby constitute ourselves as the National Organization for Women, believe that the time has come for a new movement toward true equality for all women in America, and toward a fully equal partnership of the sexes, as part of the world-wide revolution of human rights now taking place within and beyond our national borders.

The purpose of NOW is to take action to bring women into full participation in the mainstream of American society now, exercising all the privileges and responsibilities thereof in truly equal partnership with men.

We believe the time has come to move beyond the abstract argument, discussion and symposia over the status and special nature of women which has raged in America in recent years; the time has come to confront, with concrete action, the conditions that now prevent women from enjoying the equality of opportunity and freedom of choice which is their right, as individual Americans, and as human beings.

NOW is dedicated to the proposition that women, first and foremost, are human beings, who, like all other people in our society, must have the chance to develop their fullest human potential. We believe that women can achieve such equality only by accepting to the full the challenges and responsibilities they share with all other people in our society, as part of the decision-making mainstream of American political, economic and social life.

We organize to initiate or support action, nationally, or in any part of this nation, by individuals or organizations, to break through the silken curtain of prejudice and discrimination against women in government, industry, the professions, the churches, the political parties, the judiciary, the labor unions, in education, science, medicine, law, religion and every other field of importance in American society.

Enormous changes taking place in our society make it both possible and urgently necessary to advance the unfinished revolution of women toward true equality, now. With a life span lengthened to nearly 75 years it is no longer either necessary or possible for women to devote the greater part of their lives to child- rearing; yet childbearing and rearing which continues to be a most important part of most women's lives—still is used to justify barring women from equal professional and economic participation and advance.

Today's technology has reduced most of the productive chores which women once performed in the home and in mass-production industries based upon routine un-skilled labor. This same technology has virtually eliminated the quality of muscular strength as a criterion for filling most jobs, while intensifying American industry's need for creative intelligence. In view of this new industrial revolution created by au-tomation in the mid-twentieth century, women can and must participate in old and new fields of society in full equality—or become permanent outsiders.

Despite all the talk about the status of American women in recent years, the ac-tual position of women in the United States has declined, and is declining, to an alarming degree throughout the 1950's and 60's. Although 46.4% of all American women between the ages of 18 and 65 now work outside the home, the overwhelming majority—75%—are in routine clerical, sales, or factory jobs, or they are household workers, cleaning women, hospital attendants. About two-thirds of Negro women workers are in the lowest paid service occupations. Working women are becoming in-creasingly—not less—concentrated on the bottom of the job ladder. As a consequence full-time women workers today earn on the average only 60% of what men earn, and that wage gap has been increasing over the past twenty-five years in every major in-dustry group. In 1964, of all women with a yearly income, 89% earned under $5,000 a year; half of all full-time year round women workers earned less than $3,690; only 1.4% of full-time year round women workers had an annual income of $10,000 or more.

Further, with higher education increasingly essential in today's society, too few women are entering and finishing college or going on to graduate or professional school. Today, women earn only one in three of the B.A.'s and M.A.'s granted, and one in ten of the Ph.D.'s. In all the professions considered of importance to society, and in the executive ranks of industry and government, women are losing ground. Where they are present it is only a token handful. Women comprise less than 1% of federal judges; less than 4% of all lawyers; 7% of doctors. Yet women represent 51% of the U.S. population. And, increasingly, men are replacing women in the top positions in secondary and elementary schools, in social work, and in libraries—once thought to be women's fields.

Official pronouncements of the advance in the status of women hide not only the reality of this dangerous decline, but the fact that nothing is being done to stop it. The excellent reports of the President's Commission on the Status of Women and of the State Commissions have not been fully implemented. Such Commissions have power only to advise. They have no power to enforce their recommendation; nor have they the freedom to organize American women and men to press for action on them. The reports of these commissions have, however, created a basis upon which it is now pos-sible to build. Discrimination in employment on the basis of sex is now prohibited by federal law, in Title VII of the Civil Rights Act of 1964. But although nearly one-third of the cases brought before the Equal Employment Opportunity Commission during the first year dealt with sex discrimination and the proportion is increasing dramati-cally, the Commission has not made clear its intention to enforce the law with the same seriousness on behalf of women as of other victims of discrimination. Many of these cases were Negro women, who are the victims of double discrimination of race and sex. Until now, too few women's organizations and official spokesmen have been willing to speak out against these dangers facing women. Too many women have been restrained by the fear of being called "feminist." There is no civil rights movement to speak for women, as there has been for Negroes and other victims of discrimination. The National Organization for Women must therefore begin to speak.

We believe that the power of American law, and the protection guaranteed by the U.S. Constitution to the civil rights of all individuals, must be effectively applied and enforced to isolate and remove patterns of sex discrimination, to ensure equality of opportunity in employment and education, and equality of civil and political rights and responsibilities on behalf of women, as well as for Negroes and other deprived groups.

We realize that women's problems are linked to many broader questions of social justice; their solution will require concerted action by many groups. Therefore, convinced that human rights for all are indivisible, we expect to give active support to the common cause of equal rights for all those who suffer discrimination and deprivation, and we call upon other organizations committed to such goals to support our efforts toward equality for women.

We do not accept the token appointment of a few women to high-level positions in government and industry as a substitute for serious continuing effort to recruit and advance women according to their individual abilities. To this end, we urge American government and industry to mobilize the same resources of ingenuity and command with which they have solved problems of far greater difficulty than those now impeding the progress of women.

We believe that this nation has a capacity at least as great as other nations, to innovate new social institutions which will enable women to enjoy the true equality of opportunity and responsibility in society, without conflict with their responsibilities as mothers and homemakers. In such innovations, America does not lead the Western world, but lags by decades behind many European countries. We do not accept the traditional assumption that a woman has to choose between marriage and motherhood, on the one hand, and serious participation in industry or the professions on the other. We question the present expectation that all normal women will retire from job or profession for 10 or 15 years, to devote their full time to raising children, only to reenter the job market at a relatively minor level. This, in itself, is a deterrent to the aspirations of women, to their acceptance into management or professional training courses, and to the very possibility of equality of opportunity or real choice, for all but a few women. Above all, we reject the assumption that these problems are the unique responsibility of each individual woman, rather than a basic social dilemma which society must solve. True equality of opportunity and freedom of choice for women requires such practical, and possible innovations as a nationwide network of child-care centers, which will make it unnecessary for women to retire completely from society until their children are grown, and national programs to provide retraining for women who have chosen to care for their children full-time.

We believe that it is as essential for every girl to be educated to her full potential of human ability as it is for every boy—with the knowledge that such education is the key to effective participation in today's economy and that, for a girl as for a boy, education can only be serious where there is expectation that it will be used in society. We believe that American educators are capable of devising means of imparting such expectations to girl students. Moreover, we consider the decline in the proportion of women receiving higher and professional education to be evidence of discrimination. This discrimination may take the form of quotas against the admission of women to colleges, and professional schools; lack of encouragement by parents, counselors and educators; denial of loans or fellowships; or the traditional or arbitrary procedures in graduate and professional training geared in terms of men, which inadvertently discriminate against women. We believe that the same serious attention must be given to high school dropouts who are girls as to boys.

We reject the current assumptions that a man must carry the sole burden of supporting himself, his wife, and family, and that a woman is automatically entitled to lifelong support by a man upon her marriage, or that marriage, home and family are primarily woman's world and responsibility—hers, to dominate—his to support. We believe that a true partnership between the sexes demands a different concept of marriage, an equitable sharing of the responsibilities of home and children and of the economic burdens of their support. We believe that proper recognition should be given to the economic and social value of homemaking and child-care. To these ends, we will seek to open a reexamination of laws and mores governing marriage and divorce, for we believe that the current state of "half-equity" between the sexes discriminates against both men and women, and is the cause of much unnecessary hostility between the sexes.

We believe that women must now exercise their political rights and responsibilities as American citizens. They must refuse to be segregated on the basis of sex into separate-and-not-equal ladies' auxiliaries in the political parties, and they must demand representation according to their numbers in the regularly constituted party committees—at local, state, and national levels—and in the informal power structure, participating fully in the selection of candidates and political decision-making, and running for office themselves.

In the interests of the human dignity of women, we will protest, and endeavor to change, the false image of women now prevalent in the mass media, and in the texts, ceremonies, laws, and practices of our major social institutions. Such images perpetuate contempt for women by society and by women for themselves. We are similarly opposed to all policies and practices—in church, state, college, factory, or office—which, in the guise of protectiveness, not only deny opportunities but also foster in women self-denigration, dependence, and evasion of responsibility, undermine their confidence in their own abilities and foster contempt for women.

NOW will hold itself Independent of any political party in order to mobilize the political power of all women and men intent on our goals. We will strive to ensure that no party, candidate, president, senator, governor, congressman, or any public official who betrays or ignores the principle of full equality between the sexes is elected or appointed to office. If it is necessary to mobilize the votes of men and women who believe in our cause, in order to win for women the final right to be fully free and equal human beings, we so commit ourselves.

We believe that women will do most to create a new image of women by acting now, and by speaking out in behalf of their own equality, freedom, and human dignity—not in pleas for special privilege, nor in enmity toward men, who are also victims of the current, half-equality between the sexes—but in an active, self-respecting partnership with men. By so doing, women will develop confidence in their own ability to determine actively, in partnership with men, the conditions of their life, their choices, their future and their society.

Equal Rights Amendment

SECTION 1. Equality of Rights under the law shall not be denied or abridged by the United States or any state on account of sex.

SECTION 2. The Congress shall have the power to enforce, by appropriate legislation, the provisions of this article.

SECTION 3. This amendment shall take effect two years after the date of ratification.

Title IX of The Education Amendments (1972)

SEC. 1681. SEX **(a) Prohibition against discrimination; exceptions**

No person in the United States shall, on the basis of sex, be excluded from participation in, be denied the benefits of, or be subjected to discrimination under any education program or activity receiving Federal financial assistance, except that:

(1) Classes of educational institutions subject to prohibition in regard to admissions to educational institutions, this section shall apply only to institutions of vocational education, professional education, and graduate higher education, and to public institutions of undergraduate higher education;

(2) Educational institutions commencing planned change in admissions in regard to admissions to educational institutions, this section shall not apply

(A) for one year from June 23, 1972, nor for six years after June 23, 1972, in the case of an educational institution which has begun the process of changing from being an institution which admits only students of one sex to being an institution which admits students of both sexes, but only if it is carrying out a plan for such a change which is approved by the Secretary of Education

or

(B) for seven years from the date an educational institution begins the process of changing from being an institution which admits only students of only one sex to being an institution which admits students of both sexes, but only if it is carrying out a plan for such a change which is approved by the Secretary of Education, whichever is the later;

(3) Educational institutions of religious organizations with contrary religious tenets this section shall not apply to an educational institution which is controlled by a religious organization if the application of this subsection would not be consistent with the religious tenets of such organization;

(4) Educational institutions training individuals for military services or merchant marine this section shall not apply to an educational institution whose primary purpose is the training of individuals for the military services of the United States, or the merchant marine;

(5) Public educational institutions with traditional and continuing admissions policy in regard to admissions this section shall not apply to any public institution of undergraduate higher education which is an institution that traditionally and continually from its establishment has had a policy of admitting only students of one sex;

(6) Social fraternities or sororities; voluntary youth service organizations this section shall not apply to membership practices

(A) of a social fraternity or social sorority which is exempt from taxation under section 501(a) of title 26, the active membership of which consists primarily of students in attendance at an institution of higher education, or

(B) of the Young Men's Christian Association, Young Women's Christian Association, Girl Scouts, Boy Scouts, Camp Fire Girls, and voluntary youth service organizations which are so exempt, the membership of which has traditionally been limited to persons of one sex and principally to persons of less than nineteen years of age;

(7) Boy or Girl conferences this section shall not apply to

(A) any program or activity of the American Legion undertaken in connection with the organization or operation of any Boys State conference, Boys Nation conference, Girls State conference, or Girls Nation conference; or

(B) any program or activity of any secondary school or educational institution specifically for—

(i) the promotion of any Boys State conference, Boys Nation conference, Girls State conference, or Girls Nation conference; or

(ii) the selection of students to attend any such conference;

(8) Father-son or mother-daughter activities at educational institutions this section shall not preclude father-son or mother-daughter activities at an educational institution, but if such activities are provided for students of one sex, opportunities for reasonably comparable activities shall be provided for students of the other sex; and

(9) Institution of higher education scholarship awards in "beauty" pageants this section shall not apply with respect to any scholarship or other financial assistance awarded by an institution of higher education to any individual because such individual has received such award in any pageant in which the attainment of such award is based upon a combination of factors related to the personal appearance, poise, and talent of such individual and in which participation is limited to individuals of one sex only, so long as such pageant is in compliance with other nondiscrimination provisions of Federal law.

(b) Preferential or disparate treatment because of imbalance in participation or receipt of Federal benefits; statistical evidence of imbalance

Nothing contained in subsection (a) of this section shall be interpreted to require any educational institution to grant preferential or disparate treatment to the members of one sex on account of an imbalance which may exist with respect to the total number or percentage of persons of that sex participating in or receiving the benefits of any federally supported program or activity, in comparison with the total number or percentage of persons of that sex in any community, State, section, or other area: *Provided*, That this subsection shall not be construed to prevent the consideration in any hearing or proceeding under this chapter of statistical evidence tending to show that such an imbalance exists with respect to the participation in, or receipt of the benefits of, any such program or activity by the members of one sex.

(c) "Educational institution" defined

For purposes of this chapter an educational institution means any public or private preschool, elementary, or secondary school, or any institution of vocational, professional, or higher education, except that in the case of an educational institution composed of more than one school, college, or department which are administratively separate units, such term means each such school, college, or department.

GLOSSARY

A Vindication of the Rights of Woman Treatise by Mary Wollstonecraft published in 1792 in England arguing for the intellectual equality and rights of women.

abroad marriage Marriage of slaves who live on two different plantations.

age of consent Phrase referring the minimum age at which a person is considered capable of giving informed consent to any contract or behavior, with particular reference to sexual acts.

Aid to Dependent Children (ADC) A program that gave grants to states to use for the support of dependent children.

All American Girls Baseball League (AAGBL) Women's professional baseball league that began as a response to the lack of young male athletes who had joined the armed services.

American and Foreign Anti-Slavery Society Organization created in 1840 to oppose slavery through political channels but to ignore other issues such as the right of women to lead the reform movement.

American Anti-Slavery Society Organization founded by William Lloyd Garrison in 1833 committed to an immediate end to slavery.

American Birth Control League Founded in 1921 to provide services to women in need; later became Planned Parenthood.

American Woman Suffrage Association (AWSA) Formed in 1869 in Cleveland and led by Lucy Stone and Henry Blackwell to work for woman suffrage at all levels.

antebellum period Period in U.S. history extending roughly from 1830 to 1860.

antimiscegenation laws State legislation enacted to prevent interracial marriage.

Articles of Confederation Document adopted by Second Continental Congress in 1777 to create first government of the United States as a loose confederation of states.

Association for the Advancement of Women (AAW) Formed in October 1873 to promote the formation of women's clubs and to showcase women's accomplishments.

Association of Southern Women to Prevent Lynching (ASWPL) Founded by Jessie Daniel Ames in 1930 to mobilze white southern women to oppose lynching.

baby boom The cohort of babies born in the United States between 1946–1964.

back-alley abortions Illegal abortions, done in unsanitary and often dangerous nonmedical settings.

Baltimore and Ohio Railroad First railroad built in the United States, opening in 1830.

Beats A group of mostly male writers and poets centered in Greenwich, who rebelled against 1950s social and sexual conventions.

Beecher-Tilton scandal The furor created by the revelation of the Rev. Henry Ward Beecher's affair with Elizabeth Tilton, one of his parishioners.

belles Wealthy young southern women of marriageable age presented to society in a series of balls.

Big House African American description of the house on the plantation where the master lived.

Black Codes Legislation enacted by former Confederate states, 1865–1866, to define the rights and limits of freedom of former slaves.

Black Death Bubonic plague that swept Europe beginning in the 1340s and continuing particularly through the seventeenth century.

Black Power movement A younger and more militant phase of the civil rights movement that highlighted the importance of black masculinity.

bond marriage Legal agreement to marry that was used as a substitute for marriage in the early days of settlement in Texas.

Boston marriage A term popular in the late nineteenth century that referred to women who set up housekeeping together and lived in a marriage-like relationship.

Brown v. Board of Education of Topeka The 1954 Supreme Court case overturning the "separate but equal" doctrine established in *Plessy v. Ferguson*.

Californios/Californias Men and women of Spanish descent in California.

camp meetings Religious revival meetings held in open fields, usually during the summer.

casta Person of mixed heritage.

Chamberlain-Kahn Act Passed in July 1819, this legislation established federal grants for state venereal disease programs aimed to protect men serving in the armed forces.

charity girls A reference used in the early twentieth century for young women who traded sexual favors for treats and amusements.

Child Support Enforcement Amendments Act This act strengthened child support agencies' abilities to get money from the nonresidential parent of children on Aid to Families with Dependent Children (AFDC) for medical expenses and cost of living.

children's crusade Plan to send the children of the textile strikers to temporary homes outside Lawrence.

Christian Coalition A group formed by Roman Catholic and Evangelical Protestants to influence Republican party politics.

Civilian Conservation Corps (CCC) Program was designed to tackle the problem of unemployed young men from ages 18 to 25.

coartacion Ability of a slave to purchase his or her freedom under Spanish law.

cold war The foreign policy of containment directed at Communist Soviet Union and includes the alignments between foreign policy abroad and the expression of anti-Communism throughout U.S. culture.

Commission on Interracial Cooperation (CIC) Established in Atlanta in 1921 the Commission worked with white and black leaders to bring an end to lynching and improve the conditions of poor African Americans.

communitarian Referring to experimental collective communities meant to demonstrate how societies could be constructed around shared property and social responsibilities rather than around individual property.

companionate marriage A new style of marriage that emphasized companionship and compatability between spouses, as well as sex education, birth control, and easier access to divorce.

complementarity Idea that men and women have different characteristics that complement one another.

complex marriage Form of marriage promoted in the Oneida community in which every man and every woman in the community were considered married to one another.

Compromise of 1850 Congressional act allowing New Mexico and Utah to decide if they will be free or slave but also allowing California to be admitted to the Union as a free state.

Comstock Act The 1873 law that forbade the use of the U.S. Postal Service to mail "obscene" materials, which included contraceptive information and devices.

Confederate States of America The union of the eleven southern states that seceded to preserve slavery and protect states rights.

Congress of Industrial Organizations (CIO) The labor union formed in 1935 by John L. Lewis as the result of a dispute with the American Federation of Labor.

consciousness raising A popular practice of groups of women sharing intimate details of their lives to study them for the effects of sexism and gender oppression.

consumption The purchasing of consumer goods.

Contraband Relief Association Formed in August 1862 to provide food and relief to destitute former slaves.

contrabands of war Term for escaped slaves who sought refuge behind Union lines during the Civil War.

Council of National Defense Created by the U.S. Congress during World War I to manage the domestic aspects of the nation's war effort.

counterculture The youth culture of the mid-1960s that grew out of the student protest movements, with a focus on lifestyle liberation.

coureurs de bois French trappers.

coverture Legal status of a woman upon marriage under common law, in which her legal identity is merged with that of her husband.

crillo Person of Spanish heritage born in a colony.

cross-class alliance A concept referring to the joint projects of middle- and upper-class women and working-class women based on the assumption of "sisterhood."

Cullom Bill Introduced into Congress in 1870 to strengthen the provisions of the Morrill Anti-Bigamy Act, which had been largely ignored during the Civil War.

cult of domesticity Ideology suggesting that women's work within the home was crucial to society, particularly because of its moral rather than economic value

culture wars A set of clashes between conservative and liberal Americans over issues pertaining to private life.

Daughters of Bilitis A political group formed by lesbians to promote greater tolerance of homosexuality.

Daughters of Liberty Women who organized to support the Patriot cause.

Daughters of St. Crispin Formed in 1869 as the woman's branch of the all-male Knights of St. Crispin, which supported the principle of equal pay for equal work.

Dawes Severalty Act Also called the Indian Allotment Act, this 1887 legislation divided reservation land in an effort to assimilate tribal members into the general American population as "responsible farmers."

de facto segregation Racial segregation based on social practice, not enforced by law.

de jure segregation Racial segregation based on law.

Declaration of Independence Written by the Second Continental Congress in 1776 rejecting the King of England as the leader of the British colonies and asserting the right of men to form their own government.

Declaration of Sentiments Statement produced at the Seneca Falls convention in 1848 listing injustices faced by women and rights they deserved.

Democratic Party Political party that formed around Andrew Jackson in the 1820s, supporting his policies of limited federal government.

deputy husband Position assumed by a woman who took on the responsibilities of her husband while he was gone.

do-everything policy This policy provided an umbrella for the promotion of a multitude of programs beyond temperance.

domestic feminism Coined by historian Daniel Scott Smith, refers to the increasing power of married women to control reproduction.

double V campaign Winning the fight against racial segregation, or Jim Crow, and against fascism.

Dred Scott decision Decision by the Supreme Court that Dred Scott could not sue for his freedom even though he lived in a free state because slaves were not citizens.

Eagle Forum Pro-family organization founded by Phyllis Schlafly in 1972.

Edmunds-Tucker Act Legislation disincorporating the Mormon church and disenfranchising supporters of polygamy, including women.

elect People chosen by God to be saved.

Ellis Island Located in the New York Harbor, the main port of entry for immigrants in the late nineteenth and early twentieth centuries.

Emancipation Proclamation Issued by President Lincoln on January 1, 1863, freeing slaves in the Confederate states.

empressarios Agents who brought parties of immigrant settlers from the United States to Texas.

Enlightenment Intellectual movement stressing human reason and the ability to achieve progress by applying reason to problems of science and society.

Equal Employment Opportunity Commission (EEOC) The federal agency charged with enforcing employment antidiscrimination laws.

Equal Opportunity Act This act legislated a broader jurisdiction for the EEOC and strengthened its ability to enforce its rulings.

Equal Pay Act of 1963 Federal legislation that prohibited pay differentials based on sex.

Equal Rights Amendment (ERA) A proposed constitutional amendment outlawing discrimination "on account of sex."

Erie Canal First canal built in the United States, connecting New York City with upstate New York.

Executive Order 8802 This order prohibited government contractors from engaging in employment discrimination based on race, color, or national origin.

Exodusters A term for the nearly 15,000 African Americans who moved to Kansas at the close of Reconstruction.

Fair Labor Standards Act of 1938 The federal law establishing minimum wages, standards for overtime work and pay, and restrictions on child labor.

Family and Medical Leave Act (FMLA) Passed in 1993, the Act provided twelve weeks of unpaid family leave for workers.

family system of labor The practice of employing entire families, including young children, common in the production of textiles.

Family Violence Prevention and Services Act The 1984 Act provided funds for shelters and family violence programs.

family wage The idea that a man should earn sufficient wages to provide the sole support of his family.

family-wage economy Term for the situation in which all members of a family must earn wages and share them in order for the family to survive.

Farm Security Administration (FSA) Created to assist poor farmers during the dust bowl and the Great Depression.

Farmers' Alliance Organized in the 1880s as the political wing of the Granger movement and became the backbone of Populism by the end of the decade.

Federal Emergency Relief Administration (FERA) Passed in 1933, the agency gave direct aid to the states, which funneled funds through such local agencies as home relief bureaus and departments of welfare for poor relief.

Federalists Political faction that supported the Constitution and a strong central government.

feme covert Status of married woman under common law in which her legal identity is merged with that of her husband.

feme sole Status of a single woman under common law in which her legal identity is independent of a man.

feminism A term introduced into the United States around 1910 to augment the demands for voting rights and economic equality with a psychological dimension akin to "self-realization."

feminist art movement A movement in the 1970s to redefine women's art and women's place in the art world.

feminization of poverty The gradual and proportionate increase of women living in poverty in the 1970s.

fictive kin People with strong emotional ties similar to those of family members but not related to each other through marriage or birth.

Fifteenth Amendment Prohibits the denial of suffrage because of race, color, or previous condition of servitude and leaves out "sex."

filibustering Private military adventures to take over foreign governments with whom the United States is not at war.

Florence Crittenton Mission A refuge for prostitutes and safe haven for women without homes named for the recently-deceased daughter of founder Charles Crittenton.

Fourierists Followers of Charles Fourier who participated in his communitarian experiment in France and the United States.

Fourteenth Amendment Confers national citizenship on all persons born or naturalized in the United States and introduces the word "male" into the Constitution.

Free Soil Party Political party created in the 1840s around a belief that slavery should not be allowed in the territories acquired by the United States.

Freedmen's Bureau Established by Congress in March, 1865 to provide assistance to Civil War refugees; the federal agency that coordinated relief efforts for former slaves and established schools for black children.

French and Indian War Also known as the Seven Years' War in Europe, it was fought between France and England from 1754 to 1763 in both Europe and North America.

gang system System for organizing slave labor that groups slaves together to work on successive tasks.

General Federation of Women's Clubs Formed in 1890 as a federation of local women's clubs.

genizaros and genizaras Male and female Indian captives held as slaves in New Mexico.

GI Bill or the Servicemen's Readjustment Act of 1944 Provided college or vocational education, one year of unemployment compensation, and loans for returning veterans.

glass ceiling A term that refers to situations in which the advancement of a qualified person stops at a particular level because of some form of discrimination, most commonly sexism or racism.

Grange The popular term for the Patrons of Husbandry, an organization of family farmers that formed in 1867.

Great Awakening Series of religious revivals that swept the colonies in the middle of the eighteenth century.

Great Migration Movement of Puritans from England to New England between the 1620s and 1650s as a result of religious persecution.

Great Migration The migration of thousands of African Americans from the rural South to the urban North, which was especially pronounced during World War I when job opportunities opened up.

Henry Street Settlement Founded in New York City in 1893 by Lillian Wald to provide social and health services to mainly immigrant families.

Heterodoxy A club of "unorthodox women" formed by Marie Jenny Howe in 1912 that included the cream of New York's literary, artistic, and political activists.

heterosociality When women and men socialize together, as opposed to single-sex or homosocial settings.

Hollywood Production Code "Morality" codes imposed on Hollywood films in between 1930 and 1960.

home economics Originated in the 1880s as an academic discipline devoted to the care of home and family.

home protection The slogan promoted by WCTU president Frances E. Willard to secure the organization's endorsement of woman suffrage.

Homestead Act of 1862 Legislation allowing a household head, male or female, to obtain land in the public domain to establish a family farm.

Hospital Act of September 1862 Legislation by the Confederacy that allowed women to serve as nurses in hospitals.

Hull-House One of the first settlement houses in the United States, founded in Chicago in 1889 by Jane Addams and Ellen Gates Starr.

Hyde Amendment A 1976 law that reframed the government's responsibility to offer abortion services and restricted abortion from the health care provided by Medicaid.

identity politics Political action to advance the interests of members of groups that share a marginalized identity, such as race or gender.

Illinois Factory Inspection Act Passed in 1893, this landmark act specified conditions of labor in sweatshops in the state of Illinois; it was declared unconstitutional the following year.

Illinois Woman's Alliance Formed in 1888 to assist working women and their children.

indentured servant Person bound to work for a master for four to seven years as payment for transportation to the New World.

Indian Country Land in British territory west of the Proclamation Line of 1763 reserved for Indians.

Indian Removal Act Act passed by both houses of Congress in 1830 allowing the president to negotiate treaties that would exchange Indian lands east of the Mississippi River for new territory west of the Mississippi.

Indian Territory Unorganized territory west of the Mississippi River where Indians were forced to relocate in the 1830s.

Industrial Revolution Transformation from craft-based system to mass production of goods.

Industrial Workers of the World Founded in Chicago in 1905, represented the radical wing of the labor movement and organized workers into "one big union" without regard to skill.

inner light Quaker belief that Jesus is a guiding light within each person.

International Council of Women Formed in 1888 as a counterpart to the National Council of Women with delegates representing women activists from nine nations.

International Council of Women of the Darker Races of the World Founded by African American Mary Talbert in 1922 to promote Pan-African activism.

International Ladies' Garment Workers' Union Founded in Chicago in 1905, the "Wobblies" represented the radical wing of the labor movement and organized workers into "one big union" without regard to skill.

Jane Club The Chicago cooperative housekeeping arrangement for a group of working women who wished to avoid boarding-houses.

Jeffersonian Republicans Political faction that opposed the Federalists and favored limited government and an agrarian republic.

jezebel White southern stereotype of young slave woman who was thought to seek out sexual relationships with white men.

juvenile court system Special courts established to handle children under the age of 18 who commit acts that would be crimes if committed by adults as well as children who run away from home or engage in behaviors dangerous to themselves or others.

juvenile delinquency Antisocial or criminal acts performed by juveniles.

Kansas-Nebraska Act Act that repealed the Missouri Compromise by allowing the residents of Kansas and Nebraska to choose whether to be slave or free.

la familia Spanish expression denoting the enduring bonds of affection and duty extending from biological kin to close friends.

labor segmentation A practice by employers that governs the corporate labor market, opening up jobs to only specific groups by race, ethnicity, or gender.

Ladies' Federal Labor Union Chicago union of women working in several trades that did much of the campaigning for the passage of the Illinois Factory Inspection Act of 1893.

Ladies Industrial Aid Association of Union Hall Organized to provide aid to soldiers and their families in the Boston area only.

Liberty Party Political party created in 1840 around opposition to slavery in the United States.

libre Freed slaves and free persons of color in Louisiana Territory, particularly New Orleans.

Loyalists Colonists who sided with Britain during the American Revolution.

lyceums Lecture series or other forms of popular education.

mammy Stereotype of southern female slave who identified with the interests of her white charges and exercised great authority in their lives.

Manifest Destiny Belief that the borders of the United States were destined to spread westward.

Mann Act Also known as the White-Slave Traffic Act of 1910, banned the interstate transport of women for "immoral purposes."

manumission Granting of freedom to a slave.

Mariolatry Worship of the Virgin Mary as religious practice within the Roman Catholic Church.

maternalism A term used by historians to describe the emphasis of Progressive Era reformers on the health and welfare of women and children.

matrilineal Tracing inheritance and descent through the female line.

matrilocal Living with the wife's family.

medium A person who facilitates communication between the living and the dead.

mestizo Person of mixed Spanish and Indian heritage.

metis Mixture of French and Indian cultures.

Minor v. Happersett U.S. Supreme Court ruling in 1784 that allowed states to restrict the right to vote to male citizens.

miscegenation A term introduced into the United States in 1863, refers to an alleged mixing of "races" through sexual relations and provided the basis for laws prohibiting interracial marriage and cohabitation.

Missouri Compromise Agreement admitting Maine as a free state and Missouri as a slave state and stipulating that slavery not exist north of the 36° 30' parallel in the states created out of the Louisiana Territory.

modern welfare state Federal and state programs that offer working populations protections against unemployment, sickness, old-age insecurity, and the loss of a family breadwinner. FDR hoped the New Deal would create cradle-to-grave security against "the hazards and vicissitudes of life."

momism The tendency in the 1950s to blame all social ails and psychological problems on bad mothers and failed mothering.

monogamous Marriage to one spouse.

Morrill Anti-Bigamy Act Passed by Congress in 1862, this legislation made plural marriage a federal crime.

mothers' pensions State legislation established to subsidize the domestic work of poor women with dependent children.

Muller v. Oregon The landmark U.S. Supreme Court ruling that upheld Oregon state law restricting the hours a woman may work on the grounds that the state has an interest in protecting a woman's health.

municipal housekeeping A phrase popular during the Progressive Era to connote the extension of women's domestic skills to urban affairs.

National American Woman Suffrage Association Formed in 1890 to promote the ballot for women.

National Association of Colored Women Established in 1896 as the merger of the National Federation of Afro-American Women and the National League of Colored Women.

National Association Opposed to Woman Suffrage Formed in New York City in 1911 as a federation of state antisuffrage groups, which included both men and women.

National Birth Control League Founded in 1916 to advocate changes in legislation that restricted the dissemination of birth control information and devices.

National Congress of Mothers Founded in 1897, the organization promoted education for child-rearing and infant health; later became the Parent-Teaching Association.

National Consumer's League Founded in 1899 by a group of women affiliated with Hull-House to lobby for improved conditions in the manufacture of consumer goods.

National Council of Negro Women (NCNW) Founded to bring together many different national and local organizations serving or representing African American women.

National Council of Women Formed in 1888 in commemoration of the fortieth anniversary of the woman's rights meeting at Seneca Falls, New York, as a representative body of women's reform organizations.

National Labor Union A federation of trade assemblies formed in 1866 that supported woman's right to labor.

National League for the Protection of Colored Women Formed in 1906 as a federation of organizations established to assist young African American women migrating to northern cities.

National Organization for Women (NOW) The feminist organization founded in 1966 to promote women's equality.

National Recovery Administration (NRA) The government agency established to coordinate businesses who voluntarily drew up "codes of fair competition" to enhance economic recovery. These codes were intended to help workers by setting minimum wages and maximum hours, and help consumers by setting fair prices.

National Urban League A nonpartisan civil rights organization formed to give support to newly arrived migrants from the South to northern cities.

National Woman Suffrage Association (NWSA) Formed in 1869 in New York City and led by Elizabeth Cady Stanton and Susan B. Anthony to advance a strategy to introduce a federal amendment to grant women the right to vote.

National Woman's Alliance A short-lived organization led by Populist women and their allies in the temperance and suffrage movements.

National Woman's Party Succeeded the Congressional Union as the militant wing of the woman suffrage movement and focused on amending the Constitution.

National Women's Political Caucus Founded as a bipartisan organization whose goal was to increase the number of women in politics.

National Women's Trade Union League Founded in Boston in 1903 to "assist in the organization of women wage workers into trade unions."

National Youth Administration A program to devise useful work for young people who were on relief in 1935.

nativist A person who supports the interest of native inhabitants against those of immigrants.

Neighborhood Union A social settlement founded in Atlanta in 1908 by Lugenia Burns Hope in response to the impoverished conditions of African Americans.

neophytes Indian converts in California missions.

New Left A loosely connected network of campus groups that sought an immediate end to the Vietnam War and broad and wide-reaching reforms of U.S. society.

New Lights People converted to evangelical religious beliefs in the Great Awakening.

Nineteenth Amendment The so-called "Susan B. Anthony Amendment," which granted women the right to vote, was endorsed by the Senate on June 4, 1919 and became law on August 26, 1920.

Office of War Information (OWI) Created in 1942 and served as an important U.S. government propaganda agency during World War II.

Old Lights People who supported the status quo in churches and opposed the religious changes promoted by New Lights.

open marriage Refers to an agreement that recognizes the right of husbands and wives to engage in extramarital sexual relationships without the stigma of infidelity.

Operation Wetback A 1954 federal program to close the border between Mexico and Texas, California, and Arizona.

Owenites Followers of Robert Owen who participated in his communitarian experiment in England and the United States.

Page Act of 1875 Enacted by the U.S. Congress to restrict immigration from Asian countries, especially women identified as prostitutes.

Pan-African movement An international movement to promote unity among people of African nations and of African descent.

Panic of 1837 Economic depression in 1837 tied to the widespread failure of banks and businesses in the United States.

patriarchal order Society in which the father is the head of the family and the rest of the society is based on this hierarchy.

patrilineal Tracing inheritance and descent through the male line.

patrilocal Living with the husband's family.

Patriots Colonists who opposed Britain during the American Revolution.

pawn A person who is held as security for a debt.

Personal Responsibility and Work Opportunity Act Passed in 1996, the Act ended welfare as an entitlement program.

pessary Glass shield inserted in a woman's vagina to hold the uterus in place or for contraceptive purposes.

phalanx A Fouierist community.

Phyllis Wheatley Home Named after the famous African American poet, homes that were established to assist African American working women searching for work and residences.

pink-collar job A type of employment traditionally held by women, especially relatively low-paying office work.

plaçage Relationship in which a white man legally agreed to support a libre woman as part of an ongoing sexual relationship.

Plessy v. Ferguson The 1896 Supreme Court decision that established "Jim Crow" as the law of the land by condoning "separate but equal" facilities for black and white people.

plural marriage The Mormon custom of taking more than one wife in order to maximize the number of children.

polygamy Marriage to more than one spouse.

Populism Radical agrarians who sought political office in the 1890s to challenge corporate control.

President's Commission on the Status of Women (PCSW) A committee established by President John F. Kennedy to advise him on pending legislative issues concerning women.

presidio Spanish military garrison.

Proclamation Line of 1763 Boundary line designating British territory west of the Appalachian Mountains as Indian land.

Progressive movement A broad coalition of reformers who advocated efficiency in government and various legislative measures to alleviate the social injustices that accompanied the second industrial revolution.

public work A common phrase for wage labor in the postbellum South.

putting-out system Form of industrialization in which the owner of raw materials distributes the materials to workers who are paid by the piece to assemble them in their homes.

race suicide A phrase attributed to President Theodore Roosevelt heralding the demise of "civilization" caused by the dropping birth rate among Americans of Anglo-Saxon ancestry.

race women A term that denoted politically active African American women.

Reconstruction The period 1865–1877 that reintegrated the former Confederate states into the Union and established the terms of freedom for former slaves.

regent Person who rules when a king or monarch is too young or enfeebled to do so.

Retirement Equity Act Attempted to meet the needs of women in the work force and those women married to, or divorced from, working men by providing more benefits for surviving spouses, lowering the age for participation to 55, and granting the divorce spouse rights to retirement pension if stipulated in the separation papers.

revival An intense religious awakening taking place in a series of evangelical services meant to promote conversion.

Roe v. Wade The 1973 Supreme Court case that established women's right to have an abortion.

Salon Regular reception, usually held in the home of a wealthy woman, where social, intellectual, and political leaders mixed.

sanitary fairs Extravaganzas organized mainly by women to raise funds for the Union troops during the Civil War.

Scottish Enlightenment Intellectual movement centered in Scotland that assumed inequalities and hierarchies were natural and necessary in society.

Second Continental Congress Representatives of the thirteen colonies in rebellion against England, meeting as a government body from 1775 to 1781 to direct the Patriot cause.

Second Great Awakening Series of religious revivals throughout the United States that spanned the first half of the nineteenth century.

second industrial revolution The major advances in the technical aspects of industrial production, including consumer goods, that occurred in the last half of the nineteenth century.

second shift The full-time and unpaid domestic work women did when they came home from work.

second-wave feminism The surge of feminist activism that took place in the late 1960s and early 1970s.

sectarian medicine Originated as an alternative to the harsh or "heroic" practices of mainstream or "allopathic" medicine and included such movements as homeopathy, hydrotherapy, and eclecticism.

separate spheres the idea that men and women operate in different worlds: women in the private world of the home and men in the public world of business and politics

sex-segregated labor market The division of job classification along gender lines.

sexual inversion An early sexological term for same-sex desire.

sexual revolution The liberalization of U.S. attitudes toward sexuality that took place in the 1960s and 1970s.

shaman Spiritual leader, often with the power to heal.

social purity The ideal of a single standard of sexual morality for both men and women, advocating abstinence before marriage and restrained behavior after.

Social Security Act of 1935 A governmental program that created pensions for the elderly.

socialist In the antebellum period, a belief in collective sharing of wealth and work rather than a reliance on individual property holding as a basis of society and government.

Sojourner Truth Home for Working Girls Formed in 1895 for African American working women.

Soldiers' Aid Societies Woman's voluntary associations organized to assist the troops from their communities.

Sons of Liberty Organization of Patriots opposed to British taxes.

soral polygamy Marriage to two sisters by the same man.

Southern Christian Leadership Conference (SCLC) A principal organization of the civil rights movement that formed out of the Montgomery bus boycott of 1955–1956; led by Martin Luther King Jr.

sovereign Autonomous ruler or chief of state.

Spanish American War A short war between Spain and the United States in 1898 that liberated Cuba and the Philippines from Spanish rule.

specie Coin rather than paper money.

speedup Increase in the speed of machinery in a factory to produce greater output.

Spiritualism A loosely organized movement around the belief that the living can communicate with the dead.

State Children's Health Insurance Program (SCHIP) Established in 1997 to provide health insurance for families who earned too much to qualify for Medicare.

stretch-out Increase in the number of machines a factory worker tends in order to increase output.

Student Nonviolent Coordinating Committee (SNCC) A principal organization of the civil rights movement that formed in 1960 from student meetings led by Ella Baker.

Students for a Democratic Society (SDS) The main organization of the New Left.

Susan B. Anthony amendment Introduced in January 1886, the amendment specifies that the right to vote shall not be "denied or abridged" on account of sex.

sweatshop A workshop is supervised by a middleman, the sweater, whose employees produce mainly clothing under harsh conditions.

task system System for organizing slave labor that delegates to an individual slave entire responsibility for production of a crop, such as rice, on a particular plot of land.

Tejanos/Tejanas Men and women of Spanish heritage who settled in Texas.

The International Ladies Garment Workers Union (ILGWU) Formed in 1900 by the amalgamation of seven local unions.

the Negro's hour Phrase used to describe the subordination of woman's rights to the campaign to advance the political rights of African American men.

the personal is political One of the founding principles of second-wave feminism; the phrase captured feminists' attention to the psychological, sexual, and privately experienced aspects of women's oppression.

Thirteenth Amendment Extended the terms of the Emancipation Proclamation to free slaves throughout the United States; ratified in 1865.

Title IX of the Education Amendments of 1972 Passed on June 23, 1972, the law forbid sex discrimination in any educational program or activity funded by the federal government, including athletics.

tobacco brides Young women brought to Virginia in the 1620s who promised to marry men who would pay for their passage.

Trail of Tears Westward journey of sixteen thousand Cherokee Indians from Georgia to Oklahoma in 1838.

trash gang Gang of slaves composed of pregnant and older women as well as children, delegated to do lighter field tasks such as weeding and collecting trash.

Treaty of Paris Treaty that ended the French and Indian War between France and England.

truancy Process of a slave absenting himself or herself from a plantation for days or months as a form of protest.

U.S. Children's Bureau Created in 1912 within the federal government to investigate and report *"upon all matters pertaining to the welfare of children and child life among all classes of our people."*

United Cannery, Agricultural, Packing and Allied Workers of America A labor union that made the greatest inroads with Mexican cannery workers and African American tobacco workers, many of whom were women.

United Electrical, Radio and Machine Workers of America One of the first unions to affiliate with the Congress of Industrial Organization in 1936.

United Packinghouse Workers of America A union was committed to organize all workers in the meatpacking industry, regardless of skill or trade.

United States Constitution Document adopted by Constitutional Convention in 1787 to replace Articles of Confederation and to provide for a stronger centralized government of the United States.

United States v. One Package of Japanese Pessaries This case challenged the Comstock Act and made it legal for medical professionals to ship and receive contraceptives.

Uprising of 30,000 Popular name for the strike of the shirtwaist makers who shut down the New York garment industry for several months beginning in November 1909.

War Advertising Council Charged with the task of selling wartime government programs and war bonds to the American public.

war bonds Issued by the government and purchased by civilians, war bonds functioned as a loan to the government to help finance the war effort.

War Brides Act The 1945 Act that allowed Chinese American veterans to bring brides into the United States.

War Manpower Commission The federal agency charged with balancing the labor needs of agriculture, industry, and the armed forces.

War of 1812 War between the United States and England over trade restrictions, fought between 1812 and 1815.

welfare state Reference to a system of government in which the state assumes primary responsibility for the *welfare* of its *citizens* and accords them services as a matter of entitlement.

Whig Party Political party formed in opposition to the Democrats supporting an active role for the federal government in economic development.

White Rose Home and Industrial Association Formed in 1897 to assist African American women coming to New York in search of work.

white slavery panic A moral panic based on the assumption that thousands of young women were being lured into prostitution and held against their will.

winning plan Formally adopted by the NAWSA in 1916, this strategy introduced targeted key state woman suffrage referenda and simultaneously supported an amendment to the Constitution.

Woman's Central Relief Association Served as the foundation for the United States Sanitary Commission.

Woman's Christian Temperance Union (WCTU) Founded in November 1874 to curtail the use of alcohol and became the largest organization of women in the nineteenth century.

Woman's Convention Organized by women to carry out their social service within the black Baptist Church.

woman's crusade The grassroots component of the temperance campaign that erupted in 1873–1874 that brought thousands of women into activism.

Woman's Peace Party Founded in Chicago in 1915 and chaired by Jane Addams, the WPP formed to protest World War I.

Woman's Work for Woman A phrase representing the agenda of the Woman's Foreign Missionary Society.

women adrift Common reference to women who set up households outside marriage or family.

Women of the Ku Klux Klan (WKKK) the women's auxilary of the racist and nativist Ku Klux Klan

Women Strike for Peace (WSP) A group formed in the 1950s to protest nuclear weapons.

Women's Convention of the Black Baptist Church The locus of the women's movement within the Black Baptist Church.

Women's Division of the Democratic National Committee The group within the National Democratic Party that organized and coordinated women's volunteer efforts for Democratic candidates.

Women's Educational and Industrial Union Founded in 1877 to help women support themselves by offering social services and practical vocational training.

Women's Health Movement (WHM) A movement in the 1970s to bring women greater knowledge of and control over their own health.

women's health protective associations Local groups that sponsored public health initiatives and raised money for building and maintaining hospitals.

Women's International League for Peace and Freedom Formed in 1919, WILPF succeeded the Woman's Peace Party in advocating the end of militarism and world peace.

women's liberation movement The burst of radical feminist groups that formed in the mid- to late 1960s that pioneered an analysis of sexuality and private life.

Women's National Indian Association Founded in 1879 to promote assimilationist policies among Native American women.

Working Women's Protective Union Organized in New York to assist wage-earning women during the Civil War.

Works Progress Administration (WPA) A massive federal relief program launched that created paying jobs for unemployed.

World WCTU Organized in 1891 as a federation of national affiliates of the WCTU to proselytize temperance and woman's rights throughout the world.

World YWCA The U.S. YWCA extended its representation around the world to improve the conditions of women by providing social services and education.

Wounded Knee Massacre The attack by the U.S. 7th Calvary on December 29, 1890 that resulted in the deaths of nearly 190 Indians, the majority of whom were women and children.

yeoman farmer Independent farmer who owns a small plot of land that he works himself.

Young Women's Christian Association Formed in several cities shortly after the Civil War to offer social services to young wage-earning women.

Photo and Text Credits

Introduction: xxxiv–xxxv: Reprinted with the permission of The Women's College Coalition; xxxiv (bottom); Courtesy of Library of Congress; xxxvi: Corbis/Bettmann; xxxix: New York Times Co./Hulton/Archive; xl: © Bettmann/CORBIS; xlvi: Corbis/SABA Press Photos, Inc.

Chapter 1 *Photos:* 2-3: Service Historique de la Marine, Vincennes, France/The Bridgeman Art Library; 6: The Granger Collection, New York; 9(top): Cahokia Mounds State Historic Site, painting by Michael Hampshire; 9(bottom): Museum HIP; 13: Justin Kerr Associates;17: The Pinpoint Morgan Library/Art Resource, NY; 19: Musée Conde, Chantilly, France, The Bridgeman Art Library; 22: Seattle Art Museum; 27: Courtesy of Library of Congress. *Text:* 16: Richard L. Kagan and Abigail Dyer, eds. and trans. *Inquisitorial Inquiries: Brief Lives of Secret Jews and Other Heretics*, pp. 40–49. Baltimore, Maryland: The Johns Hopkins University Press. Reprinted by permission of The Johns Hopkins University Press.

Chapter 2 *Photos:* 32-33: Breamore House, Hampshire, England; 37: Courtesy of the Library of Congress; 38: "Human Races (Las Castas)," 18th century, oil on canvas, 1.04 x 1.48m. Museo Nacional del Virreinato, Tepotzotlan, Mexico. Schmliwijk/Art Resource, NY; 39: Courtesy of the John Carter Brown Library at Brown University; 42: Thomas Fisher Rare Book Library, University of Toronto; 44: The Public Archives of Canada; 46: © Bettmann/CORBIS; 51: National Potrait Gallery, Smithsonian Instituition, Washington DC/Art Resource, NY; 56: Mrs. Elizabeth Freake and Baby Mary (American), oil on canvas, 1963. 134. Worcester Art Museum, Worcester Massachusetts, Gift of Mr. and Mrs. Albert W. Rice.

Chapter 3 *Photos:* 71: Getty Images Inc.—Hulton Archive Photos; 78: Corbis/Bettmann; 79: Courtesy of the Library of Congress; 82: The Granger Collection, New York; 83: North Wind Picture Archives; 87: Library of Congress; 88: Private Collection/The Bridgeman Art Library. *Text:* 65-66: Quoted in Cynthia Kierner. *Southern Women in Revolution, 1776–1800, Personal and Political Narratives*, pp. 63–64. Columbia: University of South Carolina Press, 1998. Reprinted by permission of University of South Carolina Press; 85: Sharon Harris, ed. Letter of Molly Brandt to Judge Daniel Claus. In *American Women Writers to 1800*, pp. 280–281. New York: Oxford University Press. Reprinted by permission of Oxford University Press, Inc.

Chapter 4 *Photos:* 98-99: Smithsonian Art Museum, Washington, D.C., Art Resource, NY; 101: Courtesy of the Bancroft Library. University of California, Berkeley; 103: Getty Images Inc.—Hulton Archive Photos; 110: Woolaroc Museum; 113: US Mint; 117: Paul and Lulu Hilliard University Art Museum University of Louisiana at Lafayette; 121: Courtesy of the Ohio Historical Society.

Chapter 5 *Photos:* 130-131: Courtesy of the Library of Congress; 133: National Museum of American History Smithsonian; 134: American Textile History Museum, Lowell, Mass.; 141: Dr. Leo Hershkowitz; 143: © American Antiquarian Society; 144: © Courtesy of the Ohio Historical Society; 156: Courtesy of the Library of Congress; 158: © Historical Picture Archive/CORBIS. *Text:* 131-132: Mary H. Blewett. *We Will Rise in Our Might: Working-women's Voices from Nineteenth-Century New England*. Ithaca, NY: Cornell University Press, 1991. Reprinted by permission of Cornell University Press; 147: Lucille Salitan and Eve Lewis Perara, eds. Letter from Elizabeth Chace to Samuel Chace, dated 1854. In *Virtuous Lives: Four Quaker Sisters Remember Family Life, Abolitionism, and Women's Suffrage*. Reprinted by permission of The Continuum International Publishing Group, 1994.

Chapter 6 *Photos:* 164-165: Corbis/Bettmann; 169: From "A House Divided: America in the Age of Lincoln" by Eric Foner, published by Norton and the Chicago Historical Society in 1990. Courtesy of the Library of Congress; 170 (top): © Bettmann/CORBIS All Rights Reserved; 170 (bottom): Courtesy of the Library of Congress; 176: Courtesy of the Library of Congress; 179: Dover Publications, Inc.; 186: Moorland-Spingham Research Center. *Text:* 192: Richard C. Lounsbury, ed. *Louisa S. McCord: Poems, Drama, Biography, Letters*, pp. 293–294. Charlottesville: University of Virginia Press, 1996.

Chapter 7 *Photos:* 196-197: Getty Images Inc.—Hulton Archive Photos; 202: © Southern Baptist Historical Library and Archives; 206: Rosenbach Museum & Library, Philadelphia; 208: The Maryland Historical Society, Baltimore Maryland; 211: From the Collection of the Oneida Community Mansion House, Oneida, NY; 215: Courtesy of the Library of Congress; 217: Courtesy American Antiquarian Society; 219: The University of Massachusetts Lowell, Center for Lowell History; 221: © Punch Limited. *Text:* 212: "E.E. Porter to the New York Female Moral Reform Society Corresponding Secretary, April 21, 1838." *Advocate of Moral Reform.* June 15, 1838. Reprinted in Daniel Wright and Kathryn Kish Sklar. "What Was the Appeal of Moral Reform to Antebellum Northern Women 1835-1841?" Women and Social Movements Website. Alexander Street Press. http://wasm.alexanderstreet.com.

Chapter 8 *Photos:* 228-229: Bibliothèque Nationale, Paris France/The Bridgeman Art Library; 232: © Queen Mary, University of London; 234: Mary Evans/Fawcett Library; 236: Getty Images Inc.—Hulton Archive Photos; 238: Courtesy of the Library of Congress; 241: Brown Brothers; 244 (top): Courtesy of Library of Congress; 244 (bottom): Courtesy of Library of Congress; 246: Courtesy Earl Vandale Collection, CN09569, Center for American History,

University of Texas at Austin; 251: Corbis/Bettmann; 252: © The Harper's Magazine Foundation. All rights reserved; 253: Courtesy of the Library of Congress. *Text:* 240: "Sally Rudd to Caroline Mary Rudd, March 26, 1836." Oberlin College Archives. Reprinted in Carol Lasser and the Students of History 266 at Oberlin College. "How Did Oberlin Women Students Draw on Their College Experience to Participate in Antebellum Social Movements, 1831-1861?" Women and Social Movements Website. Alexander Street Press. http://wasm.alexanderstreet.com.

Chapter 9 *Photos:* 260-261: The Granger Collection, New York; 265: Courtesy of the Library of Congress; 267: Getty Images Inc.—Hulton Archive Photos; 271: Provided courtesy HarpWeek., LLC; 272: Getty Images Inc.—Hulton Archive Photos; 273: Corbis/Bettmann; 276: © Bettmann/CORBIS; 278 (left): © National Portrait Gallery, Smithsonian Institution/Art Resource; 278 (right): Courtesy of the Library of Congress; 281: Courtesy of the Library of Congress; 284: Courtesy of the Library of Congress; 285: Courtesy of the Library of Congress; 287: © Mary Evans Picture Library/Edwin Wallace/The Image Works. *Text:* 275-276: Kate Cumming. A *Journal of Hospital Life in the Confederate Army of Tennessee from the Battle of Shiloh to the End of the War* , 44-45. Louisville, KY: John P. Morton & Co., 1966.

Chapter 10 *Photos:* 294-295: Courtesy of the Library of Congress; 299: Library of Congress; 305: Courtesy of the Library of Congress; 308: Courtesy of the Library of Congress; 311: Courtesy of the Library of Congress; 313: The Brechin Group Inc.; 314: © Bettmann/CORBIS All Rights Reserved; 316: Courtesy of the Library of Congress; 317: Picture History; 318: Courtesy of the Library of Congress; 323: Courtesy of the Library of Congress; 324: Courtesy of the Library of Congress.

Chapter 11 *Photos:* 333: Courtesy of the Library of Congress; 337: Photo Researchers Inc.; 340: Used by Permission, Utah State Historical Society, all rights reserved; 343: Courtesy of the Library of Congress; 346: Courtesy of the Library of Congress; 348: Nebraska Historical Society, Solomon T. Butcher Collection; 349: © Bettmann/CORBIS All Rights Reserved; 353: Courtesy of the Library of Congress; 356 (left and right): National Anthropological Archives; 357: Courtesy of the Library of Congress.

Chapter 12 *Photos:* 366: Courtesy of the Library of Congress; 369: Courtesy of the Library of Congress; 372: North Baker Research Library/California Historical Society; 373: Courtesy of the Library of Congress; 375: Courtesy of the Library of Congress; 382: Courtesy of the Library of Congress; 383: Schlesinger Library, Radcliffe Institute, Harvard University; 385: © CORBIS/All Rights Reserved; 387: Courtesy of the Library of Congress; 391: Duke University.

Chapter 13 *Photos:* 398-399: Photograph courtesy of the Pocumtuck Valley Memorial Association, Memorial Hall Museum, Deerfield, Massachusetts; 401: © CORBIS/All Rights Reserved; 403: Courtesy of Teachers College, Columbia University; 404: University of Delaware Library, Special Collections Department; 405: Special Collections, Cleveland State University Library; 407: Courtesy of the Library of Congress; 409: Courtesy of the Library of Congress; 412: Schlesinger Library, Radcliffe Institute, Harvard University; 417: © CORBIS/All Rights Reserved; 419: The Granger Collection; 423: Courtesy of the Library of Congress; 427: Courtesy of the Library of Congress.

Chapter 14 *Photos:* 435: Courtesy of the Library of Congress; 438: Courtesy of the Library of Congress; 441: Courtesy of the Library of Congress; 442: Photograph courtesy Newberry Library, Congress; 444: Swathmore College Peace Collection; 446: Courtesy of the Library of Congress; 448: Carlson Library, University of Toledo; 449: Courtesy of the Library of Congress; 452: Courtesy of the Library of Congress; 453: © Bettmann/CORBIS All Rights Reserved; 459: Lebrecht Music & Arts Photo Library. *Text:* 436-437: Sherna Gluck, ed. *From Parlor to Prison: Five American Suffragists Talk about Their Lives*, pp. 98–103. New York: Vintage Books, 1976.

Chapter 15 *Photos:* 464-465: Courtesy of the Library of Congress; 469 (top): © Bettmann/CORBIS; 469 (bottom): Courtesy of the Library of Congress; 471: Courtesy of the Library of Congress; 473: Courtesy of the Library of Congress; 475: Courtesy of the Library of Congress; 476: Courtesy of the Library of Congress; 480: Courtesy of the Library of Congress; 483: Courtesy of the Library of Congress; 485: Courtesy of the Library of Congress; 487: Courtesy of the Library of Congress; 490: Courtesy of the Library of Congress; 496: Courtesy of the Library of Congress. *Text:* 478-479: Rosey Safran. "The Washington Place Fire." *The Independent* 70 (April 20, 1911). 840–841.

Chapter 16 *Photos:* 502-503: Courtesy of the Library of Congress; 506: Courtesy of the Library of Congress; 507: Corbis/Bettmann; 510: Courtesy of the Library of Congress; 515: Courtesy of the Library of Congress; 517: Courtesy of the Library of Congress; 520: The Granger Collection; 522: Courtesy of the Visiting Nurse Association of Boston; 526: The Marcus Garvey & UNIA Papers; 527: Corbis/Bettmann; 529: Courtesy W.A. Swift Photograph Collection, Archives and Special Collections, Ball State University; 534: Getty Images Inc.—Hulton Archive Photos. *Text:* 519-520: Dorothy Dunbar Bromley. "Feminist-New Style." *Harper's Magazine* (October 1927).

Chapter 17 *Photos:* 540-541: The Granger Collection, New York; 543:Courtesy of the Library of Congress; 544: National Archives and Records Administration Special Collections & Archives; 553: Special Collections & Archives, Georgia State University Library; 557: © Bettmann/CORBIS All Rights Reserved; 559: Courtesy Virginia S. Bourne, Castine, ME; 561: Corbis/Bettmann;

562: Courtesy of the Library of Congress; 563: Courtesy of the Library of Congress; 566: Courtesy of the Library of Congress; 568: Margaret Bourke-White/LIFE Magazine © TimePix; 571: Corbis/Bettmann.

Chapter 18 *Photos:* 576-577: Courtesy of the Library of Congress; 579: Courtesy of the Library of Congress; 583: Courtesy of the Library of Congress; 590: Studio X, Getty Images, Inc.; 593: Corbis/Bettmann; 599: National Archives and Records Administration; 600: UCLA Library; 604: Courtesy of the Library of Congress; 606: Courtesy of the Library of Congress; 607: Getty Images Inc.—Hulton Archive Photos; 609: Courtesy of the Library of Congress. *Text:* 594: Steven L. Isoardi, interviewer. Oral History interview with Clora Bryant from Central Avenue Sounds. UCLA Oral History Program conducted on March 29, 1990 (120 mins); April 4, 1990 (104 mins.); April 18, 1990 (133 mins.).

Chapter 19 *Photos:* 616-617: Courtesy of the Library of Congress; 620: National Archives and Records Administration; 623: Courtesy of the Library of Congress; 625: Penguin Group USA, Inc.; 628: Courtesy of the Library of Congress; 630: Bernard Hoffman/Life Magazine/© 1950 TimePix; 633: Getty Images Inc.—Hulton Archive Photos 635: © Independent Productions/Photofest; 637: Courtesy of the Library of Congress; 639: Getty Images/Time Life Pictures; 640: Courtesy of the Library of Congress; 642: Corbis/Bettmann. *Text:* 636: Jessie Lopes de la Cruz. Excerpt from Ellen Cantarow. *Moving the Mountain: Women Working for Social Change.* Reprinted by permission of The Feminist Press at the City University of New York, 1980. http://www.feministpress.org. All rights reserved.

Chapter 20 *Photos:* 652-653: Roger Sandler/Pictor; 655: Getty Images/Time Life Pictures; 658: AP World Photos; 659: George Ballis, Take Stock-Images of Change; 661: Corbis/Bettmann; 668: Courtesy of Aileen C. Hernandez;

669: Courtesy of the Library of Congress; 674: Courtesy of the Library of Congress; 678: Courtesy of the Library of Congress; 679: Bill Janscha, AP Wide World Photos; 681: Reprinted by permission of Ms. Magazine, © 1972; 682: Courtesy of the Library of Congress. *Text:* 663: Interview with Hattye Gatson from the Civil Rights Documentation Project. The Tougaloo College Oral History Collection, Tougaloo College Archives, Tougaloo, Mississippi.; 677: From the Routledge Historical Atlas of Women in America, edited by Sandra Opdycke (New York: Routledge, 2000), page 112.

Chapter 21 *Photos:* 688-689: Joseph De Sciose, Aurora Photos Inc.; 692: Corbis/Bettmann; 693: © Bettmann/CORBIS All Rights Reserved; 697: Corbis/Bettmann; 702: Courtesy of the Library of Congress; 703: Cynthia Black; 704: Nancy Crampton; 708: Time & Life Pictures/Getty Images; 709: Laima Druskis/Pearson Education/PH College; 717: David Young-Wolff.

Chapter 22 *Photos:* 724-725: Reuters/Landov; 728: © Bettmann/CORBIS All Rights Reserved; 730: AP Wide World Photos; 733: CORBIS-NY; 734: Corbis/Bettmann; 735: Courtesy of the Library of Congress; 739: Joe Marquette, AP Wide World Photos; 744: Haraz N. Ghanbari, AP Wide World Photos; 747: A. Lichtenstein, The Image Works; 750: A Ramey, PhotoEdit Inc.; 753: Lance Corporal Clifton D. Sams/U.S. Department of Defense; 756: John Neubauer, PhotoEdit Inc.; 759: Skjold Photographs. *Text:* 724-725: "More and More, Women Risk All to Enter U.S." *The New York Times*, National Section, January 10, 2006. All rights reserved. Used by permission and protected by the Copyright Laws of the United States. The printing, copying, redistribution, or retransmission of the material without express written permission is prohibited.

INDEX

A

Abbot, Grace, 565
Abolition, 197–198
  gender and, 222–223, 252–253
  moral crusade, 286–288
  politics and gender, 222–223
  race and hierarchy, 220–222
  women's suffrage and, 306–309
Abortion
  activism (anti), 739–741
  antebellum period, 149
  Europe, 19
  law, 739–741
  Native Americans, 12
  prostitution, 335
  second wave feminism, 679–680, 714–715
  third wave feminism, 759
  twentieth century (early), 451–452
  See also Rights
Abortion rights, 737–738c
Abroad marriage, 172
Abuse. See Domestic violence; Rape
Abzug, Bella, 681, 730
Activism
  abortion, 714–715
  African American women, 414–416, 470–471, 524–528
  American Revolution, 86–88
  antebellum period, 247, 289
  antiabortion, 739–741
  antilynching, 419–420, 526–528
  antiprostituion, 213
  antislavery, 220–223
  birth control, 452–454
  Cherokee, 111
  conservative, 727–741
  Europe (early), 19–20
  global feminism and, 755–757
  Great Depression, 550–556
  labor, 107, 217–219, 318–321, 472–479, 522–523, 551–556, 665–673
  medical rights, 712–715
  nineteenth century (late), 416–422
  peace, 485–486
  pensions, 482–483
  populism, 416–418
  property rights, 236
  protesting Indian removal, 218–220
  reproductive rights, 679–680
  Seneca women, 104–105
  suffrage, 305–314, 410–413, 489–496

  temperance movement, 213–215, 217, 321–324, 408–410
  twentieth century (early), 466–472
  Vietnam, 696–700
  wage discrimination, 237
  women's health, 522–523
  See also Feminism; Organizations; Rights; Unions
Adams, Abigail, 78
Addams, Jane, 422, 437, 443–444, 466, 467–468, 486
Adoption. See Children
Advocate, The, 695
AFL–CIO, 665–666. See also American Federation of Labor
Africa, 21–25
African Americans
  activism (Jazz Age), 524–528
  antebellum North, 151–152
  authors, 532
  black feminism, 700–701
  blues, 533–534
  cities, 596–597
  domestic service, 378
  emancipation, 298–302
  employment, 584–586, 620–621
  Great Migration, 484–485
  Harlem Renaissance, 532
  heartland, 347
  marriage, 298–301, 440–441
  motherhood, 627–629
  music, 531–532
  New South, 376–377
  population (reconstruction), 297t
  rights, 295–297
  tobacco economy, 48
  unions, 622–624
  World War II, 594, 608–610
  See also Freedpeople; Slavery
Age of consent, 446
Agriculture
  colonies, 28
  Native Americans, 7
  Europe, 14
  fur trade, 41–42
  hunting and gathering societies, 6
  Mississippian cultures, 7–8
  New Netherland, 45
  Pueblo cultures, 8–9
Aid to Families with Dependent Children (AFDC), 564, 672–673, 718, 734, 743

Acquired Immune Deficiency Syndrome (AIDS), 732, 755–756
Air force, 607–608
Alcott, Louisa May, 288
Algonquin, 27
All American Girls Baseball League, 592
Allen, Fredrick Lewis, 504
Allotment, 352
Al-Qaeda, 753
American Anti-Slavery Society, 223
American Association of Retired Persons, 747
American Birth Control League, 454
American Colonization Society, 220
American Federation of Labor (AFL), 472, 476, 477, 551
American Federation of Musicians, 593
American Frontier. See Frontier
American Home Economics Association, 391
American Indians. See Native Americans; specific tribes
American Medical Association, 381
American Psychological Association, 695
American Red Cross, 274
American Revolution, 77–88
American Woman's Home, 143, 390
American Woman Suffrage Association, 309–314, 340
Aminatau, Queen (Zazzau), 22
Anderson, Mary, 521
Androgyny. See Transgender
Anne of Austria, 19
Annexation of Texas, 101
Antilynching, 419–420, 526–528
Antebellum period, 137–150
Anthony, Susan B. 251, 252, 264–265, 306, 308, 309, 313, 318–319, 340, 400, 421, 447, 491
Antiabortion. See Abortion
Antifeminism, 512, 726–741
Antimiscegenation laws, 371
Antislavery movement. See Abolition
Antiwar movement, 696–700
Appalachian women, 551–553
Appeal to the Women of the Nominally Free States, 243–244
Armistice, 488
Army, 699; See also Women's Army Corps
Art, 386–388, 566–567, 710–712. See also Authors; Literature; Movies; Photography

Articles of Confederation, 88
Asian Americans, 677, 678, 702–705
Assimilation, 352
Association for the Advancement of
Women, 316–318
Association of Southern Women to
Prevent Lynching, 528
Athletics, 676–679. *See also specific
sports*
Atkinson, Ti-Grace, 695
Atlantic colonies
class, 49–50, 52–53
family structure, 54, 55–57, 72–77
intermarriage, 50
marriage, 54
patriarchy, 52–53
pilgrims, 53
puritans, 53, 57
race, 50, 52
religion, 53–59
slavery, 50
witchcraft, 58–59
See also Tobacco economy
Atlantic trade, 25m
Austin, Mary, 458
Authors, 156–157, 177, 188–191,
286–289, 458–459, 532, 642–643
Aztecs, 7, 10

B

Baby boom, 625–629
Bache, Sarah Franklin, 80
Backlash. *See* Antifeminism
Bacon, Nathaniel, 52
Bacon's Rebellion, 52–53
Bad girls, 641
Bagley, Sarah, 219
Baker, Ella, 658–660
Baltimore and Ohio Railroad, 132
Barbie, 637–638
Barcelo, Gertrudis, 120–121
Barrios, 634–635
Barry (Lake), Leonora, 419
Barton, Clara, 274–276, 316
Baseball, 592
Basement workshop, 704
Battle of the sexes, 681
Battuta, Ibn, 23
Beal, Frances, 700
Beat generation, 641
Beecher, Catherine, 143, 218–220,
239, 243–244, 316, 390
Beecher-Tilton scandal, 312
Belles, 180
Bell Jar, The, 642
Beloved, 177
Benton, Thomas Hart, 220
Berdache, 27

Bethune, Mary McLeod, 560–561, 608
Bickerdyke, "Mother" Mary Ann, 274
Big house, 170
Bin Laden, Osama, 754–755
Birth control
activism, 434, 452–454
black feminism, 700–701
cold war, 639–640
condemnation, 451
Europe, 19
Great Depression, 544–547
Jazz Age, 510–512
prostitution, 335
twentieth century (early), 451–452
voluntary motherhood, 451
Birth rate, 451–452, 545, 715–716
Black bottom stomp, 532
Black Cabinet, 560
Black Code, 115, 296–297
Black Death, 13
Black feminism, 700–701
Black Metropolis, 627
Black power, 700
Blackwell, Elizabeth, 241, 266, 272,
316, 381
Blackwell, Emily, 266
Blackwell, Henry, 309
Blanchard, Elizabeth, 433–434
Blavatsky, Helena Petrova, 386
Bloomer, Amelia, 251
Bloomers, 251
Blues, 533–534
Body image, 637
Bohemians, 454–459
Bond marriage, 119
Bonnin, Gertrude Simmons (Zitkala
Sa/Red Bird), 354
Boone, Daniel, 102, 103
Boone, Jemima, 103
Boston marriage, 443, 558
Boston Women's Health Book Collec-
tive, 712
Bourke-White, Margaret, 568–569
Boycott, 657
Boyd, Belle, 288–289
Boyd, Fraces Mullen, 331–333
Boyd, Maria Isabella ("Belle"), 278
Boyfriends, 438
Boynton v. Virginia, 662
Bradstreet, Anne, 55
Bradwell, Myra Colby, 317
Bride price, 23
Brimson, Mosel, 565
British colonies, 46–59, 77m. *See also*
Colonization
Bromley, Dorothy Dunbar, 518,
519–520
Brothels. *See* Prostitution

Brown, Charlotte Hawkins, 527–528
Brown, Helen, 588
Brown, Helen Gurley, 691
Brown, Rita Mae, 695
Brownell, Katy, 277
Brown v Board of Education of Topeka,
628, 629, 656
Bryan, William Jennings, 418
Bryant, Clora, 594
Bryn Mawr, 381–382, 470
Bubonic Plague, 13
Bunting, Mary, 667
Burns, Lugenia, 470
Burroughs, William, 694
Burst of Light, A, 702
Burton, Annie L, 300–301
Bush, George H.W., 751
Bush, George W., 752–753
Business and Professional Women's
Foundation, 747
Businesswomen, 68–69, 516–517
Bust, 759

C

Cahokia, 7–8, 9. *See also* Mississippian
cultures
Calderone, Mary Steichen, 640
California, 122–124
Californias, 123
California trail, 124–126
Californios, 123
Calvin, John, 20
Camp meetings, 199
Campbell, Helen Stuart, 402
Canning industry, 555–556
Capitalism, 67, 68–69. *See also* Con-
sumerism; Market economy; Mar-
ket revolution
Captivity, 103, 118, 123
Carter, Jimmy, 754
Carter, Rosalyn, 730
Cary, Mary Ann Shad, 313
Casta, 38
Cather, Willa, 458
Catherine de Medici, 19
Catholicism
abortion, 679, 739–741
antebellum, 207–209
colonization, 123
gender roles, 207–209, 385
marriage, 18–19
southwest frontier, 344–345
Catt, Carrie Chapman, 419, 490–491,
492–494
Cayton, Horace, 627
Cayugas, 7. *See also* Iroquois
Cayuse, 125

Cazneau, Jane, 246–247
Celibacy, 209
Cession, 104m
Chace, Elizabeth Buffam, 147
Chamberlain-Kahn act, 488
Charity girls, 439–440
Charleston (dance), 532
Chatty Cathy, 638
Chavez, Caesar, 636
Cher, 639
Cherokee, 107–111, 220
Cherokee War, 102
Cherokee war woman, 107
Chesapeake region. See Atlantic colonies
Chesnut, Mary, 190–191
Chicago, Judy, 712
Chicanas, 701–703
Chief Joseph, 352
Child, Lydia Marie, 142–143
Childbirth, 713
Childcare, socialization of, 480
Children, 10–11, 56, 443. See also Family structure; Mothering
Children's Bureau, 482–483
Children's Crusade, 476–477
Child Support Enforcement Amendments Act, 734
Chinese, 335, 553–555, 371–373
Chinese Americans, 508–510, 581, 632–634
Chinese Exclusion Act, 371–372
Chisholm, Shirley, 669–670, 681
Chopin, Kate, 442
Christian Coalition, 731
Christian Congregationalists, 385
Christianity, 40
  colonization and, 42–45
  sex, 44–45
Christianization, 38, 105
Christian Science, 386
Christian Values in Action Coalition, 731
CIO, 554
Cities, 132, 138–140. See also Urban development
Citizenship, 66, 86, 313
Civil Rights Act of 1871, 307
Civil Rights Act of 1875, 307
Civil Rights Act of 1964, 665
Civil rights movement, 655–665
Civil war
  Army nurses, 272–276
  bonnet brigades, 265–266
  Confederate women, 279–280
  gender roles, 264–280
Slavery, 280–282
Civilian Conservation Corps, 560

Clark, Kenneth Phipps, 627–628
Clark, Mamie Phipps, 627–628
Clark, William, 111
Clarke, Edward H., 450–451
Class, 11–12, 49–50, 52–53, 82, 142–150, 622
Clerical work, 367–369
Clinton, William J. 732, 743
Clinton, Hillary Rodham, 744–745
Clothing, 251, 438. See also Fashion; Shopping
Coartacion, 115
Cold war, 624–629, 635–643
Colleges, 380t
Collins, Jenny, 320
Colonization
  Atlantic colonies, 47m, 67
  British, 46–59
  Catholicism, 123
  Christianity, 42–45
  disease, 36
  Dutch, 40–41
  French, 40–46
  mining, 35, 40
  Native American women, 36, 102
  New Mexico, 35–40
  religion and, 38–40
  southwest, 35–40
  Spain, 35–40
Colorado, 418
Colored American, The, 151
Colored Women's League, 415
Columbus, Christopher, 26
Comanches, 118
Combahee River Collective, 701
Comfort, Alex, 694
Commission on Interracial Cooperation, 526–527
Commission on Obscenity and Pornography, 694
Committee for the Protection of Women and Girls, 488
Committee on Political Education, 666
Common law, 17
Common Sense, 77
Communism, 618–619, 622, 624, 626, 629, 643, 645–646
Communitarian, 231
Companionate marriage, 510–512
Complementarity, 76
Complex marriage, 210–211
Compromise of 1850, 167
Comstock Act, 445, 452, 546, 694
Concerned Women for America, 730, 732
Concubines, 18, 36, 37
Condoms. See Birth control

Confederate States of America (Confederacy), 263m, 279
  readmission to Union, 298m
Congregationalist, 74
Congress of Industrial Organizations, 551
Congress of Racial Equality, 661
Conquest, 25–26, 38. See also Colonization; Discovery
Consciousness-raising, 705–707, 712
Conservativism, 729–731
Constitution, 88
Consumer economy. See Capitalism
Consumerism, 391–392, 514, 601, 619, 630–631
Contraband Relief Association, 270
Contrabands of war, 269
Contraception. See Birth control
Convents, 20, 207–209
Corn-woman (Corn mother), 3–4, 39
Cortes, Hernan, 26, 36
Cosmopolitan, 691
Cotton Club, 533
Cotton gin, 166
Council of National Defense, 487
Counterculture, 692
Coureurs de bois, 45
Courts. See Law; Rights
Courtship. See Dating; Marriage
Coverture, 17
Cowboys, 333
Crawford, Joan, 532
Crillo, 38
Cross-class alliance, 406
Cross-dresing. See Transgender
Cullom Bill, 339
Cult of domesticity, 145
Culture. See Art; Authors; Movies
Culture wars, 731–733
Cumming, Kate, 275–276
Cushman, Charlotte, 155
Cushman, Pauline, 279
Custody rights, 242–243, 717–718

D
Dall, Caroline Healey, 314
Dame schools, 54
Dance crazes, 531–532
Dance halls, 438–439
Dance on the Tortoise, 512
Date rape, 736
Dating, 691–693
Daughters of Liberty, 78–79
Daughters of St. Krispin, 321
Davis, Katherine Bement, 510–511
Davis, Paulina Wright, 251
Dawes Severalty Act, 352, 355, 357
De Aviles, Pedro Menendez, 35, 38

De Carranza, Maria, 34
De Cespedes, Elena, 16
Declaration of Independence, 77
Declaration of Sentiments, 249
De Coronado, Francisco Vasquez, 35, 38
De facto segregation, 655
Defense of Marriage Act, 733
De jure segregation, 655
De la Cruz, Jessie Lopez, 635, 636
De l'Incarnation, Marie, 42, 43
Democracy, 88
Democratic Party, 230, 245, 520, 562, 666, 681
De Onate, Juan, 35, 36
Depression. See Great Depression
Desegregation, 655–662
De Soto, Antonia, 39
De Soto, Hernando, 12
Devil's Lake Reservation, 353
Dewson, Mary Williams (molly), 559
Diaphragm. See Birth control
Dias, Bartholomeu, 26
Dickenson, Emily, 148
Di Prima, Diane, 641
Discovery (of Americas by Europeans), 25, 27
Discrimination, 676–679. See also Gender roles; Racism; Wage discrimination
Disease, 6–7, 28, 36
Dives, 439
Division of labor. See Gender roles
Divorce
  Africa, 23
  antebellum period, 241–243
  enlightenment, 74
  law, 254–255
  mining frontier, 336
  movies, 570
  Native Americans, 10
  second wave feminism, 717–718
  slavery, 174
  Texas (early), 119
  twentieth century (early), 441–443
  United States (early), 92
  World War II, 601
Dix, Dorothea L., 272–273, 274
Dobson, James, 730, 731
Doctors. See Medicine
Dodge, Grace Hoadley, 403–404
Dodge, Mary, 286
Doe v. Bolton, 679
Do-everything policy, 408–409
Domestic life, 143–146, 387–392
Domestic service, 370, 377–378. See also Housework
Domestic violence, 215–217, 242, 756

"Don't ask, don't tell," 732
Double V campaign, 584–586, 608
Douglass, Frederick, 249, 308–309
Drake, St. Clair, 627
Dred Scott decision, 248
Dress. See Clothing
Dubois, W.E.B., 527
Duncan, Isadora, 459
Dust bowl, 544–546, 568
Duston, Hannah, 103
Dutch. See Netherlands
Dutch West India Company, 41
Dworkin, Andrea, 736
Dyer, Mary, 58
Dykes, 606

E
Eagle forum, 730
Early Childhood Education Act, 678
Eastern European immigrants, 374–376
Eastman, Crystal, 521
Eastman, Max, 455
Eddy, Mary Baker, 386
Edmunds-Tucker Act, 340, 419
Education, 90–92, 238–241, 304, 450–451, 676–679, 90–92
Elder care, 747–748
Elizabeth I (England), 14, 19
Ellis, Havelock, 434, 510
Ellis Island, 374
Emancipation, 264, 282, 298–302
Employment
  African American women, 517
  discrimination, 548
  Great Depression, 547–550
  Jazz Age, 513–517
  law, 548
  medicine, 381–382
  ministry, 384–386
  New South, 377–379
  "pink collar" work, 513–515
  post-Civil War, 336–370, 380–387
  post-WWII, 579–586, 619–624
  professional, 516–517
  second wave feminism, 715–716
  sex segregation (second wave), 716
  teachers, 380–381
  twentieth century (late), 743–747
  wage discrimination, 667
  See also Discrimination; Gender roles
Empressarios, 118
Engel v. Vitale, 731
England, 17, 46–59
Enlightenment, 66, 72, 74–77
Ensler, Eve, 757
Equal Employment Opportunity Commission, 668

Equal Opportunity Act, 675
Equal pay, 400. See also Wage discrimination
Equal Pay Act of 1963, 667–668
Equal Rights Amendment, 521–522, 667, 674–676, 727–729
Erie Canal, 132
Europe, 13–20
Evangelicalism, 199–201, 739–741
Eva site (Tennessee), 5
Eve (Genesis), 58
Executive Order 8802, 585
Executive Order 9066, 597
Exodusters, 347
Expediency, 489

F
Factory families, 150
Factory work, 133–136
Fair Labor Standards Act, 562
Family and Medical Leave Act, 745
Family planning, 19 149, 335, 545–547. See also Abortion; Birth control
Family Research Council, 730
Family structure
  Africa, 23
  American Revolution, 82
  Atlantic colonies, 48–49, 54, 55–57, 59
  Cherokee, 107
  Chinese, 371–373
  Christianity, 40
  cold war, 624–629
  conservativism, 729–731
  eastern Europeans, 374–376
  eighteenth century, 72–77
  emancipation, 299–301
  Europe, 19
  factory work, 133–136
  globalization, 749–751
  Great Depression, 544–547
  heartland frontier, 347–351
  internment camps, 597–601
  Italian immigrants, 373–374
  market economy, 67–68, 69
  mills, 379
  Native Americans, 10–11
  New Netherland, 45
  New South, 376–377
  Nez Perce, 352–353
  nineteenth century, 146
  plantations, 180–183
  Second Great Awakening, 201–203
  second wave feminism, 716–717
  Seneca, 104–106
  sexual revolution, 691–694

Sioux, 353–355
slavery, 166–167, 169, 171–174
Southern Ute, 355–377
United States (early), 92
World War II, 601–602
Family system of labor, 379
Family Violence Prevention and Services Act, 737
Family wage, 314
Family-wage economy, 137
Fanny, Fern (sara parton), 158–159
Farmer's Alliance, 416
Farming. See Agriculture
Farnham, Marynia, 626
Fascism, 585
Fashion, 437–438. 591–592, 637–638
Fatherhood, 626–627
Faubus, Orval, 656
Fauset, Jesse, 532
Federal Emergency Relief Administration, 560
Federalists, 86
Feldman, Maxine, 710
Female genital cutting, 756
Feme covert, 17, 56
Feme sole, 17
Feminine mystique, 631–632
Femininity. See Gender roles; Transgender
Feminism
  Asian Americans, 702–705
  Black feminism, 700–701
  first wave, 457–458
  global, 755–757
  Latinas, 701–703
  new style (1920s), 518, 519–520
  third wave, 757–759
  See also Liberal feminism; Radical feminism; Second wave
Feminist Art Journal, 712
Feminist art movement, 712
Feministas, 701–703
Feminization of poverty, 718–719
Ferraro, Geraldine, 734
Fertility myths, 3–4, 39
Fictive kin, 172
Fields, Maime Garvin, 503–504
Fifteenth Amendment, 297, 306–307, 309
Filibustering, 245
Firestone, Shulamith, 698
First cities, 702
First wave feminism, 457–458. See also Seneca Falls Convention
Fitzgerald, F. Scott, 504
Flapper, 505–506, 532
Flint, Larry, 694

Florence Crittenton mission, 447
Flower children, 692
Flynn, Elizabeth Gurley, 452, 476–477
Focus on the Family, 731–733
Foot binding, 372, 423
Foote, Mary Hallock, 387
Forced labor, Native Americans, 36. See also Slavery
Ford, Betty, 730
Ford, Henry, 486
Forty acres and a mule, 301
Fourierists, 231–233
Fourteenth Amendment, 297, 306, 307
Fox, George, 58
Freedman's Bureau, 270, 298, 303, 304
Freedom riders, 661–662
Freedom summer, 664
Freedpeople, 283–286, 301–302, 304
Free love, 312, 454–459, 692
Free Soil party, 247
Free-will Baptists, 385
Fremont, Jesse Benton, 126
French, Marilyn, 642, 643
French and Indian war, 67, 77
French colonization, 40–45
Freud, Sigmund, 434, 510, 512
Friedan, Betty, 631–632, 681, 715
Frontier
  activism, 337
  California, 122–124
  colonization, 117–126
  gender roles, 333–334
  mining, 335–337
  New Mexico, 119–122
  overland trails, 124–126
  prostitution, 333–335
  See also Mormons; Southwest America
Furies, 708
Fur trade, 41–46

G
Gadsden Purchase, 101
Gang system (slavery), 169, 172
Garment industry, 553–555
Garner, Margaret, 176–177
Garrison, William Lloyd, 219, 220, 222
Garvey, Marcus, 524
Gatson, Hattie, 663
Gay marriage, 732–733
Gender roles
  Africa, 4, 21
  African Americans, 72, 151, 168–171, 252–253
  antebellum North, 151
  antislavery movement, 222–223
  Atlantic colonies, 54
  Aztecs, 10

Catholicism, 207–209
Cherokee, 107–111
Chinese Americans, 508–509
Chinese immigrants, 371–373
Christianity, 40
cities (early nineteenth century), 138–140
cold war, 629–635
colonization, 26
communitarianism, 232
conservativism, 731–733
dating (early twentieth century), 438–440
dress, 251
eastern European, 374–376
eighteenth century, 66
employment, 547–550
enlightenment, 74–77
Europe, 4, 14
factory work, 133–136
freedpeople, 301–302
frontier, 333–334
fur trade, 41–42
Germans, 154–155
Great Depression, 547–550
heartland, 347–351
hunting and gathering societies, 5
internment camps, 597–601
Irish immigration, 152–154
Iroquois, 7
Italian immigrants, 373–374
Jazz Age, 505–510, 513–517
Judaism, 206–207
manufacturing, 366–367
market revolution, 67–72
maternalism, 479–483
Mexican Americans, 508
military, 603–611
mining frontier, 336
Mississippian cultures, 7–8
Mormonism, 338–339
music, 593–595
Native Americans, 4, 7
New Deal, 560–566
New Netherland, 46
New Spain, 36
Nez Perce, 352–353
nineteenth century, 142–146
plantations, 177–180
post-WWII, 619–624
Pueblo cultures, 8–9
Puritans, 54
Quakers, 205–206
Reconstruction cities, 302–305
religion, 203–205, 385
rural areas (early nineteenth century), 141–142

Gender roles—*continued*
  Second Great Awakening, 199–205
  second wave feminism, 680–682,
    716–717
  Seneca tribes, 104–106
  Shawnee, 106
  Sioux, 353–355
  Southern Ute, 355–377
  southwest, 343–346
  Spanish, 36
  tobacco economy, 47–48
  United States (early), 89–90
  World War I, 486–488
  World War II, 580–587, 589–591,
    601–602
  writing, 156–157
  See also Homemaking; Transgender
General Federation of Women's Clubs,
  413–414, 523
Generation of Vipers, 626
Genizaras, 120
Genizaros, 120
Gentlemen friends, 438
German immigration, 154–155
GI Bill, 610
Gilder, Helena de Kay, 387
Gilman, Charlotte Perkins, 390, 480, 491
Ginsberg, Alan, 641, 694
Glasgow, Ellen, 458
Glaspell, Susan, 458
Glass ceiling, 746
Global feminism, 755–757
Gold rush, 335–336
Goldman, Emma, 452–454, 456–457
Gollup, R., 368–369
Gompers, Samuel, 474
Good girls, cold war, 641
Goodwives, 54
Grable, Betty, 589
Graham, Sylvester, 213
Grange, 351, 416
Grant, Ulysses, 309
Gratz, Rebecca, 206
Great Awakening, 66, 74–75. *See also*
  Second Great Awakening
Great Depression, 540–543
  activism, 550–556
  cultures during, 566–572
  impact of, 543–550
  New Deal and women, 556–566
Great Migration, 57, 484–485
Greenberger, Marcia, 677
Greenwich Village, 455, 695
Grey, Willie Ann, 295–296
Grimke, Angelina, 197–198, 243–244
Grimke, Sarah, 243–244
Guadalupe, Diego Sanchez, 34
Guilds, 15

Gulf wars, 751–753
Gynecology, 451

H

Hagood, Margaret Jarman, 550
Hair, 503–504
Hall, Radcliffe, 512
Hamer, Fannie Lou, 659–660
Hamilton, Gail (Mary Dodge), 286
Hariot, Thomas, 27
Harlem renaissance, 532
Harris v. MacRae, 715
Haver, Jesse, 436–437
Hawaii, 202
Hays, Mary Ludwig, 82
Hayworth, Rita, 589
Health, 522–523, 712–715, 755. *See
  also* Abortion; Birth control;
  Medicine
Heartland, 347–357
Hefner, Hugh, 638, 691
Height, Dorothy, 667
Henry Street settlement, 469–470
Hepburn, Katherine, 570
Hermaphrodite, 16
Hernandez, Aileen, 668
Hernandez, Leticia, 703
Herttell, Thomas, 236
Heterodoxy, 457
Heterosociality, 435–439, 506
Hickock, Lorena, 558
Hicks, Elias, 205
Hill, Anita, 737
Hippies, 692
Hiroshima, 610
Hitler, Adolf, 578, 610
Hobbes, Thomas, 17
Hobby, Oveta Culp, 605
Hollywood. *See* Movies
Hollywood Production Code, 569
Home economics, 390–391, 544–545
Homemakers, 387–392, 630–632,
  544–545. *See also* Housekeeping
Home protection, 323–324, 416
Homestead Act of 1862, 346–347
Homosexuality, 156
  antebellum period, 148–149
  communitarianism, 232
  conservatism, 732
  Jazz Age, 512–513
  lesbian feminism, 707–710
  medicalization of, 443–444
  momism, 626
  New Deal, 558
  post-Civil War, 387
  sexual revolution, 695–696
  twentieth century (early), 443–444,
    470

Women's Army Corps, 606–607
Hoofs, Kerstine and Sophia, 19
Hoover, Herbert, 543
Hoover, J. Edgar, 626
Hospital Act of September 1862, 274
Houdewin, Zoetin, 20
Housekeeping, 391–392, 390
Houses, 630
House servants, 170–171, 172
Housework, 142, 150, 232–233, 480,
    621, 717. *See also* Gender roles;
    Homemaker
Houston, Jeanne Wakatsuki, 598
Howard University, 380
Howe, Julia ward, 286, 316, 406
Howl, 694
Hughes, Langston, 532
Hull-house, 444, 465–468, 469, 481, 482
Human Sexual Inadequacy, 694
Human Sexual Response, 693
Hundred Years' War, 13
Hunt, Jane, 248
Hunter, Jane Edna, 405
Hunting and gathering societies, 5–7, 21
Hurston, Zora Neale, 532
Hussein, Saddam, 751
Hustler, 694
Hutchinson, Anne, 58
Hyde Amendment, 714–715, 739

I

Identity politics, 701
Idia (Benin), 22
Illinois Factory Inspection Act, 408
Illinois Woman's Alliance, 407–408
Illness. *See* Disease
Immigrants
  1860–1930, 508*t*
  Chinese, 371–373
  eastern Europeans, 374–376
  globalization, 749
  Italians, 373–374
  Jazz Age, 508
  Post-Civil War, 370–376
  See also Slavery; *specific countries*
Imperialism, 421–427
Indentured servants, 45, 48
Independence (from Britain), 77–88
Indian Allotment Act, 352
Indian Country, 101–111
Indian removal, 218–220
Indian Removal Act, 111
Indian reservations, 102
Indian schools. *See* Reservation board-
    ing schools
Indian territory, 101–102
Industrial revolution, 132, 133–137,
    142–150

Industrial Workers of the World,
476, 477
Infant Care, 389
Infanticide, 19
Inheritance, 17, 56, 69–70, 74, 92,
107–111, 235–236
Inner light, 205
Inquisition, 16
Integration, 624. *See also* Segregation
Intermarriage
antebellum south, 187
colonization, 28, 35, 36–37, 38, 41,
42, 44, 50, 51–52
frontier, 118, 120, 343–345
law, 50, 117, 449–450
See also Miscegenation
International Association of Machin-
ists, 583
International Council of Women,
400–401
International Council of Women of
the Darker Races of the World,
525–526
International feminism. *See* Global
feminism
International Ladies Garment Workers
Union, 474–476, 554
International Women's Year, 730
Internet, 755
Internment camps, 577–578,
597–601
Interracial relationships. *See* Inter-
marriage
Interracial Women's Committee, 528
Iraq, 751
Irish, 152–153
Iroquois, 7
Isabella of Castile, 14, 19
Islam, 23
Issei, 597
Italians, 373–374

J
Jackson, Andrew, 229
Jackson, Helen Hunt, 351
Jackson, Thomas "Stonewall", 278
Jacobs, Harriet, 188, 270, 286
Jacques-Garvey, Amy, 524–526
James I (England), 46
Jamestown (colony), 46
Jane, 759
Jane club, 437
Japanese Americans, 577–578,
597–601, 608–610
Jay, Karla, 695
Jazz Age, 502–505
manners and morals, 505–513
modernity, culture of, 530–533

Rainey, Gertrude "Ma," 534
woman's movement during, 517–523
women and work, 513–517
women's activism during, 524–530
Jefferson, Thomas, 111
Jeffersonian Republicans, 86
Jewish immigrants, 374–376
Jezebel, 175
Jim Crow, 655
woman movement (1880–1900) and,
401, 405, 410, 415, 419–420
work segregation, 623, 627
World War II and, 585, 595
Job discrimination, 580–586, 619–621
Johnson, Andrew, 296
Johnson, Joyce, 617–618, 641
Johnson, Lady Bird, 730
Johnson, Lyndon, 668, 694, 718
Johnson, Virgina, 693
Jones, Hettie, 641
Jong, Erica, 642
Jook joints, 439
Joplin, Janice, 641
Jordan, Ann Haseltine, 202
Jordan, Barbara, 730
Joy of Sex, 694
Judaism, 206–207
Juvenile court system, 481
Juvenile delinquency, 602

K
Kanal Ikal (Mayan princess), 12
Kansas-Nebraska act, 167
Keckley, Elizabeth, 186, 188–189
Kelley, Florence, 491
Kemble, Fanny, 155, 251, 286
Kennedy, John F., 666, 667
Kennedy, Robert, 662
Kenney, Lucy, 245
Kerouac, Jack, 641
Keys, Elizabeth, 50
King, Billie Jean, 681
King, Martin Luther, Jr., 657–658, 662
Kingston, Maxine Hong, 704–705, 757
Kinsey, Alfred, 511, 601, 639, 693
Kitchen Table: Women of Color Press,
702
Kivas, 9
Knights of St. Krispin, 321
Koedt, Anne, 707
Komarovsky, Mirra, 621
Koop, C. Everett, 732
Korean War, 632
Ku Klux Klan, 303, 449, 524, 528–530

L
L-85, 591
Labor protests, 217–218

Labor rights, 318–321, 665–673. *See
also* Unions
Labor segmentation, 367
Ladies Industrial Aid Association of
Union Hall, 272
Ladies Federal Labor Union, 407
Lady of Cofachiqui, 12
Lady Xoc, 12, 13
La familia, 343
LaHaye, Beverly, 730, 732
Lake, Handsome, 106
Lake, Veronica, 589
La malinche, 37
Lange, Dorothea, 567–568
Lange, Sister Mary Elizabeth, 208
Larson, Nella, 532
Las Hijas de Cuauhtemoc, 701–703
Lathrop, Julia, 483
Latinas/Latina women
feminism, 701–703
unions, 555–556
Lauber, Lynn, 637
Law
abortion, 739–741
domestic violence, 216
employment, 548, 585, 622–624, 667,
743–747
health, 522–523
obscenity, 445–446, 694–695
prostitution, 446–448
rape, 736
reproductive rights, 679–680
slavery, 115, 117, 185–188
women's gossip, 52
See also Abortion; Rights; Women's
Rights
Lawrence Textile Strike, 476–477
League of Women Voters, 518–521
Leary, Timothy, 692
Lease, Mary. E., 417–418
Lee, Jarena, 204
Legal status of women. *See* Rights;
Women's Rights
Legislation, 477–479, 673–682
Le Jeune, Father Paul, 41, 42
Le Moyne, Jacques, 12
Lesbian. *See* Homosexuality
Lesbian feminism, 707–710
Lesbian threat, invention of, 512–513
Leviathan, 17
Levitt houses, 630
Lewis, Meriwether, 111
Liberal feminism, 668–671. *See also*
Second wave feminism
Liberty party, 247
Libres (freed slaves), 115–117
Liliuokalani (Queen), 203
Lincoln, Abraham, 296

Lindsey, Ben, 511
Literacy, 158–159
Literature. *See* Authors
Little House on the Prairie, 349
Little Rock nine, 656–657
Little women, 288
Livermore, Mary Rice, 267–269, 273–274, 276, 289, 316, 322, 406, 422
Locke, John, 72, 76, 77
Lorde, Audre, 702, 757
Louisiana purchase, 101, 112m
Louisiana territory, 111–117
Low, Anne Marie, 545, 546
Lowell, Massachusetts, 133–136
Lowell Female Labor Reform Association, 218
Loyalist, 80
Luso-Africans, 28–29
Luther, Martin, 20
Lynching, 419–420, 526–528
Lynd, Robert and Helen, 506, 550
Lyon, Mary, 239

M

Machismo, 701–703
Mackinnon, Catherine, 736
Magawley, Elizabeth, 76
Makeup, 437–438
Mammy, 171
Manifest destiny, 126
Mann Act, 448
Manufacturing, 366–367
Manumission, 115
Marina, Dona, 36, 37
Mariolatry, 345
Marital rape, 736
Market economy revolution, 67–77
Marriage
   Africa, 23–24
   antebellum South, 185–188
   art, 387
   Atlantic colonies, 54
   Aztecs, 10
   career versus (early twentieth century), 436–437
   Catholicism, 18–19
   cold war, 625–626, 629–632
   communitarianism, 232
   conservatisim, 732–733
   critique of, 312–313, 314
   England, 17
   enlightenment, 74, 76
   Europe, 17–19
   freedmen/women, 298–301
   frontier, 119, 123, 343–345
   German immigrants, 154
   global feminism, 756

globalization, 751
   Great Depression, 545–546
   independence and, 436–437
   Jazz Age, 510–512
   mining and, 336
   Mormons, 338–339
   movies, 570
   Native Americans, 10–11
   nineteenth century, 146, 148
   plantations, 180–183
   Protestantism, 19
   reform efforts, 254–255
   rights, 296
   second wave, 717–718
   sex (late nineteenth century), 454–457
   sexual revolution, 691–694
   Shawnee, 106
   slavery, 171–174
   social construction of, 433–434
   Spain, 17
   tobacco economy
   twentieth century (early), 440–441
   women's rights, 312–313
   women's work and, 514
   World War II, 601–602
   See also Family structure; Intermarriage
Married Women's Property Act, 248
Marshall, General George c. 603–605
Mary I (England), 19
Mary Tyler Moore Show, 682
Masculinity. *See* Gender roles; Transgender
Masters, William, 693
Maternalism, 479–484
Maternity leave, 666
Matriarch, black, 700
Matrilineal, 7
Matrilocal, 7
Maude, 682
Mayans, 7, 12
McCarthy, Margaret, 153
McClintok, Mary Ann, 248
McCord, Louisa, 192
McCovery, Norma, 679
McDowell, John, 211–213
McKay, Claude, 532
Media, 680–682
Medicaid, 714, 739
Medicine, 356, 381–382, 450–454, 712–715
Medium, 205–206
Men-women. *See* Two-spirit people
Merrit, Anna Lee, 388–389
Mestizo, 36, 37, 38
Metalious, Grace, 642
Methodists, 74

Metis, 45
Mexican Americans, 508, 581, 634–635. *See also* Chicanas; Latinas
Mexican cession, 101
Mexico
   colonization, 35, 36
   discovery, 36
   independence, 118
   Native Americans in, 5, 6, 7, 9, 11, 12, 29
Mickey Mouse Club, 638
Middle class, 142–150
Middle East. *See* Gulf wars
Middle passage, 29
Middletown, 506
Midwest. *See* Heartland
Midwifery, 54, 171, 713
Migrant mother, 568
Migration. *See* Frontier; Great Migration; Immigration; Indian migration
Military service, 602–611, 732, 751–753. *See also specific branches*
Mill, Harriet Taylor, 253–254
Millett, Kate, 680, 707, 708–709
Mill girls, 134, 150, 217–218
Mills, 378–379
Mining, 35, 40, 335–337
Mink, Patsy, 677, 678
Minor v. Happersett, 313
Miscegenation, 449–450
Miss America, 638, 706
Missionaries, 201–203, 422–427
Missions, in California, 122–124
Mississippi Freedom Democratic Party, 659–660
Mississippian cultures, 7–12
Missouri Compromise, 167
Moctezuma, Isabel (Aztec), 38
Model minority, 704
Modern teen, 637
Modern welfare state, 562
Modest chastisement, 215–216
Mohawks, 7. *See also* Iroquois
Momism, 626–627
Monogamy, 19, 211
Montagnais, 41
Montagu, Ashley, 627
Montgomery Improvement Association, 657
Moody, Anne, 662–665
Moraga, Cherrie, 757
Morality, 445–446
Moral majority, 732
Moral reform, 211–213
Morehouse University, 380
Morgan, Elizabeth, 407

Mormons, 337–342
Morrill Anti-Bigamy Act, 340
Morrison, Toni, 177
Morton, Jelly Roll, 532
Motherhood
  activism, 482–483
  cold war, 624–629
  health, 522–523
  internment camps, 599–601
  post-Civil War, 389
  third wave feminism, 759
  See also Family structure
Motherhood penalty, 746
Mother's pensions, 481–482
Motion pictures. *See* Movies
Mott, Lucretia, 248–249, 252
Movies, 439, 531, 569–572, 694,
  589–591
Moynihan, Patrick, 700
Ms., 681–682, 690
Muhammad, Askia (Songhay), 24
Mulatto, 221
Mullaney, Kate, 319–321
Muller v. Oregon, 477
Municipal housekeeping, 470
Murray, Judith Sargent, 91
Murray, Pauli, 668
Music, 593, 710
Myhrem, Jennifer, 758
Myth of the vaginal orgasm, 707

N

Nagasaki, 610
Naked Lunch, 694
Nash, Diane, 660, 662, 653–654
National American Woman Suffrage
  Association, 385, 410–413, 490,
  492–494, 520
National Association of Colored
  Women, 561
National Association for the Advance-
  ment of Colored People
  (NAACP), 524, 656
National Association for the Repeal of
  Abortion Laws, 679
National Association of Colored
  Women, 414–416, 446
National Association of Women
  Painters and Sculptors, 387
National Association Opposed to
  Woman Suffrage, 491
National Birth Control League, 454
National Black Feminist Organization,
  670–671
National Campaign to Protect Mar-
  riage, 732
National Conference of Puerto Rican
  Women, 671

National Congress of Mothers, 482
National Consumer's League, 472, 523
National Council of Negro Women,
  561, 667
National Council of Women, 400–401
National Defense Act, 484
National Federation of Republican
  Women, 728
National Labor Union, 318, 319, 321
National League for the Protection of
  Colored Women, 405
National Organization for Women
  (NOW), 668–671, 718
National Recovery Administration,
  553
National Socialist Party (Germany),
  578
National Urban League, 517
National Welfare Rights Organization,
  671–673
National Woman's Alliance, 418
National Woman's Party, 492
National Woman's Trade Union
  League, 472–474
National Woman Suffrage Association,
  309–314
National Women's Political Caucus,
  670, 681
National Women's Trade Union
  League, 477–479
National Youth Administration, 560
Native Americans
  acculturation, 102
  agriculture, 7
  American revolution, 83–86
  captivity, 103
  cessions, 104m
  colonization, 36
  culture areas, 5–13
  displacement, 102
  divorce, 10
  family structure, 10–11
  forced labor, 36
  fur trade, 41
  gender identity, 11
  heartland, 351–357
  Indian removal, 218–220
  marriage, 10–11
  Mexico, 5, 6, 7, 9, 11, 12, 29
  slavery, 103–104, 111–115
  territory, 101–102
Nativist, 530
Nat Turner's Rebellion, 184
Natural childbirth, 713
Natural Superiority of Women, The,
  627
Negro's hour, 306
Neighborhood union, 470

Neophytes, 123
Nestle, Joan, 696
Netherlands (Dutch), 45–46
New deal, 553, 560–562, 566–572
New England. *See* Atlantic colonies
New England Women's Club, 315–318
New France, 40–45
New Left, 696–700
New lights, 74
New Mexico, 35–40, 119–122
New Netherland, 45–46, 67
New Orleans, 41, 115–116
New South, 376–379
New Thought, 386
New World. *See* Discovery
New York Infirmary for Women and
  Children, 266
Nez Perce tribe, 352–353
Nichols, Mary Grove, 213–214
Nieto-Gomez, Anna, 701
Nightingale, Florence, 272
Nineteenth Amendment, 313–314,
  494–496, 523. *See also* Suffrage;
  Voting rights
Nisei, 598
Nixon, Richard, 694
No-fault divorce, 717
Nongovernmental organization, 755
North (antebellum), 151–154, 239
Northside Center for Child Develop-
  ment, 627–628
Novelists. *See* Authors
Noyes, John Humphrey, 210
Nuns, 20
Nurses, 272–276, 288–289, 516

O

Oakley, Annie, 333
Oaks, Gladys, 459
Oberlin College, 239–241
Objectification of women, 680–682
Obscenity, 445–446, 694–695
O'Connor, Sandra Day, 734, 735–736
Office of Civil Rights, 677
Office of War Information, 586
Office work, 514–515
O'Keeffe, Georgia, 507, 710
Okubo, Mine, 598, 600
Old Lights, 74
Olivia Records, 710
Olmecs, 7
One Day at a Time, 682
Oneida, 7, 210–211. *See also* Iroquois
Onondagas, 7. *See also* Iroquois
Open marriage, 455
Operation Rescue, 740
Operation Wetback, 634
Oregon territory, 101

Oregon trail, 124–126
O'Reilly, Leonora, 473, 474, 491
Organization of Petroleum Exporting
　　Countries, 715
Our Bodies, Ourselves, 712–713
Out, 695
Overland trails, 124–126
Owen, Robert, 231
Owenites, 231–233

P

Page Act of 1875, 449–450
Paine, Thomas, 77
Pamela, 72
Pan-African movement, 524
Panic of 1837, 235
Panic of 1873, 321
Parent-Teacher Association (PTA),
　　482
Parks, Rosa, 657
Parton, Sara, 158–159
Patriarchy, 15–19, 52–53, 55, 66,
　　178–180, 338–339
Patrilineal, 9, 21, 23
Patrilocal, 9
Patriots, 77
Patrons of Husbandry, 351
Paul, Alice, 492–494, 521
Pawns, 24
Pay. *See* Wages
Peace movement, 485–486
Pearce, Diana, 718
Pearl Harbor, 578–579, 586, 597
Peirce, Melusina Fay, 390
Perez, Eulalia, 99–101
Perkins, Frances, 561–562, 563
Personal is political, 458, 705–715
Personal Responsibility and Work Op-
　　portunity Act, 743
Pessary, 149. *See also* Birth control
Peterson, Esther, 665, 667
Petitioning, 86–88
Phalanx, 231, 233
Phelps, Elizabeth Stuart, 286, 287, 316
Phillips, Wendell, 255
Photography, 567–569
Phyllis Wheatley home, 405–406
Picotte, Susette La Flesche, 356
Pilgrims, 53
Pink-collar job, 513
Pitcher, Molly, 83
Placage, 117
Plains Indians, 353–355
Plantation novels, 188–189
Plantations, 177–183, 280–282,
　　302–303
Plath, Sylvia, 642
Playboy, 638, 691

Plessy v. Ferguson, 419, 654
Plural marriage, 338. *See also* Polygamy
Pocahontas, 51–52
Polacheck, Hilda Satt, 465–466
Political consciousness. *See* Activism
Political office, women in, 312,
　　561–562, 666, 676, 677, 734–738
Political participation, antebellum
　　women, 244–247
Politics, as personal, 705–715
Polygamy, 10, 23, 44, 232, 337–342
Pontiac's Uprising, 102
Pope (Pueblo shaman), 40
Populism, 416–418
Pornography, activism (anti), 736
Poverty, 70, 402, 562–563, 671–673,
　　718–719, 741–743, 748
Preachers, women as, 203–205, 241
Pregnancy, premarital, 445c
Presbyterians, 74
President's Commission on the Status
　　of Women, 667
Presidios, 118
Privacy rights, 679–680
Proclamation Line of 1763, 101
Professional employment, 516–517,
　　581–582, 746–747
Progressive movement, 466–472
Prohibition, 532
Propaganda, 586–587
Property rights, 10, 17, 23, 119,
　　229–236, 233–236
Prostitution, 140–141, 150, 211–213,
　　333, 334–335, 446–448, 487–488
Protestantism, 19, 20, 385, 402–404,
　　530
Protestant Reformation, 20
Public work, 379
Pueblo cultures, 7–10, 119–120
Pueblo Revolt, 40, 119
Puertocarrero, Alonzo Hernandez, 37
Puritans, Atlantic colonies, 53–58
Putos, 27
Putting-out system, 137, 150

Q

Quakers, 58, 105, 197–198, 203,
　　205–206, 385
Quartering act, 78
Queers, 606
Quicksand, 532

R

Race, 50, 53, 220–223, 564
Race literature, 525
Race songs, 533
Race suicide, 452
Race women, 524

Racial discrimination, 50, 624
Racism, 548–586, 595, 608–610,
　　627–628
Radical feminism, 680–682, 705–707
Railroad, transcontinental, 332, 339,
　　344, 346–347
Rainey, Gertrude "Ma", 534
Raleigh, Sir Walter, 26
Randolph, Mary, 179
Rape
　American Revolution and, 83
　California missions, 122
　divorce and, 242
　feminism and, 736
　global feminism and, 756–757
　mestizo society and, 37, 38
　miscegenation and, 449
　slavery and, 174–175, 177, 188
Rape, Abuse and Incest National Net-
　　work, 756–757
Rations, 595–596
Rauh, Ida, 455, 457
Readers, women as, 157–159
Reagan, Ronald, 730
Reaganomics, 741
Reconstruction amendments, 311
Reconstruction era, 296
　gender roles, 298–303
　temperance movement, 321–324
　unions, 318–321
　wage discrimination, 314
　women's organizations, 314–318
　women's suffrage movement, 305–314
Red Bird (Gertrude Simmons Bonnin),
　　354
Reed, Donna, 589
Reed, Esther De Berdt, 80
Regent, 19
Religion
　colonization, 38–40, 53–59
　women and, 20, 44, 57, 75,
　　384–386
　conservatvism, 729–731
　enlightenment, 74–75
　ERA, 727–729
　female seminaries, 238–239
　gender roles, 4, 12, 74–75, 203–205
　imperialism, 422–427
　Native Americans, 12
　sex, 209–211
　temperance movement, 321–324
　*See also specific faith/practice/
　　denomination*
Relocation. *See* Internment
Removal. *See* Indian removal
Representation, of women, 680–682
Reproduction. *See* Birth control
Republican Party, 520, 728

Reservation boarding schools, 355, 356, 357
Retail sales, 367–369
Retirement Equity Act, 734
Revivals, 199–200
Reynolds, Mary, 165–166
Richards, Ellen Swallow, 391
Richardson, Samuel, 72
Riggs, Bobby, 681
Rights
  African Americans, 295–297
  internment camps, 577–578
  labor, 318–321
  marriage, 732–733
  privacy, 679–680
  reproductive rights, 679–680
  See also Women's rights
Right-to-life, 739
Ringgold, Faith, 710–711
Roanoke colony, 27
Rockwell, Norman, 587
Roe v. Wade, 679, 714–715, 734, 739
Rogers, Edith Nourth, 603–605
Rogers, Ginger, 570, 589
Rolfe, John, 51
Roman law, 17, 45
Roosevelt, Eleanor, 541–543, 556–559, 667
Roosevelt, Franklin Delano, 557, 597
Roosevelt, Theodore, 468, 486
Root doctors, 171
Rose, Ernestine, 235
Rosie the Riveter, 580, 587, 588
Roth v. United States, 694
Rowlandson, Mary, 57, 103
Rural life, 141–142, 344–345
Russell, Jane, 637

S

Sacagawea, 111, 113–114
Safran, Rosey, 478–479
St. Augustine (Florida), 35, 38
Salem witch trials, 58–59
Salons, 76
Sambo, 308
Same-sex marriage, 732–733
Same-sex relationships. *See* Homosexuality
Samson, Deborah, 83
Sanger, Margaret, 450, 452–453, 455, 546
Sanitary fairs, 267
Santa Fe Trail, 124–126
Schlafly, Phyllis, 675, 731, 760–761, 727–728
Schniederman, Rose, 473
Scottish enlightenment, 76
Scribbling women, 156

Seamstresses, 138–139
Second Continental Congress, 77
Second Great Awakening, 198–205, 239
Second industrial revolution, 365
Second shift, 716
Second wave feminism
  athletics and education, 676–679
  employment activism, 665–673
  ERA, 674–676
  gender roles, 680–682
  medicine, 680–682
  reproductive rights, 679–680, 714–715
  unions, 665–666
  poverty, 671–673
Secretarial work, 514–515
Sectarian medicine, 381
Sedgwick, Catherine Maria, 157
Seminaries (female), 238–239
Seneca, 7, 104–106. *See also* Iroquois
Seneca Falls, 253
Seneca Falls convention, 248–249
Separate but equal, 654
Separate spheres, 145
September 11, 2001, 754
Serra, Father Junipero, 122
Servants, 138–139
Servicemen's Readjustment Act of 1944, 610
Service work, 514–515
Settlement houses (early twentieth century), 468–470
Seventeen, 637
Sex
  antebellum period, 148
  Atlantic colonies, 56
  Beat generation, 641
  Catholicism, 43
  Civil War spies, 277–279
  cold war, 635–643
  communitarianism, 232
  differences between cultures, 27
  enlightenment, 74
  Europe, 17
  Jazz Age, 505–512
  movies, 569–572
  Native Americans, 10–11
  nineteenth century, 148, 454–459
  Puritans, 57–58
  Radical feminism, 707–710
  religion, 56
  sexual revolution, 691–693
  Shakers, 209–210
  Shawnee, 106
  slavery, 174–175
  twentieth century (early), 433–444
  United States (early), 92–93

Women's Army Corps, 606
women's bodies, 450–451
women's drive, 433–434
World War I, 487–488
World War II, 601–602
Sex and the Single Girl, 691
Sex-segregated labor market, 622
Sex segregation, employment, 619–624
Sexual Behavior of the Human Female, 639
Sexual Behavior of the Human Male, 639
Sexual harassment, 737
Sexual inversion, 512
Sexuality Information and Education Council of the United States, 641
Sexually-transmitted diseases. *See* Venereal disease
Sexual politics, 707, 708–709
Sexual revolution, 691–696
Shakers, 203, 209–210
Shaman, 12, 40
Shapiro, Miriam, 712
Shaw, Anna Howard, 385
Shawnee, 106–107
Sheppard-Towner Maternity and Infancy Protection Act, 483, 522, 564
Sheweth, Mary Prat, 65–66
Shield Jaguar, 12, 13
Shock troops, 661
Shopgirls, 138–139
Shopping, 391–392. *See also* Consumerism; Fashion
Shulman, Alix Kates, 642
Silent films. *See* Movies
Sister Outsider, 702
Sisters of Charity, 274
Sisters of Mercy, 274
Sit-ins, 660–661
Slater, Samuel, 133
Slave law, 50
Slavery
  Africa, 24
  antislavery movement, 220–223
  Atlantic colonies, 50, 52, 70–72
  Catholicism, 208
  Civil War, 280–282
  divorce, 174
  escape from, 269–270, 282–286
  family structure, 166–167, 169, 171–174
  free African Americans (antebellum), 184–185
  gender roles (African American), 72, 168–171
  house servants, 170–171

Slavery—*continued*
  infanticide, 176
  law, 115, 117
  libres (freed slaves), 115–117
  Louisiana territory, 111–117
  market economy, 70–72
  marriage and, 171–174
  marriage as, 312–313
  marriage rights, 296
  Native Americans, 103–104
  New Mexico, 120
  plantation life, 177–183
  property law, 235
  rape, 174–175, 177, 188
  resistance to, 175–177
  sex, 24, 174–175
  tobacco economy, 48
  underground railroad, 283–284
  women, 24, 35–36, 115–116
Slave states, 182*m*
Slave trade, 4–5, 25, 28–30
Slave women, in American Revolution, 83–86
Smith, Amanda Berry, 424–425
Smith, Bessie, 533
Smith, John, 51
Smith, Joseph, 337
Smith College, 468–469
Socialism, 232
Socialist feminism, 699–700
Socialization of housework/childcare, 480
Social purity campaigns, 445–446
Social Security Act of 1935, 563
Social Security Disability Insurance, 665
Social work, 516
Society for Encouraging Industry and the Employment of the Poor, 70
Sojourner Truth Home for Working Girls, 405
Soldiers. *See* Military service
Soldiers' Aid Societies, 265
Sons of Liberty, 78
Soral polygamy, 10
Sorosis, 315–316
Souder, Emily Bliss Thacher, 261–262
South (antebellum), 185–188, 238. *See also* New South
Southern Christian Leadership Conference, 658
Southern Ute, 355–357
Southwest America, settlement, 342–346
Sovereign, 12
Spain, 17, 18, 35–40, 36, 117–124
Spanish American War, 421–422
Specie, 80

Speedup, 218
Spelman Seminary, 391
Spencer, Lily Martin, 144
Spinsters, 512
Spiritualism, 205–206, 386
Spock, Benjamin, 625
Sports. *See specific sports*
Spousal abuse. *See* Domestic violence
Spying, 277–279
Stamp act, 78
Stanton, Elizabeth Cady, 239, 249, 251, 254–255, 264–265, 306–311, 313–318, 340, 400, 421, 451
State Children's Health Insurance Program, 743
Statutory rape, 446
Steinem, Gloria, 680, 681–682
Stenographers, 369
Stewart, Maria, 221
Stimson, Henry L., 605
Stone, Lucy, 229–230, 252, 255, 309, 323, 406
Stop ERA, 727–729
Stowe, Harriet Beecher, 143–145, 157, 316, 351, 390
Stretch-out, 218
Strike. *See* Unions
Student Nonviolent Coordinating Committee, 661, 700
Students for a Democratic Society, 697–698
Sub-Saharan Africa, 21
Suffrage movement, 305–314
Suffrage rights, Utah, 340–342
Sweating system, 271
Sweatshop, 367
Swett, Anne, 131–132
Swisshelm, Jane, 252
Syracuse Convention, 251

T
Taft, William Howard, 483
Taliban, 754–755
Tariff act, 547
Task system, 169, 172
Tea Act of 1773, 78, 79
Teachers, 380–381, 516
Technology, homemaking, 389–391
Tejanas, 118
Tekakwitha, Kateri, 44
Television, 682
Temperance movement, 213–215, 321–324, 337, 350
Temple, Shirley, 570
Temporary Assistance to Needy Families, 743
Tenant farming, 376–377
Tenskwatawa, 107

Terrell, Mary Church, 414–415, 526
Terrorism, 753–755
Texas, 117–119
Textile industry, 551–553. *See also* Mills
Theatre, 155–156
Third Reich, 579
Third-wave feminism, 757–759
Third World Women's Alliance, 700
Thirteenth Amendment, 265, 296, 307
Thomas, Carence, 737
Thomas, M. Carey, 382
Tibbles, Susette La Flesche, 356
Tignon, 116
Till, Emmett, 653, 657
Tillmon, Johnnie, 672
Title VII, 667–668
Title IX of the education amendments of 1972, 675
Tobacco brides, 49
Tobacco economy, 47–48
Townshend acts, 78
Trade, 40–42, 47–48
Trade unions, in reconstruction era, 319–321
Tragic mulatta, 221
Trail of Tears (Cherokee), 102, 111
Trans-Atlantic trade. *See* Atlantic trade
Transcontinental railroad, 332, 339, 344, 346–347
Transgender, 11, 27, 39–40, 44, 82, 276–277, 279, 334, 444, 512–513
Trash gangs, 169
Treatise on Domestic Economy, 143
Treaty of Guadalupe Hidalgo, 342–343
Treaty of Paris, 67, 89*m*, 101
Truancy, 176
Truth, sojourner, 252–253, 313, 597
Tuatara, Fusa, 577–578
Tubman, Harriet, 283–284
Two-spirit people, 127
Tyler, Elizabeth, 529

U
Unbound Feet, 704
Uncle Tom's Cabin, 351
Underground railroad, 282–284
Unions
  Activism, 472–479, 522–523
  Great Depression, 551–556
  Illinois Women's Alliance, 407–408
  International Ladies' Garment Workers Union, 474–476
  Latina women, 555–556
  Lawrence textile strike, 476–477
  Mexican Americans, 635, 636
  post-WWII, 622–624

reconstruction era, 318–321
second-wave feminism, 665–666
textile industry, 551–553
twentieth century (early), 472–479
women's educational and industrial
    union, 406–407
World War II, 582–584
Union states, 263
Unitarians, 385–386
United Auto Workers, 583
United Cannery, Agricultural, Packing
    and Allied Workers of America,
    555
United Electrical, Radio, and Machine
    Workers of America, 624
United Mexican American Students,
    701
United Nations World Conference on
    Women (1995), 756
United Packinghouse Workers of
    America, 622
United States Constitution, 88
United States-Mexican war, 343, 344
United States Sanitary Commission,
    266–269, 289
United States v. One Package of Japanese
    Pessaries, 546
United Textile Workers, 552
Universalists, 385–386
Universal Negro Improvement Associ-
    ation, 524–526
Uprising of 30,000, 474
Urban development
  globalization, 750
  homosexuality, 512–513
  post-Civil war, 366
  reconstruction, 303–305
  sex (early twentieth century),
    435–440
  southwest frontier, 345–346
  World War II, 596–597
USS Maine, 421
Jte, 355–357

rinal orgasm, myth of, 707
na Monologues, 757
Cortlandt, Maria, 46
Devanter, Lynda, 699
Wassenaer, Nicholas, 27
r, 469
real diseases, 487–488, 602
cci, Amerigo, 26
y films, 589
y gardens, 596
m War, 696–700
tion of the Rights of Women,
91

Virginia Company, 46
Virginity, 638–639
Virgin Mary, 39, 43–44
Virgin of Guadalupe, 39, 40
Voting, 86
Voting rights
  activism, 229–230, 236, 313
  League of women voters, 518–521
  South, 491–492
  West, 418–429
  women, 489–496

W
Wage discrimination
  1990s, 745–746
  charity girls, 439–440
  family wage and, 314
  Jazz Age, 514
  labor activism and, 666–668
  media and, 681
  post-WWII, 619–621
  property rights and, 236–238
  World War II, 580, 583
Wages
  activism, 522–523
  Civil War, 270–271
  communitarianism, 233
  Europe, 15
  factory work, 136
  gender difference, 137
  internment camps, 598–599
  law, 236–238
  market economy, 70
Wage work, in industrial revolution,
    133–137
Wal-Mart, 742
Walker, Madam C.J., 503–504, 517
Walker, William, 245
Walker system, 503–504
War Advertising Council, 586
War Brides Act, 632
Ward, Nancy, 107–108
Ware, Caroline, 667
War Manpower Commission, 580
War of 1812, 132
War on poverty, 718
Warren, Mercy Otis, 81
Wartime newsreels, 589
Wayne, John, 589
Webster v. Reproductive Health Services,
    740
Welfare, 564, 671–673, 719, 741–743
Welfare queen, 742
Welfare state, 479, 562–566
Wellesley, 469
Well of Loneliness, The, 512
Wells-Barnett, Ida B, 419–420, 526
West. See Frontier

West, Mae, 570, 571
West Africa, 21–22
Wetsy, Betsy, 638
Wheatley, Phyllis, 87
Whig party, 230, 245
White, John, 27
White feminists, 701
White Rose Home and Industrial Asso-
    ciation, 405
White slavery panic, 448
White women, 49, 302–303, 335, 401
Whitman, Marcus, 125
Whitman, Narcissa, 125–126
Wiebusch, Wilhelmine, 364–365
Wife beating. See Domestic violence
Wilder, Laura Ingalls, 349
Willard, Frances E., 322–324, 399–400,
    384, 408–410, 418
Wilson, Woodrow, 484
Winning Plan, 492
Witchcraft, 39–40, 58–59
Witch hunts, 15
Witch trials, 58–59
Wittenmyer, Annie, 322, 350
Wives. See Family Structure; Gender
    Roles; Marriage
Wollstonecraft, Mary, 91
Woman's Christian Temperance
    Union, 322–324, 350, 384,
    408–410, 416, 425–426,
    445–446
Woman's Convention, 385
Woman's crusade (temperance), 322
Woman's Peace Party, 485–486
Woman's Work for Woman, 423
Woman Warrior, Memoirs of a Girlhood
    among Ghosts, 704–705
Women adrift, 435
Women and Economics, 390
Women Artists in Revolution, 711
Women of the KKK, 529–530
Women's Action Alliance, 682
Women's Air Force Service Pilots,
    607–608
Women's Army Auxiliary Corps,
    603–605
Women's Army Corps, 605–607,
    608–611
Women's associations, 387
Women's bodies, medical construction
    of, 450–451
Women's Bureau, 521
Women's Central Relief Association,
    266
Women's Convention of the Black
    Baptist Church, 470
Women's Division of the Democratic
    National Committee, 557

Women's Educational and Industrial Union, 406–407
Women's Educational Equity Act, 675–676
Women's Equity Action League, 675
Women's Health Movement, 7ßπ12–715
Women's Health Protective Association, 471
Women's International League for Peace and Freedom, 486
Women's International Terrorist Conspiracy from Hell, 706
Women's Liberation Movement, 689–690
Women's National Indian Association, 352
Women's National Loyal League, 264–265, 306
Women's network, 556–559
Women's organizations, 314–318. See also specific organizations
Women's Political Council, 657
Women's rights, 66
  activism, early, 248–249
  African American women, 252–253
  antislavery movement, 252–253
  citizenship, 86
  Civil War, 264–265
  court (eighteenth century), 70
  divorce, 254–255
  dress, 251
  movement, 1850s, 243–255
  education, 91
  internationally, 253–254
  marriage, 312–313
  new Mexican frontier, 120
  Nineteenth Amendment, 494–496
  property, 119, 229–236
  slavery, 185–188
  suffrage movement, 305–314
  Thirteenth Amendment, 265
  voting, 86, 229–230, 236, 244–247
  white women, 401
Women's shelters, 736
Women's suffrage movement, 306–309. See also Voting rights
Women Strike for Peace, 698
Women writers. See Authors
Woodhull, Victoria C. 309–313, 451
Work. See Employment; Gender roles
Working Women's Association, 318
Working Women's Protective Union, 272
Works Progress Administration, 560, 562–564
World War I, 484–496
World War II
  employment, 579–586
  family structure, 601–602
  fashion, 591–592
  military service, 602–611
  post-war employment, 619–624
World Women's Christian Temperance Union, 425–426
Wounded Knee massacre, 355
Wright, Frances (Fanny), 234–235, 237
Wright, Martha C., 248
Writing. See Authors; Literature
Wylie, Philip, 626
Wyoming, 418

Y
Yamada, Mitsuye, 704
Yankee schoolmarms, 304
Yellow peril, 449
Yeoman farmer, 183–184
Yoruba, 21
Young, Brigham, 338
Young ladies' Academy of Philadelphia, 91
Young Women's Christian Association, 402–406, 426–427, 597

Z
Zak-Kuk (Mayan princess), 12
Zakrzewska, Marie, 381, 383–384
Zami: A New Spelling of my Name, 702
Ziegfeld follies, 532
Zines, 759
Zitkala Sa (Gertrude Simmons Bonnin), 354